beauty therapy

THE FOUNDATIONS

HAIRDRESSING AND BEAUTY INDUSTRY
AUTHORITY SERIES – RELATED TITLES

HAIRDRESSING

Mahogany Hairdressing: Steps to Cutting, Colouring and Finishing Hair *Martin Gannon and Richard Thompson*

Mahogany Hairdressing: Advanced Looks *Richard Thompson and Martin Gannon*

Essensuals, Next Generation Toni & Guy: Step by Step

Professional Men's Hairdressing *Guy Kremer and Jacki Wadeson*

The Art of Dressing Long Hair *Guy Kremer and Jacki Wadeson*

Patrick Cameron: Dressing Long Hair *Patrick Cameron and Jacki Wadeson*

Patrick Cameron: Dressing Long Hair Book 2 *Patrick Cameron*

Bridal Hair *Pat Dixon and Jacki Wadeson*

Trevor Sorbie: Visions in Hair *Kris Sorbie and Jacki Wadeson*

The Total Look: The Style Guide for Hair and Make-up Professionals *Ian Mistlin*

Art of Hair Colouring *David Adams and Jacki Wadeson*

Begin Hairdressing: The Official Guide to Level 1 *Martin Green*

Hairdressing – The Foundations: The Official Guide to Level 2 *Leo Palladino* (contribution Jane Farr)

Professional Hairdressing: The Official Guide to Level 3 4e *Martin Green, Lesley Kimber and Leo Palladino*

Men's Hairdressing: Traditional and Modern Barbering 2e *Maurice Lister*

African-Caribbean Hairdressing 2e *Sandra Gittens*

Salon Management *Martin Green*

eXtensions: The Official Guide to Hair Extensions *Theresa Bullock*

BEAUTY THERAPY

Beauty Therapy – The Foundations: The Official Guide to Level 2 *Lorraine Nordmann*

Beauty Basics – The Official Guide to Level 1 *Lorraine Nordmann*

Professional Beauty Therapy: The Official Guide to Level 3 *Lorraine Nordmann, Lorraine Appleyard and Pamela Linforth*

Aromatherapy for the Beauty Therapist *Valerie Ann Worwood*

Indian Head Massage *Muriel Burnham-Airey and Adele O'Keefe*

The Official Guide to Body Massage *Adele O'Keefe*

An Holistic Guide to Anatomy and Physiology *Tina Parsons*

The Encyclopedia of Nails *Jacqui Jefford and Anne Swain*

Nail Artistry *Jacqui Jefford, Sue Marsh and Anne Swain*

The Complete Nail Technician *Marian Newman*

The World of Skin Care: A Scientific Companion *Dr John Gray*

Safety in the Salon *Elaine Almond*

An Holistic Guide to Reflexology *Tina Parsons*

Nutrition: A Practical Approach *Suzanne Le Quesne*

An Holistic Guide to Massage *Tina Parsons*

beauty therapy

THE FOUNDATIONS

THE OFFICIAL GUIDE TO NVQ LEVEL 2   THIRD EDITION

LORRAINE NORDMANN

habia
standards · information · solutions

THOMSON

Australia · Canada · Mexico · Singapore · Spain · United Kingdom · United States

THOMSON
™

Beauty Therapy – The Foundations: Third Edition

For more information, contact Thomson Learning, High Holborn House, 50-51 Bedford Row, London WC1R 4LR or visit us on the World Wide Web at: http://www.thomsonlearning.co.uk

British Library Cataloguing-in-Publication Data
A catalogue record for this book is available from the British Library

ISBN-13: 978-1-86152-910-7
ISBN-10: 1-86152-910-4

First edition published 1995 by Macmillan
Second edition published 1999 by Macmillan
Third edition published 2004 by Thomson Learning
Reprinted 2004 and 2005 by Thomson Learning

Text design by Design Deluxe
Illustrations on pages 50, 90, 92, 93, 94, 95, 98, 101, 102, 104, 106, 107, 109, 110, 111, 113, 114, 115, 116, 117, 118, 119, 120, 121, 123, 124, 125, 126, 127, 128, 129, 130, 131,132, 133, 134, 135, 136, 137, 141, 149, 240, 241, 406, 410, 411, 420, 421, 451, 456, 457, 459, 469 by Oxford Designers and Illustrators
Typeset by Meridian Colour Repro Ltd, Pangbourne-on-Thames, Berkshire, RG8 7HY

Printed in Singapore by Seng Lee Press

contents

GENERAL BEAUTY THERAPY UNITS 139

acknowledgements

HMSO (Her Majesty's Stationery Office)

Chubb Fire Ltd

Dream Workwear

Depilex

Sorisa: Adam Birtwistle

Jacqui Jefford and Anne Swain: with great appreciation for allowing us to reproduce images from their book: *The Encyclopedia of Nails*

Jacqui Jefford, Sue Marsh and Anne Swain for allowing us to use an image from their book: *Nail Artistry*

Dr M. H. Beck

Dr A. L. Wright

Dr John Gray

Hair And Beauty Industry Authority

Saks: Covent Garden

American Express

Ellisons

Hugh Rushton

Unilever

Depilex/RVB

Helinova Ltd

Elemis

Salon System

Sukar: many thanks to Roger and Nagwa Stanforth of Nagwa Trading Co. Ltd for supplying the images of sugaring and strip sugar

Precious Professional (Courtesy of Ellisons)

Ballets

Derrick Mulligan/Media Image

NSI UK

Activewise (www.activewise.co.uk)

Floataway (www.floataway.co.uk)

Many thanks to Spirit Health Club, Holiday Inn Hotel, Lodge Lane, Newton-le-Willows for allowing us to reproduce their safety check sheets in Chapter 15. Contact: spirit.haydock@IChotelsgroup.com

Jonathan Knott and staff at Spirit Health Club, Holiday Inn Hotel, Lodge Lane, Newton-le-Willows

Finders International Ltd (www.findershealth.com)

Sameer Arain: professional photographer

Elizabeth and Norman Whiteside

Jane Critchley and Emma Tonkin: models at Spirit Health Club Beauty Salon, Haydock, Holiday Inn

Janine Rigby: beauty therapist

Leah Park: beauty therapy lecturer and freelance make-up artist Lee@graduate-centre.com

Nicola Hulbert: beauty therapist, New Woman, Westhoughton

Vicki Kennedy: salon owner and beauty therapist, New Woman, Westhoughton

Photographers: Anderson and Ian Littlewood; make-up artist: Jo Crowder; and illustrator: Pam Young

Elaine Almond

Lorraine Williamson

Pamela Linforth

foreword

1997 was an auspicious year for me. Not only was it the year when the Beauty Industry Authority was created, but it was also when the second edition of Lorraine Nordmann's excellent book *Beauty Therapy – the Foundations Level 2* was published.

At that time it was a real pleasure to write the foreword for the second edition, as it was the very first endorsement by the then Beauty Industry Authority.

So here we are seven years on and the Beauty Industry Authority is now part of HABIA. The industry has expanded and become more professional, and has seen changes not only in technology, but also in aesthetics and style. Could we put all this down to Lorraine Nordmann's second edition?

If I could sum up Lorraine Nordmann in one word, it would be professional. Her career progression and dedication to continuing professional development shows a wealth of experience, knowledge and understanding of the industry. Lorraine exudes personal warmth and is appreciative of her colleagues. Her commitment to the development and introduction of innovative learning support and guidance is clearly reflected in the third edition.

Without a doubt, *Beauty Therapy – the Foundations* third edition, is the most informative book to cover the Level 2 Beauty Therapy Standards as laid down by HABIA.

Alan Goldsboro
Chief Executive Officer, HABIA

note from the author

Writing the third edition of *Beauty Therapy – the Foundations* has been an enjoyable task. This is because the content highlights the exciting developments and continued growth of the beauty therapy industry, including the options to specialise in skill areas such as make-up.

The book remains true to its original concept in providing the learner with the clear and concise guidance notes that are needed to develop and improve practical skills and underpin knowledge. Since the last edition, the presentation has been improved and developed to take into account the individual learning style of students, with text and images used to their best educational effect.

The updates in this edition reflect the current trends and training requirements in beauty therapy. With this in mind, the text has been written to fully support the NVQ Level 2 Beauty Therapy Standards, as written by The Hairdressing And Beauty Therapy Industry Association (HABIA). For ease of reference, the chapter headings match the NVQ unit titles.

I hope that *Beauty Therapy – the Foundations* will help you gain the practical skills and personal qualities that you will need to succeed in this service industry, and encourage your progression to NVQ Level 3.

Good luck in you future beauty therapy career.

Lorraine Nordmann

introduction

AN INTRODUCTION TO NVQS

National Vocational Qualifications (NVQs) are nationally recognised qualifications that have a common structure and design. They follow a similar format for all occupational and vocational sectors. The award of an NVQ/SVQ demonstrates that the person has the competence (sufficient skill and knowledge) to perform job roles/tasks effectively in their occupational area. An NVQ at Level 2 covers a wide range of varied work activities, some of which are complex and require that the candidate uses their initiative and makes independent decisions.

Each NVQ/SVQ is structured in the same way, and is made up of a number of units and elements.

The **unit** relates to a specific task or skill area of work. It is the smallest part of an award, which can be accredited separately.

The **element/s** describe/s in detail the skill and knowledge components of the unit.

An example from NVQ Level 2 Beauty Therapy is shown below.

The title of the unit is: **Unit BT 5 Provide eyelash and eyebrow treatments**.

The elements for the unit detail the practical skills and underpinning knowledge essential to provide eyelash and eyebrow treatments.

The *elements* which detail the *unit* components include:

Unit BT 5

Provide eyelash and eyebrow treatments

1 Consult with the client

2 Prepare for the treatment

3 Plan the treatment

4 Shape the eyebrows to meet client requirements

5 Tint eyebrows and lashes to meet client requirements

6 Perm eyelashes to meet client requirements

7 Complete the treatment

Units and elements

For each unit, when all competence requirements have been achieved, a unit of certification may be awarded, such as Unit BT5 Provide eyelash and eyebrow treatments.

Each NVQ is made up of a specific number of units required for the occupational area. Some of the units are termed **mandatory** (compulsory) some are termed **optional** (not compulsory).

Mandatory units must be competently achieved to gain the NVQ/SVQ award.

Optional units may be selected by the candidate to study in addition to the mandatory units.

The NVQ/SVQ will state the mandatory (compulsory) units required to achieve the qualification plus the number of optional units, which must be completed in order to achieve the full NVQ/SVQ award.

There are three training routes to achieve NVQ/SVQ Beauty Therapy Level 2:

1 Beauty Therapy General

2 Beauty Therapy Make-up

3 Nail Services

Whichever route you choose, you must achieve the mandatory units plus one optional unit from the selection of units provided.

The **core mandatory** units are fundamental, essential units to be achieved whichever route is chosen. These are as follows:

● G1 Ensure your own actions reduce risks to health and safety

● G6 Promote additional products or services to clients

● G8 Develop and maintain your effectiveness at work

Note that G4 Fulfil salon reception duties has been placed in the core section of the book, even though it is not actually mandatory. This is because it was felt that this is where lecturers would want to deliver this course content, as opposed to with the later, more practical units.

BEAUTY THERAPY NVQ/SVQ – LEVEL 2
NVQ/SVQ Qualification Structure

Candidates will need to achieve the 'core' mandatory units, plus the mandatory units from one of the two routes, and the specified number of optional units for that route.

'Core' Mandatory Units (all units must be achieved)

G1 Ensure your own actions reduce risks to health and safety

G6 Promote additional products or services to clients

G8 Develop and maintain your effectiveness at work

Beauty Therapy General (mandatory units)	Beauty Therapy Make-up (mandatory units)
BT4 Improve and maintain facial skin condition	BT4 Improve and maintain facial skin condition
BT5 Provide eyelash and eyebrow treatments	BT9 Provide make-up treatment
BT6 Remove hair using waxing techniques	BT10 Plan and promote make-up activities
BT7 Provide manicure treatment	BT11 Enhance the appearance of eyebrows and lashes
BT8 Provide pedicure treatment	
Plus one optional unit (see below)	*Plus* one optional unit (see below)

Optional Units (the relevant number of optional units must be achieved)

G4 Fulfil salon reception duties

BT5 Provide eyelash and eyebrow treatments

BT6 Remove hair using waxing techniques

BT7 Provide manicure treatment

BT8 Provide pedicure treatment

BT9 Provide make-up treatment

BT10 Plan and promote make-up activities

BT12 Extend and maintain nails

BT13 Provide nail art service

BT14 Pierce ears

BT15 Assist with spa treatments

Note: Where units are achieved as mandatory units in either of the two routes, these do not count as optional units as well.

NAIL SERVICES NVQ/SVQ – LEVEL 2
NVQ/SVQ Qualification Structure

Candidates will need to achieve all of the mandatory units and one optional unit

Mandatory Units (all units must be achieved)

G1   Ensure your own actions reduce risks to health and safety

G6   Promote additional products or services to clients

G8   Develop and maintain your effectiveness at work

BT7   Provide manicure treatment

BT8   Provide pedicure treatment

BT12 Extend and maintain nails

BT13 Provide nail art service

Optional Units

G4   Fulfil salon reception duties

BT4   Improve and maintain facial skin condition

BT5   Provide eyelash and eyebrow treatments

BT6   Remove hair using waxing techniques

BT9   Provide make-up treatment

BT10 Plan and promote make-up activities

BT14 Pierce ears

BT15 Assist with spa treatments

Performance criteria

The performance criteria lists the necessary actions that you must achieve to complete the task competently (demonstrating adequate practical skill and experience to the assessor).

The **performance criteria** requirements for BT5 Element 1 Consult with the client are listed below:

- using consultation techniques in a polite and friendly manner to determine the client's treatment plan
- discussing and agreeing the service and outcomes that are acceptable to your client and meets their needs
- maintaining the client's modesty and privacy at all times
- recognising contra-indications and taking the necessary action.

Range

Range statements are often identified for each element. The assessment range relates to the different conditions under which a skill must be competently demonstrated for the element.

For example the **range** assessment requirements for **Unit BT5 element 5**, Tint eyebrows and lashes to meet client requirements, are to cover all the hair colourings shown below:

- fair
- red
- dark
- white/grey

Range: Your performance must cover the following situations
a   Fair
b   Red
c   Dark
d   White/Grey

It is not sufficient to be able to only practically perform the task – you must understand why you are doing it, and be able to transfer your competence to a variety of situations. This is referred to as your knowledge and understanding. Further assessment of your **knowledge and understanding** of the skill, the knowledge specification, may be assessed through theoretical tasks such as written tests, assignments and oral questioning.

The **knowledge and understanding** requirements that you are required to know for **Unit BT5 Client consultation** are listed below:

- how to use effective communication and consultation techniques

- the reasons why it is important to encourage clients with contra-indications to seek medical advice
- the importance of, and reasons for, not naming specific contra-indications when referring clients to a general practitioner
- why it is important to maintain the client's modesty and privacy.

What often occurs is that the same knowledge and understanding may be necessary for similar units. This can be seen, for example, in the knowledge and understanding for **Organisational and Legal Requirements**. This duplication is necessary as some units may be studied and accredited as an individual skill, i.e. BT14 Pierce ears.

Where evidence has been achieved, this is cross-referenced (directed) in the portfolio (a file that holds your assessment evidence) to where the evidence can be found.

To achieve unit competence, all performance criteria, range, and knowledge and understanding requirements must have been met and evidence presented as necessary. Evidence is usually provided in your assessment book and portfolio.

Where there is evidence of previous experience and achievement, this may be presented to the assessor for consideration for accreditation. This is called Accreditation of Prior Learning (APL).

Beauty Therapy – the Foundations follows the Beauty Therapy NVQ/SVQ Level 2 format and covers both the practical and theoretical requirements for both the mandatory and optional units.

about the book

The book relates to the NVQ/SVQ Level 2 qualification structure and has been divided into three parts:

1 Core units
2 Anatomy and physiology
3 General beauty therapy units

CORE UNIT CHAPTERS

The core units relate to the three core mandatory units required for Beauty Therapy NVQ/SVQ Level 2, for both the Beauty Therapy general route and the Beauty Therapy make-up route.

The core unit chapters cover:

- G1 Ensure your own actions reduce risks to health and safety
- G6 Promote additional products or services to clients
- G8 Develop and maintain your effectiveness at work

Note that G4 Fulfil salon reception duties has been placed in the core section of the book, even though it is not actually mandatory. This is because it was felt that this is where lecturers would want to deliver this course content, as opposed to with the later, more practical units.

ANATOMY AND PHYSIOLOGY CHAPTER

Certain units have an anatomy and physiology knowledge requirement.

This chapter provides the essential knowledge, and also contains a useful reference chart that states the specific anatomy and physiology requirements to be studied for each unit. In addition, anatomy and physiology is discussed within the general beauty therapy units to aid understanding.

GENERAL BEAUTY THERAPY

These chapters discuss the beauty therapy technical skills in the NVQ, including both the mandatory and optional units.

The general beauty therapy chapters cover the following units:

- G4 Fulfil salon reception duties – an essential skill requirement for some workplaces
- BT4 Improve and maintain facial skin condition
- BT5 Provide eyelash and eyebrow treatments
- BT6 Remove hair using waxing techniques
- BT7 Provide manicure treatment
- BT8 Provide pedicure treatment
- BT9 Provide make-up treatment – including BT10 Plan and promote make-up activities
- BT11 Enhance the appearance of eyebrows and lashes
- BT12 Extend and maintain nails
- BT13 Provide nail art service
- BT14 Pierce ears
- BT15 Assist with spa treatments

FEATURES WITHIN CHAPTERS

Common features appear within each chapter. An explanation for each is provided below:

Learning objectives

Learning objectives

This unit describes how to provide a variety of nail art techniques for clients. It describes the competencies to enable you to:

- consult with the client
- prepare the service
- plan the service
- provide nail art service to clients
- complete the service

When providing nail art service it is important to use the skills you have learnt in the following core mandatory units:

Unit G1 – Ensure your own actions reduce risks to health and safety
Unit G6 – Promote additional products or services to clients
Unit G8 – Develop and maintain your effectiveness at work

Learning objectives introduce each chapter and list the elements that make up the unit which must be achieved in order to be accredited with the NVQ unit.

When you feel confident and competent with the skills/knowledge requirements you are ready to be assessed.

Spidergrams

Spidergrams are provided in each chapter to summarise the skills/knowledge requirement for each element, with the title of the element in the centre of the spidergram. These provide a useful checklist for you to refer to.

Activity boxes

Activity boxes feature within chapters and provide additional tasks for you to complete to assess and further your understanding of the unit content.

Health and safety boxes

In addition to the core chapter, G1 Ensure your own actions reduce risks to health and safety, health and safety boxes are provided in each chapter. They serve to draw your attention to related health and safety information for each technical skill.

Tip boxes

The authors experience is shared through tip boxes, which provide positive suggestions to improve your knowledge and skills for each unit.

Assessment of knowledge and understanding

In addition to the activity boxes in each chapter, questions are provided at the end of each chapter. These questions relate to the specific essential knowledge and understanding requirements for the unit. You can use the questions to prepare you for oral and written assessments. Seek guidance from your supervisor/assessor if there are any areas that you are unsure of. Remember also to check the anatomy and physiology chapter, referring to the chart, to include revision in the related anatomy and physiology requirement as applicable.

ACTIVITY

Explaining poor results
What reasons can you think of to explain why a permanent tint applied to the eyelashes or eyebrows has not coloured the hair successfully? Discuss your answers with your tutor.

HEALTH AND SAFETY

Fire exits
Fire-exit doors must be clearly marked and remain unlocked during working hours, and be free from obstruction.

TIP

Male facials
Recommend that the male client shaves before facial treatment. This will soften the skin and facilitate skin cleansing.

Assessment of knowledge and understanding

You have now learnt about the related anatomy and physiology for the beauty therapy units with an essential knowledge requirement.

To test your level of knowledge, answer the following short questions. These will prepare you for your summative (final) assessment.

Skin structure and function

1 Referring to the cross section of the skin, name and briefly describe the functions of the structures shown in 1–4.

2 Name six functions of the skin.

3 Name the layers of the epidermis shown in 1–7.

A concealer is applied with a brush underneath the eyes to disguise the darker skin tone.

A liquid foundation matched to the client's skin tone is applied. Application is over the whole face, including the eyelids and lips, as this gives an even skin tone.

Following the application of loose powder, again matched to the client's skin tone, excess powder is removed using a large powder brush. Application is upwards and outwards.

Blusher colour is applied to accentuate the cheek area and add colour to the face.

Colour applied to the eye emphasises the eye area. We used complementary colours in a purple range. A highlighting colour accentuates the brow-bone.

The eyebrows are accentuated using a dark matt brown colour applied with a stiff eyebrow brush. This gives definition to the eyebrow, disguising sparse hair and gaps.

Step-by-step photo sequences

Each chapter aims to demonstrate the featured practical skill using colour photographs to enhance your understanding.

Equipment lists

To assist you preparing for each practical treatment an essential equipment list is provided, supported with images of treatment tools, materials and products required. These are also useful to provide to a Level 1 beauty therapist if assisting you to prepare the work area.

EQUIPMENT LIST

headband

skin cleansing preparations

cottonwool

tissues

waste bin

spatulas

see opposite for complete list of materials required

Treatment cards

Client treatment record cards are featured in each of the general beauty therapy units. They illustrate the information that you need to assess and gain from the client at consultation in order to establish client suitability and treatment aim. It also provides guidance on information that should be provided following treatment, including aftercare advice and the promotion of additional products and services.

Use of bold terms

The text highlights certain terms in bold lettering. These often denote important technical terms which are explained and that you must become familiar with to gain knowledge competence for the unit.

Glossary of terms

There is a glossary at the back of the book, which explains technical terms found within the book.

beauty therapy

THE FOUNDATIONS

core units

chapter 1

ENSURE YOUR OWN ACTIONS REDUCE RISKS TO HEALTH AND SAFETY

Learning objectives

This chapter covers health and safety duties and responsibilities for everyone in the workplace. It describes the competencies required to ensure that:

- **you identify the hazards and evaluate the risks in your workplace**
- **you reduce the risks to health and safety in your workplace**

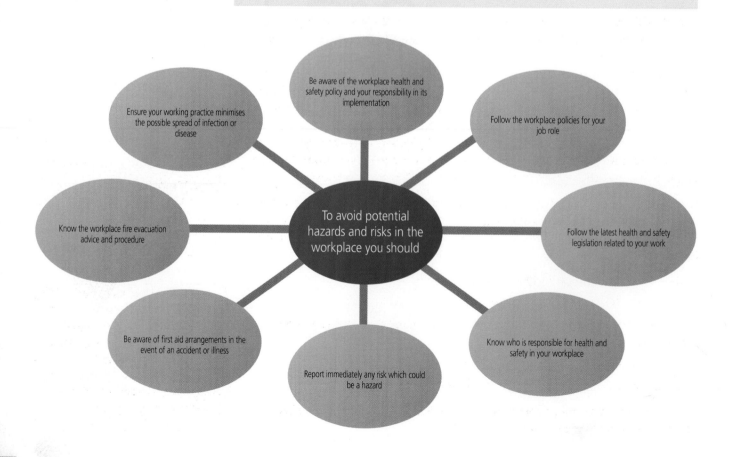

Be aware of the workplace health and safety policy and your responsibility in its implementation

Ensure your working practice minimises the possible spread of infection or disease

Follow the workplace policies for your job role

Know the workplace fire evacuation advice and procedure

To avoid potential hazards and risks in the workplace you should

Follow the latest health and safety legislation related to your work

Be aware of first aid arrangements in the event of an accident or illness

Report immediately any risk which could be a hazard

Know who is responsible for health and safety in your workplace

TAKING CARE OF ALL IN THE WORKPLACE

When working in a service industry, you are legally obliged to provide a **safe and hygienic environment**. This applies whether you are working in a hotel, a department store, a leisure centre or a private beauty salon, or operating a mobile beauty therapy service. You must pay careful attention to health and safety to minimise risk. Exactly the same is true when working in clients' homes: it is essential to follow the normal health and safety guidelines, just as you would when working in a salon.

This chapter is for everyone at work whatever their status: paid, unpaid, part-time or full-time.

Legal responsibilities

If you cause harm to your client, or put her at risk, you will be held responsible and you will be liable to **prosecution**, with the possibility of being fined.

There is a good deal of **legislation** relating to health and safety. Details are widely available, and you must be aware of your responsibilities and your rights. It is important that you obtain and read all relevant publications from your local Health and Safety Executive offices.

The Health and Safety at Work Act 1974

The **Health and Safety at Work Act 1974** is the main piece of legislation affecting these issues. It was developed from experience gained over 150 years, and now incorporates earlier legislation including the Offices, Shops and Railway Premises Act 1963 and the Fire Precautions Act 1971. It lays down the minimum standards of health, safety and welfare required in each area of the workplace – for example, it requires that business premises and equipment be safe and in good repair. It is the employer's legal responsibility to implement the Act and to ensure, so far as is reasonably practicable, the health and safety at work of the people for whom they are responsible and those who may be affected by the work they do.

Each employer of more than five employees must formulate a written **health and safety policy** for that establishment. The policy must be issued to each employee and should outline their safety responsibilities. It should include items such as:

- details of the storage of chemical substances
- details of the stock cupboard or dispensary
- details and records of the checks made by a qualified electrician on specialist electrical equipment
- names and addresses of the keyholders
- escape routes and emergency evacuation procedures.

Regular health and safety checks should be made to ensure that safety is being satisfactorily maintained.

ACTIVITY

Health and safety information
Write to your local Health and Safety Executive (HSE) office to ask for a pack of relevant health and safety information.

ACTIVITY

Health and safety rules
Discuss the rules which you feel should appear in a salon's health and safety policy.

HEALTH AND SAFETY

Health and Safety (Information for Employees) Regulations 1989: Health and safety notice
Every employer is obliged by law to display a health and safety notice in the workplace.

Removing hot wax

Employees must co-operate with their employer to provide a safe and healthy workplace. As soon as they observe any **hazard**, this must be reported to the designated authority so that the problem can be put right. Hazards include:

- obstructions to corridors, stairways and fire exits (an obstruction is anything that blocks the traffic route in the salon work environment);
- spillages and breakages.

In 1992 European Union (EU) directives updated the legislation on health and safety management. Current legislation at the time of writing (2003) is outlined below.

The Management of Health and Safety at Work Regulations 1999

These require employers to make formal arrangements for maintaining and improving safe working conditions and practices. This includes training for employees to improve competency and to monitor risk in the workplace (including product use), known as **risk assessment**. This requires:

- identification of potential hazards;
- an assessment of the potential risks associated with the hazard;
- identifying who is at risk from the hazard;
- identifying how risk is to be minimized or eliminated;
- training staff to identify and control risks;
- reviewing regularly the risk assessment process.

The Personal Protective Equipment (PPE) at Work Regulations 1992

The **Personal Protective Equipment (PPE) at Work Regulations 1992** require managers to identify through a **risk assessment** those activities or processes which require special protective clothing or equipment to be worn. This clothing and equipment must then be made available, in adequate supplies. Employees must wear the protective clothing and use the protective equipment provided, and make employers aware of any shortage so that supplies can be maintained.

The Workplace (Health, Safety and Welfare) Regulations 1992

The **Workplace (Health, Safety and Welfare) Regulations 1992** require all at work to maintain a safe, healthy and secure working environment. The regulations include legal requirements in relation to the following aspects of the working environment:

- maintenance of the workplace and equipment;
- ventilation to ensure the air is changed regularly;
- working temperature;
- lighting;
- cleanliness and handling of waste materials;
- safe salon layout;
- falls and falling objects;

HEALTH AND SAFETY

Protective equipment: gloves
If you are to come into contact with body tissue fluids or with chemicals, wear protective disposable surgical gloves. Latex gloves can cause allergic reactions and in some cases the development of asthma.
An alternative glove that provides adequate protection from contamination should be used.

ACTIVITY

Risk assessment
Carry out your own risk assessment. List the potentially hazardous substances handled in beauty therapy. What protective clothing should be available?

HEALTH AND SAFETY

European directives
As a result of directives adopted in 1992 by the European Union, health and safety legislation has been updated.
1 Obtain a copy of the eight directives. *Workplace (Health, Safety & Welfare) Regulations 1992.*
2 Look through the publication, and make notes on any information relevant to you in the workplace.

- windows, doors, gates and walls;
- safe floor and traffic routes;
- escalators and moving walkways;
- sanitary conveniences;
- washing facilities;
- drinking water;
- facilities for changing clothing;
- facilities for staff to rest and eat meals.

Manual Handling Operations Regulations 1992

These regulations apply in all occupations where manual lifting occurs. The employer is required to carry out a risk assessment of all activities undertaken which involve manual lifting.

The risk assessment should provide evidence that the following have been considered:

- risk of injury;
- the manual movement involved in performing the activity;
- the physical constraint the load incurs;
- the environmental constraints imposed by the workplace;
- workers' individual capabilities;
- action taken in order to minimise potential risks.

Manual lifting and handling

Always take care of yourself when moving goods around the salon. Do not struggle or be impatient: get someone else to help. When **lifting**, lift from the knees, not the back. When **carrying**, balance weights evenly in both hands and carry the heaviest part nearest to your body.

> **TIP** ✓
>
> The salon temperature should be a minimum of 16°C within one hour of employees arriving for work. The salon should be well ventilated, or carbon dioxide levels will increase, which can cause nausea. Many substances used in the salon can become hazardous without adequate ventilation.
>
> If the working environment is too warm this can cause heat stress, a condition that is recognised by the HSE.
>
> Lighting should be adequate to ensure that treatments can be carried out safely and competently, with the minimum risk of accident.

> **TIP** ✓
>
> When you unpack a delivery, make sure that the product packaging is undamaged, to avoid possible personal injury from broken goods.

left Lifting a box
centre Carrying several boxes
right Carrying equal weights in both hands

ACTIVITY

Identifying hazards
Make a list of potential electrical hazards in the workplace e.g. damaged plugs. Who should these be reported to?

ACTIVITY

COSHH assessments
Carry out a COSHH assessment on selected treatment products used in the salon. Consider manicures, nail extensions, waxing, and facial and eye treatments.

HEALTH AND SAFETY +

COSHH assessment
All hazardous substances must be identified when completing the risk assessment. This includes cleaning agents such as a wax equipment cleaner.

High-risk products should where possible be replaced with lower risk products.

COSHH assessment should be reviewed on a regular basis, and updated to include any new products.

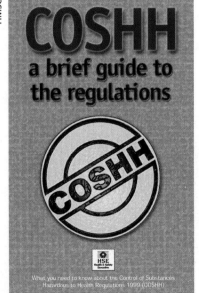

Provision and Use of Work Equipment Regulations 1992

These regulations lay down the important health and safety controls on the provision and use of work equipment. They state the duties for employers and for users, including the self-employed. They affect both old and new equipment. They identify the requirements in selecting suitable equipment and in maintaining it. They also discuss the information provided by equipment manufacturers, and instruction and training in the safe use of equipment. Specific regulations address the dangers and potential risks of injury that could occur during operation of the equipment.

Health and Safety (Display Screen Equipment) 1992

These regulations cover the use of visual display units (VDUs) and computer screens. They specify acceptable levels of radiation emissions from the screen and identify correct posture, seating position, permitted working heights and rest periods.

Control of Substances Hazardous to Health (COSHH) Regulations 1999 (recently consolidated in 2002)

These regulations were designed to make employers consider the substances used in their workplace and assess the possible risks to health. Many substances that seem quite harmless can prove to be hazardous if used or stored incorrectly. Hazardous substances are anything that can harm your health.

Employers are responsible for assessing the risks from hazardous substances and controlling exposure to them to prevent ill health. Any hazardous substances identified must be formally recorded in writing, and given a hazard risk rating. Safety precaution procedures should then be implemented and training given to employees to ensure that the procedures are understood and will be followed correctly.

Hazardous substances are identified through the use of known symbols, examples of which are shown on the right. Any substance in the workplace that is hazardous to health must be identified on the packaging and stored and handled correctly.

Hazardous substances may enter the body via:

● the eyes;
● the skin;
● the nose (**inhalation**);
● the mouth (**ingestion**).

Each beauty product supplier is legally required to make available guidelines, on how materials should be used and stored, called material safety data sheets (MSDSs); these will be supplied on request.

Electricity at Work Regulations 1989

These regulations state that every piece of electrical equipment in the workplace should be tested every 12 months by a qualified electrician.

In addition to annual testing, a trained member of staff should regularly check all electrical equipment for safety. This is recommended every three months. Report to your supervisor if you see any of these potential hazards:

- exposed wires in flexes;
- cracked plugs or broken sockets;
- worn cables;
- overloaded sockets.

Although it is the responsibility of the employer to ensure all equipment is safe to use, it is also the responsibility of the employee to always check that equipment is safe before use, and to never use it if it is faulty.

Any pieces of equipment that appear faulty must immediately be checked and, if necessary, repaired before use. If faulty they must be labelled to ensure that they are not used by accident.

Accidents

Accidents in the workplace usually occur through negligence by employees or unsafe working conditions.

Any accidents occurring in the workplace must be recorded on a **report form**, and entered into an **accident book**. The report form requires more details than the accident book – you must note down:

- the date;
- the name of the person or people involved;
- the accident details;
- the injuries sustained;
- the action taken.

Accidents can damage stock, resulting in breakage of containers and spillage of contents. Breakage of glass can cause cuts; spillages may cause somebody to slip and fall. Any breakages or spillages should therefore be dealt with immediately and in the correct way.

You must determine whether the spillage is a potential hazard to health, and what action is necessary. To whom should you report it? What equipment is required to remove the spillage? How should the materials be disposed of?

Always consider your COSHH data and check to see how the product should be handled and disposed of.

Reporting of Injuries, Diseases and Dangerous Occurrences Regulations (RIDDOR) 1995

RIDDOR requires the employer to notify the local enforcement officer, in writing, in cases where employees or trainees suffer personal injury at work. When this occurrence results in death, major injury or more than 24 hours in hospital, it must be reported by telephone first, and followed by a written report within seven days. In all cases where personal injury occurs, an entry must be made in the workplace accident book. Where visitors to the work premises are injured this must be reported also.

This information assists the HSE in investigation of serious accidents.

HEALTH AND SAFETY

Potentially hazardous substances include:

- aerosols
- disinfectants
- water treatment chemicals used in spa pools.

HIGHLY FLAMMABLE | TOXIC

HARMFUL | CORROSIVE

EXPLOSIVE | OXIDIZING

ACTIVITY

Avoiding accidents
Discuss potential causes of accidents in the workplace. How could these accidents be prevented?

HEALTH AND SAFETY

Breakages and spillages
When dealing with hazardous breakages and spillages, the hands should always be protected with gloves. To avoid injury to others, broken glass should be put in a secure container prior to disposing of it in a waste bin.

First aid

The **Health and Safety (First Aid) Regulations 1981** state that workplaces must have first-aid provision. Employers must have appropriate and adequate first-aid arrangements in the event of an accident or illness occurring.

All employees should be informed of the first-aid procedures, including:

● where to locate the first-aid box;

● who is responsible for the maintenance of the first-aid box;

● which staff member to inform in the event of an accident or illness occurring;

● the staff member to inform in the event of an accident emergency.

An adequately stocked first-aid box should be available. This should contain as a minimum level of equipment:

● basic first-aid guidance leaflet (1);

● assorted sterile adhesive dressings (20);

● individually-wrapped triangular bandages (6);

● safety pins (6);

● sterile eyepads, with attachments (2);

● medium-sized individually-wrapped sterile unmedicated wound dressings, 10cm × 8cm (6);

● large individually-wrapped sterile unmedicated wound dressings, 13cm × 9cm (2);

● extra-large sterile individually-wrapped medicated wound dressings, 28cm × 17.5cm (3);

● individually-wrapped medical wipes;

● antiseptic cream or liquid.

If bathing eyes where tap water is not readily available, sterile water should be stored in sealed containers.

First-aid kits

Disposal of waste

Waste should be disposed of in an enclosed waste bin fitted with a polythene bin liner, durable enough to resist tearing. The bin should be regularly sanitised with disinfectant in a well-ventilated area: wear protective gloves while doing this. Hazardous waste must be disposed of following the COSHH procedures and training by the employer.

Contaminated waste, such as wax strips, should be disposed of as recommended by your local authority. Items which have been used to pierce the skin, such as disposable milia extractors, should be safely discarded in a disposable **sharps container**. Again, contact your local authority to check on disposal arrangements.

Inspection and registration of premises

The Local Authority Environmental Health Department enforces the Health and Safety at Work Act, and a local authority authorised **officer** visits and inspects local business premises.

If the officer identifies any area of danger, it is the responsibility of the employer to remove this danger within a designated period of time. The inspector issues an **improvement notice**. Failure to comply with the notice will lead to prosecution. The inspector also has the authority to *close* a business until he or she is satisfied that all danger to employees and public has been removed. Such closure involves the issuing of a **prohibition notice**.

Certain treatments carried out in beauty therapy, such as ear piercing, pose additional risk as they may produce blood and body tissue fluid. Inspection of the premises is necessary before such services can be offered to the public. The inspector will visit and observe that the guidelines listed in the **Local Government (Miscellaneous Provisions) Act 1982** relating to this area are being complied with. When the inspector is satisfied, a certificate of registration will be awarded.

Fire

The **Fire Precautions Act 1971** states that all staff must be aware of and trained in fire and emergency evacuation procedures for their workplace. The **emergency exit route** will be the easiest route by which staff and clients can leave the building safely.

A **fire certificate** is a compulsory requirement of the Act if there are more than 20 employees, or more than 10 employees are on different floors at any one time.

The Fire Precautions (workplace) Regulations 1997

This requires that every employer must carry out a risk assessment for the premises, under the **Management of Health and Safety Regulations 1999**.

- Any obstacles that may hinder fire evacuation should be identified as problem areas.
- Suitable fire detection equipment should be in place, such as a **smoke alarm** to forewarn you of a fire.

ACTIVITY

Fire drill
Each workplace should have a fire drill regularly. This enables staff to practise so that they know what to do in the event of a real fire. What is the fire drill procedure for *your* workplace?

- A method to warn of a fire should be in place, this may be an automatic alarm or a trained employee shouting to raise the alarm.
- All escape routes should be clearly marked and free from obstacles.
- Fire-fighting equipment should be available and maintained, to be used only by those trained in its use.
- All employees should be trained in fire evacuation practice and procedures.
- Fire evacuation procedure should be reviewed regularly to account for changes to the staffing or premises. A fire drill should be carried out at least once a year to monitor evacuation procedures.

Fire-fighting equipment

Fire-fighting equipment must be available, located in a specified area. The equipment includes fire extinguishers, blankets, sand buckets, and water hoses. Fire-fighting equipment should be used only when the cause of the fire has been identified – using the *wrong* extinguisher could make the fire worse.

Never use fire-fighting equipment unless you are trained in its use.

Cause of fire and choice of fire extinguisher

Cause	Extinguisher	Label colour
Electrical fire	Carbon dioxide (CO_2) extinguisher	Black
Solid material fire (paper, wood, etc.)	Water extinguisher	Red
Flammable liquids	Foam extinguisher	Cream/yellow
Vaporising liquids	BCF extinguisher	Green
	Dry-powder extinguisher	Blue

Note: green and blue extinguishers can be used with all types of fire except flammable metal fires.

Fire extinguisher symbols

Fire blanket

Fire extinguishers

Fire extinguishers are available to tackle different types of fire. These should be located in a set place known to all employees. It is important that these are checked and maintained as required.

Fire blankets are used to smother a small, localised fire or if a person's clothing is on fire. **Sand** is used to soak up liquids if these are the source of the fire, and to smother the fire. **Water hoses** are used to extinguish large fires caused by paper materials and the like – buckets of water may be used to extinguish a small fire. *Turn off the electricity first!*

Never put yourself at risk – fires can spread quickly. Leave the building at once if in danger, and raise the alarm by telephoning the emergency services on the emergency telephone number, **999**.

Other emergencies

Other possible emergencies that could occur relate to fumes and flooding. Learn where the water and gas stopcocks are located. In the event of a gas leak or a flood, the stopcocks should be switched off and the appropriate emergency service contacted.

In the event of a bomb alert staff must be trained in the appropriate emergency procedures. This will involve recognition of a suspect package, how to deal with a bomb threat, evacuation of staff and clients and contacting the emergency services. Your local Crime Prevention Officer (CPO) will advise on bomb security.

Insurance

Public liability insurance protects employers and employees against the consequences of death or injury to a third party while on the premises. Professional indemnity insurance extends public liability insurance to cover named employees against claims.

Product and **Treatment Liability Insurance** is usually included with your public liability insurance, but should be checked with the insurance company. Product Liability Insurance covers you for risks which might occur as a result of the products you are using and/or selling.

Second, it is a legal requirement that every employer must have **employer's liability insurance**. This provides financial compensation to an employee should they be injured as a result of an accident in the workplace.

PERSONAL HEALTH, HYGIENE AND APPEARANCE

Your appearance enables the client to make an initial judgement about both you and the salon, so make sure that you create the correct impression! Employees in the workplace should always reflect the desired image of the profession that they work in.

HEALTH AND SAFETY

Using fire extinguishers
The vapours emitted when using vaporising liquid extinguishers 'starve' a fire of oxygen. They are therefore dangerous when used in confined spaces, as people need oxygen too!

ACTIVITY

Causes of fires
Can you think of several potential causes of fire in the salon? How could each of these be prevented?

Dream Workwear

Dream Workwear

Professional appearance

Assistant therapist

The assistant therapist qualified to Level 1 will be required to wear a clean protective overall as they will be preparing the working area for client treatments, and they may be involved in preparing clients also.

Beauty therapist

Due to the nature of many of the services offered, the beauty therapist must wear protective, hygienic clothing. The cotton overall is ideal; air can circulate, allowing perspiration to evaporate and discouraging body odour. The use of a colour such as white immediately shows the client that you are clean. A cotton overall may comprise a dress, a jumpsuit or a tunic top, with coordinating trousers.

Overalls should be laundered regularly, and a fresh, clean overall worn each day.

Receptionist

If a receptionist is employed solely to carry out reception duties, she may wear a different salon dress, complementary to those worn by the practising therapists. As she will not be as active, it may be appropriate for her to wear a smart jacket or cardigan. If on the other hand she is also carrying out services at some times, the standard salon overall must be worn.

General rules for employees

Make-up

Wear an attractive make-up, and use the correct skin-care cosmetics to suit your skin type. A healthy complexion will be a positive advertisement for your work.

HEALTH AND SAFETY ✚

Aprons and The Personal Protective Equipment (PPE) at Work Regulations 1992
For certain treatments, such as waxing, it is necessary to wear a protective apron over the overall. Assistant therapists may wear an apron whilst preparing and cleaning the working area, to protect the overall and keep it clean.

ACTIVITY

Personal Appearance
1 Collect pictures from various suppliers of overalls. Select those that you feel would be most practical for an assistant therapist and for a Level 2 beauty therapist. Briefly describe why you feel these are the most suitable.
2 Design various hairstyles, or collect pictures from magazines, to show how the hair could be smartly worn by a therapist with medium-length to long hair.

Jewellery

Keep jewellery to a minimum, such as a wedding ring, a watch, and small earrings.

Nails

Nails should be short, neatly manicured, and free of nail polish unless the employee's main duties involve nail treatments or reception duties. Flesh-coloured tights may be worn to protect the legs.

Shoes

Wear flat, well-fitting, comfortable shoes that enclose the feet and which complement the overall. Remember that you will be on your feet for most of the day!

Ethics

Beauty therapy has a **code of ethics**. Although not a legal requirement, this code may be used in criminal proceedings as evidence of improper practice.

Diet, exercise and sleep

A beauty therapist requires stamina and energy. To achieve this you need to eat a healthy, well-balanced diet, take regular exercise, and have adequate sleep.

Posture

Posture is the way you hold yourself when standing, sitting and walking. *Correct* posture enables you to work longer without becoming tired; it prevents muscle fatigue and stiff joints; and it improves your appearance.

Good standing posture

If you are standing with good posture, this will describe you:

- head up, centrally balanced;
- shoulders slightly back, and relaxed;
- chest up and out;

ACTIVITY

Code of ethics
As a professional beauty therapist it is important that you adhere to a code of ethical practice. You may wish to join a professional organisation, which will issue you with a copy of its agreed standards.

ACTIVITY

Building stamina
Ask your tutor for guidelines before beginning this activity.
1 Write down all the foods and drinks that you most enjoy. Are they healthy? If you are unsure, ask your tutor.
2 How much exercise do you take weekly?
3 How much sleep do you regularly have each night?
4 Do you think you could improve your health and fitness levels?

- abdomen flat;
- hips level;
- fingertips level;
- bottom in;
- knees level;
- feet slightly apart, and weight evenly distributed.

Good sitting posture

Sit on a suitable chair or stool with a good back support:

- sit with the lower back pressed against the chair back;
- keep the chest up and the shoulders back;
- distribute the body weight evenly along the thighs;
- keep the feet together, and flat on the floor;
- do not slouch, or sit on the edge of your seat.

Personal hygiene

It is vital that you have a high standard of personal **hygiene**. You are going to be working in close proximity with people.

Bodily cleanliness is achieved through daily showering or bathing. This removes stale sweat, dirt and bacteria which cause body odour. An anti-perspirant or deodorant may be applied to the underarm area to reduce perspiration and thus the smell of sweat.

Clean underwear should be worn each day.

Hands

Your hands and everything you touch are covered with germs. Although most are harmless, some can cause ill health or disease. Wash your hands regularly, especially after you have been to the toilet and before eating food. You must also wash your hands before and after treating each client, and during treatment if necessary. Washing the hands before treating a client minimises the risk of cross-infection, and presents to the client a hygienic, professional, caring image.

HEALTH AND SAFETY	

Soap and towels
Wash your hands with liquid soap from a sealed dispenser. Don't refill disposable soap dispensers when empty: if you do they will become a breeding ground for bacteria.
Disposable paper towels or warm-air hand dryers should be used to dry the hands.

Feet

Keep your feet fresh and healthy by washing them daily and then drying them thoroughly. Deodorising foot powder may then be applied.

ACTIVITY

The importance of posture
1 Which treatments will be performed sitting, and which standing?
2 In what way do you feel your treatments would be affected if you were not sitting or standing correctly?

ACTIVITY

Hand hygiene
What further occasions can you think of when it will be necessary to wash your hands when treating a client?

Teeth

Avoid bad breath by brushing your teeth at least twice daily and flossing the teeth frequently. Use breath fresheners and mouthwashes as required to freshen your breath. Visit the dentist regularly, to maintain healthy teeth and gums.

Hair

Your hair should be clean and tidy. Have your hair cut regularly, and shampoo and condition your hair as often as needed.

If your hair is long, wear it off the face, and taken to the crown of the head. Medium-length hair should be clipped back, away from the face, to prevent it falling forwards.

Hygiene in the workplace

Infections

Effective hygiene is necessary in the salon to prevent *cross-infection* and *secondary infection*. These can occur through poor practice, such as the use of implements that are not sterile. Infection can be recognised by the skin being red and inflamed, or pus being present.

Cross-infection occurs because some micro-organisms are contagious – they may be transferred through personal contact or by contact with an infected instrument that has not been sterilised. **Secondary infection** can occur as a result of injury to the client during the treatment, or if the client already has an open cut, if bacteria penetrate the skin and cause infection. **Sterilisation** and **sanitisation** procedures (below) are used to minimise or destroy the harmful micro-organisms which could cause infection – bacteria, viruses and fungi.

Infectious diseases that are contagious **contra-indicate** beauty treatment: they require medical attention. People with certain other skin disorders, even though these are not contagious, should likewise not be treated by the beauty therapist, as treatment might lead to secondary infection.

Sterilisation and sanitisation

Sterilisation is the total destruction of all living micro-organisms.
Sanitisation is the destruction of some, but not all, micro-organisms.

HEALTH AND SAFETY ✚

Sterilisation Record
Ultraviolet light is dangerous, especially to the eyes. The lamp must be switched off before opening the cabinet. A record must be kept of usage, as the effectiveness of the lamp decreases with use.

Sterilisation and sanitisation techniques practised in the beauty salon involve the use of *physical* agents, such as radiation and heat; and *chemical* agents, such as antiseptics, disinfectants and vapour fumigants.

Radiation A quartz mercury-vapour lamp can be used as the source for **ultraviolet light**, which destroys micro-organisms. The object to be sanitised must be turned regularly so that the UV light reaches all surfaces. (UV light has limited effectiveness, and cannot be relied upon for sterilisation.)

The UV lamp must be contained within a closed cabinet. This cabinet is an ideal place for storing sterilised objects.

An ultraviolet light cabinet

An autoclave

Sterilisation tray with liquid

Heat Dry and moist heat may both be used in sterilisation. One method is to use a dry **hot-air oven**. This is similar to a small oven, and heats to 150–180°C. It is seldom used in the salon.

More practical is a **glass-bead steriliser**. This is a small electrically-heated unit which contains glass beads: these transfer heat to objects placed in contact with them. This method of sterilisation is suitable for small tools such as tweezers and scissors.

Water is boiled in an **autoclave** (similar to a pressure cooker): because of the increased pressure, the water reaches a temperature of 121–134°C. Autoclaving is the most effective method for sterilising objects in the salon.

HEALTH AND SAFETY ✚

Using an autoclave
- Not all objects can safely be placed in the autoclave. Before using this method, check whether the items you wish to sterilise can withstand this heating process.
- To avoid damaging the autoclave, always use distilled de-ionised water.
- To avoid rusting, metal objects placed in the sterilising unit must be of good-quality stainless steel.

Gases Gases used in sterilising include **ethylene oxide** and **formaldehyde**. These chemicals are hazardous to handle, however, and are therefore unpopular.

Disinfectants and antiseptics If an object *cannot* be sterilised, it should be placed in a chemical **disinfectant** solution such as **quaternary ammonium compounds (quats)** or **glutaraldehyde**. A disinfectant destroys most micro-organisms, but not all. Hypochlorite is a disinfectant – bleach is an example of a hypochlorite. Hypochlorite is particularly corrosive and unsuitable for use with metals – use as directed by the manufacturer.

An **antiseptic** prevents the multiplication of micro-organisms. It has a limited action, and does not kill all micro-organisms. Because it is milder than a disinfectant, it can be used directly on the skin.

All sterilisation techniques must be carried out safely and effectively:

1 Select the appropriate method of sterilisation for the object. *Always* follow the manufacturer's guidelines on the use of the sterilising unit or agent.
2 Clean the object in clean water and detergent to remove dirt and grease. (Dirt left on the object may prevent effective sterilisation.)
3 Dry it thoroughly with a clean, disposable paper towel.
4 Sterilise the object, allowing sufficient time for the process to be completed.
5 Place tools that have been sterilised in a clean, covered container.

Keep several sets of the tools you use regularly, so that you can carry out effective sterilisation.

General salon hygiene rules

- *Health and safety* Follow the health and safety policies for the workplace.
- *Personal hygiene* Maintain a high standard of personal hygiene. Wash your hands with a detergent containing **chlorhexidine**.
- *Cuts on the hands* Always cover any cuts on your hands.
- *Cross-infection* Take great care to avoid cross-infection in the salon. *Never* treat a client who has a contagious skin disease or disorder, or any other contra-indication.
- *Use hygienic tools* Never use an implement unless it has been effectively sterilised or sanitised, as appropriate.
- *Disposable products* Wherever possible, use disposable products.
- *Working surfaces* Clean all working surfaces (such as trolleys and couches) with a chlorine preparation, diluted to the manufacturer's instructions. Cover all working surfaces with clean, disposable paper tissue.
- *Gowns and towels* Clean gowns and towels must be provided for each client.
- *Laundry* Dirty laundry should be placed in a covered container.
- *Hazardous waste* Must be disposed of following the COSHH procedures and training by the employer.

HEALTH AND SAFETY

Using disinfectant
Disinfectant solutions should be changed as necessary.
After removing the object from the disinfectant, rinse it in clean water to remove traces of the solution. (These might otherwise cause an allergic reaction on the client's skin.)

TIP

Before sterilisation, surgical spirit may be used to clean small objects.

HEALTH AND SAFETY

Damaged equipment
Any equipment in poor repair must be repaired or disposed of. Such equipment may be dangerous and may harbour germs.

HEALTH AND SAFETY

Cuts on the hands
Open, uncovered cuts provide an easy entry for harmful bacteria, and may lead to infection. Always cover cuts.

HEALTH AND SAFETY

Using chemical agents
Always protect your hands with gloves before immersing them in chemical cleaning agents, to minimise the risk of an allergic reaction.

- *Waste* Put waste in a suitable container lined with a disposable waste bag. A yellow **'sharps' container** should be available for waste contaminated with blood or tissue fluid.
- *Eating and drinking* Never eat or drink in the treatment area of the salon. Not only is it unprofessional, but also harmful chemicals may be ingested.
- *Smoking* Never smoke in the treatment area of the salon or other prohibited areas.
- Never carry out treatments in the workplace under the influence of drugs or alcohol. Your competence will be affected putting both yourself, clients and possibly colleagues at risk.

SKIN DISEASES AND DISORDERS

The beauty therapist must be able to distinguish a healthy skin from one suffering from any skin disease or disorder. Certain skin disorders and diseases **contra-indicate** a beauty treatment: the treatment would expose the therapist and other clients to the risk of cross-infection. It is therefore vital that you are familiar with the skin diseases and disorders with which you may come into contact in the workplace.

Bacterial infections

Bacteria are minute single-celled organisms of varied shapes. Large numbers of bacteria inhabit the surface of the skin and are harmless (**non-pathogenic**); indeed some play an important positive role in the health of the skin. Others, however, are harmful (**pathogenic**) and can cause skin diseases.

Impetigo

An inflammatory disease of the surface of the skin.

Infectious? Yes.

Appearance: Initially the skin appears red and is itchy. Small thin-walled blisters appear; these burst and form into crusts.

Site: The commonly affected areas are the nose, the mouth and the ears, but impetigo can occur on the scalp or the limbs.

Treatment: Medical – usually an antibiotic or an antibacterial ointment is prescribed.

Conjunctivitis or pink eye

Inflammation of the mucous membrane that covers the eye and lines the eyelids.

Infectious? Yes.

Appearance: The skin of the inner conjunctiva of the eye becomes inflamed, the eye becomes very red and sore, and pus may exude from the area.

Site: The eyes, either one or both, may be infected.

Treatment: Medical – usually an antibiotic lotion is prescribed.

Dr M. H. Beck

Impetigo

Hordeola or styes

Infection of the sebaceous glands of eyelash hair follicles.

Infectious? Yes.

Appearance: Small lumps containing pus.

Site: The inner rim of the eyelid.

Treatment: Medical – usually an antibiotic is prescribed.

Furuncles or boils

Red, painful lumps, extending deeply into the skin.

Infectious? Yes.

Appearance: A localised red lump occurs around a hair follicle; it then develops a core of pus. Scarring of the skin often remains after the boil has healed.

Site: The back of the neck, the ankles and the wrists.

Treatment: Medical.

Carbuncles

Infection of numerous hair follicles.

Infectious? Yes.

Appearance: A hard, round abscess, larger than a boil, which oozes pus from several points upon its surface. Scarring often occurs after the carbuncle has healed.

Site: The back of the neck.

Treatment: Medical – usually involving incision, drainage of the pus, and a course of antibiotics.

Paronychia

Infection of the tissue surrounding the nail.

Infectious? Yes.

Appearance: Swelling, redness and pus in the cuticle and in the area of the nail wall.

Site: The cuticle and the skin surrounding the nail.

Treatment: Medical.

Viral infections

Viruses are minute entities, too small to see even under an ordinary microscope. They are considered to be **parasites**, as they require living tissue in order to survive. Viruses invade healthy body cells and multiply within the cell: in due course the cell walls break down, liberating new viral particles to attack further cells, and thus the infection spreads.

HEALTH AND SAFETY

Boils
Boils occurring on the upper lip or in the nose should be referred immediately to a physician. Boils can be dangerous when near to the eyes or brain.

Dr A. L Wright

Boil

Dr M. H. Beck

Herpes Simplex

Herpes simplex

This is a recurring skin condition, appearing at times when the skin's resistance is lowered through ill health or stress. It may also be caused by exposure of the skin to extremes of temperature or to ultraviolet light.

Infectious? Yes.

Appearance: Inflammation of the skin occurs in localised areas. As well as being red, the skin becomes itchy and small vesicles appear. These are followed by a crust, which may crack and weep tissue fluid.

Site: The mucous membranes of the nose or lips; herpes can also occur on the skin generally.

Treatment: There is no specific treatment. A proprietary brand of anti-inflammatory antiseptic drying cream is usually prescribed.

Herpes zoster or shingles

In this painful disease, the virus attacks the sensory nerve endings. The virus is thought to lie dormant in the body and be triggered when the body's defences are at a low ebb.

Infectious? Yes.

Appearance: Redness of the skin occurs along the line of the affected nerves. Blisters develop and form crusts, leaving purplish-pink pigmentation.

Site: Commonly the chest and the abdomen.

Treatment: Medical – usually including antibiotics. Any lasting pigmentation may be camouflaged with cosmetics.

Dr A. L Wright

Verucca – plantar warts

Verrucae or warts

Small epidermal skin growths. Warts may be raised or flat, depending upon their position. There are several types of wart: plane, common, and plantar.

Infectious? Yes.

Appearance: Warts vary in size, shape, texture and colour. Usually they have a rough surface and are raised. If the wart occurs on the sole of the foot it grows inwards, due to the pressure of body weight.

Site:
- plane wart: the fingers, either surface of the hand, or the knees;
- common wart: the face or hands;
- plantar wart: the sole of the foot.

Treatment: Medical – using acids, solid carbon dioxide, or electrocautery.

Dr M. H. Beck

Infestations

Scabies or itch mites

A condition in which an animal parasite burrows beneath the skin and invades the hair follicles.

Infectious? Yes.

A wart

Appearance: At the onset, minute papules and wavy greyish lines appear, where dirt has entered the burrows. Secondary bacterial infection may occur as a result of scratching.

Site: Usually seen in warm areas of loose skin, such as the webs of the fingers, and the creases of the elbows.

Treatment: Medical – an anti-scabetic lotion.

Dr M. H. Beck

A scabies burrow

Pediculosis capitis or head lice

A condition in which small parasites infest scalp hair.

Infectious? Yes.

Appearance: The lice cling to the hair of the scalp. Eggs are laid, attached to the hair close to the skin. The lice bite the skin to draw nourishment from the blood; this creates irritation and itching of the skin, which may lead to secondary bacterial infection.

Site: The hair of the scalp.

Treatment: Medical – an appropriate lotion.

Pediculosis pubis

A condition in which small parasites infest body hair.

Infectious? Yes.

Appearance: The lice cling to the hair of the body. Eggs are laid, attached to the hair close to the skin. The lice bite the skin to draw nourishment from the blood; this creates irritation and itching of the skin, which may lead to secondary bacterial infection.

Site: Pubic hair, eyebrows and eyelashes.

Treatment: Medical – an appropriate lotion.

Pediculosis corporis

A condition in which small parasites live and feed on body skin.

Infectious? Yes.

Appearance: The lice cling to the hair of the body. Eggs are laid, attached to the hair close to the skin. The lice bite the skin to draw nourishment from the blood; this creates irritation and itching of the skin, which may lead to secondary bacterial infection. Where body lice bite the skin, small red marks can be seen.

Site: Body hair.

Treatment: Medical – an appropriate lotion.

Fungal diseases

Fungi are microscopic plants. They are parasites, dependent upon a host for their existence. Fungal diseases of the skin feed off the waste products of the skin. Some fungi are found on the skin's surface; others attack the deeper tissues. Reproduction of fungi is by means of simple cell division or by the production of spores.

Dr A. L Wright

Tinea pedis

Dr A. L Wright

Tinea corporis

Tinea pedis or athlete's foot

A common fungal foot infection.

Infectious? Yes.

Appearance: Small blisters form, which later burst. The skin in the area can then become dry, giving a scaly appearance.

Site: The webs of skin between the toes.

Treatment: Thorough cleansing of the area. Medical application of fungicides.

Tinea corporis or body ringworm

A fungal infection of the skin.

Infectious? Yes.

Appearance: Small scaly red patches, which spread outwards and then heal from the centre, leaving a ring.

Site: The trunk of the body, the limbs and the face.

Treatment: Medical – using a fungicidal cream, griseofluvin.

Tinea unguium

Ringworm infection of the fingernails.

Infectious? Yes.

Appearance: The nail plate is yellowish-grey. Eventually the nail plate becomes brittle and separates from the nail bed.

Site: The nail plates of the fingers.

Treatment: Medical application of fungicides.

Sebaceous gland disorders

Milia

Keratinisation of the skin over the hair follicle occurs, causing sebum to accumulate in the hair follicle. This condition usually accompanies dry skin.

Infectious? No.

Appearance: Small, hard, pearly-white cysts.

Site: The upper face or close to the eyes.

Treatment: The milium may be removed by the beauty therapist or by a physician, depending on the location. A sterile needle is used to pierce the skin of the overlying cuticle and thereby free the milium.

Dr A. L Wright

Comedones or blackheads

Comedones or blackheads

Excess sebum and keratinised cells block the mouth of the hair follicle.

Infectious? No.

Site: The face (the chin, nose and forehead), the upper back and chest.

Treatment: The area should be cleansed, and an electrical vapour treatment or other pre-heating treatment should be given to relax the mouth of the hair follicle; a sterile comedo extractor should then be used to remove the blockage. A regular cleansing treatment should be recommended by the beauty therapist to limit the production of comedones.

Seborrhoea

Excessive secretion of sebum from the sebaceous gland. This usually occurs during puberty, as a result of hormonal changes in the body.

Infectious? No.

Appearance: The follicle openings enlarge and excessive sebum is secreted. The skin appears coarse and greasy; comedones, pustules and papules are present.

Site: The face and scalp. Seborrhoea may also affect the back and the chest.

Treatment: The area should be cleansed to remove excess grease. Medical treatment may be required – this would use locally applied creams.

Steatomas, sebaceous cysts or wens

Localised pockets or sacs of sebum, which form in hair follicles or under the sebaceous glands in the skin. The sebum becomes blocked, the sebaceous gland becomes distended, and a lump forms.

Infectious? No.

Appearance: Semi-globular in shape, either raised or flat, and hard or soft. The cysts are the same colour as the skin, or red if secondary bacterial infection occurs. A comedo can often be seen at the original mouth of the hair follicle.

Site: If the cyst appears on the upper eyelid, it is known as a **chalazion** or **meibomian cyst**.

Treatment: Medical – often a physician will remove the cyst under local anaesthetic.

Acne vulgaris

Hormone imbalance in the body at puberty influences the activity of the sebaceous gland, causing an increased production of sebum. The sebum may be retained within the sebaceous ducts, causing congestion and bacterial infection of the surrounding tissues.

Infectious? No.

Appearance: Inflammation of the skin, accompanied by comedones, pustules and papules.

Site: Commonly on the face, on the nose, the chin and the forehead. Acne may also occur on the chest and back.

Treatment: Medical – oral antibiotics may be prescribed, as well as medicated creams. With medical approval, regular salon treatments may be given to cleanse the skin deeply, and also to stimulate the blood circulation.

Dr M. H. Beck

Acne vulgaris

Acne rosacea

Acne rosacea

Excessive sebum secretion combined with a chronic inflammatory condition, caused by dilation of the blood capillaries.

Infectious? No.

Appearance: The skin becomes coarse, the pores enlarge, and the cheek and nose area become inflamed, sometimes swelling and producing a butterfly pattern. Blood circulation slows in the dilated capillaries, creating a purplish appearance.

Treatment: Medical – usually including antibiotics.

Pigmentation disorders

Pigmentation of the skin varies, according to the person's genetic characteristics. In general the darker the skin, the more pigment is present, but some abnormal changes in skin pigmentation can occur.

- **hyperpigmentation** – increased pigment production;
- **hypopigmentation** – loss of pigmentation in the skin.

TIP

Hypopigmentation may result from certain skin injuries, disorders or diseases.

Ephelides or freckles

Multiple small pigmented areas of the skin. Exposure to ultra-violet light (as in sunlight) stimulates the production of melanin, intensifying their appearance.

Infectious? No.

Appearance: Small, flat, pigmented areas, darker than the surrounding skin.

Site: Commonly the nose and cheeks of fair-skinned people. Freckles may also occur on the shoulders, arms, hands and back.

Treatment: Freckles may be concealed with cosmetics if required. A sun block should be recommended, to prevent them intensifying in colour.

Lentigines

Pigmented areas of skin, slightly larger than freckles, which do not darken on exposure to ultra-violet.

Infectious? No.

Appearance: Brown, slightly raised, pigmented patches of skin.

Site: The face and hands.

Treatment: Application of cosmetic concealing products.

Chloasmata or liver spots

Increased skin pigmentation in specific areas, stimulated by a skin irritant such as ultraviolet. The condition often occurs during pregnancy, and usually disappears soon after the birth of the baby. It may also occur as a result of taking oral contraceptive pills. The female hormone oestrogen is thought to stimulate melanin production.

Infectious? No.

Appearance: Flat, smooth, irregularly shaped, pigmented areas of skin, varying in colour from light tan to dark brown. Chloasmata are larger than ephelides, and of variable size.

Site: The back of the hands, the forearms, the upper part of the chest, the temples and the forehead.

Treatment: A barrier cream or a total sun block will reduce the risk of the chloasmata increasing in size or number, and thereby becoming more apparent.

Dermatosis Papulosa Nigra

Often called flesh moles, this is characterised by multiple benign, small brown to black hyperpigmented papules, common among black skinned people.

Infectious? No.

Appearance: Raised pigmented markings resembling moles.

Site: Usually seen on the cheeks and forehead, although they may appear on the neck, upper chest and back.

Treatment: Medical by drug therapy or surgery.

Vitiligo or leucoderma

Patches of completely white skin which have lost their pigment, or which were never pigmented.

Infectious? No.

Appearance: Well defined patches of white skin, lacking pigment.

Site: The face, the neck, the hands, the lower abdomen, and the thighs. If vitiligo occurs over the eyebrows, the hairs in the area will lose their pigment also.

Treatment: Camouflage cosmetic concealer can be applied to give even skin colour; or skin-staining preparations can be used in the de-pigmented areas. Care must be taken when the skin is exposed to ultra-violet light, as the skin will not have the same protection in the areas lacking pigment.

Dr M. H. Beck

Vitiligo

Albinism

The skin is unable to produce the melanin pigment, and the skin, hair and eyes lack colour.

Infectious? No.

Appearance: The skin is usually very pale pink and the hair is white. The eyes also are pink, and extremely sensitive to light.

Site: The entire skin.

Treatment: There is no effective treatment. Maximum skin protection is necessary when the client is exposed to ultraviolet light, and sunglasses should be worn to protect the eyes.

Vascular naevi

There are two types of naevus of concern to beauty therapists: vascular and cellular. **Vascular naevi** are skin conditions in which small or large areas of skin pigmentation are caused by the permanent dilation of blood capillaries.

TIP	

If there is a vascular skin disorder, avoid overstimulating the skin or the problem will become more noticeable and the treatment may even cause further damage.

Erythema

An area of skin in which blood capillaries have dilated, due either to injury or inflammation.

Infectious? No.

Appearance: The skin appears red.

Site: Erythema may affect one area (locally) or all of the skin (generally).

Treatment: The cause of the inflammation should be identified. In the case of a skin allergy, the client must not be brought into contact with the irritant again. If the cause is unknown, refer the client to their physician.

Dilated capillaries

Capillaries near the surface of the skin that are permanently dilated.

Infectious? No.

Appearance: Small red visible blood capillaries.

Site: Areas where the skin is neglected, dry or fine, such as the cheek area.

Treatment: Dilated capillaries can be concealed using a green corrective camouflage cosmetic, or removed by a qualified electrologist using diathermy.

Spider naevus

Spider naevi or stellate haemangiomas

Dilated blood vessels, with smaller dilated capillaries radiating from them.

Infectious? No.

Appearance: Small red capillaries, radiating like a spider's legs from a central point.

Site: Commonly the cheek area, but may occur on the upper body, the arms and the neck. Spider naevi are usually caused by an injury to the skin.

Treatment: Spider naevi can be concealed using a camouflage cosmetic, or treated by a qualified electrologist with diathermy.

Benign pigmented naevus

Naevi vasculosis or strawberry marks

Red or purplish raised marks which appear on the skin at birth.

Infectious? No.

Appearance: Red or purplish lobed mark, of any size.

Site: Any area of the skin.

Treatment: About 60 per cent disappear by the age of 6 years. Treatment is not usually necessary; concealing cosmetics can be applied if desired.

Strawberry naevus

Capillary naevi or port-wine stains

Large areas of dilated capillaries, which contrast noticeably with the surrounding areas.

Infectious? No.

Appearance: The naevus has a smooth, flat surface.

Site: Some 75 per cent occur on the head; they are probably formed at the foetal stage. Naevi may also be found on the neck and face.

Treatment: Camouflage cosmetic creams can be applied to disguise the area.

Cellular naevi or moles

Cellular naevi are skin conditions in which changes in the cells of the skin result in skin malformations.

Malignant melanomas or malignant moles

Rapidly-growing skin cancers, usually occurring in adults.

Infectious? No.

Appearance: Each melanoma commences as a bluish-black mole, which enlarges rapidly, darkening in colour and developing a halo of pigmentation around it. It later becomes raised, bleeds, and ulcerates. Secondary growths will develop in internal organs, if the melanoma is not treated.

Site: Usually the lower abdomen, legs or feet.

Treatment: Medical – *always* recommend that a client has any mole checked if it is changing in size, structure or colour, or if it becomes itchy or bleeds.

Dr M. H. Beck

Malignant melanoma

HEALTH AND SAFETY

Moles
If moles change in shape or size, if they bleed or form crusts, seek medical attention.

Junction naevi

Localised collections of naevoid cells that arise from the mass production locally of pigment-forming cells (melanocytes).

Infectious? No.

Appearance: In childhood junction naevi appear as smooth or slightly raised pigmented marks. They vary in colour from brown to black.

Site: Any area.

Treatment: None.

Dermal naevi

Localised collections of naevoid cells.

Infectious? No.

Appearance: About 1cm wide, dermal naevi appear smooth and dome-shaped. Their colour ranges from skin tone to dark brown. Frequently one or more hairs may grow from the naevus.

Site: Usually the face.

Treatment: None.

Hairy naevi

Moles exhibiting coarse hairs from their surface.

Infectious? No.

Appearance: Slightly raised moles, varying in size from 3cm to much larger areas. Colour ranges from fawn to dark brown.

Site: Anywhere on the skin.

Treatment: Hairy naevi may be surgically removed where possible, and this is often done for cosmetic reasons. Hair growing from a mole should be cut, not plucked: if plucked, the hairs will become coarser and the growth of further hairs may be stimulated.

Dr M. H. Beck

Psoriasis

Skin disorders involving abnormal growth

Psoriasis

Patches of itchy, red, flaky skin, the cause of which is unknown.

Infectious? No. Secondary infection with bacteria can occur if the skin becomes broken and dirt enters the skin.

Appearance: Red patches of skin appear, covered in waxy, silvery scales. Bleeding will occur if the area is scratched and scales are removed.

Site: The elbows, the knees, the lower back and the scalp.

Treatment: There is no known treatment. Medication including steroid creams can bring relief to the symptoms.

Seborrheic or senile warts

Raised, pigmented, benign tumours occurring in middle age.

Infectious? No.

Appearance: Slightly raised, brown or black, rough patches of skin. Such warts can be confused with pigmented moles.

Site: The trunk, the scalp, and the temples.

Treatment: Medical – the warts can be cauterised by a physician.

Verrucae filliformis or skin tags

These verrucas appear as threads projecting from the skin.

Infectious? No.

Appearance: Skin-coloured threads of skin 3–6mm long.

Site: Mainly seen on the neck and the eyelids, but may occur in other areas such as under the arms.

Treatment: Medical – cauterisation with diathermy, either by a physician or by a qualified electrologist.

HEALTH AND SAFETY ✚

Skin Tags
Skin tags often occur under the arms. In case they are present, take care when carrying out a wax depilation treatment in this area: do not apply wax over tags.

Xanthomas

Small yellow growths appearing upon the surface of the skin.

Infectious? No.

Appearance: A yellow, flat or raised area of skin.

Site: The eyelids.

Treatment: Medical – the growth is thought to be connected with certain medical diseases, such as diabetes or high or low blood pressure; sometimes a low-fat diet can correct the condition.

Keloids

Keloids occur following skin injury and are overgrown abnormal scar tissue which spreads, characterised by excess deposits of collagen. To avoid skin discolouration the keloid must be protected from UV exposure.

Infectious? No.

Dr John Gray

Keloids

Appearance: The skin tends to be red, raised and ridged

Site: Located over the site of a wound or other lesion

Treatment: Medical by drug therapy or surgery.

Malignant tumours

Squamous cell carcinomas or prickle-cell cancers

Malignant growths originating in the epidermis.

Infectious: No.

Appearance: When fully formed, the carcinoma appears as a raised area of skin.

Site: Anywhere on the skin.

Treatment: Medical – by radiation.

Dr A. L. Wright

Squamous cell carcinoma

Basal-cell carcinomas or rodent ulcers

Slow-growing malignant tumours, occurring in middle age.

Infectious? No.

Appearance: A small, shiny, waxy nodule with a depressed centre. The disease extends, with more nodules appearing on the border of the original ulcer.

Site: Usually the face.

Treatment: Medical.

Dr A. L. Wright

Basal cell carcinoma

Skin allergies

The skin can protect itself to some degree from damage or invasion. **Mast cells** detect damage to the skin; if damage occurs, the mast cells burst, releasing the chemical **histamine** into the tissues. Histamine causes the blood capillaries to dilate, giving the reddening we call 'erythema'. The increased blood flow transports materials in the blood which tend to limit the damage and begin repair.

If the skin is sensitive to and becomes inflamed on contact with a particular substance, this substance is called an **allergen**. Allergens may be animal, chemical or vegetable substances, and they may be inhaled, eaten, or absorbed following contact with the skin. An **allergic skin reaction** appears as irritation, itching and discomfort, with reddening and swelling (as with nettle rash). If the allergen is removed, the allergic reaction subsides.

Each individual has different tolerances to the various substances we encounter in daily life. What causes an allergic reaction in one individual may be perfectly harmless to another.

Here are just a few examples of allergens known to cause allergic skin reactions in some people:

- metal objects containing nickel;
- sticking plaster;
- rubber;

HEALTH AND SAFETY

Record any known allergies
When completing the client record card, always ask whether your client has any known allergies.

HEALTH AND SAFETY +

Hypoallergenic products
The use of hypoallergenic products minimises the risk of skin contact with likely irritants.

HEALTH AND SAFETY

Allergies
You may suddenly become allergic to a substance that has previously been perfectly harmless. Equally, you may over time cease to be allergic to something.

- lipstick containing eosin dye;
- nail polish containing formaldehyde resin;
- hair and eyelash dyes;
- lanolin, the skin moisturising agent;
- detergents that dry the skin;
- foods – well-known examples are peanuts, cow's milk, lobster, shellfish, and strawberries;
- plants such as tulips and chrysanthemums.

HEALTH AND SAFETY

Infection following allergy
Following an allergic skin reaction in which the skin's surface has become itchy and broken, scratching may cause the skin to become infected with bacteria.

Dermatitis

An inflammatory skin disorder in which the skin becomes red, itchy and swollen. There are two types of dermatitis. In *primary dermatitis* the skin is irritated by the action of a substance upon the skin, and this leads to skin inflammation. In *allergic contact dermatitis* the problem is caused by intolerance of the skin to a particular substance or group of substances. On exposure to the substance the skin quickly becomes irritated and an allergic reaction occurs.

Infectious? No.

Appearance: Reddening and swelling of the skin, with the possible appearance of blisters.

Site: If the skin reacts to a skin irritant outside the body, the reaction is localised. Repeated contact with the allergen will lead to a general hypersensitivity. If the irritant gains entry to the body it will be transported in the bloodstream and may cause a general allergic skin reaction.

Treatment: Barrier cream can be used to help avoid contact with the irritants. When an allergic dermatitis reaction occurs, however, the only 'cure' is the absolute avoidance of the substance. Steroid creams such as hydrocortisone are usually prescribed, to sooth the damaged skin and reduce the irritation.

Allergic contact dermatitis

Eczema

Inflammation of the skin caused by contact, internally or externally, with an irritant.

Infectious? No.

Appearance: Reddening of the skin, with swelling and blisters. The blisters leak tissue fluid which later hardens, forming scabs.

Site: The face, the neck and the skin, particularly at the inner creases of the elbows and behind the knees.

Dr M. H. Beck

Dr A. L. Wright

Eczema

Treatment: Refer the client to their physician. Eczema may disappear if the source of irritation is identified and removed. Steroid cream may be prescribed by the physician, and special diets may help.

Urticaria (nettle rash) or hives

A minor skin disorder caused by contact with an allergen, either internally (food or drugs) or externally (for example, insect bites).

Infectious? No.

Appearance: Erythema with raised, round whitish skin weals. In some cases the lesions can cause intense burning or itching, a condition known as **pruritis**. Pruritis is a *symptom* of a disease (such as diabetes), not a disease itself.

Site: At the point of contact.

Treatment: Antihistamines may be prescribed to reduce the itching. The visible skin reaction usually disappears quickly, leaving no trace. Complete avoidance of the allergen 'cures' the problem.

Dr M. H. Beck

Urticaria

Assessment of knowledge and understanding

You have now learnt about the health and safety responsibilities for everyone in the workplace. This will enable you to ensure your own actions reduce risks to health and safety.

To test your level of knowledge, answer the following short questions. These will prepare you for your summative (final) assessment.

Action to avoid health and safety risks

1 What are your main legal responsibilities under the Health and Safety at Work Act 1974?

2 What is the purpose of a salon health and safety policy? What sort of information does it include?

3 What is the importance of personal presentation in maintaining health and safety in the salon?

4 Why is your personal conduct important to maintain the health and safety of yourself and colleagues and clients?

5 Why must regular health and safety checks be carried out in the workplace?

6 When completing a client's record card you recognise that treatment is contra-indicated as the client has impetigo, an infectious skin disorder. What action do you take and why?

7 Effective sterilisation methods prevent cross-infection and secondary infection. What do you understand by the following terms?
- sterilisation
- cross-infection
- secondary infection.

8 How should a large box be lifted from floor level to be placed on the work surface?

Dealing with significant risks in your workplace

1 What hazards may exist in the beauty therapy workplace?

2 Why must you always be aware of potential hazards?

3 In your role in the salon, what are the main risks that could occur, and what precautions do you take?

4 Whilst cleaning a wax heater you notice that the wires in the lead are exposed. What action should you take?

5 If you were unable to deal with a risk as it was outside of your responsibility what action would you take?

6 What does the abbreviation COSHH stand for? Why is it important to follow the suppliers' and manufacturers' instructions for the safe use of materials and products?

7 When preparing a trolley for an eyelash tint, you drop and break a bottle of hydrogen peroxide. How would you deal with this spillage? How would you dispose of the broken glass?

Taking the right action in the event of danger

1 What is the procedure for dealing with an accident in the workplace?

2 What is a fire drill? What is the fire evacuation procedure in your salon? How often should this be carried out?

3 In the event of a real fire, after having safely evacuated the building, how would you contact the appropriate emergency service?

4 In reception, you discover a smoking bin, in which the fire has been caused by an un-extinguished cigarette. How should this fire be extinguished?

5 What action should be taken in the event of a bomb alert?

6 The air conditioning system in the salon has broken. Who should be contacted to deal with this? And what would be the potential risk of inadequate ventilation?

chapter 2

FULFIL SALON RECEPTION DUTIES G4

Learning objectives

This chapter covers the skills required to ensure clients are greeted and dealt with efficiently through the salon reception. It describes the competencies to enable you to:

- **maintain the reception area**
- **attend to clients and enquiries**
- **make appointments for salon services**
- **handle payments from clients**

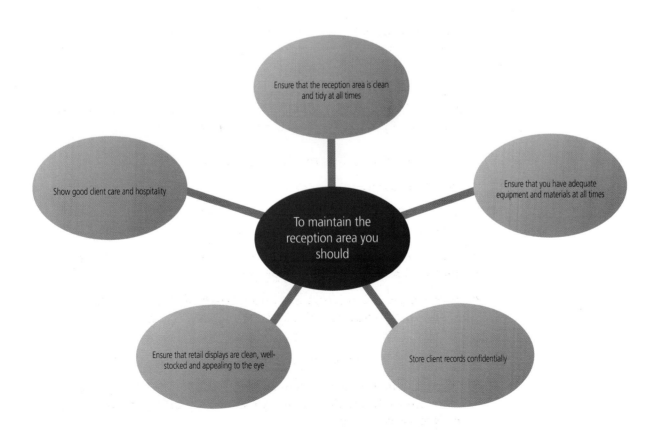

Ensure that the reception area is clean and tidy at all times

Ensure that you have adequate equipment and materials at all times

Show good client care and hospitality

To maintain the reception area you should

Ensure that retail displays are clean, well-stocked and appealing to the eye

Store client records confidentially

RECEIVING CLIENTS

The client's **reception** gives her her first and also her final impression of the salon, whether this is on the telephone or in person when she visits the salon. First impressions count, so ensure that the client gets the *right* impression!

The design of the reception area

Location

Reception is usually situated at the front of a beauty salon; in a large department store, reception may be a cosmetic counter. It should be clean, uncluttered and inviting.

With a salon, the advantage of having reception at the front is that the window can be used to attract and capture the attention and interest of potential clients. Clients who are waiting in reception, however, may seek privacy, so the window should be attractively curtained and the seating should be situated away from the view of the main window if possible.

Size

The entrance to reception should be large enough for wheelchair access. There should be adequate seating, and an area in which to hang clients' coats.

Saks Covent Garden

It may be that small treatments, such as manicures, are carried out at reception. These treatments can then be seen by others, and may attract further clients.

Hospitality is important and shows the salon's commitment to client care. If the client arrives early or is likely to be delayed, offer her a magazine or refreshment such as coffee or water. Magazines should be renewed regularly. It is also a pleasant gesture to have boiled sweets on reception for the client to take.

Smoking

The smoking policy is determined by each salon. If smoking is allowed in reception, adequate ashtrays should be provided. These should be emptied and cleaned after each use.

Decoration

The reception area should be decorated tastefully, in keeping with the décor in the rest of the salon. Attractive posters promoting proprietary cosmetic ranges may be displayed on the walls. Framed certificates of the staff's professional qualifications can be displayed, as well as health-legislation registration certificates.

Equipment

The reception area should be uncluttered. The main equipment and furnishings required for an efficient reception include the following:

- *A reception desk* The size of the desk will depend on the size of the salon; some salons may have several receptionists. The desk should include shelves and drawers; some have an in-built lockable cash or security drawer. The desk should be at a convenient height for the client to write a cheque, etc. It should also be large enough to house the appointment book or computer (or both).
- *A comfortable chair* The receptionist's chair should provide adequate back support.
- *A computer* Computers are becoming more and more popular in the salon as they can perform many functions. They can be used to store data about clients, to keep appointment schedules, to carry out automatic stock control, and to record business details such as accounts and marketing information. They can also be programmed to recommend specific treatments on the basis of personal data about the client!
- *A calculator* This is used for simple financial calculations, especially if the salon does not have a computer.
- *Stationery* This should include price lists, gift vouchers, appointment cards, and a receipt pad.
- *A notepad* This is for taking notes and recording messages.
- *An address and telephone book* This should hold all the frequently-used telephone numbers.

ACTIVITY

Magazines
What magazines do you think would be appropriate for the beauty salon?

TIP

Video facilities in reception may be used to promote salon services. Many suitable videos are available from beauty manufacturers and suppliers.

HEALTH AND SAFETY

Ventilation
To avoid losing the custom of non-smoking clients, ensure that the air is fresh and the room adequately ventilated to remove the smell of stale tobacco.

TIP

Client attention
It is important to give the right amount of attention to all clients according to their specific requirements to ensure client satisfaction. This must always be considered in a busy situation where a client may be kept waiting.

HEALTH AND SAFETY

Eating and drinking
The receptionist and other employees should not eat or drink at reception, nor should they smoke.

TIP

Some salons' price lists are in booklet form, detailing the treatments offered and explaining their benefits.

TIP

Electronic mail (e-mail)
E-mail is a more popular method of telecommunication today and requires a computer. E-mail can only be sent if the other person has a computer with this facility and an e-mail address.

HEALTH AND SAFETY ✚

Contact numbers
Just in case a client should become ill whilst in the salon, a contact number should be recorded on the client's card.

TIP

Visitors to the salon may leave a business card, stating the name of the company, and the representative's name, address and telephone number. These cards should be filed by the receptionist for future reference.

- *A telephone and an answering machine* The answering machine allows clients to notify you, even when the salon is closed, of an appointment request, or an unavoidable change or cancellation: you can then re-schedule appointments as quickly as possible. If you are working on your own, the answering machine avoids interruptions during a treatment, yet without losing custom.

- *A fax* may be available at reception. The fax is capable of transmitting text and image via a telephone line to another fax machine. This is useful when information needs to be passed on quickly.

- *Record cards* These confidential cards record the personal details of each client registered at the salon. They should be kept in alphabetical order in a filing cabinet or a card-index box, and should be ready for collection by the therapist when treating new or existing clients. See the general beauty therapy units of this book for complete unit specific examples of record cards. Each card records:
  - the client's name, address and telephone number;
  - any medical details;
  - any contra-indications (such as allergies and contra-actions);
  - treatment aims and outcomes;
  - a base on which to plan future treatments;
  - services received, products used, and merchandise purchased.

- *Pens, pencils and an eraser* Make sure these stay at the desk!

- *A display cabinet* This may be used to store proprietary skin-care and cosmetic products, and any other merchandise sold by the salon.

A record card

BEAUTY WORKS

Date	Beauty therapist name	
Client name		Date of birth
Address		Postcode
Evening phone number	Day phone number	
Name of doctor	Doctor's address and phone number	

Related medical history (conditions that may restrict or prohibit treatment application)

Are you taking any medication (esp. antibiotics, steriods, the pill)

CONTRA-INDICATIONS REQUIRING MEDICAL REFERRAL
(Preventing facial treatment application)

- ☐ bacterial infection (e.g. impetigo)
- ☐ viral infection (e.g. herpes simplex)
- ☐ fungal infection (e.g. tinea corporis)
- ☐ eye infections (e.g. conjunctivitis)
- watery eyes

CONTRA-INDICATIONS WHICH RESTRICT TREATMENT
(Treatment may require adaption)

- ☐ cuts and abrasians
- ☐ recent scar tissue
- ☐ skin allergies
- ☐ styes
- tery eyes
- ☐ bruising and swelling
- ☐ eczema
- ☐ vitiligo
- ☐ hyper keratosis

ACTIVITY

Designing record cards
Design a card to be used to record the clients' requirements and the treatment details related to NVQ Level 2 treatments.

ACTIVITY

Planning a reception area
Design a reception area, to scale, appropriate to a small or large beauty salon. Discuss the choice of wall and floor coverings, furnishings and equipment, and give the reasons for their selection. Consider clients' comfort, and health and safety.

HEALTH AND SAFETY

Cleaning
In a large salon a cleaner may be employed to maintain the hygiene of the reception area. In a smaller salon this may be the responsibility of an apprentice, the receptionist, or a therapist. Reception must be maintained to a high standard at all times.

DATA PROTECTION ACT 1998

This legislation is designed to protect the client's privacy and confidentiality. It is necessary to ask the client questions before the treatment plan can be finalised.

The relevant information gathered on the client is confidential and should be stored in a secure area following client treatment.

Inform the client that their personal details are being stored and will only be accessed by those individuals who are authorised to do so.

THE RECEPTIONIST

Receptionists should have a smart appearance and be able to communicate effectively and professionally, thereby creating the right impression.

The receptionists' duties include:

- maintaining the reception area:
- looking after clients on arrival and departure;
- scheduling appointments;
- dealing with enquiries;
- telling the appropriate therapist that a client or visitor has arrived;
- assisting with retail sales;
- operating the payment point and handling payments.

TIP

It is a good idea for the receptionist to wear a badge indicating her name and position.

TIP

If you are engaged on the telephone when a client arrives, look up and acknowledge her presence. This is positive body language which makes the client feel welcome.

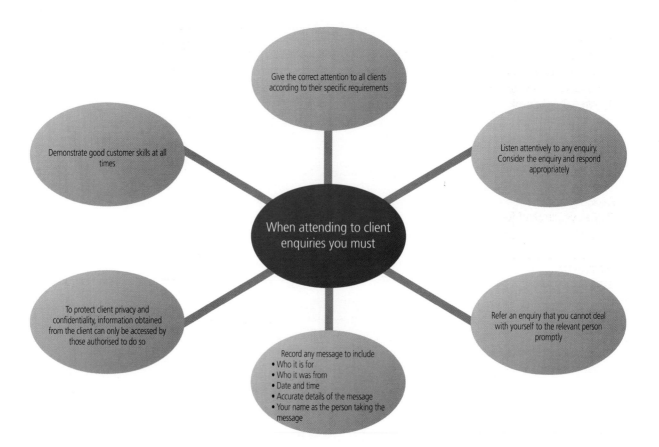

When attending to client enquiries you must

- Give the correct attention to all clients according to their specific requirements
- Listen attentively to any enquiry. Consider the enquiry and respond appropriately
- Refer an enquiry that you cannot deal with yourself to the relevant person promptly
- Record any message to include
  - Who it is for
  - Who it was from
  - Date and time
  - Accurate details of the message
  - Your name as the person taking the message
- To protect client privacy and confidentiality, information obtained from the client can only be accessed by those authorised to do so
- Demonstrate good customer skills at all times

HEALTH AND SAFETY

Fire drill
As the receptionist you should be familiar with the emergency procedure in case of fire.

The receptionist should know:

- the name of each member of staff, her role and her area of responsibility;
- the salon's hours of opening, and the days and times when each therapist is available;
- the range of services or products offered by the salon, and their cost;
- who to refer different types of enquiries to;
- the person in your salon to whom you should refer reception problems;
- any current discounts and special offers that the salon is promoting;
- the benefits of each treatment and each retail product;
- the approximate time taken to complete each treatment;
- how to schedule follow-up treatments.

Qualities of a receptionist

All clients need to feel valued. The following **interpersonal skills** are essential in a receptionist:

- act positively and confidently;
- speak clearly;
- be friendly, and smile;
- look at the customer and maintain eye contact;
- good listening skills;
- be interested in everything that is going on around the reception area;
- give each client individual attention and respect.

ACTIVITY

Reception
Pair with a colleague and share your experiences of a well managed and a badly managed reception.

ACTIVITY

Non-verbal communication
In conversation you give signals that tell others whether you are listening or not.
1 What do you think the following signals indicate?
- A smile.
- Head tilted, and resting on one hand.
- Eyes looking around you.
- Eyes semi-closed.
- Head nodding.
- Fidgeting.
2 Can you think of further body signals that indicate whether you are interested or not?

ACTIVITY

Do's and don'ts
List *five* important do's and *five* don'ts for the receptionist. Think also of things that *should not* be discussed.

Dealing with a dissatisfied client

Occasionally a client may be dissatisfied. The receptionist is usually the first contact with the client, and may have to deal with dissatisfied, angry or awkward customers. Considerable skill is needed if you are to deal constructively with a potentially damaging situation.

Never become angry or awkward yourself. Always remain courteous and diplomatic, and communicate confidently and politely.

1 Listen to the client as she describes her problems, without making judgement. Do not make excuses, for yourself or for colleagues.

2 Ask questions to check that you have the full background details.

3 If possible, agree on a course of action, offering a solution if you can. Check that the client has agreed to the proposed course of action. It may be necessary to consult the salon manager before proposing a solution to the client: if you're not sure, always check first.

4 **Log** the complaint: the date; the time; the client's name; the nature of the complaint; and the course of action agreed.

ACTIVITY

Reception role-play
With colleagues, act out the following situations, which may occur when working as a receptionist. You may wish to video the role-plays for review and discussion later.
1 A client arrives very late for an appointment but insists that she be treated.
2 A client questions the bill.
3 A client comes in to complain about a treatment given previously. (Choose a particular service.)

APPOINTMENTS

Making correct entries in the **appointment book** or salon **computer** is one of the most important duties of the receptionist. As receptionist you must familiarise yourself with the salon's appointment system, column headings, treatment times, and any abbreviations used.

Each therapist will usually have her name at the head of a column. Entries in columns must not be reallocated without the consent of the therapist, unless she is absent.

Bookings

When a client calls to make an appointment, her name and the treatment she wants should be recorded. Allow adequate time to carry out the required service (as indicated in the following chapters). Take the client's telephone number in case the therapist falls ill or is unable to keep the appointment for some other reason. If the client requests a particular therapist, be sure to enter the client's name in the correct column.

The hours of the day are recorded along the left-hand side of the appointment page, divided into fifteen-minute intervals. You must know how long each treatment takes so that you can allow sufficient time for the therapist to carry out the treatment in a safe, competent, professional manner. If you don't allow sufficient time, the therapist will run late, and this will affect all later appointments. On the other hand, if you allow too much time, the therapist's time will be wasted and the salon's earnings will be less than they could be. Suggested times to be allowed for each service are given in the treatment chapters.

Confirm the name of the therapist who will be carrying out the treatment, the date and the time.

Finally, confirm or estimate the cost of the treatment to the client.

Treatments are usually recorded in an abbreviated form. All those who use the appointment page must be familiar with these abbreviations.

Treatment	Abbreviation	Treatment time allowed*
Cleanse and make-up	C/M/up	45 mins
Eyebrow shaping	E/B reshape or trim	15 mins
Eyebrow tint	EBT	10 mins
Eyelash tint	ELT	20 mins
Eyelash perm	ELP	45 mins
Manicure	Man	45 mins
Nail art	N/Art	5–10 mins per nail
Pedicure	Ped	45 mins

Treatment	Abbreviation	Treatment time allowed*
Waxing: half,	$^1/_2$ leg wax	30 mins
three-quarter	$^3/_4$ leg wax	30–40 mins
full	Full leg wax	50 mins
Bikini wax	B/wax	15 mins
Underarm wax	U/arm wax	15 mins
Arm wax	F/arm wax	30 mins
Eyebrow wax	E/B wax	15 mins
Ear pierce	E/P	15 mins
Facial	F	60 mins
False lashes	F/Lash	20 mins

*Treatment time does not include preparation for treatment and consultation

If an appointment book is used, write each entry neatly and accurately. It is preferable to write in pencil: appointments can be amended by erasing and rewriting, keeping the book clean and clear.

Appointment cards may be offered to the client, to confirm the client's appointment. The card should record the treatment, the date, the day and the time. The therapist's name may also be recorded.

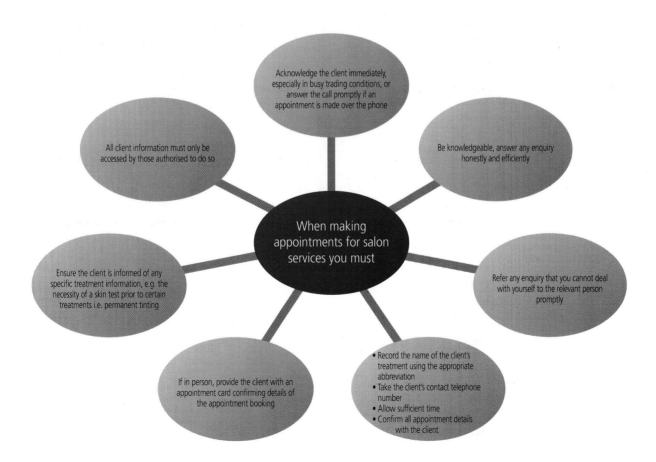

Appointments may be made up to six weeks in advance. Often clients will book their next appointment whilst still at the salon. How far ahead the receptionist is able to book appointments will vary from salon to salon.

When the client arrives for her treatment, draw a line through her name to indicate that she has arrived.

An appointment page

DAY SATURDAY		DATE 15th JANUARY	
THERAPIST	JAYNE	SUE	LIZ
9.00	Mrs Young		
9.15	½ leg wax	Jenny Kran	
9.30	Carol Green	ELT EBT	
9.45	F leg wax	trim	
10.00	B / wax		
10.15		Sandra Smith	Fiona Smith
10.30	Mrs Lord E/BWax	C / M / UP	C / M / UP
10.45			strip lash
11.00		Mrs Jones	
11.15		U/arm wax	
11.30		F/arm wax	Carol Brown
11.45			DNA
12.00			
12.15			
12.30	Nina Farrel		
12.45	man .		
1.00	Ped.		
1.15		Sue Yip E/P	
1.30	½ leg wax	T. Scott	
1.45		3/4 leg wax	
2.00	Karen Davies	U/arm wax	
2.15	facial		
2.30			
2.45			Pat King
3.00			C / M / UP
3.15	Anna Wood		Man
3.30	Man .		
3.45	E/B Reshape		
4.00			

If the client cancels indicate this on the appointment page *immediately*, usually with a large C, placed through the booking. This enables another client to take the appointment.

If a client fails to arrive the abbreviation DNA (did not arrive) is usually written over the booking. The client's telephone number should then be used to see if a re-booking is required.

Some salons will have a policy to charge for a missed appointment.

SKIN TESTS

Before clients receive certain treatments it may be necessary to carry out **skin tests**. The skin test is often carried out at reception, and the receptionist or assistant therapist will be able to perform the test once she has been trained. Every client should undergo a skin test before a permanent tinting treatment to the eyelashes or eyebrows. Further tests may be necessary, depending on the sensitivity of the client, before treatments such as artificial eyelash treatment, eyelash perming, bleaching or wax depilation. Refer to the relevant chapters to familiarise yourself with the test required.

TELEPHONE CALLS

In building new relationships, first impressions count. Good telephone technique can win clients; poor technique can lose them. Here are some guidelines for good technique:

- *Answer quickly* On average, a person may be willing to wait up to 9 rings: try to respond to the call within 6 rings.
- *Be prepared* Have information and writing materials ready to hand. It should not normally be necessary to leave the caller waiting while you find something.
- *Be welcoming and attentive* Speak clearly, without mumbling, at the right speed. Pronounce your words clearly, and vary your tone. Sound interested, and never abrupt.

Remember: the caller may be a new client ringing several salons, and her decision whether to visit *your* salon may depend on your attitude and the way you respond to her call.

Here are some more ideas about good telephone technique:

- Smile – this will help you put across a warm, friendly response to the caller.
- Alter the pitch of your voice as you speak, to create interest.
- As you answer, give the standard greeting for the salon – for example. 'Good morning, visage Beauty Salon, Susan speaking. How may I help you?'

TIP

Don't regard the phone ringing as an interruption. Always remember that clients matter – it is they who ensure the success of your business!

TIP

A client who has received a poor response to her telephone call may tell others about it.

TIP

If the salon uses a cordless phone or a mobile phone, keep it in a central location where it can easily be found when it rings. After each call, be sure to return the phone to its normal location.

ACTIVITY

Communicating with clients
Listen to experienced receptionists and notice how they communicate with clients.

ACTIVITY

Listening to yourself
A pleasant speaking voice is an asset. Do you think you could improve your speech or manner?
Record your voice as you answer a telephone enquiry, then play it back. How did you sound? This is how others hear you!

TIP ✔

Check the salon's policy on personal calls. Usually they are permitted only in emergencies. This is so that staff are not distracted from clients, and to keep the telephone free for clients to make appointments.

ACTIVITY

What do you need to know?
Think of different questions that you might be asked as a receptionist. Then ask an experienced receptionist what the most common requests are.

TIP ✔

Telephone directories, codebooks and guides to charges provide a great deal of useful information. Read them carefully to make yourself familiar with the telephone services that are available.

- Listen attentively to the caller's questions or requests. You will be speaking to a variety of clients: you must respond appropriately and helpfully to each.
- Evaluate the information given by the caller, and be sure to respond to what she has said or asked.
- Use the client's name, if you know it; this personalises the call.
- In your mind, summarise the main requests from the call. Ask for further information if you need it.
- If you have an enquiry that you cannot deal with yourself, refer to the relevant person promptly for assistance. Tell the client what you are doing.
- At the end, repeat the main points of the conversation clearly to check that you and the client have understood each other.
- Close the call pleasantly – for example, 'Thank you for calling, Mrs Smith. Goodbye.'

If you receive a business call, or a call from a person seeking employment, always take the caller's name and telephone number. Your supervisor can then deal with the call as soon as she is free to do so.

ACTIVITY

Finding the right approach
What telephone manner should you adopt when dealing with people who are:
- angry?
- talkative?
- nervous?

Transferring calls

If you transfer a telephone call to another extension, explain to the caller what you are doing and thank her for waiting. If the extension to which you have transferred the call is not answered within 9 rings, explain to the caller that you will ask the person concerned to ring back as soon as possible. Take the caller's name and telephone number.

Taking messages

Messages should be recorded on a memorandum ('memo') pad. Each message should record:
- who the message is for:
- who the message was from;
- the date and the time the message was received;
- accurate details of the message;
- the telephone number or address of the caller;
- the signature of the person who took the message.

A memo

```
TELEPHONE MESSAGE RECEIVED

To      Angela                      Date    10.7.04
From    Jenny Heron                 Time    9:30 am
Number  273451                      Taken by Sandra

Please could you ring Jenny Heron
regarding her appointment on
Saturday.
```

When taking a message, repeat the details you have recorded so that the caller can check that you've got it right. Pass the message to the correct person as soon as possible.

THE PAYMENT POINT

Every beauty therapy or cosmetic business will have a policy for handling cash and for operating the payment point.

It is important that you have received training and are confident to take payment in the client's preferred method, which may be cash (or cash equivalent, i.e. gift voucher) cheque or payment card.

Kinds of payment point

Manual tills

With **manual tills** a lockable drawer or box is used to store cash: this may form part of the reception desk. Each transaction must be recorded by hand.

At the end of the working day, record the total cash register in a book, to ensure that accurate accounts are kept. Records of petty cash must also be kept so that the final totals will balance.

Automatic tills

Modern electrical **automatic tills** use codes, one for each kind of treatment or retail sale. These are identified by keys on the till. Using these with each transaction makes it possible to analyse the salon's business each day or each week.

A computerised till

With each sale during the day a receipt is given to the client; the total is also recorded on the till's **audit roll**.

Automatic tills also provide **subtotals** of the amounts taken: these can be cross-checked against the amount in the till, to determine the daily **takings**:

- the **X reading** provides subtotals throughout the day, as required;
- the **Z reading** provides the overall figures at the end of the day.

Computerised cashdesks

Computerised cashdesks provide the same facilities as automatic tills, with additional features to help with the business's record-keeping, including client treatment cards and stock records.

Equipment and materials required

TIP

If there is too little change in the till, inform the relevant person. Running out of change would disrupt service and spoil the impression clients receive.

- *Calculator* This is useful in totalling large amounts of money or when using a manual till.
- *Credit-card equipment* If your business is authorised to accept credit cards you may use either an *imprinter* or *electronic terminal*. An imprinter is a manual system whereby the client's credit card is placed on a self-carbonating voucher within the machine and a manual sliding mechanism imprints the details of the card upon the voucher. If this system is used you require a supply of vouchers. Alternatively, where an electronic payment system is used a special till roll which provides a printout for yourself and a copy for the client is required.
- *A cash float* At the start of each day you need a small sum of money, comprising coins and perhaps a few notes, to provide change: this is called the **float**. (At the end of the day there will be money surplus to the float: if no mistakes have been made, this should match the takings.)

- *A till roll* This records the sales and provides a receipt. Keep a spare to hand. If you're using a manual cash drawer, you'll need a **receipt book**.
- *An audit roll* The retailer's copy of the till roll.
- *A cash book* This is a record of income and expenditure, for a manual till.
- *Other stationery* A date stamp and a salon name stamp (for cheques), pens, pencils and an eraser, and a container to hold these.

Security at the payment point

Having placed money in the cash drawer and collected change as required, always close the cash drawer firmly – never leave it open. Do not leave the key in the drawer, or lying about reception unattended.

Some members of staff will be appointed to **authorise** cheques and credit-card payments; one of these should initial each cheque.

Errors may occur when handling cheques or when operating an electronic or computerised payment point. Don't panic! If you can't correct the error yourself, seek assistance – but don't leave the cash drawer unattended and open.

Methods of payment

Cash

When receiving payment by **cash**, follow this sequence:

1 Accurately total the charge for the services/products received. Inform the client of the amount to be paid.

2 Check that the money offered is **legal tender** – that is, money you will be able to pay into your bank. (Your salon will probably not accept foreign currency, for example.)

3 Place the customer's money on the till ledge until you have given change, or at least state to the customer verbally the sum of money that she has given you.

4 Aloud, count the change as you give it to the client. This will help avoid payment disputes.

5 Thank the client, and give her a receipt.

6 If a client disputes the change given as too little, ask how much money she is missing. Inform the client that when the takings are cashed at the end of the day if there is a surplus and it matches that amount she will be reimbursed. Ensure that you have the client's details so that you can inform her of the outcome the next day.

Cheques

Cheques are an alternative form of payment, and must be accompanied by a **cheque-guarantee card**. This has a spending limit, usually £50 or £100. Your salon may be willing to accept cheques for larger amounts if the client can show some other identification, such as a driving licence, but you must always check first with your supervisor.

ACTIVITY

Fraud
Find out about your salon's policy in the case of fradulent monetary transactions, using either cash or cards. What actions should you take?

TIP

Hold notes to the light to check for forgeries. You should be able to see the watermark and the metal strip that runs through the note.

TIP

A cheque is only valid for 6 months from the date on the cheque.

A cheque

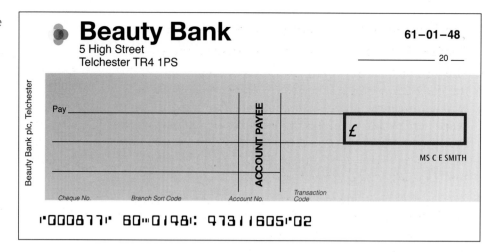

When receiving payment by cheque, follow this sequence of checks:

1 the cheque must be correctly dated;
2 the cheque must be made payable to the salon (you may have a salon stamp for this);
3 the words and figures written on the cheque must match those in the box;
4 any errors or alterations must have been initialled by the client;
5 the signature on the back of the cheque card must match that on the cheque – compare these as the customer writes her signature on the cheque;
6 the bank's 'sort code' numbers on the cheque must match those on the card;
7 the date on the cheque card must be valid;
8 the value on the cheque must not exceed the cheque card limit;
9 the cheque card number must be recorded on the back of the cheque;
10 the cheque must be signed by the client.

Debit cards

Some businesses accept **debit cards** such as Delta, Switch or Connect. The card authorises immediate debit of the cash amount from the client's account. (This card may also be a cheque-guarantee card.) You cannot perform this kind of transaction unless your salon has an electronic terminal.

Credit cards

Credit cards can be used only if your business has an arrangement with the relevant credit-card company. In this case the company will give the salon a credit limit (a **ceiling**), the maximum amount that may be accepted with the card. Any amount greater than this must be individually authorised by the credit-card company. (This is done by telephone at the time of transaction.)

Electronic payment systems

An electronic computerised terminal may be used for payment by both credit and debit cards.

A credit card

1 Check that the terminal display is in 'SALE' mode.

2 Confirm that a sale is to be made by pressing the YES button.

3 The terminal will request that you **swipe** the card. Do this, ensuring that the magnetic strip passes over the reader head and that you retain the card in your hand. In some cases the magnetic strip cannot be read by the swipe card reader: in this situation you will have to key the complete card number into the terminal manually. This does not necessarily mean that there is any reason for suspicion, but do look carefully at it for any signs that the card has been tampered with.

4 When prompted, enter the 'AMOUNT' using the keypad to input the purchases and total them. (If you make a mistake, you can clear the figures using the CLEAR button.)

5 Press ENTER, which will automatically connect the terminal to the credit card company. A message will indicate first 'DIALLING', and then 'CONNECTION MADE'.

6 Customer details are accessed automatically. After a few moments you should receive one of two messages. If the payment is authorised you will see 'AUTH CODE', and a code number will be printed on the receipt with the other purchase details. If the transaction is declined, you will see 'CARD NOT ACCEPTED'.

7 While holding the card, check the details and tear off the two-part receipt and ask the cardholder to sign in ballpoint pen, in the space provided.

8 Check the signature matches the signature on the card, and give the customer the top, signed copy, with the card.

9 Place the copies in the till. One copy is for the debit/credit card company the other for your records.

Sharp

Swiping a card through an electronic terminal

TIP
If cards are accepted as a method of payment, those that are accepted by the business will usually be displayed at the payment point.

When receiving payment by credit card, check these points:

1 the card logo is at the upper right corner on the front of the card;

2 the hologram should have a clear, sharp image and be in the centre right of the card;

3 the date on the credit card must be valid: if it is out of date ask for another form of payment;

4 the sex (Ms, Miss, Mrs, Mr, etc.) and the name of the customer must fit your client;

5 the cardholder's signature on the card must match the name on the front of the card;

6 the cardholder's account number should be embossed and across the width of the card;

7 the cardholder's account number must not be one of those on the credit-card company's warning list.

If you receive a card that is on a credit-card warning list, politely detain the customer, hold onto the card, and contact your supervisor, who will implement the salon's procedure. If the card is unsigned, do not allow the cardholder to sign the card unless you first get authorisation from the credit-card company's service provider. (The service provider's telephone number should be kept near the telephone.)

Credit card payment using an imprinter

1 Prepare the **sales voucher**, which comprises three copies. Complete the sales details on the appropriate credit-card voucher, using ballpoint pen so that the bottom copy is legible.

2 Place the card in the transaction printer, with the front (embossed side) facing upwards.

3 Place the voucher over the card, and under the voucher guide.

4 Slide the handle from left to right, and back to its original position.

5 Remove the voucher and check that the recorded details are clear and on all copies of the voucher.

6 Ask the customer to sign the voucher. Check that the signature on the voucher matches that on the credit card.

7 Give the customer the top copy as a receipt, with their credit card.

A copy of the sales voucher is sent to the credit-card company; the third copy is kept by the salon.

Travellers' cheques

Travellers' cheques also may be acceptable, provided they are in particular currencies (usually sterling). Such cheques must be compared with the client's **passport**.

A travellers' cheque

American Express

A charge card

Charge cards

Some businesses accept **charge cards** such as American Express. These differ from credit cards in that the account holder must repay to the card company the complete amount spent each month.

Gift vouchers

Gift vouchers are purchased from the salon as pre-payments for beauty therapy services or retail sales.

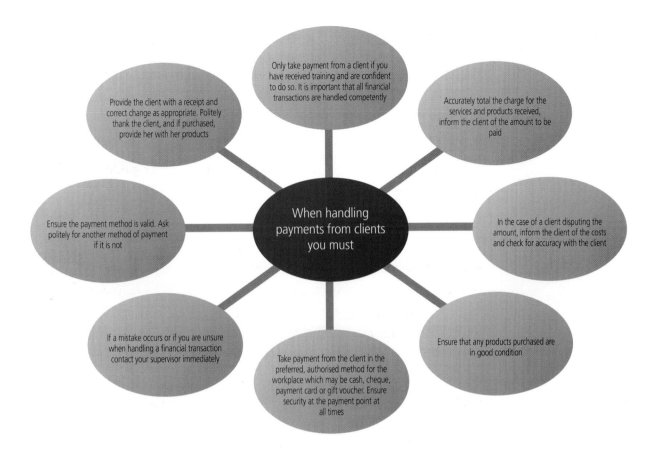

When handling payments from clients you must

Only take payment from a client if you have received training and are confident to do so. It is important that all financial transactions are handled competently

Accurately total the charge for the services and products received, inform the client of the amount to be paid

In the case of a client disputing the amount, inform the client of the costs and check for accuracy with the client

Ensure that any products purchased are in good condition

Take payment from the client in the preferred, authorised method for the workplace which may be cash, cheque, payment card or gift voucher. Ensure security at the payment point at all times

If a mistake occurs or if you are unsure when handling a financial transaction contact your supervisor immediately

Ensure the payment method is valid. Ask politely for another method of payment if it is not

Provide the client with a receipt and correct change as appropriate. Politely thank the client, and if purchased, provide her with her products

A gift voucher

BEAUTY WORKS

3 Market Street
Whitely

Tel: 39473

This voucher entitles

....

to the value of £ ....

Signed:

Date:

Valid for six months from date of purchase

Check the following

- there is usually a specific time period in which gift vouchers must be used. Check to see if this is the case and if they are still valid;
- check the value of the voucher, and remember to request another form of payment if the cost of the treatment is higher than the voucher.

It is important that all financial transactions are handled competently. However busy you are always follow the guidelines for handling each method of payment.

If you are ever unsure when handling a financial transaction or make a mistake inform your supervisor immediately. It may be that you have to be discreet when doing this, for example if a client has handed you a forged bank note!

Assessment of knowledge and understanding

You have now learnt about the skills required to ensure clients are greeted and dealt with efficiently at the salon reception, to enable you to fulfil salon reception duties.

To test your level of knowledge, answer the following short questions. These will prepare you for your summative (final) assessment.

Maintain the reception area

1 What are the main duties of the salon receptionist?

2 Hospitality is important to show the salon's commitment to customer care. What examples of hospitality may be offered to clients at reception?

3 What equipment and materials do you need at the reception desk?

4 How should the reception be maintained?

5 What is a float? When must this be checked, and why?

6 Client records are often stored at reception. How should this information be used and stored to comply with the Data Protection Act 1998?

Attend to clients and enquiries

1 What interpersonal skills are essential in a receptionist?

2 How should clients be greeted on arrival?

3 What information should be sought by the receptionist from a visitor to the reception desk?

4 What are the important details to record when taking a message?

5 If as receptionist you were unable to give appropriate information to a client, what action should you take?

6 For what different reasons may people telephone the salon?

7 A client rings up to check the time of an appointment. What information do you need from her?

8 A client complains at reception about a leg wax treatment she has received. What questions should you ask? What action should you take?

Make appointments for salon services

1 A client telephones the salon, how should you:

- answer the telephone and introduce yourself?
- speak on the telephone?
- seek information from the client?
- finish the telephone conversation?

2 What are the common systems used in salons to make appointments?

3 Why is it necessary to confirm an appointment with a client verbally before she leaves the salon?

4 A client wishes to make an appointment for an eyelash tint. What information is required from the client before making the appointment?

5 How long should you allow when making an appointment for the following treatments/services?

- full leg wax
- ear piercing
- nail art
- pedicure including a foot conditioning treatment
- full facial and eyelash tint.

Handle payment from clients

1 If you make an error when operating the till, why must you report this?

2 When taking cash from a client, what is the correct procedure to follow?

3 Why is it important to inspect the quality and condition of goods before payment is processed?

4 If you made a mistake in giving the client her change, how would you deal with this?

5 What would you check when receiving payment by cheque?

6 What is the procedure for receiving payment by credit card?

7 If a client presented an invalid cheque card, what should you say to her?

8 If your salon accepts vouchers in exchange for salon treatment/services, how are these handled?

chapter 3

PROMOTE ADDITIONAL PRODUCTS OR SERVICES TO CLIENTS

G6

Learning objectives

This chapter discusses ways to promote products and services to clients. It describes the competencies to enable you to:

- identify additional products or services that are available
- inform clients about additional products or services
- gain client commitment to using additional products and services

THE IMPORTANCE OF RETAIL SALES

Retail sales are of considerable importance to the beauty salon: they are a simple way of greatly increasing the income without too much extra time and effort. Beauty therapy treatments are time-consuming and labour-intensive; selling a product in addition to providing the treatment will greatly increase the profitability.

Clients need to be regularly informed about what products and services the business is promoting. Often this will improve their experience of the salon or spa visit. In Chapter 1 we looked at the importance of creating an initial positive impression to the client. Staff knowledge of products and services is vital to ensure personal effectiveness and helps in gaining client loyalty.

If you have got it right the client will maintain their loyalty to you and this enables the business to grow. For example: a facial treatment might take 1 hour and cost the client £20. You might then sell the client moisturiser costing £20, of which £10 might be clear profit. Supposing that you sold eight products each day, each yielding £10 profit. That would be a profit of £80 per day, or £400 per week, or £1600 each month – and thus, £19200 profit over the whole year: a significant sum.

HEALTH AND SAFETY

Contra-indications
If the client has any contra-indication to the product, recommend she seeks her doctor's approval before using it.

TIP

Encourage your client to try the testers out. Make-up can look very different on the face compared with its appearance on the palette.

SELLING PRODUCTS

When selling a client products, first find out about her needs. Consider the following:

- Is she allergic to any particular substance, contact with which should be avoided?

- Has she a skin disorder or nail disease which might contra-indicate use of a particular product? Contra-indication to products must always be noted and explained to the client.

- Is she planning to use the product over cuts and abrasions, or over areas with warts and moles? If so, is this safe?

- How much is she used to spending on products? Ask about what she is presently using: this will give you an idea of the types of product she has experience of using, and the sort of prices she is used to paying.

Bearing in mind her needs, you can now guide her to the most suitable product. This is where your expertise and your product knowledge are so important: you can describe fully and accurately the features, functions and benefits of the products you stock.

The products themselves must be presented to the client in such a way that they seem both attractive and desirable: the presentation should encourage her to purchase them. The packaging and the product should be clean and in good condition, and **testers** should be available wherever possible so that the client can try the product on herself before purchasing it.

The final choice of product is with the client, of course, but often she will ask for a recommendation, for example if she cannot decide between two

A nail polish display

A nail product display

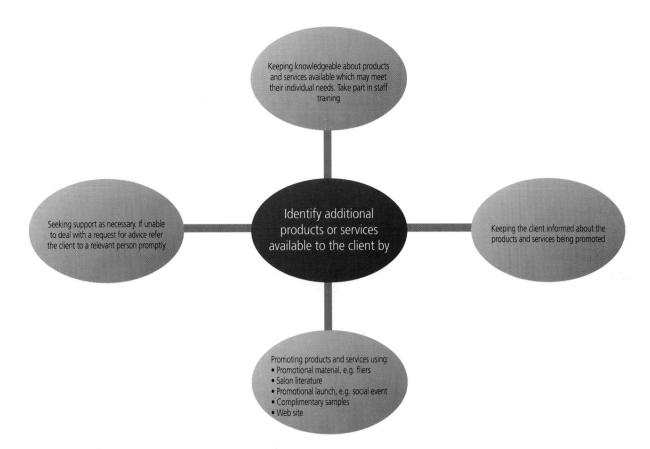

possibilities. It is in these circumstances that your ability to answer technical questions fully, from a complete knowledge of the product, will help in closing the sale. Speaking with confidence and authority on the one product that will particularly suit her requirements may well persuade her to buy it.

If the client does not know what an **allergic reaction** is – or how to recognise an allergy – it is important that you describe it to her (red, itchy, flaking and even swollen skin). If she experiences this sort of contra-action she should immediately stop applying the product she suspects is producing it.

HEALTH AND SAFETY

Patch tests

If the client has not tried a product before, or if there is doubt as to how her skin will react, a skin patch test must be carried out.

1 Select either the inner elbow or the area behind the ear.
2 Make sure the skin is clean.
3 Apply a little of the product, using a spatula.
4 Leave the area alone for 24 hours.
5 If there is no reaction after 24 hours, the client is not allergic to the product: she can go ahead and use it.

   If there has been any itching, soreness, erythema, or swelling in the area where the product has been applied, the client is allergic to it and should not use it.

TECHNIQUES IN SELLING

The first rule of selling is: *know your products*. This applies to all retail products and to all salon services.

Staff training

It is important that everybody is knowledgeable and able to answer the clients' questions – this includes the receptionist who is often the first and last person the client comes into contact with. In conversation, especially during quieter periods, they have opportunities to discuss products and services informally.

Often product companies provide training either at the salon or at another venue. This is a great opportunity to update your knowledge and skills, which you will be able to share enthusiastically with your clientele. Often certificates to prove training are issued and these should be professionally displayed in the salon.

If not all staff can participate it is important that new information is passed on to them to make them effective in their job. Team meetings are a good opportunity to discuss salon policy and new products and promotions.

Information must be supplied for clients to read, and **displays** must be set up. Be aware of your **competitors** and their current advertising displays and campaigns.

Promoting products and services

When promoting products and services it is good to use the following:

- Eye-catching promotional material (usually provided by the product supplier). Display in the window to encourage new clients!
- Updated salon literature discussing benefits and costs
- A promotional launch event, where clients can enjoy a social event and perhaps book services or buy products at discounted prices
- Promotional packages may be presented
- Samples may be given following a service
- If you have a web site you may wish to promote products and services on your homepage.

Know your products

Product usage must be discussed with clients, as necessary, and advice given on which product will best suit each of them. The only way to be able to do this is to memorise the complete range: all your products, including which skin types or treatment conditions each is for, what the active ingredients are, when and how each should be used, and its cost. Any questions asked must be answered with authority and confidence. Clients expect the staff in the beauty salon to be professionals, able to provide expert advice.

TIP

Use the products on yourself. It is always good to be able to speak from experience.

ACTIVITY

Increasing product knowledge
With colleagues, discuss and note down the features, functions and benefits of a range of cosmetic products sold in your training establishment.

ACTIVITY

Learning the product range
Learn about and memorise the product range sold in the training establishment you attend.

If the client requests advice on products that are outside of your responsibilities you could suggest alternatives or refer her to another source for information.

Information to read

The **information** available to clients can start from the window display. Use the **window stickers** if supplied with product ranges, and include stickers that advertise the salon's treatments. Few salons use windows for product displays, but you could consider doing so.

Posters are supplied with good-quality product ranges, and most suppliers provide **information leaflets** for clients. Use the posters and **display cards** in the reception area; clients can then help themselves, and read about the products. This will generate questions – and sales.

Product and retail displays

Two types of display can be used in the beauty salon. In the first, the display is there simply to be looked at, and seen as part of the decor. It should be attractive and artistically arranged, and can use dummy containers. It is not meant to be touched or sold from, so it can be behind glass or in a window display.

In the second, on the other hand, products are there to be sold. In this case products must be attractive but also accessible. The display should include testers so that clients can freely smell and touch. Each product must be clearly priced, and small signs placed beside the products or on the edge of the shelves to describe the selling points of each product.

This sort of active display must always be in the part of the salon where most people will see and walk past it – the area of 'highest traffic'. A large proportion of cosmetic and perfume sales are **impulse buys**. It is no accident that perfumery departments are beside the main entrances to department stores, or right beside access points such as escalators.

Product displays must always feature in the beauty treatment area. As the beauty therapist uses the products, she can discuss and recommend them for the client. If displays are there to see and to take from, the sale can be closed even before the client returns to reception. Although in theory clients can of course change their minds between the treatment area and actually paying, in practice once they have the product in their hands they will go on to buy it.

Ellisons

A range of skin care products for retail

Displays

Most small salons will design and create their own displays using the counter **display packs** provided by the product companies. Some will have a professional **window dresser** to regularly change the window displays for the best effect.

Displays should be well stocked, with smart undamaged packaging. Eye-level displays are best and ideally should be accessible. Change the display regularly according to the promotion, for example UV skin protection products in summer.

Displays must be checked and cleaned regularly – in busy salons this will usually mean daily. A window display will need to be dusted, straightened, and looked at from outside to make sure that it looks its best. The display from which products are being sold will also need to be dusted, perhaps wiped over (if testers have dripped), and straightened up. Testers need to be checked to make sure they are not sticky and spilt, and that no one has left dirty fingerprints on them.

ACTIVITY

Evaluating displays
Whenever you can, look at displays and make a note of neatness, cleanliness, availability, pricing and information. Compare the best with the worst.

ACTIVITY

Siting of displays
In your nearest large town, go into the big department stores and note where the cosmetic and perfumery department displays are situated.

Ellisons

A range of cosmetics

Ellisons

Make-up palettes available for retail

The range of products

It is not enough to stock just a few items and expect clients to fit in with the range you carry: different ranges must be available for each skin type, and a number of products – such as eye gel or throat cream – that will suit all skin types. Make-up and nail enamels should be attractive to all ages and types of customer. Sales must not be lost because of a lack of product range.

CONSUMER PROTECTION LEGISLATION

The salon has a legal obligation to implement and/or abide by the following legislation, designed to protect the rights of clients.

Consumer Protection Act 1987

This Act follows European Union (EU) directives to protect the customer from unsafe, defective services and products that do not reach safety standards. It also covers misleading price indications about goods or services available from a business. Dissatisfied clients may contact a number of organisations dealing with consumer protection for legal advice. If proven at fault the business may face legal action.

Consumer Safety Act 1978

This Act aims to reduce risk to consumers from potentially dangerous products.

Prices Act 1974

The price of products has to be displayed in order to prevent the buyer being misguided.

Trades Description Act 1968 and 1972

These Acts prohibit the use of false descriptions of goods and services provided by a business. Products must be clearly labelled. When retailing, the information supplied both in written and verbal form must always be accurate. The supplier must not:

● Supply misleading information
● Describe products falsely
● Make false statements.

In addition they must not:

- Make false comparisons between past and present services
- Offer products at what is said to be a 'reduced' price, unless they have previously been on sale at the full price quoted for a 28 day minimum
- Make misleading price comparisons.

Resale Prices Act 1964 and 1976

The manufacturer can supply a recommended price (MRRP), but the seller is not obliged to sell at the recommended price.

Sale and Supply of Goods Act 1994

This Act has replaced the Supply of Goods Act 1982.

Goods must be as described, of merchantable quality and fit for their intended purpose. The Act also covers the conditions under which customers can return goods.

Data Protection Act 1998

Through communication with your client it is necessary to ask clients a series of questions before the treatment plan can be finalised. Client details are recorded on the client record card. This information is confidential and should be stored in a secure area. The client should understand the reason behind the questions asked of them. Confidential information on staff or clients should only be made available to persons to whom consent has been given.

Consumer Protection (Distance Selling) Regulations 2000

These regulations are derived from a European Directive and cover the supply of goods/services made between suppliers acting in a commercial capacity and consumers. They are concerned with purchases made by telephone, fax, internet, digital television, and mail order, including catalogue shopping. Consumers must receive:

- Clear information on goods or services, including delivery arrangements and payment, suppliers' details and consumers' cancellation rights which should be made available in writing.
- The consumer also has a seven working day cool-off period where they may cancel their purchase.

The Disability Discrimination Act 1996

Under the DDA from 1996 as a provider of goods, facilities and services your workplace has the duty to ensure that clients are not discriminated against on the grounds of disability. It is unlawful to use disability as a reason or justification to:

- Refuse to provide a service
- Provide a service to a lesser standard
- Provide a service on worse terms
- Fail to make reasonable adjustments to the way services are provided.

From 2004 this will include failure to make reasonable adjustments to the physical features of service premises, to overcome physical barriers to access. Service can be denied to a disabled person if justified and if any other client would be treated in the same way. Your employer has a responsibility under the DDA to ensure that you receive adequate training to prevent discrimination in practice, and as such is responsible for your actions. Also they must make reasonable adjustments to the premises to facilitate access for disabled persons.

EQUAL OPPORTUNITIES POLICY

The Equal Opportunities Commission (EOC) states it is best practice for the workplace to have a written **Equal Opportunities Policy**. This will include a statement of the commitment to equal opportunities by the employer and the details of structure for implementing the policy.

All employees should know this policy and it should be monitored regularly to review effectiveness.

TIP

Create your own selling opportunity
- If the client is having a manicure and has weak nails, you could recommend a course of nail treatments and an appropriate nail strengthener
- If the client is going away on holiday tell her about the special 'holiday treatment package promotion'
- If the client is having an eyelash tint, tell her how quick and simple an eyebrow wax is and the difference it can make!

INFORMING CLIENTS ABOUT ADDITIONAL PRODUCTS OR SERVICES

Choose the most appropriate time to inform the client about additional products and services. If the client is receiving a treatment service this may be at the consultation, when you are getting to know the client, during the treatment when you have the opportunity to share advice, or when discussing aftercare. Here you will be able to reinforce the importance of further products and services to enhance the treatment benefits gained. This may be further use of products or services that the client has used before or those that are new to the client.

Client suitability

Following the consultation, you may feel that the client is unsuitable for treatment. Tactfully explain to the client why this is and ask her to seek permission from her GP before the treatment is given. The expectations of some clients may be unrealistic. If this is the case, patiently and diplomatically explain why and aim to agree to a realistic treatment programme. Remember your legal duty under the **Health and Safety at Work Act 1974** to take reasonable care to avoid harm to yourself and others.

Communication

Communication with your client, both verbal and non-verbal, is important. Listen to your client; this will help you to identify their treatment requirements and personality.

Observe her body language, is she interested in what you are telling her? If the client is interested, she will agree with you and her body language will be relaxed yet attentive.

If she is not interested she will probably not agree, and will not appear to be interested in what you are saying. If this occurs go back to the beginning and suggest alternatives to attempt to regain her interest, but avoid pressurising the client.

If a sale is achieved, be positive – smile, this will help to make her feel she has made a good decision.

PRODUCT PROMOTION

Planning the demonstration

Demonstrating to an audience needs particularly careful planning if the demonstration is to achieve the maximum benefit. Everything required must be in place: the products, the means to apply them, and all the relevant literature to be given out to the audience or clients.

Consider all possibilities in your planning. What type of demonstration is required? Will you be working on one client, to demonstrate and sell a product, or demonstrating to a group? Is a range of products to be demonstrated, or just one item?

Single client

When demonstrating on a client have a mirror in front of her so that you can explain as you go along and the client can watch. She can then see the benefit of the product and learn how to use it at the same time. This is a simple but effective way to sell products.

TIP

An effective demonstration will always create sales. Have the product ready to sell, or give out vouchers to encourage clients to come to the counter.

A group

The presentation should include an introduction to the demonstrator and the product, the demonstration itself, and a conclusion with thanks to the audience and model. Written **promotional material** can be placed on the seats before the audience arrives, or handed out at an appropriate point during the demonstration; **samples** can be handed around the audience for them to try.

The demonstration itself must be clear, simple and not too long. The audience *must* be able to see what is being done and hear the commentary. Maximise the impact of the demonstration by giving the audience the opportunity to buy the product immediately.

If this is not possible – because the demonstration is in another room, away from the products, or at another venue, such as at a woman's club meeting – ensure that members of the audience leave with a **voucher** to exchange for the product. This should offer some incentive, such as a **discount**, to encourage potential buyers to make the effort to come to the salon and buy. Never sell the features and benefits to potential customers, creating the desire for the product, without also giving them the chance to buy it.

Questions must be accurate and detailed. You are the expert: show your knowledge. Do not ask the client what sort of skin she has – she is not the expert, and will probably give the wrong answer. Instead, ask more detailed questions, such as 'Does your skin feel tight?' (which may indicate dryness), or 'Do you have spots in a particular area?' (which may indicate an oily patch).

Listening is a skill. Always listen carefully to the answers your customer gives: do not talk over her answer or interrupt. Only when she has finished should you give a considered, informed reply. You may need to ask another question, or you may be able straightaway to direct her to the best product for her needs.

TARGETS

The setting of financial targets for the business and for individuals is important to enable analysis of overall performance. The salon owner must have an overall idea of productivity against the targets set. Targets may vary for different employees depending upon experience, length of service and workload.

Productivity

Levels of performance will take into account expected treatment and retail sales. Treatments are normally costed on the products used, including consumables such as cottonwool and tissues, and should include other hidden costs such as laundering of towels.

Productivity can be increased through:

- Incentives
- Promotions
- Personal targets.

Poor levels of performance and productivity may indicate a need for additional training. Some companies provide rewards for employees who develop ideas for increased productivity and commission is one method of rewarding individuals who achieve and exceed targets.

Gaining client feedback

As a service industry, feedback from clients is important when measuring levels of service. It enables you to evaluate marketing methods, salon image and service.

Client feedback can be gathered in a variety of ways, both formally and informally.

Client questionnaires can be used at random to evaluate performance, for example following a promotion. The results should be analysed and appropriate action taken to improve areas of weakness, build on strengths and investigate potential areas of development.

Simply asking the client if she has enjoyed or been satisfied with the treatment received is another method of service evaluation.

Assessment of knowledge and understanding

You have now learnt about methods to promote sales of products and services to clients. This will enable you to promote additional products and services to clients, thus increasing salon income.

To test your level of knowledge, answer the following short questions. These will prepare you for your summative (final) assessment.

Identify additional products or services that are available

1 Why are retail sales important to the beauty salon?

2 Why is it important that you have a good knowledge about the products and services available in your salon?

3 How can you ensure that you are up to date with the beauty products and service you have on offer? Why is this important?

4 What are the opportunities that occur where you can promote a product or service? Think of examples from your experience.

Inform clients about additional products or services

1 Communication is important when selling. Why is it important to observe the client's body language?

2 As well as direct advice, what other ways can you make clients aware of the products and services available in your salon?

3 If the client required advice about a product or service on which you were not qualified to advise, what action would you take?

4 How must displays of retail stock be kept? Why is this important?

5 Clients have 'consumer rights'. Why is it important to give accurate information about products or services?

6 Name three pieces of legislation/regulations relating to the way products or services are delivered to clients which protect their legal rights.

Gain client commitment to using additional products and services

1 Why must the client's needs be ascertained before selling her products or services?

2 What are the benefits to the client of using additional products, as advised by the therapist?

3 Why is it important to stock a range of products?

4 How do you think speaking with confidence and authority on a product will influence the client?

5 Staff training is important to ensure that everybody is knowledgeable and able to advise clients on their questions. What other benefit does this have to the clients, employees and salon?

DEVELOP AND MAINTAIN YOUR EFFECTIVENESS AT WORK

Learning objectives

This chapter covers the importance of taking personal responsibility to improve your performance at work. This also includes ensuring effective relationships are established with colleagues so as to make a positive contribution to the effectiveness of the business. It describes the competencies required to ensure that you:

- **improve your personal performance at work**
- **work effectively as part of a team**

WORKING RELATIONSHIPS

For any beauty therapy business to be a success requires the commitment of each employed individual to ensure quality at all levels and in all services.

For this to occur it is important both that you are effective in your job role and that you have positive **working relationships** with your colleagues and with clients.

Good working relationships in the workplace are essential. Each employee, whatever their role, is valuable as part of the team in ensuring the success of the business. All staff at **induction** should be told of the function of the business, and of their role in this. They should also be told about relevant **codes of conduct**.

Your workplace will have certain salon service standards with regard to appearance and behaviour whilst in the working environment.

General codes of conduct

- Have a smart, professional appearance at all times – it creates an impression of the quality standard that can be expected

- Always have high standards of personal hygiene
- Never, eat, drink, chew gum or smoke in front of the client
- Ensure that you follow your health and safety responsibilities, never putting yourself or anybody else at risk through your actions
- Communicate clearly
- Be polite and courteous at all times to both clients and colleagues
- Never lose your temper, or swear in front of a client
- Avoid controversial and personal topics of conversation
- If you are unable to give the client information they need, quickly find somebody suitably qualified to assist
- If there are any personal issues amongst staff or towards a client, do not let these show in front of a client. Settle the grievances (reasons for complaint) as soon as possible, to avoid job satisfaction and productivity being affected.

Job roles and responsibilities

Each team member should have a **job description** (see opposite page). This details:

- the job's title;
- the specific job role;
- the duties and responsibilities;
- the work location;
- any extra special circumstances affecting duties, such as attending salon promotional events.

The job description enables each employee to know what is expected of them and to whom and for what they are responsible.

For reasons of safety and effectiveness it is important that you know what jobs and roles you are qualified to undertake.

An efficient working environment

Support and guidance should be requested, but only when needed. It is important to use your initiative whenever possible whilst operating within your job role. When seeking support or guidance, any request should be courteously asked for at an appropriate time from the appropriate person, this may be the senior therapist, trainer or supervisor.

Any request for support or guidance should be responded to clearly and courteously.

Use your time effectively, if you are not busy work on other tasks or offer to help your colleagues.

Don't ignore problems – always report these to the relevant person.

Punctuality

It is important to the efficient working of the salon that you are punctual for work. This ensures that you are composed, that clients are not kept waiting,

---

Job description – Beauty Therapist

Location:	Based at salon as advised
Main purpose of job:	To ensure customer care is provided at all times To maintain a good standard of technical and client care, ensuring that up-to-date methods and techniques are used following the salon training practices and procedures
Responsible to:	Salon manager
Requirements:	To maintain the company's standards in respect of hairdressing/beauty services
	To ensure that all clients receive service of the best possible quality
	To advise clients on services and treatments
	To advise clients on products and after-care
	To achieve designated performance targets
	To participate in self-development or to assist with the development of others
	To maintain company policy in respect of: • personal standards of health/hygiene • personal standards of appearance/conduct • operating safely whilst at work • public promotion • corporate image as laid out in employee handbook
	To carry out client consultation in accordance with company policy
	To maintain company security practices and procedures
	To assist your manager in the provision of salon resources
	To undertake additional tasks and duties required by your manager from time to time.

---

and that you are able to support other members of the team. You thereby minimise stress for yourself and for your colleagues.

Absence from work

If a member of staff is absent from work, other staff will need to review the daily work schedule to minimise disruption. In the case of holiday cover this can be planned for, but if a staff member is absent unexpectedly, teamwork will be needed to get the work done.

When you learn that someone is to be absent, find out, if you can, for approximately how long. Then:

● Check the work schedule of the person who is absent.
● Reschedule clients, but without affecting the quality of the salon's service.

- Determine whether any clients' appointments can or must be cancelled, especially if there are double bookings or if the client must be treated specifically by the person who is away. Contact clients as soon as possible, so that they can reschedule their own time.

If you yourself are ill, to minimise disruption you must report your sickness as early as possible to the relevant person. You may be required to complete sickness forms.

Effective communication between staff

Personnel problems may occur if there are ineffective communication systems. Time should be made to hold regular staff meetings where any concerns can be shared. A staff meeting can also be an exciting opportunity to share ideas to improve the efficiency of the job role and to look together at ways of improving the business.

Positive relationships with colleagues

There can be no place in a customer care industry for poor working relationships. A great portion of your time is spent in the workplace alongside your colleagues, and if the environment becomes stressful this will affect your effectiveness. It will also be apparent to clients, and relationships between staff members should not trouble them. Disputes must be resolved immediately.

Grievances

It is important that you understand the salon's **staffing structure**. You need to know who is responsible for what, and who you should approach in various circumstances, for example if you felt that you were being treated unfairly. Any grievances should be reported to a supervisor, and you should familiarise yourself with the **grievance and appeals procedure**.

This includes what action to take if you:

- have a disagreement with a colleague that you cannot resolve
- feel you are being treated unfairly
- are being discriminated against
- are working outside the limitations of your job role.

The grievance and appeals procedure should ensure that the issue is fully investigated and appropriate action is taken or implemented. In some cases this will mean that disciplinary action against an individual is taken. For a team to work effectively problems should be addressed as soon as they arise and it is important that harmonious relationships are rebuilt.

Effective teamwork

An effective team member:

- Knows who to report to for guidance
- Is supported in their job role by their supervisor and other colleagues

ACTIVITY

What personal characteristics do you need to work effectively in a team? From your own experience, discuss times when you have worked in a team. What was your role?

Ask a colleague: are you seen by others as a team player? If not, how can you develop the necessary skills?

- Communicates freely
- Has targets to work towards that are regularly reviewed
- Is flexible and willing to change to meet organisational needs
- Operates in a supportive, friendly atmosphere
- Feels valued.

EFFECTIVE COMMUNICATION WITH CLIENTS

Customer care

Many organisations have a **customer care statement** which outlines the standards of service customers can expect.

Clients want to enjoy their visits to the beauty salon and they are paying for a service. It is important that during each visit they are made to feel relaxed and comfortable.

Client care

Remember that each client has a different personality and different treatment needs, requiring an individual treatment approach.

A client can be made to feel intimidated, uncomfortable or ignored – and this can happen without your saying anything! Even without speaking you

ACTIVITY

Client care
Find out whether your organisation has a customer care statement. If so, how well do you do in providing that level of customer care? Monitor yourself against the statement, and ask colleagues for feedback.

76

LEVEL 2 CORE UNITS

ACTIVITY

Telephone calls
A telephone call is often the first contact the client has with the salon and is an important method of communication.
- How should the phone be answered?
- What should you confirm if the client requires an eyelash tint?
- What action would you take if there was not sufficient time for the appointment at the time requested?
- How would you handle a complaint about a service?

TIP

Using the correct title
It is important that a client is greeted appropriately according to their expectations.
   Never use a client's first name unless invited to do so.

communicate with your eyes, your face and your body, transmitting some of your feelings. This is called **non-verbal communication**. How you look and how you behave in front of your clients is important.

Positive relationships with clients

On meeting a client, always smile, make eye contact, and greet her cheerfully – however bad your own day is! As you communicate you can:

- promote yourself, and gain the client's confidence in your professionalism and technical expertise;
- develop a professional relationship with the client;
- establish the client's needs;
- promote services and treatments.

Verbal communication occurs when you talk directly to another person, either face to face or over the telephone. Always speak clearly and precisely, and avoid slang. It is important to be a good listener: this will help you identify the client's treatment requirements and understand her personality. You can then guide the conversation appropriately.

Responding appropriately

It may be that the client requests information that you are unable to help her with or which lies outside your responsibility. If this occurs politely inform her that you are not able or qualified to deal with her request but will get somebody else to assist. Always indicate how long this will take if it will not be immediately.

Keeping your client informed is reassuring and important to avoid dissatisfaction with the service provided.

Body language

Interpreting **body language** is an important skill: learn to notice how the client is behaving, including her voice, her eyes, her body, and her arm and hand movements. An instinctive 'feel' for customers' behaviour can be developed with experience.

Noticing client behaviour will help you to recognise the client's different needs and expectations. You must be able to adapt to these.

When approaching potential customers in a situation such as a department store, be aware that conflicting signals may be given. For example, a person may smile and nod as if interested but, in fact, walk straight past. On the other hand, if the customer makes the first approach then she obviously has an active interest already.

Initially the customer may be formal and may even have a stiff body posture and a reserved manner. As she becomes more interested, however, her posture will relax: she may begin to lean forward. It will become obvious at this stage that she is interested, and she then will go on to nod and agree, and to listen actively.

You must use your own body language to good effect. You must be relaxed but attentive, and listen actively – nodding and shaking your head, and smiling in agreement. Use relaxed, gentle hand movements: do not twitch or turn away from the customer.

If the customer is not agreeing with you, or is not interested, she may look bored, tap her fingers, fiddle with her shopping, look away, or even look at her watch. If these signs are evident, go back to the beginning and try to find out why she is not interested. This is important when selling. Perhaps she does not want the product you have recommended? Or perhaps it is too expensive? Suggest alternatives and see whether you can get her interest again.

When the customer has decided to buy, smile – help her to feel that she has made an excellent decision. She should leave feeling proud to have purchased the product.

Conversing with a client

Having developed a professional relationship with your client, centre the conversation on her, so that she feels special. Avoid interrupting the client whilst she is speaking – be patient. A nervous client may need to be reassured. Gain her confidence by being pleasant and cheerful without chattering constantly. When asking questions, don't interrogate your client. Never talk down to her, and avoid technical jargon – instead, use commonly understood words.

Certain technical information may not appear complicated, but if for example a client has bought several skin care products it is important that they know how to use them safely and efficiently. Always check tactfully with the client to ensure that they have fully understood the information provided.

> **TIP**
>
> Make notes on the client's record card of topics that interest her. You can introduce these topics in conversation next time the client receives a treatment, and she will be pleased that you have taken the trouble to remember.

> **TIP** ✔
>
> **Client confusion**
> If a client is confused about the information you have given her, identify which part is confusing.
>   Repeat the information clearly and logically to clarify your instructions, checking for understanding.
>   Always allow time for clients to consider your response and provide further explanation as necessary.
>   Confirm the client's understanding with her and ensure that she is now clear and satisfied. Remember always to be patient and respectful.

Avoid all controversial topics, such as sex, religion and politics! When a relationship has been established, value it but be discreet – clients will often share confidences with you. Never pass judgement, and ensure that you deserve clients' trust by maintaining confidentiality.

Working under pressure

Sometimes you will be extremely busy and you may be feeling tired and weary. This is not the client's problem, however! Remain cheerful, courteous and helpful. You should also use your initiative in helping others, for example by preparing a colleague's work area when you are free and she is busy.

You must be able to cope with the unexpected:

- clients arriving late for appointments;
- clients' treatments overrunning the allocated treatment times;
- double bookings, with two clients requiring treatment at the same time;
- the arrival of unscheduled clients;
- changes to the bookings.

With effective teamwork such situations can usually be overcome.

Avoiding client dissatisfaction

Some dissatisfied clients will voice their dissatisfaction; others will remain silent and simply not return to the salon. This situation can often be prevented through good customer care and effective communication.

- Always ensure that the client has a thorough consultation before any new service. This should be carried out by a colleague with the appropriate technical expertise.
- Regularly check the client's satisfaction. If there is any concern, make the supervisor aware of this immediately.
- Inform the client of any disruption to service – do not leave her wondering what the problem may be. Politely inform her of the situation, for example 'I'm sorry but we are running 10 minutes late – are you able to wait?' If your salon has the facilities, you may offer her a drink.
- Inconvenience caused by disruption to service can usually be compensated in some way. It is important to resolve problems and keep clients satisfied.

Customer care is vital: clients provide the salon's income and your wages. The success of the business depends upon satisfied clients.

Complaints procedure

Unfortunately problems do sometimes arise in which the client cannot be appeased. A **complaints procedure** is a formal, standardised approach adopted by the organisation to handle any complaints. It should also be used to handle complaints of discrimination.

Dealing with client dissatisfaction

If a client is dissatisfied she may appear angry and complain or she may say nothing. However she reacts, remember that a dissatisfied client is bad for business.

You may be required to deal with an angry client:

- Stay calm and listen to the client's complaint.
- If you are unable to handle it refer it as quickly as possible to somebody who can. Inform her of your actions at all times.
- Establish the facts and take appropriate action as laid down in your client complaints procedure.
- Always aim to repair the relationship, although at times this may not be possible.
- Not all clients are always genuine in their complaint – establish the facts and tactfully advise the client of the outcome.
- Always remain courteous, professional and create a positive impression.

Legal requirements

The salon has a legal obligation to implement legislation designed to protect client's rights.

Health and safety

Following the consultation you may feel that the client is unsuitable for treatment. Explain tactfully why this is and ask her to seek permission from her GP before the treatment is given. The expectations of some clients may be unrealistic. If this is the case, tactfully explain why and aim to agree to a realistic treatment programme.

Remember your legal duty under the **Health and Safety at Work Act 1974** to take reasonable care to avoid harm to yourself and others. Never use equipment for which you do not have the professional expertise. As well as the obvious potential hazards, you would not have the expertise to adapt the treatment to suit the client's treatment needs, and you would not be able to provide the relevant treatment advice in order to obtain the optimum treatment results.

Data Protection Act 1998

Before treating your client it is necessary to ask them a series of questions so that a treatment plan can be finalised.

Client details are recorded on the client record card. This information is confidential and should be stored in a secure area. The client should understand the reason behind the questions asked of them.

Confidential information on staff or clients should only be made available to persons to whom consent has been given.

Equal opportunities

The United Kingdom has specific legislation on equality that outlaws discrimination, protecting employees. This legislation also covers the provision of goods and services.

The **Race Relations Act 1976** makes it unlawful to discriminate on the grounds of colour, race, nationality, ethnic or national origin.

The **Commission for Racial Equality** has produced a code of conduct to eradicate racial discrimination.

The **Disability Discrimination Act (DDA) 1995** makes it unlawful to discriminate on the grounds of disability.

The **Sex Discrimination Act 1975 and 1985**, and the **Equal Pay Act 1970**, prevent discrimination or less favourable treatment of men or women on the basis of gender. This covers pay and conditions as well as promotion.

IMPROVING PERSONAL EFFECTIVENESS

In order to develop personally and to improve your skills professionally, it is important to set yourself targets against which you can measure your achievement.

To an employer it is important that you are *consistent*. You must always perform your skills to the highest standard, and present and promote a positive image of the industry and the organisation in which you are employed and which you represent.

Performance review or appraisal

Appraisal is a process whereby a supervisor identifies and discusses with individuals their strengths and weaknesses, and areas within their professional role that require further training and development. The job description is used as a key document during appraisal.

This may seem daunting, but it is an important and useful process. You can also use it to your advantage to:

- identify opportunities for further or specialist training;
- identify obstructions which are affecting progression;
- identify and amend any changes to your role;
- identify and focus on your achievements to date against targets set;
- make an action plan which will help you achieve your targets.

At the next appraisal the agreed objectives and targets set for the previous period are reviewed and the results measured. Additional accomplishments and contributions should also be looked at. A revised action plan will then be set for review at the next performance review or appraisal.

TIP

Internal verification
When you are being assessed, all assessment is checked for validity using a process called *internal verification*. An appointed person titled *internal verifier* will investigate an appeal if it is thought by the candidate that the assessment decision outcome by the assessor was incorrect.

Performance Appraisal	
Name:	Jeanette Manners
Job Title:	Trainee beauty therapist
Date of Appraisal:	19 February 2004
Objectives:	To obtain competence within:- Improving facial skin condition across the range.
Notes on Achievement:	Competence has been achieved for most facial skin condition range requirements.
Training Requirements:	Further training and practice is needed within the area of facial massage.
Any Other Comments on Performance by Appraiser:	Jeanette has achieved most of the objectives set out during the last appraisal.
Any Comments on the Appraisal by the Staff Member Appraised:	I feel that this has been a fair appraisal of my progress although I did not achieve all of my performance targets. *J Manners*
Action Plan:	- To achieve occupational competence across the range for facial skin condition (i.e. facial massage). - To undergo training and practice in hair removal techniques. - To take assessment for hair removal.
Date of Next Appraisal:	20 October 2004

Targets

Targets to be achieved may be set by the employer either for individuals or for the team as a whole. These may review quality, efficiency and results. Computer systems are often able to provide relevant data about the salon.

You should set your *own* targets, however, to monitor your effectiveness and performance. In training situations trainees undergo a programme which states:

- what training activities will take place and when;
- what tasks need to be performed;
- what standards are expected to be reached;
- when assessment should be expected;
- when a review of progress towards the agreed targets is to take place.

In the same way, you can set targets for yourself.

Personal effectiveness against targets set

Your ability to meet the expected standards is referred to as personal effectiveness.

Standards that you are assessed against include:

- The National Occupational Standards for Beauty Therapy
- Organisational Codes of Conduct
- Personal targets and their achievement, identified in appraisal and short- and long-term reviews
- Your productivity targets, i.e. with regard to technical and retail sales

If you meet the standards before the due target date, your trainer should be informed to review new targets for completion. This will ensure that you remain motivated in your work role and it will enable you to progress more quickly.

If personal targets are not being met it is important to identify the problem and constructive performance targets should be put in place to resolve unsatisfactory performance.

Your future personal objectives targets should be agreed with a date set for completion. At the next appraisal the agreed objectives and targets set for the previous period will be reviewed.

Being positive about negative feedback

Your appraisal may not always be a positive experience. It is important to be positive about recommendations to improve your performance and work towards achieving these. Not meeting targets may ultimately result in disciplinary procedure which may lead to dismissal. Your achievements of the productivity targets set leads to the financial effectiveness of the business.

TIP

National Occupational standards for Beauty Therapy
The NVQ/SVQ level 2 Beauty Therapy qualification is used to plan your training needs and assessment requirements.

The National Occupational Standards are identified in the examination-awarding body's candidate logbook. They can also be obtained from the Hairdressing and Beauty Therapy Industry Authority (HABIA).

An *individual learning plan*, negotiated with your assessor, sets short-term targets for completion and records valuable feedback on assessment completion and where there is a need for further training to meet the expected standards. This may be used when reviewing your personal performance.

Developing within the job role

There will be many opportunities to develop your skills and experience, and your understanding of your work:

- by attending trade seminars;
- by subscribing to professional trade magazines;
- by watching colleagues who have more advanced qualifications or experience;

TIP

Internal promotion may require an employee to put in extra work, take on more responsibility or come up with new ideas.

ACTIVITY

Evaluating customer care
Visit a local salon. Beforehand, think of questions you would like to ask in relation to treatments. Then evaluate the customer care and services you received. Were the staff:

- friendly?
- dressed smartly?
- knowledgeable?
- efficient and eager to assist you?
- helpful?

If you answered 'no' to any of these questions, discuss your reasons with your colleagues. What have you learnt from this experience?

- by developing your portfolio to include evidence and examples of experience gained;

- by using time effectively, and by practising – all tasks take time to master: the more you practise, the more skilled and efficient you will become.

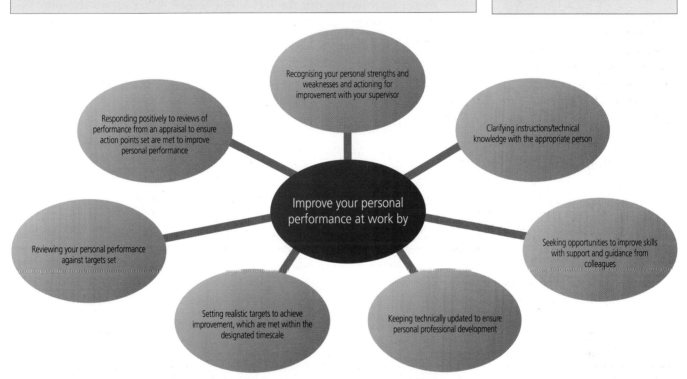

Assessment of knowledge and understanding

You have now learnt about the importance of making a good impression and your part in building up the success of the business organisation. This included the need for continuous professional development and the importance of good teamwork. This enables you to develop and maintain your effectiveness at work.

To test your level of knowledge, answer the following short questions. These will prepare you for your summative (final) assessment.

Salon roles, procedures and targets

1 It is necessary to ask a client a series of questions to finalise a treatment plan. Confidential information should only be available to persons to whom consent has been given. What is the name of the Act that implements this legislation?

2 List five important service standards to be followed with regard to appearance and behaviour whilst in the salon environment.

3 How can you make a client feel welcome?

4 Following the consultation you feel that the client is unsuitable for treatment. How would you handle this situation?

5 A client requests a service that you are not qualified to offer. She insists that she receives the treatment. You have seen other therapists carrying out the treatment before. What action should you take and why?

6 If a beauty therapist had an unprofessional attitude, how would this affect the reputation of the salon?

7 What could be a reason for client dissatisfaction? How could client dissatisfaction be avoided?

8 What steps need to be taken if a client makes a complaint?

9 If a client requested information that was outside your responsibility, how would you respond to ensure that dissatisfaction was avoided?

10 How will achievement of your training targets improve your personal performance?

11 Why is it important to have an awareness of and allocate the appropriate amount of time when booking and performing different Beauty Therapy services?

Improving your performance

1 All colleagues should be treated equally. The Equal Opportunities Commission (EOC), states that it is best practice to have a written Equal Opportunities Policy. What should this include?

2 Why are positive working relationships with your colleagues important?

3 If you have a dispute with a colleague why is it important that it is quickly resolved?

4 What are the main methods of communication?

5 Give three examples of positive body language.

6 Give three examples of negative body language.

7 A client arrives for a treatment to find that there has been a mistake with the booking and she has not been made an appointment. What action should be taken?

8 Action points for your personal development are identified at performance review or appraisal. Why is it important to respond positively to reviews and feedback on your performance?

9 Why is it important to keep up-to-date with current trends, products and services in Beauty Therapy?

anatomy
and
physiology

chapter 5

ANATOMY AND PHYSIOLOGY

As a beauty therapist it is important that you have a good understanding of anatomy and physiology, as many of your treatments aim to improve the particular functioning of systems of the body. For example a facial massage will improve blood and lymph circulation locally, as you massage the skin's surface, increase cellular renewal as you improve nutrition to the living cells, and remove dead skin cells. The result is a healthier looking skin.

ANATOMY AND PHYSIOLOGY KNOWLEDGE REQUIREMENTS

It is necessary for you to know and understand anatomy and physiology as relevant to each beauty therapy unit. This may be assessed through oral questioning, written test or assignment. To guide you in your studies the essential anatomy and physiology you need to know and understand for each unit has been identified with a ✓ symbol.

The beauty therapy units with an essential anatomy and physiology knowledge requirement are:

BT4 Improve and maintain facial skin condition

BT5 Provide eyelash and eyebrow treatments

BT6 Remove hair using waxing techniques

BT7 Provide manicure treatment

BT8 Provide pedicure treatment

BT9 Provide make-up treatment

BT12 Extend and maintain nails

BT13 Provide nail art service

BT15 Assist with spa treatments

Anatomy and physiology knowledge and understanding is located in this unit, but it can also be found within each of the beauty therapy units where essential anatomy and physiology knowledge are identified as above.

Anatomy and Physiology ✓ essential knowledge for unit

UNIT	BT4	BT6	BT7	BT8	BT9	BT12	BT13	BT15
Skin structure & function	✓	✓	✓	✓	✓	✓	✓	✓
Factors affecting skin condition	✓		✓	✓	✓	✓		✓
Structure of hair and type		✓						
Hair growth cycle		✓						
Nail structure and function			✓	✓		✓	✓	
Nail growth			✓	✓		✓	✓	
Muscle groups in parts of the body, position, structure and function	✓		✓	✓				
Muscle tone	✓							
Bones in parts of the body , position, structure and function	✓		✓	✓				
Composition and function of blood and lymph	✓		✓	✓				
Blood flow and pulse rate			✓	✓				✓
Central nervous system and autonomic system								✓

CARING FOR THE SKIN

The skin varies in appearance, according to our race, sex and age. It also alters from season to season and from year to year, and reflects our general health, lifestyle and diet.

At puberty the chemical substances (**hormones**) that control many of our bodies' activities become very active. Amongst other effects, this activity causes the skin to become more oily, and often blemishes appear on the skin's surface. Seven out of ten teenagers find that their skin becomes blemished with blackheads, inflamed angry spots and even scars at this time: a skin disorder called **acne vulgaris**.

During the twenties the skin should look its best; any hormonal imbalance that occurred at puberty should by now have stabilised. As we grow older, the skin ages too. In our late twenties and early thirties we will see fine lines appearing on the skin's surface, especially around the eyes where the skin is thinner and the skin gradually becomes drier.

At around the age of forty, hormone activity in the body becomes slower and the skin begins to lose its strength and elasticity. The skin becomes increasingly drier, and lines and wrinkles appear on the surface. In the late fifties brown patches of discoloured skin (**lentigines**) may appear: these are commonly seen at the temple region of the face and on the backs of the hands.

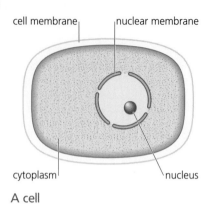

cell membrane   nuclear membrane

cytoplasm   nucleus

A cell

Fortunately help is at hand: there is an ever-increasing number of skin-care products from a vast and highly profitable cosmetics industry, and there are the skill and expertise of the qualified beauty professional.

If it is *your* intention to become a qualified beauty professional – whether make-up artist or beauty therapist – you need to learn about skin: its construction, its function, and how and why it is changed by both internal and external influences.

BASIC STRUCTURES

The human body consists of many trillions of microscopic **cells**. Each cell contains a chemical substance called **protoplasm**, which contains various specialised structures whose activities are essential to our health. If cells are unable to function properly, a disorder results.

Surrounding the cell is the **cell membrane**: this forms a boundary between the cell contents and their environment. The membrane has a porous surface which permits food to enter and waste materials to leave.

In the centre of the cell is the **nucleus**, which contains the **chromosomes**. On these are the **genes** we have inherited from our parents. The genes are ultimately responsible for cell reproduction and cell functioning.

The liquid within the cell membrane and surrounding the nucleus is called **cytoplasm**. Scattered throughout this are other small bodies, the **organelles**; each has a specific function within the cell.

Cells in the body tend to specialise in carrying out particular functions. Groups of cells which share function, shape, size or structure are called **tissues**. Tissues, in turn, may be grouped to form the larger functional and structural units we know as **organs**.

TIP

The skin accounts for one-eighth of the body's total weight. It measures approximately 1.5m² in total, depending on body size. It is thinnest on the eyelids (0.05 mm), and thickest on the soles of the feet (approximately 5 mm).

Types of tissue and general function

Name of tissue	Examples	General functions
Epithelial	Epidermis	Forms surfaces and linings for protection
Connective	Bone, cartilage, areolar	A structural tissue that supports, surrounds and connects different parts of the body
Muscular	Voluntary or skeletal, involuntary	Contracts and produces movement
Nervous	Neurones	Forms a communication system between different parts of the body

The skin

The human skin is an organ – the largest of the body. It provides a tough, flexible covering, with many different important functions.

FUNCTIONS OF THE SKIN

Protection

The skin protects the body from potentially harmful substances and conditions.

- The outer surface is **bactericidal**, helping to prevent the multiplication of harmful micro-organisms. It also prevents the absorption of many substances (unless the surface is broken), because of the construction of the cells on its outer surface which form a chemical and physical barrier.
- The skin cushions the underlying structures from physical injury.
- The skin provides a **waterproof coating**. Its natural oil, **sebum**, prevents the skin from losing vital water, and thus prevents skin dehydration.
- The skin contains a pigment called **melanin**. This absorbs harmful rays of ultraviolet light.

HEALTH AND SAFETY	

Skin protection
Although the skin is structured to avoid penetration of harmful substances by absorption, certain chemicals can be absorbed through the skin. Always protect the skin when using potentially harmful substances.

Heat regulation

Body **temperature** is controlled in part by heat loss through the skin and by sweating.

Excretion

Small amounts of certain **waste products**, such as water and salt, are removed from the body by excretion through the surface of the skin.

Warning

The skin affords a warning system against outside invasion. **Redness** and **irritation** of the skin indicate that the skin is intolerant to something, either external or internal.

Sensitivity

The skin allows the feelings of **touch**, **pressure**, **pain**, **heat** and **cold**, and allows us to recognise objects by their feel and shape.

Nutrition

The skin provides storage for **fat**, which provides an energy reserve. It is also responsible for producing a significant proportion of our **vitamin D**, which is created by a chemical action when sunlight is in contact with the skin.

Moisture control

The skin controls the movement of moisture from within the deeper layers of the skin.

THE STRUCTURE OF THE SKIN

If we looked within the skin, using a microscope, we would be able to see two distinct layers: the **epidermis** and the **dermis**. Between these layers is a specialised layer which acts like a 'glue', sticking the two layers together: this is the **basement membrane**. If the epidermis and dermis become separated, body fluids fill the space, creating a **blister**.

Situated below the epidermis and dermis is a further layer, the **subcutaneous layer** or **fat layer**. The fat layer consists of cells containing fatty deposits, called adipose cells. The thickness of the subcutaneous layer varies according to the body area, and is, for example, very thin around the eyes.

The fatty layer has a protective function and:

- acts as an insulator to conserve body heat;
- cushions muscles and bones below from injury;
- acts as an energy source as excess fat is stored.

epidermis

basement membrane

dermis

subcutaneous layer

Skin

THE EPIDERMIS

The epidermis is located directly above the dermis. It is composed of five layers, with the surface layer forming the outer skin – what we can see and touch. The main function of the epidermis is to protect the deeper living structures from invasion and harm from the external environment.

Nourishment of the epidermis, essential for growth, is received from a liquid called the **interstitial fluid**.

Each layer of the epidermis can be recognised by its shape and by the function of its cells. The main type of cell found in the epidermis is the **keratinocyte**, which produces the protein **keratin**. It is keratin that makes the skin tough and that reduces the passage of substances into or out of the body.

Over a period of about four weeks, cells move from the bottom layer of the epidermis to the top layer, the skin's surface, changing in shape and structure as they progress. The process of cellular change takes place in stages.

TIP

The epidermis is the most significant layer of the skin with regard to the external application of skin-care cosmetics and make-up.

TIP

Every five days we shed a complete surface layer. About 80 per cent of household dust is composed of dead skin cells.

- *The cell is formed* – by division of an earlier cell.
- *The cell matures* – it changes structure and moves upwards and outwards.
- *The cell dies* – it moves upwards and becomes an empty shell, which is eventually shed.

The layers of the epidermis

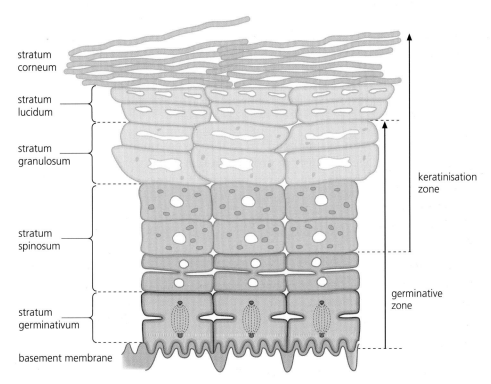

The layers of the epidermis

HEALTH AND SAFETY

Psoriasis
With the skin disorder *psoriasis*, cell division occurs much more quickly, resulting in clusters of dead skin cells appearing on the skin's surface.

The germinative zone

In the **germinative zone** the cells of the epidermis are living cells.

Stratum germinativum

The **stratum germinativum**, or **basal layer**, is the lowermost layer of the epidermis. It is formed from a single layer of column-shaped cells joined to the basement membrane. These cells divide continuously and produce new epidermal cells (keratinocytes). This process of cell division is known as mitosis.

Stratum spinosum

The **stratum spinosum**, or **prickle-cell layer**, is formed from two to six rows of elongated cells; these have a surface of spiky spines which connect to surrounding cells. Each cell has a large nucleus and is filled with fluid.

Langerhan cells and melanocyte cells

Two other important cells are found in the germinative zone of the epidermis.

HEALTH AND SAFETY

Allergic reactions
Most people will be unaware that a foreign body has invaded the skin. Sometimes, however, the skin's surface intolerance to a substance is apparent. It shows as an allergic reaction, in which the skin becomes red, itchy and swollen.

melanocyte

basement membrane

A melanocyte

Langerhan cells **Langerhan cells** absorb and remove foreign bodies that enter the skin. They then move from the epidermis to the dermis below, and finally enter the lymph system (the body's waste-transport system).

Melanocytes **Melanocytes** are the cells that produce the skin pigment **melanin**, which contributes to our skin colour. About one in every ten germinative cells is a melanocyte. Melanocytes are stimulated to produce melanin by ultra-violet rays, and their main function is to protect the other epidermal cells in this way from the harmful effects of ultra-violet.

The quantity and distribution of melanocytes differs according to race. In a white Caucasian person the melanin tends to be destroyed when it reaches the granular layer (see below). With stimulation from artificial or natural ultra-violet light, however, melanin will also be present in the upper epidermis.

In contrast a black skin has melanin present in larger quantities throughout *all* the epidermal layers, a level of protection that has evolved to deal with bright ultra-violet light. This increased protection allows less ultra-violet to penetrate the dermis below, reducing the possibility of premature ageing from exposure to ultra-violet light. The more even quality and distribution of melanin also means that people with dark skins are less at risk of developing skin cancer.

Another pigment, **carotene**, which is yellowish, also occurs in epidermal cells. Its contribution to skin colour lessens in importance as the amount of melanin in the skin increases.

Skin colour also increases when the skin becomes warm. This is because the **blood capillaries** at the surface dilate, bringing blood nearer to the surface so that heat can be lost.

> **TIP** ✔
>
> Many skin-care products and cosmetics, including lipsticks and mascaras, now contain *sunscreens*. This is because research has shown that ultra-violet exposure is the principal cause of skin ageing.

Stratum granulosum

The **stratum granulosum**, or **granular layer**, is composed of one, two or three layers of cells which have become much flatter. The nucleus of the cell has begun to break up, creating what appear to be granules within the cell cytoplasm. These are known as **keratohyaline granules** and later form keratin. At this stage the cells form a new, combined layer.

The keratinisation zone

The **keratinisation zone**, or **cornified zone**, is where the cells begin to die and where finally they will be shed from the skin. The cells at this stage become progressively flatter, and the cell cytoplasm is replaced with the hard protein keratin.

Stratum lucidum

The **stratum lucidum**, **clear layer** or **lucid layer**, is only seen in non-hairy areas of the skin such as the palms of the hands and the soles of the feet. The cells here lack a nucleus and are filled with a clear substance called **eledin**.

Stratum corneum

The **stratum corneum**, or **cornified layer**, is formed from several layers of flattened, scale-like overlapping cells, composed mainly of keratin. These help to reflect ultra-violet light from the skin's surface; black skin, which evolved to withstand strong ultra-violet, has a thicker stratum corneum than does Caucasian skin.

It takes about three weeks for the epidermal cells to reach the stratum corneum from the stratum germinativum. The cells are then shed, a process called **desquamation**.

TIP ✔

The skin will become much thicker in response to friction. A client with a manual occupation may therefore develop hard skin (calluses) on her hands. The skin condition can be treated with an *emollient* preparation, which will moisturise and soften the dry skin.

THE DERMIS

The dermis is the inner portion of the skin, situated underneath the epidermis and composed of dense **connective tissue**. It is much thicker than the epidermis.

The dermis

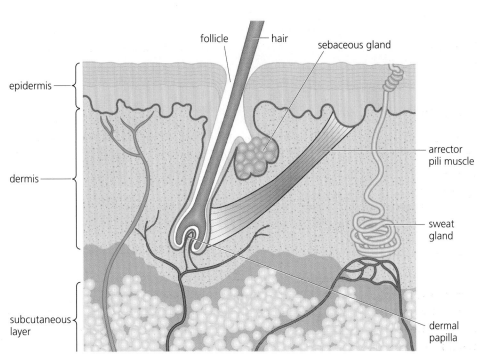

follicle — hair   sebaceous gland

epidermis

dermis

subcutaneous layer

arrector pili muscle

sweat gland

dermal papilla

The reticular layer

The dermis contains a network of protein fibres called the **reticular layer**. These fibres allow the skin to expand, to contract, and to perform intricate, supple movements.

This network is composed of two sorts of protein fibre, yellow **elastin** fibres and white **collagen** fibres: elastin fibres give the skin its elasticity, and collagen fibres give it its strength. The fibres are produced by specialised cells called **fibroblasts**, and are held in a gel called the **ground substance**.

While this network is strong, the skin will appear youthful and firm. As the fibres harden and fragment, however, the network begins to collapse, losing its elasticity. The skin then begins to show visible signs of ageing.

A major cause of damage to this network is unprotected exposure of the skin to ultraviolet light and to weather. Sometimes, too, the skin loses its elasticity because of a sudden increase in body weight, for example at puberty or pregnancy. This results in the appearance of **stretch marks**, streaks of thin skin which is a different colour from the surrounding skin: on a white skin they appear as thin reddish streaks; on a black skin they appear slightly lighter than the surrounding skin. The lost elasticity cannot be restored.

Collagen and elastin fibres

Hugh Rushton

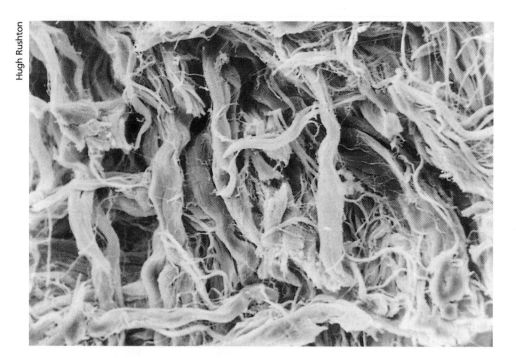

Nerve endings

The dermis contains different types of sensory **nerve endings**, which register touch, pressure, pain and temperature. These send messages to the **central nervous system** and the **brain**, informing us about the outside world and what is happening on the skin's surface. The appearance of each of these nerve endings is quite varied.

The papillary layer

Near the surface of the dermis are tiny projections called **papillae**; these contain both nerve endings and blood capillaries. This part of the dermis is known as the **papillary layer**, and it also supplies the upper epidermis with its nutrition.

Growth and repair

The body's blood system of arteries and veins continually brings blood to the capillary networks in the skin and takes it away again. The blood carries the nutrients and oxygen essential for the skin's health, maintenance and growth, and takes away waste products.

TIP

Appropriate external massage movements can be used to increase the blood supply within the dermis, bringing extra nutrients and oxygen to the skin and to the underlying muscle. At the same time, the lymphatic circulation is increased, improving the removal of waste products that may have accumulated.

HEALTH AND SAFETY

Scars
When the surface has been broken, the skin at the site of the injury is replaced but may leave a scar. This initially appears red, due to the increased blood supply to the area, required while the skin heals. When healed, the redness will fade.

Defence

Within the dermis are the structures responsible for protecting the skin from harmful foreign bodies and irritants.

One set of cells, the **mast cells**, burst when stimulated during inflammation or allergic reactions, and release **histamine**. This causes the blood vessels nearby to enlarge, thereby bringing more blood to the site of the irritation.

In the blood, and also in the lymph and the connective tissue, are another group of cells: the **macrophages**. These destroy micro-organisms and engulf dead cells and other unwanted particles.

Waste products

Lymph vessels in the skin carry a fluid (**lymph**) containing waste products such as used blood cells. The waste products are eliminated, and usable protein is recycled for further use by the body.

Control of functioning

Hormones are chemical messengers transported in the blood. They control the activity of many organs in the body, including the cells and glands in the skin. These include **melanosomes**, which produce skin pigment, and the **sweat glands** and **sebaceous glands**.

Hormone imbalance at different times of our life may disturb the normal functioning of these cells and structures, causing various **skin disorders**.

ACTIVITY

The emotions
Emotions can affect blood supply to the skin: blood vessels in the dermis may enlarge or constrict. Think of different emotions, and how these might affect the appearance of the skin.

Skin appendages

Within the dermis are structures called **skin appendages**. These include:

- sweat glands;
- hair follicles, which produce hair;
- sebaceous glands;
- nails.

Sweat glands

Sweat glands or **sudoriferous glands** are composed of **epithelial tissue**, which extends from the epidermis into the dermis. These glands are found all over the body, but are particularly abundant on the palms of the hands and the soles of the feet. Their function is to regulate body temperature through the evaporation of sweat from the surface of the skin. Fluid loss and control of body temperature are important to prevent the body overheating, especially in hot, humid climates. For this reason, perhaps, sweat glands are larger and more abundant in black skins than white skins.

sweat pore

epidermis

sweat duct

coiled tube of sweat gland

blood supply

An eccrine sweat gland

There are two types of sweat glands: *eccrine glands* and *apocrine glands*. **Eccrine glands** are simple sweat-producing glands, found over most of the body, appearing as tiny tubes (**ducts**). The eccrine glands are responsive to heat. These are straight in the epidermis, and coiled in the dermis. The duct opens directly onto the surface of the skin through an opening called a **pore**.

Eccrine glands continuously secrete small amounts of sweat, even when we appear not to be perspiring. In this way they maintain the body temperature at a constant 36.8°C.

Apocrine glands are found in the armpit, the nipples, and the groin area. This kind of gland is larger than the eccrine gland, and is attached to a hair follicle. Apocrine glands are controlled by hormones, becoming active at puberty. They also increase in activity when we are excited, nervous or stressed. The fluid they secrete is thicker than that from the eccrine glands, and may contain urea, fats, sugars and small amounts of protein. Also present are traces of aromatic molecules called **pheromones** which are thought to cause sexual attraction between individuals.

An unpleasant smell – **body odour** – develops when apocrine sweat is broken down by skin bacteria. Good habits of personal hygiene will prevent this.

Unilever

Sweat pores

Cosmetic perspiration control To extend hygiene protection during the day, apply either a deodorant or an anti-perspirant. **Anti-perspirants** reduce the amount of sweat that reaches the skin's surface: they have an astringent action which closes the pores. **Deodorants** contain an active antiseptic ingredient which reduces the skin's bacterial activity, thereby reducing the risk of odour from stale sweat.

HEALTH AND SAFETY

Anti-perspirants
The active ingredient in most anti-perspirant products is *aluminium chlorhydrate*. This is known to cause contact dermatitis in some people, especially if the skin has been damaged by recent removal of unwanted hair. Bear this in mind if you are performing an underarm depilatory wax treatment. (See the aftercare instructions, page 260.)

THE HAIR

The structure and function of hair and the surrounding tissues

A hair is a long, slender structure which grows out of, and is part of, the skin. Each hair is made up of dead skin cells, which contain the protein called keratin.

Hairs cover the whole body, except for the palms of the hands, the soles of the feet, the lips, and parts of the sex organs.

Hair has many functions:

- *scalp hair* insulates the head against cold, protects it from the sun, and cushions it against bumps;
- *eyebrows* cushion the browbone from bumps, and prevent sweat from running into the eyes;
- *eyelashes* help to prevent foreign particles entering the eyes;
- *nostril hair* traps dust particles inhaled with the air;
- *ear hair* helps to protect the ear canal;
- *body hair* helps to provide an insulating cover (though this function is almost obsolete in humans), has a valuable sensory function, and is linked with the secretion of sebum onto the surface of the skin.

Hair also plays a role in social communication.

The structure of hair

Most hairs are made up of three layers of different types of epithelial cells: the *medulla*, the *cortex*, and the *cuticle*.

The **medulla** is the central core of the hair. The cells of the medulla contain soft keratin, and sometimes some pigment granules. There is usually no medulla in thinner hairs.

The **cortex** is the thickest layer of the hair, and is made up of several layers of closely-packed elongated cells. These contain pigment granules and hard keratin.

The **cuticle** is the protective outer layer of the hair, and is composed of thin, unpigmented flat cells. These contain hard keratin, and overlap from the base to the tip of the hair.

It is the **pigment** in the cortex that gives hair its colour. When this pigment is no longer made, the hair appears white. As the proportion of white hairs rises, the hair seems to go 'grey': in fact, however, each individual hair is either coloured as before, or white.

The parts of the hair

Each hair is recognised by three parts: the *root*, the *bulb*, and the *shaft*:

- the **root** is the part of the hair that is in the follicle;
- the **bulb** is the enlarged base of the root;
- the **shaft** is the part of the hair that can be seen above the skin's surface.

The structure of skin

Each hair grows out of a tube-like indentation in the epidermis, the **hair follicle**. The walls of the follicle are a continuation of the epidermal layer of the skin.

The **arrector pili muscle** is attached at an angle to the base of the follicle. Cold, aggression or fright stimulates this muscle to contract, pulling the follicle and the hair upright.

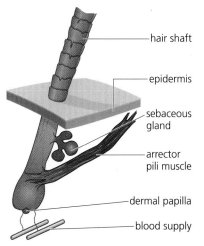

A cross-section of the hair follicle and hair

The **sebaceous gland** is attached to the upper part of the follicle; from it, a duct enters directly into the hair follicle. The gland produces an oily substance, **sebum**, which is secreted into the follicle. Sebum waterproofs, lubricates and softens the hair, and the surface of the skin; it also protects the skin against bacterial and fungal infections. The contraction of the arrector pili muscle aids the secretion of sebum.

The **dermal papilla**, a connective tissue sheath, is surrounded by a hair bulb. It has an excellent blood supply, necessary for the growth of the hair. It is not itself part of the follicle, but a separate tiny organ which serves the follicle.

The **bulb** is the expanded base of the hair root. A gap at the base leads to a cavity inside, which houses the papilla. The bulb contains in its lower part the dividing cells that create the hair. The hair continues to develop as it passes through the regions of the upper bulb and the root.

The **matrix** is the name given to the lower part of the bulb, which comprises actively dividing cells from which the hair is formed.

The hair follicle The hair follicle extends into the dermis, and is made up of three sheaths: the *inner epithelial root sheath*, the *outer epithelial root sheath*, and the surrounding *connective-tissue sheath*.

The **inner epithelial root sheath** grows from the bottom of the follicle at the papilla; both the hair and the inner root sheath grow upwards together. The inner surface of this sheath is covered with cuticle cells, in the same way as the outer surface of the hair: these cells lock together, anchoring the hair firmly in place. The inner root sheath ceases to grow when level with the sebaceous gland.

The hair bulb

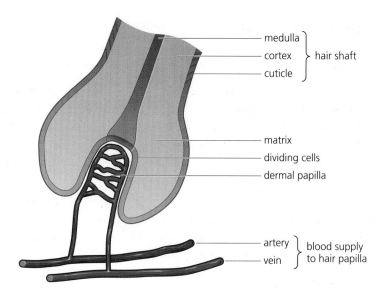

The **outer epithelial root sheath** forms the follicle wall. This does not grow up with the hair, but is stationary. It is a continuation of the growing layer of the epidermis of the skin.

The **connective-tissue sheath** surrounds both the follicle and the sebaceous gland, providing both a sensory supply and a blood supply. The connective-tissue sheath includes, and is a continuation of, the papilla.

The *shape* of the hairs is determined by the shape of the hair follicle – an angled or bent follicle will produce an oval or flat hair, whereas a straight follicle will produce a round hair. Flat hairs are curly, oval hairs are wavy, and round hairs are straight. As a general rule, during waxing curly hairs break off more easily than straight hairs.

TIP

When hairs break off due to incorrect waxing technique, they will break at the level at which they are locked into the follicle by the cells of the inner root sheath.

TIP

An angled follicle may cause the hair to be broken off at the angle during waxing, instead of being completely pulled out with its root. If this happens, broken hairs will appear at the skin's surface within a few days.

By causing damage to the follicle and changing its shape, waxing can cause the regrowth of hairs to be frizzy or curled where previously the hairs have been straight.

The nerve supply   The number, size and type of nerve endings associated with hair follicles is related to the size and type of follicle. The follicles of vellus hairs (see below) have the fewest nerve endings; those of terminal hairs have the most.

The nerve endings surrounding hair follicles respond mainly to rapid movements when the hair is moved. Nerve endings that respond to touch can also be found around the surface openings of some hair follicles, as well as just below the epidermis.

The three types of hair

There are three main types of hair: *lanugo*, *vellus* and *terminal*.

Lanugo hairs are found on foetuses. They are fine and soft, do not have a medulla, and are often unpigmented. They grow from around the third to the fifth month of pregnancy, and are shed to be replaced by the secondary vellus hairs around the seventh to the eighth month of pregnancy. Lanugo hairs on the scalp, eyebrows and eyelashes are replaced by terminal hairs.

Vellus hairs are fine, downy and soft, and are found on the face and body. They are often unpigmented, rarely longer than 20mm, and do not have a medulla or a well-formed bulb. The base of these hairs is very close to the skin's surface. If stimulated, the shallow follicle of a vellus hair can grow downwards and become a follicle that produces terminal hairs.

Terminal hairs are longer and coarser than vellus hairs, and most are pigmented. They vary greatly in shape, in diameter and length, and in colour and texture. The follicles from which they grow are set deeply in the dermis and have well-defined bulbs.

> **TIP**
>
> Some areas of the body – for example, the bikini line and underarm areas – often have terminal hairs with very deep follicles. When these hairs are removed, the resulting tissue damage may cause minor bleeding from the entrance of the follicle. Removal of these deep-seated hairs is obviously more uncomfortable than the removal of shallower hairs.

Hair growth

All hair has a cyclical pattern of growth, which can be divided into three phases: *anagen*, *catagen* and *telogen*.

Anagen **Anagen** is the actively growing stage of the hair – the follicle has re-formed; the hair bulb is developing, surrounding the life-giving dermal papilla; and a new hair forms, growing from the matrix in the bulb.

Catagen **Catagen** is the stage when the hair separates from the papilla. Over a few days it is carried by the movement of the inner root sheath, up the follicle to the base of the sebaceous gland. Here it stays until it either falls out or is pushed out by a new hair growing up behind it.

This stage can be very rapid, with a new hair growing straight away; or slower, with the papilla and the follicle below the sebaceous gland degenerating and entering a resting stage, telogen.

Telogen **Telogen** is a resting stage. Many hair follicles do not undergo this stage, but start to produce a new hair immediately. During resting phases, hairs may still be loosely inserted in the shallow follicles.

> **TIP**
>
> A hair pulled out at the *anagen* stage will be surrounded by the inner and outer root sheaths and have a properly formed bulb.

> **TIP**
>
> A hair pulled out at the *catagen* or *telogen* stage can be recognised by the brush-like appearance of the root.

The hair growth cycle

> **TIP**
>
> Because of the cyclical nature of hair growth, the follicles are always at different stages of their growth cycle. When the hair is removed, therefore, the hair will not all grow back at the same time. For this reason, waxing can appear to reduce the quantity of hair growth. This is not so; given time, all the hair would regrow. Waxing is classed as a temporary means of hair removal.

Speed of growth

The anagen, catagen and telogen stages last for different lengths of time in different hair types and in different parts of the body:

> **TIP**
>
> Vellus hairs grow slowly and take 2–3 months to return after waxing. They can remain dormant in the follicle for 6–8 months before shedding.

- *scalp hair* grows for 2–7 years, and has a resting stage of 3–4 months;
- *eyebrow* hair grows for 1–2 months, and has a resting stage of 3–4 months;
- *eyelashes* grow for 3–6 weeks, and have a resting stage of 3–4 months.

After a waxing treatment, body hair will take approximately 6–8 weeks to return.

Because hair growth cycles are not all in synchronisation, we always have hair present at any given time. On the scalp, at any one time for example, 85 per cent of hairs may be in the anagen phase. This is why hair growth after waxing starts within a few days: what is seen is the appearance of hairs that were already developing in the follicle at the time of waxing.

Types of hair growth

Hirsutism **Hirsutism** is a term used to describe a pattern of hair growth that is abnormal for that person's sex, such as when a woman's hair growth follows a man's hair-growth pattern.

Hypertrichosis **Hypertrichosis** is an abnormal growth of excess hair. It is usually due to abnormal conditions brought about by disease or injury.

Superfluous hair **Superfluous hair** (excess hair) is perfectly normal at certain periods in a woman's life, such as during puberty or pregnancy. Terminal hairs formed at these times usually disappear once the normal hormonal balance has returned. Those newly formed during the menopause are often permanent unless treated with a permanent method of hair removal, such as electrical depilation.

Factors affecting the growth rate and quantity of hair

Hair does not always grow uniformly:

- *Time of day* Hair grows faster at night than during the day.
- *Weather* Hairs grow faster in warm weather than in cold.
- *Pregnancy* In women, hairs grow faster between the ages of 16 and 24, and (frequently) during mid-pregnancy.
- *Age* The rate of hair growth slows down with age. In women, however, facial hair growth continues to increase in old age, while trunk and limb hair increases into middle age and then decreases.
- *Colour* Hairs of different colour grow at different speeds – for example, coarse black hair grows more quickly than fine blonde hair.
- *Part of the body* Hair in different areas of the body grows at different rates, as do different types and thicknesses of hair. The weekly growth rate varies from approximately 1.5mm (fine hair) to 2.8mm (coarse hair), when actively growing.
- *Heredity* Members of a family may have heritable growth patterns, such as excess hair that starts to grow at puberty and increases until the age of 20–25.
- *Health and diet* Health and diet are crucial in the rate of hair growth.
- *Stress* Emotional stress can cause a temporary hormonal imbalance within the body, which may lead to a temporary growth of excess hair.
- *Medical conditions* A sudden unexplained increase of body hair growth may indicate a more serious medical problem, such as malfunction of the ovaries; or result from the taking of certain drugs, such as corticosteroids.

The quantity as well as the type of hair present may vary with race:

- *People of Latin extraction* tend to possess heavier body, facial and scalp hair, which is relatively coarse and straight.
- *People of Eastern extraction* tend to possess very little or no body and facial hair growth, and usually their scalp hair growth is relatively coarse and straight.
- *People of Northern European and Caucasian extraction* tend to have light to medium body and facial hair growth, with their scalp hair growth being wavy, loosely curled, or straight.
- *People of African-Caribbean extraction* tend to have little body and facial hair growth, but usually their scalp hair growth is relatively coarse and tightly curled.

> **HEALTH AND SAFETY**
>
> **African-Caribbean clients**
> The body hair of African-Caribbean clients is prone to breaking during waxing, and to ingrowing after waxing. Skin damage can result in the loss of pigmentation (hypopigmentation).

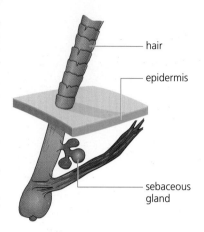

- hair
- epidermis
- sebaceous gland

A sebaceous gland

Sebaceous glands

The **sebaceous gland** appears as a minute sac-like organ. Usually it is associated with the hair follicle with which it forms the **pilosebaceous unit**, but the two can appear independently.

Sebaceous glands are found all over the body, except on the palms of the hands and the soles of the feet. They are particularly numerous on the scalp, the forehead, and in the back and chest region. The cells of the glands decompose, producing the skin's natural oil, **sebum**. This empties directly into the hair follicle.

The activity of the sebaceous gland increases at puberty when stimulated by the male hormone, **androgen**. In adults activity of the sebaceous gland gradually decreases again. Men secrete slightly more sebum than women; and on black skin the sebaceous glands are larger and more numerous than on white skin.

Sebum is composed of fatty acids and waxes. These have **bactericidal** and **fungicidal** properties, and so discourage the multiplication of micro-organisms on the surface of the skin. Sebum also reduces the evaporation of moisture from the skin, and so prevents the skin from drying out.

TIP

Cosmetic moisturisers mimic sebum in providing an oily covering for the skin's surface to reduce moisture.

HEALTH AND SAFETY

The lips
Sebaceous glands are not present on the surface of the lips. For this reason the lips should be protected with a lip emollient preparation, to prevent them from becoming dry and chapped.

HEALTH AND SAFETY

Using alkaline products
Because the skin has an acid pH, if alkaline products are used on it the acid mantle will be disturbed. It will take several hours for this protective film to be restored: during this time, the skin will be irritated and sensitive.

Acid mantle Sweat and sebum combine on the skin's surface, creating an acid film. This is known as the **acid mantle**, and discourages the growth of bacteria and fungi.

Acidity and alkalinity are measured by a number called the pH. An *acidic solution* has a pH of 0–7; a *neutral solution* has a pH of 7; and an *alkaline solution* has a pH of 7–14. The acid mantle of the skin has a pH of 5.5–5.6.

THE NAILS

The structure and function of the nail

- stratum corneum
- nail plate

The nail

Nails grow from the ends of the fingers and toes and serve as a form of protection. They also help when picking up small objects. Dark streaks caused by pigmentation are common on the nail plate of black skinned clients. These tend to increase with age.

The nail plate

The **nail plate** is composed of compact translucent layers of keratinised epidermal cells: it is this that makes up the main body of the nail. The layers of cells are packed very closely together, with fat but very little moisture.

The nail gradually grows forward over the nail bed, until finally it becomes the free edge. The underside of the nail plate is grooved by longitudinal ridges and furrows, which help to keep it in place.

In normal health the plate curves in two directions:

- transversely – from side to side across the nail;
- longitudinally – from the base of the nail to the free edge.

There are no blood vessels or nerves in the nail plate: this is why the nails, like hair, can be cut without pain or bleeding. The pink colour of the nail plate derives from the blood vessels that pass beneath it.

Function: To protect the living nail bed of the fingers and toes.

The free edge

The **free edge** is the part of the nail that extends beyond the fingertip; this is the part that is filed.

Function: To protect the fingertip and the hyponychium (see below).

The matrix

The **matrix**, sometimes called the **nail root**, is the growing area of the nail. It is formed by the division of cells in this area, which is part of the germinating layer of the epidermis. It lies under the eponychium (see below), at the base of the nail, nearest to the body. The process of keratinisation takes place in the epidermal cells of the matrix, forming the hardened tissue of the nail plate.

Function: To produce new nail cells.

The nail bed

The **nail bed** is the portion of skin upon which the nail plate rests. It has a pattern of grooves and furrows corresponding to those found on the underside of the nail plate; these interlock, keeping the nail in place, but separate at the end of the nail to form the free edge. The nail bed is liberally supplied with blood vessels, which provide the nourishment necessary for continued growth; and sensory nerves, for protection.

Function: To supply nourishment and protection.

The nail mantle

The **nail mantle** is the layer of epidermis at the base of the nail, before the cuticle.

Function: To protect the matrix from physical damage.

Dr M. H. Beck

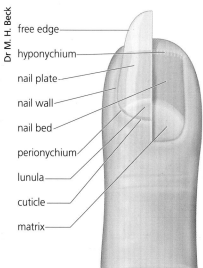

free edge
hyponychium
nail plate
nail wall
nail bed
perionychium
lunula
cuticle
matrix

The structure of the nail

TIP ✔

Fingernails grow more quickly than toenails. Fingernails grow about 0.1mm each day, and grow faster in summer than in winter.

The lunula

The **lunula** is located at the base of the nail, lying over the matrix. It is white, relative to the rest of the nail, and there are two theories to account for this:

- newly formed nail plates may be more opaque than mature nail plates;
- the lunula may indicate the extent of the underlying matrix – the matrix is thicker than the epidermis of the nail bed, and the capillaries beneath it would not show through as well.

Function: None.

The hyponychium

The **hyponychium** is part of the epidermis under the free edge of the nail.

Function: To protect the nail bed from infection.

The nail grooves

The **nail grooves** run alongside the edge of the nail plate.

Function: To keep the nail growing forward in a straight line.

The perionychium

The **perionychium** is the collective name given to the nail walls and the cuticle area.

Function: To protect the nail.

The nail walls

The **nail walls** are the folds of skin overlapping the sides of the nails.

Function: To protect the nail plate edges.

The eponychium

The **eponychium** is the extension of the cuticle at the base of the nail plate, under which the nail plate emerges from the matrix.

Function: To protect the matrix from infection.

The cuticle

The **cuticle** is the overlapping epidermis around the base of the nail. When in good condition, it is soft and loose.

Function: To protect the matrix from infection.

ACTIVITY

Recognising nail structure
With a colleague, try to identify the structural parts of each other's nails. Write down both the parts that you can see and the parts that you cannot.

Nail growth

Cells divide in the matrix and the nail grows forward over the nail bed, guided by the nail grooves, until it reaches the end of the finger or toe, where it becomes the free edge. As they first emerge from the matrix the translucent cells are plump and soft, but they get harder and flatter as they move toward the free edge. The top two layers of the epidermis form the nail plate; the remaining three form the nail bed.

The nail plate is made up of a protein called keratin, and the hardening process that takes place in the nail cells is known as **keratinisation**.

The nail bed has a pattern of grooves and furrows corresponding to those found on the underside of the nail plate: the two surfaces interlock, holding the nail in place.

Fingernails grow at approximately twice the speed of toenails. It takes about 6 months for a fingernail to grow from cuticle to free edge, but about 12 months for a toenail to do so.

THE NERVOUS SYSTEM

The neurological system transmits messages between the brain and other parts of the body. The nervous system is made up of a network of nerve cells and fibres which transmits nerve impulses between parts of the body.

The neurological system of the body has two main divisions:

1 The central nervous system (CNS)
2 The autonomic nervous system

The central nervous system

The central nervous system (CNS) is composed of the brain and spinal cord.

The brain transmits impulses to all parts of the body in order to stimulate other organs to act and is protected by the bones of the cranium. The spinal cord extends downwards through the vertebral column and is protected by the bones (vertebrae) of the spinal column. The brain is composed of several parts, each of which performs special functions.

Nerves

A nerve is a whitish fibre or bundle of fibres in the body that transmits impulses of sensations between the brain or spinal cord and other parts of the body. All nerves emerge from the CNS. Sensory (receptor) nerves are linked to sensory receptors, while motor (effector) nerves end in a muscle or gland. Twelve pairs of cranial nerves emerge from the brain; thirty-one pairs of spinal nerves emerge from between the vertebrae of the spinal column.

The CNS transmits instructions to organs through nerve impulses that pass along nerve fibres made up of nerves. Each nerve consists of a nerve cell and its parts, axons and dendrites. Axons carry nerve impulses away from the cell; dendrites carry impulses towards the cell.

When an impulse reaches the end of a nerve fibre a chemical called a *neurotransmitter substance* is released. This chemical passes across a tiny gap called a *synapse* and is taken up by an adjacent neuron, generating an electrical impulse in the neuron.

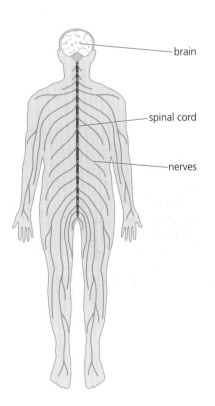

brain

spinal cord

nerves

The nervous system

Passage of an impulse across a synapse

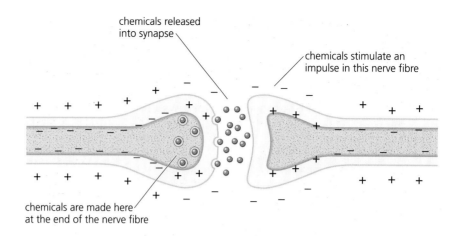

chemicals released into synapse

chemicals stimulate an impulse in this nerve fibre

chemicals are made here at the end of the nerve fibre

Neurons can stimulate muscles fibres to contract. The *motor point* is where a motor nerve enters a muscle. When stimulated by a motor nerve muscle contraction occurs.

The autonomic nervous system

The autonomic nervous system controls those body structures over which there is no conscious control, the involuntary activities. It regulates the functioning of organs such as the heart, the stomach, the lungs and the secretion of most glands. There are two divisions of the autonomic nervous system – the *sympathetic* and *parasympathetic nervous systems*.

Many organs receive a supply from each division. Fibres from one division stimulate the organ while fibres from the other division inhibit it, thus ensuring balance in the body.

The sympathetic nervous system is stimulated in periods of stress or danger and prepares the body for physical activity. Fibres of the sympathetic division increase blood flow by causing the heart to beat faster and the blood vessels in the muscles to widen. Activities that are not essential in this stressful situation are inhibited.

The parasympathetic nervous system is associated with resting and causes the blood flow to slow by causing the heart to beat slower and the blood vessels in the muscles to contract (go smaller). Fibres of this division stimulate digestion and absorption of food.

The nervous system therefore co-ordinates the activities of the body by responding to stimuli received by sense organs, including the nose, tongue, eyes, ears and skin.

> **TIP** ✓
>
> The sympathetic division is associated with **stress**.
> The parasympathetic system is associated with **peace**.

THE MUSCLES

Muscles are responsible for the movement of body parts. Each is made up of a bundle of elastic fibres bound together in a sheath, the **fascia**. Muscular tissue contracts (shortens) and produces movement. Muscles never completely relax – there are always a few contracted fibres in every muscle. These make the muscles slightly tense and this tension is called muscle tone.

Muscle tissue has the following properties:

● It has the ability to contract

● It is extensible (when the extensor muscle in a joint contracts the corresponding flexor muscle will be stretched or lengthened)

● It is elastic – following contraction or extension it returns to its original length

● It is responsive – it contracts in response to nerve stimulation.

A muscle is usually anchored by a strong tendon to one bone: the point of attachment is known as the muscle's origin. The muscle is likewise joined to a second bone: the attachment in this case is called the muscle's **insertion**. It is this second bone that is moved: the muscle contracts, pulling the two bones towards each other. (A different muscle, on the other side of the bone, has the contrary effect.) Not all muscles attach to bones, however: some insert into an adjacent muscle, or into the skin itself. The muscles with which we are concerned here are those of the face, the neck and the shoulders.

Facial muscles

Many of the muscles located in the face are very small and are attached to ('insert into') another small muscle or the facial skin. When the muscles contract, they pull the facial skin in a particular way: it is this that creates the facial expression.

With age, the facial expressions that we make every day produce lines on the skin – frown lines. The amount of tension, or **tone**, also decreases with age. When performing facial massage, the aim is to improve the general tone of the facial muscles.

Muscles of facial expression

Muscle	Expression	Location	Action
Occipito-frontalis	Surprise	The forehead	Raises the eyebrows
Corrugator	Frown	Between the eyebrows	Draws the eyebrows together
Orbicularis oculi	Winking	Surrounds the eyes	Closes the eyelid
Risorius	Smiling	Extends diagonally, from the corners of the mouth	Draws mouth corners outwards
Buccinator	Blowing	Inside the cheeks	Compresses the cheeks
Zygomaticus	Smiling, laughing	Extends diagonally from the corners of the mouth	Lifts the mouth corners upwards and outwards
Zygomaticus, major and minor	Smiling, laughing	Extend diagonally upwards from the corners of the mouth	Lifts the corners of the mouth
Procerus	Distaste	Covers the bridge of the nose	Wrinkling of the skin over the bridge of the nose
Nasalis	Anger	Covers the front of the nose	Opens and closes the nasal openings
Quadratus labii superioris	Distaste	Surrounds the upper lip	Raises and draws back the upper lips and nostrils
Depressor labii	Sulking	Surrounds the lower lip	Depresses the lower lip and draws it slightly to one side
Orbicularis oris	Pout, kiss, doubt	Surrounds the mouth	Purses the lip, closes the mouth
Triangularis	Sadness	The corner of the lower lip extends over the chin	Draws down the mouth's corners
Mentalis	Doubt	Chin	Raises the lower lip, causing the chin to wrinkle
Platysma	Fear, horror	The sides of the neck and chin	Draws the mouth's corners downwards and backwards

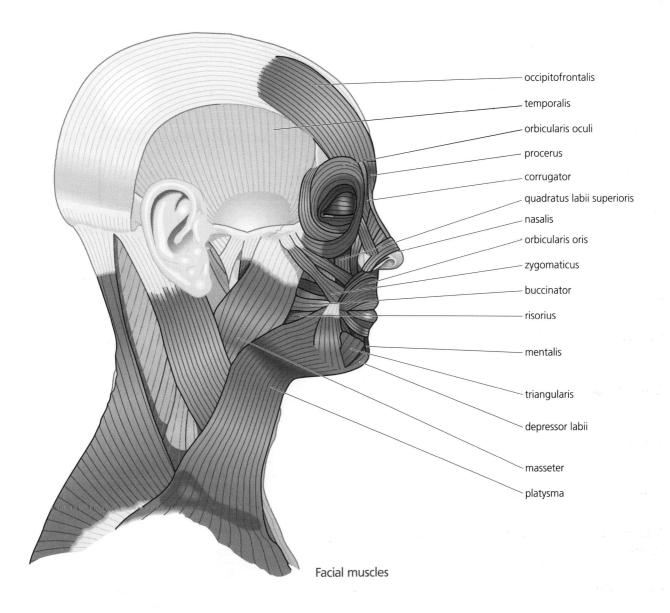

- occipitofrontalis
- temporalis
- orbicularis oculi
- procerus
- corrugator
- quadratus labii superioris
- nasalis
- orbicularis oris
- zygomaticus
- buccinator
- risorius
- mentalis
- triangularis
- depressor labii
- masseter
- platysma

Facial muscles

Muscles of mastication

The muscles responsible for the movement of the lower jawbone (the **mandible**) when chewing are called the **muscles of mastication**.

Muscle	Location	Action
Masseter	The cheek area: extends from the zygomatic bone to the mandible	Clenches the teeth; closes and raises the lower jaw
Temporalis	Extends from the temple region at the side of the head to the mandible	Raises the jaw and draws it backwards, as in chewing

Muscles that move the head

Muscle	Location	Action
Sterno-cleido-mastoid	Runs from the sternum to the clavicle bone and the temporal bone	Flexes the neck; rotates and bows the head
Trapezius	A large triangular muscle, covering the back of the neck and the upper back	Draws the head backwards and allows movement at the shoulder
Occipitalis	Covers the back of the head	Draws scalp backwards

Muscles that move the head

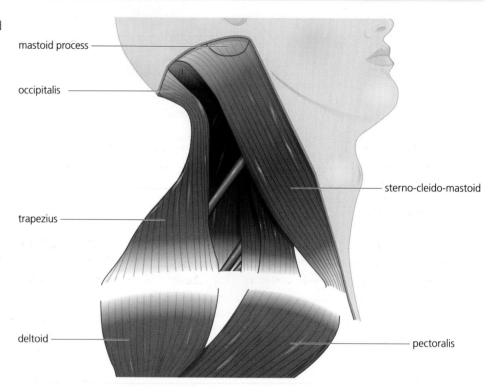

mastoid process

occipitalis

sterno-cleido-mastoid

trapezius

deltoid

pectoralis

Muscles of the upper body

When massaging the shoulder area you will cover the following muscles of the upper body.

Muscle	Location	Action
Pectoralis major	The front of the chest	Moves the arm towards the upper body
Deltoid	A thick triangular muscle, covering the shoulder	Takes the arm away from the side of the body

The muscles of the hand and arm

The hand and fingers are moved primarily by muscles and tendons in the forearm. These muscles contract, pulling the tendons, and thereby move the fingers much as a puppet is moved by strings.

Muscles of the arm and hand

The muscles that bend the wrist, drawing it towards the forearm, are **flexors**; other muscles, **extensors**, straighten the wrist and the hand.

The muscles of the foot and lower leg

The muscles of the foot work together to help move the body when walking and running. In a similar way to the movement of the hand, the foot is moved primarily by muscles in the lower leg; these pull on tendons, which in turn move the feet and toes.

ACTIVITY

Observing the tendons
Hold your palm face upwards, with your sleeve pulled back so that you can see your forearm. Move the fingers individually towards the palm. Can you see the tendons moving?

Muscles of the foot

Muscles of the lower leg

THE BONES

When carrying out a facial massage you will feel below your hands the underlying bones. **Bone** is the hardest structure in the body: it protects the underlying structures, gives shape to the body, and provides an attachment point for our muscles, thereby allowing movement.

Kinds of bones

flat

short

irregular

long

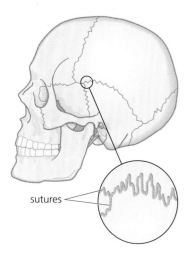

A ball and socket joint, as in the shoulder

The skeleton is made up of many bones. Each bone is connected to its neighbour by *connective tissue*, a structural tissue that supports, surrounds and links different parts of the body. Fibrous connective tissue is used for immovable joints such as those of the cranium. *Fibro-cartilage* is used for semi-immovable joints such as those between the bones of the vertebrae. The most common joints – *synovial joints* – are freely moveable and are loosely held together by a form of connective tissue called a *ligament*.

Bones have different shapes, according to their function.

Bones of the head

The bones which form the head are collectively known as the **skull**. The skull can be divided into two parts, the face and the cranium, which together are made up of 22 bones:

- the 14 facial bones form the face;
- the 8 cranial bones form the rest of the head.

As well as forming our facial features, the facial bones support other structures such as the eyes and the teeth. Some of these bones, such as the nasal bone, are made from **cartilage**, a softer tissue than bone.

The cranium surrounds and protects the brain. The bones are thin and slightly curved, and are held together by connective tissue. After childhood, the joints become immovable, and are called **sutures**.

sutures

Sutures

facial bones (14)

Bones of the face

- 2 lacrimal
- 2 nasal
- 2 turbinate
- 1 vomer
- 2 maxillae
- 1 mandible

2 malar (zygomatic)

2 palatine

Facial bones

Bone	Number	Location	Function
Nasal	2	The nose	Form the bridge of the nose
Vomer	1	The nose	Forms the dividing bony wall of the nose
Palatine	2	The nose	Form the floor and wall of the nose and the roof of the mouth
Turbinate	2	The nose	Form the outer walls of the nose
Lacrimal	2	The eye sockets	Form the inner walls of the eye sockets; contain a small groove for the tear duct
Malar (zygomatic)	2	The cheek	Form the cheekbones
Maxillae	2	The upper jaw	Fused together, to form the upper jaw, which holds the upper teeth
Mandible	1	The lower jaw	The largest and strongest of the facial bones; holds the lower teeth

---

ACTIVITY

Facial expressions
In front of a mirror, move the muscles of your face to create the expressions that you might form each day.

What expressions can you make? Which part or parts of the face are moving? Which facial muscles do you think have contracted to create these expressions?

TIP

Crow's feet
To avoid the premature formation of 'crow's feet':
- avoid squinting in bright sunlight – wear sunglasses;
- have your eyes tested regularly;
- if you use a visual display unit, ensure that you take regular breaks, and have a protective filter screen to remove glare.

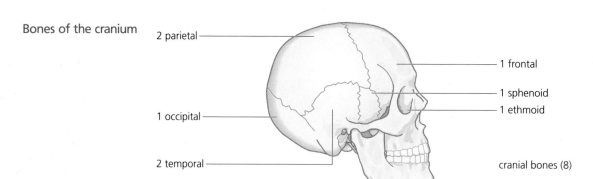

Bones of the cranium

2 parietal

1 frontal

1 sphenoid

1 ethmoid

1 occipital

2 temporal

cranial bones (8)

Cranial bones

Bone	Number	Location	Function
Occipital	1	The lower back of the cranium	Contains a large hole called the *foramen magnum*: through this pass the spinal cord, the nerves and blood vessels
Parietal	2	The sides of the cranium	Fused together to form the sides and top of the head (the 'crown')
Frontal	1	The forehead	Forms the forehead and the upper walls of the eye sockets
Temporal	2	The sides of the head	Provide two muscle attachment points: the mastoid process and the zygomatic process
Ethmoid	1	Between the eye sockets	Forms part of the nasal cavities
Sphenoid	1	The base of the cranium the back of the eye sockets	A bat-shaped bone which joins together all the bones of the cranium

Bones of the neck, chest and shoulder

Bone	Number	Location	Function
Cervical vertebra	7	The neck	These vertebrae form the top of the spinal column: the *atlas* is the first vertebra, which supports the skull; the *axis* is the second vertebra, which allows rotation of the head
Hyoid	1	A U-shaped bone at the front of the neck	Supports the tongue
Clavicle	2	Slender long bones at the base of the neck	Commonly called the *collar bones*: these form a joint with the sternum and the scapula bones, allowing movement at the shoulder
Scapula	2	Triangular bones in the upper back	Commonly called the *shoulder blades*: the scapulae provide attachment for muscles which move the arms. The *shoulder girdle*, which allows movement at the shoulder, is composed of the clavicles and the scapulae
Humerus	2	The upper bones of the arms	Form ball-and-socket joints with the scapulae: these joints allow movement in any direction
Sternum	1	The breastbone	Protects the inner organs; provides a surface for muscle attachment; and supports muscle movement

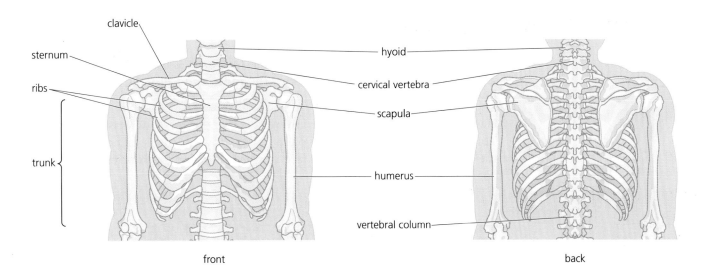

front

back

Bones of the neck, chest and shoulder

THE HAND AND THE FOREARM

The bones of the hand

The wrist consists of 8 small **carpal** bones, which glide over one another to allow movement. This is called a **condyloid** or **gliding joint**.

There are then 5 **metacarpal** bones that make up the palm of the hand.

The fingers are made up of 14 individual bones called **phalanges** – 2 in each of the thumbs, and 3 in each of the fingers.

ACTIVITY

Identifying bones in the hand
Look very closely at your hand. Can you identify where the bones are? Try feeling the bones with your other hand. How many can you feel?

Bones of the hand

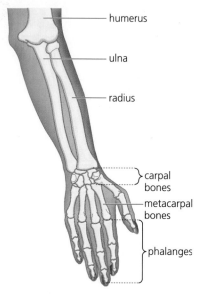

Bones of the arm

The bones of the arm

The arm is made up of 3 long bones: the **humerus** is the bone of the upper arm, from the shoulder to the elbow; the **radius** and **ulna** lie side by side in the lower arm, from the elbow to the wrist.

Having two bones in the lower arm makes it easier for your wrist to rotate. This movement that causes the palm to face downwards is called **pronation**; the movement that causes it to face upwards is called **supination**.

THE FOOT AND THE LOWER LEG

The bones of the foot

The foot is made up of 7 **tarsal** bones, **5 metatarsal** bones, and 14 **phalanges**. These bones fit together to form arches which help to support the foot and to absorb the impact when we walk, run and jump.

Bones of the foot

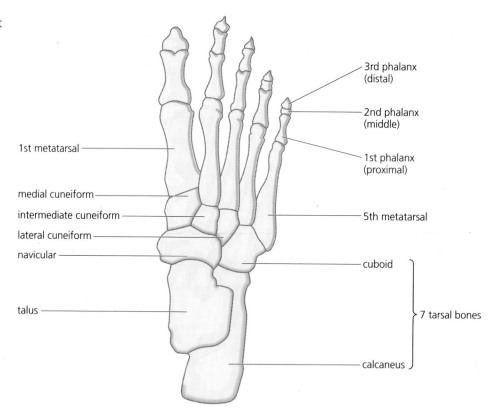

The arches of the foot

The **arches** of the foot are created by the formation of the bones and joints, and supported by ligaments. These arches support the weight of the body and help to preserve balance when we walk on even surfaces.

Arches of the foot

The bones of the lower leg

The lower leg is made up of 2 long bones, the **tibia** and the **fibula**. These bones have joints with the upper leg (at the knee) and with the foot (at the ankle). Having two bones in the lower leg – as with the forearm – allows a greater range of movement to be achieved at the ankle.

Bones of the lower leg

THE BLOOD SUPPLY

A healthy muscle is activated by a nerve supply, which effects movement; the necessary oxygen and nutrients are brought by the blood.

Blood transports various substances around the body:

- It carries oxygen from our lungs, and nutrients from our digested food to supply energy – these allow the cells to develop and divide, and the muscles to function.

- It carries waste products and carbon dioxide away for elimination from the body.
- It carries various cells and substances which allow the body to prevent or fight disease.

The main constituents of blood

Blood consists of the following:

- **Plasma** A straw-coloured liquid: mainly water, with foods and carbon dioxide.
- **Red blood cells (erythrocytes)** These cells appear red because they contain **haemoglobin**; it is this that carries oxygen from the lungs to the body cells.
- **White blood cells (leucocytes)** There are several types of white blood cells: their main role is to protect the body, destroying foreign bodies and dead cells, and carrying away the debris (a process known as **phagocytosis**).
- **Platelets (thrombocytes)** When blood is exposed to air, as happens when the skin is injured, these cells bind together to form a clot.
- **Other chemicals** Hormones also are transported in the blood.

The circulation

The circulation of blood is under the control of the **heart**, a muscular organ which pumps the blood around the body.

TIP

The pumping of the blood under pressure through the carotid arteries can be felt as a pulse in the neck. Press gently on the neck just inside the position of the sternomastoid muscle.

Pulse rate relates to the speed of the heartbeat. The strength of the pulse is affected by the pressure of the blood flow leaving the heart.

Blood pressure increases during activity and decreases during rest.

Relaxing treatments such as facial massage lower blood pressure.

Blood leaving the heart is carried in large, elastic tubes called **arteries**. The blood to the head arrives via the **carotid arteries**, which are connected via other main arteries to the heart. There are two main carotid arteries, one on each side of the neck.

These arteries divide into smaller branches, the *internal carotid* and the *external carotid*. The **internal carotid artery** passes the temporal bone and enters the head, taking blood to the brain. The **external carotid artery** stays outside the skull, and divides into branches:

- the **occipital branch** supplies the back of the head and the scalp;
- the **temporal branch** supplies the sides of the face, the head, the scalp and the skin;
- the **facial branch** supplies the muscles and tissues of the face.

small arteries to hair follicles

temporal branch

facial branch

external carotid artery

blood flow

occipital branch

internal carotid artery

common carotid artery

The blood supply to and from the head

veins to hair follicles

facial branch

internal jugular vein

blood flow

temporal branch

occipital branch

external jugular vein

These arteries also divide repeatedly, successive vessels becoming smaller and smaller until they form tiny blood **capillaries**. These vessels are just one cell thick, allowing substances carried in the blood to pass through them into the **tissue fluid** which bathes and nourishes the cells of the various body tissues.

The blood capillaries begin to join up again, forming first small vessels called **venules**, then larger vessels called **veins**. These return the blood to the heart.

Veins are less elastic than arteries, and are closer to the skin's surface. Along their course are **valves** which prevent the backflow of blood.

The main veins are the external and internal jugular veins. The **internal jugular vein** and its main branch, the **facial vein**, carry blood from the face and head. The **external jugular vein** carries blood from the scalp and has two branches: the **occipital branch** and the **temporal branch**. The jugular veins join to enter the **subclavian vein**, which lies above the clavicle.

Blood returns to the heart, which pumps it to the lungs, where the red blood cells take on fresh oxygen, and where carbon dioxide is expelled from

HEALTH AND SAFETY

Capillaries
The strength and elasticity of the capillary walls can be damaged, for example by a blow to the tissues.

the blood. The blood returns to the heart, and begins its next journey round the body.

The arteries of the arm and hand

The arm and hand are nourished by a system of arteries which carry blood to the tissues. You can see the colour of the blood from the capillaries beneath the nail: it is these that give the nail bed its pink colour.

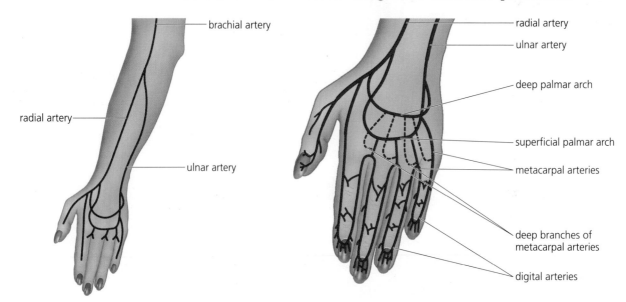

Arteries of the arm and hand

The arteries of the foot and lower leg

The skin and nails of the feet are nourished by a system of arteries which bring blood to the tissue.

When it is cold, and when the circulation is poor, insufficient blood reaches the feet and they feel cold. Severe circulation problems in the feet may lead to **chilblains**.

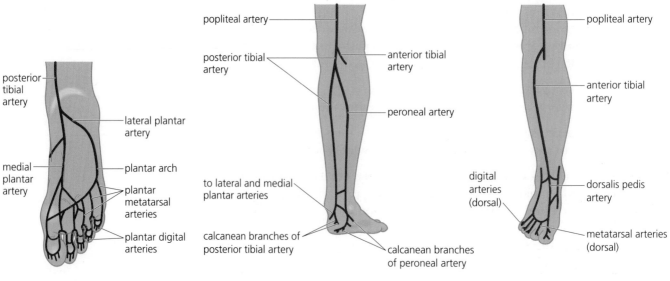

Arteries of the foot

Arteries of the lower leg

THE NERVE SUPPLY

All muscles are made to work by electrical stimulation via the nerves. These, together with the **brain** and the **spinal cord**, form the nervous system.

Kinds of nerve

There are two types of nerve: *sensory nerves* and *motor nerves*. Both are composed of white fibres enclosed in a sheath.

- **Sensory nerves** These receive information and relay it to the brain. They are found near to the skin's surface and respond to touch, pressure, temperature and pain.
- **Motor nerves** These are situated in muscle tissue and act on information received from the brain, causing a particular response, typically muscle movement.

Appropriate massage manipulations, when applied to the skin, produce a stimulating or relaxing effect on nerves.

HEALTH AND SAFETY

Nerve damage
Nerve cells do not reproduce; when damaged, only a limited repair occurs.

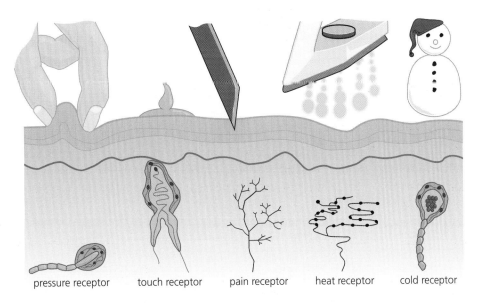

Sensory nerves

pressure receptor   touch receptor   pain receptor   heat receptor   cold receptor

Nerves of the face and neck

These nerves link the brain with the muscles of the head, face and neck.

There are 12 pairs of **cranial nerves**. Those of concern to the beauty therapist when performing a facial massage are as follows:

- the 5th cranial nerve, or **trigeminal**;
- the 7th cranial nerve, or **facial**;
- the 11th cranial nerve, or **accessory**.

5th cranial nerve

7th cranial nerve

5th cranial nerve

This nerve carries messages to the brain from the sensory nerves of the skin, the teeth, the nose and the mouth. It also stimulates the motor nerve to create the chewing action when eating. The 5th cranial nerve has three branches:

- the **ophthalmic nerve** serves the tear glands, the skin of the forehead, and the upper cheeks;
- the **maxillary nerve** serves the upper jaw and the mouth;
- the **mandibular nerve** serves the lower jaw muscle, the teeth and the muscle involved with chewing.

7th cranial nerve

This nerve passes through the temporal bone and behind the ear, and then divides. It serves the ear muscle and the muscles of facial expression, the tongue and the palate.

The 7th cranial nerve has five branches:

- the **temporal nerve** serves the orbicularis oculi and the frontalis muscles;
- the **zygomatic nerve** serves the eye muscles;
- the **buccal nerve** serves the upper lip and the sides of the nose;
- the **mandibular nerve** serves the lower lip and the mentalis muscle of the chin;
- the **cervical nerve** serves the platysma muscle of the neck.

11th cranial nerve

This nerve serves the sternomastoid and trapezius muscles of the neck and its function is to move the head and shoulders.

THE LYMPHATIC SYSTEM

The **lymphatic system** is closely connected to the blood system, and can be considered as supplementing it. Its primary function is defensive: to remove bacteria and foreign materials, thereby preventing infection. It also drains away excess fluids for elimination from the body.

The lymphatic system consists of the fluid **lymph**, the **lymph vessels**, and the **lymph nodes** (or glands). You may have experienced swelling of the lymph nodes in the neck when you have been ill.

Unlike the blood circulation, the lymphatic system has no muscular pump equivalent to the heart. Instead, the lymph moves through the vessels and around the body because of movements such as contractions of large muscles. Facial massage can play an important part in assisting this flow of lymph fluid, thereby encouraging the improved removal of the waste products transported in the lymph.

Lymph

Lymph is a straw-coloured fluid, derived from blood plasma, which has filtered through the walls of the capillaries. The composition of lymph is similar to that of blood, though less oxygen and fewer nutrients are available. In the spaces between the cells where there are no blood capillaries, lymph provides nourishment. It also carries **lymphocytes** (a type of white blood cell).

Lymph travels only in one direction: from body tissues back towards the heart.

Lymph vessels

Lymph vessels often run very close to veins, forming an extensive network throughout the body. The lymph moves quite slowly, and there are valves along the lymph vessels to prevent backflow of the lymph.

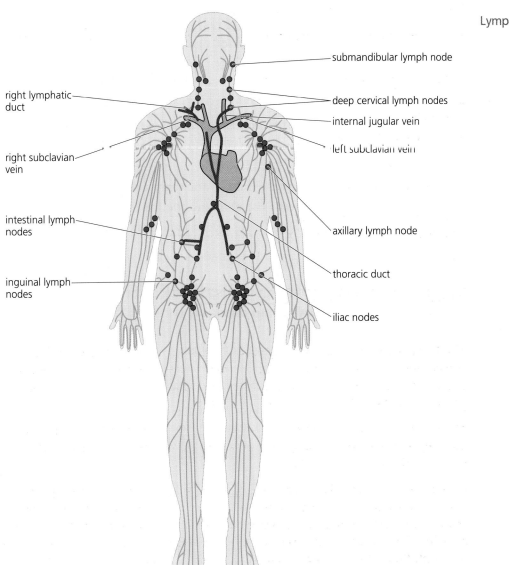

Lymph vessels

right lymphatic duct

right subclavian vein

intestinal lymph nodes

inguinal lymph nodes

submandibular lymph node

deep cervical lymph nodes

internal jugular vein

left subclavian vein

axillary lymph node

thoracic duct

iliac nodes

The lymph vessels join to form larger lymph vessels, which eventually flow into one or other of two large lymphatic vessels: the **thoracic duct** (or **left lymphatic duct**) and the **right lymphatic duct**. The thoracic duct receives lymph from the left side of the head, neck, chest, abdomen and lower body; the right lymphatic duct receives lymph from the right side of the head and upper body.

These principal lymphatic vessels then empty their contents into a vein at the base of the neck, which in turn empties into the **vena cava**. The lymph is mixed into the venous blood as it is returned to the heart.

Lymph nodes

Lymph nodes or **glands** are tiny oval structures which filter the lymph, extracting poisons, pus and bacteria, and thus defending the body against infection by destroying harmful organisms. **Lymphocytes**, found in the lymph glands, are special cells which produce **antibodies** which enable us to resist invasion by micro-organisms.

When performing massage, the hands should be used to apply pressure to direct the lymph towards the nearest lymph node: this encourages the speedy removal of waste products. Various groups of lymph nodes drain the lymph of the head and neck.

Lymph nodes of the head

- The **buccal group** drains the eyelids, the nose and the skin of the face.
- The **mandibular group** drains the chin, the lips, the nose and the cheeks.
- The **mastoid group** drains the skin of the ear and the temple area.
- The **occipital group** drains the back of the scalp and the upper neck.
- The **submental group** drains the chin and the lower lip.
- The **parotid group** drains the nose, eyelids and ears.

Lymph nodes of the neck

- The **superficial cervical group** drains the back of the head and the neck.
- The **lower deep cervical group** drains the back area of the scalp and the neck.

Lymph nodes of the head and neck

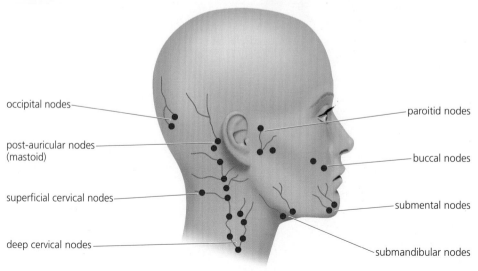

occipital nodes

post-auricular nodes (mastoid)

superficial cervical nodes

deep cervical nodes

paroitid nodes

buccal nodes

submental nodes

submandibular nodes

Lymph nodes of the chest and arms

● The nodes of the armpit area drain various regions of the arms and chest.

Assessment of knowledge and understanding

You have now learnt about the related anatomy and physiology for the beauty therapy units with an essential knowledge requirement.

To test your level of knowledge, answer the following short questions. These will prepare you for your summative (final) assessment.

Skin structure and function

1 Referring to the cross section of the skin, name and briefly describe the functions of the structures shown in 1–4.

2 Name six functions of the skin.

3 Name the layers of the epidermis shown in 1–7.

4 The skin can become dehydrated at times. What does this term mean and what factors can cause it? What treatments and advice could be given to a client with dehydrated skin?

5 What skin disorders can occur due to an imbalance of hormones, (chemical messengers) in the skin?

6 Describe erythema. What are its possible causes?

7 How does the natural ageing process affect the skin?

8 How do the following affect the skin:
- alcohol
- caffeine
- smoking
- medication
- stress

9 How does the physiological functioning of the skin differ between skin types?

Structure of hair

1 Referring to the cross section of the hair follicle, briefly describe the name and function of each numbered area.

2 What is the soft downy hair on the face called?

3 What is coarse pigmented hair called?

4 What is the name of the protein found in skin cells?

5 Why does spot bleeding occasionally occur with wax/sugar depilation?

Hair growth cycle

1 What are the different stages of the hair growth cycle called?

2 What happens to the hair at each stage?

3 What relevance has the hair growth cycle for a wax depilation treatment?

4 What is the difference in the time between the hair growth cycle anagen to telogen for scalp hair and eyebrow hair?

Nail structure and function

1 Referring to the cross section of the nail, briefly describe the name and function of each of the numbered areas.

2 Why does the nail bed appear pink?

3 Why does the nail bed contain nerve endings?

Nail growth

1 In which part of the nail structure do the cells divide to form the nail?

2 As the nail cells grow forward they harden; what is this process called?

3 How long does it take for a fingernail to grow from cuticle to free edge?

4 When do nails grow faster – in summer or winter?

5 What is the difference in growth rate between fingernails and toenails?

6 Why does localised massage to the hand and foot encourage healthy nail growth?

7 What other factors affect nail growth?

Muscle groups in parts of the body, position structure and function

1 What happens when muscles contract?

2 What structure attaches a muscle to a bone?

3 On the diagram of the muscles of the face, name muscles 1–6. What are the actions of these muscles?

4 On the diagram of muscles that move the head and neck, name muscles 1–5. What are the actions of these muscles?

5 What is the collective name for the group of muscles that bend the wrist, drawing it towards the forearm?

6 What is the collective name for the group of muscles that straighten the wrist and the hand?

Muscle tone

1 What is muscle tone?

2 Name four properties of muscle tissue.

3 With age, the facial expressions that we make every day produce lines on the skin – frown lines. What happens to the tone of the muscles with age?

4 What effect does massage have on the tone of muscles?

Bones in parts of the body, position structure and function

1 What is the function of bone?

2 Bones have different shapes according to their function. Name three shapes of bones and where they are found.

3 What attaches bones to different parts of the body?

4 On the diagram of the cranium name the bones numbered 1–8.

5 Name three facial bones to which you may apply contouring products during make-up.

6 Which of the bones form the:
   ● face
   ● cranium?

7 Which bones or bones form the
   ● forehead
   ● cheekbones
   ● jawbone?

8 On the diagram of the bones of the neck, chest and shoulder name the bones and their functions (items 1–7).

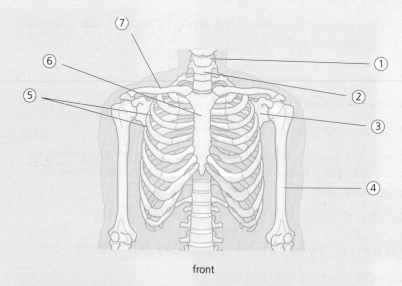

front

9 The wrist is made up of eight small carpal bones which glide over one another to allow movement. Name them.

10 What type of joint is found in the wrist?

11 How do the fingers move?

12 What is the function of the arches of the foot?

13 How does the foot move?

Composition and function of blood and lymph

1 What are the main constituents of blood?

2 What are the main constituents of lymph?

3 What does blood transport around the body?

4 What is the difference in function in the body between blood and lymph?

5 What is the function of lymph nodes or glands?

6 On the diagram of the head, name the lymph nodes numbered 1–5.

7 Blood helps to maintain body temperature. What is normal body temperature?

8 How does massage affect the circulation of lymph?

Blood flow and pulse rate

1 The circulation of the blood is under the control of the heart, which pumps blood around the body.
On the illustration below label the arteries that transport blood to the head and veins that return blood from the head.

blood supply to the head

blood supply from the head

2 How does the pressure of blood leaving the heart affect pulse rate?

3 How does activity affect blood pressure?

4 How does massage affect blood flow and pulse rate?

Central nervous system and autonomic nervous system

1 The neurological system transmits messages between the brain and other parts of the body. There are two main divisions, what are they called?

2 What is the central nervous system composed of?

3 What is the difference between sensory nerves and motor nerves?

4 To what are the main sensory nerve endings in the skin receptive?

5 How do nerve impulses pass along nerve fibres?

6 How do nerves stimulate muscles to contract?

7 What is meant by the autonomic nervous system?

8 How many pairs of cranial nerves emerge from the brain?

9 Those of concern to the beauty therapist when performing facial massage are the 5th, 7th and 11th.
   What is the function of the:
   - 5th, known as trigeminal nerve
   - 7th, known as the facial nerve
   - 11th, known as the accessory nerve?

10 Name the main branches of the 7th cranial facial nerve, items 1–5 in the diagram.

general
beauty
therapy
units

chapter 6

BT4 IMPROVE AND MAINTAIN FACIAL SKIN CONDITION

Learning objectives

This unit describes how to improve and maintain the facial skin condition using a variety of treatments.

It describes the competencies to enable you to:

- **consult with the client**
- **prepare for the treatment**
- **plan the treatment**
- **improve and maintain skin condition**
- **complete the treatment**

When providing facial treatments it is important to use the skills you have learnt in the following core mandatory units:

Unit G1 – Ensure your own actions reduce risks to health and safety

Unit G6 – Promote additional products or services to clients

Unit G8 – Develop and maintain your effectiveness at work

BASICS OF SKIN CARE

Nutrition

If the skin is to function efficiently, the skin must be cared for both internally and externally.

Internally, a nutritionally balanced diet is vital to the health and appearance of the skin. A number of skin allergies and disorders are in part the result of a poorly balanced diet.

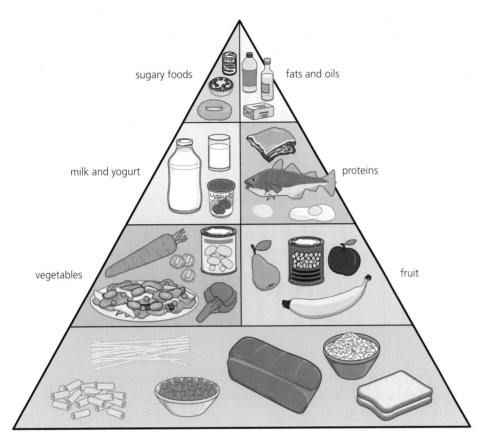

Foods contain the chemical substances we need for health and growth, the **nutrients**: a healthy diet contains all the essential nutrients. The nutrients are carried to the skin in the blood, where they nourish the cells in the processes of growth and repair.

There are six principal groups of nutrients.

Carbohydrates

Carbohydrates provide energy quickly. They are either simple sugars or starches that the body can turn into simple sugars.

Food sources: Carbohydrates are found in fruit, vegetables, milk, grains, and honey.

Fats

Fats provide a concentrated source of energy, and are also used in carrying certain vitamins (see below) around the body. Fat is stored in the body around organs and muscles and under the skin. However, if too much fat is deposited under the skin, the elastic fibres there may be damaged by the expansion of the 'adipose' tissue. Fat is also used in the formation of sebum, the skin's natural lubricant.

Food sources: Although this is not always evident, fats are present in almost all foods, from plants and from animals.

Proteins

Proteins provide material for the growth and repair of body tissue, and are also a source of energy. Severe protein deficiency in children gives the skin a yellowish appearance, known as **jaundice**.

Food sources: Proteins are found in meat, fish, eggs, dairy products, grains, and nuts.

Minerals

Minerals provide materials for growth and repair and for regulation of the body processes. The major minerals are calcium, iron, phosphorus, sulphur, sodium, potassium, chlorine, and magnesium. Of these, the most important to the skin is iron. A pale, dry skin may indicate **anaemia**, caused by a shortage of iron.

Food sources: Fruit and vegetables; iron is found in liver, egg yolks, and green vegetables.

Vitamins

Vitamins regulate the body's processes and contribute to its resistance to disease. Vitamins are divided into two groups, according to whether they are soluble in water or in fat:

- the fat-soluble vitamins are A, D, E, and K;
- the water-soluble vitamins are B and C.

The vitamins most important to the condition of the skin are vitamins A, B_2, B_3 and C.

Vitamin A Insufficient vitamin A in the diet leads to **hyperkeratinisation** (production of too much keratin). This causes blockages in the skin tissue. The skin becomes rough and dry, and eye disorders such as styes may occur.

Food sources: Vitamin A is found in red, yellow and green vegetables, and in egg yolk, butter and cheese.

Vitamin B_2 Vitamin B_2 (also called **riboflavin**) helps to break down other foodstuffs, releasing energy needed by cells to function efficiently. A deficiency of vitamin B_2 causes the skin at the corners of the mouth to crack.

Food sources: Vitamin B_2 is found in brewer's yeast, milk products, leafy vegetables, liver, and whole grains.

Vitamin B_3 Vitamin B_3 (also called **niacin**) has the same function as vitamin B_2, but is also vital in the maintenance of the tissues of the skin.

Food sources: Vitamin B_3 is found in meat, brewer's yeast, nuts, and seeds.

Vitamin C Vitamin C (also called **ascorbic acid**) maintains healthy skin. A lack of vitamin C causes the capillaries to become fragile, and haemorrhages of the skin, such as bruising, may occur. Severe deficiency results in **scurvy**.

Food sources: Vitamin C is found in fruit and vegetables.

Water

Water forms about two-thirds of the body's weight, and is an important component both inside and outside the body cells. At least one litre of water should be drunk every day, to avoid dehydration of the body and the skin.

Food sources: Water is also a constituent of many foods, including fruits and vegetables.

Fibre

Fibre is not broken down into nutrients, but it is very important for effective digestion.

Food sources: Fibre is found in fruit, vegetables and cereals.

Threats to the skin

Internal

Alcohol **Alcohol** deprives the body of its vitamin reserves, especially vitamins B and C, which are necessary for a healthy skin. Alcohol also tends to dehydrate the body, including the skin.

Caffeine Coffee, tea, cocoa and soft fizzy drinks contain a mild drug called **caffeine**. In moderate doses, such as two or three cups of coffee per day, caffeine is safe. If you drink too much, however, caffeine can cause nervousness, interfere with digestion, block the absorption of vitamins and minerals, and spoil the appearance of the skin.

Smoking **Smoking** interferes with cell respiration and slows down the circulation. This makes it harder for nutrients to reach the skin cells and for waste products to be eliminated. Cigarette smoking also releases a chemical that destroys vitamin C. This interferes with the production of collagen, and thereby contributes to premature wrinkling. Nicotine is a **toxic** substance – a poison!

Medication Certain **medicines** taken by mouth can cause skin dehydration, oedema – swelling of the tissues – (this may for example be caused by steroids) or irregular skin pigmentation (sometimes caused by the contraceptive pill). During the initial consultation with the client, find out whether she is taking any medication – and take this into account in your diagnosis and treatment plan.

Stress **Stress** is shown in the face as tension lines where the facial muscles are tight. Because blood and lymph cannot circulate properly, this causes a 'sluggish' skin condition and poor facial nutrition. A person suffering from stress usually experiences disturbed sleep or sleeplessness (**insomnia**). Lack of sleep causes the skin to become dull and puffy, especially the tissue beneath the eyes, where dark circles also appear. Too *much* sleep also can

HEALTH AND SAFETY

Weight loss
If you lose weight too quickly, your skin will sag and wrinkle.

TIP

Advise your clients to replace tea with herbal infusions and to drink decaffeinated coffee (in moderation) rather than regular coffee.

TIP

Some cosmetic companies offer bath preparations that aid relaxation by the inhalation of aromatic ingredients. These ingredients, combined with the warm water, may help a client who has difficulty in sleeping.

cause the facial tissue to become puffy – because the circulation is less active, body fluids collect in the tissues.

If someone is suffering from stress, they may drink more tea, coffee or alcohol, or smoke more cigarettes: this too damages the skin.

Stress and anxiety are often the underlying cause of certain skin disorders. Some skin conditions, such as boils and styes, appear at times of stress; others, such as psoriasis and eczema, may become much worse. At the consultation, try to determine whether the client is suffering from stress: if she is, make sure that the salon treatments promote relaxation.

External

As well as looking after the skin from the *inside*, by diet, it needs care from the *outside* – it must be kept clean, and it must be nourished.

With normal physiological functioning, the skin becomes greasy, and sweat is deposited on its surface. The skin's natural oil (**sebum**) can easily build up and block the natural openings, the hair **follicles** and **pores**: this may lead to infection. Facial cosmetics too affect the health of the skin; if not regularly removed, they may cause congestion. Skin-care treatments help to maintain and improve the functioning of the skin.

Ultraviolet light Although recently **ultraviolet** (**UV**) has been identified as a hazard to skin, it also has some *positive* effects. One of these is its ability to stimulate the production of **vitamin D**, which is absorbed into the bloodstream and nourishes and helps to maintain bone tissue. Second, UV light activates the pigment **melanin** in the skin, and thereby creates a **tan**. Many people feel better when they have a tan, as it gives a healthy appearance.

Ultraviolet light is divided into different bands. The most important to skin tanning are UVA and UVB. **UVA** stimulates the melanin in the skin to produce a rapid tan, which does not last very long. UVA penetrates deep into the dermis where it can cause premature ageing of the skin. **Free radicals** – highly reactive molecules which cause skin cells to degenerate – are also formed. These molecules disrupt production of collagen and elastin, the fibres that give skin its strength and elasticity. Reduced elasticity leads to wrinkling.

UVB stimulates the production of vitamin D. Melanin activation by UVB produces a longer-lasting tan than that produced by UVA. UVB is partially absorbed by the atmosphere – it has a shorter wavelength than UVA – and only 10 per cent reaches the dermis. UVB causes thickening of the stratum corneum layer, which reflects ultra-violet away from the skin's surface.

UVB causes **sunburn**: the skin becomes red as the cells are damaged, and the skin may blister. UVB is also implicated in skin cancers, especially malignant melanoma.

HEALTH AND SAFETY

Sunbathing
Never wear perfume, cosmetic products or deodorants when sunbathing, either in natural sunlight or in artificially produced (sun-canopy) ultraviolet. The chemicals in these products can sensitise the skin, causing an allergic skin reaction.

TIP

Pigmentation marks caused by repeated exposure to UV light eventually remain, even without the exposure to UV. Some clients dislike such marks, and you could advise them on camouflage make-up.

The relaxing, warming effect of the sun is caused by the **infra-red** (**IR**) light. This penetrates the skin to the subcutaneous layer and is thought to speed skin ageing and possibly to cause a cancer called squamous cell carcinoma. The tan is actually a sign of skin damage, therefore, and both UV and IR probably contribute to photo-ageing – the premature ageing of the skin by light.

Although black skin has a high melanin content, which absorbs more ultra-violet and allows less to reach the dermis, it is not fully protected against the UV and still requires additional protection.

Chemical skin protection, or sunscreens, are designed to absorb ultra-violet light (UVA and UVB), reducing the rate of skin ageing in all skin types. Various sunscreens are available, classified by numbers according to their sun-protection factor (SPF). This is the amount of protection that the sunscreen gives you from the sun. The application of the sunscreen extends your natural skin protection, allowing you to stay in the sun for longer without burning. For example, if normally you can be in the sun for 10 minutes before the skin begins to go red, a sunscreen with an SPF of 10 will allow you 10 × 10 minutes' – 100 minutes' – safe exposure in the sun.

Artificial UV light produced by sunbeds, used for cosmetic skin tanning, also causes premature ageing. Most sunbeds use concentrated UVA, which causes dermal tissue damage resulting in lines and wrinkles.

It may take years to see the effects of the dermal damage caused by unprotected UV exposure, but once they have occurred the effects are irreversible. UVA rays are present all year round, so to prevent premature ageing cosmetic preparations containing sunscreens should be worn at all times.

TIP

Ultraviolet can penetrate water to a depth of 1 metre, so even when swimming you need to wear a sunscreen. Special waterproof products are designed for this purpose.

Climate Sebum, the skin's natural grease, provides an oily protective film over the surface of the skin which reduces evaporation. Despite this, unprotected exposure of the skin to the environment allows evaporation from the epidermis which results in a dry, dehydrated skin condition.

The climate has several effects on the skin:

- *Sebum production* When the skin is exposed to the cold, less sebum is produced. The skin has reduced protection, allowing moisture to evaporate.

- *Perspiration* In very hot weather more moisture is lost as **perspiration**: perspiration increases, to cool the skin and regulate the body's temperature.

- *Humidity* Moisture loss from the skin is also affected by the **humidity** (water content) of the surrounding air. In hot, dry weather humidity will

TIP

To acquire a tan without the damaging effects of the sun or sunbeds, use a *fake tanning* preparation. This treatment is becoming popular in the beauty therapist's salon.

be low, so water loss will be high. In temperate, damp conditions humidity will be high, so water loss will be low.

- *Extremes of temperature* Alternating heat and cold often leads to the formation of **broken capillaries**. These appear as fine red lines on Caucasian skin, and as discoloration on black skin.

- *Stratum corneum* The cells of the stratum corneum multiply with repeated unprotected exposure to the climate, as the body's natural defence.

The damaging effects caused by the climate can be reduced by using protective skin-care preparations such as moisturisers. These spread a layer of oil over the skin's surface, reducing evaporation.

Environmental stress and pollution Further causes of moisture loss include harsh alkaline chemicals such as detergents and soaps – which remove sebum from the skin's surface – and air conditioning and central heating.

Environmental **pollutants** such as lead, mercury, cadmium and aluminium can accumulate in the body. One result is the formation of dangerous chemicals that attack proteins in the cells. Such pollutants find their way into food through polluted waters, rain and dust. To protect the body, always wash vegetables thoroughly, and eat a diet rich in vitamins C and E.

Air pollution, involving carbon from smoke, chemical discharges from factories, and fumes from car exhausts, should be removed from the skin by effective cleansing. Absorption of these pollutants is reduced by the application of moisturiser: this forms a barrier over the skin's surface.

SKIN-CARE TREATMENTS

The beauty therapist has the professional expertise to help each client improve the appearance and condition of her skin by the application of appropriate cosmetic treatments and preparations. The facial skin services she offers include:

- consultation and skin analysis;
- skin cleansing;
- specialised skin-care treatments;
- the application of face masks or face packs;
- manual massage of the face, neck and shoulders;
- facial cosmetic make-up.

The beauty therapist cannot change the underlying skin type, which is genetically determined, but she can keep the physiological characteristics of each skin type in check.

SKIN TYPES

The basic structure of the skin does not vary from person to person, but the physiological functioning of its different features does; it is this that gives us **skin types**.

The first and most important part of a facial treatment is the correct diagnosis of the skin type. This is carried out at the beginning of each facial treatment. The beauty therapist must choose the correct skin-care products and facial treatments for the client's skin type. This assessment is called a **skin analysis**.

Basic types

There are four main skin types:

- normal;
- dry;
- greasy;
- combination.

Normal skin

Normal skin is often referred to as **balanced**, because it is neither too oily nor too dry. Because when young this skin type seldom has any problems, such as blemishes, it is often neglected. Neglect causes the skin to become dry, especially around the eyes, cheeks and neck, where the skin is thinner.

A normal skin type in adults is very rare. It has these characteristics:

- the pore size is small or medium;
- the moisture content is good;
- the skin texture is even, neither too thick nor too thin;
- the colour is healthy (because of good blood circulation);
- the skin elasticity is good, when young;
- the skin feels firm to the touch;
- the skin pigmentation is even-coloured;
- the skin is usually free from blemishes.

Dry skin

Dry skin is lacking in either sebum or moisture, or both. Because sebum limits moisture loss by evaporation from the skin, skin with insufficient sebum rapidly loses moisture. The resulting dry skin is often described as **dehydrated**.

Dry skin has these characteristics:

- the pores are small and tight;
- the moisture content is poor;
- the skin texture is coarse and thin, with patches of visibly flaking skin;
- there is a tendency towards sensitivity (broken capillaries often accompany this skin type);
- premature ageing is common, resulting in the appearance of wrinkles, seen especially around the eyes, mouth and neck;
- skin pigmentation may be uneven, and disorders such as ephelides (freckles) usually accompany this skin type;
- milia are often found around the cheek and eye area.

Greasy skin

In **greasy skin** the sebaceous glands become very active at puberty, when stimulated by the male hormone **androgen**. An increase in sebum production often causes the appearance of skin blemishes. Sebaceous gland activity begins to decrease when the person is in their twenties.

Greasy skin has these characteristics:

- the pores are enlarged;
- the moisture content is high;
- the skin is coarse and thick;
- the skin is sallow in colour, as a result of the excess sebum production, dead skin cells become embedded in the sebum, and the skin has sluggish blood and lymph circulation;
- the skin tone is good, due to the protective effect of the sebum;
- the skin is prone to shininess, due to excess sebum production;
- there may be uneven pigmentation;
- certain skin disorders may be apparent – comedones, pustules, papules, milia, or sebaceous cysts.

Acne vulgaris and **seborrhoea** are skin disorders that occur when the skin becomes excessively greasy due to the influence of hormones. Treatment of these skin disorders should be carried out to control sebum flow (see page 25).

Combination skin

Combination skin is partly oily and partly dry. The oily parts are generally the chin, nose and forehead, known as the **T-zone**. The upper cheeks may show signs of oiliness, but the rest of the face and neck area is dry.

Combination skin is the commonest skin type. It has these characteristics:

- the pores in the T-zone are enlarged, while in the cheek area they are small to medium;
- the moisture content is high in the oily areas, but poor in the dry areas;
- the skin is coarse and thick in the oily areas, but thin in the dry areas;
- the skin is sallow in the oily areas, but shows sensitivity and high colour in the dry areas;
- the skin tone is good in the oily areas, but poor in the dry areas;
- there is uneven pigmentation, usually seen as ephelides and lentigines;
- there may be blemishes such as pustules and comedones on the oily skin at the T-zone;
- milia and broken capillaries may appear in the dry areas, commonly on the cheeks and near the eyes.

Additional characteristics

Whilst looking closely at the skin, further skin characteristics may become obvious. The skin may be:

- sensitive;
- dehydrated;
- moist;
- oedematous (puffy).

Sensitive skin

Sensitive skin usually accompanies a dry skin type, but not always.

The characteristics of sensitive skin are these:

- the skin may show high colouring;
- there are usually broken capillaries in the cheek area;
- the skin feels warm to the touch;
- there is superficial flaking of the skin;
- the skin may show high colouring after skin cleansing, if it is sensitive to pressure.

In a black skin, instead of the redness shown by a Caucasian skin, irritation shows up as a darker patch.

ACTIVITY

Recognising skin types
Refer to the illustration below. What skin characteristics would you expect to see in each of the numbered areas? Consider each of the skin types discussed.

HEALTH AND SAFETY

Sensitive skin
Use hypoallergenic products – these do not contain any of the known common skin sensitisers.
A skin that is sensitive may also be allergic to certain substances.

TIP ✓

Encourage clients with dehydrated skin to drink 6–8 glasses of water a day to replenish the moisture in the body.

Allergic skin **Allergic skin** is irritated by external **allergens**, including chemicals in some cosmetics. The allergens inflame the skin and may damage its protective function. At the consultation, always try to discover whether the client has any allergies, and if so, to what.

The allergies of most concern to the beauty therapist are those caused by substances applied to the skin. The therapist must be aware of such substances and avoid their use. Contact with an allergen, especially if repeated, may cause skin disorders such as eczema or dermatitis (see pages 32–3).

Dehydrated skin

Dehydrated skin is skin that has lost water from the skin tissues. The condition can affect any skin type, but most commonly accompanies dry or combination skin types. The problem may be related to the client's general health. If she has recently been ill with a fever, for example, the skin will have lost fluid through sweating. If she is taking medication, this too may cause dehydration, as may drastic dieting. In many cases the dehydration is caused by working in an environment with a low humidity, or in one that is air-conditioned. You must try to discover the cause, and provide both corrective treatment and advice.

The characteristics of dehydrated skin are as follows:

- the skin has a fine orange-peel effect, caused by its lack of moisture;
- there is superficial flaking;
- fine, superficial lines are evident on the skin;
- broken capillaries are common.

Moist skin

Moist skin appears moist and feels damp: this is due to the over-secretion of sweat. The beauty therapist cannot correct this skin condition, which is often caused by some internal physiological disturbance such as a hormonal or metabolic imbalance.

Advise the client to use lightweight cleansing preparations. She should avoid skin-toning preparations with a high alcohol content; these would stimulate the skin, causing yet further perspiration and skin sensitivity. She should avoid highly spiced food, and be aware that alcoholic or hot drinks will cause dilation of the skin capillaries, thereby increasing the skin's temperature.

Oedematous (puffy) skin

TIP ✓

Whilst completing the record card you may be able to recognise aspects of your client's lifestyle that probably contribute to the oedematous skin. If so, you can advise the client accordingly.

Oedematous skin is, and appears, swollen and puffy: this is because the tissues are retaining excess water. The condition may be caused by a medical disorder, or may be a side-effect of medication. Hot weather can cause temporary swelling of the tissues, as can local injury to the tissues. Poor blood circulation and lymphatic flow may cause puffy skin, too; this is often seen around the eyes. In this case the condition may benefit from gentle massage around the eye area. Tissue-fluid retention in the facial skin may be caused by an incorrect diet, such as one that includes too much salt or the drinking of too much alcohol, tea or coffee.

Unless you are quite sure about the cause of the oedema, always seek permission from your client's doctor before treating the skin.

The sex of the client

Men have a more acidic skin surface than females and the stratum corneum is thicker on males than females. However, males have coarse facial hair and shaving daily removes cells of the stratum corneum before they are ready to desquamate naturally. This can sensitise and dry the skin, especially if after-shave lotions with a high alcohol content are directly applied. A moisturiser should be applied to protect the skin.

The collagen content of the skin is different in men and women. Collagen and sebum production falls in menopausal women causing skin ageing. Skin does not appear to age as quickly in males as females because collagen and sebum production remain constant.

The main reason males choose to have a facial is for relaxation and to improve the appearance of the skin, rather than for the anti-ageing benefits.

> **TIP**
>
> **Male facials**
> Recommend that the male client shaves before facial treatment. This will soften the skin and facilitate skin cleansing.

The age of the skin

Having identified the skin type, the beauty therapist must classify the age of the skin.

Often the age of a client will relate to skin problems that are evident. A young client, for example, may have skin blemishes such as comedones, pustules and papules. These disorders are caused by overactivity of the sebaceous gland at puberty, when the body is developing its secondary sexual characteristics. It is at this time that acne vulgaris is most likely to occur, due to the hormonal imbalance. The skin of clients aged over 25 years, however, is generally termed **mature skin**.

The beauty therapist should also consider the client's skin tone and muscle tone in relation to her age. A young skin will probably have good skin tone, and the skin will be supple and elastic. This is because the collagen and elastin fibres in the skin are strong. Poor skin tone, on the other hand, is recognised by the appearance of facial lines and wrinkles.

A healthy young skin will also have good muscle tone, and the facial contours will appear firm. With poor muscle tone, the muscles becomes slack and loose.

> **TIP**
>
> To test skin tone, gently lift the skin at the cheeks between two fingers and then let go. If the skin tone is good, the skin will spring back to its original shape.

Mature skin

The change in appearance of women's skin during ageing is closely related to the altered production of the hormones oestrogen, progesterone and androgen at the menopause.

Mature skin has the following characteristics:

- The skin becomes dry, as the sebaceous and sudoriferous glands become less active.

ACTIVITY

The ageing process
Cut out photographs from magazines or newspapers showing men and women of different cultures and various ages.
1 Can you identify the visible characteristics of ageing?
2 Does ageing occur at the same rate in men and women and in different cultures?
3 Discuss your findings with your tutor.

Aged skin

Dr John Gray

- The skin loses its elasticity as the elastin fibres harden, and wrinkles appear due to the cross-linking and hardening of collagen fibres.
- The epidermis grows more slowly and the skin appears thinner, becoming almost transparent in some areas such as around the eyes, where small veins and capillaries show through the skin.
- Broken capillaries appear, especially on the cheek area and around the nose.
- The facial contours become slack as muscle tone is reduced.
- The underlying bone structure becomes more obvious, as the fatty layer and the supportive tissue beneath the skin grow thinner.
- Blood circulation becomes poor, which interferes with skin nutrition, and the skin may appear sallow.
- Due to the decrease in metabolic rate, waste products are not removed so quickly, and this leads to puffiness of the skin.
- Patches of irregular pigmentation appear on the surface of the skin, such as lentigines and chloasmata.

The skin may also exhibit the following skin conditions, although these are not truly *characteristic* of an ageing skin:

- Dermal naevi may be enlarged.
- Sebhorrheic warts may appear on the epidermal layer of the skin.
- Verruca filiformis warts may increase in number.
- Hair growth on the upper lip or chin, or both, may become darker or coarser, due to hormonal imbalance in the body.
- Dark circles and puffiness may occur under the eyes.

HEALTH AND SAFETY

UV light and ageing
The ageing process is accelerated when the skin is regularly exposed to ultraviolet light.

TIP

Skin appearance
As the surface of the skin reflects light and shows the skin colour, the therapist's aim is for the skin surface to be smooth and healthy. This is achieved by the removal of dead skin cells and ensuring it is adequately moisturised.

DIFFERENCES IN SKIN

Although there is no difference between skin functions such as sweat and sebaceous gland activity in white and black skin, the amount of pigment, called *melanin*, varies, resulting in different skin and hair colour.

There are two forms of the melanin pigment: *eumelanin*, produced in black and brown skin colours, and *phaeomelanin*, found in lighter skins. Both forms of pigment can be present together but the amount of each can vary.

People who originate from hot countries have more melanin and a darker skin pigment, whilst those who originate from cooler countries have less melanin and a lighter skin pigment.

African-Caribbean

The skin colour is dark and ranges in tone to almost black. This is because it has more melanin, which absorbs ultraviolet (UV) light. As black skin is exposed to UV light it becomes darker and darker. This causes hyperpigmentation – uneven patches of skin tone which are darker than the surrounding skin.

Care must be taken when dealing with blemishes on darker skins as scars may occur as the skin heals. The scars may become keloids, scarring that becomes enlarged and projects above the skins surface. Even minor scratches may result in keloid formation.

Hyperpigmentation may also occur. It is more common in darker skinned people due to increased melanin. Hyperpigmentation most commonly occurs following skin inflammation, such as acne vulgaris. Keloids may become hyperpigmented if exposed to the sun in the early stages of their formation.

Vitiligo (loss of skin pigment) is a considerable problem when it occurs in dark skin, as it is very obvious. Cosmetics may be applied as a corrective technique.

Male clients may have a tendency towards *pseudo folliculitis*, an inflammatory skin disorder. This occurs as the hair is coarser and curly and has a tendency as it grows out of the skin to curl back and re-enter it, becoming ingrown. This foreign object in the skin becomes irritated and inflamed. Hyperpigmentation may also accompany this condition.

Dermatosis papulosis nigra, also called flesh moles, can occur. These are brown or black hyperpigmented markings, resembling moles, usually seen on the cheeks. Their cause is unknown but they are sometimes found to be hereditary. They also occur more frequently in females than males.

Hair colour is dark brown to black.

African-Caribbean skin

Dr John Gray

> **TIP** ✔
>
> Hyper and hypopigmentation can affect the skin of any race.
>   Chloasma or liver spots are an example of hyperpigmentation. These occur as a result of skin damage and are commonly seen as dark brown marks on the backs of the hands.
>   Freckles or ephelides are another example of hyperpigmentation. These become darker when the skin is exposed to the sun.
>   Prescription creams containing hydroquinone bleach and laser treatment may be used to lighten the skin. However, care must be taken using hydroquinone bleach on black skin as hypopigmentation can occur.

Asian

The skin colour has a light to dark tone due to increased melanin, with yellow undertones. There is a tendency towards hyperpigmentation, appearing as dark patches of skin, and scarring can appear following skin inflammation. Dermatosis papulosis nigra can occur. In females there is a normal tendency towards superfluous facial hair.

Hair colour is dark brown to black.

Asian skin

Dr John Gray

Dr John Gray

Caucasian skin

Dr John Gray

Oriental skin

Caucasian

The skin colour is white. This skin has less melanin and so less defence in the presence of UV light; sun damage results in skin burning and premature ageing. Caucasian skin has a tendency to show freckles (ephelides), as a result of uneven melanin distribution in the skin.

Hair colour is usually fair, red or brown.

TIP
Skin and UV light defence Very dark skin offers up to 30 times more protection against the sun than lighter skin.

Oriental

The skin colour has more melanin present and has a yellowish tone. Oriental skin is usually oily and prone to hyperpigmentation. Blemishes should be treated with caution as hyperpigmentation and scarring could result due to increased levels of melanin. Female skin generally appears smooth and has little facial hair.

Hair colour is usually mid-brown to black.

ACTIVITY
Which countries do the skin types listed below originate from: ● Caucasian ● Oriental ● Asian ● African-Caribbean

RECEPTION

Before carrying out *any* facial treatments, the beauty therapist must consult with the client to determine their treatment needs and to discuss the services that are available. **Consultation** is a service that should be offered separately: there should be no pressure on the client to book a treatment following the consultation.

Making the appointment

When a new client telephones to make an appointment for a service, always allocate extra time for the consultation beforehand. Explain to the client how long they should allow for the appointment. For example, if a client is seeking a basic skin cleansing and mask treatment, allow 30 minutes; if they are a new client allow 45 minutes so that there is time for the consultation and filling in the record card. If it is necessary to remove facial blockages and to carry out other specialised treatments, allow 45 minutes to 1 hour.

BEAUTY WORKS

Date	Beauty therapist name	
Client name		Date of birth (identifying client age group)
Address		Postcode
Evening phone number	Day phone number	
Name of doctor	Doctor's address and phone number	
Related medical history (conditions that may restrict or prohibit treatment application)		
Are you taking any medication (this may affect the appearance of the skin or skin sensitivity)		

CONTRA-INDICATIONS REQUIRING MEDICAL REFERRAL
(Preventing facial treatment application)

- ☐ bacterial infection (e.g. impetigo)
- ☐ viral infection (e.g. herpes simplex)
- ☐ fungal infection (e.g. tinea corporis)
- ☐ eye infections (e.g. conjunctivitis)
- ☐ watery eyes
- ☐ systemic medical conditions
- ☐ severe skin condition

SKIN GROUP

- ☐ oily
- ☐ dry
- ☐ combination
- ☐ young
- ☐ mature

FACIAL PRODUCTS

- ☐ cleanser
- ☐ toner
- ☐ eye cleanser
- ☐ exfoliant
- ☐ mask – setting
- ☐ mask – non-setting
- ☐ massage medium
- ☐ moisturiser
- ☐ specialist skin treatments (e.g. eye cream)

MASSAGE MEDIUMS

- ☐ oil
- ☐ cream

CONTRA-INDICATIONS WHICH RESTRICT TREATMENT
(Treatment may require adaptation)

- ☐ cuts and abrasions
- ☐ bruising and swelling
- ☐ recent scar tissue
- ☐ eczema
- ☐ skin allergies
- ☐ vitiligo
- ☐ styes
- ☐ hyper keratosis
- ☐ watery eyes

SKIN CONDITION

- ☐ sensitive
- ☐ mature
- ☐ dehydrated
- ☐ milia
- ☐ broken capillaries
- ☐ comedones
- ☐ pustules
- ☐ papules
- ☐ open pores
- ☐ hyperpigmentation
- ☐ hypopigmentation
- ☐ dermatitis papulosa nigra
- ☐ keloids
- ☐ ingrowing hairs

EQUIPMENT AND MATERIALS

- ☐ magnifying light
- ☐ skin warming devices
- ☐ protective covering
- ☐ consumables

MASSAGE TECHNIQUES

- ☐ effleurage
- ☐ petrissage
- ☐ friction
- ☐ tapotement
- ☐ vibrations

Beauty therapist signature (for reference)
Client signature (confirmation of details)

PRESENT SKIN-CARE ROUTINE

This information includes
- what products the client is currently using to cleanse and care for the skin of the face and neck
- how regularly the products are used
- how the products are applied and removed

TREATMENT ADVICE

This information includes
- what products have been used in the facial treatment
- advice re products that would be suitable for the client to use at home to care for their skin
- advice on product application and removal in order to gain maximum benefit from their use
- contra-action advice, action to be taken in the event of an unwanted skin reaction
- use of make-up following facial treatment
- recommendations for further facial treatments
- the recommended time intervals between treatments

On arrival

When the client arrives for the treatment, the **record card** is completed. Record the client's personal details, such as her name and address. Check that there are no contra-indications to facial treatment.

The beauty therapist will add further information to the record card at the consultation and during treatment.

The consultation

The consultation is the time when the beauty therapist can assess whether the client is actually suited to treatment. The therapist must look for contra-indications, and must give no treatment if there are any – this is to safeguard the therapist, the client herself and, in the case of a client with a contagious skin disorder, other clients who would be at risk of cross-infection.

The beauty therapist's knowledge of facial treatments and advice on skin care will instil confidence in the client. Explain what is involved with each treatment, how long it takes, the aftercare involved and any home care that is required. This will demonstrate your professional expertise.

The client is likely to ask which is the most suitable treatment for her, and you must advise her as to which would best meet her needs.

Make the client aware of the cost of the individual treatment – or treatment programme, if necessary – so that she can decide whether or not to undertake the financial commitment involved.

Invite the client to ask questions during the consultation. By the end, she should understand fully what the proposed treatment involves.

TIP

Never make assumptions about what the client can afford. Usually the client will indicate to you what she is prepared to spend.

She may receive the treatment immediately, following the consultation, or go away to consider the proposals.

During the consultation, details are noted on the client's record card. You can fill this in as you speak to her, without diverting your attention away from her.

CONTRA-INDICATIONS

The consultation and skin analysis will draw your attention to any contra-indications or aspects that require special care and attention.

Remember that not all contra-indications are visible – a current bone fracture, for example, would not be. Refer to the checklist of contra-indications on the client's record card.

The following contra-indications are relevant to *all* facial treatments:

- *Skin disorder*, such as acne vulgaris (unless medical approval has been sought and given).
- *Skin disease*, such as impetigo.
- *Bruising* in the area.
- *Haemorrhage*, if recent – wait until the condition has healed.
- *Operation* in the area, if recent – wait for 6 months.

HEALTH AND SAFETY

Herpes simplex
A small skin lesion due to herpes simplex may initially appear to be simply a pustule with a scab. At the consultation, always check whether the client knows if she suffers from some skin disease or disorder.

- *Fracture*, if recent – wait for 6 months.
- *Furuncle* (boil).
- *Inflammation or swelling* of the skin.
- *Scar tissue*, if recent – wait for 6 months.
- *Sebaceous cyst*.
- *Eye disorder*, such as conjunctivitis.

Certain contra-indications restrict treatment; that is, the treatment may have to be adapted or delayed until the contra-indication has gone. For example, if eczema is present but the skin is not broken, the treatment can proceed but the area should be avoided as much as possible.

If the client has an allergy to an ingredient in the cosmetic preparations used, treatment cannot proceed until an alternative, non-allergenic product suited to the client is obtained. If the client has a stye, treatment cannot proceed. However, when the eye disorder has gone treatment may be carried out.

EQUIPMENT AND MATERIALS

Beauty salons differ in how much floor space is available and how much of that is allocated to each beauty service. There may be one or several facial-treatment cubicles. In the case of a salon having only one such cubicle, it is important that the range of facial services offered can all be delivered safely and hygienically.

Basic equipment

Each treatment cubicle should have the following basic equipment.

Treatment couch or beauty chair

A treatment couch

The **couch** or **chair** should be covered with easy-to-clean upholstery: it must withstand daily cleaning with warm water and detergent. It must have an adjustable **back rest**, for the comfort of both the client and the therapist. If possible, purchase a couch that also has an adjustable **leg rest**, as this allows treatments such as pedicure to be carried out.

Ellisons

Beauty stools

Sorisa

A magnifying lamp

Equipment trolley

The **equipment trolley** should be large enough to accommodate all the necessary equipment and products; trolleys are usually of a two- or three-shelf design. Like the chair or couch, the trolley should be made of a material that will withstand regular cleaning. Some models have restraining bars to prevent objects sliding off the trolley. Drawers are useful in storing tools and small consumables. The trolley should have securely fixed easy-glide castors.

Beauty stool

The **stool** should be covered in a fabric similar to that covering the treatment couch. It may or may not have a back rest; in some designs the back rest is removable. For the comfort of the therapist, it should be adjustable in height; to allow mobility, it should be mounted on castors.

Magnifying lamp

The **magnifying lamp** is available in three models: floor-standing, wall-mounted, and trolley-mounted.

Covered waste-bin

A **covered waste-bin** should be placed unobtrusively within easy each. It should be lined with a disposable bin-liner. You should also have a 'sharps' box for the disposal of contaminated equipment.

Arrangements for the collection and disposal of contaminated waste should be made with your local environmental health office.

Sorisa

Covered waste-bins

EQUIPMENT LIST

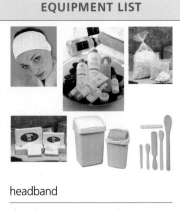

headband

skin cleansing preparations

cottonwool

tissues

waste bin

spatulas

see opposite for complete list of materials required

TIP ✔

Disposable paper roll may be placed over the surface of the treatment couch if desired. This should be changed for each client.

TIP ✔

Wall-mounted towel racks save storage space.

HEALTH AND SAFETY ✚

Containers
Bottles and other containers should be clean and clearly labelled.

Preparing the cubicle

The following guidelines describe the basic preparation of the **facial treatment cubicle**. Further equipment and materials relevant to other beauty services are discussed within the appropriate chapters.

- **Towel drapes** There should be a *large towel* to cover the client's body, and a *small hand towel* to drape across the client's chest and shoulders.

- **Headband** A clean material headband should be provided for each client.

- **Skin-cleansing preparations** The trolley should carry a display of facial skin-cleansing preparations to suit all skin types.

- **Trolley** The surface of each shelf can be protected with a sheet of 500mm disposable bedroll.

- **Towel** A clean towel should be placed on the trolley for the therapist to wipe her hands on as necessary.

- **Gown** A clean gown should be provided for each client as necessary.

- **Cottonwool** There should be a plentiful supply of both damp and dry cottonwool, sufficient for the treatment to be carried out. *Dry* cottonwool should be stored in a covered container; *damp* cottonwool is usually placed in a clean bowl.

- **Tissues** Facial tissues should be large and of a high quality. They should be stored in a covered container.

- **Mirror** A clean hand mirror should be available, for use in consulting with the client before, during and after her treatment.

- **Waste** A covered container for waste may be placed on the bottom shelf of the trolley or it can be put into the waste bin at once.

- **Container for jewellery** A container may be provided in which the client can place her jewellery if she needs to remove it prior to treatment.

- **Spatulas** Several clean spatulas (preferably disposable) should be provided for each client. One should be used in tucking any stray hair beneath the headband. Others will be used in removing products from their containers.

TIP ✔

It is bad practice to leave the client in order to fetch more cottonwool. It is also bad practice to prepare too much and be wasteful!

Pre-shaped cottonwool discs are ideal for facial treatments. Alternatively, cut high-quality cottonwool into squares (6cm × 6cm).

PREPARING THE CLIENT

By the time the client is shown through to the treatment cubicle, the record card will already have been partly filled in at reception. The card should be collected by the beauty therapist, who will add to it during and after the treatment.

In the privacy of the treatment cubicle, carry out the consultation. This takes place when the client first meets the therapist and again whenever a new treatment is to be carried out.

The consultation

The consultation enables the therapist:

- to assess whether the client is suited to treatment or whether treatment is contra-indicated in some way;
- to ask the client specific questions about her present skin-care routine and her general health.

The client's answers will indicate to the therapist what is required, and what is achievable, from a skin-care programme.

During the consultation the therapist can also:

- explain what is involved in each treatment, how long it takes, and what aftercare and home care are required (if relevant);
- assess how much the client is willing to spend, and design a treatment programme within her budget.

The consultation is also helpful to the client. She can:

- discover what the beauty therapist can offer;
- ask questions, and receive honest professional advice concerning the most appropriate choice of skin-care treatment;
- decide how much she is willing to spend.

At the end of the consultation the client should understand fully what the proposed treatment involves.

HEALTH AND SAFETY

Poor health
If the client is in poor health, or is taking medication that affects her skin condition, it may not be possible to treat her until the medical condition has been treated by her physician.

TIP

Compliance with the Data Protection Act 1998
Ensure all client records are stored securely, with only those staff who have the client's permission having access to them.

ACTIVITY

Answering questions
You should be able to answer honestly, competently and tactfully any questions related to the beauty services you offer. Below are examples of the questions you may be asked at consultation.

- 'I have always used soap and water upon my face. Is this a satisfactory way to cleanse my face?'
- 'Why do I need to use a separate night cream as well as a day moisturiser?'
- 'How often should I have a facial?'
- 'I have extremely oily skin. Why do I need to wear a moisturiser?'
- 'What can I do to treat these fine lines around my eyes?'

What answers would you give? Think of further questions you might be asked with regard to skin care. An experienced beauty therapist will be able to advise you.

Prior to treatment

Depending on the treatment to be carried out, the client may need to remove some clothing. Offer her a **gown** to wear.

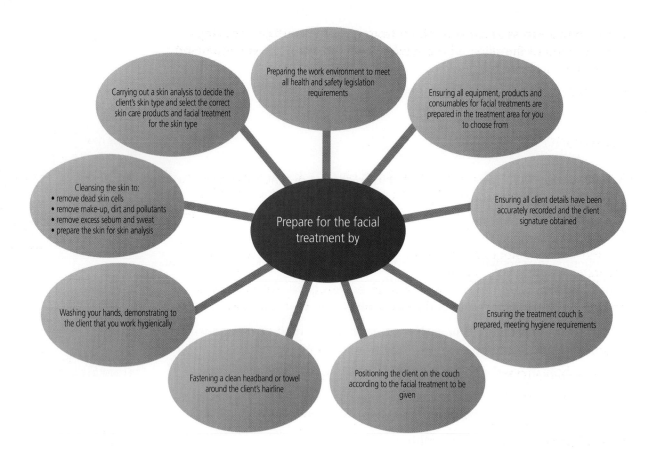

Prepare for the facial treatment by

Preparing the work environment to meet all health and safety legislation requirements

Ensuring all equipment, products and consumables for facial treatments are prepared in the treatment area for you to choose from

Carrying out a skin analysis to decide the client's skin type and select the correct skin care products and facial treatment for the skin type

Ensuring all client details have been accurately recorded and the client signature obtained

Cleansing the skin to:
• remove dead skin cells
• remove make-up, dirt and pollutants
• remove excess sebum and sweat
• prepare the skin for skin analysis

Ensuring the treatment couch is prepared, meeting hygiene requirements

Washing your hands, demonstrating to the client that you work hygienically

Positioning the client on the couch according to the facial treatment to be given

Fastening a clean headband or towel around the client's hairline

TIP

Always give clear instructions to your client. This will help to ensure that she is not embarrassed or uncomfortable at any time.

TIP

Check that the headband is comfortable. A tight headband will cause tension and eventually a headache.

1 Position the client on the couch according to the treatment to be given. Cover the client with the large bath towel. If necessary, drape a small hand towel across her shoulders.

2 If facial, neck and shoulder massage is to be given, ask the client politely to remove her arms from her bra straps in preparation: this avoids disturbance later.

3 Fasten a clean headband around the client's hairline. Position the headband so that it does not cover the skin of the face. If using steam, cover the hair to stop it getting damp.

4 After preparing the client, wash your hands: this demonstrates to the client your concern to work hygienically.

CLEANSING

Skin cleansing is essential in promoting and maintaining a healthy complexion. There are various cleansing preparations to choose from; basically their action is the same in each case:

● to gently exfoliate dead skin cells from the stratum corneum, exposing younger cells and improving the skin's appearance;

● to remove make-up, dirt and pollutants from the skin's surface, reducing the possibility of blemishes and skin irritation;

- to remove excess sweat and sebum from the skin's surface, reducing congestion of the skin and the subsequent formation of comedones and pustules;
- to prepare the skin for further treatments.

Cleansing preparations

A cleanser is required that will remove both oil-soluble and water-soluble substances. Oil is capable of dissolving grease; water will dissolve other substances. Usually, therefore, a cleanser is a combination of both oil and water.

Oil and water do not combine: if you simply mix the two together they separate again, with the oil floating on the top of the water. If the two substances are shaken together vigorously, however, one substance will break up and become suspended in the other. The result is known as an **emulsion**.

Emulsions are used in many cosmetic preparations. They are either:

- **oil-in-water** (O/W) – minute droplets of oil, surrounded by water;
- **water-in-oil** (W/O) – minute droplets of water, surrounded by oil.

To give the emulsion stability, and to stop it separating out again, an **emulsifier** is added.

Various cleansing preparations are available to the beauty therapist, with formulations designed to suit the different skin types. They include:

- cleansing milks;
- cleansing creams;
- cleansing lotions;
- facial foaming cleansers;
- cleansing bars;
- eye make-up removers.

Whichever cleanser is chosen, it should have the following qualities:

- it should cleanse the skin effectively, without causing irritation;
- it should remove all traces of make-up and grease;
- it should feel pleasant to use;
- it should be easy to remove from the skin;
- ideally, it should be pH-balanced.

The **pH scale** is used to measure the **acidity** or **alkalinity** of a substance. Using a numbered scale of 1–14, acids have a pH less than 7; alkalis have a pH greater than 7. Substances with a pH of 7 are **neutral**.

> **TIP**
>
> Seasonal changes affect the skin. You may need to alter the client's basic skin-care routine through the year.

The pH scale

ACTIVITY

Acidic or alkaline?
To discover whether a liquid product is acidic or alkaline, carry out a simple test using litmus paper. Litmus changes colour according to the pH:

- litmus paper turns *blue* if an *alkali* is present;
- litmus paper turns *red* if an *acid* is present.

Test the pH of various cleansing preparations.

The skin is naturally slightly acidic: it has an **acid mantle**. Alkalis strip the skin of its protective film of sebum, making it feel dry and taut. To avoid skin irritation it is preferable to use a product that matches the acid mantle, a product whose pH is 5.5–5.6.

Cleansing milks

Cleansing milks are usually oil-in-water emulsions, with a relatively high proportion of water to oil, making the milk quite fluid in its consistency.

Cleansing milks have these specific treatment uses:

- treating dry skin that is prone to sensitivity;
- treating sensitive skin.

Cleansing creams

Cleansing creams have a relatively high proportion of oil to water, making the emulsion thicker and richer in its consistency than cleansing milks. The high oil content allows the product to be massaged over the skin surface without dragging the tissues. The cream is also more effective in removing grease and oil-based make-up from the skin.

Cleansing creams have these specific treatment uses:

- removing facial cosmetics;
- treating by deep cleansing massage;
- treating very dry skin.

Cleansing lotions

Cleansing lotions are solutions of detergents in water. They do not usually contain oil, and are therefore unsuitable for the removal of facial cosmetics.

Cleansing lotions have these specific treatment uses:

- cleansing a normal to combination skin type;
- treating greasy skin (where a high oil content could aggravate the skin, causing yet further sebum production).

Medicated ingredients may be included in a cleansing formulation: these are only suitable for greasy, congested, spotty skin types.

If the client has a mature, normal or combination skin, a cleansing lotion may not be effective because of the reduced oil content.

> **TIP**
>
> If a client has a very dry skin, advise her to avoid the use of tap water on the face – tap water contains salts and chlorine, which can dry the skin.

Facial foaming cleansers

Facial foaming cleansers usually contain a mild detergent which foams when mixed with water. Additional ingredients are selected for the treatment of different skin types. These cleansers are quick to use and afford a suitable alternative for the client who likes to cleanse her face with soap and water. If the client wears an oil-based make-up, advise her to use a cleansing cream first to remove make-up thoroughly before using this cleanser.

Facial foaming cleansers have a general application:

- treating most skin types except very dry or sensitive skin.

Cleansing bars

Although it is efficient as a cleanser, **soap** is usually considered unsuitable for use on the skin. It has an *alkaline* pH, which disturbs the skin's natural *acidic* pH balance. Soap strips the skin of its protective acid mantle, leaving insoluble salts on the skin's surface. The skin may be left feeling itchy, taut and sensitive.

Cleansing bars are a milder alternative to soap, and are specially formulated to match the skin's acidic pH of 5.5–5.6. They are less likely to dry out the skin.

Cleansing bars have this specific application:

- treating greasy to normal skin which is not sensitive.

> **TIP**
>
> Cleansing rinse-off formulations are very popular with male clients.

Eye make-up remover

Eye tissue is a lot finer than the skin on the rest of the face. It readily puffs if aggravated by oil-based cleansing preparations, and becomes very dry if harsh cleansing preparations are used.

To remove make-up from this area, use an **eye make-up remover**. This product cleanses the eyelid and lashes, gently emulsifying the make-up. It also conditions the delicate skin. Formulated as a lotion or a gel, it is designed to remove either water-based or oil-based products (or both) from the eye area.

Oily eye make-up removers have these specific treatment uses:

- treating clients who wear waterproof mascara;
- removing wax or oil-based eyeshadow.

Non-oily eye make-up removers have these applications:

- treating clients with sensitive skin around the eyes;
- treating clients who wear contact lenses;
- treating clients who wear individual false eyelashes.

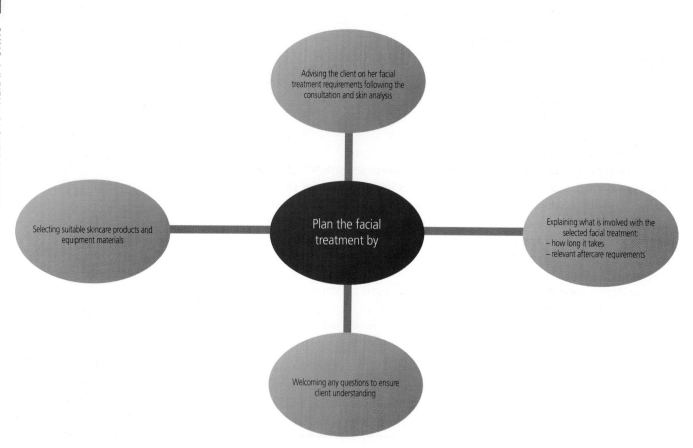

Plan the facial treatment by

Advising the client on her facial treatment requirements following the consultation and skin analysis

Selecting suitable skincare products and equipment materials

Explaining what is involved with the selected facial treatment:
– how long it takes
– relevant aftercare requirements

Welcoming any questions to ensure client understanding

Cleansing treatment

There are two manual processes involved in the cleansing routine: the *superficial cleanse* and the *deep cleanse*.

The superficial cleanse uses lightweight cleansing preparations to emulsify surface make-up, dirt and grease. This is followed by the more thorough deep cleanse, in which a heavier cleansing cream is applied to the face. The high percentage of oil contained in the cream formulation allows the cream to be massaged over the skin's surface without evaporation of the product.

Superficial cleansing

Each part of the face requires a special technique in the application and removal of the cleansing product. The face is cleansed in the following order:

- the eye tissue and lashes;
- the lips;
- the neck, chin, cheeks, and forehead.

HEALTH AND SAFETY

Eye care
Never apply pressure over the eyeball when cleansing the eye area.

TIP

Unlike the muscles of the body, which attach to bones, most of the facial muscles are attached to the facial skin itself. You should therefore avoid stretching the skin unnecessarily – if you do, you may also stretch the facial muscles and contribute to premature ageing.

Sequence for superficial cleansing

1 Wash your hands.

2 Cleanse the eye area, using a suitable eye make-up remover. Each eye is cleansed separately. Your non-working hand lifts and supports the eye tissue whilst the working hand applies the eye make-up remover.

If a water-based eye make-up remover is used, this is applied directly to a clean piece of cottonwool. Stroke down the length of the eyelashes, from base to points. Next, cleanse the eye tissue in a sweeping circle, outwards across the upper eyelid, circling beneath the lower lashes towards the nose. Repeat, regularly changing the cottonwool until the eye area and the cottonwool show clean.

Sometimes a cleansing milk is used to remove eye make-up. In this case, apply a little of the product to the back of one hand. The ring finger is then used to apply the cleansing milk to the lashes.

Use damp cottonwool to remove the emulsified product.

Repeat the cleansing process until the eye area is clean.

Cleansing the eye area

TIP ✔
The ring finger is always used as it provides the least pressure.

TIP ✔
If there is any make-up left at the base of the lower lashes after eye cleansing, this may be removed with a cotton bud or a thin piece of clean cottonwool. Ask the client to look upwards, and gently draw the cottonwool along the base of the lower lashes, towards the nose.

HEALTH AND SAFETY ✚
Hygiene Never use the reverse side of the cottonwool pad – this is unhygienic.

3 Cleanse the lips, preferably with a cleansing milk or lotion (as this readily emulsifies the oils or waxes contained in lipstick).

Apply a little of the product to the back of your non-working hand. Support the left side of the client's mouth with this hand. With the

Cleansing the lips

Cleansing the face

Removing cleanser

TIP

When cleansing, be careful that cleanser does not enter the eyes or mouth.

TIP

If the client is wearing facial make-up, it is usual to perform the superficial cleanse twice.

HEALTH AND SAFETY ✚

Safe pressure
Reduce pressure when working over the *hyoid bone* at the throat and bony prominences such as the *zygomatic bone* (the cheekbone) and the *frontal bone* (the forehead).
   Pressure must always be *upwards* and *outwards*, to avoid stretching the tissues.

working hand, apply the product in small circular movements across the upper lip, from left to right; and then across the lower lip, from right to left.

   Remove the cleanser from the lips. Support the corner of the mouth; using a clean damp piece of cottonwool wipe across the lips.

   Repeat the cleansing process as necessary, until the lips and the cottonwool show clean.

4 Select a cleansing milk or lotion to suit your client's skin type.

   Pour the product into one hand – sufficient to cover the face and neck, and to massage gently over the surface of the skin. Massage the surface of the hands together: this warms the product (so that it isn't cold on the client's skin) and distributes it over your hands.

   Clasp the fingers together at the base of the neck, and unlink them as you move up the neck.

   Clasp the fingers together again at the chin, drawing the fingers outwards to the angle of the jawbone.

   Stroke up the face, towards the forehead, with your fingertips pointing downwards and your palms in contact with the skin.

   Using a series of light circular movements of your fingertips, gently massage the product into the skin, beginning at the base of the neck and finishing at the forehead.

   Remove the cleanser thoroughly with clean damp cottonwool, simultaneously stroking over the skin surface, upwards and outwards in a rolling motion. Repeat this process as necessary, using clean cottonwool each time.

HEALTH AND SAFETY ✚

Client comfort
When cleansing around the nose, avoid restricting the client's nostrils.

Applying cleanser

Deep cleansing

The deep cleanse involves a series of massage manipulations which reinforce the cleansing achieved with the cleansing product. Blood circulation is increased to the area: this has a warming effect on the skin which relaxes the skin's natural openings, the hair follicles and pores. This aids the absorption of cleanser into the hair follicles and pores, where it can dissolve make-up and sebum.

There are various deep-cleansing sequences; all are acceptable if carried out in a safe, hygienic manner, and all can achieve the desired outcomes. Here is one sequence for deep cleansing.

1 Select a cleansing cream to suit your client's skin type. The procedure for application is the same as that for the superficial cleanse.

2 Stroke up either side of the neck, using your fingertips. At the chin, draw the fingers outwards to the angle of the jaw, and lightly stroke back down the neck to the starting position.

3 Apply small circular manipulations over the skin of the neck.

Stroking up the sides of the neck

Circular manipulations of the neck

Stroking the jawbone and chin

Circular manipulations of the chin, nose and temples

Running movement on the nose

Eye circling

4 Draw the fingertips outwards to the angle of the jaw. Rest each index finger against the jawbone (you will be able to feel the lower teeth in the jaw). Place the middle finger beneath the jawbone. Move the right hand towards the chin where the index finger glides over the chin; return the fingers, beneath the jawbone, to the starting position. Repeat with the left hand.

Repeat step 4 a further 5 times.

5 Apply small circular manipulations, commencing at the chin working up towards the nose, and finishing at the temples. Slide the fingers from the temples back to the chin, and repeat.

Repeat step 5 a further 5 times.

6 Position the ring finger of the right hand at the bridge of the nose. Perform a running movement, sliding the ring, middle and index fingers off the end of the nose. Repeat immediately with the left hand.

Repeat step 6 a further 5 times with each hand.

7 With the ring fingers, trace a circle around the eye orbits. Begin at the inner corner of the upper browbone; slide to the outer corners of the browbone, around and under the eyes, and return to the starting position.

Repeat step 7 a further 5 times.

Circling manipulation of the forehead

Criss-cross stroking of the forehead

Lifting the eyebrows

> **TIP** ✔
>
> Check that the brow hair and the skin beneath the chin are free of grease: it is easy to overlook some cleansing product in these areas.

8 Using both hands, apply small circular manipulations across the forehead. *Repeat step 8 a further 5 times.*

9 Open the index and middle fingers of each hand and perform a criss-cross stroking movement over the forehead.

10 Slide the index finger upwards slightly, lifting the inner eyebrow. Lift the centre of the eyebrow with the middle finger. Finally, lift the outer corner of the eyebrow with the ring finger. Slide the ring fingers around the outer corner and beneath the eye orbit. *Repeat step 10 a further 5 times.*

11 With the pads of each hand, apply slight pressure at the temples. This indicates to the client that the cleansing sequence is complete.

12 Remove the cleansing cream from the skin, using damp cottonwool.

TONING

Toning

After the skin has been cleansed it is then toned with an appropriate lotion.

Toning preparations

Toning lotions remove from the skin all traces of cleanser, grease and skin-care preparations. The toning lotion's main action is as follows.

● It produces a cooling effect on the skin when the water or alcohol in the toner evaporates from the skin's surface. (When a liquid evaporates it changes to a gas, which takes energy. In the case of toner, the energy is taken from the skin, which therefore feels cooler.)

● It creates a tightening effect on the skin, because of a chemical within the toner called an astringent. This causes the pores to close, thereby reducing the flow of sebum and sweat onto the skin's surface.

- It helps to restore the acidic pH balance of the skin. Milder skin toners have a pH 4.5–4.6; stronger astringents disturb the pH more severely, and may cause skin irritation and sensitivity.

There are three main types of toning lotions, the main difference being the amounts of alcohol they contain. They include:

- bracers and fresheners;
- tonics;
- astringents.

Skin bracers and fresheners

Skin bracers and **skin fresheners** are the mildest toning lotions: they contain little or no alcohol. They consist mainly of purified water, with floral extracts such as **rose water** for a mild toning effect.

Skin bracers and fresheners are recommended for:

- dry, delicate skin;
- sensitive skin;
- mature skin.

Skin tonics

Skin tonics are slightly stronger toning lotions. Many contain a little of some astringent agent such as witchhazel.

Skin toners are recommended for:

- normal skin.

Astringents

Astringents are the strongest toning lotions; they have a high proportion of alcohol. They may contain antiseptic ingredients such as **hexachlorophene**; these are for use on a blemished skin, to promote skin healing.

Astringents are recommended for:

- oily skin with no skin sensitivity;
- mild acne in young skin.

Application

Toning lotion may be applied in several ways. Whichever method you choose, it should leave the skin thoroughly clean and free of grease.

The most popular method of application is to apply the toner directly to two pieces of clean damp cottonwool, which are wiped gently upwards and outwards over the neck and face.

Alternatively, the toner may be applied under pressure as a fine spray, using a vaporiser. This produces a fine mist of the toning lotion over the skin. If using this method, always protect the eye tissue with cottonwool pads and

TIP

All toning lotions have some astringent effect on the skin, but those that contain a relatively high alcohol content are actually marketed as astringents.

Do not use toning lotions that contain more than 20 per cent alcohol on a dry skin – they may cause skin irritation.

Avoid the excessive use of astringent on a greasy skin – the astringent will make the skin dry, and it will then produce more sebum.

TIP

When applying toning lotion to a combination skin, you may need to apply different toning lotions to treat separate skin conditions.

TIP

Before facial application it is a good idea to spray the mist onto the back of the client's hand: this helps her to relax.

hold the vaporiser about 30cm from the skin, directing the spray across the skin in a sweeping movement.

To produce a stimulating effect, the toning lotion can be applied to dampened cottonwool: hold this firmly at one corner, and gently tap it over the skin.

After applying toning lotion, immediately blot the skin dry with a soft facial tissue to prevent the toner evaporating from the skin's surface (which would stimulate the skin).

Blotting the skin

Make a small tear in the centre of a large facial tissue, for the client's nose. Place the tissue over her face and neck, and mould it into position to absorb excess moisture.

Blotting the skin

HEALTH AND SAFETY

Client comfort
To avoid claustrophobia and discomfort, tell the client before you start how and why facial blotting is carried out.

MOISTURISING

The skin depends on water to keep it soft, supple and resilient. Two-thirds of our body is composed of water and the skin is an important reservoir, containing about 20 per cent of the body's total water content. Most of the fluid is in the lower layers of the dermis, but it circulates to the top layer of the epidermis, where it evaporates.

The skin protects its water content in these ways:

- sebum keeps the skin lubricated, and reduces water loss from skin;
- the skin cells have **natural moisturising factors** (**NMFs**), a complex mix of substances which are able to fix moisture inside the cells;
- a 'cement' of fats (lipids) between the skin cells forms a watertight barrier.

The natural moisture level is constantly being disturbed. The application of a cosmetic **moisturiser** helps to maintain the natural oil and moisture balance by locking moisture into the tissues, offering protection and hydration.

The basic formulation of a moisturiser is oil and water to make an oil-in-water emulsion. The water content helps to return lost moisture to the surface layers; the oil content prevents moisture loss from the surface of the skin. Often a **humectant**, such as **glycerine** or **sorbitol**, is included: this attracts moisture to the skin from the surrounding air and stops the moisturiser from drying out. If a humectant is included, less oil is used in the formulation: this results in a lighter cream.

Moisturiser also has the following benefits:

- it protects the skin from external damage caused by the environment;
- it softens the skin and relieves skin tautness and sensitivity;
- it plumps the skin tissue with moisture, which minimises the appearance of fine lines;
- it provides a barrier between the skin and make-up cosmetics;
- it may contain additional ingredients which improve the condition of the skin (such as vitamin E, which has a humectant action and is an excellent skin conditioner);
- it may contain ultraviolet filters, which protect the skin against the age-accelerating sunlight.

Moisturisers are available for wear during the day or the night. These are available in different formulations, to treat all skin types and conditions.

Moisturisers for daytime use

Moisturising lotions

Moisturising lotions contain up to 85–90 per cent water and 10–15 per cent oil. They have a light, liquid formulation, and are ideal for use under make-up.

Moisturising lotions have these specific applications:

- greasy skin;
- young combination skin;
- dehydrated skin;
- normal skin.

Moisturising creams

Moisturising creams contain up to 70–85 per cent water and 15–30 per cent oil. They have a thicker consistency, and cannot be poured.

Moisturising creams have these specific applications:

- mature skin;
- dry skin.

TIP

Even on an overcast day, as much as 80 per cent of the sun's age-accelerating UVA can penetrate the skin.

TIP

Some clients dislike the heavier cream, feeling that it is too heavy for their skin. Offer them a suitable moisturising lotion alternative.

HEALTH AND SAFETY

Allergies
Hypoallergenic moisturisers are available for clients with sensitive skin. These are screened from all common sensitising ingredients, such as lanolin and perfume, and they also have soothing properties.

ACTIVITY

Moisturisers
Collect information on different moisturisers from various skin-care suppliers. You could visit local beauty salons, retail stores or beauty wholesale suppliers, or write to professional skin-care companies.

Application

Moisturiser is applied after the final application of toning lotion. If the moisturiser is being applied before make-up, use a light formulation so that it does not interfere with the adherence of the foundation.

1 Remove some moisturiser from the jar, using a disposable spatula or sanitised plastic spatula. Place it on the back of the non-working hand, then take it on the fingertips of your working hand.

2 Apply the moisturiser in small dots to the neck, chin, cheeks, nose and forehead. Quickly and evenly spread it in a fine film over the face, using light upward and outward stroking movements.

3 Blot excess moisturiser from the skin using a facial tissue.

Applying moisturiser

TIP ✓

If the moisturiser is very fluid, apply it directly to the fingertips of the non-working hand – it would run if applied to the back of the hand.

Moisturisers for night-time use

Moisturisers are applied to the skin in the evening, after the skin has been cleansed, toned and blotted dry.

An emulsion **night cream** with a higher proportion of oil is the most effective for application in the evening: by this time the surrounding air is dry and warm, which encourages water loss from the skin; the oil seals the surface of the skin, preventing this water loss.

A small amount of **wax** (such as beeswax) may be included in the formulation: this improves the 'slip' of the product, making it easier to apply and helping its skin-conditioning effect.

Throat creams

The neck can become dry as it is exposed to the weather, often without the protection of a moisturiser. As a client ages, the collagen molecules in the dermis become increasingly cross-linked; they are then unable to retain the same volume of water, and the skin loses its plump appearance.

The formulation for a **throat cream** is similar to that for a night cream; it also contains various skin conditioning supplements, such as collagen or vitamin E, which help maintain moisture in the stratum corneum.

Encourage your client to include the neck in her cleansing routine, applying facial moisturiser to the neck during the day and either a night cream or specially formulated throat cream in the evening. Recommend that she always applies the throat cream gently in an upward and outward direction, using her fingertips.

To improve the appearance of the neck, good posture is important. If the client is round-shouldered the head often drops forwards, putting strain on the muscles of the neck. This causes tension in the muscles, which become tight and painful. Correct the client's posture, and advise her to massage the neck when applying the throat cream to relieve tension.

Eyecreams

The eye tissue is very thin and readily becomes very dry, emphasising fine lines and wrinkles (**crow's feet**). Special care must be taken when applying products near this area: it contains a large number of **mast cells**, the cells that respond to contact with an irritant by causing an allergic reaction.

Eye cream is a fine cream formulated specifically for application to the eye area. A small quantity of the product is applied to the eye tissue using the ring finger of one hand, gently stroking around the eye, inwards and towards the nose. Support the eye tissue with the other hand. Do not apply the product too near to the inner eyelid or you will cause irritation to the eye.

Further skin-care preparations

Eye gel

Eye gel is usually applied in the morning: it has a cooling, soothing, slightly astringent effect. (This is caused partly by the evaporation of the water in the gel, and partly by the inclusion of plant extracts such as **cornflower** or **camomile**.)

Eye gel is recommended for all clients, but especially for those suffering with slightly puffy eye tissue. It may also be applied following a facial treatment, to normalise the pH of the skin.

Eye gel may be applied with a light tapping motion, using the pads of the fingers. This will mildly stimulate the lymphatic circulation in the area and help to reduce any slight swelling.

Ampoule treatment

Serums are chemicals used to revitalise the skin. They are supplied in **ampoules**, sealed glass or plastic phials which prevent the content from evaporating and losing their effectiveness. Serums are usually applied for 7–28 days as a skin-tonic course for the treatment of different skin types and conditions.

TIP

Advise the client against losing weight quickly, especially when older – the neck tissue can look loose and very wrinkled as the underlying fat is lost.

ACTIVITY

Eye conditions
Think of different *non-medical* eye conditions for which a client might seek your advice. Discuss with colleagues the possible cause of these conditions, and what you could recommend to improve the appearance in each case.

Ampoule application

Sorisa

A vapour unit

REMOVING SKIN BLOCKAGES

After the skin has been cleansed, you may wish to remove minor skin blemishes such as comedones (blackheads) and milia (whiteheads). It is preferable to warm the tissues first: this softens the skin and relaxes the openings of the skin which are blocked.

Warming the skin

Steam is the ideal means of producing the required warming effect on the skin to achieve both cleansing and stimulation. Skin warming is often incorporated into a facial treatment after the manual cleansing, so as to stimulate the skin and make it more receptive to subsequent treatments.

The effects are these:

- the pores are opened;
- locally the blood circulation and the lymphatic circulation are stimulated;
- the surface cells of the epidermis are softened, which helps desquamation;
- sebaceous gland activity is improved, which benefits a dry, mature skin type;
- skin colour is improved.

Steam is provided by an electric **vapour unit**. In this, distilled water is heated electrically.

The resulting steam is applied as a fine mist over the facial area. As the steam settles upon the skin it is absorbed by the surface epidermal cells. These cells are softened and can be gently loosened with exfoliation treatment.

HEALTH AND SAFETY

Vapour application
Keep the vapour directed away from the client's face until a visible jet of steam can be seen. To avoid skin sensitisation, consider carefully where to position the steam so as to ensure even heat distribution.

Contra-indications

Although the treatment is suitable for most clients, do not use steam if you discover that the client has any of the following:

- *Respiratory problems*, such as asthma or a cold.
- *Vascular skin disorders*, such as acne rosacea.
- *Claustrophobia*.
- *Excessively dilated arterioles*.
- *Skin with reduced sensitivity*.
- *Diabetes*, unless the client's GP has given permission.

Application

The duration of the application and the distance differ according to the skin type.

Before applying steam, protect the client's eyes with damp cottonwool. Areas of delicate skin should be protected with damp cottonwool and if necessary a barrier cream.

Explain to the client:

- for how long the treatment is to be applied;
- the sensations that will be experienced;
- the physical effect on the skin.

If you are using ozone, this is applied following the steam application for the final few minutes, as directed by the manufacturer. The steam will change in appearance to a bluish-white cloud.

HEALTH AND SAFETY

Steam application
A greasy skin will tolerate a shorter application distance and a longer application time. For a sensitive skin type, increase the application distance and reduce the time. What are the manufacturer's guidelines for your equipment? Remember that these are only *guidelines* – observe the skin's reaction and check that the client is comfortable.

Applying steam to the back

HEALTH AND SAFETY ✚

Ozone
Most vapour units produce ozone when the oxygen in the steam is passed over a high-intensity quartz mercury arc tube. Ozone is thought to be beneficial in the treatment of a blemished skin, as it kills many bacteria, but it may also be carcinogenic (liable to cause cancer) if inhaled. Use a vapour unit only in a well-ventilated room, and only for short periods of time.

After applying steam vapour, blot the skin dry with a soft facial tissue and proceed to remove any blockages.

At the end of the treatment, turn off the machine and unplug it. Check that you have tidied away the trailing lead so that there is no risk of it causing an accident.

Contra-actions

Contra-actions to steaming include the following:

- *over-stimulation of the skin*, caused by incorrect application distance and duration of the steam;
- *scalding*, caused by spitting from a faulty steam jet or by the vessel being over-filled;

ACTIVITY

Vapour units
Collect literature on different vapour units. Compare their efficiencies and features. Which would be the best buy? Consider:

- Is the unit transportable, for marketing demonstrations?
- Is it height-adjustable, to suit the height of the treatment couch?
- Is it easy to clean?
- If floor-standing, does it move easily?
- Does it allow the addition of aromatic oils?
- Has it safety features to prevent overheating or the vessel running dry?

Towel steaming

● *discomfort*, caused by the steam being too near the skin, leading to breathing difficulties, or by the treatment being applied for too long.

Towel steaming

Towel steaming is an alternative to steaming which can be used if an electrical vapour unit is not available to achieve the same beneficial effects. Several clean small towels are required: these are heated in a bowl of clean hot water, or specialised unit, and are then applied to the face.

Application Seat the client in a semi-reclined position. Neatly fold a small clean towel and immerse it in very warm water. Wring it out quickly and, standing behind the client, transfer it to her face – with the towel folded in half, place it over the lower half of the face, directly under the client's lower lip; then unfold it to cover the upper face, leaving the mouth and nostrils uncovered.

Press the towel gently against the face for 2 minutes; during this time the towel will begin to cool. Remove the towel and replace it with another heated towel. Continue in this way, heating and replacing the towels, for approximately 10 minutes.

> **HEALTH AND SAFETY**
>
> **Treatment programme**
> If the client suffers from severe congestion, do not attempt to carry out all the removals in one session. This would sensitise the skin, making it appear very red, and would be most uncomfortable for the client. Instead she should visit the salon weekly for you to clear the skin gradually as part of an overall treatment programme.

> **TIP**
>
> Provided that you have received instruction in the use of aromatic oils, and provided that the client has no contra-indications to them, you may add oils to the water.

Equipment and materials

> **EQUIPMENT LIST**
>
>
>
> disposable rubber gloves
>
> medical swabs
>
> facial tissues
>
> stainless steel comedo extractor
>
> disposable individual milium extractor needle
>
> 'sharps' disposal container

You will need the following equipment and materials:

● *Disposable rubber gloves.*
● *Medical swabs*, impregnated with isopropyl alcohol or antiseptic lotion.
● *Facial tissues* – soft and white.
● *Stainless steel comedo extractor* and a *disposable individual milium extractor needle* (sterile), or combined *stainless steel comedo and milium extractor.*
● *'Sharps' disposal container* – for the contaminated needles.

Sterilisation and sanitisation

You must put the disposable milium extractor in a 'sharps' container. All waste material from this treatment (such as facial tissues and gloves) should be disposed of in an identified waste container, as directed by your local health authority.

After use the stainless steel comedo extractor should be cleaned with an alcohol preparation and then sterilised in an autoclave.

Wear disposable rubber gloves whilst carrying out the treatment.

Treatment

Comedo removal

Using the loop end of the extractor, apply gentle pressure around the comedo. The comedo should leave the skin, apparent as a plug. You may need to apply gentle pressure with your fingers at the sides of the comedo to ensure that it is effectively removed; when doing this, wrap a tissue around the pads of the index fingers.

Contra-actions:

- Skin bruising could occur if too much pressure is applied.
- Capillary damage could result if too much force is used when squeezing the comedo. The surrounding blood capillaries can rupture, causing permanent skin damage.

Milium extraction

Hold the point of the extractor parallel with the skin's surface, and *superficially* pierce the epidermis. This makes an opening through which the sebaceous matter can pass to the skin's surface. Using either the comedo extractor or tissue wrapped around the index fingers, apply gentle pressure. A mild antiseptic soothing lotion applied after extraction will help the skin to heal.

Comedo extractors

Milium extraction

HEALTH AND SAFETY	+
Client comfort	
- Never obstruct the client's nostrils when removing a comedo from the nose area. - Never apply pressure on the soft cartilage of the nose.	

HEALTH AND SAFETY	+
Avoiding infection Ensure that *all* contents of the skin blockage are removed, or infection may occur.	

EXFOLIATION

The natural physical process of losing dead skin cells from the stratum corneum layer of the epidermis is called **desquamation**. **Exfoliation** is a salon technique used to accelerate this process. It is normally carried out after the skin has been cleansed and toned, and before further facial treatments.

Exfoliation has the following benefits:

- dead skin cells, grease and debris are removed from the surface of the skin;
- fresh new cells are exposed, improving the appearance of the skin;
- skin preparations such as moisturising lotions are more easily absorbed;
- the blood circulation in the area is mildly stimulated, bringing more oxygen and nutrients to the skin cells and improving the skin colour.

TIP	
Exfoliation should be strongly recommended for the mature client. The removal of the surface dead cells has a rejuvenating effect on the skin's appearance.	

Mechanical exfoliation

Contra-indications

Exfoliation is beneficial for most skin types; however, avoid application if the client has the following:

- highly sensitive skin;
- a vascular skin disorder such as telangiectases or damaged broken veins in the area of treatment application.

Exfoliants

Various exfoliants are available; they may be of chemical or vegetable origin. Alternatively, mechanical exfoliation may be used.

Biochemical skin peel

Natural acids (alpha-hydroxy acids – AHAs), derived from fruits, sugar cane and milk, are applied to the skin as a face mask. The natural acids dissolve dead surface cells and stimulate circulation in the underlying skin. These masks are available to suit all skin types.

When you apply this type of face mask, warn the client that there will be a stinging sensation and then a tightening effect as the mask sets.

Pore grains

Pore grains are the most popular exfoliants: a base of cream or liquid containing tiny spheres of polished plastic or crushed nuts is gently massaged over the skin's surface.

Clay exfoliants

Gentler **clay exfoliants** have a clay base which is applied like a face mask. As it dries, the clay absorbs dead skin cells and sebum. The mask is then gently stroked away, using the pads of the fingers.

Mechanical exfoliation

Mechanical exfoliation, or 'facial brushing', softens and cleanses the skin. Dead skin cells and excess sebum are removed as the soft hair bristles rotate over the skin's surface. The rotary action also increases the cleansing action of exfoliation.

If steam is applied before mechanical exfoliation, this will soften the dead skin cells, and **skin peeling cream** may be applied: together these will maximise the result of exfoliation.

Be careful to avoid over-stimulation, sensitising the skin's surface, or disturbing the skin's natural protective qualities.

Advice on home use

The client can be advised to use exfoliants at home as a specialised cleansing treatment after normal cleansing and toning. Exfoliants should be applied once a week for all skin types except greasy, for which it may be applied twice a week.

Advise the client to massage the product gently over the skin using her fingertips. Application should always be upwards and outwards.

After application, any product residue should be thoroughly rinsed from the face using clean, tepid water. The client may then apply a face mask or tone the skin and apply a nourishing skin moisturiser.

TIP

Point out to clients that exfoliants designed for use on the *body* are unsuitable for use on the *face* – their action is not as gentle.

TIP

To encourage sales of this skin-care product, demonstrate the product on the back of one of the client's hands. She will be amazed when she compares the appearance of her hands.

HEALTH AND SAFETY +

Exfoliants

- Tell the client how the skin should look after exfoliation treatment. The skin's colour should be *slightly* heightened; but too vigorous a massage application may cause the formation of broken capillaries.
- Tell the client to avoid contact with the delicate eye tissue.
- A client with a pustular skin should not use exfoliant products – they would probably cause discomfort, and any lesions present might burst.

MASK TREATMENT

The **face mask** is a skin-cleansing preparation which may contain a variety of different ingredients selected to have a deep cleansing, toning, nourishing or refreshing effect on the skin. The mask achieves this through the following actions:

- if it contains *absorbent* materials, dead skin cells, sebum and debris will adhere to it when it is removed;
- if it contains *astringent* ingredients, the pores and the skin will tighten;
- if it contains *emollient* ingredients, the skin will be softened and nourished;
- if it contains *soothing* ingredients, the skin can be desensitised to reduce skin irritation.

TIP

The term *face pack* is sometimes used instead of *face mask*: a face pack does not set, but remains soft; a face mask sets and becomes firm.

Mask preparations

There are basically two types of mask: setting and non-setting.

Setting masks

Setting masks are applied in a thin layer over the skin and then allowed to dry. The mask need not necessarily set solid – a solid mask can become uncomfortable, and be difficult to remove.

A face mask

Depilex/RVB

Setting masks come in these varieties:

- clay packs;
- peel-off masks – gel, latex, or paraffin wax;
- thermal masks.

Clay masks The **clay mask** absorbs sebum and debris from the skin surface, leaving it cleansed. It can also stimulate or soothe the skin, according to the ingredients chosen. Various clay powders are available – select from these according to the physiological effects you require:

- **Calamine** A light pink powder which soothes surface blood capillaries. *Uses in treatment*: for sensitive or delicate skin.
- **Magnesium carbonate** A very light, white powder which creates a temporary astringent and toning effect. *Use in treatment:* for open pores on dry and normal skins.
- **Kaolin** A cream-coloured powder which has a very stimulating effect on the skin's surface capillaries, thereby helping the skin to remove impurities and waste products. *Use in treatment*: for congested, greasy skin.
- **Fuller's earth** A green, heavy clay powder. It has a very stimulating effect, such that the skin will show slight reddening. It also produces a whitening, brightening effect. *Use in treatment*: for greasy skin with a sluggish circulation. Due to its strong effect, it is *not* suitable for a client with a sensitive skin.
- **Flowers of sulphur** A light, yellow clay powder, which has a drying action on pustules and papules. *Use in treatment*: applied only to specific blemishes (pustules).

To activate these masks it is necessary to add a liquid – an **active lotion** – which turns the powder to a liquid paste. Active lotions are selected according to the skin type of the client and the mask to be used; they reinforce the action of the mask.

- **Rose water and orange-flower water** These are very popular; they have a very mild stimulating and toning effect.
- **Witchhazel** This has a soothing effect on blemished skin; it is also an astringent and is suitable for use on greasy skin.
- **Distilled water** This is used on highly sensitive skins.
- **Almond oil** This is mildly stimulating. Because it is an oil, it does not allow the mask to dry: it is therefore recommended for highly sensitive skin or dehydrated skin.
- **Glycerol** A humectant, which prevents the mask drying and is suitable for a dry, mature skin.

Clay masks have the disadvantage when treating a black skin that they tend on removal to leave streaks of white residue. Choose a mask that does not have this effect.

The mask should be kept in place for about 10–15 minutes.

Peel-off masks **Peel-off masks** may be made from gel, latex or paraffin wax. Because perspiration cannot escape from the skin's surface, moisture

---

HEALTH AND SAFETY

Avoiding infection
Clay mask ingredients must always be made from sterilised materials, because of the danger from tetanus spores.

HEALTH AND SAFETY

Allergies
When treating a sensitive skin, remove the mask before it has set to avoid the stimulating action of the mask sensitising the skin.

TIP

Ensure that you position the gauze correctly so that the nose and eye holes are properly placed.

ACTIVITY

Choosing face masks
Which clay powder and which active lotion would you mix for clients with the following skin types?
1 A mature, sensitive skin type.
2 A young, normal skin type.
3 A combination skin type: cheeks, neck area dry; forehead, nose and chin area greasy.

is forced into the stratum corneum. The mask also insulates the skin, causing an increase in temperature.

The **gel mask** is either a suspension of biological ingredients, such as starches, gums or gelatin, or a mixture of synthetic non-biological resin ingredients. The mask is applied over the skin; on contact with the skin it begins to dry. When dry it is peeled off the face in one piece. *Uses in treatment*: depending on the biological ingredients added, the gel mask can be used to treat all skin types. (If the client has excessive facial hair, such as at the sides of the face, this mask may cause discomfort on removal. To avoid this place a lubricant under the mask, or use a different sort of mask.)

The **latex mask** is an emulsion of latex and water: when applied to the skin, the water evaporates to leave a rubber film over the face. This produces a rise in temperature, thereby stimulating the skin. In alternative peel-off masks, latex is replaced by a synthetic resin emulsion such as **polyvinyl acetate** (PVA) resin. *Uses in treatment*: latex masks tighten the skin temporarily, and are suitable for a mature skin; they can also be used with dry skin.

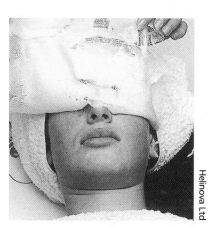

The **paraffin-wax mask** is stimulating in its action. The paraffin wax is blended with petroleum jelly or acetyl alcohol which improve its spreading properties. The wax is heated to approximately 37°C and is then applied to the skin as a liquid. It sets on contact, so speed is essential if the mask is to be effective. The wax mask is loosened at the sides and removed in one piece after 15–20 minutes. *Use in treatment*: the paraffin-wax mask is suitable for dry skin. Because of its stimulating action, it is unsuitable for greasy skin or highly sensitive skin.

A paraffin-wax mask

Helinova Ltd

Thermal masks The **thermal mask** contains various minerals. The ingredients are mixed and applied to the face and neck, avoiding the mouth and eye tissue. The mask warms on contact with the skin: this causes the pores to enlarge, thereby cleansing the skin. As the mask cools it sets, and the pores constrict slightly. The mask is removed from the face in one piece. *Uses in treatment*: thermal masks have a stimulating, cleansing action, suitable for a normal skin or for a congested, greasy skin with open pores.

Non-setting masks

Some **non-setting masks** stay soft on application; others become firm, but they do not tighten like a setting mask. For this reason they do not tone the skin as effectively as setting masks. Non-setting masks include:

- warm oil;
- natural masks – fruit, plant and herbal;
- cream.

> **HEALTH AND SAFETY**
>
> **Client comfort**
> Before applying the wax to the client's skin always test the temperature of the wax on your own inner wrist.

> **HEALTH AND SAFETY** +
>
> **Contra-indications**
> Do not use thermal masks on a client with a circulatory disorder or one who has lost tactile sensation.

> **HEALTH AND SAFETY** +
>
> **Client comfort**
> If a client is particularly nervous, choose an effective non-setting mask. Some clients feel claustrophobic when wearing a setting mask.

EQUIPMENT LIST

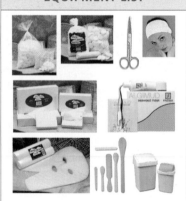

dampened clean cottonwool

cottonwool eye pads

scissors

facial tissues

protective headband

clean spatulas

face mask ingredients

gauze

waste bin

see top of opposite page for complete list of materials required

Warm-oil masks A plant oil, typically **olive oil** or **almond oil**, is warmed and then applied to the skin. It softens the skin and helps to restore the skin's natural moisture balance.

A **gauze mask** is cut to cover the face and neck, with holes for the eyes, nostrils and lips. This is then soaked in warm oil. A dampened cottonwool eye pad is placed over each eye. The gauze is then placed over the face and neck. It is usually left in place for 10–20 minutes. *Uses in treatment*: warm-oil masks are recommended for mature skin and dry or dehydrated skin.

Natural masks **Natural masks** are made from natural ingredients rich in vitamins and minerals. Fresh **fruit** and **vegetables** have a mildly astringent and stimulating effect. Usually the fruit is crushed to a pulp and placed between layers of gauze which are laid over the face.

Honey is used for its toning, tightening, antiseptic and hydrating effect. **Egg white** has a tightening effect and is said to clear impurities from the skin. **Avocados** have a nourishing effect; **bananas** soften the skin, and are used for sensitive skins.

ACTIVITY

Creating natural masks
Create some masks, listing the ingredients to suit each of the following skin types:
- dry;
- greasy;
- mature, with superficial wrinkling;
- sensitive.

If possible, arrange to carry out one of the masks on a suitable client in the workplace. Evaluate the natural face mask. Consider: cost, preparation, application, removal and effectiveness. Remember to ask your client for *her* opinion!

Cream masks **Cream masks** are pre-prepared for you. They have a softening and moisturising effect on the skin. Each mask contains various biological extracts or chemical substances to treat different skin types or conditions. Instructions will be provided with the mask, stating how the product is to be used professionally.

These masks are popular in the beauty salon: they often complement a particular facial treatment range used by the salon, and they are available for retail sale to clients.

Contra-indications

The contra-indications to general skin care apply also to face-mask application. In addition, observe the following:

- *Allergies* Check whether your client knows that she has allergies. If so, avoid all contact with known allergens.
- *Claustrophobia* Do not use a setting mask on a particularly nervous client. Some clients feel claustrophobic under its tightening effect.
- *Sensitive skins* Do not use stimulating masks on clients with highly sensitive skin.

Equipment and materials

When applying masks you will need the following equipment and materials:

- *Disposable tissue roll* – such as bedroll.
- *Towels (2)* – freshly laundered for each client.
- *Flat mask brushes (3)* – sanitised.
- *Trolley*.
- *Client's record card*.
- *Dampened clean cottonwool*.
- *Cottonwool eye pads (2)* – pre-shaped round and dampened.
- *Scissors* – to cut cottonwool eye pads (if cottonwool discs are not to be used).
- *Facial tissues (white)* – to blot the skin dry after applying toner following mask removal.
- *Protective headband (clean)*.
- *Clean spatulas (several)* – to mix individual masks (if required).
- *Facial toning lotions (a selection)* – to suit various types of skin.
- *Sterilised mask-removal sponges (2)* – for use when removing the mask using clean warm water.
- *Large bowl* – to hold warm water during removal of the mask.
- *Lukewarm water* – if required for mask removal.
- *Moisturisers (a range)* – to suit different skin types for use after mask removal.
- *Hand mirror (clean)* – to show the client her skin following the facial treatment.
- *Face-mask ingredients*.
- *Gauze* – used in applying certain masks.
- *Waste bin (covered and lined)* – for waste consumables.

Sterilisation and sanitisation

After applying the mask, clean the mask brush thoroughly in warm water and detergent. Next, place it in a chemical sanitising agent; rinse it in clean water; allow it to dry; and then store it in the ultra-violet cabinet.

When you use a paraffin-wax mask, remove as much mask residue as possible from the brush, then place the brush in boiling water to completely remove all the wax. Sanitise the brush as usual before use.

If you use sponges to remove the mask, place them in warm water and detergent. After rinsing them in clean water, place them ready for sterilisation in an autoclave. (With repeated sanitisation, sponges will begin to break up.)

A large high-quality cottonwool disc may be purchased to use in mask removal.

Preparing the cubicle

Check that you have all the materials you need to carry out the treatment. You may like to place a paper roll at the head of the couch, underneath the client's head, to collect any mask residue on mask removal.

The head of the couch should be flat or slightly elevated. Don't have it in a semi-reclined position during the mask application, as some masks are liquid in consistency and may run into the client's eyes and behind her neck.

Treatment

Preparing the client

For maximum effect, the mask must be applied on a clean, grease-free surface. If the mask application follows a facial massage, ensure that the massage medium has been thoroughly removed.

Select the appropriate mask ingredients to treat the skin type and the facial conditions that require attention.

Applying the mask

The mask is usually applied as the *final* facial treatment, because of its cleansing, refining and soothing effects upon the skin. The methods of preparation, application and removal are different for the various face-mask types, so the guidelines below are a general outline of effective treatment technique.

1 Having determined the client's treatment requirements, select the appropriate mask ingredients. If you use a commercial mask, always read the manufacturer's instructions first.

2 Discuss the treatment procedure with the client. Tell her:
   - what the mask will feel like on application;
   - what sensation, if any, she will experience;
   - how long the mask will be left on the skin.
   Generally the mask will be left in place for 10–20 minutes, but the exact time depends on the type and effect required.

3 Prepare the mask ingredients for application.

4 Using the sterilised mask brush or spatula, begin to apply the mask. The usual sequence of mask application is neck, chin, cheeks, nose, and forehead.
   If you are using more than one mask to treat different skin conditions, apply first the one that will need to be on longest.

TIP

If you are using paraffin wax, remember to heat it in advance.

HEALTH AND SAFETY

Allergies
When using a commercial mask, try to find out *exactly* what it contains, so that you don't apply a sensitising ingredient to an allergic skin type.

HEALTH AND SAFETY

Client comfort
It is important to check that your client is comfortable whilst the mask is on her face. (She will suffer discomfort if her skin is intolerant to a particular mask.)

TIP

Don't mix the mask with the mask brush – if you do, the solid contents will tend to collect in the bristles, the mask won't be mixed effectively, and the brush won't spread the mask evenly.

Apply the mask quickly and evenly so that it has maximum effect on the whole face. Don't apply it too thickly; as well as making mask removal difficult, this is wasteful as only the part that is in contact with the skin has any effect.

Keep the mask clear of the nostrils, the lips, the eyebrows and the hairline.

5 To relax the client, apply cottonwool eye pads dampened with clean water.

6 Leave the mask for the recommended time or according to the effect required. Take account also of the sensitivity of the skin and your client's comfort.

> **TIP**
>
> While the mask is on the face you can tidy the working area and collect together the materials required for mask removal. Do not disturb the client, who will be relaxing at this time.

7 Wash your hands.

8 When the mask is ready for removal, remove the eyepads.

Explain to the client that you are going to remove the mask. Briefly describe the process, according to whether this is a setting or a non-setting mask.

Remove the mask. Mask sponges, if used, should be damp, not wet, so that water doesn't run into the client's eyes, nose or mouth.

9 When the mask has been completely removed, apply the appropriate toning lotion using dampened cottonwool. Blot the skin dry with a facial tissue.

10 Apply an appropriate moisturiser to the skin.

11 Remove the headband, and tidy the client's hair.

12 With a mirror, show the client her skin. Evaluate the treatment.

13 Record the results on her record card.

Contra-actions

Before you apply the mask, explain to the client what the action of the mask will feel like on the skin. This will enable her to identify any undesirable skin reaction, evident to her as skin irritation – a burning sensation.

Ask the client initially whether she is comfortable: this will give her the opportunity to tell you if she is experiencing any discomfort. Should there be a contra-action to the mask, remove the mask immediately and apply a soothing skin-care product.

If on removal of the mask you can see that there has been an unwanted skin reaction (that is, if you see inflammation), apply a soothing skin-care product. In either case, note the skin reaction on the record card, and choose a different mask next time.

> **HEALTH AND SAFETY**
>
> **Setting masks**
> When using a setting mask, ensure that the mask is evenly applied or it will dry unevenly.

> **HEALTH AND SAFETY**
>
> **Peel off masks**
> When using a peel-off mask, make sure that the border of the mask is thick enough – if it isn't, it will be difficult to remove and the client may experience discomfort.

> **TIP**
>
> When using water to remove a mask you may need to renew the water as you work.

Advice on home use

The client may be given a sample of the face mask for use at home. Explain to her the procedure for application and removal, so that she achieves maximum benefit from the mask. Encourage her to apply a mask once or twice a week depending on her skin type, to dislodge dead skin cells and to cleanse and stimulate the skin.

Advise the client not to apply the mask directly before a special occasion, in case it causes blemishes, as sometimes happens.

The skin should be toned and moisturised after removing the mask.

FACIAL MASSAGE

Manual massage is the external manipulation using the hands, of the soft tissues of the face, neck and upper chest. Massage can improve the appearance of the skin and promote a sensation of stimulation or relaxation.

Each massage performed is adapted to the client's physiological and psychological needs. The skin's physiological needs are observed during the skin analysis; the client's psychological needs are usually discovered during the consultation.

The benefits of the facial massage include the following:

- Dead epidermal cells are loosened and shed. This improves the appearance of the skin, exposing fresh, younger cells.
- The muscles receive an improved supply of oxygenated blood, essential for cell growth. The tone and strength of the muscles are improved, firming the facial contour.
- The increased blood circulation in the area warms the tissues. This induces a feeling of relaxation which is particularly beneficial when treating tense muscles.
- As the blood capillaries dilate and bring blood to the skin's surface, the skin colour improves.
- The lymphatic circulation and the venous blood circulation increase. These changes speed up the removal of waste products and toxins, and tend therefore to purify the skin. The removal of excess lymph improves the appearance of a puffy oedematous skin (provided that this does not require medical treatment).
- The increased temperature of the skin relaxes the pores and follicles. This aids the absorption of the massage product, which in turn softens the skin.
- Sensory nerves can be soothed or stimulated, depending on the massage manipulations selected.
- Massage stimulates the sebaceous and sudoriferous glands and increases the production of sebum and sweat. This increase helps to maintain the skin's natural oil and moisture balance.

Depilex/RVB

Facial massage

Reception

Facial massage is carried out as required, usually once every 4–6 weeks. Before the facial massage is given, the skin is cleansed; afterwards it is usual to apply a cleansing face mask, which absorbs any excess grease from the skin.

When booking a client for this treatment, allow one hour. The facial massage itself should take approximately 20 minutes, but this may vary according to the client's skin type.

Warn the client that the skin may appear slightly red and blotchy after treatment, due to the increase in blood circulation to the area: this reaction will normally subside after 4–6 hours.

Because of the stimulating effect on the skin recommend to the client that she receives this service when she does not have to apply any cosmetic products directly afterwards.

Sometimes the skin develops small blemishes after facial massage; this is due to its cleansing action. If the client is preparing for a special occasion, therefore, such as her wedding, make the appointment for at least 5 days in advance.

ACTIVITY

Planning a massage
How will observations from the skin analysis and the client consultation influence the facial massage treatment?

TIP

The headband can spoil the hair, and the massage medium may enter the hairline. Recommend that the client does not style her hair directly before the facial treatment.

Massage manipulations

The facial massage is based on a series of classic massage movements, each with different effects. There are four basic groups of massage movements:

- effleurage;
- petrissage;
- percussion (also known as tapotement);
- vibrations.

The therapist can adapt the way each of these movements is applied, according to the needs of the client. Either the *speed of application* or the *depth of pressure* can be altered.

Effleurage

Effleurage is a stroking movement, used to begin the massage, as a link manipulation, and to complete the massage sequence. This manipulation is light, has an even pressure, and is applied in a rhythmical, continuous manner to induce relaxation.

The pressure of application varies according to the underlying structures and the tissue type, but it must *never* be unduly heavy.

Effleurage has these effects:

- desquamation is increased;
- arterial blood circulation is increased, bringing fresh nutrients to the area;
- venous circulation is improved, aiding the removal of congestion from the veins;

- lymphatic circulation is increased, improving the absorption of waste products;
- the underlying muscle fibres are relaxed.

Uses in treatment: to relax tight, contracted muscles.

Petrissage

> **TIP**
>
> Pressure may be increased when working on larger muscles in the neck or shoulders.

Petrissage involves a series of movements in which the tissues are lifted away from the underlying structures and compressed. Pressure is intermittent, and should be light yet firm.

Petrissage has these effects:

- improvement of muscle tone, through the compression and relaxation of muscle fibres;
- improvement in blood and lymph circulation, as the application of pressure causes the vessels to empty and fill;
- increased activity of the sebaceous gland, due to the stimulation.

Movements include picking up, kneading, knuckling, pinching, rolling, frictions, and scissoring.

Uses in treatment: to stimulate a sluggish circulation; to increase sebaceous gland and sudoriferous gland activity, when treating a dry skin condition.

Percussion

> **HEALTH AND SAFETY** +
>
> **Contra-indications**
> Do not apply percussion over highly sensitive or vascular skin conditions.

Percussion, also known as **tapotement**, is performed in a brisk, stimulating manner. Rhythm is important as the fingers are continually breaking contact with the skin; irritation could occur if the movement were performed incorrectly.

Percussion has these effects:

- a fast vascular reaction because of the skin's nervous response to the stimulus – this reaction, erythema, has a stimulating effect;
- increased blood supply, which nourishes the tissues;
- improvement in muscle and skin tone in the area.

> **TIP**
>
> When a stimulating massage is required, incorporate more petrissage and tapotement into the massage sequence.

Movements include clapping and tapping. In facial massage, only light tapping should be used.

Uses in treatment: to tone areas of loose, crepey skin around the jaw or eyes.

Vibrations

Vibrations are applied on the nerve centre. They are produced by a rapid contraction and relaxation of the muscles of the therapist's arm, resulting in a fine trembling movement.

Vibration has these effects:

- stimulation of the nerves, inducing a feeling of wellbeing;
- gentle stimulation of the skin.

Movements include *static* vibrations, in which the pads of the fingers are placed on the nerve, and the vibratory effect created by the therapist's arms and hands is applied in one position; and *running* vibrations, in which the vibratory effect is applied along a nerve path.

Uses in treatment: to stimulate a sensitive skin in order to improve the skin's functioning without irritating the surface blood capillaries.

Equipment and materials

The massage is carried out using a **massage medium** which acts as a lubricant. A massage cream or oil may be used; these are slightly penetrating, and soften the skin. Choose a product that contains ingredients to suit the client's skin type and the age of the skin.

Whichever product you choose, it should provide sufficient slip whilst allowing you to control the massage movements.

ACTIVITY

Choosing a massage medium
Compare two professional skin-care ranges. Look at:
1 the choice of facial-massage preparations;
2 the ingredients used in their formulation, and the effects claimed.

Treatment

There are many different massage sequences, but each uses one or all of the massage manipulations discussed above. What follows is a basic sequence for facial massage.

1 **Effleurage to the neck and shoulders** Slide the hands down the neck, across the pectoral muscles around the deltoid muscle, and across the trapezius muscle. Slide the hands up the back of the neck to the base of the skull.
    Repeat step 1 *a further 5 times.*

2 **Thumb kneading to the shoulders** Using the pad of both thumbs, make small circles (frictions) along the trapezius muscle, working towards the spinal vertebrae.
    Apply each movement 3 times; then repeat the sequence (step 2) *a further 2 times.*

TIP ✔

It is important to maintain good posture during facial massage. If you slouch, you will experience muscle fatigue!

Effleurage to the shoulders

Effleurage to the shoulders

Thumb kneading to the shoulders

3 **Finger kneading to the shoulders** Position the fingers of each hand behind the deltoid, and make large rotary movements along the trapezius.

Apply each rotary movement 3 times; repeat the sequence (step 3) a further 2 times.

4 **Vibrations** Place the hands, cupped, at the base of the neck: perform running vibrations up the neck to the occipital bone.

Repeat step 4 a further 6 times.

5 **Circular massage to the neck** Perform small circular movements over the platysma and the sternomastoid muscle at the neck.

6 **Hands cupped to the neck** Cup your hands together. Place the hands at the left side of the neck, above the clavicle. Slide the hands up the side of the neck, across the jawline, and down the right side of the neck; then reverse.

Repeat step 6 a further 2 times.

7 **Knuckling to the neck** Make a loose fist: rotate the knuckles up and down the neck area.

Repeat step 7 to cover, a further 2 times.

8 **Up and under** Place the thumbs on the centre of the chin, and the index and middle fingers under the mandible. Slide the thumbs firmly over the chin. Bring the index finger onto the chin, and place the middle finger under the mandible forming a V shape. Slide along the jawline to the ear.

Finger kneading to the shoulders

Vibrations to the shoulders

Circular massage to the neck

Hands cupped to the neck

Knuckling to the neck

Up and under

HEALTH AND SAFETY ✚

The trachea
Never apply pressure when working on the neck over the trachea.

HEALTH AND SAFETY ✚

Sensitive skin
Do not use knuckling on sensitive skin.

Up and under

Circling to the mandible

Flick-ups

Half face brace

Lifting the eyebrows

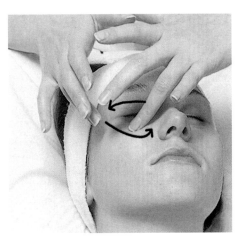

Inner and outer eye circles

Replace the index finger with the thumb, and return along the jaw to the chin.
Repeat step 8 a further 5 times.

9 **Circling to the mandible** Place the thumbs one above the other on the chin, and proceed with circular kneading along the jawline towards the ear. Reverse and repeat.
Repeat step 9 a further 2 times.

10 **Flick-ups** Place the thumbs at the corners of the mouth. Lift the orbicularis oris muscle, with a flicking action of the thumbs.
Repeat step 10 a further 5 times.

11 **Half face brace** Clasp the fingers under the chin; turn the hands so that the fingers point towards the sternum. Unclasp, and slide the hands up the face towards the forehead.
Repeat step 11 a further 2 times.

12 **Lifting the eyebrows** Place the right hand on the forehead at the left temple, and stroke upwards from the eyebrow to the hairline. Repeat the movement with the left hand. Alternate each hand; repeat the movement across the forehead.
Repeat step 12 a further 2 times.

13 **Inner and outer eye circles** Using the ring finger, *gently* draw 3 outer circles and 3 inner circles on each eye, following the fibre direction of the orbicularis oculi muscle.
Repeat step 13 a further 2 times.

HEALTH AND SAFETY +

The lips
Do not flick the lips. Position the thumbs 5 mm from the corner of the mouth to avoid this.

14 **Half face brace** Repeat step **11**.

15 **Circling to the chin, the nose and the temples** Apply circular kneading to the chin, the nose and the temples. Return to the starting position.
*Repeat step **15** a further 2 times.*

16 **Thumb kneading under the cheeks** Place the thumbs under the zygomatic bones. Carry out a circular kneading over the muscles in the cheek area.
*Repeat step **16** a further 5 times.*

17 **Tapping under the mandible** Tap the tissue under the mandible, using the fingers of both hands. Work from the left side of the jaw to the right; then reverse.
*Repeat step **17** a further 5 times.*

18 **Lifting the masseter** Cup the hands. Using the hands alternately, lift the masseter muscle.
*Repeat step **18** a further 5 times.*

19 **Rolling and pinching** Using a deep rolling movement, draw the muscles of the cheek area towards the thumb in a rolling and pinching movement.
*Repeat step **19** a further 5 times.*

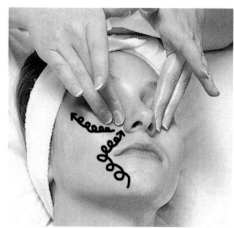

Circling to the chin, nose and temple

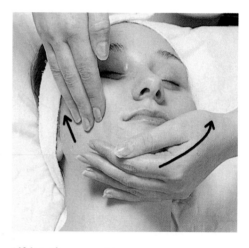

Tapping under the mandible

Lifting the masseter

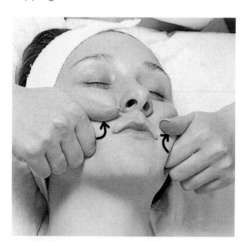

Rolling and pinching

HEALTH AND SAFETY	

Sensitive skin
Avoid the use of tapotement over areas of sensitivity.

TIP	

If the skin appears to drag during massage, stop and apply more massage medium. If you keep going you may cause skin irritation or discomfort.

TIP	

During the facial massage, the client's face should relax. If there are evident signs of tension, such as vertical furrows between the eyebrows, check that the client is warm and comfortable.

Lifting the mandible

Knuckling along the jawline

Upward tapping

The scissor movement

Tapotement around the eyes

20 **Lifting the mandible** Place the pads of the fingers underneath the mandible and pivot diagonally. Lifting the tissues work towards the ear.
Repeat step 20 a further 2 times.

21 **Knuckling along the jawline** Knuckle along the jawline and over the cheek area.
Repeat step 21 a further 2 times.

22 **Upwards tapping on the face** Using both hands, gently slap along the jawline from ear to ear, lifting the muscles.
Repeat step 22 a further 5 times.

23 **Full face brace** Place the fingertips under the chin, and slide both hands up the face to the forehead, lifting all the facial muscles.
Repeat step 23 a further 2 times.

24 **Scissor movement to the forehead** Open the index and middle fingers to make a V shape at the outer corner of each eyebrow. Open and close the fingers in a scissor action towards the inner eyebrow.
Repeat step 24 a further 2 times.

25 **Tapotement movement around the eyes** Using the pads of the fingers, tap gently around the eye area.
Repeat step 25 a further 2 times.

ACTIVITY

Designing mobility exercises
Devise *ten* exercises to increase the strength and mobility of your hands and wrists.

26 **Eye circling** Repeat step **13**, 3 times.

27 **Effleurage** Repeat step **1**.

Eye circling

Effleurage

> **TIP**
>
> When learning the facial massage you need to practise. Practise the movements on a styrofoam headblock with facial features, or mannequin head as used in hairdressing, to perfect the manipulations. If these are unavailable, practise each manipulation on your knee – this will increase the agility and strength of your fingers and wrists.

Improve and maintain facial skin condition by

- Sanitising the hands following client preparation and as necessary during treatment application
- Giving due care and consideration to health and safety legislation throughout the treatment
- Using facial products following manufacturer's guidelines and treatment requirements
- Removing dead skin cells using an exfoliant product or manual or mechanical treatment
- Warming the skin using a technique suitable for the skin type to achieve a cleansing and stimulating action
- Performing extraction of sebaceous blockages without causing excessive skin damage
- Manipulating the soft tissues of the face, neck and upper chest by applying facial massage techniques adapted to the clients physiological/psychological needs
- Selecting a massage medium to perform facial massage suited to the skin type
- Applying a face mask to achieve a desirable effect on the skin:
  – cleansing
  – toning
  – nourishing
  – refreshing
- Toning the skin using a suitable lotion to remove excess skincare preparations and grease, and restore the skins acidic pH balance
- Applying specialised skin preparations
  – eye gels/creams
  – serums
  – neck cream
- Applying moisturiser to
  – keep the skin lubricated and prevent water loss
  – reduce sensitivity
  – protect it from external environmental damage
  – provide a barrier between the skin and facial cosmetics
- Allowing treatment time of 60 minutes
- Recording details of the treatment on the client record card

> **TIP**
>
> Massage medium can easily be overlooked in the following areas: the eyebrows; the base of the nostrils; under the chin; in the creases of the neck; behind the ear; and on the shoulders.

After the massage

After the facial massage, remove the massage medium thoroughly using clean, damp cottonwool. Check thoroughly that all product has been removed.

Apply toner to remove traces of oil, leaving the skin grease-free. Finally, blot the skin dry.

You may then proceed with further skin treatments, such as a face mask, or simply apply an appropriate moisturiser to conclude the treatment.

Advice on home care

Encourage your client to use massage movements when applying emollient skin-care products. Show her how to perform such movements correctly.

Facial exercises may be given to the client for her to practise at home. These should be carried out at least four times per week.

ACTIVITY

Massage at home
Design a simple massage routine that a client could be taught to use at home.

Which type of manipulation is involved in each movement in your sequence? What effect do you wish to achieve by incorporating it?

ACTIVITY

Facial exercises at home
Think of *ten* facial exercises that you could teach a client, to improve the muscle tone of the face and neck.

Teach these to a client after carrying out a facial massage treatment. At a later stage, evaluate the exercises and discuss with her their effectiveness.

Elemis

SPECIALIST FACIAL TREATMENT

Specialist treatments should be offered to your client when there is a specific need or if she feels she would like to benefit from such a treatment. Specialist training in these advanced techniques is usually offered by the main product companies.

The model for this specialist facial treatment is a mature client with dry, dehydrated skin with areas of sensitivity. One hour and 15 minutes was allowed for this facial.

The following facial treatment will:

- Stimulate the blood circulation
- Aid with the removal of toxins and waste products
- Have a skin cleansing action
- Remove dead skin cells (desquamation)
- Improve the moisture content of the skin
- Firm skin tone

Cleansing the eye area

Application of facial cleanser.

The cleanser is selected to rehydrate the skin.

Removal of facial cleanser using dampened cotton-wool in an upwards and outwards direction.

Application of a hot towel, infused with lavender oil, to the face. This will have a skin cleansing action causing the pores to open. It also has therapeutic relaxation properties, as the client inhales the lavender oil.

Removal of the hot towel.

Facial massage movements are applied to the shoulders and face. Eastern massage techniques are included to rebalance the mind and body.

Pressure is applied to different points on the meridians or energy pathways based upon shiatsu massage – an ancient Eastern massage technique.

Application of a non-setting exfoliant cream mask.

This mask will gently remove dead skin cells.

Exfoliant removal using warm, damp towelling mitts.

Application of an eye serum eye-mask to relax and strengthen the delicate skin tissue around the eye.

A specialised lifting massage is applied to increase cellular renewal around the eyes.

A Japanese silk cream mask is contoured to the face and neck, feeling like a second skin.

The treatment concludes with the skin being toned and moisturised and the client being gently awakened with Japanese chimes. The treatment will give both psychological and physiological benefits.

Assessment of knowledge and understanding

You have now learnt about the different products and treatments that you can apply to the skin of the face and neck. This will enable you to improve and maintain facial skin condition.

To test your level of knowledge, answer the following short questions. These will prepare you for your summative (final) assessment.

Anatomy and physiology questions required for this unit are found on pages 129–36.

Consult with the client

1 What details should be recorded on the client's record card?

2 At the consultation you notice the client has herpes simplex. What action do you take?

3 At the consultation a client asks you your advice about a small lump on her skin that occasionally bleeds. What advice do you give her?

4 How do you identify a client's skin type and treatment requirements?

5 How should all client records be stored to comply with the Data Protection Act 1998?

Prepare for the treatment

1 How can you ensure that the client will be relaxed during the facial treatment?

2 How can you ensure that you and the client are correctly positioned for the facial treatment to avoid discomfort?

3 It may be necessary when preparing for the facial treatment to dispense products for use in the treatment. Why should these be dispensed in amounts according to your needs?

4 Taking into account health and safety requirements, how should you prepare yourself for treatment?

5 What do you understand by the terms sanitisation and sterilisation?

6 How can you ensure that skin-care products and equipment are used hygienically?

Plan the treatment

1 How long would you allow to complete a facial treatment?

2 Why is it important that the facial treatment is given in the allocated time?

3 Design a facial treatment, lasting one hour, for a client with an oily skin type. Describe:
   - the aim of the facial treatment
   - the facial treatment products you are going to use

- when and how you will apply them
- the different stages of the facial and how long each stage will last
- any specialised treatments or products you are going to use
- aftercare advice which should be given to maintain the skin condition. Consider also what products the client should be recommended to use at home.

4 Why is it important to keep accurate records of the client's treatment?

5 How does the natural ageing process affect the skin? What characteristics would you expect to see?

6 What would be your treatment aim, and how would you adapt facial massage application, for a client with a mature skin?

7 How would you select and apply skin care products for a client with an allergic skin type?

Improve and maintain the clients skin condition

1 When would you use a skin warming treatment such as facial steaming?

2 What is the purpose of the following skin care products?
- cleanser
- toning lotion
- exfoliant
- moisturiser
- face mask
- eye gel.

3 State three beneficial effects of facial massage on the skin.

4 What is the name given to the excessive erythema that can occur during a facial? What could be the cause of this?

5 What products should not be used immediately after a facial?

6 Why is the client's lifestyle an important consideration when analysing the condition of her skin?

Provide appropriate advice to the client

1 What skin-care products would you recommend that a client use as part of her home care routine?

2 How would you explain to the client the correct application – and where relevant, removal of the following products for home use?
- cleansing milk
- cream exfoliant
- toning lotion
- non-setting face mask
- eye cream
- night cream.

3 What details should be recorded on the client record card following facial skin-care treatment?

4 What improvements to lifestyle can benefit the client's skin?

5 How often would you recommend a full facial treatment?

6 A client may visit the salon for a mini-facial. What would this usually consist of, and why would you recommend this additional service?

chapter 7

ENHANCE THE APPEARANCE BT11
OF EYEBROWS AND LASHES*
PROVIDE EYELASH AND BT5
EYEBROW TREATMENTS**

Learning objectives

This unit describes how to enhance and improve the appearance of the client's eyebrows and lashes using the practical skills of brow shaping, lash and brow tinting, and eyelash perming.

It describes the competencies to enable you to:

- **consult with the client**
- **prepare for the treatment**
- **plan the treatment**
- **shape the eyebrows to meet the client's requirements**
- **tint the eyebrows and lashes to meet the client's requirements**
- **perm eyelashes to meet the client's requirements**
- **complete the treatment**

It also covers the knowledge requirements for BT11 Enhance the appearance of eyebrows and lashes. False eyelash application is found on pages 353–65.

When providing eyebrow and lash treatments it is important to use the skills you have learnt in the following core mandatory units:

Unit G1 – Ensure your own actions reduce risks to health and safety

Unit G6 – Promote additional products or services to clients

Unit G8 – Develop and maintain your effectiveness at work

*Mandatory for the BT make-up route
**Mandatory for the BT general route

TIP ✔

Whilst the client is having her eyebrows shaped, you have an ideal opportunity to discuss further possible treatments, such as an eyebrow tint.

TIP ✔

At the consultation, identify any peculiarities such as bald patches or scarring in the brow area to avoid any argument later.

Eyebrow tweezers

EYEBROW HAIR REMOVAL

The eyebrows, situated above the bony eye orbits of the face, help to protect the eyes from moisture and dust, and to cushion the skin from physical injury. Misshapen bushy brows give an untidy appearance to the face; but when correctly shaped, the brows give balance to the facial features and enhance the eyes – the most expressive feature of the face.

RECEPTION

Eyebrow shaping is offered in the salon as either an **eyebrow reshape** or an **eyebrow trim** – the former involves removing eyebrow hair to create a new shape, the latter involves removing only a few stray hairs in order to maintain the existing shape. When making an appointment it is usual to allow 15 minutes for each service.

It is wise to have a designated time between treatments so that there is no confusion between the two services. For example, under two weeks could be regarded as a trim, and over two weeks as a reshape.

If the client has thick, heavy brows, or if she does not have her brows shaped regularly, she should be encouraged to have them shaped gradually over a period of weeks, until the desired shape is achieved. This will allow the client to become accustomed to the new shape and will minimise any discomfort.

Eyebrow shaping may be carried out as an independent treatment, or combined with other treatments such as permanent tinting of the brows. In the latter case, the brows should be tinted before shaping, to avoid the tint coming into contact with the open follicle and perhaps causing an allergic reaction.

Before brow-shaping treatment commences, carry out a consultation. Discuss the shape and the effect that might be achieved. Consider such factors as age, the natural shape of the brow, and fashion.

If a client wears contact lenses, these ideally must be removed before treatment commences, as the eyes may water during treatment.

CONTRA-INDICATIONS

If whilst completing the record card or on visual inspection of the skin the client is found to have any of the following, eyebrow shaping treatment must not be carried out:

- *Hypersensitive skin.*
- *Any eye disorder*, such as conjunctivitis, styes or hordeola, watery eye, blepharitis or cysts.
- *Inflammation or swelling* of the surrounding eye tissue.
- *Skin disease* in the area.
- *Skin disorder* in the area, such as psoriasis or eczema.
- *Bruising, cuts or abrasions* in the eye area.

BEAUTY WORKS

Date	Beauty therapist name	
Client name		Date of birth (identifying client age group)
Address		Postcode

Evening phone number	Day phone number

Name of doctor	Doctor's address and phone number

Related medical history (conditions that may restrict or prohibit treatment application)

Are you taking any medication (this may affect the condition of the skin or skin sensitivity)

CONTRA-INDICATIONS REQUIRING MEDICAL REFERRAL
(Preventing eye treatment application)

☐ severe skin conditions
☐ eye infections (e.g. conjunctivitis, styes)
☐ eye disease

EYE TREATMENT

☐ shaping eyebrows
☐ tinting eyebrow hair
☐ tinting eyelashes
☐ eyelash perming
☐ false eyelashes

BROW SHAPE WORK TECHNIQUES

☐ brow shape selected following measurement of the client's natural brow and eye for brow shaping treatment
☐ opening of the pores
☐ keeping the skin taut
☐ removal of hairs in the direction of hair growth
☐ protection of the eye
☐ hair removed to complement the shape and proportions of clients natural brow, in relation to facial features and shape

CONTRA-INDICATIONS WHICH RESTRICT TREATMENT
(Treatment may require adaptation)

☐ inflammation of the skin
☐ recent scar tissue
☐ eye disorders
☐ skin allergies
☐ bruising

TINTING WORK TECHNIQUES

☐ skin test carried out
☐ tint colour selection suited to clients colouring characteristics
☐ timing, development and removal of tint adapted according to client's natural colouring characteristics
☐ manufacturer's instructions complied with

COLOURING CHARACTERISTIC

☐ fair   ☐ red   ☐ dark   ☐ grey

EYELASH PERMING

☐ skin test carried out
☐ rod size selected to suit client's lash length and effect to be achieved
☐ treatment application timed in accordance with previous treatment history
☐ manufacturer's instructions complied with

FALSE EYELASHES

☐ skin test carried out
☐ colour and length of lash type selected to meet agreed treatment requirement and effect to be achieved
☐ individual lash
☐ strip lash
☐ manufacturer's instructions complied with

Beauty therapist signature (for reference)

Client signature (confirmation of details)

TREATMENT ADVICE

This information includes
- results of treatment
- recommended time intervals between treatments
- use of aftercare products
- possible contra-actions that may occur and advice on the action to be taken in the event of an allergic or unwanted skin or eye irritation
- use of make-up and/or other services following treatment

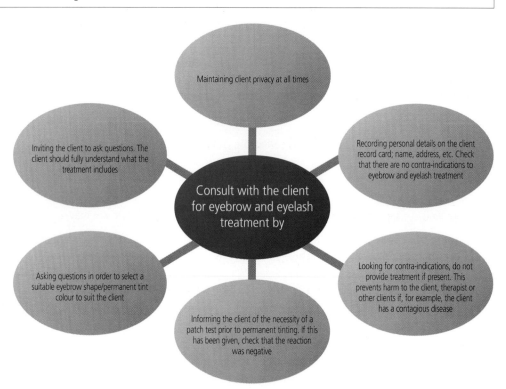

If you are unsure about the wisdom of proceeding with treatment – for example, if there is an undiagnosed lump in the area – ask your client to seek medical approval first.

EQUIPMENT AND MATERIALS

There are two sorts of tweezers. **Automatic tweezers** are designed to remove the bulk of excess hair; they have a spring-loaded action. **Manual tweezers** are used to remove stray hairs, and to accentuate the brow shape where more accurate care is required. They are available with various ends, which you use is a matter of personal preference, but slanted ends are generally considered to be the best for eyebrow shaping.

Although many therapists may complete an eyebrow shaping using only one of these – automatic or manual tweezers – it is important to be skilled in the use of both these tools.

Disposable mascara wands are ideal for brushing the hairs during brow shaping.

To carry out eyebrow shaping, you will need the following equipment and materials:

TIP

When purchasing tweezers, make sure that the ends meet accurately so they will grasp the hair effectively.

HEALTH AND SAFETY

Maintaining hygiene
Several pairs of tweezers must be purchased (perhaps five), due to the length of time required for sterilisation. Buy good-quality stainless-steel tweezers: cheaper metals rust after repeated sterilisation.

At the consultation, identify any peculiarities such as bald patches or scarring in the brow area to avoid any argument later.

- *Couch or beauty chair* – with sit-up and lie-down positions and an easy-to-clean surface.
- *Disposable tissue* – such as bed roll.
- *Towels (2)* – freshly laundered for each client.
- *Tweezers (sterilised)* – both automatic and manual.
- *Eyebrow pencil* – used to mark the skin when measuring brow length.
- *Pencil sharpener (stainless steel)* – suitable for use in the autoclave.
- *Disposable spatula*.
- *Antiseptic cleansing solution* – for use on the skin.
- *Soothing lotion or cream* – with healing and antiseptic properties, for the skin of the face.
- *Dry cottonwool* – stored in a covered jar.
- *Damp cottonwool* – prepared for each client.
- *Hand mirror (clean)* – used when discussing the brow shaping requirements and the finished result.
- *Record card*.
- *Scissors* – for trimming hairs.
- *Trolley* – on which to place everything.
- *Light magnifier (cold)*.
- *Facial tissues (white)* – for blotting the skin dry and for stretching the skin during hair removal.
- *Surgical spirit* – for cleansing the tweezers before sterilisation.
- *Disposable surgical gloves*.

EQUIPMENT LIST

couch or beauty chair

tweezers

disposable spatula

dry cottonwool

scissors

facial tissues

surgical spirit

disposable surgical gloves

see opposite for complete list of materials required

Sterilisation and sanitisation

Sterilise tweezers at an appropriate time during the working day. Ensure that you always have sterile tweezers ready for use with each client. After they have been sterilised in the autoclave, the tweezers should be stored in the ultraviolet cabinet.

A fresh disinfectant solution may be used to store a spare pair of tweezers while carrying out an eyebrow treatment. This solution is usually dispensed into a small container stored on the trolley. (Spare tweezers are necessary in case you should accidentally drop the other tweezers during the treatment.)

Disposable rubber gloves may be worn for protection during the eyebrow shaping treatment – the therapist may come into contact with tissue fluids from the client's skin.

As the waste from the treatment may contain body fluids and pose a health threat, it must be collected and disposed of carefully, in accordance with the local health officer's rules and regulations.

Automatic tweezers

Preparing the cubicle

Before the client is shown through to the cubicle, it should be checked to ensure that the required equipment and materials are available and the area is clean and tidy.

The plastic-covered couch should be clean, having been thoroughly washed with hot soapy water, or wiped thoroughly with surgical spirit or a

TIP

At the consultation, identify any peculiarities such as bald patches or scarring in the brow area, to avoid any argument later.

professional, alcohol-based cleaner. The couch or chair should be protected with a long strip of disposable paper bedroll or a freshly laundered sheet and bath towel. A small towel should be placed neatly at the head of the couch – for hygiene and protection during treatment, this will be draped across the client's chest. The tissue will need changing and the towels should be freshly laundered for each client.

The couch or beauty chair should be flat or slightly elevated.

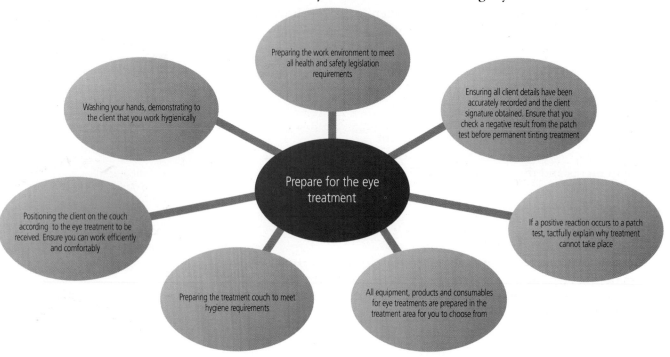

PLANNING THE TREATMENT

Factors to be considered

Before shaping the brows you must consider the following factors.

The natural shape of the brow

The natural brow follows the line of the eye socket. This varies greatly between clients, and affects what is achievable.

If the client has been shaping her own brows, it may be necessary to let them grow for a short period before shaping them professionally. If the brows are very thin or very thick, it may take several sessions before the desired shape is achieved.

If the brows have been plucked over a long period of time, they may not grow back successfully; this should be discussed with the client. In such instances, temporary eyebrow pencil or matt powder eyeshadow may be used to achieve the desired effect (see the photograph on page 349).

Fashion

Each season sees new fashion trends, which also affect eye makeup and eyebrow shapes. This should be considered before using any form of permanent hair removal to shape the brows.

TIP

A sharpened eyebrow-pencil should be used to simulate brow hairs – apply feathery strokes using the pencil point. To create a natural effect, two different pencil colours may be used, for example brown and grey.

TIP

By permanently tinting brow hair before shaping you will colour any finer lighter hairs, which will then form part of the brow.

The age of the client

The brow hair of older clients may include a few coarse, long, discoloured white or grey hairs. These may be removed provided that this does not alter the brow line or leave bald patches.

In general, thick eyebrows make the client look older, by creating a hooded appearance; and thin eyebrows will make the client look severe. Ideally the brows should therefore be shaped to a medium thickness.

The natural growth pattern

The shape and effect that the client requests may be made impossible by the pattern of the natural growth of the hair, which is genetically determined. When shaping the brows of the oriental client, for example, you will notice that the eyebrow hair grows in a downward direction. To create an arch it may be necessary to trim the hairs, using a small, sterile pair of sharp nail scissors. Alternatively, you may remove the outer eyebrow length and use a cosmetic pencil to create a new brow-line. Use your professional judgement to advise the client.

Oblique eyebrow

Arched eyebrow

Choosing an eyebrow shape

The eyebrows should be in balance with the rest of the facial features: the right brow shape for each client will depend on her facial proportions and her natural brow shape.

There is no single ideal brow shape; different brow shapes are shown on the right.

Angular

What is achievable?

Obviously not all of these brow shapes are achievable for every client, but the skilful application to the eyebrows of temporary cosmetic colour can create the illusion of the desired brow shape.

The quantity of brow hair removed during shaping produces a thin, medium or thick final shape, as illustrated opposite and on the following page. Other approaches, too, may be used:

Straight eyebrow

- *Semi-permanent tattooing* This can be used to add colour permanently to the brows, for example to disguise a bald patch.
- *Hair transplants* These are available already in the USA for the client with sparse eyebrows.
- *False individual eyebrow hairs* These are applied in the same way as individual false eyelashes.

Ideally, the distance *between* the two eyebrows should be the width of one eye. If this is not the case, the illusion may be created by removing hairs or by applying temporary brow colour to create this effect.

Rounded eyebrow

Wide-set eyes can be made to appear closer together by extending the brow-line beyond the inside corner of the eye; close-set eyes can be made to look further apart by widening the distance between them.

Thin

Medium

Thick

ACTIVITY

Correcting brow shapes (1)

You cannot change the bone structure of the facial features without cosmetic surgery, but brow shaping can create the illusion of improved facial balance and proportion. Discuss why each of the brow shapes below would complement the accompanying face shape.

Face shape   *Correct brow shape*

Square

Round

Oblong

Pear
(triangular)

Heart

ACTIVITY

Correcting brow shapes (2)
How would you correct the following eye shapes?
- Wide-set.
- Close-set.

ACTIVITY

Correcting brow shapes (3)
From magazines, collect pictures of faces showing different eyebrow shapes. Discuss which you think are correct and which incorrect, explaining why.

Measuring the eyebrows to decide length

In order to determine the correct length of the client's eyebrows, there are three main guidelines:

1 Place an orange stick or spatula beside the nose and the inside corner of the eye. This is usually in line with the tear duct. Any hairs that grow between the eyes and beyond this point should be removed. If the client has a very broad nose, however, this guide is inappropriate: tweezing would commence near the middle of the brow. In this instance, use the tear duct at the inside corner of the eye as a guide.

2 Place an orange stick or spatula in a line from the base of the nose (to the side of the nostril) to the outer corner of the eye. Any hairs that grow beyond this point should be removed.

3 Place an orange stick or spatula in a vertical line from the centre of the eyelid. This is where the highest point of the arch should be.

Initially these guidelines will be needed to ensure that the correct length and brow shape are achieved, but the experienced therapist will recognise the corrective work to be carried out without the need for measuring.

PREPARING THE CLIENT

The client should be shown through to the cubicle after the record card has been completed.

Consult the record card and check the area for any contra-indications to treatment.

HEALTH AND SAFETY

Cross-infection
Use a fresh cottonwool pad for each eyebrow to avoid cross-infection.

SHAPING THE EYEBROWS

1 Position the cold-light magnifying lamp to give maximum visibility of the area.

2 Position the client on the couch.

3 Wash your hands.

4 Working from behind the client, cleanse the eyebrow area, using a lightweight cleansing lotion or eye make-up remover. Apply a mild antiseptic lotion to two damp cottonwool pads, then gently wipe each eyebrow. (This removes all grease from the area, so that the tweezers will not slip.) The brow area should then be blotted dry, using a clean, folded facial tissue.

5 Brush the brow hair with the disposable brush, firstly *against* the natural hair growth, then with it. This enables you to define the brow shape and to observe the natural line.

6 Measure the brows (using the guidelines on page 213).

TIP

It is often stated, that before beginning shaping, the brows should be prepared with warm, damp cottonwool pads, to relax the hair follicles and soften the eyebrow tissue, thus making hair removal easier. During treatment, however, you will be wiping over the area with an antiseptic lotion which has a cooling, soothing and tightening effect on the skin, so this preparation is ineffectual.

7 Place a clean piece of cottonwool in a convenient position for collecting the removed hairs, for instance at the top of the couch next to the client's head.

8 Put on disposable gloves, as you may come into contact with body tissue fluid.

9 Begin tweezing, using a sterilised pair of automatic tweezers. These are designed to remove hairs quickly and efficiently, and are therefore used for the bulk of the hair identified for removal. It is usual to start at the bridge of the nose: the skin here is less sensitive than under the brow line.

TIP

Occasionally clients start sneezing when you tweeze hairs at the bridge of the nose. If this happens, leave this area till last.

10 Gently stretch the skin between the index and middle fingers, pressing lightly onto the skin. This will help you to avoid accidentally nipping the skin; it will also open the mouth of the hair follicle and minimise discomfort to the client.

11 Remove the hairs quickly, in the direction of growth. This prevents the hairs from breaking off at the skin's surface. Hair breakage can be seen to have occurred if a stubbly regrowth appears 1 or 2 days after shaping. Incorrect removal may also cause distortion of the hair follicle, or result in the hair becoming trapped under the skin as it starts to regrow (*ingrowing hair* – see page 258).

Hairs should be removed individually, and the tweezers should be wiped regularly on the pad of clean cottonwool used to collect the removed hairs.

Measuring the eyebrow: the inner eye

Measuring the eyebrow: the outer eye

Cleansing the eyebrow

Brushing the eyebrow

Tweezing at the bridge of the nose, using automatic tweezers

Tweezing at the outer corner of the eyebrow

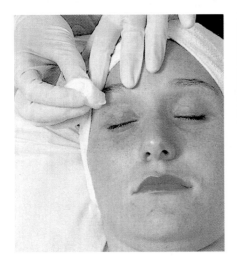

Applying antiseptic and soothing lotion

Brushing the eyebrow into shape

The completed eyebrow after shaping

TIP

Twenty per cent of hairs are not visible above the skin's surface at any one time. Explain this to the client so that she understands why stray hairs may appear shortly after treatment.

HEALTH AND SAFETY

Contra-action: using ice
To maintain hygiene, place the ice cube in a new small freezer foodbag. Dispose of the bag hygienically after use.

HEALTH AND SAFETY

Soothing lotion
Care should be taken when applying soothing lotion. If too much is applied it may run and enter the eye causing further discomfort.

It is often best to apply a small amount of soothing lotion to a clean cottonwool pad, using a separate one for each eye to avoid cross-infection.

12 Remove the hairs from underneath the outer edge of the brow, working inwards towards the nose. It is advisable to work on each brow alternately. This ensures that the brows are evenly shaped; it also reduces prolonged discomfort in any one area during shaping. Hairs should ideally be removed only from *below* the brow, otherwise the natural line may be lost. It is sometimes necessary, however, to remove the odd stray hair growing *above* the natural line.

During shaping, show the client her brows and avoid removing too much hair.

13 At regular intervals during shaping, brush the brows to check their shape. Apply antiseptic lotion to a clean, dampened cottonwool pad, and wipe this gently over the eyebrow tissue to reduce sensitivity and to sanitise the area.

14 When the bulk of excess hair has been removed, manual tweezers may be used to take away any stray hairs and to define the line. Long hairs may be trimmed with scissors if necessary. Any discoloured, coarse, long, curly or wavy hairs may be removed, as long as this does not alter the line or leave a bald patch.

15 On completion of brow shaping, wipe the eyebrows with the antiseptic soothing lotion, applied with clean, damp cottonwool. Apply a mild antiseptic cream to the area, using clean, dry cottonwool, to reduce the possibility of infection.

16 Brush the brows into shape and show the client the finished effect.

17 The hairs that have been removed should be disposed of hygienically.

CONTRA-ACTIONS

Erythema is considered to be a contra-action to the treatment: it is recognised as a marked reddening of the skin seen over the whole area or specifically around one damaged follicle. It is usually accompanied by minor swelling of the area. If this occurs the therapist must try to reduce the redness by applying a soothing antiseptic lotion or cream to the area. In extreme cases it may be necessary to apply ice. Record details of any contra-action on the client's record card.

If the reddening reduces in response to your corrective action, you may decide in future to remove only a few stray hairs at each eyebrow-shaping treatment, to minimise the risk of this reaction recurring.

AFTERCARE AND ADVICE

Advise the client not to wear eye make-up for at least eight hours following the eyebrow-shaping treatment. The hair follicle has been damaged where the hair has been torn out: it will be susceptible to infection unless the area is cared for whilst it heals. It should not be necessary for the client to continue using antiseptic lotion at home, but she should be advised to carry out these instructions if discomfort or continued reddening occurs:

1 Cleanse the eyebrow area using a mild antiseptic lotion or witchhazel, applied with a small piece of clean, dampened cottonwool.

2 Apply an antiseptic soothing lotion or cream, with clean, dry cottonwool.

3 Gently remove excess antiseptic lotion or cream using a clean, soft facial tissue.

4 Repeat as necessary, approximately every 4 hours. *If the reddening does not subside in the next 24 hours, contact the salon.*

5 Eye make-up may be worn as soon as the redness has gone – usually after 8 hours.

HEALTH AND SAFETY

Avoiding infection
If excess antiseptic lotion or cream is left on the area, this may attract small particles of dust, which could cause infection.

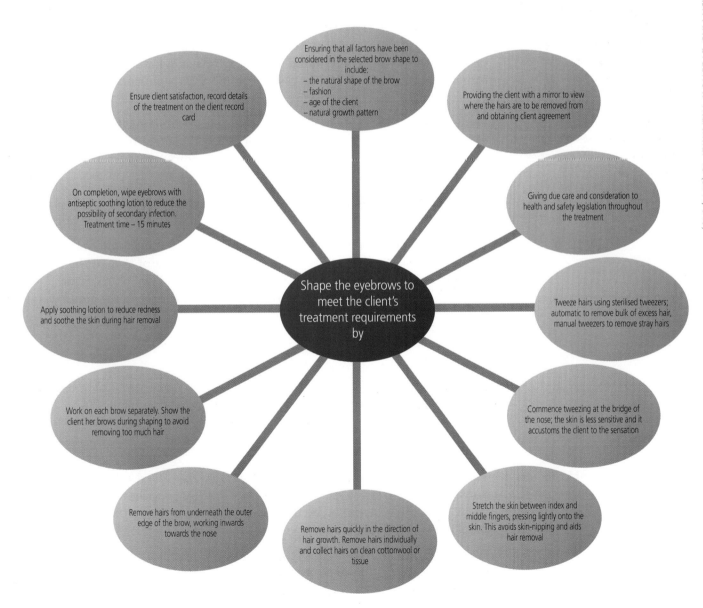

EYELASH AND EYEBROW TINTING

The hair of the eyelashes and eyebrows protects the eyes from moisture and dust, but the lashes and brows also give definition to the eye. Many clients, especially those with fair lashes and brows, feel that without the use of eye cosmetics their eyes lack this definition.

HEALTH AND SAFETY

Permanent tinting
Always use a tint that is permitted for use under EU regulations and complies with The Cosmetic Products (Safety) Regulations 1989. If you use any other tint your insurance may be invalid.

TIP

When a client requests a blue eyelash tint, make clear that this will not produce an 'electric blue' fashion colour.

PERMANENT TINTING

Further definition of the brow and lash hair can be created if a permanent dye is applied to them. Most clients will benefit from tinting because the tips and the bases of these hairs are usually lighter than the body of the hairs, causing the hairs to appear shorter than they actually are. Tinting the length of the lash or brow hair makes it appear longer and bolder, yet the effect created looks natural.

Because the skin around the eye area is very thin and sensitive, dyes designed for permanently tinting the hair in this area have been specially formulated to avoid any eye or tissue reactions. *The application of any other dye materials in this area is dangerous, and may even lead to blindness.*

Permanent tints are available in different forms, including jelly, liquid and cream tints. The most popular and acceptable permanent tinting product is the cream tint: this is thicker, so it does not run into the eye and it is easy to control during mixing, application and removal.

Several colours of permanent tint are available, including brown, grey, blue and black.

If the shade you want is not available, you can vary the shade of available tints by leaving the dye on the hair for different lengths of time, or by mixing different colours together. For example, to produce a navy blue colour; leave the tint to process for 3-5 minutes. If left to process for 10 minutes, the same tint will produce a raven blue-black colour.

The development of colour

Two products are essential for the permanent tinting treatment:

- professional **eyelash** or **eyebrow tint**;
- **hydrogen peroxide** (H_2O_2).

The tint contains small molecules of permanent dye called **toluenediamine**. These need to be 'activated' before their colouring effect becomes permanent: this is achieved by the addition of hydrogen peroxide. The peroxide is said to **develop** the colour of the tint.

Chemically, hydrogen peroxide is an **oxidant**, a chemical that contains available oxygen atoms and encourages certain chemical reactions – in this case, tinting.

HEALTH AND SAFETY

Peroxide strength
Do not use a higher strength than 10-volume or 3% hydrogen peroxide. If you do, skin irritation or minor skin burning may occur.

The hydrogen peroxide container will state either its volume or its percentage strength. To activate the tint and for safe use around the eye area, a 3% or 10-volume strength peroxide is used.

When you add the hydrogen peroxide to the tint, the small dye molecules together form large molecules which remain trapped in the cortex of the hair. The hair is thus permanently coloured, but in time, as it continues to grow, the new hair will show the natural colour.

RECEPTION

When making an appointment for this service, allow 5 minutes for a skin test, 10 minutes for an eyebrow tint, and 20 minutes for an eyelash tint. When the client is booking her treatment, ask her:

- to visit the salon 24 hours before the appointment, for a skin test;
- if she wears contact lenses, to bring her lens container so that she can place the lenses in it during the tinting treatment.

On average, a client will need her lashes tinted every 6 weeks, or sooner if for example she takes a holiday in a climate where sun bleaches them. Eyebrow tinting, on the other hand, should be repeated when the client feels it to be necessary, perhaps every 4 weeks, as eyebrows seem to lose colour intensity more quickly than lash hair

Skin tests

Some clients are sensitive to the tint, and produce an allergic reaction immediately on contact with it; others may become allergic later. For this you therefore need to carry out a skin test before each lash- or brow-tinting treatment. (The skin test is also known as a patch test, a hypersensitivity test, or a predisposition test – see page 45.)

Two responses to the skin test are possible – positive and negative:

- a *positive* result is recognised by irritation, swelling or inflammation of the skin – if this occurs, do not proceed with the treatment;
- a *negative* result produces no skin reaction – in this case you may proceed with the treatment.

TIP

Replace the cap of the hydrogen peroxide container *immediately* after use, or the peroxide will lose its strength.

TIP

It is acceptable for the salon receptionist – provided that she has been trained to do so – to carry out the skin test.

A skin test

ACTIVITY

Eyelash and eyebrow tinting
List reasons why clients would benefit from this service. Discuss the reasons with your tutor.

ACTIVITY

Allergic reactions
With colleagues, discuss the possible implications of ignoring a positive reaction to the skin test.

CONTRA-INDICATIONS

After completing the record card and inspecting the eye area, if you have found any of the following, do not proceed with the tinting treatment:

- *Inflammation or swelling* around the eye area.
- *Skin disease* in the eye area.
- *Skin disorder* in the area, such as psoriasis or eczema.
- *Cuts and abrasions* in the area.
- *Hypersensitive skin*.
- *Eye disorders*, such as conjunctivitis, blepharitis, styes or hordeola, watery eye, or cysts.
- A *positive (allergic) reaction* to the skin test.
- *Contact lenses* (unless removed).

A particularly nervous client would also be contra-indicated:

- it would be difficult for her to keep her eyes closed for 10 minutes;
- she might panic as the tint was applied, creating the possibility of tint entering the eye;
- she might blink frequently, making preparation of the eye area and application of the tint both difficult and hazardous.

EQUIPMENT AND MATERIALS

To carry out the tinting you will need the following equipment and materials:

- *Couch or beauty chair* – with sit-up and lie-down positions and an easy-to-clean surface.
- *Trolley* – on which to display everything.
- *Towels (medium-sized)* – freshly laundered for each client.
- *Headband (clean)* – to protect long hair or bleached hair from the tint.
- *Cleansing milk* – used to remove make-up from the eye area.
- *Eye make-up remover (non-oily)*.
- *Coloured tints (a selection)*.
- *Hydrogen peroxide (10-volume/3%)*.
- *Petroleum jelly* – to protect the the skin and prevent skin staining.
- *Damp cottonwool* – for cleansing the eye area and for lash and brow tint removal.
- *Eyeshields (commercial)* – to prevent skin staining during eyelash tinting.
- *Disposable brushes (2)*.
- *Facial tissues (white)* – for blotting the eye area dry.
- *Disposable spatulas* – for removing the petroleum jelly from its container.
- *Non-metallic bowl* – for mixing the permanent tint (note that some metals cause immediate release of the oxygen from the hydrogen peroxide, causing ineffective processing of the tint).

EQUIPMENT LIST

coloured tints

disposable brushes

see opposite for complete list of materials required

TIP

The brows or lash hair to be tinted must be grease-free – the grease would be a barrier to the tint.

TIP

Trimmed disposable lipbrushes can be used to apply the petroleum jelly and permanent tint.

HEALTH AND SAFETY ✚

Applicator brushes
Because it is impossible to sterilise applicator brushes effectively, use disposable brushes for the application of petroleum jelly and permanent tint.

- *Permanent tint (commercial)*.
- *Skin stain remover*.
- *Distilled (purified) water*.
- *Bottle, with a long flexible tube* – to dispense distilled water.
- *Collodion ('new skin')* – used to cover the tint when carrying out the skin test.
- *Bowl (clean)* – to hold dampened cottonwool.
- *Swing-top bin* – lined with a disposable bin-liner, for waste.
- *Hand mirror (clean)*.
- *Client's record card*.

Sterilisation and sanitisation

It is necessary to use disposable applicator brushes for the application of the petroleum jelly and the permanent tint because it is impossible to sterilise brushes effectively.

Preparing the cubicle

Before the client is shown through to the cubicle, it should be checked to ensure that the required equipment and materials are available and the area is clean and tidy.

Clean and protect the couch or beauty chair as for eyebrow-shaping treatment page 209–10). The couch or chair should be flat or slightly elevated.

The cubicle should be adequately lit to ensure that treatment can be given, safely, but avoid bright lighting that could cause eye irritation.

PLANNING THE TREATMENT

For the eyelashes and eyebrows, select a colour that complements the client's hair and skin colours, her age and her usual eye cosmetics. Always discuss the choice of colour carefully with the client to discover her preference. You may ask certain questions in order to help you in your selection:

- 'What colour mascara do you normally wear?'
- 'How dark would you like your eyelashes/eyebrows?'
- 'Do you normally wear eyebrow pencil? Of what colour?'

> **TIP**
>
> When selecting and using permanent tint for a white-haired client, note that the hair is very often resistant to colour.

ACTIVITY

Choosing lash and brow colours
Which colour do you think would be most suitable for the eyelashes and eyebrows of the following clients?
- Brunette.   ● Grey.
- Fair.   ● Elderly.
- Red.

Cleansing the eye

PREPARING THE CLIENT

The client should be shown through to the cubicle after the record card has been completed.

1 Position the client comfortably, in a flat or slightly elevated position. If she is wearing contact lenses, these must be removed.

2 Drape a towel across the client's chest and shoulders, and protect her hair with a clean headband.

3 Wash your hands, which assures the client that the treatment is beginning in a hygienic and professional manner.

4 Consult the client's record card, then check the area for any visible contra-indications or abnormalities before proceeding.

5 Cleanse the area to be treated with a cleansing milk to dissolve facial make-up. Then use a non-oily eye make-up remover to remove eye products: apply this with clean, damp cottonwool.

6 To ensure that the area is thoroughly clean and grease-free, apply a mild toning lotion, stroked over the lash or brow hair.

7 Blot the eyelashes or eyebrows dry with a clean facial tissue. This ensures that the tint is not diluted, and also prevents the tint from being carried into the eye.

8 Prepare the pre-shaped eyeshields by applying petroleum jelly to the inner surface of each eyeshield (the surface that comes into contact with the skin).

9 Ensure that the light is not shining directly into the client's eyes. If it were, the eyes might water, carrying the tint into the eye or down the face (causing skin staining).

10 Finally, check that the client is comfortable before beginning tint application.

TINTING THE EYELASHES

1 Remove some petroleum jelly from its container, using a new disposable spatula.

2 Working from behind the client, ask the client to open her eyes and to look upwards towards you. Using a disposable brush, apply petroleum jelly underneath the lower lashes of one eye, ensuring that it extends at the outer corner of the eye. (This is in case the client's eyes water slightly during treatment, which might otherwise lead to skin staining.) The petroleum jelly must not come into contact with the lash hair, where it would create a barrier to the tint.

3 Place the prepared eyeshield on the skin under the lower lashes, ensuring that it adheres to the petroleum jelly and fits 'snugly' to the base of the lower lashes.

4 Repeat the above process for the other eye.

5 Ask the client to close her eyes gently. Instruct her not to open them again until you advise her to do so, in about 10 minutes' time.

6 Apply petroleum jelly to the upper eyelid, in a line on the skin at the base of the lashes.

7 Considering the length and density of the clients eyelashes, mix the required amount of tint with 10-volume (3%) hydrogen peroxide. As a guide, a 5 mm length of tint from the tube, mixed with 2 or 3 drops of hydrogen peroxide, is usually sufficient. Mix the products to a smooth cream in the tinting bowl, using the disposable brush. Always re-cap bottles and tubes tightly after use, to avoid deterioration of materials.

8 Wipe excess tint off the brush onto the inside of the bowl. Apply the tint thinly to each hair. Work from the base of the lash to the tip, ensuring that each hair is evenly covered. Press down gently with the applicator to ensure that the lower lashes also are covered. The few inner and outer lashes should also be covered, down to the base.

HEALTH AND SAFETY

Client comfort

The client should not be left during the lash-tinting treatment. You must be available both to offer reassurance and to take the necessary action if the eyes water.

If the eyes do water whilst the eyes are closed, hold a tissue at the corner of the eye to soak up the moisture. Take further action if watering persists and the eyes begin to sting.

Eyeshields

Applying the tint

Processing the tint

Removing the tint

Soothing the eyes

The completed eyelash tint

HEALTH AND SAFETY

Using tints
Always read the manufacturer's instructions carefully before using a permanent tint.

9 Allow the tint to process, for approximately 5–10 minutes from the completion of application. Discard any unused mixture as soon as the tint has been applied.

10 On completion of processing, remove the eyelash tint by applying clean, damp cottonwool pads over each eye, wiping away most of the tint and removing the protective eyeshield in one movement, an outward sweep. Using fresh dampened cottonwool pads, gently stroke down the lashes from roots to tips, until all excess tint has been removed. With a sweeping action on each eye and using one cottonwool pad, wipe from the side to the middle against the lash growth, whilst the other hand supports the eye tissue. *All tint must be thoroughly removed before the client opens her eyes.*

11 Ask the client to open her eyes. If removal has been correctly carried out, the lashes and their bases will be free from tint. (While training, if any tint remains at the base of the lashes after the eyes have been opened, ask the client to close her eyes again and finish the removal process using clean, damp cottonwool.) Check that every lash has been tinted, especially the base of each lash and the inner and outer corner lashes.

12 Once you are satisfied that all tint has been removed, place a cool, damp cottonwool pad over each eye for 2–3 minutes to soothe the eye tissue.

13 Show the client the result, ensuring that the colour is dark enough and that she is satisfied with the final effect.

14 Complete the client's record card.

15 Take the client to reception to book her next appointment.

TINTING THE EYEBROWS

1 Remove some petroleum jelly from its container, using a new disposable spatula.

2 Brush the brow hair away from the skin, using a disposable brow brush.

3 Using a disposable brush, surround each eyebrow with petroleum jelly, as close as possible to the brow hair (to avoid skin staining).

4 Mix approximately 5 mm of the chosen tint colour with 2 or 3 drops of 10-volume (3%) hydrogen peroxide in a tinting bowl. Ensure that the tint is mixed thoroughly to a creamy consistency.

5 Wipe excess tint off the brush onto the inside of the tinting bowl. Apply the tint neatly and economically to the brow hair of the first eyebrow; ensuring that the brow hairs, from the base to the tips, are evenly covered.

Brushing the eyebrow against the growth

Applying the tint to the first eyebrow

Applying the tint to the second eyebrow

Removing the tint from the first eyebrow

Removing the tint from the second eyebrow

The completed effect, showing both eyelash and eyebrow tint

6 Apply the tint to the second eyebrow; following the same procedure.

7 Immediately after application of the tint to the second eyebrow, remove the tint from the first eyebrow. Use a clean dampened cottonwool pad. Place it on the eyebrow, then wipe it across the eyebrow in an outward sweep, removing the excess tint. Ensure that all traces of excess tint have been removed, to prevent skin staining.

   Never leave tint on the eyebrows for longer than 2 minutes. Eyebrow hair colour develops much more quickly than lash hair.

8 Remove the tint from the second eyebrow in the same way.

HEALTH AND SAFETY

Skin stains
If skin staining accidentally occurs, use a professional skin stain remover designed for this purpose. Afterwards, use plenty of clean, dampened cottonwool pads to avoid skin irritation.

ACTIVITY

Explaining poor results
What reasons can you think of to explain why a permanent tint applied to the eyelashes or eyebrows has not coloured the hair successfully? Discuss your answers with your tutor.

9 Show the client the effect of the tinted eyebrows. If the brow hair is not dark enough, re-apply the tint to the eyebrow hair; following the same application and removal procedure.

10 When you are both satisfied with the colour of the tinted eyebrows, complete the client's record card.

11 Take the client to reception to book her next appointment.

TIP

The effect of tinting depends on the natural colour:
- *Blonde hair* develops colour rapidly – if the tint is left on the eyebrow too long, a harsh appearance will be created.
- *Red hair* is more resistant to the tint, and developing will take a little longer – allow 15 minutes' processing time when tinting lash hair.
- *Dark hair* requires tinting to increase the intensity of the natural eyebrow colour, giving a glossy, conditioned appearance.

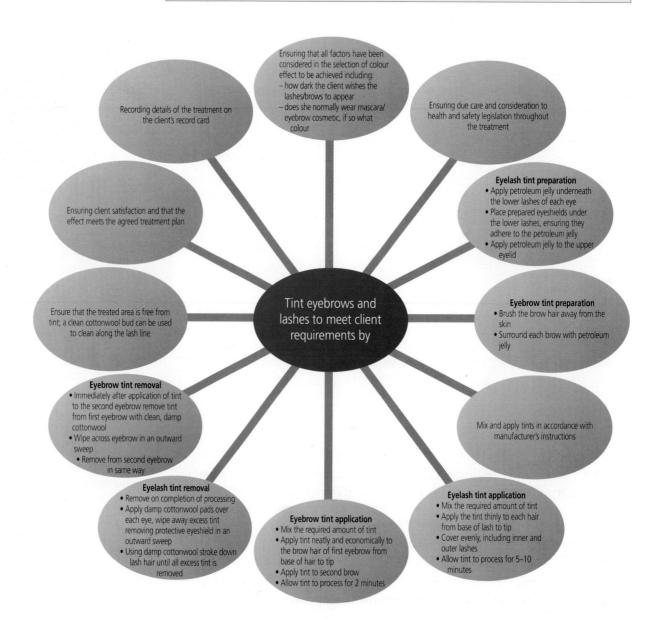

CONTRA-ACTIONS

If the client complains of discomfort during the treatment, tint may have entered the eye. Take the following action:

1 Remove the tint immediately from the eye area, using clean, damp cottonwool pads in an outward sweep.

2 When you are satisfied that all excess tint has been removed (that is, when the cottonwool shows clean), flush the eye with clean water. Repeat the rinsing process until discomfort has been relieved.

If there is a noticeable sensitivity of the eye tissue after eyebrow or eyelash tinting, recommend that the client does not receive the treatment again. Record this on her record card.

EYELASH PERMING

Eyelash perming entails permanently curling the lashes, which enhances the appearance of the eyes. The lashes immediately appear longer, which suits most clients. The treatment also suits:

- short sparse lashes, to make them appear longer and denser;
- downward-slanting eyes, as the eyes appear lifted when the outer lashes are curled;
- special occasions and holidays;
- clients who are unable to wear eye make-up at work.

The effect lasts as long as the hair growth cycle of the eyelashes.

HEALTH AND SAFETY ✚

Eyelash curling
Repeated mechanical eyelash curling is time-consuming and can weaken the lashes, causing breakage of the natural lash. Permanent curling is the ideal alternative.

RECEPTION

When making an appointment for this service, recommend that the client has a skin test. Ask her to visit the salon for this, 24 hours before the appointment.

If she wears contact lenses, ask her to bring her lens container so that she can place the lenses in it during the perming treatment.

Advise the client that the treatment requires that she keep her eyes closed for a long time. Some clients may find this uncomfortable, and may choose not to have the treatment.

The client should not have an eyelash tint immediately before perming, as the colour of the lashes will be lightened by the treatment process. However, tinting is effective *following* eyelash perming and should be promoted. Allow a minimum of 24 hours following the eyelash perming service before tinting.

On average, a client will need her eyelashes perming every 2–3 months. Treatment takes approximately 45 minutes.

Skin tests

Some clients may be sensitive to the perm solution, and may produce an allergic reaction immediately on contact with it; others may become allergic later. For this reason, a skin test must be carried out before *each* eyelash perming treatment. This is essential not just for new clients, but also if there has been a lengthy interval since the last eyelash perming service.

1 Apply a small amount of perm solution to the inside of one elbow, and a small amount of fixing lotion to the other.
2 Test the client's tolerance to the adhesive by applying a small amount of the adhesive to the inside of the elbow or behind the ear. Avoid immediate contact with clothing.
3 Advise the client how to recognise a positive skin reaction: skin reddening, itching and swelling. Advise her to apply a soothing agent if this occurs and to notify you. This reaction can then be recorded on the client's record card.

CONTRA-INDICATIONS

After completing the record card and inspecting the eye area, if you have found any of the following do not proceed with the eyelash perming treatment:

- *Inflammation or swelling* around the eye area.
- *Skin disease* in the eye area.
- *Skin disorder* in the area such as psoriasis or eczema.
- *Cuts and abrasions* in the eye area.
- *Hypersensitive skin*.
- *Eye disorders*, such as conjunctivitis, blepharitis, styes or hordeola, watery eye, or cysts.
- *Positive (allergic) reaction* to the skin test.
- *Contact lenses* – unless removed.
- *Considerable nervousness* – a particularly nervous client may make application, fixing and removal hazardous.

EQUIPMENT AND MATERIALS

To carry out the perming you will need the following equipment and materials:

- *Couch or beauty chair* – with sit-up and lie-down positions and an easy-to-clean surface.

- *Trolley* – on which to place everything.

- *Towels (medium-sized)* – freshly laundered for each client.

- *Headband (clean)* – to protect the hair.

- *Eye make-up remover (non-oily)*.

- *Mild perm solution (usually 6% thioglycollate)* – especially designed for use in the eye area. (It is this solution that curls the lash into the desired new shape.)

- *Fixing/neutralising lotion* – sodium bromate. (It is this which makes the new curl permanent.)

- *Eyelash curlers (a selection of different sizes)* – small curlers are used for fine hair, larger curlers for thicker hair.

- *Eyelash adhesive* – to secure the lashes to the curlers.

- *Lint-free pads* – to remove the perm and fixing lotion.

- *Disposable wooden cocktail or orange sticks* – to secure the natural lashes to the curlers.

- *Disposable brushes* – to apply the perm lotion and fixing lotion.

- *Damp cottonwool* – for cleansing the eye area and to remove excess products.

- *Bowls (2, clean)* – to hold damp cottonwool or lint-free pads.

- *Moisturising agent* – to facilitate removal of the curlers.

- *Timer* – to accurately time the 'curling' and 'fixing' processes

- *Swing-top bin* – lined with a disposable bin-liner, for waste.

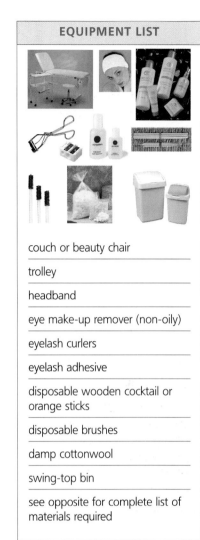

EQUIPMENT LIST

| couch or beauty chair |
| trolley |
| headband |
| eye make-up remover (non-oily) |
| eyelash curlers |
| eyelash adhesive |
| disposable wooden cocktail or orange sticks |
| disposable brushes |
| damp cottonwool |
| swing-top bin |
| see opposite for complete list of materials required |

Salon System

Perm lotions

TIP

Perm lotions for the eye area are usually of *gel* formulation: this makes the lotion easy to control. Bear this in mind when selecting this product. The bottles are small to reduce the risk of oxidation, which would make the lotion ineffective.

TIP

A specialised conditioning agent may be applied to the lashes. This would be professionally applied as part of the perming service to rehydrate the lashes.

HEALTH AND SAFETY +

Storage
Store the perm and fixing lotion in a well-ventilated area, away from direct sources of heat and light. If a spillage occurs wear gloves while you clean it up, and increase ventilation in the area.

TIP

If possible, after cleansing leave the lashes to dry for 10 minutes before perming, to ensure that the lashes are completely dry.

- *Hand mirror (clean).*
- *Record card.*

Sterilisation and sanitisation

Ideally, applicators used for the perming chemical agents should be disposable. Alternatively, several brushes must be available to allow effective sanitisation between clients.

Preparing the cubicle

Before the client is shown through to the cubicle it should be checked to ensure that the required equipment and materials are available and the area is clean and tidy.

The couch or beauty chair should be flat or slightly elevated. Clean and protect the couch or chair as for eyebrow-shaping treatment (page 183).

The cubicle should be adequately lit to ensure that the treatment can be given safely, but avoid bright lighting which might cause eye irritation.

PREPARING THE CLIENT

The client should be shown through to the cubicle after the record card has been completed.

1 Position the client comfortably, in a flat or slightly elevated position. If she wears contact lenses, these must be removed.
2 Drape a towel across the client's chest and shoulders, and protect her hair with a clean headband.
3 Wash your hands. This assures the client that the treatment is beginning in a hygienic and professional manner.
4 Consult the client's record card, then check the area for any visible contra-indications or abnormalities before proceeding.
5 Cleanse the surrounding eye area with a cleansing milk to dissolve facial make-up. Then use a non-oily eye make-up remover to remove eye products: apply this with clean, damp cottonwool.
6 Blot the eyelashes dry with a clean facial tissue. This ensures that the perm lotion is not diluted, and also prevents the perm lotion being carried into the eye.
7 Explain the procedure to the client and tell her about the sensations she may experience during eyelash perming. Warn her that she will need to keep her eyes closed for a long period. Some clients may find this difficult, while others will enjoy this as a time of relaxation!
8 Comb through the lashes to ensure they are evenly separated and dry. This will optimise the results.

PERMING THE EYELASHES

1 Select the correct size of curler for the client's lash length. Bend it so that it fits the contour of the eye. If the curler is too long it may be trimmed.

2 Place the curler at the base of the upper lashes, near the inner tear duct.

3 Gently curl the natural lashes around the curler, using the disposable stick. Ensure that the lashes do not overlap each other and are straight or the ends will be 'crooked', spoiling the overall effect and appearance.

4 When you are satisfied that the lashes are straight and that the client is comfortable, apply the perm lotion evenly to the upper lashes, using a disposable brush.

TIP	
Avoid overhandling the curler as this will affect the natural adhesion of the curler to the skin.	

TIP	
A protective damp cottonwool pad may be placed over the lower lashes to form a barrier to the perm lotion, when it is being applied to the upper lashes.	

Cleansing the eye area

Selecting the correct curler

Curling the lashes

Applying the perm lotion

Processing the perm lotion

Removing the perm lotion

Applying the fixing/neutralising lotion

Covering the lashes with lint-free pads

Removing the fixing/neutralising lotion

Removing the curler

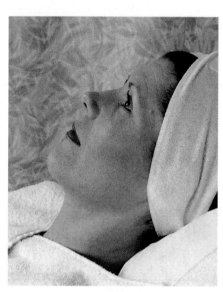

The completed effect

TIP ✔

If necessary, apply non-permanent eyelash adhesive using a fine wooden or plastic cocktail stick to secure the lashes to the curler and to keep them even and straight so that the lower and upper lashes do not stick together.

5 Cover the lashes with plastic film (clear wrap) or dry lint-free pads. This creates warmth which aids the perming process. Allow:
- 7–10 minutes for fine or previously tinted hair;
- 10 minutes for coarse hair.

Follow manufacturer's guidance on timing as this may vary.

6 Remove the perm lotion using dry lint-free pads, gently blotting the lashes.

7 Apply the fixing/neutralising lotion with a clean disposable brush.

8 Cover the lashes with plastic film (clear wrap) or dry lint-free pads for 10 minutes.

9 Gently remove the fixing/neutralising lotion from the lashes, using dry lint-free pads.

10 When all fixing/neutralising lotion has been thoroughly removed, gently remove each curler, rolling downwards. A moisturising agent may be applied with a cotton bud to the lashes to aid the removal of the curlers. Warn the client that she will feel a gentle pulling movement as the curlers are removed.

11 Wipe excess product from the lashes with damp, clean cottonwool.

12 Show the client the finished result in a mirror.

13 Wash your hands again.

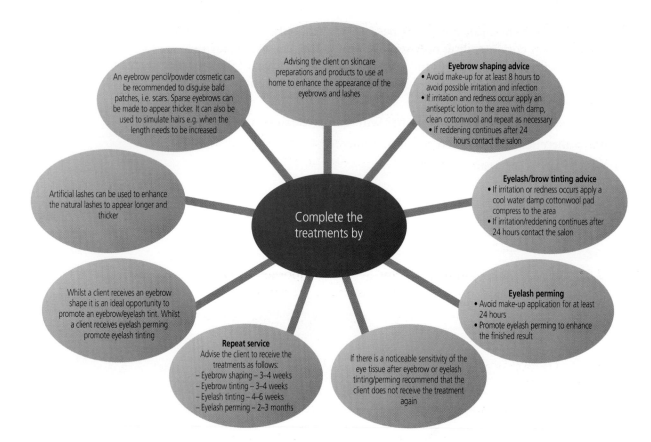

An eyebrow pencil/powder cosmetic can be recommended to disguise bald patches, i.e. scars. Sparse eyebrows can be made to appear thicker. It can also be used to simulate hairs e.g. when the length needs to be increased

Advising the client on skincare preparations and products to use at home to enhance the appearance of the eyebrows and lashes

Eyebrow shaping advice
• Avoid make-up for at least 8 hours to avoid possible irritation and infection
• If irritation and redness occur apply an antiseptic lotion to the area with damp, clean cottonwool and repeat as necessary
• If reddening continues after 24 hours contact the salon

Eyelash/brow tinting advice
• If irritation or redness occurs apply a cool water damp cottonwool pad compress to the area
• If irritation/reddening continues after 24 hours contact the salon

Artificial lashes can be used to enhance the natural lashes to appear longer and thicker

Complete the treatments by

Eyelash perming
• Avoid make-up application for at least 24 hours
• Promote eyelash perming to enhance the finished result

Whilst a client receives an eyebrow shape it is an ideal opportunity to promote an eyebrow/eyelash tint. Whilst a client receives eyelash perming promote eyelash tinting

Repeat service
Advise the client to receive the treatments as follows:
– Eyebrow shaping – 3–4 weeks
– Eyebrow tinting – 3–4 weeks
– Eyelash tinting – 4–6 weeks
– Eyelash perming – 2–3 months

If there is a noticeable sensitivity of the eye tissue after eyebrow or eyelash tinting/perming recommend that the client does not receive the treatment again

CONTRA-ACTIONS

If the client complains of discomfort during the treatment, the chemical lotion may have entered the eye. Take the following action:

1 Remove the perm or fixing lotion immediately, using clean, damp cottonwool pads.

2 When you are satisfied that all excess lotion has been removed, flush the eye if necessary with water. Repeat the rinsing process for at least 15 minutes, until discomfort has been relieved. If the irritation does not cease after rinsing, dry the eye area, protect the eye with a sterile pad, and advise the client to seek medical attention.

If there is a noticeable sensitivity or a burning sensation in the eye area after eyelash perming, recommend that the client does not receive the treatment again. Record this on her record card.

AFTERCARE AND ADVICE

Advise your client not to apply make-up for at least 24 hours. Similarly, she should not receive any other eye treatments for at least 24 hours.

Subsequently, however, eyelash tinting will enhance the effect of the newly permed lashes, so you can promote this service to the client.

Assessment of knowledge and understanding

You have now learnt about the different eye treatments available to treat the lashes and the eyebrows. These skills will enable you to enhance the appearance of the eyebrows and lashes.

To test your level of knowledge, answer the following short questions. These will prepare you for your summative (final) assessment.

Consult with the client

1 How should all client records be stored to comply with the Data Protection Act 1998?

2 Good communication is important. Why is it important to have a thorough consultation before you commence the treatment?

3 If the client is having an eyelash/brow tint why is it important to check the results of the skin test before you proceed?

4 Why is a skin sensitivity test needed before every tinting treatment?

5 What eye disorders would contra-indicate treatment?

6 What factors should you consider when deciding the correct eyebrow shape for a client?

7 How can you determine the length of a client's eyebrows that will best suit her facial features?

8 How do you select the colour when carrying out a permanent tinting treatment?

9 What details should be recorded on the client's record card?

10 Why is it important to keep a record of the treatment carried out?

Prepare for the treatment

1 What are the acceptable methods of sterilisation for tweezers?

2 How would you prepare the treatment area to ensure general client comfort during treatment application?

3 How should the client be positioned for the eye treatment to avoid discomfort and ensure effective treatment application?

4 How should the brows be prepared to minimise discomfort and the risk of infection, before shaping commences?

5 How should the lash and brow area be prepared to avoid skin staining and to ensure effective tinting?

Plan the treatment

1 Why is it important that the eye treatment is given in the allocated time?

2 Why is it important to discuss the treatment plan with the client before treatment commences?

3 It is important to select the correct and most suitable equipment and materials for the treatment. When would you use the following?
- automatic tweezers
- manual tweezers.

4 If the client wished to have her fair brows tinted, but had a positive reaction to the skin test, what could you recommend as an alternative?

Shape the eyebrows to meet the client's treatment requirements

1 How long would you allocate to carry out an eyebrow shaping treatment?

2 How can you ensure that hairs are removed at their root?

3 What factors should you consider in your approach to eyebrow shaping with the following clients?
- a client with excessively thick eyebrows who requests a thin eyebrow shape
- a client who has close-set eyes
- a client with a round face
- a client who has a few stray long, coarse hairs
- a client with sensitive skin.

4 How should consumables used during a brow shape be disposed of?

5 What hygiene and safety precautions should be followed when performing an eyebrow shape?

6 Give two examples of contra-actions that may occur following eyebrow shaping.

7 What action would you take if a skin contra-action occurred following eyebrow shaping?

Tint the eyebrows and lashes to meet the client's treatment requirements

1 How long would you allocate to carry out an eyelash and eyebrow tint?

2 Why is the quantity of tint applied to the area important in relation both to efficiency and the final result?

3 How would permanent tinting be performed when treating the following:
- a very nervous client, to ensure a safe, efficient eyelash tinting treatment
- a client who requires an eyebrow shape and an eyebrow tint. In which order should these treatments be given and why?

4 What is the difference in processing time between a brow tint and an eyelash tint?

5 How long would you allow the tint to process when treating a client with:
- blonde hair
- grey hair
- red hair
- dark hair?

6 If a client complained of irritation during an eyelash tinting treatment, what action would you take?

7 How would a contra-action to permanent tint be recognised?

Complete the treatment

1 Why is a soothing antiseptic lotion applied following an eyebrow shaping treatment?

2 What aftercare advice should be given to a client following an eyebrow shaping treatment?

3 What aftercare advice should be given to a client following a permanent tinting treatment?

4 When would you recommend that a client returns to the salon for an eyebrow trim, following an eyebrow shape?

5 When would you recommend that the client returned to the salon for a permanent tinting treatment:
- for the eyelashes
- for the eyebrows?

Perm eyelashes to meet client requirements

1 How can you ensure the eyelashes are securely attached to the curler?

2 Why should crossing the eyelashes be avoided when fixing the hair to the curler?

3 Why are the bottom lashes often protected with a protective shield during perm lotion application to the upper lashes?

4 How will timing following perm lotion application vary according to hair texture, colouring and previous treatment of the eyelashes, including perming and tinting?

5 What lotion is applied to fix the hair into its new curled shape?

6 How are the curlers removed following neutralising fixing procedure?

7 How often would you recommend a client has her eyelashes permed?

8 What other eye treatment service would enhance the effect of eyelash perming?

chapter 8

REMOVE HAIR USING WAXING TECHNIQUES

BT6

Hair removal is a popular treatment in the beauty salon, where both temporary and permanent methods of removal are usually available. Temporary removal must be repeated regularly, as the removed hair will regrow. With permanent methods, the client needs to visit the salon regularly to have the hair removed; thereafter, the part of the hair responsible for its growth has been destroyed and the hair will not grow again.

Temporary measures

Depilatory waxing

Depilatory waxing, using a warm, hot or cold wax, involves applying wax to the treatment area, embedding the hairs in it. When the wax is removed

ACTIVITY

Hair removal
Make short notes on the suitability and effectiveness of the different methods of hair removal.

from the area, the hairs are removed also, at their roots. They grow again in approximately four weeks.

Plucking

Plucking or **tweezing** uses a pair of tweezers to remove the hair. These grasp the hair near the surface of the skin, and the hair is then plucked in the direction of growth, again removing it at its root. The hair grows again in approximately four weeks.

Threading

Threading involves the use of a thread of twisted cotton, which is rolled over the area from which the hair is to be removed: the hairs catch in the cotton, and are pulled out. This skill is frequently practised by people of Asian or Mediterranean origin.

Due to the sensitive nature of the eye tissue, tweezing is often considered the most suitable choice for temporary hair removal from eyebrows.

Permanent measures

Electrical methods

Galvanic electrolysis, **electrical epilation** and the **blend epilation technique** are all techniques that use an electrical current. The current is passed to the hair root via a fine needle inserted into the hair follicle. The current destroys the hair root, preventing hair regrowth.

A cross-section of the hair follicle and hair

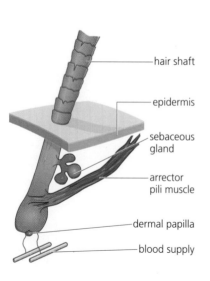

- hair shaft
- epidermis
- sebaceous gland
- arrector pili muscle
- dermal papilla
- blood supply

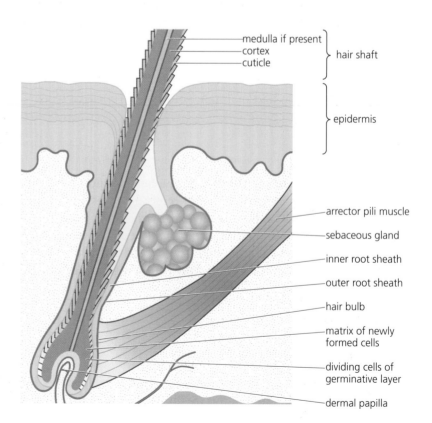

- medulla if present
- cortex
- cuticle
- } hair shaft
- } epidermis
- arrector pili muscle
- sebaceous gland
- inner root sheath
- outer root sheath
- hair bulb
- matrix of newly formed cells
- dividing cells of germinative layer
- dermal papilla

The hair bulb

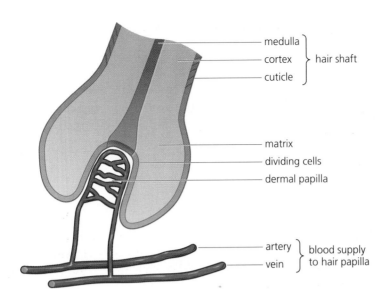

The client needs to understand that the hair will never grow back if
effectively treated with any of the above permanent methods. This is an
important consideration when treating the brow hair, as the desired shape
and thickness of the brows change frequently under the influence of fashion.

There are other methods of hair removal that the client may have used at
home previously.

- *Cutting the hairs with scissors* Scissors are used to trim the hair close to
  the skin's surface.

- *Shaving* A razor blade is stroked over the skin, against the natural hair
  growth. This removes the hair at the skin's surface.

- *Depilatory cream* A strong alkaline chemical cream is applied to the hair,
  and removed after 5–10 minutes: the hair will have been dissolved at the
  skin's surface.

The hair growth cycle

WAX DEPILATION

Wax depilation involves using wax to remove hair temporarily from the face and body. Waxing removes both the visible hair and the root, so the regrowth is of completely new hairs with soft, fine-tapered tips. It will take 4–6 weeks before the client requires the service again.

RECEPTION

When the client is booking her treatment she should be asked whether she has had a wax treatment before in the salon. If she has not, a small area of waxing should be carried out as a test patch, to ensure that she is not sensitive to the technique or allergic to any of the products used. If this test-patch causes an unwanted reaction within 48 hours, then the treatment must not be undertaken.

Advise the client not to apply any lotions or oils to the area on the day of her treatment – these could prevent the adhesion of the wax to the hairs being removed. Ask her also to allow at least one week, and preferably two, between any home shaving or other depilatory treatment and a salon waxing treatment. This is to let the hairs grow to a length sufficient to be waxed.

Treatment	Warm waxing (minutes)	Hot waxing (minutes)	Sugaring (minutes)
Half leg	30	30	20–30
Half leg and bikini	30	45	45–50
Full leg	50	60	55
Full leg and bikini	60	60–75	60–75
Bikini	15	15	15–20
Underarm	15	15	15
Half arm	15	15–20	15–20
Full arm	30	20–30	20–30
Top lip	5	5–10	5–10
Chin and throat	10	20	15–20
Top lip and chin	15	15–20	15–20
Eyebrows	15	10–15	10–15

Allow a 4–6-week interval between successive wax depilation appointments. The times to be allowed for wax treatments are as shown in the table.

It is important to complete treatment in the time allowed in order to be efficient in treatment application and to ensure the appointment schedule runs smoothly and clients are not kept waiting.

CONTRA-INDICATIONS

If the client has any of the following, wax depilation must not be carried out:

- *Skin disorders*, such as bruising or recent haemorrhage.
- *Swellings*.
- *Diabetes*.
- *Defective circulation*.
- *Folliculitis*.
- *Recent scar tissue*.
- *Fractures or sprains*.
- *Severe varicose veins*.
- *Loss of skin sensation*.

Certain contra-indications restrict treatment application. This may mean that the treatment has to be adapted for the client. For example, in the case of a small, localised bruise the area could be avoided.

Other contra-indications that restrict treatment include:

- Cuts
- Abrasions
- Self tan
- Heat rash
- Bruises
- Sunburn
- Warts
- Hairy moles
- Varicose veins (non-severe)

TIP	

Waxing a client with a recent well-established suntan may cause the loose sun-damaged epidermis to peel and be lost, along with the hair.

TIP	

Precaution if there is a restrictive contra-indication present
If there is a hairy mole or small abrasion you may apply petroleum jelly to avoid wax adherence.

Advising the client on the most appropriate temporary hair removal method, consider:
– area to be treated
– hair type, vellus/terminal
– amount of hair
– skin sensitivity

Maintaining client privacy at all times

Recording personal details on the client record card, name/address, etc. Check that there are no contra-indications to temporary hair removal

Inviting the client to ask questions. The client should fully understand what the treatment includes

Consult with the client to remove hair using temporary methods by

Looking for contra-indications, do not provide treatment if present. Not all contra-indications can be seen, for example diabetes. These are checked verbally

Completing the consultation
• Explain what is involved with the hair removal methods
• How long the treatment takes
• Expected sensations and treatment skin reactions
• Aftercare requirements
• Costs

Clients should be advised to allow preferably 2 weeks between home shaving and other temporary methods before a salon waxing treatment

Discussing what methods of hair removal have been used previously and when they were last used

BEAUTY WORKS

Date	Beauty therapist name	
Client name		Date of birth (identifying client age group)
Address		Postcode
Evening phone number	Day phone number	
Name of doctor	Doctor's address and phone number	
Related medical history (conditions that may restrict or prohibit treatment application)		
Are you taking any medication (this may affect the sensitivity and skin reaction following treatment)		

CONTRA-INDICATIONS REQUIRING MEDICAL REFERRAL
(Preventing hair removal treatment)

- ☐ bacterial infection (e.g. impetigo)
- ☐ viral infection (e.g. herpes simplex/warts)
- ☐ fungal infection (e.g. tinea corporis)
- ☐ severe skin conditions
- ☐ diabetes
- ☐ severe varicose veins

TEST CONDUCTED

- ☐ self
- ☐ client

WAX PRODUCTS

- ☐ hot wax
- ☐ warm wax – spatula method
- ☐ warm wax – roller system
- ☐ strip sugar
- ☐ sugar paste

WORK TECHNIQUES

- ☐ keep the skin taut during application and removal
- ☐ speed of product removal
- ☐ direction and angle of removal
- ☐ ongoing wax product temperature checks

CONTRA-INDICATIONS WHICH RESTRICT TREATMENT
(Treatment may require adaptation)

- ☐ cuts and abrasions
- ☐ bruising and swelling
- ☐ self tan
- ☐ skin disorders
- ☐ heat rash
- ☐ sunburn
- ☐ warts or hairy moles
- ☐ mild eczema/psoriasis

AREAS TREATED FOR HAIR REMOVAL

- ☐ eyebrows
- ☐ facial
- ☐ legs
- ☐ underarm
- ☐ bikini line
- ☐ arm

Beauty therapist signature (for reference)

Client signature (confirmation of details)

This information includes
- advice re products that would be suitable for a client to apply at home to soothe and care for her skin to reduce redness and irritation and prevent secondary infection
- advice re avoidance of activities, actions and treatments that may cause irritation and poor skin healing. These include:
  - exposure to ultra-violet treatments to avoid irritation and skin pigmentation
  - avoidance of perfumed or chemical-based products such as body lotion and fake tan preparations to avoid skin irritation
  - wearing of restrictive clothing to avoid skin irritation
  - avoidance of touching the treated area to prevent skin infection
  - avoidance of swimming and other exercise to avoid skin irritation
  - advice on the use of exfoliating products to prevent ingrowing hairs
- contra-action advice and action to be taken in the event of an unwanted skin reaction
- recommendations for further temporary hair removal treatments
- the recommended time intervals between treatments

The therapist must not carry out a wax treatment immediately after a heat treatment, such as a sauna, or steam or ultraviolet treatments, as the heat-sensitised tissues may be irritated by the wax treatment.

If you are unsure if treatment may commence, refer the client to their General Practitioner for permission to treat. If the treatment cannot be carried out for any reason, always explain why, without naming a contra-indication, as you are not qualified to do so. Clients will respect your professional advice.

EQUIPMENT AND MATERIALS

Types of wax

Warm wax

Warm wax first became available in 1975 and is now the market leader for hair removal. It is clean and easy to use; and because it is disposed of afterwards it is also hygienic. Finally, it is very economical.

Warm wax is used at a low temperature, around 43°C, so there is little risk of skin burning, and in less sensitive areas the wax can be re-applied once or even twice if necessary.

Warm wax does not set but remains soft at body temperature. It adheres efficiently to hairs and is quick to use; treatment is relatively pain-free. It can remove even very short hairs (2.5 mm) from legs, arms, underarms, the bikini line, the torso, the face and the neck.

Warm waxes are frequently made of mixtures of glucose syrup and zinc oxide. Honey (fructose syrup) can be used instead of glucose syrup, and this type is often called **honey wax**.

Hot wax

Hot wax takes longer to heat than warm wax, and is relatively slow to use, taking approximately double the time of a warm waxing.

A wax-depilation heater and trolley

As hot wax is used at quite a high temperature, 50°C, extra care must be taken to avoid accidental burns. Because of this risk, hot wax cannot be re-applied to already treated areas.

Hot wax cools on contact with the skin. It contracts around the hair shaft, gripping it firmly. This makes it ideal for use on stronger, short hairs.

Hot waxes for hair removal need to be a blend of waxes and resins so that they stay reasonably flexible when cool. **Beeswax** is a desirable ingredient, and often comprises 25–60 per cent of the finished product. **Cetiol**, **azulene** and **vitamin E** are often added to wax preparations to soothe the skin and minimise possible skin reactions.

Cold wax

Cold wax is used cold straight from its container (although some do in fact need gentle heating). It is spread with a clean spatula, and removed using a Cellophane, muslin or paper strip. This product was designed for home use by the public, and is not generally seen in salons.

Cold waxes are often natural rubber solutions in a volatile solvent. The solvent evaporates from the skin to leave a rubber film with the hairs embedded in it: this is pulled off and thrown away. The adhesion between the rubber and the hair is not sufficient for strong terminal hair or short hair growth.

Sugar wax

There are two methods of sugar wax hair removal – *sugar paste* and *strip sugar*.

Sugar paste is applied to the skin, using the hands, in the direction of hair growth. The hairs embed in the wax, which is then removed swiftly against hair growth, removing the hairs.

Strip sugar is similar in application and removal to warm wax and requires a wax removal strip to remove the wax, against hair growth. Sugar wax has pure sugar as the main ingredient, plus other natural ingredients such as lemon.

Warm waxing

To carry out warm waxing you will need the following equipment and materials:

- *Wax heater* – with a thermostatic control, a lid and a central bar.
- *Couch* – with sit-up and lie-down positions and an easy-to-clean surface.
- *Trolley* – to hold all the necessary equipment and materials.
- *Disposable tissue roll* – such as bed roll.
- *Protective plastic couch cover*.
- *Disposable wooden spatulas* – a selection of differing sizes, for use on different body areas.
- *Wax-removal strips (bonded-fibre)* – thick enough that the wax does not soak through, but flexible enough for ease of work. These strips should be cut to size and placed ready in a container.

ACTIVITY

Methods of hair removal
Other methods of temporary hair removal include the professional use of threading; and the home use of plucking, cold wax, ready-waxed strips, sugaring, electrical devices, chemical depilatory creams, shaving and pumice powder. Find out how each method works and assess its effectiveness. Are any of them potentially hazardous?

ACTIVITY

Wax heaters
Look in current beauty magazines for the different types of wax heater, including roll-ons. Try to see demonstrations of them working. Discuss size, cleaning, safety, hygiene and any other points that you think are important. Which heater would you choose, and why?

- *Talcum powder*.
- *Cottonwool pads* – for cleaning equipment and the client's skin.
- *Facial tissues (white)* – for blotting skin dry.
- *Alcohol-based skin cleanser (professional)* or *antiseptic wipes* – the cleanser is also called a pre-wax lotion.
- *Surgical spirit* – or a commercial cleaner designed for cleaning equipment.
- *Towels (medium-sized)* – for draping around the client.
- *Small scissors (curved)* – for trimming over-long hairs.
- *Disinfecting solution* – in which to immerse small metal implements.
- *Tweezers* – for removing stray hairs.
- *Wax* – see below.
- *After-wax lotion* – with soothing, healing and antiseptic qualities.
- *Mirror (clean)* – for facial waxing.
- *Apron* – to protect workwear from spillages.
- *Disposable surgical gloves*.
- *Bin (swing-top)* – lined with a disposable bin-liner.
- *Client's record card*.
- *List of contra-indications*.
- *Aftercare leaflets*.

When choosing a wax, select one with the following qualities:

- It should have a low melting temperature – the wax should be liquid at body temperature (37°C), and very runny at around 43°C.
- It should be easy to remove from equipment.
- It should be able to remove short, strong hairs (25 mm).
- It should have a pleasant fragrance or no smell.
- It should not stick to the skin, but only to the hair.

EQUIPMENT LIST

couch
trolley
disposable wooden spatulas
wax removal strips (bonded-fibre)
cottonwool pads
facial tissues
alcohol-based skin cleanser (also known as pre-wax lotion)
tweezers
wax
disposable surgical gloves
bin (swing-top)
see opposite for complete list of materials required

 HEALTH AND SAFETY

Personal Protective Equipment Act (PPE) at Work Regulations 1992
Waxing is a treatment where there is a risk of contamination and cross-infection, therefore protective equipment such as gloves should be available and worn.

Sterilisation and sanitisation

Disposable waste from waxing may have body fluids on it: potentially it is a health risk. It must be handled, collected and disposed of according to the local environmental health regulations. It is a good idea to wear disposable rubber gloves whilst carrying out the treatment, to protect yourself from body fluids.

 HEALTH AND SAFETY

Contaminated waste
Any wax waste that contains bodily fluids should be bagged separately from other regular waste and special arrangements made for its disposal.

Wash your hands regularly, before and after preparing the work area and before application of the disposable gloves. This shows the client that you have a high standard of hygiene.

An apron should be worn to protect work wear from wax spillage.

Preparing the cubicle

To enable the hairs to be removed effectively the treatment area should be well lit and warm as the client must be made as comfortable as possible when performing the treatment. If the client is cold the follicles will restrict, making hair removal more difficult.

Before the client is shown through, the cubicle and its contents should be checked to ensure that they are clean and tidy. The bins should have been emptied since the previous client.

Check the trolley to ensure that you have all that you need for carrying out the treatment, and that the wax is of a suitable consistency, i.e. ready for application.

The plastic-covered couch should be clean, having previously been washed with hot soapy water or wiped thoroughly with surgical spirit or a professional alcohol-based cleaner. The use of an additional heavy-duty plastic sheet is recommended: this is easier to wipe than the couch, and can be replaced if damaged.

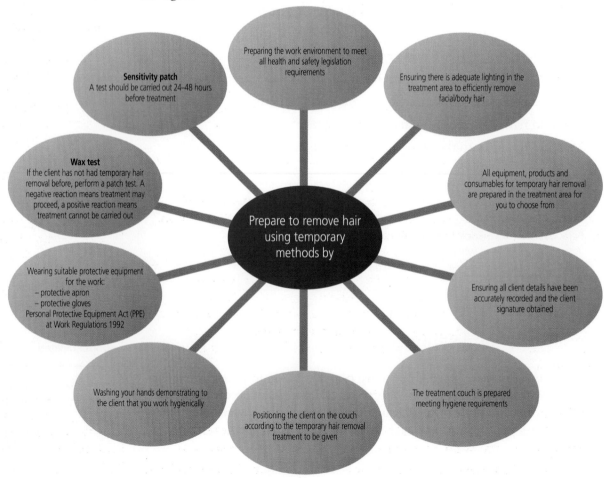

The couch should then be covered and protected with a long strip of paper-tissue bed roll. Place a towel neatly on the couch, ready to protect the client's clothing and to cover her when she has undressed. The tissue should be disposed of after use, and the towel freshly laundered for each client.

The couch should be in the sit-up position, unless the client is only having her bikini line or underarm areas waxed, in which case it should be flat.

HEALTH AND SAFETY

Couch covers
If the salon chooses to use stretch-towelling couch covers or additional towels to provide extra comfort, these must be provided clean for each client and laundered in hot soapy water after use.

PREPARING THE CLIENT

After the record card has been completed at reception, the client should be asked to read the list of contra-indications and sign to state that she is not suffering from any of the problems stated. She should then be shown through to the cubicle, and asked to remove specific items of clothing as necessary so that the treatment may be carried out.

ACTIVITY

Ensuring client comfort
Imagine that you are a client who has never had a waxing treatment before. You are shown through to a cubicle and left to 'Get yourself ready, please.' How would you feel? What would you do? What clothing would you think it necessary to remove for each area of waxing?

Ask the client whether it is the first time she has had the treatment: if it is, explain to her that the treatment can be uncomfortable, but it is quick and any discomfort experienced is tolerable.

Be efficient and quick, so that the client does not have to wait. Try to get her talking about something pleasant, such as a holiday, to take her mind off the treatment. Throughout the treatment, reassure her, praising her in order to motivate her to continue with her treatments. Do try to be sympathetic to your client's feelings, and provide support and encouragement when necessary. Waxing, although a necessity for many people, is not a particularly pleasant or relaxing treatment.

1 Use a towel to protect the client's remaining clothing.
2 Wipe the area to be waxed with a professional antiseptic pre-wax cleansing lotion on cottonwool. Blot the area dry with tissues before applying the wax. While wiping the skin, look for contra-indications.
3 Record any bruising on her record card to avoid potential problems later.

TIP

When a client books for a bikini-line wax, ask her when she comes for her treatment to wear an old pair of high-cut panties.

TIP

Client records
In accordance with the **Data Protection Act 1998**, confidential information on clients should only be made available to persons to whom consent has been given. All client records should be stored securely, and be available to refer to at any time as required.

TIP

Here are some useful explanatory phrases: 'It's a bit like ripping a plaster off, and taking the hairs with it. It isn't so bad, or so many people wouldn't have it done time and time again!'

TIP

If there is any bruising on the client's legs, tactfully draw her attention to these bruises, or she might later think that the treatment has caused them.

Cleansing the skin of the lower leg

4 If the client's skin is very greasy (she may for example have applied oil before coming to the salon), cleanse it using an astringent lotion such as witchhazel.

5 Immediately before starting the treatment, wash your hands.

TIP

A woman's pain threshold is at its lowest immediately before and during her period. The hormones which stimulate the regrowth of hair are also at their most active during this period. For these two reasons, avoid wax depilation at this time if possible.

WARM WAXING

General techniques

Warm waxing has a few basic rules which must be followed to ensure a good result.

HEALTH AND SAFETY

Temperature of wax
Before applying the wax, check its temperature. Test the wax on yourself first, to ensure that it's not too warm; then try a little on a small visible area of the client (such as the inside of the ankle) before spreading it on other areas.

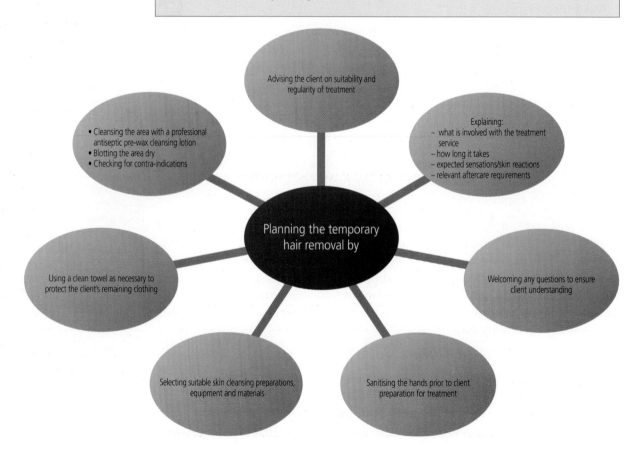

1 Observe the direction of hair growth. Warm wax must always be *applied with* the direction of hair growth, and *removed against* the direction of growth. This ensures both maximum adhesion between the hair, the strip and the wax, and that the hair will be pulled back on itself in the follicle and thus removed complete with its bulb.

2 Dip the spatula into the wax. Remove the excess on the sides and tip by wiping the spatula against the metal bar or the sides of the tub. Place the strip under the spatula while transferring it to the client: this will control dripping and improve your technique.

3 Place the spatula onto the skin at a 90° angle, and push the wax along in the direction of the hair growth. Do not allow the spatula to fall forward past 45°. The objective is to coat the area with a very thin film of wax. Quite a large area can be spread with each sweep of the spatula, as warm wax does not set. Do not attempt to smooth out or go over areas on which wax has already been spread, however, as the wax will have become cooler and will not move again, but will drag painfully on the client's skin.

4 Fold back 20 mm at the end of a strip and grip the flap with the thumb widthways across the strip. The flap should provide a wax-free handle throughout the treatment.

5 Place the strip at the bottom end of the wax-covered area, and make a firm bond between the wax and the strip by pressing firmly along the strip's length and width, following the direction of hair growth. If the strip is placed anywhere but at the *bottom* of a waxed area, the hairs at the bottom of the strip will become tangled together and held in the wax on the area below the strip: the removal of the strip will then be far more painful for the client.

6 Using the non-working hand, stretch the skin to minimise discomfort. Gripping the flap tightly, use the working hand to remove the strip against the direction of hair growth. Use a firm, steady pull. Make sure that the strip is pulled back on itself, close to the skin. (To obtain the correct angle of pull, stand at the side of the client, facing her.) Maintain this same horizontal angle of pull until the last bit of the strip has left the skin: *do not pull the strip upwards at the end of the pull*, as this would break the hairs at the end of the strip and be very painful.

7 The strip may be used many times; in fact it works best when some wax builds up on its surface. When there is too much wax on the surface it will stop picking up more: throw it away and start with a new one.

8 Do not repeatedly spread and remove wax over one area. In particular, wax should not be spread and removed more than twice on sensitive areas such as the bikini line, the face and the underarms. Any remaining stray hairs must instead be removed using sterilised tweezers.

TIP

The faults most commonly seen in warm-wax depilation are these:
- spreading the wax too thickly;
- placing the strip in the middle of a wax-spread area, instead of starting at the bottom and working up;
- pulling the strip upwards instead of backwards, away from the leg.

TIP

An angled follicle may cause the hair to be broken off at the angle during waxing, instead of being completely pulled out with its root. If this happens, broken hairs will appear at the skin's surface within a few days.

By causing damage to the follicle and changing its shape, waxing can cause the regrowth of hairs to be frizzy or curled where previously they were straight.

TIP

The thinner the wax, the easier the treatment is to carry out and the better the result. Also, less wax and fewer strips are used.

TIP

Wax spilt on carpets can be removed by placing fabric waxing strips or brown paper over the spill, and running a warm iron over them.

TIP

To take the sting out of the removal, immediately place a hand or finger over the depilated area.

Half leg treatment

The areas of the body where warm-wax hair removal is most frequently used are the lower legs. This is often referred to simply as a **half leg treatment**. A 'pair of half legs' should take 20–30 minutes to treat, and use no more than two or three strips.

1 Prior to the treatment, the area to be waxed should be cleansed as previously described.

2 Sit the client on the upraised couch, with both legs straight out in front of her.

3 Spread the wax on the *front* of the leg further away from you. Use three sweeps of the spatula: each sweep should go from just below the knee to the end of hair growth at the ankle.

   Repeat this pattern of spreading on the leg nearer to you. (By spreading the further leg first, you will not have to lean over an already waxed area.)

4 Starting with the nearer leg, remove the wax using the strip. Start at the ankle and work upwards towards the knees.

   Repeat for the other leg.

5 Ask the client to bend her legs to one side. Beginning again with the further leg, spread wax on one *side* of the leg, from the knee to the ankle, using two sweeps of the spatula.

   Repeat for the nearer leg.

6 Starting with the nearer leg, remove the wax from the bottom upwards.

   Repeat for the other leg.

Applying warm wax to the lower leg

Spreading on wax (to show the angle of the spatula)

Applying a strip

Applying warm wax to the knee

Removing the wax strip from the knee

7 Repeat steps **5** and **6** for the other side of the legs.

8 Bend one knee. Spread the wax from just above the knee, downwards.

9 Remove this wax from the bottom upwards, remembering that strips cannot pull around corners effectively. To keep the angle of the pull horizontal, remove wax below the knee first, then that above the knee.

10 Repeat steps **8** and **9** for the other knee.

11 Lower the back rest and ask the client to turn over.

12 On the *back* of the legs, the direction of hair growth is not from the top to the bottom but sweeping at an angle, from the outside to the inside of the calf muscle.

Starting with the further leg, spread wax following the direction of the natural hair growth.

Repeat for the nearer leg.

13 Starting with the nearer leg, remove the wax against the direction of the natural hair growth.

Repeat for the other leg.

14 Finally, apply after-wax lotion to clean cottonwool and apply this to the back of the client's legs. As you apply the lotion, check for hairs left behind: if there are any, remove them using tweezers.

Ask the client to turn over, and repeat application on the front of the legs. Remove any excess using a tissue.

> **TIP**
>
> The most common fault seen in half leg waxing is trying to take too big an area at once over the calf muscle and not supporting the surrounding tissues adequately. This will result in a painful treatment for the client.

Toes

Clients frequently request that their toes be waxed in conjunction with a half leg or full leg treatment. When doing this, follow the normal guidelines for waxing, but be aware that hair may grow in many directions. Cut strips into small pieces to effectively remove hair.

Wax spills

If you spill wax on the couch cover, immediately place a quarter-width facial-sized piece of strip on top of the spill. This prevents the wax from damaging the client's clothing when she moves.

Full leg treatment

A **full leg wax** should take 40–50 minutes and from four to six strips should be sufficient.

When doing a full leg wax, follow the same sequence of working as with the half leg. On the thighs, observe the direction of hair growth carefully, as the hair grows in different directions. It is best not to spread wax on too large an area at once, or you may forget the direction of growth. Each direction of hair growth should be treated as a separate area. It is of prime importance that you support the skin on the thighs as you remove the strip – the tissues in this area can bruise very easily. The two essential factors in preventing bruising, pain, and hair breakage are:

● the correct angle of pull;

● adequate support for the tissues.

Different temperatures

Summer heat and winter cold can each give rise to problems with the wax treatment. In summer, the wax stays too warm on the body, becoming sticky and difficult to work with, and tending to leave a sticky residue on the treated areas. In winter, the client's legs may be cold, causing the wax to set too quickly as you spread it, so that it becomes too thick. This prevents the efficient removal of both the wax and the hair growth.

To some extent these problems can be overcome by using thicker waxes with higher melting points in the summer, and thinner waxes with lower melting points in the winter.

Bikini-line treatment

A **bikini-line treatment** takes 10–15 minutes, and requires a new strip for each section to ensure effective hair removal from this delicate area.

1 Treat one side at a time. It is best if the client lies flat, as the skin's tissues are then pulled tighter, but the treatment can be carried out in a semi-reclining position if the client prefers. Bend the client's knee out to the side, and put her foot flat against the knee of the other leg. This is sometimes referred to as the **figure-four position**.

2 Tuck a tissue along and under the lower edge of the client's briefs. Raise this edge and agree with the client where she wants the final line to be. Hold the briefs slightly beyond this line, and ask the client to place her hand on top of the tissue to hold everything in place. This leaves you with both hands free, one to pull the strip and one to support the tissues.

3 Cleanse and dry the areas to be waxed.

4 Using sterilised scissors, trim both the hair to be waxed and the adjacent hairs down to about 5–12 mm in length. This is essential to avoid tangling, pulling and pain, and to prevent wax going onto hair that you do not want to remove.

5 Spread and remove the wax in two or three separate and distinct areas, the number depending on the directions of hair growth.

6 Use half of the strip length to remove the wax. Do not cover the whole area and tear it off at once! As soon as an area is completed, apply after-wax lotion. If necessary, use a clean tissue to remove excess lotion.

Applying warm wax to the bikini line

Applying a strip (showing the support of the skin area)

Removing the wax strip

7 With both legs straight out in front on the couch, place a tissue along the top edge of the client's briefs, against the abdomen. Lower the briefs as necessary to expose just the hair to be removed – check this with your client. Usually the direction of hair growth here sweeps in from the sides and then up to the navel.

8 Trim the hair as before.

9 Apply and remove the wax in small sections, carefully observing hair growth. On completion, apply after-wax lotion.

Underarm treatment

An underarm treatment should take 5–15 minutes and two strips, one for each underarm.

1 With her bra still on, ask your client to lie flat on her back with her hands behind her head, elbows flat on the couch.

2 Cleanse both underarms with pre-wax lotion on clean cottonwool; blot with a tissue.

3 Place a protective tissue under the edge of the bra cup on the side away from you. Ask the client to bring her opposite arm down and over, and to pull the breast away from the underarm being waxed and across towards the middle of her chest. This pulls the tissues tight, making the treatment a lot more comfortable for her; it also leaves you with both hands free, one to pull and one to support.

4 Underarm hair usually grows in two main directions. Observe the directions of hair growth, then apply and remove the wax separately for each small area.

5 Apply after-wax lotion to the treated area. Check for stray hairs; remove these with sterile tweezers.

6 Blot any excess cream with a clean tissue.

> **TIP**
>
> If certain types of water-soluble waxes are being used, perspiration may cause problems: it may prevent the wax from gripping the hair. Bear this in mind when selecting the wax to use on areas liable to perspiration such as the underarm and the top lip.

> **TIP** ✔
>
> Both bikini line and underarm waxing can be uncomfortable, especially if the hair growth is thick – always bear this in mind when carrying out the treatment. Some slight bleeding can be expected as the hairs in this area are very strong and have deep roots. Any waste contaminated by blood must be disposed of hygienically in a sealed bag.

Applying warm wax to the underarm (showing support)

Removing the wax strip

The completed area

Arm treatment

Depilation in this area should take 10–15 minutes for a **half arm treatment** and 20–30 minutes for a **full arm treatment**. Half the length of the strip should be used.

Arms are usually waxed with the client in the sitting position, her general clothing being protected with a towel. Sleeve edges can be protected with tucked-in tissues; ideally, though, upper outer clothing should be removed.

The roundness of the arm means that in order to effect a horizontal pull the work must be done in short lengths. Other than this, follow the general rules for waxing.

Face treatment

The **face treatment** must always be approached with extra care as facial skin is more sensitive than skin elsewhere on the body. Faulty technique can result in the top layer of skin being removed. (If this happens, a scab will form after about a day and the mark will take days to heal and fade completely.)

A **top-lip wax** should take approximately 5 minutes, a **chin and throat wax** approximately 10 minutes, and a **lip and chin wax** approximately 15 minutes. A removal strip of no more than one-eighth normal size should be used on the face.

1 The client should be in a semi-reclining position, with her head supported and a clean towel draped across her shoulders to protect her clothing. A clean headband can be used to keep the hair away from the face.

2 Cleanse and wipe over the area using an antiseptic cleansing lotion. Blot it dry with a tissue.

3 Spread and remove wax for small areas at a time, paying close attention to the direction of natural hair growth. (For example, you might need to spread one-half of the top lip with wax; remove this in three or four narrow strips; repeat the process on the other half; and finally treat the central section immediately under the nose.)

Do not allow wax to build up on the facial wax strips – such a build-up could lead to skin removal. Use a new strip for each area.

HEALTH AND SAFETY

The lips
The lips are extremely sensitive. To avoid possible irritation, do not allow the wax to come into contact with them.

Eyebrow treatment

Eyebrows, as a part of the face, are treated accordingly (see above). An **eyebrow wax** should take approximately 10–15 minutes.

TIP ✔

Previously bleached hair tends when waxed to break off at skin level. Clients should be told not to bleach facial hair if it is to be waxed.

HEALTH AND SAFETY ✚

Surgical spirit
Surgical spirit is too harsh for use on the face.

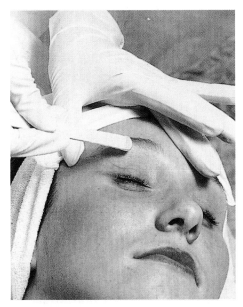

Applying warm wax to an eyebrow

Removing the wax strip

1 Study the eyebrows and decide upon their final shape and proportions.

2 Brush the eyebrows and separate the unwanted hair from the line of the other hairs.

3 Using a small spatula, apply a thin film of wax to the unwanted hairs in a small area. Remove the wax using a clean strip. Repeat in different areas, using a clean strip each time, until all the unwanted hairs have been removed.

4 Apply a soothing antiseptic cream and use sterile tweezers to remove any stray hairs.

HEALTH AND SAFETY

Sensitisation
Under no circumstances should wax be applied to facial hair, underarm hair or bikini-line hair more than twice during any one treatment. If after this any hairs remain, they must be removed with tweezers. The delicate skin in these areas readily becomes sensitised.

TIP

Other areas of the neck and face can be treated by wax depilation – for example to tidy up a haircut at the neckline, or to remove sideburns – provided that you follow the general guidelines for facial treatments.

Regrowth

Because of the cyclical nature of hair growth and the fact that follicles will be at different stages of their growth cycle when the hair is removed, the hair will not all grow back at the same time. Waxing can therefore appear to reduce the *quantity* of hair growth. This is not so, however, and the hair will all grow back eventually: waxing is therefore classed as a temporary form of hair removal.

Nevertheless, certain bodily changes (such as ageing), when *combined* with waxing, can result in permanent hair removal. This effect is so erratic and unpredictable, though, that waxing cannot reliably be sold as a permanent method of hair removal.

CONTRA-ACTIONS

Four contra-actions are quite common with waxing:

- ingrowing hairs;
- removal of skin;
- burns – both wax and friction burns;
- erythema – increased blood flow to the skin, giving a slight redness.

Ingrowing hairs

Ingrowing hairs can arise in three ways:

- *Over-reaction to damage* An excessive reaction by the skin and the follicle to the 'damage' produced by depilation may cause extra cornified cells to be made. These may block the surface of the follicle, causing the newly growing hair to turn around and grow inwards.
- *Overtight clothing* If after the treatment the client wears clothing that is too tight, this too can block the follicle.
- *Dry skin* Likewise dry skin can cause blockage of the follicle.

Ingrowing hairs can usually be recognised to be one or other of three types:

- *A hair growing along beneath the surface of the skin* Identify the tip (the pointed end); then pierce the tissues over the root end with a sterile needle. Free the tip and leave it in place so that the follicle can heal around it.
- *A coiled ingrowing hair* This looks like a small black spot or dome on the skin. If this is gently squeezed and rolled between the fingertips, using a tissue, it will release the coiled ingrowing hair and some hardened sebum. If the hair does not fall out, it should be left in place (as above).
- *An infected ingrowth* If the trapped sebum or hair starts to decay, either of the two preceding forms can become infected or begin to display an immune response. The area first becomes red (irritation); then an infected white dome-shaped pustule develops. Release the trapped tissue (as above), and cover the affected area – which may bleed, or leak tissue fluid – with a sterile non-allergenic dressing.

Skin removal

If the upper, dead, protective cornified layer of the skin is accidentally removed during a treatment – leaving the granular layer of the living, germinative layer exposed – the skin should be treated as if it has been burnt. Cool the area immediately by applying cold-water compresses for 10 minutes. Dry it carefully; then apply a dry, non-fluffy dressing to protect the area from infection. The dressing should be worn for 3–4 days, and the area then left open to the air. (Antiseptic cream by itself should be used only when the injury is very minor.) Medical attention should be sought if necessary.

Remove unwanted hair using temporary methods by

- Establishing the hair growth pattern before product application
- Ensure the treatment is cost effective and completed in a commercial time
  Eyebrow wax – 15 minutes
  Underarm wax – 15 minutes
  Half leg wax – 30 minutes
  Bikini-line wax – 15 minutes
  Arm wax – 30 minutes
  Full leg wax – 45 minutes
- Giving due care and consideration to health and safety legislation throughout the treatment
- Applying and removing depilatory products in accordance with manufacturer's instructions
- Applying a soothing antiseptic lotion following treatment to reduce redness and help skin healing
- **Roller wax, warm wax, strip sugar technique**
  - Apply with the direction of hair growth
  - Remove against the direction of hair growth
- Ensure client satisfaction and that the result meets the agreed treatment plan
- **Hot wax, sugar paste technique**
  - Apply against the direction of hair growth
  - Remove against the direction of hair growth
- If a contra-action occurred, discontinue the treatment and provide the appropriate advice
- **Warm wax, strip sugar and roller wax**
  - Aim to coat the area with a very fine film of wax
- Stray and very short hairs may be removed using a pair of sterilised tweezers
- Before after-wax lotion is applied check the treatment area is free from wax residue and stray hairs
- When removing wax use the non-working hand to stretch skin to minimise discomfort
- During hair removal treatment:
  - ensure the wax temperature is comfortable for the client
  - assess skin reaction to treatment
  - reassure the client

Burns

A burn should be treated as 'skin removal' (page 258). If blisters form, they should not be broken – they help prevent the entry of infection into the wound. Medical attention should be sought.

Erythema

Erythema is a visible redness, accompanied by an increase in warmth on the surface of the skin. It derives from increased blood flow through the capillaries near the surface of the skin, caused by the histamine reaction after waxing (page 31). Ask the client to follow the recommended aftercare advice.

AFTERCARE AND ADVICE

An **after-wax lotion** should be applied, using clean cottonwool, at the end of the treatment. This breaks down any wax residue, helps to guard against infection and irritation, and takes away any feelings of discomfort. Encourage your client to continue with the use of such a lotion at home for a few days: it will protect against dryness, discomfort and ingrowing hairs.

TIP

Before after-wax lotion is applied ensure that the treatment area is free of waxing product and hair and check that the finished result is to the client's satisfaction.

ACTIVITY

Aftercare leaflets

Discuss why aftercare leaflets should be given to clients, as well as giving them the advice verbally.

What could happen if aftercare advice is not given?

Advise the client against wearing any tight clothing (such as tights or hosiery) over the waxed areas for the 24 hours following a treatment. Such clothing could lead to irritation and ingrowing hairs.

If the client suffers from ingrowing hairs, she should **exfoliate** her skin every 4–7 days, starting two or three days after the treatment. Exfoliation prevents the build-up of dead skin cells on the surface of the skin; these would otherwise block the exit from the follicle and cause a growing hair to turn back on itself and grow inwards. Ingrowing hairs should be freed and, if possible, left in place so that the follicle exit will re-form around the hair's shaft.

Advise the client that for the 24 hours following her treatment she should not apply any talcum powders, deodorants, anti-perspirants, perfumes, self-tanning products or make-up over the treated areas. Any of these products could block the pores or cause irritation or allergy reactions on the temporarily sensitised area. During this time she must use only plain, unperfumed soap and water on the treated area.

For the same 24-hour period she should preferably avoid exercise, especially swimming, and not apply heat or ultraviolet treatments – hot baths, for example, or the use of a sunbed or sauna – as these would add to the heat generated in the skin following the treatment and would probably cause discomfort or irritation. She must also refrain from touching or scratching the area, so as to avoid infecting the open follicles.

Ensure that the client records are up to date, accurate and complete.

TIP

Aftercare leaflets should contain this information: these can be given to the client at the end of the treatment to remind her what to do at home.

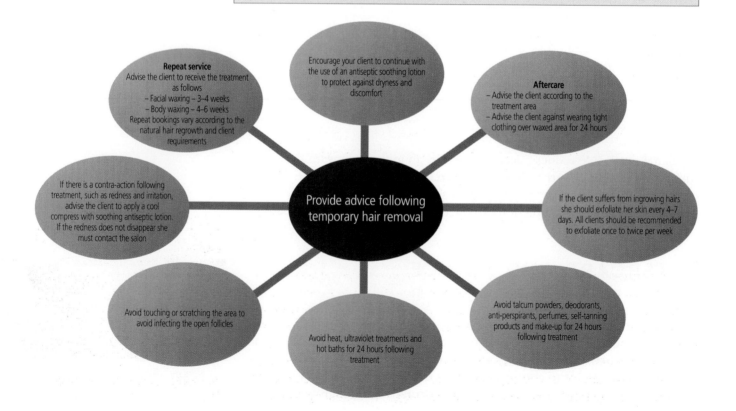

HOT WAXING

In **hot waxing**, the wax is applied at a higher temperature. The hairs embed in the wax and are gripped tightly as the wax cools and contracts. When the wax is pulled away, it removes the hair from the base of the follicle.

Equipment and materials

The equipment and materials required for hot waxing are the same as for warm waxing (page 246–7), except that:

- *a wax heater* suitable for hot wax should be selected;
- *wax-removal strips* are not necessary.

Some people prefer to apply the hot wax with disposable brushes rather than spatulas, but either can be used.

Carrying out the treatment

General technique

1 Ensure that the area to be waxed is clean and grease-free.
2 Apply a small amount of talc, against the direction of hair growth. This is to make the hairs stand on end and to stick more firmly into the wax.
3 Keep the same order of work as for warm waxing.
4 Apply wax in strips approximately 5 cm wide and 10 cm long, with about 5 cm distance between the strips.
5 Carefully observe the direction of hair growth and the size of the area to be waxed.
6 Test the heat of the wax on the inside of the wrist.

TIP ✔

If the wax is *not hot enough* when it is applied, it will not contract effectively around the hair and will therefore not grip it properly. This may result in poor depilation and possible hair breakage.

If on the other hand the wax is allowed to *overheat*, it may cause burns. Also, the quality of the wax will deteriorate and the wax will become brittle as it cools.

7 Using either a disposable spatula or a brush, apply a layer of wax about 5 cm × 10 cm *against* the direction of hair growth. Apply a second layer *with* the direction of growth; and a third layer *against* the direction of growth. (If two or three strips are applied at the same time, you can work faster.)

Keep the edges of the wax thicker than the middle, to make it easier to remove. Overlap the lower edge by about 2 cm onto a hair-free area: this makes it less painful later, when you lift the edge to make a lip to pull.

Applying hot wax to the lower leg

Removing the hot wax

TIP ✔

If the wax becomes too cool and brittle for removal, fresh hot wax may be applied with care over the area to soften it.

Curl up the lower end of the wax to make a lip, and press and mould the wax firmly onto the skin.

8 Leave the wax for a minute or so, to cool. The wax has to cool sufficiently to grip the hairs, but not so much that the wax becomes brittle and breaks on removal. As it sets, it starts to lose its gloss: it should be removed when this happens and while it is still pliable.

9 Support the area below the wax, grasp the lip, and tear the wax off the skin *against* the direction of hair growth in one movement (as with warm-wax removal). Immediately press or firmly stroke the area with your hand: this takes away some of the discomfort.

10 Check the area for any remaining wax and any stray hairs. Remove using tweezers. (Second applications are not advisable when using hot wax, because of the risk of burning.)

If this general application technique is followed, any area of the body can be depilated – use the same order of work as for warm waxing: observe the direction of hair growth and take into account the body area: use smaller strips in smaller areas; support the skin; and use the correct angle of pull for removal.

Aftercare and contra-actions

The contra-actions and aftercare are the same as for warm waxing (pages 258–60).

SUGARING AND STRIP SUGAR

Sugaring is an ancient and popular method for hair removal. The superfluous hairs become embedded in a pliable organic paste of sugar, lemon and water. The sugar paste is then removed from the skin's surface, against the hair's growth, leaving the skin hair-free.

Sugaring may be applied using a paste formulation removed with the hands, referred to as sugar paste, or in a formulation similar to warm wax, removed with material strips, referred to as **strip sugar**. Sugaring is effective on fine hair growth, and as it contains no chemicals or additives this method is unlikely to cause skin allergy.

RECEPTION

Re-book the client for sugaring hair removal every 4–6 weeks, dependent upon the hair growth rate and area. For effective hair removal, the hairs must be at least 2 mm long.

The equipment and materials required for sugaring are the same as for warm waxing (pages 246–7), except for the following differences.

Sugar paste

- *Wax heater (with a thermostatic control) or microwave* – to heat the paste.
- *Sugaring paste* – either soft or hard, depending on your personal preference and the temperature of the working environment: hard paste is a better choice in warmer temperatures and when working on coarser hair.
- *Talc (purified)*.
- *Bowl of clean water* – to remove the sugar paste from the hands, reducing stickiness.

TIP

Talc aids the sugaring treatment technique, by reducing stickiness when working with the paste, and by absorbing perspiration (particularly in areas such as the underarms).

Strip sugar

- *Wax heater (with a thermostatic control)* – to heat the strip sugar.
- *Strip sugar.*
- *Talc (purified)*.
- *Disposable wooden spatulas* – a selection of differing sizes, for use on different body areas.
- *Wax-removal strips (bonded-fibre)* – thick enough that the wax does not soak through, but flexible enough for easy working.
- *Disposable surgical gloves*.

Sterilisation and sanitisation

As sugar paste is water-soluble, it is easily cleaned from any surface. However, the wax heater containing the sugar wax must be regularly sanitised.

PREPARING THE CLIENT

1 Cleanse the area to be treated, using an antiseptic cleansing tissue.
2 Blot the skin dry.
3 Apply talc to cover the area: this prevents the sugar from sticking to the skin.

Cleaning with an antiseptic pre-wipe

Applying talc

Applying and removing sugar paste

Applying a cooling spray

Applying a soothing cream

SUGARING

Sugar paste

The sugar paste adheres to the hair and not to the skin, which allows the sugar to be reapplied to a treatment area. Technique is important and it takes practice and experience to become skilled.

1 Heat the sugar gently, to soften it.

2 Apply the sugar paste to the skin by hand. Select the amount used according to the treatment area. Draw the paste over the treatment area *in the direction* of the hair growth, embedding the hair in the paste.

3 Remove it quickly *against* the hair growth.

4 If necessary, reapply the paste to the area to remove further hairs. Continue this process until no hair remains.

5 After use, discard the paste as it will be contaminated with excess hair and dead skin cells: this affects the ease of paste removal, and presents a risk of cross-infection.

6 To complete the treatment, a cooling treatment spray may be applied to the area, followed by a soothing cream.

7 Record details of the treatment on the client's record card.

TIP

Sugar wax – both strip and paste – may be heated in a microwave to soften it. Check guidelines set by the microwave manufacturer on power and timing.

Applying strip sugar

Removing strip sugar

Strip sugar

This is similar in application and removal to warm wax.

1 The wax is gently heated until it is fluid.
2 Apply the wax using a spatula *in the direction of* the hair growth to cover the treatment area.
3 Remove the wax *against* the hair growth using a clean strip.
4 To complete the treatment, a cooling treatment spray may be applied to the area, followed by a soothing cream.
5 Record details of the treatment on the client's record card.

> **HEALTH AND SAFETY**
>
> **Temperature**
> Ensure that the temperature is correct – neither too hot, which may cause burning, nor too cool, which may make working uncomfortable and inefficient.

CONTRA-ACTIONS

General waxing contra-actions should be considered (see pages 258–9), as well as:

- *Ingrowing hairs* – caused by incorrect removal technique when using sugaring, or a build-up of dead skin cells over the hair follicle opening.
- *Discomfort* – caused by the wax being too hard, affecting application and efficient removal.
- *Burning*, of the client or the therapist – caused by the sugar paste or the strip sugar being too hot.

AFTERCARE AND ADVICE

General post-waxing advice should be offered (see pages 259–60). Appropriate aftercare retail products may be recommended such as an exfoliating body mitt, or antiseptic moisturising lotion to promote skin healing.

Disposable applicator waxing
systems

DISPOSABLE APPLICATOR ROLLER WAXING SYSTEMS

This is a hygienic method, using **disposable applicators** which are new for each client. A disposable applicator head screws onto the wax applicator tube in place of a cap. This reduces the possible risk of contamination through cross-infection. The method is considered less messy, as the wax is contained in the tube and is not exposed until application.

Each tube of wax as needed is heated to working temperature, which minimises the risk of burning.

WAXING THE LEGS

1 Follow general waxing preparation guidelines for the treatment area (see page 248).

2 Remove the disposable applicator from the right-hand heating and storage compartment.

3 Remove the cap from the tube of wax. Attach the applicator head to the tube.

Removing the applicator

Removing the cap from the tube

Releasing the applicator

Applying the wax

Returning the tube to the heat

Removing the wax from the leg

Collecting soothing lotion

Discarding the applicator

4 Release the applicator by lifting the lever upwards. Squeeze until a small amount of wax appears on the front of the applicator, then apply the wax. Hold the applicator at a 45° angle to the leg, and glide it smoothly down the leg.

5 Apply a thin film of wax to the front of both legs, then press down the closing device on the applicator to stop wax flow.

6 Wipe any wax residue from the front of the applicator and return the tube to heat.

7 Remove wax from the leg, starting at the ankle and working towards the knee. Support the skin with one hand, and firmly stretch it against the removal of the wax. Continue application and removal to the sides and back of the legs

8 When treatment is complete, apply antiseptic soothing lotion.

9 Record details of the treatment on the client's record card.

10 Remove the applicator from the tube, replacing the cap and returning the tube to the heater. Dispose of the applicator head.

AFTERCARE AND ADVICE

Follow the general aftercare and advice guidelines on pages 259–60.

LIGHTENING HAIR

Bleaching lightens the hair and is an effective way to disguise pigmented facial and body hair that the client finds unacceptable. The effect lasts up to 4 weeks.

The bleaching products, usually powder and cream, are mixed together and are immediately applied directly to the area to be lightened.

RECEPTION

The client should receive the bleaching treatment every 3–4 weeks. Allow 15–30 minutes when booking this service, according to the client's treatment requirements.

Treatment should not follow any preheating treatment such as facial steaming, as the pores would be open which could cause skin irritation.

Skin tests

1 Mix a small amount of the product, as directed by the manufacturer.

2 Apply a little of this to the inner arm, approximately 25 mm square. If there is an allergic reaction, remove the bleach product immediately.

3 After 10–15 minutes, remove the product using cool water applied with cottonwool.

4 Check the area over the next 24 hours to assess skin tolerance. Redness, itchiness and swelling indicate a positive (allergic) reaction.

5 Note the test result on the client's record card.

CONTRA-INDICATIONS

After completing the record card and inspecting the area, if you have found any of the following do not proceed with the bleaching treatment:

- *Hypersensitive skin.*
- *Dry, sensitive skin.*
- *Cuts and abrasions* in the area.
- *Skin disorder or disease.*
- *Positive reaction (allergy)* to a skin test.
- *Skin erythema.*

EQUIPMENT AND MATERIALS

- *Couch* – with sit-up and lie-down positions and an easy-to-clean surface.
- *Trolley* – to hold all the necessary equipment and materials.
- *Bleach powder* and *cream hydrogen peroxide* – in facial and body cosmetic formulations.
- *Cleansing cosmetic preparations* – to cleanse the area to be lightened.
- *Barrier cream* – to protect the surrounding areas.
- *Damp cottonwool* – to remove cleansing preparations and excess bleach from the skin and hair.

- *Bowl (clean)* – to hold the clean cottonwool.
- *Facial tissues (white)* – for blotting skin dry.
- *Headband* – to protect the scalp hair when performing facial bleaching.
- *Towels (medium-sized)* – to protect the client's clothing.
- *Non-metallic mixing dish* – metal would speed the decomposition of the product.
- *Disposable spatula* – for mixing and application.
- *Mirror (clear)* – for facial bleaching to show the client the effect produced for acceptability.
- *Soothing lotion* – to apply to the skin following bleaching.
- *Disposable surgical gloves* – to protect your hands.
- *Swing-top bin* – lined with a disposable bin-liner, for waste.
- *Client's record card*.

Sterilisation and sanitisation

Use disposable equipment where possible to avoid cross-infection. Wear protective gloves during application and removal of the bleach, to protect your hands from possible chemical contact.

Preparing the cubicle

Before the client is shown through to the cubicle, it should be checked to ensure that the required equipment and materials are available and the area is clean and tidy.

The couch or chair should be protected with a long strip of disposable tissue-paper bedroll, or a freshly laundered bedsheet and a bath towel. A small towel should be placed neatly at the head of the couch, ready to be draped across the client for protection. (The paper tissue will need replacing and the towels laundered for each client).

PREPARING THE CLIENT

Facial hair lightening

1 Protect the client's clothing with clean towels. A headband should be worn to protect the client's hair. Drape a small towel across her chest.

2 Cleanse and tone the area. Blot the skin dry with a clean facial tisssue. Ensure that the area is free of grease, which would form a barrier to the hair-lightening products.

3 For facial bleaching, the client should be slightly elevated.

> **TIP**
>
> The lightening process will vary according to the coarseness and colour of the client's hair. You should always consider this.

TIP

Advise the client that the part of the *skin* treated will be lightened slightly also. As this affects only the surface dead skin cells of the epidermis, the effect is temporary – usually 12–24 hours.

HEALTH AND SAFETY ✚

Bleaching products
Always mix the ingredients according to manufacturer's instructions.

A barrier cream may be applied to protect the surrounding area from the bleaching products.

HEALTH AND SAFETY ✚

Bleach
Never spread the bleach onto other surrounding areas unnecessarily.

Body hair lightening

1 Protect the client's clothing in the area with clean towels or disposable paper tissue.
2 Cleanse the area thoroughly, with a cleansing agent and clean cottonwool, to remove dead skin cells and any body oils or cosmetic lotions. Blot the skin dry with a clean facial tissue.
3 Position the client comfortably, in a position in which you are able to treat the area easily.

LIGHTENING THE HAIR

Facial hair

1 Place the required amount of powder and cream in a non-metallic dish, following the manufacturer's instructions. Mix well to a smooth opaque cream.
2 Using a clean, sanitised spatula, apply the bleach to the area. Cover the hair evenly.
3 Time the application accurately, taking into account:
   ● hair coarseness and pigmentation;
   ● skin type and tolerance.
4 If necessary – e.g. if the hair is very dark – apply the bleach a second time.
5 When the hair is sufficiently bleached, remove the bleaching products thoroughly, using a spatula and dampened cottonwool.

Applying bleach to the upper lip

Processing

Removing the bleach

The finished result

6 Dry the area with a facial tissue and apply an unperfumed moisturising agent.

7 Show the client the finished result in the mirror.

8 Discard the bleach and clean the mixing container.

9 Record the treatment details on the client's record card.

Eyebrows

1 The brows lighten very quickly. Lighten the brows to complement the colour of the client's scalp hair.

2 Show the client the finished result in the mirror.

3 Discard the bleach and clean the mixing container.

4 Record the treatment details on the client's record card.

Body hair: arms and legs

1 Mix sufficient bleach for one arm or one leg.

2 Allow the bleach to process, for approximately 15 minutes. If the hair is not sufficiently lightened, mix and apply the product for approximately a further 10 minutes.

3 Remove the mixture.

4 Mix new bleach and apply this to the other limb. Process and remove.

5 Discard the bleach and clean the mixing container.

6 Record the treatment details on the client's record card.

HEALTH AND SAFETY
Eye care Take great care to avoid the bleach mixture entering the eyes or sensitising the delicate eye tissue.

HEALTH AND SAFETY

Ultraviolet light
On areas that have been previously bleached, ultraviolet light may cause a reaction and hyperpigmentation in the skin.

CONTRA-ACTIONS

- *Irritation* – caused by skin intolerance. If irritation occurs, wash off the bleaching product immediately with clean water and apply a suitable soothing product. If irritation continues, obtain medical attention.

- *Erythema or skin burn* – caused by over-exposure to the bleaching agents, or using bleaching agents at an incorrect strength for the body part.

AFTERCARE AND ADVICE

A moisturising, soothing agent should be applied following treatment. For the next 24 hours the client should avoid possible sensitisers such as perfumed products and ultraviolet light.

Assessment of knowledge and understanding

You have now learnt about the different temporary hair removal methods available for the face and body. This knowledge will enable you to remove hair using temporary methods with waxing and sugaring techniques.

To test your level of knowledge, answer the following short questions. These will prepare you for your summative (final) assessment. Anatomy and physiology questions required for this unit are found on pages 129–31.

Consult with the client

1 To reassure the client, how would you explain to her the treatment sensation and expected post-treatment skin reaction?

2 It is necessary to check the hair growth before hair removal. How long should hair growth be before wax/sugar depilation can be carried out?

3 A client complains that on her previous treatment (which was her first), stubbly hairs appeared the following week. What could have been their cause?

4 When observing the area for hair removal, what conditions would contra-indicate treatment?

5 Why is diabetes normally regarded as a contra-indication to temporary hair removal methods?

Prepare for the treatment

1 What hygiene legislation should be followed in relation to wax and sugar depilation?

2 What hygiene precautions should be taken when completing wax depilation? Consider:
- the therapist's safety
- care of the client.

3 What is the recommended temperature of wax when using:
- hot wax
- warm wax – spatula method
- warm wax – roller method
- strip sugar?

4 What additional precautions should be taken to ensure that the wax is used at a comfortable temperature?

5 How should the area to be treated for wax depilation be prepared to ensure effective hair removal?

6 How would you position the client for temporary hair removal in the following areas:
- bikini wax
- underarm wax
- chin wax?

Plan the treatment

1 It is important to select the most suitable method to remove the hair type. From the following temporary hair removal methods – warm wax, hot wax, strip sugar and sugar paste – identify which you would select for:
- the face
- the underarm
- the bikini
- the legs
- the eyebrows?

2 It is necessary to consider the direction of hair growth for the hair removal technique chosen. Why is this?

3 Considering the body part to be treated, why is it important to consider the client's privacy and modesty?

4 Why is preparation of the area important in terms of lighting, heating and client comfort?

5 In compliance with your responsibilities under health and safety legislation, when should personal protective equipment be worn? Which Health and Safety Act does this come under?

6 Certain ingredients may cause an allergic reaction, therefore it is important that you know what the product contains. What are the main ingredients in:
  - warm wax
  - strip sugar.

Remove unwanted hair

1 How do hot wax and warm wax differ in relation to:
  - application
  - removal?

2 How does warm wax applied with a roller differ from that applied with a spatula in terms of:
  - application
  - removal?

3 Which contra-indications restrict treatment, meaning that the treatment may proceed, but the area contra-indicated must be avoided?

4 What would be three undesirable post-treatment skin reactions? How could these be avoided?

5 Why is it important to position yourself and the client correctly, (whilst considering her comfort) for hair removal?

6 How should contaminated waste be disposed of?

Complete the treatment

1 What aftercare instructions should be given to the client following wax depilation treatment for both the face and body?

2 If your client suffers from ingrowing hairs, what advice would you give her which could possibly prevent them reoccurring?

3 When would you book a client to return for the following repeat depilation treatments, and how long would you allow for each area:
  - eyebrow
  - full leg
  - bikini
  - underarm
  - arm?

chapter 9

PROVIDE MANICURE TREATMENT

`BT7`

THE PURPOSE OF A MANICURE

The word **manicure** is derived from the Latin words *manus*, meaning 'hand', and *cura*, meaning 'care'. A manicure therefore cares for the hands for the following reasons:

- to improve the hands' appearance;
- to keep the nails smooth;

ACTIVITY

Making appointments
What other questions could the receptionist ask in order to make the business run more efficiently? Write down your answers.

- to keep the cuticles attractive and healthy;
- to keep the skin soft.

RECEPTION

When a client makes an appointment for a manicure treatment, the receptionist should ask a few simple questions that will save time when she arrives for treatment.

- Does she require nail polish? With drying time, this part of the treatment can last up to 20 minutes, so the appropriate length of time needs to be booked out in the appointment book.
- Are any nails damaged or in need of repair? Again extra time will need to be allowed for this work.
- Does she require any services in addition to her nail treatment, such as paraffin wax or warm oil? Allow extra time accordingly.
- Has the client had artificial nails applied previously which require removal? Allow approximately 20 minutes for this process.

Allow 45 minutes for a manicure.

Allow up to 1 hour for a specialist hand-nail treatment.

BEAUTY WORKS

Date	Beauty therapist name	
Client name		Date of birth (identifying client age group)
Address		Postcode
Evening phone number	Day phone number	
Name of doctor	Doctor's address and phone number	

Related medical history (conditions that may restrict or prohibit treatment application)

Are you taking any medication (this may affect the sensitivity of the skin to the treatment)

CONTRA-INDICATIONS REQUIRING MEDICAL REFERRAL
(Preventing manicure treatment application)

- ☐ bacterial infections (e.g. paronychia)
- ☐ viral infections (e.g. plane warts)
- ☐ fungal infections (e.g. tinea unguium)
- ☐ severe nail separation
- ☐ severe eczema and psoriasis
- ☐ severe bruising

EQUIPMENT AND MATERIALS

- ☐ nail and skin treatment tools
- ☐ abrasives (e.g. buffing cream)
- ☐ cuticle softeners
- ☐ nail and skin products
- ☐ nail conditioners (e.g. cuticle cream)
- ☐ skin conditioners (e.g. hand cream)
- ☐ nail, skin and cuticle corrective treatments (e.g. paraffin wax)
- ☐ consumables

HAND AND NAIL TREATMENTS

- ☐ warm oil
- ☐ hand mask
- ☐ paraffin wax
- ☐ thermal mitts
- ☐ exfoliators

NAIL FINISH

- ☐ light colour
- ☐ dark colour
- ☐ french manicure
- ☐ buffing

CONTRA-INDICATIONS WHICH RESTRICT TREATMENT
(Treatment may require adaptation)

- ☐ minor nail separation
- ☐ minor eczema and psoriasis
- ☐ recent scar tissue
- ☐ severely bitten
- ☐ severely damaged nails
- ☐ broken bones
- ☐ minor cuts or abrasions
- ☐ minor bruising or swelling

COURSE OF TREATMENT

	Date	Date	Date
☐ improvement of skin condition products used	——	——	——
☐ improvement of nail condition products used	——	——	——

NAIL, CUTICLE AND SKIN CONDITION

nails	cuticle	skin
☐ normal	☐ dry	☐ dry
☐ brittle	☐ split	☐ hard
☐ dry	☐ overgrown	
☐ weak		
☐ ridged		

MASSAGE MEDIUMS

- ☐ creams
- ☐ oils

Beauty therapist signature (for reference)

Client signature (confirmation of details)

PRESENT NAILCARE ROUTINE

This information includes
- what products the client is currently using to care for her nails and hands and the regularity of their use
- how the client protects the hands to prevent dryness, such as wearing gloves when washing with a detergent-based cleaning agent
- details that may influence the clients nail condition, e.g. occupation

TREATMENT ADVICE

This information includes
- what products have been used in the manicure treatment
- advice re products that would be suitable for the client to use at home to care for the skin of her hands and nails
- advice on general care of the skin of the hands and nails
- advice on product application and removal in order to gain maximum benefit from their use
- contra-action advice, action to be taken in the event of an unwanted skin reaction
- recommendations for further manicure treatments
- the recommended time intervals between treatments

HEALTH AND SAFETY

You are not qualified to diagnose, this is the job of the GP.
Therefore if you are unsure about any nail or skin condition present refer the client to their GP.

TIP

Artificial nails
If the client has had several new sets of artificial nails applied this will damage the natural nail.

The nail plate may be thin, ridges may appear upon the nail plate and the removal technique, using acetone, will cause dehydration. All of these effects will need to be discussed with your client at consultation and an appropriate treatment plan discussed.

TIP

Removal of artificial nails
These are removed using a solvent containing acetone that softens the product, allowing removal from the natural nail. However, it is particularly drying to the natural nail which will later require rehydrating.
Procedure
Remove any nail polish, trim any excess length.
Soak the nails in acetone for approximately 20 minutes, until the product has thoroughly softened.
Remove the softened product with an orange stick.
Wash the hands and nails thoroughly to remove acetone.
Continue with manicure treatment.

SKIN AND NAIL DISORDERS OF THE HANDS

When a client attends for a manicure treatment, the therapist should always look at the client's skin and nails to check that no infection or disease is present which might contra-indicate treatment. Below is a list of common disorders that may be seen on the hands. Not all of these contra-indicate treatment.

Other bacterial, fungal and viral infections that relate to this unit are located in Chapter 1, where contra-indications are illustrated and discussed.

Disorder	Cause	Appearance	Salon treatment	Home-care advice
Onychophagy	Excessive nail-biting	Very little nail plate; bulbous skin at the fingertip; nail walls often red and swollen, due to biting of the skin surrounding the nails	Regular weekly manicures Cuticle treatment to maximise the visible nail-plate area	Bitter-tasting preparations painted onto the nail plate Wear gloves to avoid biting
Onychorrhexis	Using harsh detergents without wearing gloves Poor diet Not wearing gloves in cold weather	Split, flaking nails	Warm-oil manicures on a weekly basis	Regular use of a rich handcream Always wear rubber gloves when cleaning or washing up Always wear warm gloves in cold weather Ensure a balanced diet
Hangnail	Biting the skin around the nails Cracking of the dry skin or cuticle	Epidermis around the nail plate cracks and a small piece of skin protrudes between the nail plate and the nail wall, sometimes accompanied by redness and swelling: this condition can be extremely painful	Warm-oil treatments to soften the skin and cuticles Remove the protrusion of dead skin with cuticle nippers: do not cut into live tissue	Regular use of a rich handcream Wear rubber gloves when cleaning and washing up Wear warm gloves in cold weather Ensure a balanced diet
Longitudinal ridges in the nail plate (corrugated nails)	Illness Damage to the matrix Age	Grooves in the nail plate running from the cuticle to the free edge: may affect one or all nails	Abrasive buffing to smooth out the ridges Use of a ridge-filling base coat prior to nail polish application	General manicure advice

Dr A.L. Wright

Disorder	Cause	Appearance	Salon treatment	Home-care advice
Pterygium	Neglect of the nails	Overgrown cuticles, often tightly adhered to the nail plate: if left untreated, this may lead to splitting of the cuticle and subsequent infection	Warm-oil treatments weekly Once softened, remove excess cuticle with cuticle nippers	Regular use of a rich cuticle cream Wear rubber gloves when cleaning and washing up
Transverse furrows in the nail plate (Beau's lines)	Temporary arrested development of the nail in the matrix, due to illness or trauma of the nail	Groove in the nail plate, often on all nails simultaneously, running from side to side: this will grow out with the nail	General manicure regularly	General manicure advice
Leuconychia	Trauma to the nail plate or matrix, due to pressure or hitting with a hard object	White spots or marks on the nail plate: will grow out with the nail	General manicure treatment	Be careful with the hands Wear protective gloves when doing housework or gardening
Bruised nails	Trauma to the nail (e.g. trapping it in a door); severe damage can result in loss of the nail	Part of the nail plate may appear blue or black	Although this disorder does not contra-indicate treatment, it is advisable to postpone manicuring the nails until the condition is no longer painful Nail polish may be used to disguise the damaged nail	Be careful with the hands and nails Seek medical advice if swelling is present or if pain persists
Minor nail separation	Lifting of the nail plate from its bed	Where separation has occurred this appears as a greyish-white area	It is advisable to postpone manicuring for this nail until the condition is corrected	Be careful to avoid infection of the nail bed. Protect the nail with a protective dressing and gloves as applicable

Dr A.L. Wright

CONSULTATION

Before carrying out a manicure treatment, it is necessary to assess the condition of the client's skin, nails and cuticles. This is done in order that the most appropriate equipment and products may be chosen. Also, by correctly assessing and analysing the client's hand condition and writing this on her record card, you will be able to see over a period of time how the condition is progressing.

Assessing the hands

The parts to assess are these:

- *The cuticles* Are they dry, tight or cracked, or are they soft and pliable?
- *The nails* Are they strong or weak, brittle or flaking? Are they discoloured or stained? What shape are they – square, round, oval? Are they long or short? Are they bitten?
- *The hands* Is the skin dry, rough or chapped, or is it soft and smooth? Is the colour even?

Whilst assessing the client's hands or feet for treatment, you should also be looking for any *contra-indications* to treatment.

ACTIVITY

Assessing the hands
Look closely at your own hands. Assess their condition and make notes about everything you see.
Then assess the hands of a colleague. How do they differ from your own?

Treatment plan

After analysing the client's nails and adjacent skin, a treatment plan should be considered. In order to correct nail problems the client should attend the salon weekly. She should also be advised of the appropriate treatment preparations to use at home, so as to support the salon treatment. Specialist nail treatments include:

- **Nail strengthener** This is used on brittle, damaged nails, to strengthen, condition and protect them against breaking, splitting or peeling.
- **Ridge filler** This is used on nails with ridges to provide an even surface, allowing a smoother application of polish.

EQUIPMENT AND MATERIALS

Before beginning the manicure, check that you have the necessary equipment and materials to hand.

Next to each piece of equipment the purpose is discussed, as in other chapters.

- *Manicure table or trolley* – on which to place everything.
- *Medium-sized towels (3)* – to dry the skin, nails etc.
- *Small bowls (3)* – lined with tissues.
- *A finger bowl* – to place the hand into a nail cleansing agent.
- *Emery board* – used to shape the new free edge.
- *Orange sticks* – tipped at either end with cottonwool. (Orange sticks should be disposed of after each client, as they cannot be effectively sterilised.) Used to remove products from containers, to ease the cuticle back and clean under the free edge.

Ellisons

A manicure station

Salon System

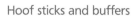

Hoof sticks and buffers

Ellisons

Cuticle knives

Ellisons

Cuticle nippers

Ellisons

Scissors

EQUIPMENT LIST

manicure table or trolley

emery board

orange sticks

hand cream or oil

base coat

coloured nail polish

top coat

nail polish remover

hoof stick

cuticle nippers

nail scissors

cuticle remover

cuticle oil or cream

cottonwool

tissues

see opposite for complete list of materials required

- *Hand cream or oil* – to massage the skin of the hand and arm.
- *Base coat* – to prevent nail staining and improve the appearance of the nail.
- *Coloured nail polish* – a selection for the client to choose from.
- *Top coat* – to provide shine and strength to the nail polish. Reduces peeling and chipping.
- *Cuticle knife* – to remove excess eponychium from the nail plate.
- *Hoof stick* – to gently push back the cuticles.
- *Cuticle nippers* – to remove excess cuticle and dead, torn skin surrounding the nail.
- *Nail scissors* – to shorten nail length.
- *Buffers* – to improve nail shine, stimulate blood circulation and remove surface ridges when used with a buffing paste.
- *Buffing paste* – used to reduce the appearance of ridges on the nail plate surface.
- *Cuticle remover* – used to soften the skin cells and cuticle before treatment.
- *Cuticle oil or cream* – used to condition the skin of the cuticle, especially beneficial for dry nails.
- *Cottonwool* – to remove nail polish and excess nail treatment products used.
- *Tissues* – to protect clean clothing in the area etc.
- *Sanitising solution*.
- *Antiseptic* – to cleanse the skin.

- *Four-sided buffer* – to impact shine and improve nail appearance.
- *Client's record card* – to record the personal details and products used.
- *Nail polish remover* – to remove nail polish and excess nail care and skin care preparations.
- *Nail polish drier* – an aerosol preparation applied to speed the drying process of nail polish.

Products used in manicure and pedicure treatments

Product	Ingredients	Use
Nail polish remover	Acetone or ethyl acetate Perfume Colour Oil	To remove nail polish To remove grease from the nail plate prior to applying polish
Hand lotion/oil	Vegetable oils (e.g. almond oil) Perfume Emulsifying agents (e.g. beeswax or gum tragacanth) Emollients (e.g. glycerine or lanolin) Preservatives	To soften the skin and cuticles To provide slip during hand massage
Nail bleach	Citric acid or hydrogen peroxide Glycerine Water	To whiten stained nails and the surrounding skin
Nail polish	Formaldehyde Solvent Colour pigments Resin Toluene Nitrocellulose Plasticisers Pearlised particles	To colour nail plates To provide some protection
Cuticle cream	Emollients (e.g. lanolin or glycerine) Perfume Colour	To soften the cuticles
Cuticle oil	Oils such as lanolin	To condition the nail and surrounding skin
Nail strengthener	Formaldehyde	To harden soft nails
Cuticle remover	Potassium hydroxide Glycerine	To soften dead cuticles
Buffing paste	Perfume Colour Abrasive particles (e.g. pumice, talc or silica)	To shine the nail plate (used with a buffer)
Nail polish drier	Mineral oil Oleric acid or silicone	Increases the speed at which the polish hardens
Nail polish solvent	Ethyl acetate Toluene	Thins nail polish that has thickened

Sterilisation and sanitisation

(Note: These instructions apply to pedicure also.)

Hygiene must be maintained in a number of ways:

- ensure that tools and equipment are clean and sterile before use;
- disinfect work surfaces regularly;
- use disposables wherever possible;
- always follow hygienic working practices;
- maintain a high standard of personal hygiene.

Manicure and pedicure tools and equipment can be sterilised or sanitised by the following methods:

TIP

Any metal to be placed in the autoclave should be of a high-quality stainless steel, to prevent rusting

HEALTH AND SAFETY

You can buy sterilising sprays to sterilise the surface of the tools that the chemical agent comes into contact with.

Use in a well-ventilated area and avoid contact with flame and excessive heat.

Tool/Equipment	Method	Term used
Cuticle knife	Autoclave	Sterilisation
Cuticle nippers	Autoclave	Sterilisation
Orange stick	Throw away after use	Disposable
Callus file	Autoclave	Sterilisation
	Chemical (e.g. disinfectant)	Sanitisation
Overall	Wash in hot soapy water (60°C)	Sanitisation
Bowl	Chemical (e.g. disinfectant)	Sanitisation
Emery board	Throw away after use	Disposable
Buffer	Wipe handle with surgical spirit	Sanitisation
	Wash buffing cloth in hot (60°C) soapy water	
Towel	Wash in hot soapy water (60°C)	Sanitisation
Spatula	Throw away after use	Disposable
Nail clippers	Autoclave	Sterilisation
Scissors	Autoclave	Sterilisation
Hoof stick	Immerse in chemical (e.g. disinfectant)	Sanitisation
Trolley	Wipe with chemical (e.g. disinfectant)	Sanitisation

Preparing the working area

Ensure that all manicure tools and equipment are sanitised, and that all necessary materials are neatly organised on the trolley.

Keeping the working area tidy promotes an organised and professional image, and prevents time being wasted as you try to find materials.

Place a towel over the work surface, then fold another towel into a pad and place it in the middle of the work surface. The pad helps to support the client's forearm during treatment. Place the third towel over the pad, with more of the towel on the manicurist's side – this is used to dry the client's hands during treatment.

A tissue or disposable manicure mat should then be placed on top of the towels, to catch any nail clippings or filings. This can be thrown away later, avoiding irritation to the client from filings.

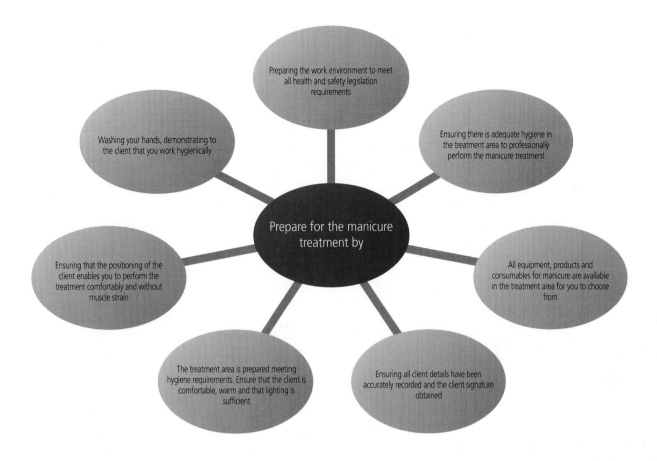

Prepare for the manicure treatment by

- Preparing the work environment to meet all health and safety legislation requirements
- Ensuring there is adequate hygiene in the treatment area to professionally perform the manicure treatment
- All equipment, products and consumables for manicure are available in the treatment area for you to choose from
- Ensuring all client details have been accurately recorded and the client signature obtained
- The treatment area is prepared meeting hygiene requirements. Ensure that the client is comfortable, warm and that lighting is sufficient
- Ensuring that the positioning of the client enables you to perform the treatment comfortably and without muscle strain
- Washing your hands, demonstrating to the client that you work hygienically

PREPARING THE CLIENT

Ensure that the client is warm and comfortable when preparing them for a manicure.

Lighting must be efficient to avoid eyestrain and to allow the treatment to be performed competently.

Offer the client a lightweight gown to cover her clothing. This will prevent damage to her clothes from accidental spillage of products during treatment. Ask her to remove any jewellery from the area to be treated, to prevent the jewellery being damaged by creams and to avoid obstructing massage movements. Put the jewellery in a tissue-lined bowl where the client can see it. Ensure that the client is seated at the correct height, and close enough to the manicurist to avoid having to lean forward.

When the client is comfortably seated, wash your hands – preferably in view of the client, who will then observe hygienic procedures being carried out. This will assure her that she is receiving a professional treatment.

Consult the client's record card, and begin the treatment.

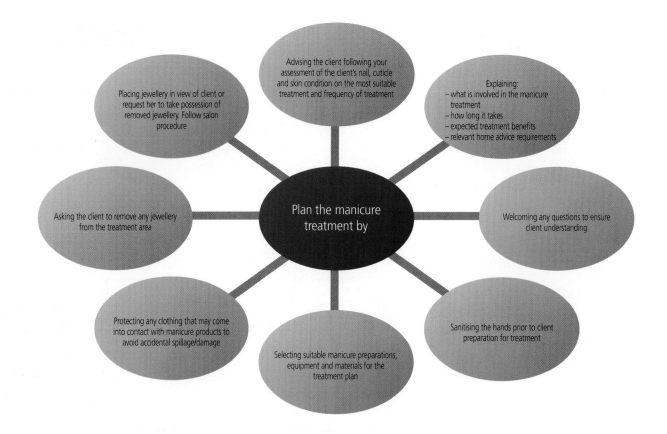

Placing jewellery in view of client or request her to take possession of removed jewellery. Follow salon procedure

Advising the client following your assessment of the client's nail, cuticle and skin condition on the most suitable treatment and frequency of treatment

Explaining:
– what is involved in the manicure treatment
– how long it takes
– expected treatment benefits
– relevant home advice requirements

Asking the client to remove any jewellery from the treatment area

Plan the manicure treatment by

Welcoming any questions to ensure client understanding

Protecting any clothing that may come into contact with manicure products to avoid accidental spillage/damage

Selecting suitable manicure preparations, equipment and materials for the treatment plan

Sanitising the hands prior to client preparation for treatment

THE MANICURE PROCEDURE

Removing nail polish

This procedure shows briefly the stages in the manicure. Each step is discussed in detail later in the chapter.

1 Remove any existing nail polish, using fresh cottonwool for each hand.
2 File and buff the nails of the left hand.
3 Apply cuticle cream.
4 Place the left hand in a manicure bowl containing warm water and a little antiseptic liquid soap.
5 Repeat steps 2 and 3 for the right hand.
6 Remove the left hand from the manicure bowl and dry with a towel.
7 Place the right hand into the manicure bowl.
8 Apply cuticle remover to the left hand, and push back the cuticle with a cottonwool-tipped orange stick or hoof stick.

Filing

Buffing

Applying cuticle cream

The hand in a bowl

Applying cuticle remover

Pushing back cuticles

Using a cuticle knife

Massaging in cuticle oil

Applying the base coat

Applying nail polish

The completed manicure

9 Remove excess cuticle with nippers, and excess eponychium with a knife.

10 Wipe the nails with cottonwool to remove the cuticle remover.

11 Apply cuticle oil and massage it in with your thumbs.

12 Repeat steps **8–11** for the right hand.

13 Massage both hands.

14 Remove grease from the nail plate with a cottonwool pad soaked in nail polish remover.

15 The client may find it convenient to pay for her treatment at this stage, to avoid smudging her polish later.

16 Apply the polish: base coat (once); polish (twice); and top coat (once). If the client doesn't want polish, buff to a shine with paste or use a four-sided buffer.

TIP

Keep the client's jewellery in full view throughout the treatment, so that she doesn't forget it when she leaves.

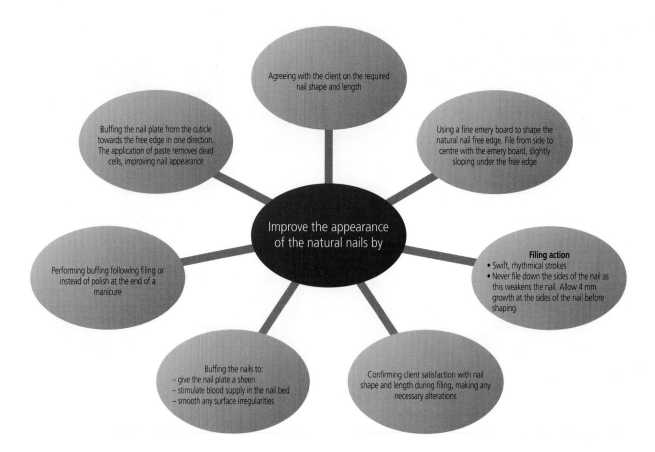

Improve the appearance of the natural nails by

Agreeing with the client on the required nail shape and length

Using a fine emery board to shape the natural nail free edge. File from side to centre with the emery board, slightly sloping under the free edge

Filing action
• Swift, rhythmical strokes
• Never file down the sides of the nail as this weakens the nail. Allow 4 mm growth at the sides of the nail before shaping

Confirming client satisfaction with nail shape and length during filing, making any necessary alterations

Buffing the nails to:
– give the nail plate a sheen
– stimulate blood supply in the nail bed
– smooth any surface irregularities

Performing buffing following filing or instead of polish at the end of a manicure

Buffing the nail plate from the cuticle towards the free edge in one direction. The application of paste removes dead cells, improving nail appearance

Filing

A selection of files

The part of the nail that is filed is the free edge. When filing the natural nail, use a fine emery board. Very often emery boards have different degrees of coarseness on either side, indicated by different colours. Use the darker, rougher side to remove excess length, and the lighter, smoother side for shaping and removing rough edges. A flexible emery board is preferable to a stiff one as it generates less friction.

Always file the nails from the side to the centre, with the emery board sloping slightly under the free edge. Use swift, rhythmical strokes. Avoid a sawing action – this would generate friction and might cause the free edge to split.

Never file completely down the sides of the nail, as strength is required here to balance the free edge. Always allow about 4 mm of nail growth to remain at the sides of the nail.

TIP	

When filing the nails ensure that the finished appearance complements the client's nail/hand.

If the fingers are long and thin, select a rounded/square shape and keep the nail length short.

If the fingers are short and fat, the nails should be filed into an oval shape and the nail length should be longer to elongate the fingers.

Cutting the nails

Where it is necessary to reduce nail length, it is more efficient to do so by cutting the nail free edge. This is performed using nail scissors, which have been sterilised before use on each client. Support the nail wall with one hand on the free edge being cut. This minimises client discomfort. Dispose of the trimmed nail plate hygienically.

Oval

The ideal nail shape is oval. This is the shape that offers the most strength to the free edge.

Oval

Square

A recent trend from America is to have the free edge square. The client should be informed, however, that if she has severe corners on the nails she will be more likely to catch and break them.

Square

Pointed

One nail shape that should never be recommended is the pointed nail. This leaves the nail tip very weak and likely to break.

Pointed

Buffing

In manicure, **buffing** is used for these reasons:

- to give the nail plate a sheen;
- to stimulate the blood supply in the nail bed, increasing nourishment and encouraging strong, healthy nail growth;
- to smooth any surface irregularities.

A **buffer** should have a handle made of plastic and a replaceable convex pad covered with chamois or soft leather. **Buffing paste** is the cream used to help smooth out surface irregularities, and thereby give the nail a shine. It contains abrasive particles such as pumice, talc or kaolin.

The **four-sided buffer**: this is shaped like a thick emery board and has four types of surface, ranging from slightly abrasive to very smooth. It can be used to bring the nail to a shine without the need for buffing paste. It cannot be effectively sterilised, however, and must therefore be discarded after use on one client.

Buffing is carried out after filing and before the nails are soaked in the finger bowl. It could also be used instead of polish at the end of the manicure, or on a man's nails.

If it is being used, **buffing paste** is applied by taking a small amount out of the pot with a clean orange stick and applying this to each nail plate. With the fingertip, use downward strokes from the cuticle to the free edge to spread the paste without getting it under the cuticle (which would cause irritation). With the buffer held loosely in the hand, buff in one direction only from the base of the nail to the free edge, using smooth, firm, regular strokes. Use approximately six strokes per nail.

Cuticle work

Cuticle work is carried out to keep the cuticle area attractive and also to prevent cuticles from adhering to the nail plate, which could lead to splitting of the cuticle as the nail grows forward, and subsequently to infection of the area.

The work is carried out after soaking the nails in warm soapy water. This step loosens dirty particles from the free edge and softens the skin in the cuticle area.

Procedure

1 Take the fingers from the soapy water and pat them dry with a soft towel.

2 Apply cuticle remover to the cuticle and nail walls, using the applicator brush. (**Cuticle remover** is a slightly caustic solution that helps soften and loosen the cuticles and the eponychium from the nail plate.)

3 Gently push back the cuticle with a cottonwool-tipped orange stick. This is tipped with cottonwool to avoid splinters from the wood, and also so that the cottonwool may be replaced if necessary.) Use a gentle, circular motion to push back the cuticle, holding the orange stick like a pen.

   Use a fresh orange stick for each part of the manicure treatment, and when working on different hands, to prevent cross-infection.

4 Hold the cuticle knife at 45° to the nail plate and stroke it in one direction only, gently loosening any eponychium that has adhered to the nail plate: do not scratch it backwards and forwards. The cuticle knife should have a fine-ground flat blade which can be resharpened when

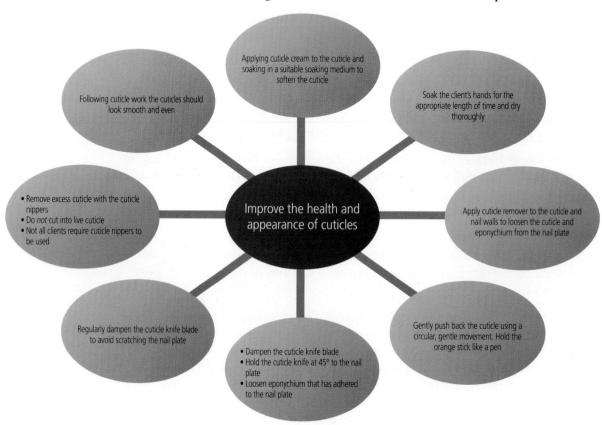

necessary. Dampen it regularly in the manicure bowl to prevent scratches occurring on the nail plate.

5 Hold the nippers comfortably in the palm of the hand, with the thumb resting just above the blades – this gives firm control over what can be a dangerous instrument. Use the cuticle nippers to remove any loose or torn pieces of cuticle, and to trim excess dead cuticle. *Do not cut into live cuticle*: if you do, it will bleed profusely and will be very uncomfortable for the client. Not every client will require the use of cuticle nippers – use them only when needed. (Cuticle nippers should have finely-ground cutting blades to give a clean cut and to avoid tearing the cuticle.)

Hand massage

Hand massage is generally carried out near the end of the manicure treatment, just prior to nail polish application. It can also be carried out on its own if the client wants the effects of the massage but does not need or want treatment to her nails.

The reasons for offering a hand massage during a manicure are as follows:

● to moisturise the skin with hand cream;

● to increase circulation;

● to keep a range of movement in the joints;

● to ease discomfort from arthritis or rheumatism;

● to relax the client;

● to help remove any dead skin cells (desquamation)

Hand massage sequence

1 **Effleurage to the whole hand and forearm** Use long sweeping strokes from the hand to the elbow, moving on both the outer and the inner sides of the forearm.
   Repeat step **1** *a further 5 times.*

2 **Thumb kneading to the back of the hand and the forearm** Use the thumbs, one in front of the other, and move backwards and forwards in a gently sawing action. Move from the hand to the elbow, then slide the thumbs back down to the hands.
   Repeat step **2** *a further 2 times.*

Effleurage to the hand and forearm

Thumb kneading to the back of the hand

Thumb kneading to the palm   Finger circulations

3 Thumb kneading to the palm and the inner forearm Use the same movements as in step 2.

4 Finger circulations, supporting the joints Supporting the knuckles with one hand, hold the fingers individually and gently take each through its full range of movements, first clockwise and then anticlockwise. Move from the little finger to the thumb.

  *Repeat step **4** a further 2 times.*

5 Wrist circulations, supporting the joints Support the wrist with one hand and put your fingers between the client's gently grasping her hand. Move the wrist through its full range of movement, first clockwise and then anticlockwise.

  *Repeat step **5** a further 2 times.*

6 Effleurage to the whole hand and forearm Use the same movement as in step 1.

  *Repeat step **6** a further 5 times*

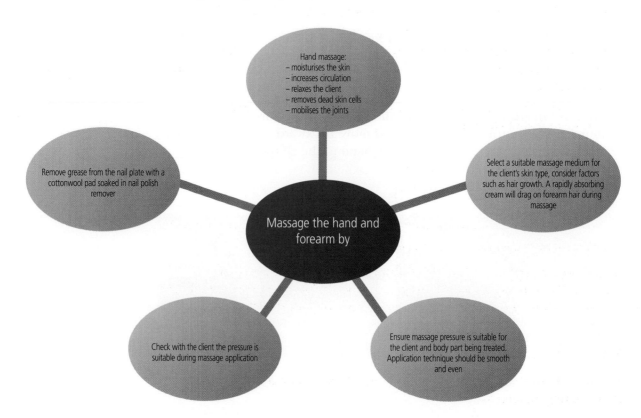

Hand massage:
– moisturises the skin
– increases circulation
– relaxes the client
– removes dead skin cells
– mobilises the joints

Remove grease from the nail plate with a cottonwool pad soaked in nail polish remover

Select a suitable massage medium for the client's skin type, consider factors such as hair growth. A rapidly absorbing cream will drag on forearm hair during massage

Massage the hand and forearm by

Check with the client the pressure is suitable during massage application

Ensure massage pressure is suitable for the client and body part being treated. Application technique should be smooth and even

Treatment plan

After analysing the client's nails and adjacent skin, a treatment plan should be considered. In order to correct nail problems the client should attend the salon weekly. She should also be advised of the appropriate treatment preparations to use at home, so as to support the salon treatment.

Specialist nail treatments include base coats such as:

- **Nail strengthener** This is used on brittle, damaged nails, to strengthen, condition and protect them against breaking, splitting or peeling.
- **Ridge filler** This is used on nails with ridges to provide an even surface, allowing a smoother application of polish.

Nail polish application

Nail polish is used to coat the nail plate for a number of reasons:

- to adorn the nail;
- to disguise stained nails;
- to add temporary strength to weak nails;
- to coordinate with clothes or make-up.

Types of polish

- **Cream** This has a matt finish, and requires a top coat application to give a sheen.
- **Crystalline** This is pearlised by the addition of natural fish scales or synthetic ingredients such as bismuth oxychloride.
- **Base coat** This protects the nail from staining by a strong-coloured nail polish; it also gives a good grip to polish, and smooths out minor surface irregularities.
- **Top coat** This gives a sheen to cream polish, and adds longer wear as it helps to prevent chipping.

Contra-indications to nail polish

Do not apply polish in these circumstances:

- if there are diseases and disorders of the nail plate and surrounding skin;
- if the client is allergic to nail polish.

In addition, crystalline nail polish should not be applied to excessively ridged nails as it may appear to exaggerate the problem. Short or bitten nails should be painted only with pale polishes, to avoid attracting attention.

How to apply nail polish

Before nail polish is applied the client's hand jewellery may be replaced, to avoid smudging afterwards.

1 After ensuring that the nail plate is free from grease, start with the thumb and apply three brush strokes down the length of the nail from the cuticle to the free edge, beginning in the centre, then down either side close to the nail wall.

Take care to avoid touching the cuticle or the nail wall. If flooding occurs, remove the polish immediately with an orange stick and polish remover.

2 Apply one base coat, two coats of coloured polish, and one top coat. Top coat is required only after using cream polish; pearl polish does not need a top coat.

Styles of application

- **Traditional application** This style is the one most commonly requested by clients: the entire nail plate is covered with polish.
- **French application** This style involves painting the nail plate of the nail bed pink or pale beige, and the free edge white.
- **Free lunula application** This style involves applying polish over the whole nail plate except the area of the lunula.
- **Application to give the appearance of longer nails** This style creates an optical illusion that the nails are longer than they really are. The whole nail plate is painted, leaving a slightly larger gap than usual along the nail walls.

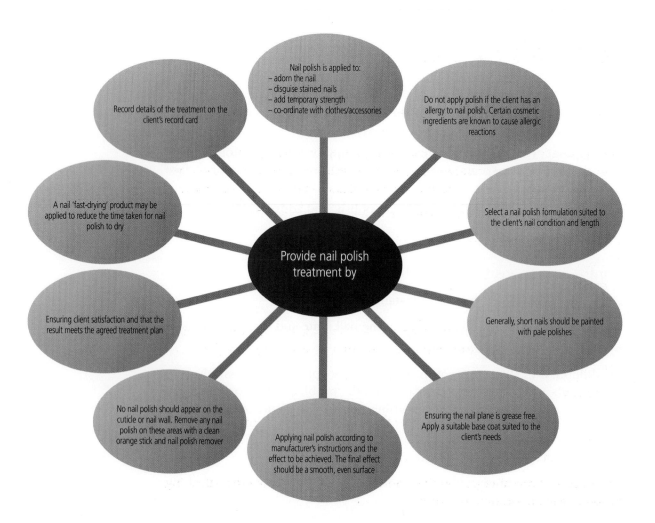

Reasons for peeling and chipping nail polish

Chipping may be explained by any of the following:

- The nail polish was not thick enough because of over-thinning with solvent.
- No base coat was used.
- Grease was left on the nail plate prior to painting.
- The nail plate is flaking.
- The polish was dried too quickly by artificial means.

Peeling polish may have the following explanations:

- No top coat was used.
- Successive coats were not allowed to dry between applications.
- The nail polish was too thick, due to evaporation of the solvent.
- Grease was left on the nail plate prior to painting.

Nail polish should be stored in a cool, dark place, to avoid separation and fading. The caps and the rims of bottles *must* be kept clean, not only for appearance but also to ensure that the bottle is airtight.

If polish does thicken, **solvent** may be added to restore the correct consistency. This should be done twenty minutes prior to use, to ensure an even consistency.

Nail art

CONTRA-ACTIONS

Certain cosmetic ingredients are known to cause allergic reactions in some people.

The client – or the manicurist – may at some time develop an allergy to a manicure product that has been successfully used previously. This could be for a number of reasons, including new medication being taken or illness.

The symptoms of an allergic reaction could be as follows:

- redness of the skin (erythema);
- swelling;
- itching;
- raised blisters.

The symptoms do not necessarily appear on the hands. In the case of nail polish allergy, the symptoms often show up on the face, which the hands are continually touching.

In the case of an allergic reaction:

- Remove the offending product immediately, using water or, in the case of polish, solvent.
- If symptoms persist, seek medical advice.

Always record any allergies on the client's record card, so that the offending product may be avoided in future.

AFTERCARE AND ADVICE

It is important when carrying out a manicure that the client knows how to care for her nails at home. It is your duty as a therapist to ensure that the correct aftercare advice is given. If it isn't, the client may unwittingly undo all the good work you have done during the treatment.

When giving aftercare advice you have a good opportunity to recommend retail products, such as nail polish or hand cream, thereby enhancing retail sales and the salon's profit.

Aftercare advice will differ slightly for each client, according to individual needs, but generally it will be as follows:

- Wear rubber gloves when washing up.
- Wear protective gloves when gardening or doing housework.
- Always wear gloves in cold weather.
- Dry the hands thoroughly after washing, and apply hand cream.
- Avoid harsh soaps when washing hands.
- Do not use the fingernails as tools (for instance, to prise lids off tins).
- Advise on appropriate nail/skin-care products to remedy the problems present, i.e dry skin, weak nails.
- Advise the client on what other professional treatments you could recommend.
- Advise the client on a treatment plan to improve the nail/skin condition and the time intervals recommended between each treatment.

It is also advisable to tell the client what to do in the event of a contra-action.

Exercises for the hands

Hand exercises play an important role in the home-care advice given to clients, for the following reasons:

- They keep the joints supple, allowing greater movement.
- Circulation is increased, encouraging healthy nail and skin growth.
- Good circulation helps to prevent cold hands.
- Exercises keep the client interested in her hands, and so more likely to keep regular salon appointments.

Exercise routine

1 Rub the palms together, back and forth, until warm.
2 Make a tight fist with each hand, then slowly stretch out all the fingers as far as possible.
   Repeat step 2 a further 3 times.
3 With the fingers extended, rotate the wrists slowly in large clockwise circles.
   Repeat step 3 a further 3 times.
4 With the fingers extended, rotate the wrists slowly in large anticlockwise circles.
   Repeat step 4 a further 3 times.

ACTIVITY

Designing an aftercare leaflet
Devise an aftercare leaflet for clients, advising a suitable home-care routine.

5 Play an imaginary piano vigorously with the fingers for 10 seconds.

6 With the hands together as if praying, gently widen the fingers as far as possible, then relax.

Repeat step 6 a further 3 times.

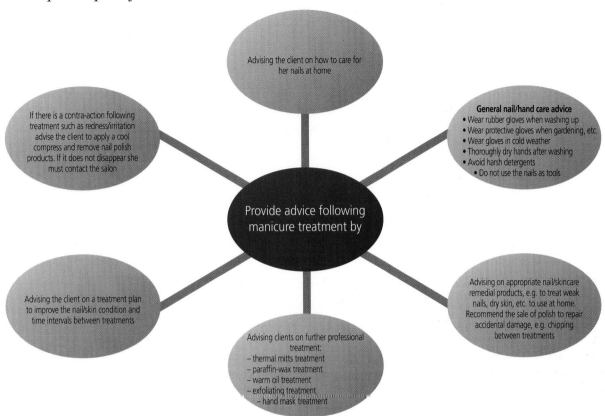

Advising the client on how to care for her nails at home

General nail/hand care advice
- Wear rubber gloves when washing up
- Wear protective gloves when gardening, etc.
- Wear gloves in cold weather
- Thoroughly dry hands after washing
- Avoid harsh detergents
  - Do not use the nails as tools

If there is a contra-action following treatment such as redness/irritation advise the client to apply a cool compress and remove nail polish products. If it does not disappear she must contact the salon

Provide advice following manicure treatment by

Advising the client on a treatment plan to improve the nail/skin condition and time intervals between treatments

Advising clients on further professional treatment:
– thermal mitts treatment
– paraffin-wax treatment
– warm oil treatment
– exfoliating treatment
– hand mask treatment

Advising on appropriate nail/skincare remedial products, e.g. to treat weak nails, dry skin, etc. to use at home. Recommend the sale of polish to repair accidental damage, e.g. chipping between treatments

MANICURE FOR A MALE CLIENT

A man's hands differ slightly from a woman's so some adaptations to the basic manicure are necessary if the treatment is to be effective:

- File the nails to a shorter length.
- Omit the coloured nail polish.
- Shape the nails square rather than oval.
- Buff the nails with paste, if a shine is required.
- Use unperfumed lotion for massage.
- Use a lotion or an oil rather than cream for massage.
- Use deeper movements during hand and arm massage.

ACTIVITY

Comparing hands
Carefully look at and touch a man's hands, then look at and touch those of a woman. Write down as many differences as you can.

From your observations, can you think of any further adaptations that may be necessary in manicuring a man's hands?

HAND AND NAIL TREATMENTS

In addition to a manicure, further treatments may be added as appropriate. Here are some examples.

Warm-oil treatment

Warm-oil treatment involves gently heating a small amount of vegetable oil (such as almond oil) and soaking the cuticles in it for five minutes. This softens the cuticles and the surrounding skin, and is an excellent treatment for clients with dry, cracked cuticles.

Exfoliating treatment

Ellisons

Exfoliating treatment is carried out as part of the massage routine. The massage is performed as usual, using a mildly abrasive cream. This offers the following benefits:

- the removal of dead skin cells;
- improvement of the skin texture;
- improvement of the skin colour;
- increased circulation.

The abrasive particles must be thoroughly removed with hot, damp towels before continuing with the rest of the manicure.

An exfoliating treatment

Hand treatment mask

Ellisons

An appropriate **treatment mask** may be applied, according to the client's treatment requirements. This may be either stimulating and rejuvenating, or moisturising. The hands may be placed inside warm hand gloves for 10 minutes to enable the mask to penetrate the epidermis. The mask is then removed, and followed with treatment massage cream.

- **Paraffin-wax treatment** The wax is heated in a special bath to a temperature of 50–55°C. It is then applied to the hands with a brush and left to set for 10–15 minutes. The heating effect stimulates the blood circulation, eases discomfort of arthritic and rheumatic conditions and softens the skin, improving the appearance and condition of the nails and dry skin.

A hand treatment mask

After use the wax is disposed of.

Thermal mitts

These are electrically heated gloves in which the hands are placed for approximately 15 minutes.

They are usually used following the application of hand oil/lotion within the manicure routine. The hands are prepared by wrapping them in cling film.

The treatment has the following benefits:

- Decreases joint stiffness in the case of a client suffering from arthritis.
- Improves the condition of dry skin of the cuticles and hands, by increasing the absorption of moisturising products.
- Improves skin colour and circulation.

Specialist hand and arm treatment

ACTIVITY

Researching treatments
Research other types of hand and nail treatments. Write down the details of your research, and try out the treatments on clients.

Specialist treatments should be offered to your client when there is a specific treatment need or if she feels she would like to benefit from such a treatment.

Specialist training in these advanced techniques is usually offered by major product companies.

The model for this specialist hand and arm treatment is a mature client who suffers from the medical condition rheumatoid arthritis where the joints become inflamed and painful.

The following hand and arm treatment will:

- Stimulate the blood circulation.
- Have a skin cleansing action.
- Remove dead skin cells (desquamation).
- Improve the moisture content of the skin.
- Minimise discomfort caused by an arthritic, rheumatic condition.

Your treatments should be adapted the meet the treatment objectives for the client.

Allow 30 minutes for this specialist hand and arm treatment.

The hands and arms are cleansed using warm towelling mitts infused with lime oil for its therapeutic, refreshing and energising properties.

The hands are exfoliated to remove all dead skin cells and brighten the skin. A salt-based preparation with emollient, skin-softening ingredients is applied to each hand.

Towelling mitts are used to remove the exfoliating treatment. These have been steamed and are warm when used.

A skin-nourishing milk lotion is applied to each arm using a 'drizzling' technique. The milk is particularly beneficial for dry, sensitive skin.

Massage movements are applied using effleurage and petrissage massage manipulations.

A further skin treatment product oil is applied and massaged into the skin. This will act as a treatment mask for the skin.

The hands are then placed in steamed towels and encased in a plastic bag and dry towelling mitten for 10–15 minutes. Remove mittens and continue with nail polish application if desired.

Assessment of knowledge and understanding

You have now learnt about the different manicure treatments available to improve the condition of the hands, nails and surrounding skin. These skills will enable you to professionally provide manicure treatment.

To test your level of knowledge, answer the following short questions. These will prepare you for your summative (final) assessment.

Additional anatomy and physiology questions required for this unit are found on pages 129–30, 131–2.

Anatomy and physiology

1 How many bones form the hand? Name them.

2 Name the bones of the forearm.

3 Name the main arteries of the arm and hand.

4 Name two muscles of the hand.

5 What are the group of muscles called that bend the wrist, drawing it towards the forearm?

Consult with the client

1 Communication is important. Give three examples of good communication techniques.

2 Why should the manicurist consult the client's record card prior to treatment?

3 Why is it important to assess the condition of the client's hands and nails before treatment commences?

4 Why is it important to discuss and agree the treatment service and outcomes with your client at consultation?

5 Name three contra-indications observed at consultation, which would prevent treatment being carried out.

Prepare for the treatment

1 Personal appearance is important to make a good impression. Give three examples of good personal appearance relevant to the manicurist and to organisational requirements.

2 How can cross-infection be avoided when performing manicure treatment? Give examples of three preventative measures.

3 Why is it important that the client is warm and comfortable when having a manicure?

4 Why is good lighting important?

Plan the treatment

1 Why would you choose to include the following hand and nail treatments in your treatment plan?
- paraffin-wax therapy
- hand mask
- warm oil
- thermal mitts
- exfoliators.

2 Why are several treatments often necessary to improve the condition of the nails and skin to their full potential?

3 Why is it important to complete your treatment plan in the allocated time?

4 What is the commercially acceptable time for a manicure?

Improve the appearance of the natural nails

1 How can the buffing improve the appearance of the natural nails?

2 How would you recognise each of the following, and what could you recommend to improve the appearance and condition?
- weak nails
- dry nails
- brittle nails
- ridged nails
- dry cuticles

- overgrown cuticles
- dry skin
- hard skin.

Improve the health and appearance of the cuticles and surrounding skin

1 Which manicure tools are used to improve the appearance of the cuticles?

2 Describe how a cuticle knife should be used to avoid damage to the surface nail plate and cuticle.

3 If used incorrectly cuticle remover can cause drying of the cuticle. Explain how this could occur.

4 What products used on the cuticles help to prevent them from drying and splitting?

Massage the hand and forearm

1 What are the differences in formulation and treatment benefits for the massage mediums:
- cream
- oil.

2 How would you adapt your hand and arm massage technique when treating a male client?

3 What are the terms used for the different types of massage applied in a manicure?

4 State four benefits of hand and arm massage.

5 What would be the benefit of massaging cream into the hands at home?

Provide nail polishing treatments

1 What is the difference between a base coat and a top coat in terms of purpose and application technique?

2 What is the nail polish application technique for a 'French manicure'?

3 If a client had badly bitten nails, what type and colour of polish would you suggest that she tried?

4 When would the appearance of the client's natural nails be unsuitable for the application of a dark nail polish?

5 Which nail polish product would reduce the appearance of ridges on the nail plate?

6 If a client has her nails polished professionally, what would be the recommended time interval between treatments?

7 Why is it a good idea to retail the nail polish colours used within the treatment?

Complete the treatment

1 What general advice should be given to a client on maintaining the condition and appearance of her nails following a manicure?

2 Why is it important to advise the client to avoid a sawing action when filing the nails?

3 What aftercare advice would you give to a client with very dry hands and cuticles?

4 List three retail products that you could recommend to a manicure client.

5 For each of the clients below, suggest a treatment routine. Detail the treatment plan to include: cause of the condition, aims of the treatment, products used, treatments recommended, relevant retail sales and homecare advice.
- a hairdresser with very soft, weak, stained nails
- an engineer, with a bruised nail, overgrown cuticles and cracked skin on the fingers
- a teenager who has badly bitten nails
- an elderly client with strong, ridged nails and dry skin on the hands.

PROVIDE PEDICURE TREATMENT

BT8

Learning objectives

This unit describes how to provide pedicure treatments for client's to improve the appearance and condition of the foot, nails and surrounding skin.

It describes the competencies to enable you to:

- **consult with the client**
- **prepare for the treatment**
- **plan the treatment**
- **improve the appearance of the natural nails and cuticles**
- **massage the foot and lower leg**
- **provide nail polishing treatments**
- **complete the treatment**

When providing manicure treatment it is important to use the skills you have learnt in the following core mandatory units:

Unit G1 – Ensure your own actions reduce risks to health and safety

Unit G6 – Promote additional products or services to clients

Unit G8 – Develop and maintain your effectiveness at work

THE PURPOSE OF A PEDICURE

The word **pedicure** is derived from the Latin word *pedis*, meaning 'foot' and *cura*, meaning 'care'. The treatment is very similar to manicure except that it is carried out on the feet instead of the hands. A pedicure is carried out for many reasons:

- to improve the appearance of the foot;
- to reduce the amount of hard skin;
- to relax tired, aching feet;
- to keep the nails smooth and healthy.

CONSULTATION

Before carrying out a pedicure treatment, it is necessary to assess the condition of the client's skin, nails and cuticles. This is done in order that the most appropriate equipment and products may be chosen. Also, by correctly assessing and analysing the client's foot condition and writing this on her record card, you will be able to see over a period of time how the condition is progressing.

The parts to assess are these:

- *The cuticles* Are they dry, tight or cracked, or are they soft and pliable?
- *The nails* Are they strong or weak, thickened, discoloured or stained? Sometimes this may indicate a nail disorder. The nails of the foot should be filed straight across into a square shape. Shaping the nails at the corners can cause ingrowing toenails.
- *The skin* Is the skin dry, rough or cracked, or is it soft and smooth. Is the colour even?

Treatment plan

After analysing the client's nails and adjacent skin, a treatment plan should be considered. In order to correct any problems the client should attend the salon weekly. She should also be advised of the appropriate treatment preparations to use at home, so as to support the salon treatment.

- **Revitalising foot spa agents** These may be in tablet form or as a foaming soak. They are dissolved in warm water, in which the feet are then immersed.
- **Exfoliator** This is used following immersion of the feet in the foot spa. It removes surface dead skin cells, preventing the formation of callus tissue.
- **Massage lotion** This is a massage preparation which includes refreshing essential oils such as peppermint. It is recommended for the relief of tired, aching feet.
- **Foot mask** A mask may be applied to cool and to refresh the feet. Booties may be worn while the mask penetrates the epidermis.
- **Foot gel or spray** This may be applied to create an immediate cooling effect.

Whilst assessing the client's feet for treatment, you should also be looking for any contra-indications to treatment.

Ellisons

Pedicure equipment

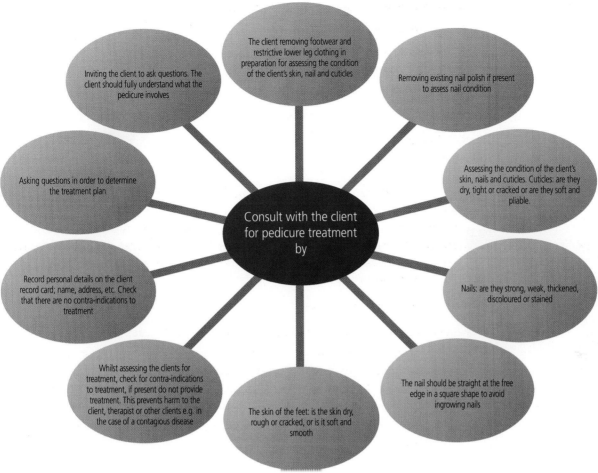

The client removing footwear and restrictive lower leg clothing in preparation for assessing the condition of the client's skin, nail and cuticles

Inviting the client to ask questions. The client should fully understand what the pedicure involves

Removing existing nail polish if present to assess nail condition

Asking questions in order to determine the treatment plan

Assessing the condition of the client's skin, nails and cuticles. Cuticles: are they dry, tight or cracked or are they soft and pliable.

Record personal details on the client record card; name, address, etc. Check that there are no contra-indications to treatment

Nails: are they strong, weak, thickened, discoloured or stained

Consult with the client for pedicure treatment by

Whilst assessing the clients for treatment, check for contra-indications to treatment, if present do not provide treatment. This prevents harm to the client, therapist or other clients e.g. in the case of a contagious disease

The skin of the feet: is the skin dry, rough or cracked, or is it soft and smooth

The nail should be straight at the free edge in a square shape to avoid ingrowing nails

RECEPTION

When a client makes an appointment for a pedicure treatment, the receptionist should advise the client how long the treatment will take. This will include sufficient time for the nail polish to dry before replacing footwear.

Ask the client whether she is currently receiving treatment from a chiropodist for conditions such as verrucas or athlete's foot. These would contra-indicate treatment: the receptionist should advise the client to wait until the condition has cleared.

Allow 45 minutes for a pedicure.

Allow up to 1$\frac{1}{2}$ hours for a specialist foot treatment.

TIP

Advise the client booking a pedicure treatment that she will have to allow the nail polish to dry thoroughly before replacing footwear. It is a good idea to wear footwear that will enable her toes to dry thoroughly to avoid spoiling the nail polish.

CONTRA-INDICATIONS

When a client attends for a pedicure treatment, the therapist should always look at the client's skin and nails to check that no infection or disease is present which might contra-indicate treatment.

If a client has any of the following conditions, a pedicure treatment must not be carried out:

- *Athlete's foot* – tinea pedis.
- *Verrucas* – plantar warts.
- *Diabetes*.
- *Cuts or abrasions* on the feet or legs.
- *Infectious skin disease*, such as ringworm.

Below is a list of common disorders that may be seen on the feet. Not all of these contra-indicate treatment.

Disorder	Cause	Appearance	Salon treatment	Home-care advice
Calluses Dr A.L. Wright	Incorrect footwear	Thick, yellowish, hardened patches of skin, usually found on prominent areas of the foot such as the heel and the ball of toe: may be painful	Use a rasp or pumice stone gently to remove any build-up of hard skin: painful calluses should be treated by a chiropodist	Ensure that shoes fit correctly Avoid standing for long periods Alternate style of footwear regularly
Corns Dr A.L. Wright	Incorrect footwear (corns are often found on toes which have been squeezed together by tight shoes)	Similar to calluses except that the affected area is smaller and more compact; corns often look white, and may be extremely painful	Small corns may be treated in the same way as a callus, but if the client has large or painful corns she should be treated by a chiropodist	Ensure that shoes fit correctly Avoid standing for long periods Alternate style of footwear regularly
Bunions	Long-term wear of ill-fitting shoes, especially those with high heels or pointed toe areas A weakness in the arches of the feet	The large joint at the base of the big toe protrudes, forcing the big toe inwards towards the other toes	None – refer the client to a chiropodist if the bunion is painful; gentle massage may help to ease any pain or discomfort	Try to keep pressure off the affected area
Chilblains	Poor blood supply to the hands and feet, aggravated in cold weather	Fingers and toes may be red, blue or purple in colour; the client may complain of painful or itchy areas	Regular manicures or pedicures, with special attention paid to massage which will help to improve the circulation	Keep affected areas warm and dry Avoid tight footwear, which might restrict the circulation If the condition is severe, seek medical advice
Ingrowing toenails Dr A.L. Wright	Ill-fitting shoes Cutting toenails too far down at the sides	The side of the nail penetrates the nail wall: redness, inflammation and pus may be present, depending on the severity of the condition	None – refer client to a chiropodist	Avoid tight footwear Do not cut the toenails too short, particularly at the sides

Other bacterial, fungal and viral infections that relate to this unit are located in Chapter 1, where contra-indications are illustrated and discussed.

BEAUTY WORKS

Date	Beauty therapist name

Client name	Date of birth (identifying client age group)
Address	Postcode

Evening phone number	Day phone number
Name of doctor	Doctor's address and phone number

Related medical history (conditions that may restrict or prohibit treatment application)

Are you taking any medication (this may affect the sensitivity of the skin to the treatment)

CONTRA-INDICATIONS REQUIRING MEDICAL REFERRAL
(Preventing pedicure treatment application)

☐ bacterial infections (e.g. paronychia)
☐ viral infections (e.g. plantar warts)
☐ fungal infections (e.g. tinea unguium)
☐ severe nail separation
☐ severe eczema and psoriasis
☐ severe bruising

EQUIPMENT AND MATERIALS

☐ nail and skin treatment tools
☐ abrasives (e.g. buffing cream)
☐ cuticle softeners
☐ nail and skin products
☐ nail conditioners (e.g. cuticle cream)
☐ skin conditioners (e.g. hand cream)
☐ nail, skin and cuticle corrective treatments (e.g. paraffin wax)
☐ consumables

FEET AND NAIL TREATMENTS

☐ heat treatments
☐ skin conditioners
☐ paraffin wax
☐ foot masks
☐ thermal boots
☐ exfoliators

NAIL FINISH

☐ light colour
☐ dark colour
☐ french manicure

CONTRA-INDICATIONS WHICH RESTRICT TREATMENT
(Treatment may require adaptation)

☐ mild nail separation
☐ minor eczema and psoriasis
☐ recent scar tissue
☐ severely damaged nails
☐ broken bones
☐ minor cuts or abrasions
☐ minor bruising or swelling

COURSE OF TREATMENT

	Date	Date	Date
☐ improvement of skin condition products used	—	—	—
☐ improvement of nail condition products used	—	—	—

NAIL, CUTICLE AND SKIN CONDITION

nails	cuticle	skin
☐ normal	☐ dry	☐ dry
☐ brittle	☐ split	☐ hard
☐ dry	☐ overgrown	
☐ weak		
☐ ridged		

MASSAGE MEDIUMS

☐ creams
☐ oils

Beauty therapist signature (for reference)

Client signature (confirmation of details)

PRESENT NAILCARE ROUTINE

This information includes
- what products the client is currently using to care for her nails and feet and the regularity of their use
- details that may influence the clients nail/foot condition, e.g. occupation

TREATMENT ADVICE

This information includes
- what products have been used in the pedicure treatment
- advice re products that would be suitable for the client to use at home to care for the skin of her feet and nails
- advice on general care of the skin of the feet and nails
- advice on product application and removal in order to gain maximum benefit from their use
- use of home-care products
- contra-action advice, action to be taken in the event of an unwanted skin reaction
- recommendations for further pedicure treatments
- the recommended time intervals between treatments

EQUIPMENT LIST

dry cottonwool

nail polish remover

scissors or toenail clippers

emery board

cuticle oil

cuticle remover

cuticle nippers

hoof stick

callus file

massage lotion or oil

base coat

coloured nail polish

top coat

tissues

foot spa

see opposite for complete list of
materials required

EQUIPMENT AND MATERIALS

Before beginning the pedicure, check that you have the necessary
equipment and materials to hand. The purpose of each piece of equipment
is discussed as in other chapters.

- *Pedicure bowl (1)* – to soak and cleanse the foot.
- *Small towels (5)* – to protect and dry the client's skin.
- *Small bowls (3)* – for storage.
- *Sanitising fluid solution.*
- *Dry cottonwool* – to remove nail polish and excess nail preparations.
- *Antiseptic* – to cleanse and sanitise the clean skin.
- *Nail polish remover.*
- *Scissors or toenail clippers* – to shorten nail length.
- *Emery board* – to shorten and shape the nail free edge.
- *Cuticle oil* – used to condition the skin of the cuticle, especially beneficial for dry cuticles.
- *Cuticle remover* – used to soften the skin cells and the cuticle before treatment.
- *Cuticle knife* – to remove excess eponychium from the nail plate.
- *Cuticle nippers* – to remove excess cuticle and dead, torn skin surrounding the nail.
- *Hoof stick* – to gently push back the cuticles.

- *Callus file* – or exfoliating scrub to remove excess dead skin from the foot.

- *Massage lotion or oil* – to massage the skin of the foot and lower leg.

- *Base coat* – provides an even surface to improve nail polish application and prevent skin staining.

- *Coloured nail polish* – a selection for the client to choose from.

- *Top coat* – to provide shine to nail polish. Adds strength and reduces peeling and chipping.

- *Tissues* – to protect client's clothing and the area etc.

- *Client's record card* – to record the personal details and products used.

- *Foot spa* – optional, to revitalise and refresh the skin by stimulation of the blood and circulation.

- *Nail polish drier* – an aerosol preparation applied to speed the drying process of nail polish.

- *Toe separators* – are used to keep the toes separated during nail polish application. Alternatively disposable items such as cottonwool or tissues may be used for this purpose, as they are more hygienic.

Ellisons

A foot spa

Ensure that the client is warm and comfortable when preparing for the pedicure. Client privacy and modesty should also be considered. Not all clients would be happy to be on view while receiving the treatment. Ensure that lighting is efficient to avoid eye strain and to enable the treatment to be performed competently.

Products used in pedicure treatments

Product	Ingredients	Use
Nail polish remover	Acetone or ethyl acetate Perfume Colour Oil	To remove nail polish To remove grease from the nail plate prior to polishing
Hand lotion/oil	Vegetable oils (e.g. almond oil) Perfume Emulsifying agents (e.g. beeswax or gum tragacanth) Emollients (e.g. glycerine or lanolin) Preservatives	To soften the skin and cuticles To provide slip during foot massage
Nail bleach	Citric acid or hydrogen peroxide Glycerine Water	To whiten stained nails and the surrounding skin

Product	Ingredients	Use
Nail polish	Formaldehyde Solvent Colour pigments Resin Toluene Nitrocellulose Plasticisers Pearlised particles	To colour nail plates To provide some protection
Cuticle cream	Emollients (e.g. lanolin or glycerine) Perfume Colour	To soften the cuticles
Nail strengthener	Formaldehyde	To harden soft nails
Cuticle remover	Potassium hydroxide Glycerine	To soften dead cuticles
Buffing paste	Perfume Colour Abrasive particles (e.g. pumice, talc or silica)	To shine the nail plate (used with a buffer)
Nail polish drier	Mineral oil Oleric acid or silicone	Increases the speed at which the polish hardens
Nail polish solvent	Ethyl acetate Toluene	Thins nail polish that has thickened
Exfoliating scrub	Abrasive ingredients such as pumice, sea salt, detergent, water and water-soluble ingredients, added moisturisers, refreshing agents, e.g. peppermint oil	To remove dead skin cells, cleanse the skin, condition, soften and refresh the skin, improving blood circulation in the area

Preparing the working area

All metal instruments should be sterilised in the autoclave prior to use. Non-metal instruments should be sanitised by immersing them in a suitable disinfecting fluid. Prepare the equipment neatly on a trolley so that everything you need is to hand and the client need not be disturbed during treatment.

Place a towel on the floor between you and the client. The foot bowl containing warm, soapy water should be placed on this towel.

Towels should be placed on your lap: one is for protection, the other is for drying the client's feet. Keep the other towels close by, for wrapping the client's feet.

When cutting the client's nails and removing hard skin, a tissue should be placed on your lap and then removed before continuing treatment.

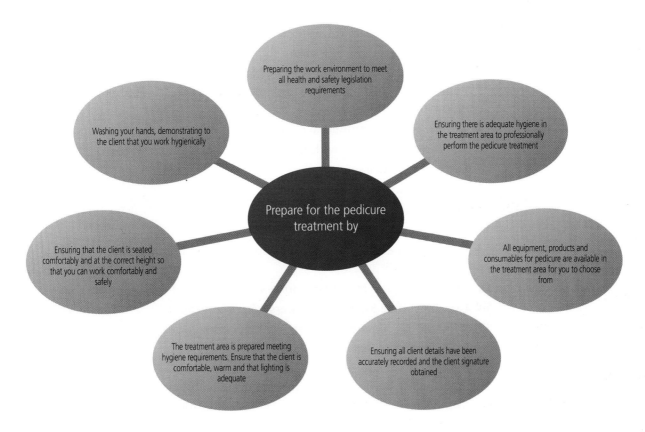

Prepare for the pedicure treatment by

Preparing the work environment to meet all health and safety legislation requirements

Ensuring there is adequate hygiene in the treatment area to professionally perform the pedicure treatment

Washing your hands, demonstrating to the client that you work hygienically

All equipment, products and consumables for pedicure are available in the treatment area for you to choose from

Ensuring that the client is seated comfortably and at the correct height so that you can work comfortably and safely

Ensuring all client details have been accurately recorded and the client signature obtained

The treatment area is prepared meeting hygiene requirements. Ensure that the client is comfortable, warm and that lighting is adequate

CONSULTATION

The procedure for this is discussed with that for manicure – see page 281.

PREPARING THE CLIENT

Ensure that the client has a comfortable chair at the correct height, so that you can work comfortably and the client can enjoy her treatment without strain to the muscles and joints of the leg.

Before treatment begins, ask the client to remove her tights or socks, and any clothing that might restrict her lower leg movement, such as jeans or trousers. Cover her upper legs with a clean towel. This will help her to be more comfortable and allow you to work without restriction.

Consult the client's record card and begin treatment.

THE PEDICURE PROCEDURE

1 Wash your hands.
2 Wipe both feet with cottonwool soaked in surgical spirit (separate pieces for each foot).

TIP

A *foot spa* may be used instead of an ordinary foot bowl, adding a touch of luxury to the pedicure treatment.

3 Soak both feet in warm water to which a mild antiseptic liquid soap has been added.

4 Take out the left foot and towel-dry it.

5 Remove any existing nail polish, and check again for contra-indications below the nail plate.

6 Cut the toenails straight across, using toenail clippers or scissors.

7 File the nails smooth with the coarse side of the emery board.

8 Apply cuticle massage cream.

9 Place the foot back in the water.

10 Remove the right foot and repeat procedures **4–9**.

11 Dry the right foot and apply cuticle remover.

12 Push back the cuticles with a cottonwool-tipped orange stick or hoof stick.

13 Clean under the free edge with a separate tipped orange stick.

14 Use the cuticle knife and nippers where indicated.

15 Wipe off the remaining cuticle remover with cottonwool, and file the nails again if necessary.

16 Apply cuticle oil.

17 Remove any hard skin. This may be done with exfoliating cream or a rasp, depending on the severity of the condition.

18 Wrap the foot in a dry towel and place it on the floor.

19 Repeat procedures **11–18** for the left foot.

20 Remove the foot bowl from the working area.

21 Perform a foot and lower leg massage.

22 Remove any grease from the nail plates with nail polish remover on cottonwool.

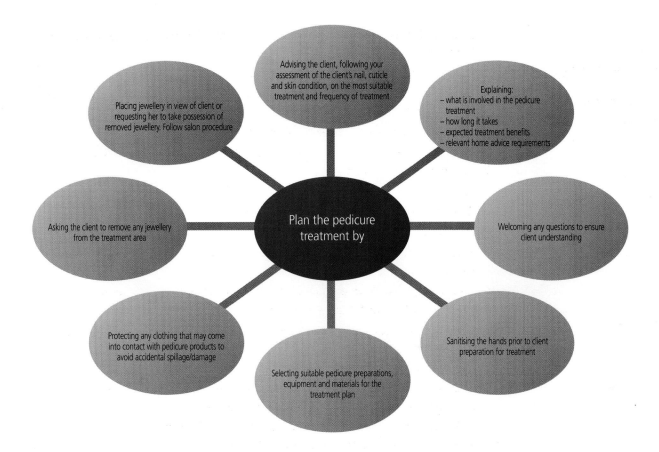

Plan the pedicure treatment by

- Advising the client, following your assessment of the client's nail, cuticle and skin condition, on the most suitable treatment and frequency of treatment
- Explaining:
  – what is involved in the pedicure treatment
  – how long it takes
  – expected treatment benefits
  – relevant home advice requirements
- Placing jewellery in view of client or requesting her to take possession of removed jewellery. Follow salon procedure
- Welcoming any questions to ensure client understanding
- Asking the client to remove any jewellery from the treatment area
- Sanitising the hands prior to client preparation for treatment
- Protecting any clothing that may come into contact with pedicure products to avoid accidental spillage/damage
- Selecting suitable pedicure preparations, equipment and materials for the treatment plan

Wiping the feet with surgical spirit

Drying the feet

Filing the toenails

Applying cuticle massage cream

Applying cuticle remover

Pushing back the cuticles

23 Place tissue between the toes.

24 Apply base coat, polish and top coat where indicated.

Using a cuticle knife

Using cuticle nippers

Removing hard skin with a rasp

Applying polish to the toenails

The completed pedicure

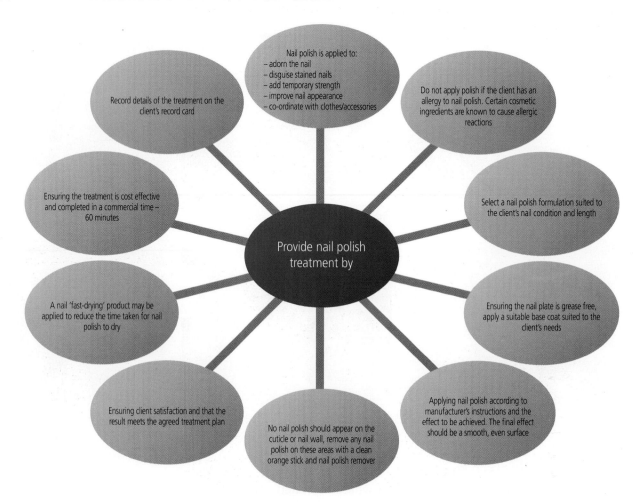

Nail polish is applied to:
– adorn the nail
– disguise stained nails
– add temporary strength
– improve nail appearance
– co-ordinate with clothes/accessories

Do not apply polish if the client has an allergy to nail polish. Certain cosmetic ingredients are known to cause allergic reactions

Record details of the treatment on the client's record card

Select a nail polish formulation suited to the client's nail condition and length

Ensuring the treatment is cost effective and completed in a commercial time – 60 minutes

Provide nail polish treatment by

Ensuring the nail plate is grease free, apply a suitable base coat suited to the client's needs

A nail 'fast-drying' product may be applied to reduce the time taken for nail polish to dry

Applying nail polish according to manufacturer's instructions and the effect to be achieved. The final effect should be a smooth, even surface

Ensuring client satisfaction and that the result meets the agreed treatment plan

No nail polish should appear on the cuticle or nail wall, remove any nail polish on these areas with a clean orange stick and nail polish remover

Cutting and filing toenails

Toenails should be cut straight across, using nail clippers or strong sharp scissors, then filed smooth using the coarse side of the emery board.

Removing hard skin

Hard skin develops on the feet as a form of protection, either from friction from footwear or from standing for long periods of time.

It is therefore not advisable to remove *all* the hard skin from an area, as this would remove the protective pad. Hard skin should be removed only to improve the appearance of the feet. Hard-skin build-up that causes pain or discomfort should be referred to a chiropodist for treatment.

Excess hard skin may be removed from the feet in a number of ways, including exfoliators, pumice stones, callus files, chiropody sponges, and corn planes. Exfoliators should be used with a deep circular massage movement: they are ideal when only a very small build-up of hard skin is present. Files, pumice stones and the rest should be used with a swift stroking movement in one direction only (similar to buffing). Sawing back and forth would lead to friction, and discomfort for the client.

Always finish off a hard-skin removal procedure with a lot of moisturiser or foot massage lotion, to soften the newly exposed skin.

HEALTH AND SAFETY

Cutting toenails
Never cut toenails down at the sides. This increases the chance of ingrowing toenails, and may lead to infection.

Removing hard skin with a rasp

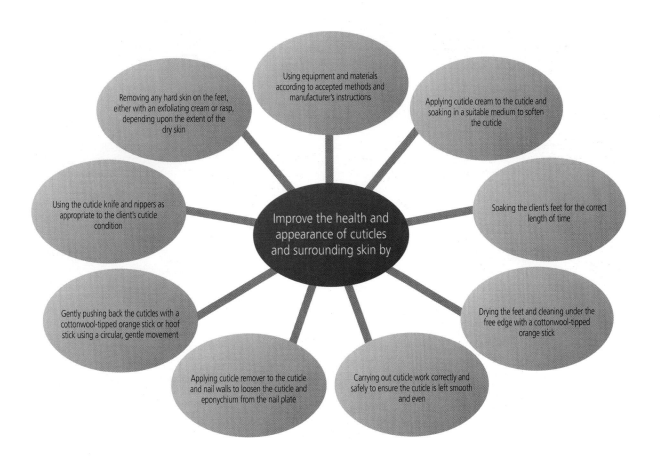

Improve the health and appearance of cuticles and surrounding skin by

- Using equipment and materials according to accepted methods and manufacturer's instructions
- Applying cuticle cream to the cuticle and soaking in a suitable medium to soften the cuticle
- Soaking the client's feet for the correct length of time
- Drying the feet and cleaning under the free edge with a cottonwool-tipped orange stick
- Carrying out cuticle work correctly and safely to ensure the cuticle is left smooth and even
- Applying cuticle remover to the cuticle and nail walls to loosen the cuticle and eponychium from the nail plate
- Gently pushing back the cuticles with a cottonwool-tipped orange stick or hoof stick using a circular, gentle movement
- Using the cuticle knife and nippers as appropriate to the client's cuticle condition
- Removing any hard skin on the feet, either with an exfoliating cream or rasp, depending upon the extent of the dry skin

Foot massage

As with a manicure massage, the pedicure massage is carried out near the end of the treatment, prior to nail polishing. The pedicure massage includes the foot and the lower leg, and offers benefits to the client comparable with those of the manicure massage.

Foot massage sequence

1 **Effleurage from the foot to the knee** Use long sweeping strokes from the toes to the knee, moving on both the back and the front of the leg.
   Repeat step 1 a further 5 times.

2 **Thumb frictions to the dorsal aspect of the foot** Use the thumbs, one in front of the other, and move backwards and forwards in a gentle sawing action. Move from the toes to the ankle, then slide back down to the toes.
   Repeat step 2 a further 2 times.

3 **Thumb frictions to the plantar aspect of the foot** Use the same movement as in step 2, but on the sole of the foot, moving from the toes to the heel.
   Repeat step 3 a further 2 times.

4 **Toe circulating** Supporting the base of the toes with one hand, hold the toes individually with the other and move them through their full range of movement, first clockwise and then anticlockwise.
   Repeat step 4 a further 2 times.

Effleurage to the lower leg

Thumb frictions to the dorsal aspect of the foot

Thumb frictions to the plantar aspect of the foot

Toe circling

Palm kneading to the plantar surface of the foot

Finger kneading around the malleolus

5 Palm kneading to the bottom surface of the foot Place the heel of the hand into the arch of the foot and massage with deep circular movements.

Repeat step 5 a further 5 times.

6 Finger kneading around the ankle bone Using two fingers of each hand, use small circular movements to knead around the ankle bone. Massage both sides of the ankle bone at the same time.

Repeat step 6 a further 2 times.

7 Deep stroking to the top and bottom of the foot simultaneously Cup the foot with the whole of the hand, so that the thumb is on the sole of the foot and the fingers on top of the foot. Firmly stroke the foot from toe to ankle, using alternate hands.

Repeat step 7 a further 5 times.

8 Effleurage from the foot to the knee Use the same movement as in step 1.

Repeat step 8 a further 5 times.

Deep stroking to the foot

Effleurage from foot to knee

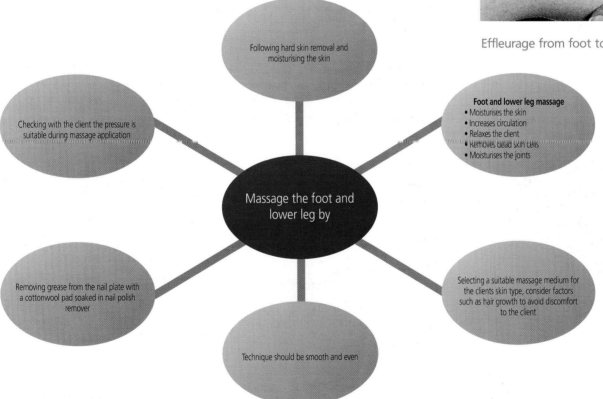

Massage the foot and lower leg by

Following hard skin removal and moisturising the skin

Foot and lower leg massage
• Moisturises the skin
• Increases circulation
• Relaxes the client
• Removes dead skin cells
• Moisturises the joints

Checking with the client the pressure is suitable during massage application

Removing grease from the nail plate with a cottonwool pad soaked in nail polish remover

Selecting a suitable massage medium for the clients skin type, consider factors such as hair growth to avoid discomfort to the client

Technique should be smooth and even

CONTRA-ACTIONS

The client – or the manicurist – may at some time develop an allergy to a manicure product that has been successfully used previously. This could be for a number of reasons, including new medication being taken or illness.

The symptoms of an allergic reaction could be as follows:

- redness of the skin;
- swelling;
- itching;
- raised blisters.

The symptoms do not necessarily appear on the hands. In the case of nail polish allergy, the symptoms often show up on the face, which the hands are continually touching.

In the case of an allergic reaction:

- Remove the offending product immediately, using water or, in the case of polish, solvent.
- If symptoms persist, seek medical advice.

Always record any allergies on the client's record card, so that the offending product may be avoided in future.

AFTERCARE AND ADVICE

Offering aftercare advice at the end of a pedicure treatment will help the client to look after her feet between salon visits, and is also an ideal opportunity to recommend retail products.

Aftercare advice will differ slightly for each client, but it will basically be as follows:

- Change socks or tights daily.
- Apply moisturising lotion to the feet after bathing.
- Ensure that the feet are thoroughly dry after washing, especially between the toes.
- Apply talc or a special foot powder between the toes to help absorb moisture.
- Go barefoot wherever it is safe and practical to do so.
- Ensure that footwear fits properly.
- Avoid wearing high heels for long periods of time.
- Advise on appropriate nail/skin-care products to remedy the problems present, e.g. dry skin, nails, stained nails.
- Advise the client of any other professional treatments you could recommend.
- Advise the client on a treatment plan to improve the nail/skin condition and the time intervals recommended between each treatment.
- Always file the nails straight across.
- If any pain is felt in the feet, visit a chiropodist.

It is also advisable to advise the client what to do in the event of a contra-action.

Foot treatments

In addition to the pedicure, further treatments may be added as appropriate. Here are some examples:

- **Exfoliating treatment** is carried out as part of the massage routine. An abrasive massage cream is massaged over the skin of the foot in circular movements, concentrating over the ball and heel of the foot. Exfoliation has the following effects: it removes dead skin, increases circulation and improves the condition and appearance of the skin.

- **Foot treatment mask** is applied according to the clients treatment requirements. The mask is applied to the skin and the feet can then be wrapped in warm thermal booties to aid the absorption of the mask. The mask removes dead skin cells, improves circulation and improves the condition of the skin of the feet.

- **Paraffin wax treatment**, this wax is heated in a special bath to a temperature of 50–55°C. It is then applied to the feet with a brush and left to set for 10–15 minutes. The heating effect stimulates the blood circulation, eases the discomfort of arthritic and rheumatic conditions, and softens the skin, improving the appearance and condition of dry skin. After use the wax is disposed of.

- **Thermal booties** are electrically heated booties. They are used to stimulate, rejuvenate and moisturise the skin of the feet. The feet are prepared with the application of a foot treatment mask, protected in a film wrap and placed inside warm booties for 10 minutes to enable the mask to penetrate the skin of the epidermis.

> **TIP**
>
> **Paraffin wax**
> Heat the wax at least half an hour before the client arrives to ensure it has melted properly. Paraffin wax may have essential oils added to enhance the therapeutic effects.

Specialist foot and leg treatment

Specialist treatments should be offered to your client when there is a specific need or if she feels she would like to benefit from such a treatment. Specialist treatment training in these advanced techniques is usually offered by major product companies.

The model for this specialist foot and leg treatment is a client who regularly visits the gym and wished to benefit from a spa-therapy revitalising treatment following a workout.

The following foot and leg treatment will:

- Stimulate the blood circulation
- Aid with the removal of toxins and waste products
- Have a skin cleansing action
- Remove dead skin cells (desquamation)
- Improve the moisture content of the skin
- Relax tense/stiff muscles in the foot and leg

Your treatments should be adapted the meet the treatment objectives for the client. Allow 30 minutes for the specialist foot and leg treatment below.

The skin of the feet and legs is cleansed using warm towelling mitts infused with lime oil for its therapeutic refreshing and energising properties.

The feet and legs are exfoliated to remove all dead skin cells and brighten the skin.

A sea salt-based preparation with emollient, skin softening ingredients is applied to each foot and leg.

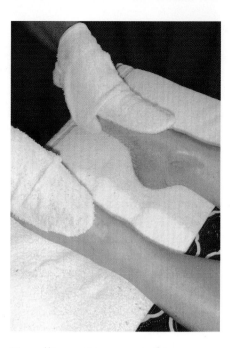

Towelling mitts are used to remove the exfoliating treatment. These have been steamed and are warm when used.

A skin-nourishing milk lotion is applied to each foot and leg using a 'drizzling' technique. The milk is particularly beneficial for dry skin.

Massage movements are applied using effleurage and petrissage manipulations to introduce the massage medium into the skin.

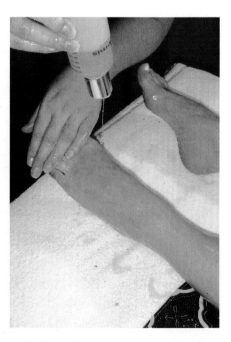

A further skin-treatment product oil is applied and massaged into the skin. This will act as a treatment mask for the skin to soften and condition.

The feet are then placed in steamed towels, encased in a plastic bag and dry towelling mitten for 10–15 minutes.

When the treatment mask is applied, a scalp massage is applied to induce client relaxation.

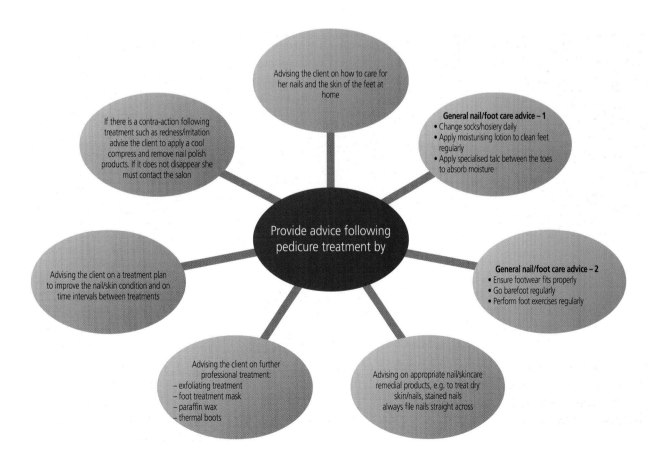

Advising the client on how to care for her nails and the skin of the feet at home

If there is a contra-action following treatment such as redness/irritation advise the client to apply a cool compress and remove nail polish products. If it does not disappear she must contact the salon

General nail/foot care advice – 1
• Change socks/hosiery daily
• Apply moisturising lotion to clean feet regularly
• Apply specialised talc between the toes to absorb moisture

Provide advice following pedicure treatment by

Advising the client on a treatment plan to improve the nail/skin condition and on time intervals between treatments

General nail/foot care advice – 2
• Ensure footwear fits properly
• Go barefoot regularly
• Perform foot exercises regularly

Advising the client on further professional treatment:
– exfoliating treatment
– foot treatment mask
– paraffin wax
– thermal boots

Advising on appropriate nail/skincare remedial products, e.g. to treat dry skin/nails, stained nails always file nails straight across

Exfoliating treatment

Exercises for the feet and ankles

As part of the home-care advice given to a pedicure client, **foot exercises** should be mentioned – these can play a very important role in keeping the client's feet healthy. They help:

- to stimulate circulation;
- to keep joints mobilised, allowing a greater range of movement in the toes and ankles;
- to keep muscles strong, reducing the chance of fallen arches (flat feet).

Here are some examples of exercises:

1 Sitting on a chair with the feet flat on the floor, raise the toes upwards and then relax.
2 Stand on tiptoes, and relax down again.
3 Sitting on a chair with the feet flat on the floor, lift one leg slightly and draw a circle with the toes so that the ankle moves through its full range of movement.
4 **Dorsiflexion**: bending the foot backwards towards the body.
5 **Plantar flexion**: pointing the foot down towards the ground.
6 **Inversion**: moving the foot inwards towards the middle of the body.
7 **Eversion**: moving the foot out towards the side of the body.

Assessment of knowledge and understanding

You have now learnt about the different pedicure treatments available to improve the condition of the feet, nails and surrounding skin. These skills will enable you to professionally provide pedicure treatment.

To test your level of knowledge, answer the following short questions. These will prepare you for your summative (final) assessment.

Additional anatomy and physiology questions required for this unit are found on pages 129–30, 131–2.

Anatomy and physiology

1 How many bones form the foot? Name them.
2 Name the bones of the lower leg.
3 Name the main arteries of the lower leg.
4 Name the two muscles of the foot.
5 Name two muscles of the lower leg.

Consult with the client

1 What is the purpose of the client consultation?
2 Why is it important to assess the condition of the client's foot and nail condition before treatment commences?

3 Name three contra-indications observed at consultation which would prevent treatment being carried out.

4 What conditions, if present, would restrict your treatment application?

5 Why is diabetes considered a contra-indication to pedicure treatment?

Prepare for the treatment

1 Taking into account client comfort and modesty, why is it important that the client is correctly prepared for treatment?

2 How can you ensure that the position of the client for pedicure minimises potential risk of injury to yourself?

3 How can cross-infection be prevented when performing pedicure treatment? State three examples.

4 Why is it important to sanitise your hands effectively before treatment commences?

Plan the treatment

1 When would you choose to include the following foot and nail treatments in your treatment plan?
- heat treatments
- skin conditioners.

2 What is the commercially acceptable time for a pedicure treatment?

3 What should be considered when designing a pedicure treatment plan for a client?

4 Why is it important to complete your treatment plan in the allocated time?

Improve the appearance of the natural nails

1 With regard to the nails, what should be agreed with the client before the nails are shaped?

2 Why should toenails be cut straight across and not oval, like fingernails?

Improve the health and appearance of the cuticles and surrounding skin

1 What is the purpose of the soaking medium usually added to the warm water to soak the client's feet?

2 Describe the methods available for removing hard skin from the feet.

3 How should the skin be left following hard skin removal?

4 Name three treatment products used in pedicure and their effect on the nail, cuticle or skin of the foot as applicable.

5 What do you understand by the term 'erythema', and its cause?

6 Give three effects on the nail and skin of the incorrect use of pedicure tools.

Massage the foot and lower leg

1 How is the quantity and type of massage medium selected for each client?

2 How and why should massage technique be adapted for each client?

3 State four benefits of foot and lower leg massage.

4 What are the terms used for the different types of massage applied in a pedicure?

Provide nail polishing treatment

1 Why should grease be removed from the nail plate prior to nail polish application?

2 How is the type of base coat selected for a client?

3 How many coats of coloured polish are usually applied with:
   - cream polish
   - pearlised polish.

4 Following nail polish application, how should the painted nail and cuticle appear?

5 Why should client records be up to date following treatment?

Complete the treatment

1 State the general aftercare advice that you would give to a pedicure client.

2 List three retail products that you would recommend to a pedicure client.

3 What possible contra-action could occur during or after a pedicure treatment? What advice would you give to client with regard to a contra-action occurring?

4 How can foot exercises be of benefit to a pedicure client?

5 How often would you recommend a pedicure to maintain the condition and appearance of the nails and feet?

6 For each of the clients below suggest a treatment routine. Detail the treatment plan to include the cause of the condition, aims of the treatment, products used, treatments recommended, relevant retail sales and home-care advice:
   - a middle-aged retail worker who has very hard, cracked skin on the soles of her feet around both heels;
   - an elderly man who has little movement in his ankle joints and slightly distorted joints in his toes;
   - a pregnant client who has tired, aching feet and swollen ankles.

chapter 11

PROVIDE MAKE-UP TREATMENT

`BT9`

PLAN AND PROMOTE MAKE-UP ACTIVITIES

`BT10`

Learning objectives

This unit describes how to provide make-up for a variety of occasions including day, evening, special occasions and photographic work. The choice and application of make-up will be applied to suit the client's skin type, colouring and condition.

Also covered is how to plan and promote make-up activities.

In addition the techniques of false lash application applied to enhance the client's natural lashes or change the look of the eye area, are discussed. For further information on eye treatments, refer to Chapter 7: Provide eyelash and eyebrow treatments.

It describes the competencies to enable you to:

- **consult with the client**
- **prepare for the treatment**
- **plan the treatment**
- **apply make-up products**
- **complete the treatment**

When providing make-up treatment it is important to use the skills you have learnt in the following core mandatory units:

Unit G1 – Ensure your own actions reduce risks to health and safety

Unit G6 – Promote additional products or services to clients

Unit G8 – Develop and maintain your effectiveness at work

MAKE-UP SERVICES

Make-up is used to enhance and accentuate the facial features to make us appear more attractive – which in turn makes us feel more confident. Make-up is used to create balance in the face, by skilful application of different cosmetic products to reduce or to emphasise facial features.

Each client is unique, so each requires an individual approach for her make-up. The overall effect should be attractive, complementing the client's personality, her lifestyle, and the context for which the make-up is to be worn.

RECEPTION

Make-up application is offered for different purposes.

- *A make-up lesson* A chance for the client to learn from a professional how to apply make-up that suits her.
- *Special occasion make-up* Make-up applied by a specialist to suit the occasion for which it is to be worn, such as a wedding. If the make-up is for a bride, advise the client to visit the salon for a consultation and a practice session so that you can decide together on an appropriate make-up. Ask the client if possible to bring a swatch of the dress material with her, so that you can select colours to complement this and to co-ordinate with the accessories.
- *Evening make-up* will be seen under artificial lighting. The effect this has on the appearance of the make-up will depend upon the source and this must be considered when applying an evening make-up. Generally evening make-up is heavier in application and stronger colours may be applied. Products to emphasise and highlight, such as frosted eye-shadows and lip-glosses, may be introduced.
- *Remedial make-up* Make-up may be applied for remedial purposes, to cover facial disfigurements or birthmarks, and the client can be taught how to do this herself.
- *Photographic make-up* is applied for many reasons including magazine shoots, portrait work and fashion shows. Make-up application must be skilful to achieve the right end-result as the location may be a photographic studio or outdoors on location.
- *A professional job* Some clients simply wish to have their make-up professionally applied.

As always, you need to know how long each service will take. Here are some suggested times:

- make-up lesson: 1 hour;
- special occasion, evening and photographic make-up: 45 minutes – 1 hour;
- straight make-up: 45 minutes.

In the salon advise the client that if she intends to have her hair washed and styled, this should be done before she has the make-up applied.

TIP

Effective communication
When applying make-up it is important that you fully understand the effect to be achieved. Good communication is essential. Ask the client/photographer what the final result should look like.

It is also important that you check that the client does not have allergies to any products to avoid a contra-action.

If a client requests a deep cleansing facial followed by make-up application, suggest that she has the facial at least five days prior to the make-up. The facial will stimulate the skin, increasing its normal physiological functioning. This will affect how long the make-up lasts; it may even cause the colour of the foundation to change.

Do not reshape the eyebrows at the same treatment as make-up application – secondary infection could occur; also the skin in the area will be very pink, altering the colour and thus the effect of eyeshadow.

CONTRA-INDICATIONS

Certain contra-indications prevent make-up application. Check for these at the consultation, and if any of the following are present on inspection of the skin, do not proceed with make-up application:

- *Skin disorders* including bacterial infections such as impetigo, viral infections such as herpes-simplex, and fungal infections such as tinea corporis.
- *Active psoriasis and eczema.*
- *Bruising* in the area.
- *Recent haemorrhage*.
- *Swelling and inflammation* in the area.
- *Recent scar tissue*.
- *Sensory nerve disorders*.
- *Cuts or abrasions* in the area.
- A *recent operation* in the area.
- *Eye disorders* such as styes, conjunctivitis and watery eyes.

Ask the client whether she has any known allergies to cosmetic preparations: note the answer on the record card. Care must be taken to avoid contact with an allergen.

The consultation

If the client is new, complete a record card noting the client's personal details. An example of a typical record card for make-up is found on page 330.

Discuss your make-up plan with the client to ensure that the make-up will meet her requirements. You may need to ask questions such as those that follow, but of course the questions depend on the purpose of the make-up application.

- 'Do you normally wear make-up?'
- 'For what occasion is the make-up to be worn?'
- 'What colour are the clothing and accessories to be worn on this occasion?'
- 'Are there any colours that you particularly like or dislike?'
- 'What effect would you like the make-up to create?' (This question may be asked in many contexts – the client/photographer may wish to achieve a natural or a glamorous effect, or to emphasise or diminish certain facial features.)

ACTIVITY
Recognising contra-indications
What skin disorders can you think of that would contra-indicate make-up application?

ACTIVITY
The record card
Why is it important to complete a record card? What information should be recorded on it?

TIP
Contra-indications
Remember – never name a contra-indication, you may be wrong. Refer the client to their GP, this is their role.
In the case of the skin disorder herpes simplex, the make-up treatment may be received when the skin is healed and clear.

BEAUTY WORKS

Date	Beauty therapist name	
Client name		Date of birth (identifying client age group)
Address		Postcode

Evening phone number   Day phone number

Name of doctor   Doctor's address and phone number

Related medical history (conditions that may restrict or prohibit treatment application)

Are you taking any medication (this may affect skin sensitivity)

CONTRA-INDICATIONS REQUIRING MEDICAL REFERRAL
(Preventing the application of make-up)

- ☐ bacterial infections (e.g. impetigo)
- ☐ viral infections (e.g. herpes simplex)
- ☐ fungal infections (e.g. tinea corporis)
- ☐ conjunctivitis   ☐ watery eyes

SKIN TYPE

- ☐ oily   ☐ dry   ☐ combination

FOUNDATION

- ☐ liquid   ☐ cream
- ☐ compact   ☐ mousse

POWDER

- ☐ loose   ☐ compact

EYE PRODUCTS FOR EYE AREA

- ☐ cream eyeshadow   ☐ liquid eyeliner
- ☐ pencil eyeliner   ☐ powder eyeshadow

EYE PRODUCTS FOR BROW AREA

- ☐ pencil   ☐ liquid
- ☐ shadow   ☐ eyebrow mascara

EYE PRODUCTS FOR EYELASHES

- ☐ mascara   ☐ false lashes
- ☐ lash curling

CONTRA-INDICATIONS WHICH RESTRICT TREATMENT
(Treatment may require adaptation)

- ☐ cuts and abrasions
- ☐ bruising and swelling
- ☐ recent scar tissue
- ☐ eczema
- ☐ skin allergies
- ☐ vitiligo
- ☐ styes

MAKE-UP CONTEXT

- ☐ day   ☐ evening
- ☐ special occasion

CHEEK PRODUCTS

- ☐ highlighter   ☐ shader
- ☐ blusher

LIP PRODUCTS

- ☐ pencil lipliner
- ☐ lipgloss
- ☐ lipstick

Beauty therapist signature (for reference)

Client signature (confirmation of details)

TREATMENT ADVICE

This information includes
- what products have been used in the make-up application
- how they have been applied to achieve the treatment effect
- how to reapply products to achieve/maintain the result
- future treatment needs. This will include other services that you would recommend to the client

PRODUCTS FOR HOME USE

This information includes
- how the make-up should be removed, referring to skin care products and how they should be used
- advice re products that would be suitable for the client to use at home to care for her skin
- also retail advice re make-up products that you would recommend for the client and how they should be used/applied

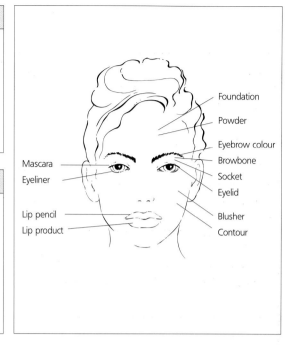

Retail advice make-up record card

Consult with the client for make-up treatment by

- Maintaining client privacy at all times
- Inviting the client to ask questions. The client should understand fully what the make-up treatment involves
- Recording personal details on the client record card, i.e. name, address, etc. Check that there are no contra-indications to make-up treatment
- Establishing the client's skin type in order to select appropriate skincare/cosmetic preparations
- Looking for contra-indications, do not provide treatment if present. This prevents harm to the client, therapist or other clients, for example in the case of a contagious disease
- Using questions in order to determine the treatment plan:
  – does the client wear make-up normally
  – what is the occasion
  – colour preferences
  – effect they wish the make-up to create
  – known allergies to cosmetics
- Discussing the purpose of the make-up application:
  – day
  – evening
  – special occasion
  – photographic

EQUIPMENT AND MATERIALS

Before beginning the make-up, check that you have to hand the necessary equipment and materials.

EQUIPMENT LIST

couch or beauty chair

trolley

headband

cleansing lotion

eye make-up remover

toning lotion

moisturiser

dry cottonwool

large white facial tissues

make-up

bright lighting

make-up brushes

disposable applicators and brushes

cosmetic sponges

make-up palette

pencil sharpener

eyelash curler

artificial eyelashes

spatulas

orange sticks

see opposite for complete list of materials required

TIP ✔

The chair must offer head support, or the client's neck will become strained during the make-up; also the head needs support if it is to be steady during the application of eye and lip make-up.

- *Couch or beauty chair* – with a reclining back and a head rest and an easy-to-clean surface.
- *Trolley or other surface* – on which to place everything.
- *Disposable tissue, (such as bedroll)* – to cover the work surface and the couch or beauty chair.
- *Towels (2)* – freshly laundered for each client – one to be placed over the head of the couch or chair, the other over the client's chest and shoulders to protect her clothing.
- *Headband, (clean)* – to protect the client's hair whilst cleansing the skin.
- *Hairclips* – to protect the client's hair during make-up application.
- *Cleansing lotion* – to prepare the skin.
- *Eye make-up remover* – to prepare the skin.
- *Toning lotion* – to prepare the skin.
- *Moisturiser (lightweight)* – to facilitate make-up application and create a barrier between the skin and make-up.
- *Magnifying lamp* – to inspect the skin after cleansing and check for areas requiring special attention e.g. broken capillaries that need concealer.
- *Damp cottonwool* – prepared for each client and used during skin cleansing.
- *Dry cottonwool* – stored in a covered jar, to apply loose face powder.
- *Large white facial tissues* – to blot the skin after facial toning, and to protect the skin during make-up application.
- *Bowls* – to hold the prepared cottonwool.
- *Bowls or lined pedal bin* – for waste materials.
- *Client's record card*.
- *Make-up (a range)* – suitable for clients with known skin allergies to cosmetics, for contact-lens wearers, for different skin types and skin colours, including:
  - concealing and contouring cosmetics (shaders, highlighters and blushers);
  - foundations;
  - translucent powders;
  - eyeshadows;
  - eyeliners;
  - browliners;
  - mascara;
  - lipsticks;
  - lipglosses;
  - lipliners.

- *Bright lighting.*
- *Make-up brushes (assorted)* – at least 3 sets, to allow for sanitisation after use.
- *Disposable applicators and brushes* where possible – for example for mascara and the application of eyeshadow.
- *Cosmetic sponges* – for applying foundation.
- *Make-up palette* – for preparing cosmetic products prior to application.
- *Hand mirror (clean).*
- *Pencil sharpener* – for cosmetic pencils.
- *Eyelash curlers.*
- *Artificial eyelashes.*
- *Spatulas (several).*
- *Orange sticks (several)* – for removing make-up products from their containers.

Ellisons

Make-up brushes

Make-up brushes

These are prepared from different fibres which may be synthetic or animal including camel, sable, ox, pony and goat.

Powder and blusher brushes may be produced from softer hair but for the purpose of contouring and blending brushes must be firmer.

- *Large face powder dusting brush*, to remove excess face powder or to apply specialised powders
- *Contouring blush brush*, to apply facial contouring products to highlight and shade areas of the face
- *Blusher brush* (large to medium), to apply powder colour to the face and for blending
- *Small flat angle-edged eye shadow brush*, to apply and blend powder eye make-up products in the socket area of the eye
- *Small rounded-edged eye shadow brush*, used to blend and shade
- *Medium firm eyeshadow blending brush*, used to blend powder eye colours and soften harsh lines and colour
- *Small concealer brush*, for exact placement of concealing product
- *Eyebrow brush*, used to remove excess make-up from the brow hair and to add colour, blend eyebrow pencil and groom the brow hair into shape
- *Eyeliner brush*, a fine brush used to apply make-up colour to contour the eyes creating a precise line
- *Mascara wand/comb*, to apply mascara and remove excess mascara to separate the lashes
- *Lip brush*, used to apply lip products and ensure a definite, balanced outline to the lips

Ellisons

Eyelash curlers

TIP

False eyelashes should be available if you are applying an evening or special occasion make-up – you may wish to apply these to enhance the final effect.

TIP

When you give a make-up lesson, do so in front of a large mirror so that the client can watch the various stages of make-up application.

Record the make-up used and the advice given on a separate record, for the client to take away with her.

TIP

Make-up brushes
When buying make-up brushes, make sure that the hairs are secure at the base of the brush.
Have more than one of set of brushes. To avoid cross-infection they must be cleaned after use.

TIP

If you intend to apply make-up at different locations, buy a large make-up case so that you can transport the make-up easily and hygienically.

HEALTH AND SAFETY

Transporting make-up
If you are transporting your make-up in a box, keep the box clean. Clients won't be impressed if they see soiled, dirty make-up containers.

HEALTH AND SAFETY

Avoiding cross-infection
To avoid cross-infection, don't use directly on a client the applicators supplied with cosmetic products.

TIP

Keep a store of spare make-up sponges – they soon crumble with repeated cleaning.

HEALTH AND SAFETY

Hygiene at home
Advise clients to keep their own make-up clean. Dirty brushes spoil effective make-up application, and offer breeding grounds for bacteria.

Sterilisation and sanitisation

Where possible, use disposable applicators during make-up application, costing these into the treatment price. Sanitise make-up brushes after each use: wash them in warm water and detergent, rinse them thoroughly in clean water, and allow them to dry naturally. Once dry, place the brushes in an ultraviolet light cabinet ready for use.

TIP

An *alcohol-based cleanser* may be used to clean make-up brushes. The brushes are first cleaned with a solution of warm water and detergent, then thoroughly rinsed in clean water and allowed to dry. They are then briefly immersed in the alcohol solution and again allowed to dry.

All cosmetic products should be removed from their containers using a clean spatula or orange stick, and placed on the clean plastic make-up palette before application. (This avoids contamination of the make-up with bacteria from unclean make-up applicators.)

The make-up palette should be cleaned with warm water and detergent, then wiped with a disinfectant solution applied using clean cottonwool. It should be stored in the ultraviolet cabinet.

Mascara should be applied using a disposable brush applicator, fresh for each client.

Sharpen cosmetic pencils with a pencil sharpener before each use.

Make-up sponges should be disposed of after use, or washed in warm water and detergent; then placed in a disinfectant solution and rinsed. Allow them to dry, then place them in the ultraviolet cabinet, with each side being exposed for at least 20 minutes.

HEALTH AND SAFETY

Maintaining hygiene
If you drop a make-up tool on the floor, discard it – don't use it again until it has been sanitised.

Make-up sponges

Preparing the cubicle

The make-up room should be decorated in light, neutral colours to avoid the creation of unnecessary shadows. The area where the make-up is to be applied should be well lit, ideally with the same kind of light as that in which the make-up will be seen.

Place all the equipment and materials required on the trolley or work surface, in front of a make-up mirror. If you are displaying the make-up on a trolley, place the cosmetic products on a lower shelf until required, when they can be moved to the top shelf. This avoids cluttering the working area.

Lighting

You need to know the *type* of light in which the proposed make-up will be seen: this is important when deciding upon the correct choice of make-up colours, because the appearance of colours may change according to the type of light. Is the make-up to be seen in daylight, in a fluorescent-lit office, or a softly-lit restaurant?

White light (natural daylight) contains all the colours of the rainbow. When white light falls on an object, it absorbs some colours and reflects others: it is the *reflected* colour that we see. Thus, an object that we see as red is an object that absorbs the colours in white light *except* red. A *white* object reflects most of the light that falls upon it; a *black* object absorbs most of the light that falls on it.

If the make-up is to be worn in natural light, choose subtle make-up products as daylight intensifies colours.

HEALTH AND SAFETY

Ventilation
Good ventilation is important so that the client's skin does not become too warm. It is easier to apply make-up effectively to a cool skin, and the make-up will be more durable.

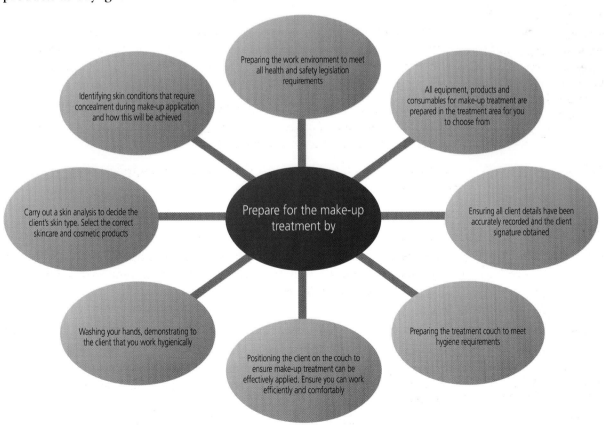

Prepare for the make-up treatment by

- Preparing the work environment to meet all health and safety legislation requirements
- All equipment, products and consumables for make-up treatment are prepared in the treatment area for you to choose from
- Identifying skin conditions that require concealment during make-up application and how this will be achieved
- Ensuring all client details have been accurately recorded and the client signature obtained
- Carry out a skin analysis to decide the client's skin type. Select the correct skincare and cosmetic products
- Preparing the treatment couch to meet hygiene requirements
- Washing your hands, demonstrating to the client that you work hygienically
- Positioning the client on the couch to ensure make-up treatment can be effectively applied. Ensure you can work efficiently and comfortably

TIP ✔

If working under artificial light, use warm white fluorescent light for day make-up, as this closely resembles natural light.

A diffuser may be used to cover the fluorescent tube, this softens the cool effect on the make-up and reduces the effects of shadows.

If the make-up is to be worn in the office, it will probably be seen under **fluorescent light**. This contains an excess of blue and green, which have a 'cool' effect on the make-up: the red in the face does not show up and the face can look drained of colour. Reds and yellows should be avoided, as these will not show up; blue-toned colours will. Don't apply dark colours, as fluorescent light intensifies these.

Evening make-up is usually seen in **incandescent light** – light produced by a filament lamp. This produces an excess of red and yellow light, which creates a warm, flattering effect. Almost all colours can be used in this light, except that browns and purples will appear darker. Choose a lighter foundation than normal to reflect the light, and use frosted highlighting products where possible for the same reason.

Because it is necessary to choose brighter colours and to emphasise facial features using contouring cosmetics, evening make-up will appear very obvious and dramatic in daylight. Explain to the client the reasons for the effect created, so that when she leaves the salon in daylight she won't feel that the make-up is inappropriate.

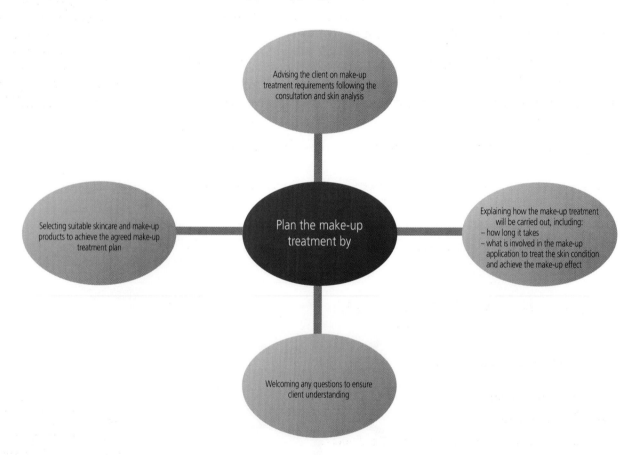

PREPARING THE CLIENT

Take the client through to the treatment area. Make-up application may take place either at the make-up chair, in front of a mirror, or at the treatment couch. Before you start the make-up, discuss and plan the make-up with the client, recording significant details on her record card.

Before preparing the client for the treatment, wash your hands. The client need remove only her upper outer clothing, to her underwear. Offer the client a gown, or drape a clean towel or make-up cape across her chest and shoulders. Place a headband or hairclip around the hairline, to protect the hair and keep it away from the face. Any jewellery in the treatment area should be removed. Refer to the record card to check for any known allergies to cosmetic products.

TIP

If a headband is used, remove it directly after the facial cleanse so that it doesn't flatten and spoil the hair.

HEALTH AND SAFETY

Contact lenses
If the client wears contact lenses, ask her whether she wishes to remove them before the skin is cleansed. (The need for this will depend on the sensitivity of the eyes.)

After preparing the client, and before touching the skin, wash your hands again. Now cleanse and tone the skin, using products appropriate to her skin type. Just as skin-care products vary in their formulation to suit the various skin types, so make-up products are designed for different skins. Record all relevant details on the record card.

Inspect the skin using a magnifying lamp. Identify any areas that require specific attention.

Apply a light-textured moisturiser before make-up application. This has the following benefits:

TIP

Existing cosmetic eyeliner is sometimes difficult to remove. Use a cotton bud soaked in eye make-up remover: gently stroke this along the base of the lower eyelashes, in towards the nose.

- it prevents the natural secretions of the skin changing the colour of the foundation;
- it seals the surface of the skin, and prevents absorption of the foundation into the skin;
- it facilitates make-up application by providing a smooth base.

Remove excess moisturiser by blotting the skin with a facial tissue.

APPLYING THE MAKE-UP

The make-up sequence

- Conceal any blemishes.
- Apply foundation.
- Contour the face (with cream liquid products).
- Apply powder.
- Contour the face (with powder products).
- Apply blusher.
- Apply eyeshadow.
- Make up the eyebrows.
- Apply mascara.
- Make up the lips.

TIP

Concealing may be completed before or after foundation application.

Applying concealer

- Contour products, used to shade and highlight the face and features, can be applied in powder or cream formulation. Application sequence for contouring will depend upon product formulation chosen.

Concealing blemishes

Before you begin to apply make-up to the face, inspect the skin and identify any areas that require concealing, such as blemishes, uneven skin colour or shadows.

Foundation may be used to disguise minor skin imperfections, but where extra coverage is required it is necessary to apply a special **concealer**, a cosmetic designed to provide maximum skin coverage. The concealer may be applied directly to the skin after skin moisturising, or following application of the foundation.

Choose a concealer that matches the client's skin tone as closely as possible. If the concealer is to be applied *after* the foundation, it should match the colour of the *foundation*.

Concealer can contain pigment to help correct skin tone.

- *Green* helps to counteract high colouring, and to conceal dilated capillaries.
- *Lilac* counteracts a sallow skin colour.
- *White or cream* helps to correct unevenness in the skin pigmentation.

Concealers come in a range of colours, to suit all skins. Mix different colours together to obtain the required colour.

Applying concealer

Remove a small quantity of the concealer from its container, using a clean disposable spatula.

Apply the concealer to the area to be disguised, using either a clean make-up sponge or a soft make-up brush. Blend the concealer to achieve a realistic effect.

Using concealer to camouflage

Specialist techniques are required to conceal problem areas; this technique is called *camouflage*. Areas that may be required to be camouflaged include:

- *Scars*: caused by injury, post-operative, keloids (lumpy scar tissue forming at the site of wounds), acne vulgaris, burns which can cause the skin to become ridged or discoloured.
- *Birthmarks*: darker pigmented areas.
- *Pigment disorders*: hypopigmentation (reduced melanin production, e.g. vitiligo); hyperpigmenation (increased melanin production), e.g. Chloasmata (brown patches), moles, dermatosis papulosa nigra, a benign (non-malignant) skin condition common among adult black-skinned people characterised by multiple small, hyperpigmented (dark brown to black) papules on the face, neck, upper back and chest.
- *Vascular disorders*: Acne Rosacea (chronic inflammation of the skin on the nose and cheeks caused by the dilation of the blood capillaries), telangiectasia (dilated capillaries appearing on the face).

TIP ✔

Common racial skin problems:
- Caucasian – easily damaged by exposure to high temperatures and ultraviolet light, leading to broken veins and pigmentation disorders.
- Oriental – prone to uneven pigmentation on ultraviolet light exposure.
- Asian – often has uneven pigmentation skin tones; darker skin is often found around the eyes.
- African-Caribbean – greater protection against ultraviolet light as melanin is present in all layers of the epidermis; tends to scar easily, possibly leading to uneven pigmentation, vitiligo and keloids.

Vitiligo

Applying concealer to camouflage

Always check the manufacturer's instructions on how to apply the camouflage/concealing product. Brands vary and some may require different preparation and setting techniques.

This type of concealer is thick and it is preferable to build up several layers to achieve the desired effect, rather than applying a thick layer.

TIP ✔

It is preferable to build up several layers to achieve the desired effect, rather than applying a thick layer.

Treatment application

1 Select the chosen colour or colour mixture which best matches the skin tone surrounding the area to be treated.

2 Using your ring and middle fingers in a patting motion, or using a dry sponge, blend the make-up thinly over the problem area, extending it approximately 2 cm past the edge. If disguising scars, a brush may be used to feather the make-up at the edges to create a natural effect. The sponge may be dampened if needed to facilitate extra blending.

3 Build up the colour depth to ensure the blemish is completely covered, thinning the colour at the edge to blend in. A small make-up brush can be used to blend in the edges of the make-up.

4 Once the required result has been achieved, apply the fixing powder generously with a large powder puff.

5 Leave the make-up to set for 5–10 minutes.

6 Gently brush off any excess fixing powder with a large, soft make-up brush, e.g. blusher/powder brush. Blot off excess powder if required with damp cottonwool. The make-up is now waterproof and rub resistant, and should not be detectable.

7 If the camouflage has been applied to the face, a full make-up may now be applied. The foundation colour selected should match the colour of the camouflage make-up.

8 Apply foundation up to the area of camouflage make-up and blend so that an invisible finish is created. Putting an oily cream foundation over the camouflage make-up will only move or remove the camouflage make-up: it is best to use a non-oily or liquid foundation.

9 Record on the client record card the make-up products selected and application technique used.

Covering a deep red mark

- *Covering a deep red mark*: use a green pigmented make-up first, then apply make-up which matches the skin tone over the top
- *Covering a dark brown mark*: use white, opaque make-up first, then apply make-up which matches the skin tone over the top.
- *Covering a lighter mark*: commence with a darker foundation and apply make-up which matches the skin tone over the top.

The foundation

Foundation is applied to produce an even skin tone, to disguise minor skin blemishes, and as a contour cosmetic. Black skin in particular often has an uneven skin tone, requiring certain parts of the face to be lightened and others darkened to produce an even skin tone.

Foundation is available as a cream, a liquid, a gel, cake or mousse. It is composed of water, powder, oil, a humectant (such as glycerol), inorganic pigments, and additives which protect the skin from the environment (such as sunscreens and moisturisers).

Some foundations contain **'anti-ageing' ingredients** such as vitamin E. These are to neutralise **free radicals**, natural chemicals thought to be responsible for damaging the skin and producing the signs of ageing – the lines and wrinkles!

Kinds of foundation

Each foundation differs in its formulation to suit a particular skin type. The correct choice will guarantee that the foundation lasts throughout the day.

Cream foundations **Cream foundations** are oil-based, and blend easily on application. They provide a heavy coverage, and have these specific treatment uses:

- dry skin;
- normal skin;
- mature skin.

Liquid foundations **Liquid foundations** are oil- or water-based, providing a light to medium coverage. Oil-based liquid foundations have these specific treatment uses:

- dry skin;
- normal skin;
- mature skin;
- combination skin (apply the foundation to the *dry* areas).

Water-based liquid foundations have the following uses:

- normal skin;
- oily skin;
- combination skin (apply the foundation to the *greasy* areas).

Water-based foundations do not spread very easily because the water content rapidly evaporates, so these foundations must be applied quickly.

Gel foundations

Gel foundations provide a sheer, non-greasy coverage. They have these specific treatment uses:

- black, unblemished skin;
- tanned skin;
- skin on which a natural effect is required.

Compact or cake foundations

Compact or cake foundations may have an oil, a wax or a powder base. They give a heavy coverage, and have these specific treatment uses:

- dry skin;
- normal skin;
- badly blemished or scarred skin.

Mousse foundation

Mousse foundation provides a light to medium coverage depending on application technique. It has a mineral oil base. Its specific treatment uses are:

- normal skin,
- combination skin.

Care must be taken to apply the mousse foundation to an area of the skin and blend quickly or it may start to dry on the face, creating a chalky appearance.

The colour of the foundation

The colour of the foundation should match the client's natural skin colour. Test the foundation for compatibility on the client's jawline or forehead. If an incorrect colour is selected, or if the foundation is insufficiently blended on application, there will be a noticeable **demarcation line**.

Skin colour	Foundation colour
Fair	Ivory or light beige, with warm tones of pink or peach
Olive	Dark beige or bronze
Suntanned	Bronze
Florid	Matt beige with a green tint
Sallow	Beige with a pink tint
Light brown	Light brown foundation with a warm tone
Medium brown	Light brown with an orange tone
Dark brown	Deep bronze foundation with an orange tone
Black	Dark golden bronze (usually a gel)

TIP

On an ebony black skin, avoid powder-based foundations as these will make the skin look grey and dull. Use a transparent gel foundation instead.

HEALTH AND SAFETY

Choosing a foundation
- If the skin is greasy and blemished, a *medicated* foundation may be used.
- If the client suffers from acne vulgaris, it is preferable not to apply foundation at all – bacterial infections might be aggravated.
- If the skin is sensitive, select a *hypoallergenic* foundation.

ACTIVITY

Selecting a foundation
Name a suitable foundation for each of the following skin types:
- normal;
- dry;
- greasy;
- combination;
- sensitive;
- blemished.

TIP

The make-up palette is useful when mixing foundations to match the colour of your client's skin.

Applying foundation

TIP ✓

Avoid applying foundation with the fingers. Apart from being less hygienic, with this method the warmth of your hands may cause streaking.

Applying the foundation

If the foundation is in a jar, remove some from its container using a clean disposable spatula. Put it on a clean make-up palette.

Foundation may be applied using either a large soft brush, which is stroked over the surface of the skin, or a cosmetic sponge. It should be applied to one area of the face at a time, with an outward stroking movement.

Use a cosmetic sponge to blend the foundation. Take care that you blend it at the hairline and at the jawline. Avoid clogging the eyebrows with foundation. The **cosmetic make-up wedge** is designed to apply varying amounts of pressure to the different areas of the face, and to ensure even coverage of the foundation.

When applying foundation around the eye area, use a small soft brush or the angular edge of a cosmetic sponge. This will help you achieve accuracy in application.

The extent of coverage can be controlled by the method of application. If the cosmetic sponge is damp, coverage is light and sheer. To achieve a heavier coverage, use a dry latex sponge.

Apply foundation to cover the entire face, including the lips and the eyelids. Do not extend the make-up past the jawline unless the occasion requires this – for example, if a bride's dress exposes part of the upper chest – as the foundation will mark clothes at the neckline.

Contouring

Contour cosmetics

Changing the shape of the face and the facial features can be achieved with the careful application of **contour cosmetics**. These products draw attention either towards or away from facial features, and can create the optical illusion of perfection.

Contour cosmetics include **highlighters**, **shaders** and **blushers**. They are available in powder, liquid and cream forms.

- Highlighters draw attention towards – they emphasise.
- Shaders draw attention away – they minimise.
- Blushers add warmth to the face, and emphasise the facial contours.

Each face differs in shape and size, so each requires a different application technique.

Applying blusher

Some blushers appear very vibrant in the container, yet when they are applied to the skin they appear very subtle.

Powder blushers

1 Stroke the contour brush over the powder blusher. Tap the brush gently, to dislodge excess blusher.

2 Apply the blusher to the cheek area, carefully placing the product according to the effect you wish to create. The direction of brush strokes

Applying blusher

should be upwards and outwards, towards the hairline. Keep the blusher away from the nose, and avoid applying blusher too near the outer eye.

3 Apply more blusher if necessary. The key to successful blusher application is to build up colour slowly until you have achieved the optimum effect.

Cream blushers Apply the cream blusher after foundation application, then place a loose translucent powder over the cream blusher.

If liquid or cream cosmetics are used, these must be applied on top of a liquid or cream foundation, *before* powder application. (If powder contour products are used, these should be applied *after* the application of the loose face powder. The rule of contour cosmetic application is: powder on powder; cream on cream.)

Before applying these products, decide on the effect you wish to achieve. Study the client's face from the front and side profiles, and determine what facial corrective work is necessary.

ACTIVITY

Facial bone structure
Draw and label the main facial bones. It is the differing sizes and proportions of these bones that give us our individual features.
   To discover the size of each facial feature, feel the bony prominences of your own face with your fingers.

Face shapes

To assess the client's face shape, take the hair away from the face – hairstyles often disguise the face shape. Study the size and shape of the facial bone structure. Consider the amount of excess fat, and the muscle tone.

Oval This is regarded as the perfect face shape. Corrective make-up application usually attempts to create the *appearance* of an oval face shape.

Draw attention to the cheekbones by applying shader beneath the cheekbone, and highlighter above. Blusher should be drawn along the cheekbone and blended up towards the temples.

TIP

Keep blusher away from the centre of the face, to avoid accentuating the breadth of the face.

Round

Bone structure Broad and short.

Corrective make-up Apply highlighter in a thin band down the central portion of the face, to create the illusion of length. Shader may be applied over the angle of the jaw to the temples. Apply blusher in a triangular shape, with the base of the triangle running parallel to the ear.

TIP

Remember – it is easier to apply more blusher than to remove excess, which would disturb the foundation!

TIP

Foundation may be suitable as a contour cosmetic. Choose a foundation either two shades lighter (as a highlighter) or two shades darker (as a shader) then the base foundation.

Oval

Round

Square

Square

Bone structure A broad forehead and a broad, angular jawline.

Corrective make-up Shade the angles of the jawbone, up and towards the cheekbone. Apply blusher in a circular pattern on the cheekbones, taking it towards the temples.

Heart

Bone structure A wide forehead, with the face tapering to a narrow, pointed chin, like an inverted triangle.

Corrective make-up Highlight the angles of the jawbone and shade the point of the chin, the temples and the sides of the forehead. Apply blusher under the cheekbones, in an upward and outward direction towards the temples.

Diamond

Bone structure A narrow forehead, with wide cheekbones tapering to a narrow chin.

Corrective make-up Apply shader to the tip of the chin and the height of the forehead, to reduce length. Highlight the narrow sides of the temples and the lower jaw. Apply blusher to the fullness of the cheekbones, to draw attention to the centre of the face.

Oblong

Bone structure Long and narrow, tapering to a pointed chin.

Corrective make-up Apply shader to the hairline and the point of the chin, to reduce the length of the face. Highlight the angle of the jawbone and the temples, to create width. Blend blusher along the cheekbones, outwards towards the ears.

Heart

Diamond

Oblong

Pear

Bone structure A wide jawline, tapering to a narrow forehead.

Corrective make-up Highlight the forehead, and shade the sides of the chin and the angle of the jaw. Apply blusher to the fullness of the cheeks; or blend it along the cheekbones, up towards the temples.

> **ACTIVITY**
>
> **Contouring**
> Study three different clients or colleagues. Identify their face shapes. Where would you apply the contouring cosmetics for each face shape, and why?

Pear

Features

Noses

- *If the nose is too broad* Apply shader to the sides of the nose.
- *If the nose is too short* Apply highlighter down the length of the nose, from the bridge to the tip.
- *If the nose is too long* Apply shader to the tip of the nose.
- *If there is a bump on the nose* Apply shader over the area.
- *If there is a hollow along the bridge of the nose* Apply highlighter over the hollow area.
- *If the nose is crooked* Apply shader over the crooked side.

> **ACTIVITY**
>
> **Correcting nose shapes**
> Think of the different nose shapes you may encounter, such as Roman, turned up, bulbous, or with a long tip. Which contour cosmetics would you select to correct each? Where would you apply them?

> **TIP**
>
> An Asian face may appear as a rather flat plane: the skilful application of shading and highlighting products can create highs and lows.

Foreheads

- *If the forehead is prominent* Apply shader centrally over the prominent area, blending it outwards toward the temples.
- *If the forehead is shallow* Apply highlighter in a narrow band below the hairline.
- *If the forehead is deep* Apply shader in a narrow band below the hairline.

Chins

- *If the jaw is too wide* Apply shader from beneath the cheekbones and along the jawline, blending it at the neck.
- *If the chin is double* Apply shader to the centre of the chin, blending it outwards along the jawbone and under the chin.
- *If the chin is prominent* Apply foundation to the tip of the chin.
- *If the chin is long* Apply shader over the prominent area.
- *If the chin recedes* Apply highlighter along the jawline and at the centre of the chin.

> **TIP**
>
> Foreheads can be improved by a flattering hairstyle.
> - Prominent forehead: choose soft, flat, textured fringes
> - Shallow forehead: choose a shorter, soft fringe. Height will make the forehead appear longer.
> - Deep forehead: choose a longer, soft fringe

Necks

- *If the neck is thin* Apply highlighter down each side of the neck.
- *If the neck is thick* Apply shader to both sides of the neck.

Powdering

Face powder is applied to set the foundation, disguising minor blemishes and making the skin appear smooth and oil-free. It also protects the skin from the environment by acting as a barrier.

Most powders are based on **talc** as the main ingredient, but talc particles are of uneven size, and substitutes such as **mica** are now becoming popular. These give a more natural, flattering effect to the skin's appearance.

Powder adheres to the foundation through the addition of **zinc**, **magnesium stearate** or **fatty esters**. These chemicals set the make-up and remove tackiness. Further powder products can then be applied to the skin.

Face powder contains absorbent materials such as **precipitated chalk** or **nylon derivatives**. These absorb sweat and sebum throughout the day, reducing shine and giving the foundation greater durability.

During manufacture, the insoluble substances in face powder go through a process called **micronisation** in which the particles are finely ground to make a powder, which is then thoroughly blended. Colour pigment may be added to produce different shades and effects.

Face powders

There are two basic products: loose powders and compact powders.

Loose powders **Loose powders** do not contain any oils or gums to bind the powder together. They are available in a range of shades, with different pastel pigments being added to counteract skin imperfections. Colours include pink and lilac, which are flattering when viewed under artificial lights; yellow, which enhances a tanned skin; and green, which counteracts a red skin. Iridescent ingredients may be included to produce shimmering and highlighting effects.

Many cosmetic products contain **titanium dioxide**, an opaque white pigment, to provide coverage. When applied to a black skin, this can give the skin a chalky appearance. When selecting products for a black skin, bear in mind not just the shade but also the ingredients.

TIP

Some powders reflect light whilst appearing subtle and non-shiny. These are most flattering for a mature skin, as wrinkles appear less obvious.

Compact powders **Compact powders** contain a gum, mixed with the ingredients to bind them together. These powders provide a greater coverage, especially if they contain titanium dioxide. Pressed powders should be recommended only for a client's personal use, and then only to remove shine from the skin during the day, as required.

Applying powder

Face powder is applied *after* the foundation, unless a water-based foundation or a combination powder foundation has been selected. Select a matt powder for a daytime make-up, and an iridescent powder for an evening make-up.

1 Remove the loose powder from its container, using a clean spatula or – if the powder is in a shaker – by sprinkling it out. Place the powder on a clean facial tissue.

2 Ask the client to keep her eyes closed. Using a clean piece of cottonwool, press the cottonwool into the powder and then press the powder all over the face.

3 Remove excess powder using a large, sterilised facial powder brush. Direct the brush strokes first up the face, which dislodges the powder, then down the face, which flattens the facial hair and removes the final residue of excess powder.

Facial contouring using powder products may now be carried out.

Applying powder

The eyes

Make-up is applied to the eye area to complement the natural eye colour, to give definition to the eye area, and to enhance the natural shape of the eye.

Eyeshadow

Eyeshadow adds colour and definition to the eye area. The different types include matt, pearlised, metallic and pastel. They are available in cream, crayon or powder form. Eyeshadows are composed of either oil-and-water emulsions or waxes containing inorganic pigments to give colour.

- **Cream eyeshadows** These contain wax and oil.
- **Crayon eyeshadows** These are composed of wax and oil, and are similar in appearance and application to an eyepencil.
- **Powder eyeshadows** These have a talc base, mixed with oils to facilitate application. Lighter shades are produced by the addition of **titanium dioxide** – avoid these on a dark skin as they contrast too harshly with the natural skin colour.

Applying eyeshadow

Pearlised eyeshadows are created by the addition of **bismuth oxychloride** or **mica**; a *metallic* effect is created by the addition of fine particles of **gold leaf**, **aluminium** or **bronze**.

Applying eyeshadow Eyeshadow application will differ according to the eye shape of the client.

1 Protect the skin beneath the eye with a clean tissue – this is to collect small particles of eyeshadow that may fall during application.

2 Lift the skin at the brow slightly to keep the eye tissue taut, enabling you to reach the skin near to the base of the eyelashes.

3 Apply the selected eyeshadow to the eyelid, using a sponge or a brush applicator.

4 Highlight beneath the browbone.

5 Using a brush, apply a darker eyeshadow to the socket area, beginning at the outer corner of the eye. Blend the colour evenly, to avoid harsh lines.

TIP	

When applying powder colours, always tap the brush before application, to remove excess eyeshadow. If too much colour is deposited on the applicator, stroke it over a clean tissue to remove the excess.

Eyeliner

Eyeliner defines and emphasises the eye area. It is available in pencil, liquid or powder form.

- **Eyepencil** This is made of wax and oil, and contains different pigments which give it its colour.
- **Liquid eyeliner** This is a gum solution, in which the pigment is suspended.
- **Powder eyeliner** This has a powder base with the addition of mineral oil.

HEALTH AND SAFETY	

Eyepencil
A good-quality eyepencil will be quite soft when applied to the skin, to avoid dragging the delicate eye tissue.

TIP	

Have a clean cotton bud available so that you can remove the powder from any minor mistakes during application.

Powder eyeliner is the most suitable choice for a client who lives in a hot country, as it will not smudge.

Applying eyeliner If you are using a powder or liquid eyeliner, apply it with a clean eyeliner brush.

1 Lift the skin gently upwards at the eyebrows, to keep the eyelid firm and make application easier.

Applying eyeliner to the upper lashline   Applying eyeliner to the base lashline

2 Draw a fine line along the base of the eyelashes, as required.

3 Lightly smudge the eyeliner to soften the effect of the line.

Eyebrow colour

Eyebrow colour emphasises the eyebrow, and can make sparse eyebrows look thicker. It is available in pencil or powder form.

- **Eyebrow pencil** This is firmer than an eyepencil, and is composed of waxes which hold the inorganic pigments.
- **Powder brow colour** This is composed of a talc base, mixed with mineral oil and pigments.
- **Liquid eyebrow** This is a fluid, quick-drying eyebrow colour to define the brows.
- **Eyebrow mascara** This is composed of mineral oil and waxes with pigment suspended in it. The mascara defines the brows and controls and shapes them.

Applying eyebrow colour

1 Select an appropriate colour of powder or eyebrow pencil. Brush the eyebrows with a clean brow brush, to remove excess face powder and eyeshadow.

2 Simulate the appearance of brow hair by using fine strokes of colour, or disguise bald patches with a denser application.

3 Brush the eyebrows into shape.

Mascara

Mascara enhances the natural eyelashes, making them appear longer, darker and thicker. It is available in liquid, cream and block-cake forms. It is composed of waxes or an oil-and-water emulsion, and contains pigments which give it its colour.

Applying eyebrow colour

HEALTH AND SAFETY

Mascara
Mascara when purchased is usually provided with a brush applicator. This applicator cannot be effectively cleaned and sanitised, however, so it should not be used. Instead use a disposable mascara brush for each client.

TIP

Clear mascara makes the lashes appear thicker, whilst appearing very natural.

TIP

Never pump the mascara wand when loading it with mascara. This encourages air to enter and makes the mascara dry out.

- **Liquid mascara** This is a mixture of gum in water or alcohol; the pigment is suspended in this. It may also contain short textile filaments which adhere to the lashes, having a thickening, lengthening effect. Water-resistant mascara contains resin instead of gum, so that it will not run or smudge.

- **Cream mascara** This is an emulsion of oil and water, with the pigment suspended in this.

- **Block mascara** This is composed of mineral oil, lanolin and waxes, which are melted together to form a block on setting. It must be dampened with water before application.

HEALTH AND SAFETY

Allergies
If the client has hypersensitive eyes or skin, use hypoallergenic cosmetics that contain no known sensitisers.

HEALTH AND SAFETY

Contact lenses
If the client wears contact lenses, don't use either lash-building filament mascaras or loose-particled eyeshadows, which have a tendency to flake and may enter the eye.

Applying mascara

Applying mascara Using a disposable mascara brush, apply mascara to the eyelashes:

1 Hold the brush horizontally to apply colour to the length of the lashes. Where the lashes are short and curly, or difficult to reach, hold the brush vertically and use the point of the brush.

2 Place a clean tissue underneath the base of the lower eyelashes, and stroke the brush down the length of the lashes from the base to the tips.

3 Lift the eyelid at the browbone. Ask the client to look down slightly whilst keeping her eyes open. From above, stroke down the length of the lashes from the base to the tips.

4 Using a zigzag motion, draw the brush upwards through the upper and lower surfaces of the lashes, from the base to the tips.

5 Finally, separate the eyelashes with a clean brush or lash comb.

TIP

Curly lashes will require brushing, using a clean brush, both before mascara application and after each coat, to separate the lashes.

ACTIVITY

Choosing mascara
What colour mascara should be applied if the client has the following hair colouring: brown, auburn, black or grey?

Eye make-up for the client who wears glasses

If the client wears glasses, check the function of the lens, as this can alter the appearance and effect of the eye make-up.

● *If the client is short-sighted, the lens makes the eye appear smaller.* Draw attention to the eyes by selecting brighter, lighter colours. When applying eyeshadow and eyeliner, use the corrective techniques for small eyes. Apply mascara to emphasise the eyelashes.

● *If the client is long-sighted, the lens will magnify the eye.* Make-up should therefore be subtle, avoiding frosted colours and lash-building mascaras. Careful blending is important, as any mistakes will be magnified!

Corrective eye make-up

Dark circles

1 Minimise the circles by applying a concealing product.

Dark circles

Wide-set eyes

1 Apply a darker eye colour to the inner portion of the upper eyelid.

2 Apply lighter eyeshadow to the outer portion of the eyelid.

3 Apply eyeliner in a darker colour to the inner half of the upper eyelid.

4 Eyebrow pencil may be applied to extend the inner browline.

Wide-set eyes

Close-set eyes

1 Lighten the inner portion of the upper eyelid.

2 Use a darker colour at the outer eye.

3 Apply eyeliner to the outer corner of the upper eyelid.

4 Pluck brow hairs at the inner eyebrow – this helps to create the illusion of the eyes being further apart.

Close-set eyes

Round eyes

1 Apply a darker colour over the prominent central upper-lid area.

2 Elongate the eyes by applying eyeliner to the outer corners of the upper and lower eyelids.

Round eyes

Prominent eyes

1 Apply dark matt eyeshadow over the prominent upper eyelid.

2 Apply a darker shade to the outer portion of the eyelid, and blend it upwards and outwards.

3 Highlight the browbone, drawing attention to this area.

4 Eyeliner may be applied to the inner lower eyelid.

TIP	✔
To make the eyes appear less prominent, select matt eyeshadows – pearlised and frosted eyeshadows will highlight and emphasise the eye.	

Prominent eyes

Overhanging lids

Deep-set eyes

Downward-slanting eyes

Small eyes

Narrow eyes

Oriental eyes

Overhanging lids

1 Apply a pale highlighter to the middle of the eyelid.

2 Apply a darker eyeshadow to contour the socket area, creating a higher crease (which disguises the hooded appearance).

Deep-set eyes

1 Use light-coloured eyeshadows.

2 Eyeshadow may also be applied in a fine line to the inner half of the lower eyelid, beneath the lashes.

3 Apply eyeliner to the outer halves of the upper and lower eyelids, broadening the line as you extend outwards.

Downward-slanting eyes

1 Create lift by applying the eyeshadow upwards and outwards at the outer corners of the upper eyelid.

2 Apply eyeliner to the upper eyelid, applying it upwards at the outer corner.

3 Confine mascara to the outer lashes.

Small eyes

1 Choose a light colour for the upper eyelid.

2 Highlight under the brow, to open up the eye area.

3 Curl the lashes before applying mascara.

4 Apply a light-coloured eyeliner to the outer third of the lower eyelid.

5 A white eyeliner may be applied to the inner lid, to make the eye appear larger.

Narrow eyes

1 Apply a lighter colour in the centre of the eyelid, to open up the eye.

2 Apply a shader to the inner and outer portions of the eyelid.

Oriental eyes

1 Divide the upper eyelid in two vertically. Place a lighter colour over the inner half of the eyelid and a darker colour at the outer half.

2 Apply a highlighter under the eyebrow.

3 White eyeliner may be applied at the base of the lashline, on the lower inner eyelid.

TIP

False eyelashes may be effective in enhancing the eye's natural shape.

The eyelashes

To emphasise the eyelashes, making them appear longer temporarily, curl them using **eyelash curlers**.

Curling the eyelashes

1 Rest the upper lashes between the upper and lower portions of the eyelash curlers.
2 Bring the two portions gently together with a squeezing action.
3 Hold the lashes in the curlers for approximately 10 seconds, then release them.
4 If the lashes are not sufficiently curled, repeat the action.

HEALTH AND SAFETY +

Eyelash curling
Repeated eyelash curling can lead to breakage. The technique should therefore be used only for special occasions.

ARTIFICIAL EYELASHES

False eyelashes are made from small threads of nylon fibre or real hair. They are attached to the client's natural lash hair imitating the natural eyelashes and making the lashes appear longer and thicker, and thereby drawing attention to the eye. There are two main types: **semi-permanent individual lashes** and **strip lashes**.

False lashes are applied for the following reasons:

- to create shape and depth in the eye area, when completing a corrective eye make-up;
- simply to add definition to the eye area;
- to enhance an evening or fantasy make-up;
- to provide thick long lashes for photographic make-up;
- to provide an alternative eyelash-enhancing effect for a client who is allergic to mascara.

False eyelashes

RECEPTION

When making an appointment for false-eyelash application, find out why the client wants false lashes and determine which type would be more appropriate.

Strip lashes

Artificial **strip lashes** are designed to be worn for a short period, either for a day or an evening. They are attached to the natural eyelashes with a soft, weak adhesive. After removal the strip must be cleaned before re-application. Allow 20 minutes for the application of strip lashes; if applying them in conjunction with a make-up, allow an additional 45 minutes for the make-up.

Individual lashes

Artificial *individual* lashes are attached to the natural lashes with a strong adhesive. They may be worn for approximately 4–6 weeks, and are therefore known as **semi-permanent lashes**. Allow 20 minutes for the application of individual eyelashes; and again allow a further 45 minutes if applying them in conjunction with a make-up.

Although individual lashes can be worn for up to 6 weeks they look effective only for approximately 3 weeks. After this time, the appearance of the artificial lashes begins to deteriorate, the lash adhesive becomes brittle, and the eyelash area may become irritated.

Due to the cyclic nature of hair replacement some individual lashes will be lost when the natural lash falls out. These lashes may be replaced each week, as necessary; the client is usually charged a price for each individual lash replaced. The client must be told of this service as part of the aftercare advice.

Booking the treatment

When a client makes an appointment for an artificial lash treatment, she should be asked the following questions:

● *Has she had a similar treatment before in this salon?* If she has not, she should visit the salon beforehand for a skin test to assess her sensitivity to the adhesive (see page 45).

● *Is she having the false eyelashes applied for any particular reason, such as a holiday or a special occasion?* In deciding which type of false eyelash would be most appropriate, take into consideration the effect required and for how long the lashes are to be worn.

If the client wears glasses, the artificial lashes must not be so long as to touch the lenses. Also, if the lens magnifies the eye, this must be taken into account. Ask the client to bring her glasses with her to the salon.

CONTRA-INDICATIONS

If following completion of the record card or inspection of the eye area you have found any of the following, do not apply false eyelashes:

- *Skin disease*.
- *Skin disorder* in the eye area, such as psoriasis or eczema.
- *Inflammation or swelling* around the eye.
- *Hypersensitive skin*.
- *Any eye disorder*, such as styes or hordeola, conjunctivitis, blepharitis, watery eye, or cysts.
- *A positive (allergic) reaction* to the adhesive skin test.
- *Contact lenses* (unless removed).

An unduly nervous client with a tendency to blink could prove hard to treat in this way. Use your discretion in deciding on the suitability of a client for treatment.

EQUIPMENT AND MATERIALS

To apply the false eyelashes you will need the following equipment and materials:

- *Couch or beauty chair* – with sit-up and lie-down positions and an easy-to-clean surface.
- *Trolley* – on which to display everything.
- *Towels (2, medium-sized)* – freshly laundered for each client.
- *Headband* – freshly laundered for each client.
- *Disposable tissue roll* – for example bed roll.
- *Cleansing milk* – used to remove facial make-up in the eye area.
- *Eye make-up remover (non-oily)*.
- *Damp cottonwool* – for removing cleansing product from the eye area.
- *Facial tissues (white)* – for blotting the eyelashes dry.
- *Disposable mascara brush*.
- *Manual tweezers (2 pairs, sterilised)* – special tweezers are available, designed specifically to assist in attaching individual eyelashes.
- *Surgical spirit* – for wiping the points of the tweezers to remove adhesive.
- *Plastic palette (sanitised)* – on which to place the artificial lashes prior to application.
- *Eyelash adhesive* – for strip lashes.

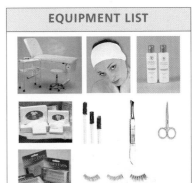

EQUIPMENT LIST

couch or beauty chair

trolley

headband

eye make-up remover

facial tissues

disposable mascara brush

manual tweezers

strip eyelash lengths

eyelash adhesive (for individual lashes)

individual eyelash lengths

eyelash adhesive solvent

sterilised scissors

see opposite for complete list of materials required

TIP

In order that you can effectively clean the dish after the treatment, you need to line the dish with a disposable lining.

- *Strip eyelash lengths (a selection)* – in a choice of colours.
- *Eyelash adhesive* – for individual lashes.
- *Individual eyelash lengths (a selection)* – in a choice of colours.
- *Eyelash adhesive solvent* – for removing and cleaning artificial lashes.
- *Sterilised dish (small)* – lined with foil, in which to place the eyelash adhesive during lash application.
- *Sterilised scissors (1 pair)* – used for trimming the length of strip lashes.
- *Hand mirrors (clean).*
- *Client's record card.*

Sterilisation and sanitisation

When preparing to apply artificial *strip* lashes, clean the surface of the palette onto which you will stick the lashes once you have removed them from their packet. Use surgical spirit, applied with clean cottonwool. The palette may be stored in the ultraviolet light cabinet until ready for use. *Individual* lashes come in a special 'contoured' package: you can hold this securely whilst removing individual lashes, so the lashes can be kept hygienically until required.

Always have a spare pair of tweezers available during application of the individual or strip false lashes. Should you accidentally drop the tweezers with which you are working, you will need a clean, sterile pair available.

Scissors, used to trim strip lashes, should be sterilised before use.

Preparing the cubicle

Before the client is shown through to the cubicle, it should be checked to ensure that the required equipment and materials are available and the area is clean and tidy. The plastic-covered couch should be clean, having been thoroughly washed with hot, soapy water, or wiped thoroughly with surgical spirit or a professional alcohol-based cleaner. The couch or chair should be protected with a long strip of disposable tissue-paper bed roll, or a freshly laundered sheet and a bath towel. A small towel should be placed neatly at the head of the couch, ready to be draped across the client's chest for protection during treatment. (The paper tissue will need changing and the towels will need to be laundered for each client.)

The couch or beauty chair should be in a slightly elevated position, to give the optimum position for the therapist when applying the false lashes. In this position, too, the client will not be staring into the overhead light (which might cause the eyes to water).

ACTIVITY

Position of client
Can you think of further disadvantages of having the client lying flat when applying false lashes?

PLANNING THE TREATMENT

A variety of false lashes is available, including lashes intended for corrective work as well as those simply intended to enhance the natural lashes. Lashes may be short, medium or long; their texture may be fine, medium or thick, with some having a feathered effect. Strips designed for use on the lower lashes are called **partial lashes**: here small groups of hairs are placed intermittently along the length of the false-lash base.

In a commercial salon, the most popular colours are usually black and brown. For special effects, however; strip lashes are available in fantasy colours, complete with glitter and jewels!

Factors when choosing false eyelashes

Before applying artificial lashes the beauty therapist should consider the following points, and advise the client accordingly.

The client's age

Artificial lashes create a very bold, dramatic effect, which can make an older client look too hard. Remember that the skin colour and the natural hair colour change with age: the lash chosen must enhance the client's appearance.

The client's natural lashes

Does the client have short or long, sparse or thick, very curly or straight lashes? Choose an artificial lash to complement the natural lash. Here are some guidelines:

- *Short and stubby lashes* These are commonly seen on older clients who have overhanging eyelids. Choose a medium lash length in a medium thickness at the outer corner of the eyelid; the lashes should become gradually shorter from the centre of the eyelid to the inner corner. Brush the artificial and natural lashes together after application to ensure that they blend.

- *Sparse lashes* Place individual short lashes along the natural lashline; or, to give a more natural appearance, you may wish to apply partial strip lashes to the upper eyelid.

- *Curly eyelashes* These are very common on African-Caribbean clients. Choose a longer, sweeping strip or individual false lashes, in black. The chosen lashes and colour should give emphasis and depth to the eye.

The natural eyelash colour

Select false lashes that complement the hair and skin tone. Natural-hair false eyelashes offer the greatest choice of colour; but these are expensive and may be difficult to purchase.

<table>
<tr><td>

TIP

In America streaked lashes are available, to give a more subtle effect for the mature client.

</td></tr>
</table>

Short and stubby lashes

Sparse lashes

Curly lashes

False eyelashes

ACTIVITY

Choosing eyelash colours
Suggest a choice of false eyelash colour for the clients below:
- a mature grey-haired client;
- a young red-haired client;
- a mature client with bleached hair;
- a mature African-Caribbean client.

TIP

Permanent waving is available as a cosmetic treatment, using a specialised perming lotion to curl the eyelashes.

Small eyes

Close-set eyes

Wide-set eyes

Downward-slanting eyes

Using false eyelashes for corrective purposes

Here are some outlines of corrective techniques for various eye shapes.

- *Small eyes* Place false lashes at the outer corners of the upper eyelid. These should be longer than the natural lashes.
- *Close-set eyes* Place fine, long, individual or partial lashes at the outer third of the eye. They may be applied to the lower lashes as well as to the upper.
- *Wide-set eyes* Apply medium-length lashes at the inner corner of the eye and to the centre, becoming slightly shorter towards the outer corner of the upper eyelid. This may be repeated on the lower lash also.
- *Downward-slanting eyes* Apply longer lashes (individual or partial strip lashes) to the outer corners of the upper eyelid.
- *Round eyes* Individual or strip lashes should be used to lengthen the lashline. Apply the false lashes from the centre of the upper eyelid outwards.
- *Deep-set eyes* Apply fine lashes to the upper and lower lashes. The upper-lid false lashes should be longer; to draw attention to the eye.
- *Overhanging lids* Apply longer lashes to the upper eyelid, from the outer corner and tapering to a shorter length at the centre of the lid and toward the inner corner.

Round eyes

Deep-set eyes

Overhanging lids

PREPARING THE CLIENT

Show the client through to the prepared treatment area after filling in the record card at reception.

1 Position the client comfortably on the treatment couch or beauty chair (which should be slightly elevated). If the client wears contact lenses, these must be removed before the treatment begins.

2 Drape a clean towel across the client's chest and shoulders. Protect her hair with a clean headband.

3 Wash your hands, which indicates to the client that treatment is beginning and in a hygienic and professional manner.

4 Consult the clients record card, then check the treatment area for visible contra-indications or abnormalities before proceeding.

5 It is usual to carry out a full facial cleanse (rather than cleansing only the eye area) as make-up is usually applied to complement the false eyelashes. Use a cleansing milk to dissolve facial make-up, followed by a non-oily eye make-up remover to cleanse the eye area. Both products should be removed with clean, damp cottonwool.

6 To ensure that the eye tissue and eyelashes are thoroughly clean and grease-free, apply a mild toning lotion: stroke this over the skin using clean, damp cottonwool.

7 Blot the lashes dry, using a fresh facial tissue for each eye. (Any moisture left on the natural lashes would reduce the effectiveness of the eyelash adhesive.)

8 Brush the natural lashes to separate them before application.

APPLYING SEMI-PERMANENT LASHES

1 Check that everything you need is on the trolley.

2 Check that the back of the couch or beauty chair is slightly raised, at a height that is comfortable for you.

3 Discuss the treatment procedure with the client. Explain that she will be required to keep her eyes open during the treatment. Reassure her that she may blink during application. Very often clients feel that they shouldn't, and their eyes begin to water.

4 Ask her to tilt her head downwards very slightly. This tends to lower the upper eyelids, making application easier.

5 Depending on the effect required, you may start application of the individual lashes at different positions along the natural lashline. In general, apply shorter lashes to the inner corners of the eyelid, and longer lashes to the outer corners; this creates a realistic effect and ensures client comfort. If you are applying individual lashes to the entire upper lid, it is practical to start application at the inner corner of the eyelid and work outwards: this follows the natural contour of the eye.

TIP

Do not prepare the lash adhesive until you are ready to use it. It tends to dry on contact with the air.

TIP

When applying the individual lashes to the inner portion of the eyelid, hold the skin taut, stretching the skin slightly. This will enable you to position the false lash more easily.

TIP

Use a clean pair of tweezers to remove the individual lashes from their container when required. Holding the tweezers firmly, grip each lash near its base (this avoids misshaping the outer lash hairs).

TIP

To ensure efficient application, don't get adhesive on the points of the tweezers.

6 With the sterile tweezers, select a lash from the package, holding it near its centre. Brush the underside of the individual lash, at the root, through the adhesive. The adhesive should extend slightly beyond the root. You need sufficient adhesive, but not too much – excess adhesive should be removed by wiping the lash against the inside of the adhesive container.

7 Working from behind the client, hold the tweezers at the angle at which the false lash will be applied to the natural lashline. Hold the brow tissue with your other hand, to steady the eyelid.

TIP

Positioning the individual lashes correctly requires experience. It is a good idea initially to practise application without adhesive.

Using a stroking movement, place the underside of the false lash on top of the natural lash. Stroke the adhesive along the length of the natural eyelash. Guide the false lash towards the base of the natural lash, so that the false lash rests along the length of the natural lash. Wait a few seconds to allow the adhesive to dry (to prevent the lashes from sticking together). Continue placing further false lashes side by side until the desired effect is achieved.

During application, keep checking your work. If a lash is out of line, remove it while the adhesive is still soft. If the adhesive has set, the lash will need to be removed using adhesive solvent – see illustration on page 364.

8 Apply the false lashes one at a time, to each eye alternately. This avoids sensitising the eye, and makes it easier for you to create a balanced effect.

9 If the client requires false lashes to be applied to the *lower* lid, the application technique is slightly different.

Work facing the client, with the client looking upwards, her eyes slightly open. Follow the same general procedure for applying the false eyelashes; here, however, the lashes curve downwards and the adhesive is applied to the *upper* surface of the lash.

Lashes applied to the lower eyelid are usually shorter than those chosen for the upper lid, and more adhesive is required for the lashes to be secure and have maximum durability.

10 When you have completed the lash application, ask the client to sit up, and show her the completed effect.

The natural lashes

Selecting a lash

Brushing through the adhesive

Applying a lash to the upper lid

The completed effect

11 If the client is satisfied with the result, you can apply a water-or powder-based eye make-up if desired. Do not apply mascara, as this will reduce the adhesion to the natural lash. Mascara also clogs the lashes together; and is difficult to remove without affecting the eyelash adhesive. On completion, the lashes can be gently brushed – using a disposable brush – to remove particles of eyeshadow.

APPLYING STRIP LASHES

Strip false eyelashes are applied *before* carrying out the eye makeup – this avoids the eye make-up being spoilt if the eyes water slightly during application.

1 Carefully apply moisturiser and foundation, taking care not to get any cosmetic products on the lashes. (If you do, gently wipe over the lashes with the non-oily eye make-up remover, and blot the eyelashes dry again with a clean facial tissue.)

2 Brush the lashes to separate them, using a clean disposable mascara brush. This makes false-lash application easier, and removes any fine particles of loose powder.

3 Remove the strip lashes from their container; and place them on a clean sanitised palette. Each strip is designed to fit either the left or the right eye: remember which is which when placing them on the palette.

4 Check the length of the strip against the client's eyelid. The strip should never be applied directly from one corner of the eyelid to the other; but should start about 2 mm from the inner corner of the eye, and end 2 mm from the outer corner. This ensures a natural effect and maximises the durability of the false lash.

   When you remove the strip lash from the package you will find that there is adhesive on the backing strip, which fixes the lash in the container: this adhesive is sufficient to hold the lash onto the client's natural lash while you measure the length.

5 To trim the false lashes you require a sharp pair of scissors. First correct the length of the *strip* if necessary. Hold the lashes securely with one hand, and then trim the strip at the outer edge.

   Then trim the lashes themselves, if necessary. Never reduce the length of the lashes by cutting straight across them: the result would not look natural. Natural eyelashes are of varying lengths, due to the nature of the hair growth cycle; it is this effect that you must simulate. To shorten the lash, 'chip' into the lash. Use the *points* of the scissors to shorten the lash length. Cut the lashes so that the shorter lashes are at the inner corner of the eyelid, gradually increasing toward the outer corner.

6 Check that everything required for the false eyelash application is available on your trolley.

Salon System

Removing the strip lashes from their container using tweezers

Salon System

Trimming the lashes

Salon System

Positioning the lash on the base of the natural lashline

Pressing the strip lash and the natural lash together

7 The couch or beauty chair should be in a slightly raised position. During the treatment you will be working from behind the client: the height must be comfortable for you.

8 Discuss the treatment procedure with the client. Explain to her that she will be required to keep her eyes open during the application. Ask her to tilt her head downwards very slightly – this lowers the upper eyelids, making application easier.

9 Using the sterile tweezers, remove one of the eyelash strips from the palette. Handle it very carefully, as it can easily become misshapen.

   Remembering that the strip is designed to fit either the right or the left eye, place it against the appropriate eyelid and check the length (with the client's eyes closed).

10 Once satisfied that the length of the strip lash is correct, remove the adhesive tape used to hold it in the container.

11 Place a small quantity of strip lash adhesive on the sanitised palette.

12 Ask the client to look down slightly, with her eyes half open. With one hand lift her brow to steady the upper eyelid.

   Holding the strip lash with the sterile tweezers at its centre, drag it at its base through the adhesive. (The adhesive must be moist.) It is usually white, but when it dries it becomes colourless.

   Position the base of the strip lash as close as possible to the base of the natural eyelash, ensuring that it is about 2 mm in from the inner and outer corners of the eye. *Gently* press the false and natural eyelashes together with your fingertips, along the length of the lash and at the outer corners.

13 When you are sure that the first strip lash is secure, apply the second in the same way.

14 If strip lashes are to be applied to the bottom lashes also, apply these now, in the same way as the upper lashes. (Strip lashes for the lower lids are fine, with an extremely thin base. These lashes should be trimmed as before to ensure comfort and durability in wear.)

15 Allow 3–5 minutes for the adhesive to dry.

16 Gently brush the lashes from underneath the natural lashline, using a clean disposable mascara brush. This will blend the natural and false lashes together Check that both sets of lashes are correctly positioned, and that a balanced look has been achieved.

17 Artificial lashes look more realistic if eyeliner is applied to the client's eyelid: this disguises the base of the strip lash.

Salon System

The completed effect

CONTRA-ACTIONS

If during application of false lashes the eye starts to water, blot the tears with the corner of a clean tissue. The tears can cause the adhesive to take on an unsightly white crystallised appearance. Any possible irritation of the eyes should therefore be avoided, during both preparation of the eye area and application itself.

Never place eyelashes *underneath* the natural eyelashes – eye irritation would occur.

While practising individual eyelash application you may find at some point that you have accidentally glued a couple of the lower and upper natural lashes together. Apply adhesive solvent to a cottonwool-tipped orange stick, and gently roll this over the lash length to dissolve the adhesive.

If solvent or adhesive should accidentally enter the eye, rinse the eye thoroughly and immediately, using clean water. Repeat this until discomfort is no longer experienced.

HEALTH AND SAFETY

Client comfort
Check the eyelash application as you work. Ensure that the lower and upper lashes are not stuck together, and that the eyelashes are accurately and evenly applied.

AFTERCARE AND ADVICE

The following aftercare instructions should be given to the client after false eyelash application:

- Avoid rubbing the eyes, or the lashes may become loosened.
- Do not use an oil-based eye make-up remover as its cosmetic constituents would dissolve the adhesive.
- Use only dry or water-based eye make-up (as these may readily be removed with a non-oily eye make-up remover).
- If the lashes are made of a synthetic material, heat will cause them to become frizzy. Advise the client to avoid extremes of temperature, such as a hot sauna.
- Do not touch the eyes for $1\frac{1}{2}$ hours after application, while the adhesive dries thoroughly.

If the client has had *individual* artificial lashes applied, the following home-care advice should be given on caring for the lashes:

- Use a non-oily eye make-up remover daily to cleanse the eyelids and eyelashes. Avoid contact with oil-based preparations in the eye area, such as moisturisers and cleansers – the oil content would dissolve the adhesive, and the lashes would become detached.
- Do not attempt to remove the artificial lashes – pulling at the artificial lash would pull out the natural eyelashes also.
- After bathing, gently *pat* the eye area dry with a clean towel.

Clients with individual false eyelashes should have the false lashes maintained by regular visits to the salon. Lost individual lashes can be replaced as necessary; this is often described as an eyelash **infill** service.

TIP

Disposable cotton buds may be used to apply eyelash adhesive solvent.

If the client wishes to have the individual false lashes removed, this should be done professionally.

Removing individual eyelashes

1 Position the client lying on the couch.

2 Wash your hands.

3 Remove make-up from the eye area, cleansing the skin with a suitable eye make-up remover.

4 While the client's eyes are open, place a pre-shaped eyeshield underneath the lower lashes of each eye. (This will protect the eye tissue from the solvent.) Position the eyeshields so that they fit snugly to the base of the lower lashes.

5 Ask the client to close her eyes gently, and not to open them again until you tell her to do so.

6 Prepare a new disposable orange stick by covering it at the pointed end with clean, dry cottonwool.

7 Moisten the cottonwool with the artificial eyelash adhesive solvent.

HEALTH AND SAFETY

Eye care

Do not allow eyelash adhesive solvent to come into excessive contact with the eye tissue – it could cause irritation of the skin. Ensure that there is sufficient solvent only on the cottonwool: it should be moist but not dripping wet or the solvent might enter the eye.

Applying adhesive solvent to remove false eyelashes

8 Treating one eye at a time, gently stroke down the false eyelashes with the adhesive solvent until the adhesive dissolves and the false eyelash begins to loosen.

9 When you are satisfied that the eyelash adhesive has dissolved, gently attempt to remove the false eyelash. Support the upper eyelid with the fingers of one hand, using the other hand to remove the eyelash with a sterile pair of manual tweezers. If the adhesive has been adequately dissolved, the eyelash will lift away easily from the natural eyelash. If there is any resistance, repeat the solvent application until the eyelash comes away readily.

HEALTH AND SAFETY

Client comfort

Never attempt to remove the artificial eyelashes until they have begun to loosen – if you do, the clients natural eyelashes will be removed also, causing her discomfort.

Soothing the eye area after removal of the lashes

10 As the artificial eyelashes are removed, collect them on a clean white facial tissue or a clean pad of cottonwool.

11 Having removed all of the artificial eyelashes from one eye, soothe the area by applying damp cottonwool pads soaked in cool water. (This will also remove any remaining solvent.) A damp cottonwool pad may be placed over the eye, while you remove the false lashes from the other eye.

Removing strip false lashes

If a client wears strip eyelashes she will need instructions on how to remove and care for the false lashes herself.

1 Use the fingertips of one hand to support the eyelid at the outer corner. With the other hand, lift the lash strip base at the outer corner of the eye. Gently peel the strip away from the natural lash, from the outer edge towards the centre of the eyelid.

2 Peel the adhesive from the backing strip, using a clean pair of manual tweezers. Take care to avoid stretching the strip lash.

3 Clean the strip lash in the appropriate way.

- *Strips made from human hair* Clean with a commercial lash cleaner or 70% alcohol. This removes the remaining adhesive and the eye make-up.
- *Synthetic strips* Place in warm, soapy water for a few minutes, to clean the lashes and remove the remaining adhesive. Rinse in tepid water.

4 After cleaning the strip lashes should be recurled.

Removing strip eyelashes

HEALTH AND SAFETY

Client comfort
When removing the strip lash, avoid pulling the natural lashes with the false lashes.

Recurling strip lashes

For reasons of hygiene and because of the time involved, this service will not be offered by the salon. The client, however; will need advice on how to recurl the lashes at home.

1 On removal from the water, place the lashes side by side, ensuring that the inner edges are together inside a clean facial tissue.

2 Wrap a tissue around an even, barrel-shaped object such as a felt-tip pen, and secure it with an elastic band.

3 The false lashes, inside the facial tissue, should then be rolled around this object. Keep the base of the lash straight, so that the whole lash length curls around the object.

Once recurled, the strip lashes can be returned to the contoured shelves in their original container; and stored for further use.

HEALTH AND SAFETY

Semi-permanent lashes
The client should be advised to return to the salon for semi-permanent lashes to be removed professionally.

Recurling strip lashes

THE LIPS

Lip cosmetics add colour and draw attention to the lips. As the lips have no protective sebum, the use of lip cosmetics also helps to prevent them from drying and becoming chapped.

It is not uncommon for the lips to be out of proportion in some way. Using lip cosmetics and corrective techniques, symmetrical lips can be created. A careful choice of product and accurate application are required to achieve a professional effect.

The main lip cosmetics are lipliner, lipsticks and lipglosses. Sometimes the lips may be unevenly pigmented. The application of a lip toner or foundation over the lips corrects this.

Lipliner

Lipliner is used to define the lips, creating a perfectly symmetrical outline. This is coloured in with another lip cosmetic, either a lipstick or a lipgloss. The lipliner also helps to prevent the lipstick from 'bleeding' into lines around the lips.

Lipliner has a wax base which does not melt and can be applied easily. It contains pigments which give the pencil its colour.

When choosing a lipliner, select one that is the same colour as, or slightly darker than, the lipstick to be used with it.

Lipsticks

Lipstick contains a blend of oils and waxes, which give it its firmness, and silicone, essential for easy application. It also contains pigment, to add colour, an emollient moisturiser, to keep the lips soft and supple and perfume, to improve its appeal. In addition it may include vitamins, to condition the lips, or sunscreens, to protect the lips from ultraviolet rays. Some lipsticks contain a relatively large proportion of water – these moisturise the lips and provide a natural look. The coverage provided by a lipstick depends on its formulation.

Lipsticks are available in the following forms: cream, matt, frosted and translucent. Frosted lipstick has good durability, as it is very dry. Some other lipsticks also offer extended durability, and are suitable for clients who are unable to renew their lipstick regularly.

When choosing the colour of lipstick, take into account the natural colour of the client's lips, the skin and hair colours, and the colours selected for the rest of the make-up.

Lipglosses

Lipgloss provides a moist, shiny look to the lips. It may be worn alone, or applied on top of a lipstick. Its effect is short-lived. Lipgloss is made of mineral oils, with pigment suspended in the oil.

Note that mature clients often have creases on the lips that extend to the surrounding skin. If lipgloss is used it will often bleed into these lines.

HEALTH AND SAFETY

Lip pencils
Always sharpen the lip pencil before use on each client, to provide a clean, uncontaminated cosmetic surface.

HEALTH AND SAFETY

Lipstick
For reasons of hygiene, remove a small quantity of lipstick by scraping the stick with a clean spatula – don't apply the lipstick directly.

HEALTH AND SAFETY

Allergies
Lipsticks often contain ingredients that can cause allergic reactions, such as lanolin and certain pigment dyes. If the client has known allergies, use a hypoallergenic product instead.

Dry lips

Sometimes the lips become dry and chapped. Recommend that the client keeps them moisturised at all times, especially in extremes of heat, cold or wind. Some facial exfoliants can be professionally applied over the lips to remove dead skin.

If the client does not like to wear make-up during the day, or if the client is male, recommend that the lips be protected with a lip-care product.

Corrective lip make-up

Thick lips

Select natural colours and darker shades, avoiding bright, glossy colours.

1 Blend foundation over the lips to disguise the natural lip line.
2 Apply a darker lipliner inside the natural lip line to create a new line.

Thick lips

Thicker upper or lower lip

1 Use the technique described above to make the larger lip appear smaller.
2 Apply a slightly darker lipstick to the larger lip.
3 If the lips droop at the corners, raise the corners by applying lipliner to the corners of the upper lip, to turn them upwards.

Thicker upper lip

Thin lips

Select brighter, pearlised colours. Avoid darker lipsticks, which will make the mouth appear smaller.

1 Apply a neutral lipliner just outside the natural lip line.

Thicker lower lip

Small mouth

1 Extend the line slightly at the corners of the mouth, with both the upper and the lower lips.

Thin lips

Uneven lips

1 Use a lipliner to draw in a new line.
2 Apply lipstick to the area.

Lines around the mouth

1 Apply lipliner around the natural lip line.
2 Apply a matt cream lipstick to the lips. (Don't use gloss, which might bleed into the lines around the mouth.)

Small mouth

Uneven lips

Lines around the mouth

Applying lipstick

1 Select a lip pencil and lipstick to complement the client's colouring and the colour theme of the make-up.

2 Using a pencil sharpener, sharpen the lip pencil to expose a clean surface.

3 Ask the client to open her mouth slightly.

4 Outline the lips, carrying out lip correction as necessary. Begin the lip line at the outer corner of the mouth, and continue it to the centre of the lips. Repeat the process on the other side of the lip, commencing at the outer corner of the mouth.

5 Remove sufficient lipstick using a clean spatula.

6 Using a sterile lipbrush, apply the lipstick to the lips.

7 Apply a clean facial tissue over the lip area, and *gently* press it onto the lips. This process, known as **blotting**, removes excess lipstick and fixes the colour on the lips.

8 A second light application of lipstick may then be applied.

9 If desired, lipgloss may be applied over the lipstick to add sheen, again using a sterile lipbrush.

HEALTH AND SAFETY +

Lipbrushes
Disposable lipbrushes are available to enable lip cosmetics to be applied hygienically.

Applying lipliner

Applying lipstick

When you have finished . . .

After applying the make-up, fix the client's hair and then discuss the finished result in front of the make-up mirror.

Wash your hands. Record details of the treatment on the client's record card.

The completed make-up

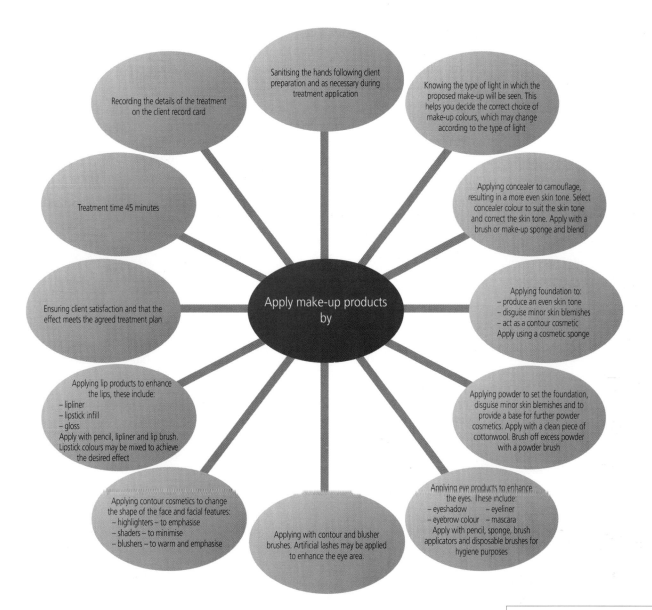

Apply make-up products by

- Recording the details of the treatment on the client record card
- Sanitising the hands following client preparation and as necessary during treatment application
- Knowing the type of light in which the proposed make-up will be seen. This helps you decide the correct choice of make-up colours, which may change according to the type of light
- Treatment time 45 minutes
- Applying concealer to camouflage, resulting in a more even skin tone. Select concealer colour to suit the skin tone and correct the skin tone. Apply with a brush or make-up sponge and blend
- Ensuring client satisfaction and that the effect meets the agreed treatment plan
- Applying foundation to:
  – produce an even skin tone
  – disguise minor skin blemishes
  – act as a contour cosmetic
  Apply using a cosmetic sponge
- Applying lip products to enhance the lips, these include:
  – lipliner
  – lipstick infill
  – gloss
  Apply with pencil, lipliner and lip brush. Lipstick colours may be mixed to achieve the desired effect
- Applying powder to set the foundation, disguise minor skin blemishes and to provide a base for further powder cosmetics. Apply with a clean piece of cottonwool. Brush off excess powder with a powder brush
- Applying contour cosmetics to change the shape of the face and facial features:
  – highlighters – to emphasise
  – shaders – to minimise
  – blushers – to warm and emphasise
- Applying with contour and blusher brushes. Artificial lashes may be applied to enhance the eye area.
- Applying eye products to enhance the eyes. These include:
  – eyeshadow – eyeliner
  – eyebrow colour – mascara
  Apply with pencil, sponge, brush applicators and disposable brushes for hygiene purposes

CONTRA-ACTIONS

Certain cosmetic ingredients are known to provoke allergic reactions in some people. These allergens may cause irritation, excessive erythema, inflammation and swelling.

Known cosmetic allergens include the following:

- *Lanolin* This is similar to sebum, and is obtained from sheep's wool. It is added to many cosmetics as an emollient.
- *Mineral oils* Examples are oleic acid and butyl stearate.
- *Eosin (bromo-acid dye)* A staining pigment, used in some lip cosmetics and perfumes.
- *Paraben* An antiseptic ingredient, used as a preservative in facial cosmetics.
- *Certain colourants* One example is carmine.
- *Perfume* This is added to most cosmetics, and is a common sensitiser.

Other contra-actions include:

HEALTH AND SAFETY

Allergies
Where possible, before using a new cosmetic, a client with known allergies should first receive a patch test, or be given a small sample of a product to try on a less sensitive area of the skin, to assess the skin's tolerance. If a severe allergic reaction occurs, medical attention must be sought immediately.

It is possible that clients may grow out of an allergy to a given product. It is also possible, however, suddenly to become allergic to a product that has not given problems before.

- *Watery eyes* The client's eyes water excessively. If the client has watery eyes a tissue may be placed at the corners until the irritation has ceased. If the client's eyes continue to water remove eye make-up and discontinue treatment.

- *Excessive perspiration* Some clients may perspire which will affect adherence of the make-up and its finished result. Blot the skin with soft facial tissue and apply more loose face powder to absorb perspiration. If the client continues to perspire discontinue treatment.

External contact with an allergen may cause urticaria (hives or nettle rash), eczema or dermatitis. If an allergy occurs, the product should be removed from the skin and a soothing substance applied. The client should be advised not to use the product again.

AFTERCARE AND ADVICE

Following make-up application, recommend the correct skin care products to remove the products you have applied. If false lashes have been applied their removal must also be discussed, see pages 364–5.

Advise the client on application procedures to maintain the effect e.g. removal of facial shine from the face with pressed powder.

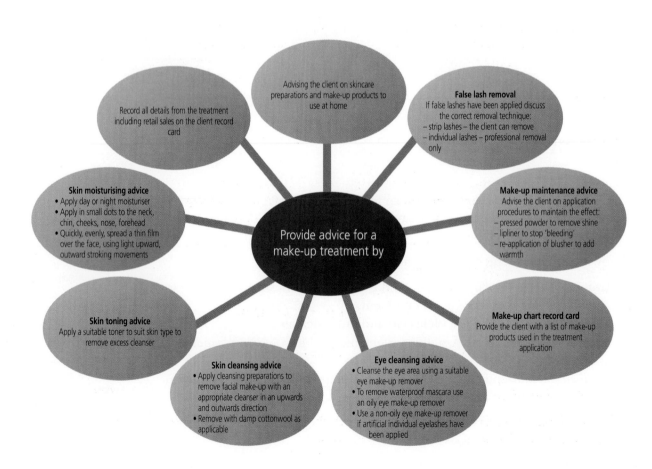

Provide advice for a make-up treatment by

Advising the client on skincare preparations and make-up products to use at home

False lash removal
If false lashes have been applied discuss the correct removal technique:
– strip lashes – the client can remove
– individual lashes – professional removal only

Make-up maintenance advice
Advise the client on application procedures to maintain the effect:
– pressed powder to remove shine
– lipliner to stop 'bleeding'
– re-application of blusher to add warmth

Make-up chart record card
Provide the client with a list of make-up products used in the treatment application

Eye cleansing advice
- Cleanse the eye area using a suitable eye make-up remover
- To remove waterproof mascara use an oily eye make-up remover
- Use a non-oily eye make-up remover if artificial individual eyelashes have been applied

Skin cleansing advice
- Apply cleansing preparations to remove facial make-up with an appropriate cleanser in an upwards and outwards direction
- Remove with damp cottonwool as applicable

Skin toning advice
Apply a suitable toner to suit skin type to remove excess cleanser

Skin moisturising advice
- Apply day or night moisturiser
- Apply in small dots to the neck, chin, cheeks, nose, forehead
- Quickly, evenly, spread a thin film over the face, using light upward, outward stroking movements

Record all details from the treatment including retail sales on the client record card

Explain to the client that you can offer a make-up lesson in which you would discuss the reason for the selection of make-up products and colours, and the techniques for applying them. Recommend the correct skin-care products to remove the products you have applied.

PROFESSIONAL MAKE-UP LESSONS AND DEMONSTRATIONS

When correctly applied, make-up increases a person's confidence whilst accentuating their best features and correcting their worst. Professional make-up lessons or demonstrations can be applied in an individual or group context. Group demonstrations are a useful method to generate further business through promotion of make-up products and services.

Before performing an individual or group make-up demonstration ensure that you are familiar with the products that you will be using. Your own personal appearance is also important to gain client confidence in the product!

For a group demonstration allow sufficient time for client questioning during the demonstration, and ensure you have available all the make-up resources required.

Consultation

At consultation identify what effect the client wishes to achieve – client preference must *always* be considered. Many clients requesting a make-up lesson have tired of their usual make-up application and require inspiration; some are unaccustomed to wearing make-up but recognise its potential to enhance. Other clients will request the service for personal special occasions.

Make-up presentations are a great way to launch a company's new season colours.

Gaining an understanding of the client's requirements is important to achieve a finished result that the client will feel comfortable to wear. Engage the client in conversation to establish her needs, likes and dislikes.

An effective consultation will have gathered important information such as:

- Is the client used to wearing make-up?
- What effect does the client wish to achieve?
- Does the client normally wear make-up? (If not, a more subtle effect should be aimed for.)
- Consider client preferences with regard to colours selected and the overall effect to be achieved.

Agree all details of the make-up plan with the client.

During a make-up lesson or presentation ensure the lighting is adequate to show each stage of make-up application effectively.

Gaining client satisfaction

Make-up application should be demonstrated in such a way that it enhances client understanding, showing cost-effectiveness. For a make-up lesson this will normally require that the make-up is completed in front of a mirror and the client has the opportunity to perform the application technique that you have demonstrated on them. For example, you demonstrate eye make-up application and then the client applies the make-up to the other eye following the same technique.

Tools of the trade are important, and the client must be shown which make-up tool/brush is selected and used to achieve a particular result. Supportive advice should be given to the client during this process, whilst responding positively to any questions with recommendations.

Make-up demonstrations can be an ideal opportunity to promote and achieve a retail sale of the products that you have selected to use. Remember it is important to promote *features* and *benefits*.

Plan and promote make-up activities including group demonstration and one-to-one demonstration by

- Prepare and plan for the make-up activity ensuring all necessary resources are available including make-up resources and promotional materials. Confirm the time and venue for make-up activity

- Determine the make-up objectves
  – to enhance the client appearance
  – to promote the business and its products and services

- Carry out the make-up activity ensuring the make-up objectives are met and the features and benefits of both products and services are effectively promoted

- Use effective communication techniques suitable to the type of make-up activity

- Make-up activities include
  – group demonstration
  – one-to-one demonstration

- During the make-up activity encourage questions to ensure client understanding of products and services. Consolidate understanding through oral explanation and practical demonstration

- During make-up activity ensure legal and hygiene requirements are met and that a clean, tidy work environment is maintained

- Confirm the client's satisfaction with the finished result. Ensure it meets the agreed treatment objective/correct make-up result accordingly

- Performing make-up activity work in a cost-effective, commercially viable time

- Record details on a client record card recording make-up products used and application techniques

- Following a group demonstration have available an appointment book and promotional materials to secure business opportunities

Ellisons

A make-up palette

A *feature* is the make-up product's specialist ingredients and the effects that their application can achieve.

A *benefit* is what the client could expect from buying the product. Be enthusiastic about the products that you are using as this will inspire the client. Knowledge will sell not only your products but you!

Aftercare and advice

Ensure that the finished result is to the client's satisfaction. This is the opportunity to demonstrate to the client how to make any necessary changes to achieve the desired result. Allow time for the client to ask further questions about the products selected and applied. The make-up record card is useful (as is a before-and-after photograph for reference) to list products used and the make-up effect achieved. A make-up chart can be given to the client, to reinforce the discussion that has taken place during any make-up lesson; it will also be invaluable if the client returns wishing to purchase any of the make-up cosmetics you have used. Following a group demonstration you may wish to make your business card or service menu available for the client's future reference. You may even wish to enable the clients to book appointments.

Promote additional services, professionally answer further questions following the make-up application and give additional tips on make-up technique as applicable – this will show your professional knowledge. Keep in contact with your client to make them aware of future product promotions.

THE CLIENT'S NEEDS

Day make-up

The effect should be natural. Any corrective work carried out should be very subtle and kept to the minimum, as natural light makes any imperfections appear obvious.

Select a foundation the same colour as the skin – aim to even out the skin tone. Set the foundation with a translucent face powder.

Apply a subtle, warm blusher to add colour to the face. Avoid strong colours of cosmetics, especially on the eyes. The mascara colour should be chosen to complement the client's natural lash and skin colours. Mascara should be used to emphasise, but not exaggerate, the length and thickness of the eyelashes. Eyeliner may be used, but it should be carefully placed and blended.

Line the lips in a colour that will coordinate with the lipstick to be applied, which again should be quite natural.

Evening make-up

This should be applied bearing in mind the type of lighting in which the client will be seen. Artificial light dulls the effect, and changes the colour of the make-up: dark shades lose their brilliance, appearing 'muddy', so you need to use brighter colours. Emphasise the facial features with the careful placement of contouring cosmetics.

Areas where shadows may be created, such as the eyes, should be emphasised using light, bright, and highlighting cosmetic products. Add warmth to the face with an intense colour of blusher placed on the cheekbones. A highlighting powder in a pearlised or metallic shade may be applied directly on top of or over the blusher. The client may like to try adventurous cosmetics such as metallics and frosted eye products.

Curl the eyelashes with eyelash curlers, or apply false eyelashes to emphasise the eyes. Fashion shades of mascara may be selected, in purples, greens and blues, to complement the make-up and produce the effect required. Light shades of eyeliner may be used to frame the eyes and to 'open' them up.

Add a lipgloss to the lips, or apply a frosted lipstick to emphasise the mouth.

Colour the eyebrows, and carefully groom them to frame the eye area.

Special occasion make-up

A special occasion is usually an important event such as a wedding, day at the races, graduation ceremony or New Year's Eve party.

Whatever the occasion, whether daytime or evening, indoors or outdoors, you will need to consider the type of lighting the make-up will be viewed in – natural or artificial – and any other factors, such as how long it is to be worn for.

> **TIP** ✔
>
> In poor lighting, face shading should be subtle as it makes shadows appear darker.

Derrick Mulligan/Media Image

The selection of colours should co-ordinate with what the client will be wearing, and finally you need to know the effect they wish the make-up to create – should it be subtle or glamorous? Make-up products can then be selected and appropriately applied to suit the occasion.

Photographic make-up

If applying make-up for photographic purposes, it is important to consider the effect to be created. This should be planned with the photographer in advance of the make-up application.

Consider the brightness of the lighting used. The brighter the lighting is the lighter the make-up pigment will appear. Make-up will therefore need to be applied more strongly. Lighting can be hot and may affect the make-up application making it melt, especially with oil-based make-up. Therefore, avoid oily make-up and regularly apply powder to remove shine.

Generally, matt colours are used, as the lighting will emphasise any shine.

For black and white photography remember dark colours will appear darker when photographed. Therefore, it may be necessary to apply lighter shades in preference to dark – for example, a dark shade of cheek colour would create a dark shadow.

Avoid lip gloss unless you wish the lips to appear full.

Photographic make-up

TIP ✔

Make-up considerations for photographic make-up
Frosted colours used on the eyes will draw attention to the eyes and emphasise problem areas such as fine lines, so be subtle in their application. Areas that you do not wish to emphasise should be matt as powder minimises flaws.
   Oily face make-up will emphasise open pores.
   Thick lashes, if required, can create shadows under the eye area. The lighting would have to be adjusted to avoid shadowing.
   Photographic make-up may be applied in a photographer's studio or on location. Ensure you are able to transport your make-up safely.

It is important to define facial features using shading and highlighting techniques, as photographic make-up removes natural shades and highlights.

Care should be taken to blend all make-up to avoid any demarcation lines, which will be emphasised in the photograph.

Make-up to suit skin and hair colouring

Fair skin and blonde hair

If the client has fair hair and fair skin, keep the skin colour natural. Apply a blusher in rose pink or beige.

Define the eyes with soft tones of browns and pinks. Apply a brown-black mascara.

Caucasian client

Philippine client

Indian client

African-Caribbean client

Colour the lips with a rose-pink or peach lip-colour. Avoid lip colours lighter than the natural skin tone.

Oriental skin and black hair

For creamy, sallow skin with dark hair, use blusher to add warmth and to brighten the skin, in either pink or brown.

The eyes are dark, with a prominent browbone. Emphasise the socket of the eye with careful shading; extend this upwards and outwards. Place highlighter along the browbone.

Pastel colours complement the eye colour. Select black mascara to emphasise the eyes. Deep pinks and orangey-reds suit the lips.

Fair skin and red hair

Redheads usually have fair skin with freckles. The skin will flush and colour easily, probably requiring the application of a green-tinted moisturiser, concealer or face powder. Apply blusher in a warm rose or peach colour. Browns, rusts, greens and peach eyeshadow colours suit this skin and complement the eyes. Brown mascara is preferable, to avoid making the eyes appear hard.

For the lips, select a lipstick in peach, golden rust or pink.

Black skin and black hair

A yellow-toned foundation is required: it may be necessary to blend foundations to obtain the correct colour. Avoid pink-toned foundations, which make the skin appear chalky.

Women with dark skin tend to have dark brown to brown-black eyes, and can use a wide range of heavily pigmented colours, especially browns and bronzes. Dark shades of blusher in red and plum may be chosen; eyeliner and mascara can be black, or any other dark shade.

Avoid lip colours lighter than the skin tone. A lipliner darker than the lip colour may be used.

Olive or fair skin and dark hair

Select a foundation to suit the basic skin tone. If the skin is fair, choose an ivory base; if it is sallow, select a foundation with a rusty, yellow tone. (With a sallow skin, avoid the use of pinks on the eyes – they make the eyes appear sore.)

A beige blusher suits this skin colour, and is complemented by the selection of brown or green shades for the eyes. Black mascara should be used for the eyelashes.

For the lips, choose warm reds or beige.

Make-up for the mature skin

As the skin ages it becomes sallow in colour and appears thinner. Small capillaries can be seen, commonly on the cheek area, and small veins may appear around the eyes. Pigment changes in the skin become obvious, and remain permanently.

At the make-up consultation, discuss your ideas with your client. Very often a mature client will have been using the same colours and the same cosmetics for many years, and they may not even be complementary. You will need to advise her tactfully on a fresh approach.

Select a foundation that matches the skin colour yet enhances the skin's appearance. An oil-based foundation is appropriate for use on a mature skin: it keeps the skin supple and prevents the foundation from settling into the creases and emphasising the lines and wrinkles.

A concealer may be applied to cover obvious capillaries and small veins, or a foundation may be selected which provides adequate coverage.

A lighter foundation may be applied over wrinkled areas, to make them less obvious. These areas include:

- around the eyes (crow's feet);
- between the brows;
- across the forehead;
- between the nose and the mouth (naso-labial folds);
- around the mouth (the lipline).

With age, the contours of the face lose their firmness as the fat cells that plump the face reduce, and the facial muscles lose tone and sag. Poor muscle tone can be seen in the following areas:

- the cheek area;
- loose skin along the jawline;

Mexican client

TIP

Dark circles under the eyes can be minimised with concealer. Select a concealer lighter than the foundation to be applied.

ACTIVITY

Shading
Where would you place the shading product in order to correct poor muscle tone in the areas discussed opposite?

- loose skin under the brow and overhanging the lid;
- loose skin on the neck.

The application of a shader, subtly blended, can improve the appearance of such areas.

Apply translucent powder. It may be preferable to avoid doing so in the eye area as it can emphasise lines around the eyes. To reduce the powdery effect – which may make the skin appear dry – you may direct a fine water spray from a suitable distance, to set the make-up.

Apply a blusher with a warm tone – avoid harsh, bright shades. A cream blusher may be applied after the foundation. Place it high on the cheekbone and blend it upwards at the temples, drawing attention upwards rather than downwards.

The lipline becomes less obvious as one grows older, and lines often appear along it. Lipliner should be applied, to redefine the lips and to prevent the lipstick from 'bleeding' into the lines. Select a lipliner that is the same colour as, or slightly lighter than, the lip colour. (A darker lip colour would create an unwanted shadow.) A special lip fixative may be recommended, and a durable cream lipstick applied. Avoid the use of a gloss lipstick which would emphasise lines around the mouth.

The angle of the mouth may droop. Corrective techniques may be used to disguise this.

Powder matt eyeshadows should be selected for use on the eyelid: these soften the appearance of any lines in the area. Choose natural, light shades. Dark colours can make the eyes appear small and tired.

Eyeliner should be used, in neutral shades of brown and grey – avoid harsh, bright colours, which will give a hard appearance.

Eyebrows should be perfectly groomed, and arched to give lift to the eye. Bushy eyebrows give the eyes a hooded appearance. If eyebrow colour is required, select a colour that is slightly lighter than the brow colour, or a blend of two colours. If the client has grey hair, use grey and charcoal to provide a natural effect.

Eyelashes should be emphasised with a natural-looking shade of mascara, lightly applied. (If the eyelashes lose their colour, you can recommend that the client has her lashes professionally – and permanently – tinted. Individual false eyelashes may be recommended for corrective purposes.)

TIP

Cream eyeshadow settles into creases, which emphasise a crepey eyelid. Frosted or pearlised eyeshadows also emphasise a crepey eyelid.

TIP ✔

If the client is visiting the salon for a make-up, you could recommend that she have a professional make-up lesson – at which you could discuss a fresh approach to her make-up.

HEALTH AND SAFETY

Allergies
Sometimes the eyes become quite sensitive with age. Apply hypoallergenic mascara in such cases.

SPECIAL OCCASION MAKE-UP

Make-up is to be applied to a Caucasian client to achieve a more glamorous look for a social lunch with friends. We allowed 45 minutes to achieve the look.

It is a dry skin type as the sebaceous and sudoriferous glands have become less active as part of the ageing process.

Other noticeable facial characteristics include:

1 Dark circles around the eye area.

2 Thin, delicate tissue around the eye with small veins and capillaries showing through the skin.

3 Habitual frown lines.

4 Poor muscle tone resulting in dropped facial contours, i.e. double chin.

5 Poor skin tone as the skin loses its elasticity resulting in wrinkling and loss of firmness.

6 Sallow skin colour due to poor blood circulation.

With ageing the skin appears much finer in this area and capillaries and veins are more noticeable. Avoid pinky concealers as these will appear grey when applied over the dark circles. Select a concealer that matches the skin tone but with some warmth, e.g. a golden colour.

Remember a little goes a long way – too much can settle in creases around the eyes emphasising them.

The client's skin has been cleansed, toned, moisturised and blotted to remove excess moisturiser.

Foundation is selected to match the client's skin tone, which has a yellow pigment. As the skin is dry and sallow a liquid formulation foundation is selected. The foundation is applied and blended with a cosmetic sponge all over the face, over the jaw line, blended into the neck and over the eyelids and lips. Sometimes foundation is all you will need to adequately conceal any blemishes.

Concealer is applied using a brush to disguise dark circles, which are usually a purplish colour, under the area.

The finger pads may be used to blend the concealer as necessary. Remember pressure must be light to avoid excess drag around this delicate area.

A translucent loose powder is used to set the foundation and remove any stickiness. This facilitates the application of further powder cosmetics and gives durability to the foundation.

Use a large powder brush to remove excess powder, brushing upwards and outwards.

Now add colour and contour to the face using blusher. Using a blusher/contour-brush stroke colour along the cheekbone towards the hairline. It can also be applied to other areas of the face such as the temples to add warmth. If a cream blusher is used apply this after foundation application and before the powder.

Apply eye shadow in a matt colour. Metallic and pearlised colours should be used sparingly as they emphasise crepey skin found on the upper eyelid, due to poor skin tone.

An ivory beige matt shadow is applied over the entire eyelid.

In contrast a matt brown eye shadow is applied at the corner of the eyes and blended into the eye socket. This draws attention to the eyes. A shading brush is used to soften and blend the colour, creating a smoky look.

Eyeliner pencil is applied at the corner edges of the upper and lower eyelids, just above and below the eyelashes. Powder colour is applied on top of the pencil using an eyeliner brush. This increases durability and softens the look.

Colour is applied to the brows. Brow pencil or powder eye shadow may be used to define the shape of the brows.

The brows are groomed by brushing them in the direction of growth using an eyebrow brush. This also ensures all eyebrow colour is blended evenly.

Mascara is applied. Additional coats have been applied at the corners of the eyes to lengthen the eyelashes and open the eyes, giving a vibrant look. A lash comb may be used to remove excess mascara if necessary.

The lips have been outlined using a lipliner pencil. The colour has been chosen to match the lipstick. The client's lips are small and the liner has been applied just outside the natural lip line for corrective purposes to create the illusion of fuller lips. Glossy lipstick should be avoided as this can bleed into fine lines around the lips.

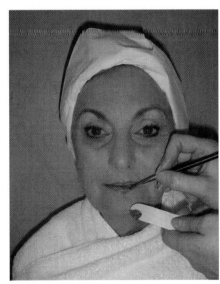

The lips are coloured using a bronze-coloured lipstick applied with a lip brush. The lipstick is chosen to complement the eye shadow.

The finished result – a make-up for a special occasion!

ASIAN CLIENT MAKE-UP APPLICATION

Day make-up

Corrective work completed is subtle, as natural daylight makes any imperfections seem more obvious.

The clients' skin has been cleansed, toned, moisturised and blotted to remove excess moisturiser. 30 minutes was allowed to achieve the look.

This is an oily skin type, where over-activity of the sebaceous glands in the skin is creating a shiny, sallow appearance.

Other noticeable facial characteristics include:

- Darker skin underneath the eye area which requires concealer correction.

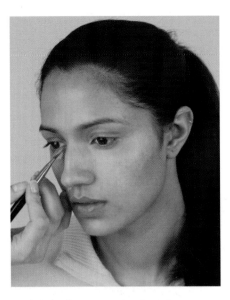

A concealer is applied with a brush underneath the eyes to disguise the darker skin tone.

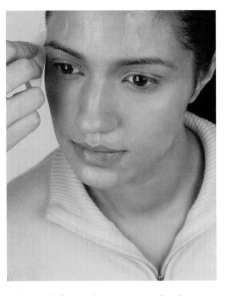

A liquid foundation matched to the client's skin tone is applied. Application is over the whole face, including the eyelids and lips, as this gives an even skin tone.

Following the application of loose powder, again matched to the client's skin tone, excess powder is removed using a large powder brush. Application is upwards and outwards.

Blusher colour is applied to accentuate the cheek area and add colour to the face.

Colour applied to the eye emphasises the eye area. We used complementary colours in a purple range. A highlighting colour accentuates the brow-bone.

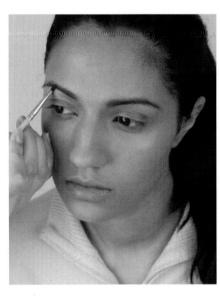

The eyebrows are accentuated using a dark matt brown colour applied with a stiff eyebrow brush. This gives definition to the eyebrow, disguising sparse hair and gaps.

The lashes are lengthened using a lash-building mascara in black.

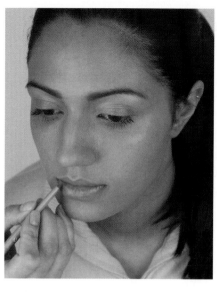

Lipliner colour is applied to define the desired lip contour. A co-ordinating lip colour is selected to match the lipliner and complement the eye make-up colour.

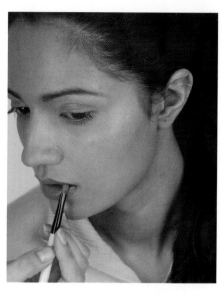

The lip colour is applied using a lip brush.

The final day make-up look.

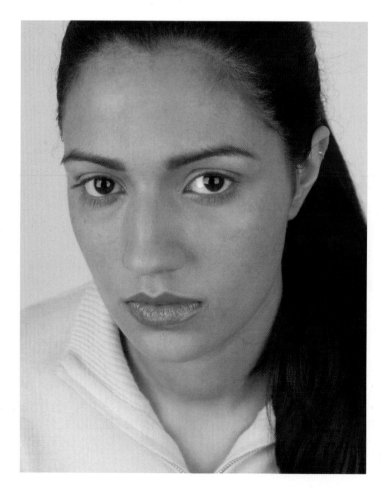

AFRICAN-CARIBBEAN CLIENT MAKE-UP APPLICATION

Evening make-up

Make-up which will be seen under artificial lighting is applied. Stronger pigmented make-up colours have been selected, and the make-up effect emphasises facial features through the choice and application of make-up products. 45 minutes was allowed to achieve the look.

The client's skin has been cleansed, tone and moisturised and blotted to remove excess moisturiser.

This is a combination skin type and the sebaceous glands are overactive in the 'T' zone – forehead, nose and chin – and the pores appear larger in this area. The sebaceous glands are less active in the cheek which results in a dry skin type with tight pores.

Other noticeable facial characteristics include:

- The skin tone of the face has uneven pigmentation.
- The face shape requires balance which can be achieved using shaded contour colour.

Foundation is selected to match the client's skin type and even the skin tone. A mousse foundation has been used to provide a medium coverage and has been blended quickly to avoid a chalky appearance.

A cream formulation shading product, in a darker shade than the foundation, is applied underneath the cheekbone and at the temples to accentuate the cheekbones and reduce the width of the face at the temples.

LEVEL 2 PROVIDE MAKE-UP TREATMENT (BT9) PLAN AND PROMOTE MAKE-UP ACTIVITIES (BT10)

Loose powder matching the client's skin tone is applied to set the foundation and facilitate application of further powder products. Powder blusher is applied to the cheekbone.

Following application of a neutral eye shadow matt colour, a darker shading product is used to emphasise the eye socket.

The natural lash line is accentuated by eyeliner application. A steady hand is required!

The brows are defined.

Mascara application draws attention to the eyes.

Lipliner is applied to define the perfect lip line.

The lips are coloured in using a matt lipstick co-ordinated to suit the lipliner. Lip gloss achieves a final touch which will focus attention and add emphasis in darker lighting.

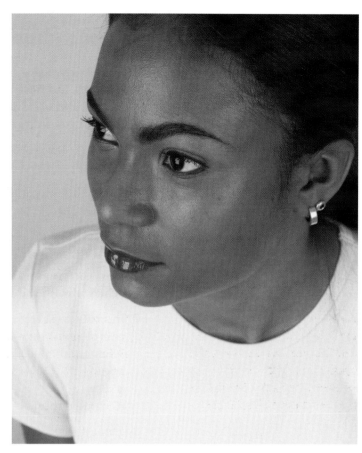

The final evening make-up look

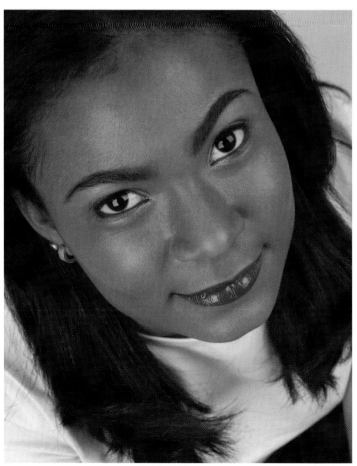

Assessment of knowledge and understanding

You have now learnt about the different make-up application techniques and how to adapt these to suit the client's skin type, colouring and condition. These skills will enable you to professionally provide make-up treatment.

To test your level of knowledge, answer the following short questions. These will prepare you for your summative (final) assessment.

Anatomy and physiology questions required for this unit are found on pages 129–30.

Consult with the client

1 How can you ensure that you fully understand the effect to be achieved with the make-up application?

2 In order to select the correct skin care and make-up products to complement the client's skin it is necessary to identify her skin type. What are the facial characteristics for the following skin types:
   - oily
   - dry
   - combination?

3 Name three skin, and three eye disorders that would contra-indicate make-up application.

4 Why is it important that you never name a contra-indication?

5 What product ingredients are known to cause allergic reactions, and should therefore not be used on a client with sensitive skin?

Prepare for the treatment

1 How can you ensure that the treatment environment is suitable for the application of make-up?

2 How should the make-up brushes be prepared for each client to avoid cross-infection?

3 Why is it important to have a variety of make-up products available?

4 How should the skin be prepared before the application of make-up?

Plan the treatment

1 What should be considered when planning a make-up with a client?

2 How should the client be positioned when applying make-up?

3 What is the difference in application technique for the following make-up contexts:
   - day
   - evening
   - special occasion?

4 How is the correct colour of foundation selected for your client?

5 Why is it important to match lighting with the occasion for which the make-up is to be worn?

Apply make-up products

1 Why is it important that make-up is applied in a suitable sequence?

2 How can you ensure hygienic practice when applying the following products:
- foundation
- face powder
- mascara
- lipstick?

3 For what purposes would you apply a concealer?

4 Describe how a minor skin imperfection may be disguised with make-up application.

5 How and why would you curl the natural lashes?

6 What is the purpose of:
- shader
- highlighter?

7 What corrective make-up techniques should be applied for each of the following?
- square face
- high forehead
- narrow eyes
- hyperpigmentation
- hypopigmentation?

8 Below is a picture of a client with a mature skin. Looking at the facial characteristics, what corrective work would require to be applied.

9 False lashes may be applied to enhance the eyes. What is the difference in each type in terms of:
- application
- how long they may be worn for
- removal?

Complete the treatment

1 What aftercare advice should be given to a client following make-up application?

2 If a client has received a make-up lesson what should she be provided with?

3 Name three contra-actions that could occur during or after make-up application. What action should be taken?

4 How can you promote the sale of skin care and make-up products during a make-up application?

5 What advice would you give with regard to the type of make-up products and application for a client who is not used to wearing make-up and is getting married abroad?

6 From a magazine, collect a photographic image from the client group below:
- African-carribean
- Asian
- Caucasian
- Oriental.

Describe how each look has been created, explaining the make-up application and products used.

EXTEND AND MAINTAIN NAILS

BT12

Learning objectives

This unit describes how to extend and maintain nails. It describes the competencies to enable you to:

- **consult with the client**
- **prepare for the treatment**
- **plan the treatment**
- **repair natural nails to improve condition and appearance**
- **apply artificial nail using the wrap system**
- **maintain and repair artificial nail structures**
- **complete the treatment**

When performing extending and maintaining nail treatments, it is important to use the skills you have learnt in the following core mandatory units:

Unit G1 – Ensure your own actions reduce risks to health and safety

Unit G6 – Promote additional products or services to clients

Unit G8 – Develop and maintain your effectiveness at work

Anatomy and physiology knowledge and understanding is located in Chapter 5. The essential knowledge requirements are listed on page 89.

Nail extensions

TYPES OF NAIL EXTENSION

Nail extensions are a rapidly growing area in the beauty industry and it is the duty of the professional beauty therapist to be aware of current trends. There are many professional methods available to enhance the length, strength, appearance or repair of the nail. These include sculptured nails, nail tips, tips and overlays and pre-formed 'stick-on' nails. To achieve sculptured nails, tips and overlays there is a choice of materials to select from including liquid/powder acrylic; fibreglass/silk wrapping system; UV gel and UV liquid/powder acrylic.

Nail tips

- **Sculptured nails** These can be achieved using a liquid and powder system or gel. The mixture is 'sculpted', built up over the natural nail plate and extends past the free edge on a nail form.

- **Nail tips** This method uses nail tips commonly made from plastic or nylon, applied to the natural nail tip only to add length. The seam area where the nail tip is attached to the natural nail plate is buffed so there is no visible line.

- **Tips and overlays** A nail tip is applied, blended to remove the visible line and is then overlaid with acrylic, gel or fibreglass. This extends the length of the nail and increases the strength of the structure.

- **Pre-formed 'stick-on' nails** A plastic nail is applied to cover the whole natural nail plate, therefore no buffing is required.

- **Nail repairs** When a nail that has been extended requires repair, it should be repaired using the relevant method. This is discussed in the section on maintenance for each nail system.

  To repair a natural nail in the case of flaking or free-edge break the beauty therapist can use a *nail wrap*.

- **Nail wrap** Material such as silk or fibreglass is attached to the nail using an adhesive and adhesive dryer. They are used to strengthen the natural nails or nail tips. Wraps are made either from tissue or fabric such as linen, silk or fibreglass.

Clients demand a high level of service when they attend a salon for nail treatments, so thorough knowledge is essential. A good trade supplier will usually offer training courses and full back-up support.

Due to the vast number of products available, however, specific application techniques may vary. To ensure a completely safe and professional-looking application, always follow the manufacturer's instructions.

Nail extension and maintenance service

These services offer the following benefits:

- improve the appearance of short, stubby fingers by lengthening the free edge;

- improve the appearance of the natural nail shape;

- to strengthen the natural nail;

- can motivate a nail-biter to break the habit. An acrylic/gel overlay or nail wrap will strengthen the nail and improve its appearance;

- provide temporary length to the nails in the case of application for a special occasion but the client does not want the nails to be permanent. Tips may be applied for this effect;

- for repair, in the case of flaking nails, free edge or flesh line break or severed free edge. The client can have the nail appearance balanced using the most appropriate nail system;

- to disguise a disfigured nail that is not contra-indicated to treat. A nail system can be applied for corrective purposes;

- if an overlay is placed over nail polish this extends its durability.

RECEPTION

The following time should be allocated for these nail extension and maintenance services:

- Sculptured nails: approximately 1 hour and 20 minutes full set
- Nail tips: approximately 45 minutes
- Tips and overlays: approximately 1 hour and 30 minutes
- Preformed stick on nails: approximately 30 minutes
- Nail repair and natural nail wraps: approximately 10 minutes per nail.

It is important that treatments are received in the given time to ensure client satisfaction, to ensure the efficiency of the reception area, and that expected income targets are met. A client who is kept waiting or finds the treatment time excessive will probably go to an alternative nail technician/salon next time.

When a client makes an appointment for a nail-extension service, the receptionist should ask a few simple questions in order to ascertain her needs. Information obtained from the client will help the nail technician to set up the working area with the appropriate equipment and materials, and will save time when the client arrives for treatment. The basic questions that the receptionist should ask are these:

- Why does she want a nail-extension treatment – is it for a special occasion, for example, or to help stop nail biting?
- Has she had nail extensions applied before?
- Does she want a temporary or permanent result?

Effective communication and questioning techniques are important to ensure that you fully understand the client's treatment requirements. A professional, friendly approach will give the client confidence in you and her expectation of the level of service she can expect.

All data on the client relating to their treatment should be recorded on the client's record card. This should be stored confidentially and accessed only by those with authority to do so to comply with the Data Protection Act 1984.

As with all beauty treatments, accurate record cards must be kept for clients having nail-extension services. If a client has had such services before, the receptionist should consult the card and tell the nail technician about these. This will give the nail technician a good idea of what to expect when the client arrives. For example, if the client has not attended for over three weeks, her nails may need a lot of maintenance work and extra time could be booked to allow for this.

Information recorded on the client's record card will include the following.

Occupation/lifestyle

The client's occupation/lifestyle will help the nail technician to decide which type of nail system to use, and how long to leave the free edge. A client with a very physically demanding occupation, for example, will need a very strong

TIP

Because of the maintenance procedures with nail-extension treatments, clients' appointments should be booked in advance. This ensures that maintenance can be carried out as required.

BEAUTY WORKS

Date	Beauty therapist name	

Client name		Date of birth (identifying client age group)

Address		Postcode

Evening phone number	Day phone number

Name of doctor	Doctor's address and phone number

Related medical history (conditions that may restrict or prohibit treatment application)

Are you taking any medication (this may affect skin sensitivity to the treatment or client suitability)

CONTRA-INDICATIONS REQUIRING MEDICAL REFERRAL
(Preventing nail extension or maintenance treatment)

- ☐ bacterial infections (e.g. paronychia/impetigo)
- ☐ viral infections (e.g. plantar warts)
- ☐ fungal infections (e.g. onychomycosis)
- ☐ onycolysis (nail separation from nail bed)
- ☐ nail/skin disorders ☐ nail/skin disease
- ☐ severe bruising ☐ severe cuts and abrasions
- ☐ medical conditions ☐ recent scar tissue
- ☐ allergic reaction ☐ diabetes
- ☐ loss of sensation in the fingers/hands

NAIL TREATMENTS ARE

- ☐ repairs
- ☐ replacement of overlay ☐ finishing ☐ balancing
- ☐ tips and overlays
- ☐ natural nail overlays

NAIL SHAPE AND NAIL/SKIN CONDITION

- ☐ nail shape e.g. round, oval, square
- ☐ natural nail shape e.g. claw, spoon, fan (this will guide you in your application technique)
- ☐ nail condition e.g. dry, damaged
- ☐ skin type e.g. dry/sensitive, moist
- ☐ cuticle condition e.g. normal, overgrown (a pre-treatment service may be necessary to improve nail/skin condition)

PRODUCTS USED

- ☐ adhesives ☐ artificial nail products
- ☐ cuticle oils ☐ dehydrators
- ☐ primers

CONTRA-INDICATIONS WHICH RESTRICT TREATMENT
(Treatment may require adaptation)

- ☐ cuts and abrasions
- ☐ bruising and swelling of nail/skin
- ☐ recent scar tissue in area (avoid area)
- ☐ eczema ☐ onychopagy (severely bitten nails)
- ☐ undiagnosed lumps, bumps, swellings
- ☐ recent injuries to the treatment area
- ☐ medication ☐ mild psoriasis/eczema

CONSULTATION TECHNIQUES

- ☐ questioning, including:
  reasons for treatment   previous nail treatments received
  occupation   hobbies
  condition of skin and nails
- ☐ visual ☐ manual
- ☐ reference to client records

OBJECTIVES OF TREATMENT

- ☐ nail length ☐ nail shape ☐ nail finish, natural/polish

RECOMMENDATIONS

- ☐ from the client's expectations, record recommendations; nail system/nail length, shape and finish

EQUIPMENT AND MATERIALS

- ☐ nail and skin treatment tools
- ☐ nail and skin products
- ☐ consumables ☐ tips
- ☐ wrap fibre-glass/silk ☐ setting agents
- ☐ forms

Beauty therapist signature (for reference)

Client signature (confirmation of details)

TREATMENT ADVICE

This information includes
- what products have been used in the nail extension/maintenance treatment
- advice re products that would be suitable for the client to use at home for hand and nail protection
- advice on how to gain maximum benefit from product use

Nail care advice
- Advice to follow immediately following treatment to include
  - possible reactions to the treatment and recommended action to take
  - dealing with accidental damage
  - wearing gloves for housework, immersing the hands in water
  - do not use the fingernails as tools
  - only use non-acetone nail polish remover
  - do not pick at the nail or surrounding skin (this may be a habit the client has)
  - return to the salon for any repairs
- contra-action advice, action to be taken in the event of an unwanted reaction, e.g. premature loss of nail extensions, lifting of products, discolouration of the natural nail plate, allergic reaction, swelling, infection

Further treatments
- recommendations for further treatments
- the recommended time intervals between maintenance treatments

---

nail extension with a medium-to-short free edge. Other things to consider include any hobbies or interests the client may have that may affect the nail system chosen, for example swimming or gardening.

Condition of natural nails and cuticles

The condition prior to nail extension will be relevant later when the nail extensions are removed. The client cannot expect her nails to be in perfect condition later if they were not so at the outset.

If the client's nails or skin are in poor condition this may mean alternative nail services, such as manicure or nail/skin conditioning treatments, should be carried out.

If the client has excessively overgrown cuticles, a manicure must be performed before nail extensions are applied. This must be carried out at a previous appointment because the nail plate will be too moist following the cuticle treatment and this will affect the adherence of the material used to the nail plate.

Type of nail system used

Should the nail technician be away for any reason, other technicians must know what type of nail system to apply. The record card will tell assisting staff which products to set out at the working area.

Size of nail tips (if used)

A record of the size of tip used will save time during repairs and maintenance – the technician will know which tip size to use, and won't have to measure each time to get the right size.

ACTIVITY

Record cards
What other information specific to the application of nail extensions do you think should be on the client record card? In what way is this information relevant?

Allergies to products

Knowing which products (if any) the client is allergic to is crucial so that these products can be avoided. An allergy to a product may cause discomfort at the nail or surrounding skin. This can result in dryness, cracking, redness and swelling.

Reason for having nail extensions

This information helps the technician to assess whether to recommend temporary or permanent extensions. It is important that the correct service is chosen for the client to ensure client satisfaction. Explain why the service is best suited to the client.

Client signature

The client must confirm that she has been informed of the treatment details and possible contra-actions.

CONTRA-INDICATIONS

Question the client to check for contra-indications. If, whilst completing the record card or on visual inspection of the skin or nail, you find the client to have any of the following nail conditions, services should not be carried out. Treating a client with a contra-indication may lead to cross-infection or a worsening of the client's condition. Refer to pages 279–80 to see pictures of these conditions.

Contra-indications to nail extension are as follows:

HEALTH AND SAFETY

Nail health
If the client has inflammation, redness and swelling or infection, or if pus is present, **never treat the client**. Refer them to their GP.

- *Onychophagy* Severely bitten nails contra-indicate extension as they do not allow sufficient nail plate for adhesion of a nail tip. Also the bulbous skin at the fingertip would cause the result to be spoon-shaped.
- *Onychorrhexis* Thin, peeling nails do not provide a secure enough base for nail extensions.
- *Onychomycosis* A fungal condition which can spread unnoticed beneath the artificial nail. As it is contagious, it may also infect the nail technician and the manicure instruments.
- *Paronychia* Inflammation and bacterial infection of the nail fold would cause discomfort for the client during any nail treatment. The products used might further irritate the condition.
- *Certain occupations* Some heavy manual occupations, such as those involving lifting, preclude nail extensions: the nails would be too easily broken. However, application in such cases would not actually be detrimental to the client's well-being, so it is at the discretion of the nail technician.
- *Allergies* If a client has suffered an allergy after a previous nail-extension application, do not repeat the application. Where possible identify the product and use an alternative.
- *Cuts and abrasions in the specific area* Applying nail extensions to a client with these conditions could result in discomfort during treatment and might lead to subsequent infection.

HEALTH AND SAFETY

Treating a diabetic client
Great care should be taken when performing nail services on a diabetic client. This is because the skin has slow healing and if the skin was accidentally broken with cuticle nippers or a file, infection could occur. It is best not to nip the cuticles on this client.

- *Bruised nail* A blood clot forms under the nail plate caused by injury.
- *Atrophy of the nail* The nail wastes away. Caused by injury or by poor health.
- *Onycholysis* Separation of the nail plate from the nail bed.
- *Onychocryptosis* Ingrowing fingernail where the nail grows into the tissue of the surrounding nail. This commonly occurs where there has been damage to the nail resulting in deformity.
- *Warts* Raised horny skin tissue with a rough surface; caused by a virus.
- *Extreme curvature of the natural nail* For nail extensions, as effective adherence would not occur.

EQUIPMENT LIST

nail workstation

lamp

waste bin

plastic glasses

manicure pads or disposable tissue

cottonwool discs

tissues

orange sticks

cuticle knife and cuticle nippers

dappen dishes

scissors

coarse file (100-grit)

medium file (180-grit)

fine file (240-grit)

1000–2000 grit file

medium-sized towels

acetone remover

non-acetone remover

see opposite for complete list of materials required

Dappen dishes

EQUIPMENT AND MATERIALS

The equipment and materials listed below are general to all applications of nail extensions, maintenance and natural nail repair. Additional specialised items are listed with the individual techniques.

- *Nail workstation.*
- *Seating* – for technician and client.
- *Lamp* – for workstation use.
- *Waste bin (with lid).*
- *Plastic glasses* – to protect the eyes.
- *Safety mask* – to avoid the inhalation of dust.
- *Manicure pads or disposable tissue.*
- *Nail preparation products.*
- *Nail wipes* – lint-free pads used to remove dust created during treatment.
- *Cottonwool discs.*
- *Cotton buds.*
- *Tissues.*
- *Orange sticks* – to loosen the cuticle at the base of the nail.
- *Cuticle knife and cuticle nippers* – to trim excess cuticle.
- *Glass bowl.*
- *Bowls (3).*
- *Dappen dish* – small glass or plastic dish to hold products during treatment application.
- *Scissors* – used to cut wrap material to size, often referred to as *stork scissors*.
- *Tip cutters* – to cut the artificial nail structure.
- *Coarse file (100-grit)* – for reducing and shaping the length of the artificial free edge.
- *Medium file (180-grit)* – for blending in the seam areas and shaping the artificial free edge.
- *Fine file (240-grit)* – to smooth the nail and remove any scratches from the nail surface.
- *1000–2000 grit file* – termed micro-abrasive and used to buff and shape the nail.

TIP	

The lower the number of grit, the coarser the file. Thus a 100-grit file is coarse; a 240-grit file is smooth.

- *Four-sided buffer* – to bring the nail surface to a shine.
- *Medium-sized towels (3).*
- *Disinfectant fluid (in a jar).*
- *Spray sanitiser* – for small pieces of equipment.
- *Nail steriliser* – alcohol based sanitising agent used to prevent bacterial and fungal growth.

- *Acetone remover* – to remove nail polish.
- *A non-acetone nail polish remover* – for clients with artificial nails or nail wraps.
- *Cuticle oil* to condition the cuticles.
- *Non-acetone nail polish remover (in a pump dispenser)*.
- *Mild antiseptic cleanser* – for hands or an anti-bacterial soap and water.
- *Aftercare leaflets*.
- *Client's record card*.

Sterilisation and sanitisation

For the health and safety of both the nail technician and the client, and to uphold the standards of the profession, you should ensure that all tools and materials are sterilised prior to use. Disposable items should be used where applicable.

Prior to treatment both the client and the technician should wash their hands with a mild antiseptic cleanser and dry them on soft disposable paper towels. This will help to prevent cross-infection, and make the working area pleasant for both.

Before artificial nails are applied, the natural nail should be sterilised using an appropriate solution such as **isopropyl alcohol**. This reduces the risk of infection from bacteria and fungi.

Allow the client to see the cleaning and sterilising procedures taking place: they will instil in her confidence in your work and professional competence as well as reassure her about her own safety.

Preparing the working area

The working area should contain all the equipment and materials necessary for the treatment: this avoids unnecessary disturbance to the client during treatment. It should be well ventilated, warm, and with a good source of light. The bulb used in the workstation lamp should be 40 watts. This will avoid excessive heat production which would affect product consistency when sculpting during nail extension treatment.

A ventilation system is required to remove fumes, vapours and dusts that could lead to eye and respiratory problems. The system used must ensure effective ventilation taking into account the number of nail technicians working in the area.

In the case of a freelance nail technician a desktop extractor may be purchased. Temperatures must not be too warm as this can affect the application and setting properties of nail materials. When carrying out nail services you will need a lamp on the work surface, in addition to general room lighting. This reduces shadows and allows you to work with precise detail.

Work surfaces should be covered with a clean, dry material capable of absorbing liquid if spilt. The material should be disposable or capable of being sterilised. Ideal materials are towels or disposable tissue.

If blood is spilt (this is often caused by using a new file) the contaminated waste should be placed in a sealed bag and incinerated and the area cleaned

A manicure and nail extension station

Ellisons

TIP

Brush cleaner is available to place the brushes in following their use. This prevents brushes becoming hard.

HEALTH AND SAFETY

Smoking
Due to the flammable nature of the products used, clients should be advised not to smoke during treatment.

using a disinfectant cleaner. Wear gloves when using disinfectants and handling contaminated waste.

Towels must be clean, dry and soft to ensure client comfort. Fresh towels must be used for each client. Place one towel flat to cover the work surface; fold the other towel into a small pad and place it beneath the client's forearm. This supports the client's arm during treatment and helps to keep her comfortable.

Disposable tissue should be placed over the top of the towel. It should be changed two or three times during treatment, to keep to a minimum the dust from filing.

The chairs for both the client and nail technician should be comfortable – they will be in use for approximately one and a half hours. The client will not be happy with her nails if she has had to sit in discomfort whilst they were being applied.

HEALTH AND SAFETY

Eye care
Like the client, the nail technician too should always wear plastic glasses to protect her eyes during the cutting of a client's artificial nails.

PREPARING THE CLIENT

The client may be given a light protective gown to wear during treatment. This will protect her clothes from the dust created during filing and from accidental spillages.

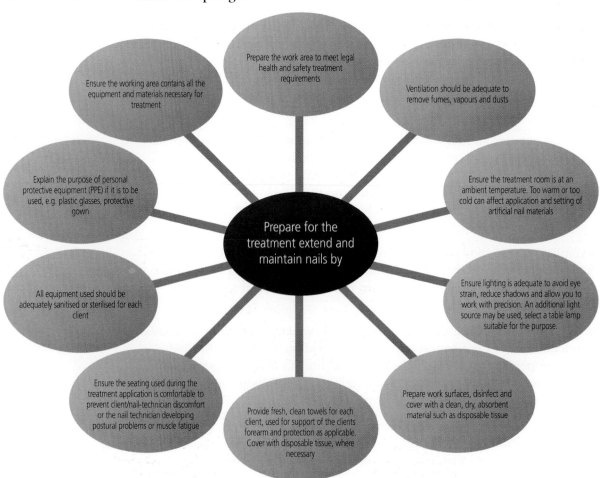

Prepare for the treatment extend and maintain nails by

- Prepare the work area to meet legal health and safety treatment requirements
- Ventilation should be adequate to remove fumes, vapours and dusts
- Ensure the treatment room is at an ambient temperature. Too warm or too cold can affect application and setting of artificial nail materials
- Ensure lighting is adequate to avoid eye strain, reduce shadows and allow you to work with precision. An additional light source may be used, select a table lamp suitable for the purpose.
- Prepare work surfaces, disinfect and cover with a clean, dry, absorbent material such as disposable tissue
- Provide fresh, clean towels for each client, used for support of the clients forearm and protection as applicable. Cover with disposable tissue, where necessary
- Ensure the seating used during the treatment application is comfortable to prevent client/nail-technician discomfort or the nail technician developing postural problems or muscle fatigue
- All equipment used should be adequately sanitised or sterilised for each client
- Explain the purpose of personal protective equipment (PPE) if it is to be used, e.g. plastic glasses, protective gown
- Ensure the working area contains all the equipment and materials necessary for treatment

When artificial nails are cut they occasionally flick towards the client's face. This could prove to be uncomfortable or dangerous should clippings get into the client's eyes, so **plastic glasses** should be available to the client whilst nail clipping is taking place. Advising the client to wear the glasses also assures her that you are taking all possible precautions to safeguard her health.

PLANNING THE TREATMENT

Before applying nail services to a client, you should first discuss what she requires. This will help you to decide which nail service best matches her needs. Points to discuss include:

- Is the client's lifestyle/occupation very physical? If so she will need her nails to be shorter and very strong.
- Is the client's hand in water a great deal?
- Is she allowed to wear nail polish at work? If not she will need a nail system that looks natural without nail polish.
- How long does she want the nails to last? Temporarily or semi-permanently?

Discovering your client's treatment requirements will help you to offer her the best possible service to meet her needs.

Explain in full why the service is recommended, what is involved and what results she can expect. Invite the client to ask questions, as this will help confirm her understanding of the treatment.

Explain the maintenance requirements of the nail service. Record details on the client record card.

> **TIP**
>
> **Record card completion**
> All details should be recorded on the record card.
> Information will be provided on:
> - The client's nail/skin condition at the time of treatment
> - The nail service selected to suit the client's treatment requirement
> - The result of the treatment
> - Aftercare advice and maintenance requirements
>
> This is useful if the client is treated by another nail technician, or if there was a need to review the previous treatment for any reason.

Plan the treatment extend and maintain nails by

- Discuss with the client the condition of their natural nails and cuticles, if in poor condition discuss alternative nail services
- The selection of the correct nail service will ensure client satisfaction
- Select and advise the client of the most appropriate treatment plan to meet their aims
- Confirm the client's understanding of the treatment plan and details, possible contra-actions and obtain the client signature on the record card
- Prepare the clients natural/artificial nails for the nail service to be received

EXTENDING THE NAILS

Applying pre-formed nails

Pre-formed nails are only a temporary way of producing attractive nails as they are designed to last only 7–14 days. Made of plastic, these nails come in many shapes and sizes, and are also available in colours to eliminate the need for nail polish.

Advantages	Disadvantages
1 Quick to apply.	1 The least natural-looking of all types of nail extension.
2 Ideal as a temporary measure for nail-biters who have insufficient nail plate for a semi-permanent nail extension.	2 Only last 7–14 days.
3 Ideal for special occasions.	3 Not suitable for matching odd broken nails, due to their own unnatural appearance.
4 Inexpensive to apply.	4 Nail polish is required to give a more natural appearance.
5 The procedure is easy to learn.	

Equipment and materials

EQUIPMENT LIST

nail tips

resin and nozzle

polishes

In addition to the basic equipment and materials (pages 398–9), you will need the following:

- *Nail tips* – assorted styles and sizes.
- *Resin and nozzle*.
- *Polishes* – a selection, including base coat and top coat.

Application

1 Wash your hands, and ask your client to wash hers. Dry thoroughly.
2 Remove any existing nail polish and check for contra-indications.
3 Spray or wipe the nails with a sanitising product and allow to dry. Wipe from the free edge towards the cuticle to avoid body oils coming into contact with the nail plate. The nail may be sterilised with isopropyl alcohol or a proprietary product designed for this purpose. Do not use surgical spirit as this would leave an oily film on the nail plate, preventing proper adhesion of the artificial nail.
4 Remove any excess cuticle with cuticle nippers. Remove excess cuticle on the nail plate with a cuticle knife.
5 Choose the style and shape of tip appropriate to the needs of the client. Measure the pre-formed nail against the natural nail. If the exact size cannot be found, choose a nail that is slightly too big and file it to the correct size with a medium-grit file.

Check the sizes of the pre-formed nails in relation to the natural nails. Shape the base of the artificial nail with a fine-grit file until it matches the shape of the cuticle. This gives a better fit and a more natural-looking result.

6 Dehydrate the nails to remove any oil or moisture. Use a cotton bud, cottonwool-tipped orange stick or spray. Attention should be paid to the side of the nail and cuticle and under the free edge.

7 Start at the little finger and work across to the thumb. Apply a line of adhesive down the centre of the natural nail plate, and spread it over the whole nail using the applicator nozzle. Leave a small gap around the edges to allow for spreading when the artificial nail is applied.

8 Holding the free edge of the pre-formed nail, apply it to the natural nail by gently sliding it towards the cuticle: hold it in place for a few seconds with your thumb, to allow the adhesive to set. Do not push the pre-formed nail *under* the cuticle area as this might cause permanent damage to the matrix and subsequent growth of the nail. If air bubbles appear under the nail, remove the nail quickly, before the adhesive begins to set, and re-apply it.

9 Repeat steps 7 and 8 for the other nails.

10 Cut the nails to the desired length with scissors or tip cutters. File them into shape, first with a coarse-grit file to reduce bulk, then with a fine-grit file to give a smooth finish. Cut the free edge with scissors, *from the side to the centre*. (Cutting straight across may result in the nail splitting or cracking.) Specially-designed clippers are available to cut artificial nails: they save time by cutting the nail in one movement, and leave the free edge with little filing to be carried out.

11 Apply polish as usual.

12 Make another appointment for the client.

13 Dispose of used materials, clean the workstation and equipment using effective sterilisation and sanitation procedures.

Aftercare and advice

Give your client the following instructions:

- Use rubber gloves when immersing the hand in water.
- Do not use the fingernails as tools!
- Use only non-acetone nail polish removers. Acetone will soften the artificial nails and lead to lifting.
- Caution should be exercised when near any naked flame, including cigarettes, as nail adhesives are flammable and plastic nails can melt.
- Advise on retail products including non-acetone polish remover.
- Contact the salon if any problems occur.

Maintenance

This type of nail extension is only temporary – it is not designed to stay on for long. The client should return to the salon after one week to allow you

TIP

The artificial free edge should be no longer than the nail plate from the cuticle to the flesh line. This will ensure that the nail is balanced, and reduces the chance of the nail coming off.

HEALTH AND SAFETY

Adhesives
Artificial nail adhesives will bond skin in seconds. If this happens, use a cotton bud to apply acetone to the bonded area to dissolve the resin, and gently ease the skin apart. If this does not work, or if the skin is sore, seek medical attention immediately.

Always read manufacturers' instructions, and follow them carefully.

to check for signs of lifting: as soon as these appear, the nails should be removed. Pre-formed nails should be removed after two weeks in any case, as after this time regrowth will have caused a noticeable gap between the cuticle and the preformed nail.

If the client desires artificial nails that will last longer, she should be advised on the application of semi-permanent extensions such as acrylic, fibreglass or gel.

APPLYING NAIL TIPS

Nail tips are a very natural-looking type of nail extension, but they are also very weak. As the name suggests, nail tips are applied only to the tip of the natural nail – approximately halfway down the natural nail – and this leaves the cuticle area free.

Nail tips can be strengthened by the overlay application of gel, fibreglass or acrylic.

Advantages	Disadvantages
1 Very natural-looking.	1 The weakest form of nail extension.
2 Ideal for special occasions such as weddings where the hands are on show.	2 Only last 7–10 days.
3 Easy to remove.	3 Easily broken.
4 Ideal for matching odd broken nails.	
5 Odourless during application.	

Kinds of nail tips

There are many different styles of nail tip, but generally they fall into two categories: *cut-out tips* and *full tips*. **Cut-out tips** are used for a client:

- with a small nail plate area;
- with an exaggerated transverse arch of the nail plate;
- who only desires short nail extensions.

Full tips are used for a client:

- who desires long nail extensions;
- who has a medium-to-large nail plate area;
- who has a regular transverse arch to the nail plate.

Equipment and materials

In addition to the basic equipment and materials (pages 398–9), you will need the following:

- *Nail tips* – assorted styles and sizes.
- *Resin and nozzle*.
- *Polishes* – a selection, including base coat and top coat.

Application

1 Wash your hands, and ask your client to wash hers. Dry thoroughly.

2 Remove any nail polish and check for contra-indications.

3 Sterilise the nail plate. (Wiping or spraying the nails with an appropriate nail steriliser will help to inhibit the growth of bacterial and fungal infections.)

4 Check the size of the nail tips. Tips are curved in their design to suit different nail plate shapes – this is the 'C' curve. The tip should be selected to suit the shape of the natural nail. The tip is also arched, and again the shape should be selected to suit the nail arch. The sidewalls of the tip are also important and should match the clients nail shape, tapered or straight and fit snugly into the nail grooves. It may be necessary to file the nail tip to achieve the correct fit. Incorrect selection will result in weakness and lifting. Place the tip against the client's nail to select the correct tip. When the nail tips have been sized correctly, lay them out on the work surface in order of application. For clients with very small nail plates (such as nail-biters), use a tip with a cut-out well area.

5 Dehydrate the nails to remove surface oils and moisture.

6 Lightly buff the distal end of the natural nail, where the tip is to be applied, with a medium-grade file (e.g. 180-grit). Buff the nail surface gently with the file to remove remaining surface oils: this promotes better adhesion of the nail tip.

7 Apply a small amount of adhesive to the *natural* nail tip. Adhesive should be applied only in the area that the well of the nail tip is to cover.

8 Apply a small amount of adhesive to the well of the tip. Apply the nail tip, at a 45° angle to the natural nail. Hold the edge of the well against the free edge, then gently press down and rock the tip into position, squeezing out all air bubbles until the tip is flat against the nail surface. Hold the tip in place for a few seconds. Firm pressure is required to ensure effective adhesion.

   If air bubbles appear or if the nail tip is not straight, remove it immediately before the adhesive starts to set; then re-apply. If the adhesive has already set, the nail will have to be carefully removed and then reapplied.

9 Remove excess adhesive from surrounding tissue. Apply a small amount of adhesive to the seam area and allow this to set. (This is to ensure that the edge of the tip is securely bonded: it also allows blending to be done more quickly.)

EQUIPMENT LIST

nail tips

resin and nozzle

polishes

ACTIVITY

Contra-indications
Make a list of all the conditions that you feel would contra-indicate the application of nail tips.

TIP

Nail tip material
ABS (acrylonitrile-butadine-styrene) is a plastic that goes through a number of drying preparations which result in it being extremely suitable as a nail tip material. It is flexible and has a natural appearance. It is also easy to work with when blending.

Nail tips

Applying adhesive to the seam area

10 Blend the seam area. Blending can be achieved manually using a file, or chemically using acetone or tip-blender agent. Begin with a fine-grit 240 file to blend the tip to the natural nail. Hold the board at a slight angle, and blend the seam area without touching the nail plate excessively. If you are using a chemical blender, it dissolves the plastic tip. This should be applied with a cotton bud or brush to the area to be blended. Apply to each nail and after a few minutes the plastic will soften. A fine file is then used to remove any excess and blend the line by removing the excess plastic. Further chemical blender may be applied if necessary. Excess plastic *must* be removed.

11 Buff the nail to a shine with a four-sided buffer, using the coarse side first and working through to the smooth side. The tip must appear like a natural nail.

12 Cut the nail tip to the desired length with tip cutters and file to shape. The client's choice must always be taken into consideration, but remember to *advise* about length.

13 Apply cuticle oil to soften the cuticles and surrounding skin.

14 Ask the client to wash her hands to remove the cuticle oil and dust particles. Wash your own hands. Change the towel on the work surface for a fresh one at this stage. This keeps dust to a minimum and prevents dust particles from spoiling the nail polish application.

15 Apply base coat over the entire nail plate.

16 Nails may be left to appear natural or painted with a coloured polish, as desired.

17 Make another appointment for the client.

18 Dispose of used materials, clean the workstation and equipment using effective sterilisation and sanitisation procedures.

Aftercare and advice

These are the same as for pre-formed nails – page 403. However, extra care must be taken when removing nail polish. Use non-acetone remover *only,* as acetone will dissolve the nail tips.

Maintenance of nail tips

Clients wearing nail tips will need to return for maintenance treatment each week. Nail tips are considered temporary and will require replacement, re-gluing and rebuffing. Glue is applied to the seam area.

APPLYING FIBREGLASS NAIL EXTENSIONS

Fibreglass nail extensions are the most natural-looking nail-extension system: the finished nail is transparent over the nail bed, allowing the natural pink colour to show through. The nails appear very thin and flexible, similar to natural nails.

Fibreglass nails are also the least damaging to the natural nails, because no primer is needed during application. This makes them an ideal choice as a temporary measure for clients who wish to grow their own nails to wear without artificial products.

Advantages	Disadvantages
1 Very natural-looking.	1 Not suitable for clients with very little nail plate (principally nail-biters), as not enough nail plate is available for adequate adhesion of the nail tip and the fibreglass overlays.
2 Ideal for matching odd broken nails.	
3 Very strong and flexible.	2 More expensive to apply than other nail systems.
4 Not porous, so do not stain.	
5 Easy and quick to remove.	3 The shape of the finished nail relies on the shape of the tip. Additional curves can be created with thicker overlay systems which can balance the nail's appearance.

Equipment and materials

In addition to the basic equipment and materials (pages 398–9), you will need the following:

- *Nail tips* – in assorted styles and sizes.
- *Scissors* – for fibreglass. The scissors should be fine and sharp bladed.
- *Resin, often referred to as a non-light gel, and nozzle*.
- *Resin activator* – which speeds the drying time.
- *Fibreglass mesh*.
- *Polishes* – a selection, including base coat and top coat.

EQUIPMENT LIST

nail tips

scissors

resin and nozzle

resin activator

fibreglass mesh

polishes

Application

In the procedure below, each step is carried out for all ten nails before proceeding to the next step.

Approximate application time: 1–1½ hours.

1 Wash your hands, and ask your client to wash hers. Dry thoroughly.
2 Remove any nail polish and check for contra-indications.
3 Sanitise the nail plate. (Wiping or spraying the nails with an appropriate nail sanitiser will help to inhibit the growth of bacterial and fungal infections.)

Sterilising the nail

Buffing the nail to remove shine

Applying resin

4 Push back the cuticles and cut the free edge to approximately 3 mm. The cuticles must be pushed back gently with a cottonwool-tipped orange stick or hoof stick. This is to ensure that as much as possible of the nail plate is uncovered to allow optimum adhesion of the nail extension. It also ensures that the nails look their best after treatment. Using cuticle nippers, remove excess cuticle.

5 Size and select tip to suit the client's natural nail shape.

6 Lightly buff the nail surface to remove shine. Use a fine-grit file to remove any surface oils and to roughen the nail plate slightly. This allows better adhesion of the nail extension. Use a dehydrator to remove excess oil and moisture.

7 Apply resin down the centre of the nail plate, and spread it in a thin layer over the whole nail using the extender nozzle. Leave a small gap all around the nail plate, to avoid resin touching the cuticle or the nail walls.

8 Spray with activator. An activator is used not only to speed up the drying time of the adhesive, but also to make the surface non-porous: this helps to prevent staining from nail polish or other dyes. Activator must be sprayed from at least 40–45 cm away to ensure even application and client comfort. A mask may be worn to avoid respiratory problems.

Depress the pump fully to ensure a fine mist of activator. (Failure to do so will result in large droplets of activator falling on the nail plate. This could cause a heat reaction, making application uncomfortable for the client and giving pitting in the resin, which would prevent even application.)

9 Lightly buff the distal end of the nail plate.

10 Apply a small drop of adhesive to the natural nail tip: adhesive should be applied only in the area that the well of the nail tip is to cover.

11 Apply the nail tip, at a 45° angle to the natural nail. Hold the edge of the well against the free edge, then gently press and rock it into position, squeezing out all air bubbles until the tip is flat against the nail surface.

12 Apply a small amount of adhesive to the seam. (This is to ensure that the edge of the tip is securely bonded: it also allows blending to be done more quickly.)

13 Spray with activator.

Buffing the nail tip

Applying the nail tip

Cutting the nail tip

Blending the seam

14 Cut the nail tip to the desired length, and file it to shape.

15 Blend the seam area. Do not buff to a shine as this would prevent further resin from adhering properly.

TIP ✔

After each use, the sides of the resin bottle should be squeezed to allow any resin in the applicator nozzle to flow back into the bottle. A 'burping' sound will be heard from the bottle if this has been done correctly. (Failure to do this will result in the nozzle becoming blocked, making application difficult.)

16 Apply adhesive to the nail plate and spread it over the nail. This must be done carefully, to avoid touching the cuticle and surrounding skin. Any product that touches the skin will allow natural oils to get underneath, resulting in lifting later.

17 Spray with activator.

18 Apply fibreglass mesh. Very sharp scissors must be used to cut the mesh, or fraying will result. Cut the fibreglass to fit the whole nail surface, leaving approximately 3 mm gap around the edges. Avoid over-handling the fibreglass mesh to prevent contamination which could affect adhesion.

Apply the mesh with the tacky side to the nail plate, and ensure that it is completely smooth with no frayed edges.

19 Repeat steps 16 and 17 twice. Allow the resin to soak into the fibreglass mesh for a few seconds before spraying with activator. This reduces the chance of the mesh showing through the finished application.

Applying fibreglass mesh

20 Gently buff the surface to remove shine. This allows step 21 to be carried out effectively. If the surface is buffed too much the fibreglass mesh will show through. If this happens, repeat steps 16 and 17 twice before continuing as usual.

21 Buff the surface to a shine. Using a four-sided buffer, bring the now dull surface to a shine. Begin with the coarsest side of the buffer and work down to the smooth.

Applying resin over the fibreglass

Buffing the nail to a shine

Applying cuticle oil

Completed fibreglass nail extensions

22 Apply cuticle oil. This is to reintroduce moisture to the area, which may have become dehydrated with all the buffing and filing. It also gives a luxurious glossy finish. Apply oil to the cuticle and the nail walls then massage in with thumbs.

23 Ask the client to wash her hands, to remove all dust particles and leave the hands feeling fresh and comfortable.

24 Nail polish may be applied, if required. Treat the nails as if they were natural: apply a base coat to avoid staining from dark colours.

Remember that only *acetone-free* nail polish remover may be used. Acetone nail polish remover would result in a softening of the nails.

25 Make another appointment for the client.

26 Dispose of used materials. Clean the workstation and equipment using effective sterilisation and sanitation procedures.

TIP	
Do not spray activator towards the adhesive bottle as it might set inside.	

TIP	
Fibreglass nails are not porous and therefore do not need a base coat under coloured polish. It is a good idea to advise the client to use it anyway, however, as this gets her into a good habit for the future when she is applying nail polish to her natural nails.	

A fibreglass stress strip

Stress strip application

A **stress strip** is simply a narrow piece of fibreglass mesh, placed across the nail where the nail tip is blended into the natural nail. This is the weakest area of the nail extension and is usually where breaks will occur if the client is careless with her nails.

Stress strips should be used on the nail of clients:

● who desire very long nail extensions;

● who are quite physical with their hands.

To apply a stress strip, simply apply the nails in the usual way but stop prior to the application of the fibreglass mesh (i.e. before step **18**). Now apply the stress strip across the nail, and coat with a layer of resin and spray activator. Then continue in the usual way, applying mesh over the whole nail plate without touching the cuticle or nail walls:

18a Apply the fibreglass stress strip.

18b Apply resin over the whole nail, and spray with activator.

18c Apply fibreglass mesh over the whole nail, without touching the cuticle or nail walls.

18d Proceed with application in the usual way.

Fibreglass mesh over the whole nail

Aftercare and advice

These are the same as for pre-formed nails – page 403.

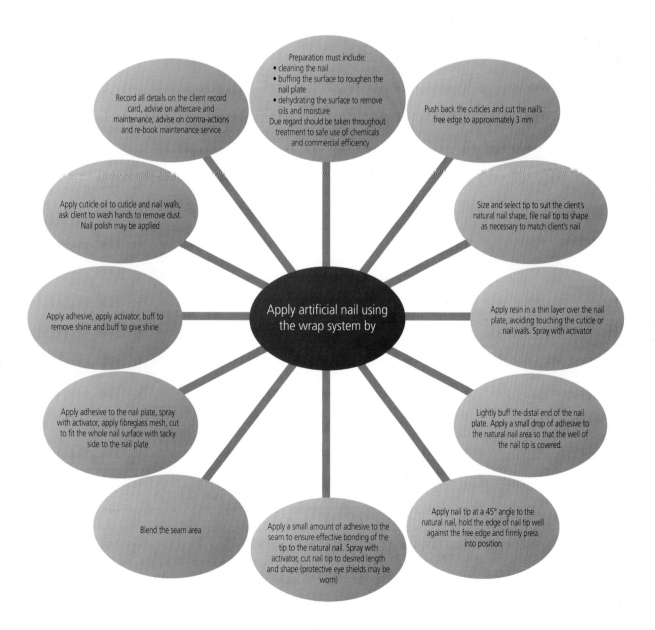

Apply artificial nail using the wrap system by

Preparation must include:
• cleaning the nail
• buffing the surface to roughen the nail plate
• dehydrating the surface to remove oils and moisture
Due regard should be taken throughout treatment to safe use of chemicals and commercial efficiency

Record all details on the client record card, advise on aftercare and maintenance, advise on contra-actions and re-book maintenance service

Push back the cuticles and cut the nail's free edge to approximately 3 mm

Apply cuticle oil to cuticle and nail walls, ask client to wash hands to remove dust. Nail polish may be applied

Size and select tip to suit the client's natural nail shape, file nail tip to shape as necessary to match client's nail

Apply adhesive, apply activator, buff to remove shine and buff to give shine

Apply resin in a thin layer over the nail plate, avoiding touching the cuticle or nail walls. Spray with activator

Apply adhesive to the nail plate, spray with activator, apply fibreglass mesh, cut to fit the whole nail surface with tacky side to the nail plate

Lightly buff the distal end of the nail plate. Apply a small drop of adhesive to the natural nail area so that the well of the nail tip is covered.

Blend the seam area

Apply a small amount of adhesive to the seam to ensure effective bonding of the tip to the natural nail. Spray with activator, cut nail tip to desired length and shape (protective eye shields may be worn)

Apply nail tip at a 45° angle to the natural nail, hold the edge of nail tip well against the free edge and firmly press into position

Maintenance

Two weeks after the initial application

1 Cleanse the hands and nails and check with the client that she has been satisfied with her nails. If not, explore why.

2 Remove any nail polish with acetone-free polish remover, and check for any signs of infection. If infection is present, remove the nails immediately and advise the client to see her GP.

3 If the nails are healthy push back the cuticles with a cottonwool-tipped orange stick or hoof stick.

4 Buff the seam area using a fine 240-grit file to remove any loose or lifting fibreglass, then buff with a fine-grit file until the seam becomes invisible. Buff the whole nail plate with a fine-grit file to remove shine.

 Do not use cuticle nippers to remove loose or lifting fibreglass: these would cause discomfort to the client and would damage the natural nail.

5 Cleanse and dehydrate the nail's new growth area.

6 Apply a small amount of resin to the regrowth area and spread it with the nozzle to cover the whole regrowth area.

7 Spray with activator from at least 40–45 cms away.

8 Apply resin to the whole nail surface, including the regrowth area.

9 Spray with activator.

10 Buff gently with a fine-grit file to remove shine.

11 With a four-sided buffer, bring the nails to a shine.

12 Apply cuticle oil.

TIP

Clients can still have a regular manicure whilst they are wearing nail extensions. Recommending a regular manicure will help to keep the client's skin and cuticles in good condition, whilst allowing you to keep a check on the condition of the nail extensions.

Four weeks after the initial application

1 Cleanse the hands and nails and check with the client that she has been satisfied with her nails. If not, explore why.

2 Remove any nail polish with acetone-free polish remover, and check for any signs of infection. If infection is present, remove the nails immediately and advise the client to see her GP.

3 If the nails are healthy push back the cuticles with a cottonwool-tipped orange stick or hoof stick.

4 Buff the seam area using a fine 240-grit file to remove any loose or lifting fibreglass, then buff with a fine-grit file until the seam becomes invisible. Buff the whole nail plate with a fine-grit file to remove shine.

 Do not use cuticle nippers to remove loose or lifting fibreglass: these would cause discomfort to the client and would damage the natural nail.

5 Cleanse and dehydrate the nail's new growth area.

6 Apply a small amount of adhesive to the regrowth area and spread it with the nozzle to cover the whole regrowth area.

7 Spray with activator from at least 40–45 cm away.

8 Apply a small piece of fibreglass to the regrowth area, slightly overlapping the old application.

9 Apply resin over the new fibreglass.

10 Spray with activator.

11 Repeat steps 8 and 9.

12 Apply adhesive to the whole nail surface, including the regrowth area.

13 Spray with activator from at least 40–45 cm away.

14 Buff gently with a fine-grit file to remove shine.

15 With a four-sided buffer, bring the nails to a shine.

16 Apply cuticle oil.

> **TIP**
>
> Alternate maintenance procedures so that one maintenance is with fibreglass, the next without. This avoids unnecessary use of fibreglass and build-up of product around the cuticle area.

Problem solving

- *White areas under the nail tip* This could be due to air bubbles trapped during application of the nail tip. Remove the tip and start again. Use slightly more adhesive, to give more time before the nail bonds.
- *Fibreglass mesh shows through the finished nail* This can happen if the first coat of adhesive did not soak through properly before the activator was sprayed, or if the fibreglass was handled too much prior to application.
- *Lifting of the fibreglass overlay* This may be due to products touching the cuticle or nail wall. Too much adhesive, or not enough, may also cause this problem.
- *Burning* If the client complains of a burning sensation, hold the activator further away to avoid this heat reaction.
- *Frayed fibreglass mesh* If the mesh has frayed through the adhesive, it could be that the scissors were not sharp enough, or that the fibreglass was not pressed smooth to the nail before the adhesive was applied.

NATURAL NAIL WRAPS

Material is attached to the natural nail, or over the nail tip to provide strength. Wraps are also popular where nail repair is required.

Advantages	Disadvantages
1 The natural nail is not damaged.	1 Paper wraps are less expensive but are temporary and can be removed with acetone.
2 Provides strength and protection whilst growing the natural nails.	2 Fibreglass is more durable but more expensive.
3 Easy to remove.	3 The thinness of the product makes it unsuitable for certain nail conditions such as bitten nails.

Equipment and materials

- *Fabric or tissue.*
- *Resin.*
- *Resin activator.*
- *If tissue wrap is used mending liquid is required to strengthen the tissue.*

Application: nail wraps

1 Wash your hands, and ask your client to wash hers. Dry thoroughly.

2 Remove any nail polish and check for contra-indications.

3 Sanitise the natural nail plate. Wiping or spraying the nails with an appropriate nail sanitiser will inhibit the growth of bacterial and fungal infections.

4 File the nails to shape and push back the cuticles gently with a cottonwool-tipped orange stick or hoof stick. This is to ensure that as much of the nail plate as possible is uncovered to allow optimum adhesion of the nail wrap. Using cuticle nippers, remove excess cuticle.

5 Lightly buff the nail surface to remove shine using a fine-grit file.

6 Use a dehydrator to remove excess oil and moisture.

7 Cut fabric to the size of the nail using very sharp scissors to avoid fraying. Fibreglass mesh usually has an adhesive backing. Attach this to the nail plate leaving a 3 mm gap round the edges, this prevents lifting.

8 If your wrap is non-adhesive, apply adhesive to the nail plate first.

9 Apply a layer of resin over the material, and allow this to dry. Apply a resin activator to speed the drying process.

10 Repeat stage 9 applying a further coat of resin. Allow the resin to soak into the fibreglass wrap for a few seconds before spraying with activator.

11 Buff the surface of the nail to remove shine and blend the nail wrap seam area into the natural nail. Avoid excessive buffing or the fibreglass mesh will show through.

12 Gently buff the surface of the nail to create shine, using a four-sided buffer.

13 Apply cuticle oil.

14 Ask the client to wash her hands to remove dust and oil.

15 Wipe over with non-acetone nail polish remover, then nail polish may be applied.

16 Make another appointment for the client.

17 Dispose of used materials, clean the workstation and equipment using effective sterilisation and sanitisation procedures.

Aftercare and advice

These are the same as for pre-formed nails, see page 403.

TIP

Resin *wets* the wrap material helping to disguise it, whilst also providing strength and flexibility.
Application
Too much will affect effective adhesion and could result in lifting.

Maintenance

Fabric wraps area maintained following the 2 week and 4-week maintenance plan listed on pages 412–13.

APPLYING SCULPTURED ACRYLIC NAILS

Liquid and **powder acrylic** can be used in two ways to produce strong, natural-looking nail extensions: they can be sculpted over a nail form, or they can be sculpted over a nail tip. Which method is used depends on the client's needs and the therapist's preference. With nail tips:

- application takes longer, as time is needed to apply and blend in the tips;
- less sculpting skill is required, as the tip provides the basis of a natural shape;
- the method is more expensive, due to the use of tips;
- less filing is required, as the need for sculpting is minimal.

With nail forms:

- once the application skill has been mastered, sculpting over a form is quicker than with application of a tip;
- the method is cheaper, as no nail tips are required;
- the technique is more difficult to learn;
- if the form is incorrectly applied or is moved during application, extensive filing is required to achieve a natural shape.
- it is easy to replace a broken nail to create a balanced look during a manicure.

Acrylic nails are very strong and durable, and are therefore ideal for clients who are very physical with their hands.

Advantages	Disadvantages
1 Very strong.	1 The need for primer means that the natural nails are weaker when acrylic nails are removed. However, this weakness is not permanent and will grow out as the nails grow forward.
2 Suitable for nail-biters, due to the strong adhesive qualities of acrylic and the fact that a large nail plate is not needed.	2 Acrylic nails are not suitable for clients who wish to grow their own nails without artificial products to strengthen them.
3 The moulding qualities of acrylic allow sculpting to be adapted to any size or shape of natural nail.	3 Products have a strong, unpleasant odour.

HEALTH AND SAFETY

Acrylic products
Products are available which can be added to acrylic liquids to eliminate the unpleasant odour. This makes the treatment much more pleasant for both the client and the nail technician.

EQUIPMENT LIST

acrylic powder

acrylic liquid

primer

nail forms

brush

polishes

Equipment and materials

In addition to the basic equipment and materials (pages 398–9), you will need the following:

- *Acrylic powder* – in a variety of colours, including white, pink and clear – often referred to as a polymer.
- *Acrylic liquid* – often referred to as a monomer.
- *Primer* – methocrylate acid which aids the adhesion of the acrylic to the natural nail.
- *Nail forms* – available in metal, plastic or paper.
- *Brush* – for use with acrylics; the best brushes are sable.
- *Polishes* – a selection, including base coat and top coat.

HEALTH AND SAFETY

Personal protective equipment (PPE)
To prevent harm to yourself or the client you may choose to wear PPE during nails services. This includes:
Glasses to prevent chemical splashes and dust entering the eyes.
Dust masks to prevent inhalation of dust, especially when filing.
Gloves to prevent absorption of chemicals through the skin or nail plate. Regular contact with skin irritants can result in irritant contact dermatitis, where the skin becomes allergic to the product.

TIP

Polymerisation
When liquid monomer and powder polymer are mixed, a chemical reaction called *polymerisation* occurs which concludes with setting.

Application: sculptured acrylic nail extensions

Approximate application time: 1¹/₂ hours.

1 Wash your hands, and ask your client to wash hers. Dry thoroughly.
2 Remove any nail polish and check for contra-indications.
3 Push back the cuticles with a cottonwool-tipped orange stick or hoof stick. Remove any excess cuticle with cuticle nippers.
4 Sanitise the natural nail plate. (This prevents the growth of bacterial and fungal infections beneath the artificial nail.)
5 Lightly buff the nail plate with a fine-grit board, to remove shine.
6 Apply primer to the nail plate and allow this to dry. Do not allow primer to touch the cuticle or the nail walls. Avoid over-use or the nail plate will become too smooth and the acrylic will lift.
7 Apply the nail form to the fingertip, beneath the free edge of the natural nail. This is the base for the extended acrylic tip. Check from all angles that the form is in the most natural position.

8 To achieve a natural look when applying acrylic nails using the two-colour acrylic method, use pink or white acrylic for clients with light skins, and ivory or peach acrylic for clients with dark skins.

   Dip the brush in the liquid rotating the brush slightly, then in acrylic powder to form a ball of medium-dry consistency the size of a small pea. Apply this to the nail form to create a free edge. Smooth and shape the acrylic using the middle and side of the brush to flatten and press the acrylic into place.

9 Dip the brush in liquid, then in powder, as before, and apply to the middle of the nail plate. Use the sides of the brush to blend the acrylic towards the free edge and the sides of the nail.

10 Dip the brush in liquid, then powder, and apply the acrylic near the cuticle. This should be a wetter, thinner application to avoid a ridge and give a more natural-looking application.

11 When the desired shape has been created, allow it to set hard. To check whether the acrylic has set, tap it with an orange stick: listen for an audible click rather than a dull sound.

   Once set, remove the nail form and shape the free edge with a coarse/medium-grit file.

12 Using a four-sided buffer, smooth the nail surface to a shine.

13 Apply cuticle oil.

14 Wash your hands, and the client should wash hers. This step is very important: you both need to remove any acrylic dust that might otherwise become irritating on the skin.

   Remove the towel from the workstation and replace it with a clean one. This prevents dust particles from ruining the nail enamel application, and makes the working environment more pleasant. Dust can also lead to irritant contact dermatitis.

15 Polish the nails as usual. Always use a base coat, as acrylic is a porous substance and nail polish might stain it.

16 Make another appointment for the client.

17 Dispose of used materials. Clean the workstation and equipment using effective sanitisation and sterilisation procedures.

Aftercare and advice

These are the same as for nail extensions on page 403.

TIP

Nail extension removal
Every 2–3 months the nails should be removed and a new set applied. This allows the new nail growth to be properly dehydrated with acetone. Failure to due this will result in repeated problems with nails lifting in the cuticle area.

TIP

Consistency control
To achieve a medium consistency of acrylic liquid (monomer) and powder (polymer), mix 1.5 parts monomer, 1 part polymer.

   To achieve a wet consistency mix 2 parts liquid, and 1 part powder.

Application: nail tips with acrylic overlay

Follow the instructions for nail-tip application up to and including step **12** (pages 405–6). Then follow this procedure:

13 Apply primer to the natural nail area only.

14 Dip the brush in liquid, then in clear powder, to form a ball the size of a large pea.

15 Apply the acrylic ball to the centre of the nail plate. Use the sides of the brush to blend acrylic over the entire nail plate, ensuring that application is thinner at the cuticle, the nail wall and the free edge areas, to give a natural appearance. Acrylic applied too thickly near the cuticle will cause lifting.

16 Re-apply acrylic if necessary to ensure adequate coverage of the nail plate.

17 Check the nail from all angles to ensure that the shape is natural.

18 Once the desired shape has been created, allow the product to set hard.

19 Remove any surface irregularities using a coarse/medium-grit file.

20 Buff the surface to a shine with a four-sided buffer.

21 Apply cuticle oil to the skin around the nail.

22 Wash your hands, and your client should wash hers.

23 Apply nail polish as desired.

24 Make another appointment for the client.

25 Dispose of used materials. Clean the workstation and equipment using effective sterilisation and sanitisation procedures.

Aftercare and advice

These are the same as for nail extensions – see page 403.

Maintenance: sculptured acrylic nail extensions

Maintenance should be carried out approximately every two weeks after the initial application. This keeps the nails strong, balanced, attractive and healthy.

1 Wash your hands, and ask your client to wash hers.
   Refer to the client's record card for details of previous nail-extension applications.

2 Remove any nail polish with acetone-free nail polish remover, and check for any signs of infection. If infection is present remove the extensions immediately and advise the client to see her GP.

3 If the nails are healthy push back the cuticles with a cottonwool-tipped orange stick or hoof stick. Use cuticle nippers to remove excess cuticle.

4 Lightly buff the seam area with a medium-grit file to remove any loose or lifting acrylic, then buff with a fine-grit file until the seam becomes invisible. Buff the whole nail plate with a medium-grit file to remove the shine. Do not try to cut off loose acrylic with cuticle nippers: this would cause damage to the natural nail plate and would be extremely uncomfortable for the client.

5 Lightly buff the new nail regrowth with a fine-grit file, and apply primer to this area only. Avoid contact with previously applied acrylic as it will weaken and discolour it.

6 Apply a small ball of pink or clear acrylic near the cuticle. This should be a thin application, to avoid a ridge and to give a more natural-looking finish.

Blend in the new application by brushing the acrylic down towards the free edge.

Dip the brush into liquid and wipe it clean on a tissue regularly throughout the application. This will prevent the acrylic from setting on the brush.

7 When the infill is finished, allow it to set hard.

8 Using a four-sided buffer, smooth the nail surface to a shine.

9 Apply cuticle oil.

10 Both of you should now wash your hands.

11 Polish the nails as usual.

12 Make another appointment for the client.

13 Dispose of used materials. Clean the workstation and equipment using effective sterilisation and sanitisation procedures.

Maintenance: tips with acrylic overlay

This procedure is carried out using exactly the same method as for sculptured acrylic nails (above).

TIP

The white free edge moves forward with the growing nail, and soon the natural nail's free edge can be seen through the acrylic. To disguise this, file the surface of the artificial free edge to form a step at the natural flesh line. Be careful not to file it right through. Fill in this step with white acrylic. Use a fine layer of clear acrylic to strengthen the join.

HEALTH AND SAFETY

Working with acrylic
The dust created during the filing of acrylic nails can lead to skin allergies and respiratory problems. Keep dust to a minimum by using an extractor fan near the workstation and changing the towels on the workstation during treatment.

Repair to acrylic nails

Due to the strength of a correctly applied acrylic nail, repairs are seldom necessary. If nails are cracked, chipped or broken, however, repairs may be carried out using the following methods.

Lifting or cracking of the product around the cuticle area

1 Repair using the general maintenance procedure.

Chip or crack in the free edge

1 Use the edge of a coarse-grit file to widen and roughen the crack. (This makes filling it in easier.)

2 Place a nail form beneath the free edge and 'fill in' the chip or crack with matching coloured acrylic. Wetting the old acrylic nail with acrylic liquid will improve adhesion.

3 File and buff the new acrylic as in original application.

Free edge broken off

1 Roughen the nail surface with a medium-grit file.

2 Place a nail form beneath the free edge. Dampen the free edge with acrylic liquid, and sculpt the free edge with white powder as in original application. Secure free edge with a thin layer of clear acrylic over the entire nail.

3 Finish off as in the original application.

Problem solving

- *Acrylic overlay lifting from the natural nail* This is probably due to incorrect preparation of the natural nail plate. Alternative reasons are that too much or too little product was used, or that the product was touching the skin.

- *Infills are obvious* Ensure a thorough blending-in of the previous application before applying new acrylic.

- *Nails break at the flesh line* Not enough product was applied in the area, or it was over-buffed.

- *Acrylic liquid is solid in the bottle* The liquid has been contaminated with powder. Never pour products back into the bottle, or put the brush in the bottle.

- *Acrylic appears frosty when set* The room is too cold. The room should be quite warm if the product is to set correctly.

- *The finished nail points upwards or downwards* This results from incorrect placing of the nail form or incorrect application of the nail tip. Check regularly from all angles during application.

- *The transverse arch of the nail is irregular* The acrylic was applied unevenly:
  - too much product at the sides of the nail;
  - too much product on the middle of the nail;
  - too much product at one side – the client's fingers were tilted before the product set, or the application was too wet (causing the product to run).

- *The longitudinal arch of the nail is irregular* The acrylic was applied unevenly:
  - too much product at the cuticle area;

Nail pointing up

Nail pointing down

Too much product at the sides

Too much product in the middle

Too much product at one side

- too much product in the centre of the nail;
- too much product at the free edge.

If you make a mistake, remove the nail using the correct procedure and re-apply it.

Too much product in the cuticle area

APPLYING GEL NAIL EXTENSIONS

Too much product in the middle

Gel can be applied over a tip or can be sculpted over a nail form, as with acrylic. Application methods are very similar to those with acrylic, but due to the self-levelling nature of the gel, the procedure is easier. Because gel is clear, the finished nail is very natural-looking and does not require nail polish. Coloured gels are also available: these give a permanently polished look which doesn't chip or fade, but clients may get bored with the colour.

Too much product at the free edge

Some gel systems require the use of an ultraviolet light to set the gel, others use a spray activator similar to that used in fibreglass application.

Advantages	Disadvantages
1 Very natural-looking and retain their surface shine.	1 Not as strong as acrylic or fibreglass.
2 Easier to apply than acrylic or fibreglass.	2 Methods using ultraviolet light are more expensive than other systems.
3 Self-levelling gel means less filing.	3 Light must penetrate the gel to harden the oligomers. The products must be thin in application and exposed to the correct UV light or uncured product will remain.
4 Less filing means less dust, so the environment is more pleasant for the client and the nail technician.	

TIP	✔

Adhesive maintenance
To ensure that adhesive is kept in optimum condition:
- Close cap securely after use
- Store upright
- Store at temperatures of 60–85°F

EQUIPMENT LIST

gel

gel-setting spray or ultraviolet light

primer

nail forms

nail tips

adhesive

brushes

polishes

Equipment and materials

In addition to the basic equipment and materials (pages 398–9), you will need the following:

- *Gel* – usually oligomers, semi-liquid in consistency, similar to monomer and polymer system.
- *Gel-setting spray or ultraviolet light* – to harden and cure the gel nail.
- *Primer*.
- *Nail forms*.
- *Nail tips*.
- *Adhesive*.
- *Brushes* – a synthetic brush may be used as it holds the gel and spreads it evenly.
- *Polishes* – a selection, including base coat and top coat.

Application: the tip and overlay method

Approximate application time: 1–1$\frac{1}{2}$ hours.

1 Wash your hands, and ask your client to wash hers. Dry thoroughly.
2 Remove any nail polish and check for contra-indications.
3 Sanitise the natural nail plate. This prevents the growth of bacterial and fungal infections beneath the artificial nail.
4 If the nails are healthy push back the cuticles and cut the free edge to approximately 3 mm.
5 Size up the nail tips.
6 Lightly buff the natural nail to remove shine.
7 Apply a small drop of adhesive to the tip of the natural nail.
8 Apply the nail tip.
9 Cut the nail tip to the desired length, and file it to shape.
10 Blend the seam area.
11 Apply primer to the natural nail plate area.
12 Apply gel according to the manufacturer's instructions. Some gels need an ultraviolet light source to cure them; others may be set with an activator spray or brush-on setting liquid.
13 Oxygen inhibits polymerisation, the chemical reaction of the gel on the nail surface, leaving a sticky layer. This usually requires the application of a base coat gel, which is cured. Followed by a building gel which again is cured. Ensure the client places the fingers and thumbs correctly when the gel is being cured.
14 Buff the nail's surface.
15 Remove any dust and finally apply a top coat from the cuticle to the free edge, which is cured.
16 Remove any sticky residue with a nail-wipe soaked in non-acetone nail polish remover.

17 Buff the surface of the nail vigorously to a shine.

18 Apply cuticle oil.

19 Ask the client to wash her hands.

20 Apply nail polish if desired.

21 Make another appointment for the client.

22 Dispose of used materials, clean the workstation and equipment using effective sterilisation and sanitisation procedures.

TIP

Because gel is semi-liquid, ask the client to keep her fingers flat until the gel is set, otherwise the gel will slide to one side of the nail resulting in an uneven application. Apply gel to the fingers and thumbs separately, so that the client can keep them level.

Application: sculptured gel nail extensions

Approximate application time: 1–1¹/₂ hours.

1 Wash your hands, and ask your client to wash hers. Dry thoroughly.

2 Remove any nail polish and check for contra-indications.

3 Sanitise the natural nail plate with sterilising solution. (This prevents the growths of bacterial and fungal infections beneath the artificial nail.)

4 Lightly buff the nail plate with a fine-grit board, to remove the shine.

5 Apply primer to the nail plate and allow it to dry. Do not allow primer to touch the cuticle or the nail walls.

6 Apply a nail form to the fingertip, beneath the free edge of the natural nail: this is the base for the extended gel tip. Check from all angles that the form is in the most natural position.

7 Dip the brush in gel to form a ball the size of a small pea. Apply this to the nail plate near the cuticle, and pull the gel towards the free edge using the brush. (Do not apply like nail polish, as this would result in too thin an application of gel.) Gel is self-levelling: push it over the nail plate, avoiding the cuticle and nail walls. Shape the gel over the nail form to create the free edge.

8 When you have created the desired shape, allow the gel to set hard. Gel may be set with an activator spray, a brush-on activator, or with an ultra-violet light, according to the manufacturer's instructions.

9 Once set, remove the nail form and shape the free edge with a coarse-grit file.

10 Remove any sticky residue on the gel with a nail wipe soaked in non-acetone nail polish remover.

11 Using a four-sided buffer, smooth the nail surface to a shine.

12 Apply cuticle oil.

13 You and your client should now wash your hands. This step is very important: it removes any dust or gel residue that might otherwise become irritating to the skin.

TIP

Every 2–3 months the nails should be removed and a new set applied. This allows the new nail growth to be properly dehydrated with acetone. (Failure to do this will result in repeated problems with nails lifting in the cuticle area.)

Sterilising the nail plate

Buffing the nail plate to remove shine

Fitting the nail forms

Applying the base coat gel

Curing the gel

Wiping with acetone

Smoothing the nail plate

Applying the cuticle oil

Remove the towel from the workstation and replace it with a clean one. This prevents dust particles from ruining the nail polish application, and makes the working environment more pleasant.

14 Apply polish to the nails as usual. Always use a base coat to prevent the polish staining the gel.

TIP

Some systems use three different gels, others only one. Always read the manufacturer's instructions carefully.

Aftercare and advice

Maintenance to the nail extensions should be carried out approximately every two weeks after the initial application. This keeps the nails strong, balanced and attractive.

Maintenance

1 Wash your hands, and ask your client to wash hers. Refer to the client's record card for details of previous nail extension applications.

2 Remove any nail polish with acetone-free nail polish remover and check for any signs of infection. If infection is present, remove the extensions immediately and advise the client to see her doctor.

3 Push back the cuticles with a cottonwool-tipped orange stick or hoof stick.

4 Buff the seam area with a medium-grit file to remove any loose or lifting gel, then buff with a fine-grit file until the seam becomes invisible. Buff the whole nail plate with a medium-grit file to remove the shine and to avoid build-up of product. Do not try to cut off loose gel with cuticle nippers: this would cause damage to the natural nail plate and would be extremely uncomfortable for the client.

5 Lightly buff nail regrowth with a fine-grit file, and apply primer to this area only.

6 Apply a small ball of gel near the cuticle. This should be a thin application to avoid a ridge and to give a more natural-looking finish. Blend in the new application by brushing the gel down towards the free edge.

7 When the infill is finished, cure it with ultraviolet light or activator spray.

8 Remove any sticky residue with non-acetone polish remover.

9 Using a four-sided buffer, smooth the nail surface to a shine.

10 Apply cuticle oil.

11 You and your client should now wash your hands.

12 Apply polish to the nails as usual.

Completed sculptured gel nail extensions

CONTRA-ACTIONS

A contra-action to artificial nail application is an adverse condition that appears after nails have been applied. Examples are:

- thinning of the natural nail plate;
- allergies;
- infection (such as paronychia, tinea unguium or onychomycosis);
- softening of the nail plate;
- physical trauma to the nail plate, bed or cuticle.

Thinning of the natural nail plate

Appearance

When artificial nails are removed, the natural free edge is very thin. It can easily be bent or torn using very light pressure.

Causes

- Excessive filing of the nail plate during preparation.
- Excessive filing whilst blending in nail tip.
- Incorrect removal of the nails.

Treatment

1 Keep the free edge short.
2 Allow the thin nail plate to grow out.
3 Apply nail strengthener to the nails.
4 Do not re-apply artificial nails until the thin nails have grown out.

Allergies

Appearance

Redness, blisters, inflammation and itching. These may appear on the cuticle or skin around the nails, or on the face and neck which the nails regularly touch.

Cause

- Exposure to a product to which the client is allergic. Allergies are specific to individual people, so what may irritate one client may prove harmless to another.

Treatment

1 Remove the artificial nails immediately, using the correct procedure. If the allergic reaction is severe, advise the client to seek medical attention.
2 Once the allergy has cleared alternative nail systems may be applied to single nails to test the client's tolerance. Do not test products on the client's skin: they are not designed for such use, and will cause an allergic response in many clients and therefore give misleading results.

Infection

Appearance

Redness, inflammation and pus in the cuticle area and surrounding skin; separation of the nail plate from the nail bed at the flesh line; or dark spots between the artificial nail and the natural nail plate.

HEALTH AND SAFETY

Allergenic products
There are many suppliers of nail-extension products. If a product regularly causes allergies among clients when being used correctly, inform the manufacturer and try alternative products to discover one that is less irritating.

Causes

- Lack of hygiene in the salon during application.
- Incorrect home care.

Treatment

1 Remove the nails immediately, using the correct method.
2 Advise the client to seek medical attention.

Softening of the natural nail plate

Appearance

When nails are removed, the natural nail plate is very soft and easily torn at the free edge.

Cause

- Prolonged exposure to the products used in artificial nail application, particularly primer.

Treatment

1 Allow the softened nail to grow out, keeping the free edge short. Apply nail strengthener, and do not re-apply artificial nails until soft nails have grown out.

Physical trauma

Appearance

Bruising, ridges in the nail plate and cuts and abrasions to cuticle and surrounding skin.

Causes

- *Bruising* Too much pressure applied to nails during treatment.
- *Ridges* Excessive filing in one place, causing thinning of the nail plate.
- *Cuts and abrasions* Careless use of files and buffers.

Treatment

1 Apply antiseptic to cuts and abrasions. Allow bruises and ridges to grow out.

Extreme care should be taken during application. Use tools correctly and do not apply too much pressure. Ensure that tools are of a high quality, with no rough or sharp edges.

HEALTH AND SAFETY

Lifting nails
If nails start to lift, moisture will get underneath: this creates an ideal breeding ground for bacteria. Always advise the clients to return to the salon immediately the nails start to lift, so that the appropriate treatment can be carried out at once to avoid infection.

HEALTH AND SAFETY

Files
If the sides of files are rough or sharp, use a fine-grit file to gently smooth them down. This will reduce the risk of cutting client's cuticles, and will also make the files more pleasant for the nail technician to work with.

REPAIRING AND STRENGTHENING THE NATURAL NAIL

If a natural nail is broken, split or cracked, it is sometimes possible to repair and strengthen the damage so that the client doesn't lose the free edge of her nail. Repairs and strengthening can be done with different types of materials, the strongest being silk, fibreglass, linen and acrylic. Once repaired, nails should be treated in the same way as artificial nails – for example, non-acetone nail polish remover must be used.

Types of nail damage that can be repaired are:

- brittle nails;
- flaking nails;
- free edge or flesh-line break;
- severed free edge.

Brittle nails

Brittle nails may be protected with a gel overlay. This will provide additional protection as the natural nail grows, whilst providing a natural appearance. A thin protective coating of a nail system is applied to the natural nail over the nail plate.

1 Remove any nail polish, and dehydrate the nail plate by wiping it with a cotton bud soaked in acetone. Check that there are no contra-indications.
2 Following manufacturer's instructions, prepare the natural nail.
3 Apply base coat gel and cure, remove tackiness.
4 Apply building gel and cure, remove tackiness.
5 File the nail to shape including the nail walls and free edge.
6 Buff and dust.
7 Apply top coat gel and cure, remove tackiness.
8 Apply cuticle oil.
9 Clean the hands and nails.
10 Apply polish if required.

Flaking nails

1 Remove any nail polish, and dehydrate the nail plate by wiping it with a cotton bud soaked in acetone. Check that there are no contra-indications.
2 Place a piece of mending material over the whole nail plate, extending over the free edge.
3 Apply a layer of resin over the material and allow this to dry. Use a resin activator, if available, to reduce the drying time. If using acrylic, allow it to dry before proceeding to step 5.
4 Repeat step 3.
5 Use a four-sided buffer to bring the nails to a shine.

TIP

Coating the whole nail with any of the materials used in repairs or extensions is known as capping. This service can be offered to clients who don't want artificial nails but who need something to keep their own nails from breaking. Capping needs to be maintained in the same ways as semi-permanent nails.

Free edge or flesh-line break

1 Remove any nail polish, and dehydrate the nail plate by wiping it with a cotton bud soaked in acetone. Check that there are no contra-indications.

2 Place a small piece of mending material over the break.

3 Apply a layer of resin over the material and allow this to dry. Use a resin activator, if available, to reduce the drying time.

4 Repeat step **3**.

5 Use a four-sided buffer to smooth the repair application and bring the nails to a shine.

Severed free edge

1 Place the severed free edge into a bowl of hot water, to soften the nail. Soak for approximately 3 minutes, then dry with a tissue.

2 Remove any nail polish, and dehydrate the nail plate by wiping it with a cotton bud soaked in acetone. Check that there are no contra-indications.

3 Lightly buff the whole nail plate to remove the shine.

4 Place a small drop of resin close to the free edge.

5 Apply the severed nail tip to the nail plate, overlapping it slightly.

6 Blend the join with a medium-grit file.

ACTIVITY

Nail services
List the different types of nail service that could be offered using the procedures detailed in this chapter.

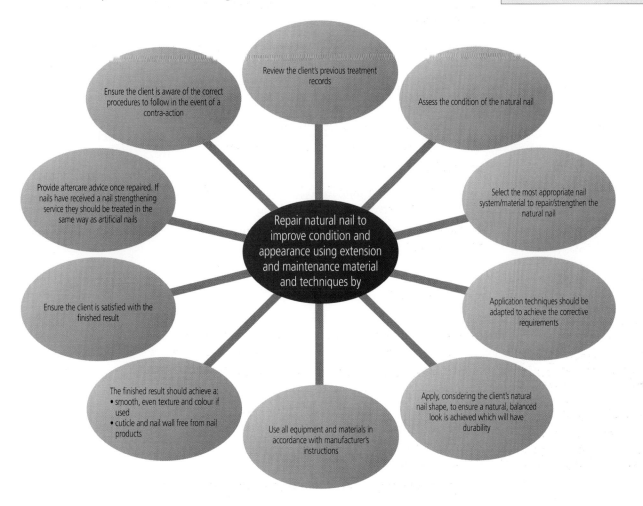

Review the client's previous treatment records

Assess the condition of the natural nail

Ensure the client is aware of the correct procedures to follow in the event of a contra-action

Select the most appropriate nail system/material to repair/strengthen the natural nail

Provide aftercare advice once repaired. If nails have received a nail strengthening service they should be treated in the same way as artificial nails

Repair natural nail to improve condition and appearance using extension and maintenance material and techniques by

Application techniques should be adapted to achieve the corrective requirements

Ensure the client is satisfied with the finished result

Apply, considering the client's natural nail shape, to ensure a natural, balanced look is achieved which will have durability

The finished result should achieve a:
• smooth, even texture and colour if used
• cuticle and nail wall free from nail products

Use all equipment and materials in accordance with manufacturer's instructions

7 Place a small piece of mending material over the join.

8 Apply a layer of resin over the material and allow this to dry. Use a resin activator, if available, to reduce the drying time.

9 Apply mending material to the whole nail plate.

10 Repeat step **8** twice.

11 Use a four-sided buffer to smooth the repair application and bring the nails to a shine.

If the client did not keep her severed free edge, the broken fingernail could be matched to the others by applying a nail extension.

REMOVING ARTIFICIAL NAILS

1 The client should wash her hands.

2 Remove any existing nail polish.

3 Cut off the artificial free edge, being careful not to cut the natural free edge.

4 Slightly roughen the surface of the nail with a medium-grit file, to encourage absorption of the solvent by the nail.

5 Place the fingertips in a glass bowl containing a solvent such as acetone to a depth of 2–3 cms. To ensure client comfort, place the hands in separate bowls. Leave to soak for 15–20 minutes. Care should be taken when using acetone. It is extremely drying to the natural nails and the nails can be dehydrated and weakened resulting in splitting and peeling. Fibreglass is the easiest nail system to remove, whilst UV gel is the hardest. This strength differs due to the bonds that form the structures.

6 Every 2–3 minutes, remove the fingers and wipe away the dissolving artificial nail with a tissue soaked in acetone. An orange stick may be used to gently buff away the artificial nail structure.

7 When the nail has completely dissolved, a full manicure, including the application of a nail strengthener, should be carried out to ensure that the client leaves the salon with her nails in the best possible condition.

8 Make another appointment for a nail service to improve the condition of the natural nail or nail extension replacement.

TIP

Every 2–3 months the nails should be removed and a new set applied. This allows the new nail growth to be properly dehydrated with acetone. (Failure to do this will result in repeated problems with nails lifting in the cuticle area.)

HEALTH AND SAFETY

Loosening nails
Never try to re-stick nails that are coming loose by applying adhesive under the false nail – this could trap bacteria beneath the nail, leading to infection.

TIP

Always recommend after nail extension removal that the client purchase a nail-strengthener for home use.

AFTERCARE AND ADVICE

It is important when carrying out nail treatments that the client knows how to care for her nails at home. It is up to you to give her the correct advice, otherwise she may unwittingly undo the work done during treatment.

When you give home-care advice you can also recommend products such as nail polish or hand cream and specialised nail treatments, enhancing retail sales and your profits.

Home-care advice will differ sightly for each client, but basically it will be as follows for nail extensions:

- Use only non-acetone nail polish remover, to avoid softening the nails.
- Have the nails regularly maintained (infilled), to keep them attractive and strong.
- Always use a base coat under nail polish, to avoid yellowing.
- Do not pull the nails off if they start to lift: have them removed professionally and safely.
- Use a pen when dialling a telephone number to avoid stress to the free edge.
- Use a nail brush to gently remove dirt from underneath the free edge.
- Contact the salon if there is any indication of infection, such as swelling, discoloration or inflammation.

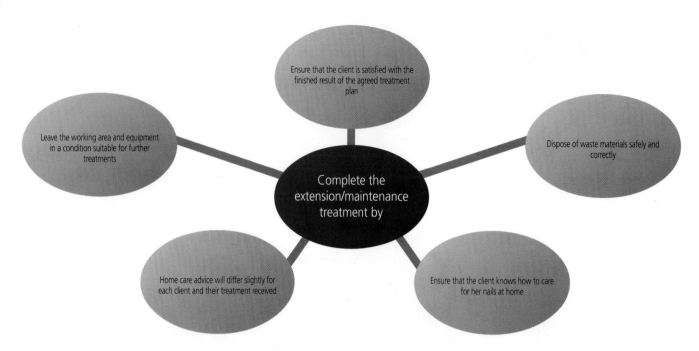

Ensure that the client is satisfied with the finished result of the agreed treatment plan

Leave the working area and equipment in a condition suitable for further treatments

Dispose of waste materials safely and correctly

Complete the extension/maintenance treatment by

Home care advice will differ slightly for each client and their treatment received

Ensure that the client knows how to care for her nails at home

Assessment of knowledge and understanding

You have now learnt about the different nail extension and maintenance services available. To be effective in your role you must be able to consult with the client and select the most appropriate nail service to meet her treatment requirements. This skill enables you to effectively extend and maintain nails.

To test your level of knowledge, answer the following short questions. These will prepare you for your summative (final) assessment.

Additional anatomy and physiology questions are found on pages 129–30, 131–2.

Structure and growth of the nails

1 What are the functions of the following nail parts:
   ● nail groove
   ● free edge
   ● matrix?
2 What factors affect the growth rate of the nail?
3 How can damage to the nail bed or matrix be recognised?
4 Name four functions of the skin.

Consult with the client

1 How can you ensure that you comply with the requirements of the Data Protection Act 1998?
2 Name three contra-indications to nail extension services.
3 Why is it important not to name specific contra-indications but to refer the client to their GP?
4 Why must an accurate record be kept for clients receiving nail extension and maintenance services?

5 How will the following information discussed and recorded on the record card help you to decide on the nail service to apply?
- occupation
- condition of the client's natural nails and cuticles
- reasons for having nail extensions.

6 Why is it important to fully explain the treatment service recommended, and what results the client can expect to achieve?

Prepare for the treatment

1 What Health and Safety legislation states how chemicals required for nail extension services should be stored and used?

2 Why is good ventilation important in the working area?

3 What other environmental conditions are important to ensure that your treatment is effective and comfortable for your client and you?

4 How may the client's clothing be protected during treatment?

5 What personal protective equipment may the client wear during the trimming of nail tip length?

6 Why should the clients nail plate be free of oil and moisture prior to the application of natural nail wraps and extensions?

7 Why is your working position important when performing nail services?

8 What equipment should be sterilised before treatment?

9 What does the term sterilisation mean?

Plan the treatment

1 Name four different nail shapes that you may expect to see.

2 Why must natural nail shape be considered during extension treatment application?

3 Why is it important to treat overgrown cuticles before nail extension treatment?

4 How could nail extension materials be used to improve the quality or appearance of the following nail conditions:
- brittle nails
- flaking/peeling nails?

5 Why is it important to spend time sizing the nail tip to match the client's natural nail shape and size?

6 Why are the nails dehydrated before wrap system treatment?

Repair natural nails to improve condition and appearance

1 If the skin is accidentally broken during treatment, how would you deal with this to ensure the safety of yourself, the client and others?

2 Why should a margin be left around the edge of the nail when applying artificial nail products to lengthen or strengthen?

3 How is the nail system for natural nail repair chosen?

4 What are the different overlay systems available?

5 How would you repair the following:
- free edge broken at flesh line
- flaking nails
- brittle nails?

Apply artificial nail using the wrap system

1 Why is the nail plate dehydrated before treatment?
2 How is the nail tip selected for the client?
3 How can damage to the natural nail be avoided when blending the nail tip?
4 Why is a free margin left around the cuticle and side of the nail wall area?
5 How would excessive resin application affect the durability of the nail?
6 What are the advantages of artificial nail application using the wrap system?

Maintain and repair artificial nail structures

1 What is the recommended time following application for a maintenance treatment for:
- natural nail wraps
- tip and overlay nail extensions?
2 What do you understand by the term *achieving* balance when applying artificial nail materials to the nails?
3 What is the purpose of nail maintenance treatment:
- two weeks after the initial application
- four weeks after the initial application?
4 Before application of repair materials how should the new natural nail be prepared?

Complete the treatment

1 How can you ensure that client satisfaction is achieved both during treatment and following nail extension treatment application?
2 What advice should be given to a client with regards to care for her nails?
3 If accidental damage occurs what actions should the client be advised to take?
4 What information should be recorded following a treatment application?
5 What do you understand by the term contra-action?
6 State the possible cause and action to take for the folliowing contra-actions:
- allergic reaction
- onycholysis (nail separation)
- lifting of the nail extension product?

chapter 13

PROVIDE NAIL ART SERVICE BT13

Learning objectives

This unit describes how to provide a variety of nail art techniques for clients. It describes the competencies to enable you to:

- **consult with the client**
- **prepare for the service**
- **plan the service**
- **provide nail art service to clients**
- **complete the service**

When providing nail art service it is important to use the skills you have learnt in the following core mandatory units:

Unit G1 – Ensure your own actions reduce risks to health and safety

Unit G6 – Promote additional products or services to clients

Unit G8 – Develop and maintain your effectiveness at work

INTRODUCTION

Nail art is an exciting and elaborate form of nail decoration, which may be applied to the hands or feet.

As the nail industry grows, nail art is becoming increasing popular, especially for special occasions, and designs are limited only by the manicurist's imagination. The artwork can be as simple as a single stripe across a painted nail, or as intricate as a detailed desert island scene.

TIP

Being creative
There are increasing opportunities for you to compete with other skilled operatives in nail art competitions. These usually occur at beauty exhibitions.

Nail trade magazines are extremely useful to keep you updated on the latest colours, nail products and designs, as many nail artists display their creations.

Christmas design

RECEPTION

When a client makes an appointment for nail art, question the client on the type of effect and design she would like. Discuss the cost of the service; prices will vary depending on the materials used, or the time involved to create the design. If the client's natural nails are in poor condition it will be necessary to allow extra time to perform a simple nail treatment, to improve the nails' natural appearance, and facilitate application. Allow extra time accordingly when booking the treatment.

The client must be aware that it takes 20–30 minutes for the polish to harden. It is also a good idea if the client pays *before* the service to prevent spoiling her painted nails.

Allow 5–10 minutes for each nail.

CLIENT CONSULTATION

Before carrying out the nail art service, it is necessary to assess the condition of the client's nails and cuticles. This is done to see if it is necessary to carry out a simple nail treatment, including file and cuticle work, beforehand.

Whilst assessing the client's hands/feet you should also be looking for any *contra-indications* to treatment.

Discuss the nail art requirements. Question the client on what type of result she wishes to achieve – are the nails to match a special outfit? If so, what colour would be most suitable, or is it for a special occasion where the nail art could match the theme!

It is a good idea to prepare a number of nail art designs to show the client. These may be applied to artificial nails, or they may be images of nail art designs that you have created and photographed.

If the client's expectations are unsuitable because of the client's natural nail shape or size, offer a suitable alternative. For example, if the client's nails were too short you could apply plastic nail tips, secured to the natural nail with nail adhesive, and paint these.

Decide upon the nail shape and length.

Nail shapes include:

Oval

Square

Pointed

Record all details on the client treatment record card. This will be useful if the client returns for this service, also it is important in the event of a contra-action such as an allergic reaction. It will inform you of those products that were used which may have caused the contra-action.

> **TIP** ✓
>
> **Colour choice**
> Choice of nail polish should suit the clients skin colouring and tone. Hold the bottle against the skin for compatibility.

> **TIP** ✓
>
> **Squoval nail shape**
> Squoval is a term used in the nail industry to describe a square nail shape which is slightly rounded at the free edge!

BEAUTY WORKS

Date	Beauty therapist name	
Client name		Date of birth
Address		Postcode

Evening phone number   Day phone number

Name of doctor   Doctor's address and phone number

Related medical history (conditions that may restrict or prohibit treatment application)

Are you taking any medication

CONTRA-INDICATIONS REQUIRING MEDICAL REFERRAL
(Preventing nail art service application)

☐ bacterial infections (e.g. paronychia)
☐ viral infections (e.g. plane or plantar warts)
☐ fungal infections (e.g. tinea ungium)
☐ severe nail separation
☐ severe eczema and psoriasis
☐ severe bruising

EQUIPMENT AND MATERIALS

☐ nail and skin treatment tools
☐ nail and skin products
☐ consumables

PRODUCTS

☐ nail conditioners e.g. cuticle cream
☐ skin conditioners e.g. hand cream
☐ nail, skin and cuticle corrective treatments e.g. paraffin wax
☐ nail polish

NAIL ART MATERIALS

☐ polishes
☐ flatstones
☐ paints
☐ glitters
☐ self-adhesive transfers
☐ topcoats
☐ foiling

☐ rhinestones
☐ polish secures
☐ basecoats
☐ blending
☐ water release transfers
☐ marbling
☐ striping

CONTRA-INDICATIONS WHICH RESTRICT TREATMENT
(Treatment may require adaptation)

☐ minor nail separation
☐ minor eczema and psoriasis
☐ severely bitten nails
☐ severely damaged nails
☐ broken bones
☐ minor cuts or abrasions
☐ minor bruising or swelling

Beauty therapist signature (for reference)

Client signature (confirmation of details)

TREATMENT ADVICE

This information includes
- what products have been used in the nail art service
- advice re products that would be suitable for the client to use at home to care for the skin of her hands/feet and nails
- advice on general care of the skin of the hands/feet and nails
- advice on product application and removal in order to gain maximum benefit from the use of home care products
- contra-action advice, action to be taken in the event of an unwanted skin reaction
- recommendations for further manicure/pedicure nail art treatments
- the recommended time intervals between treatments

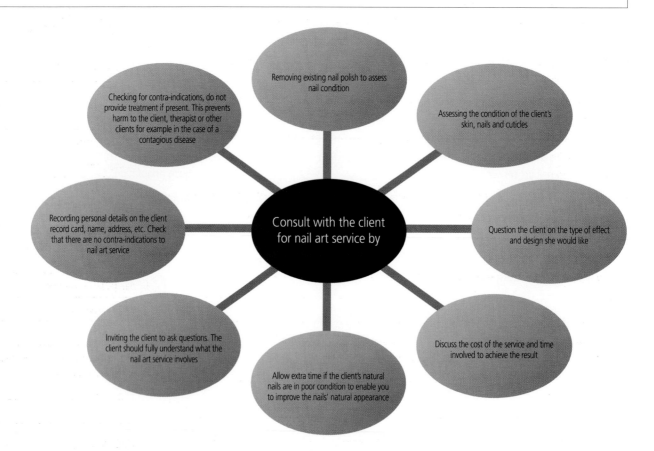

Consult with the client for nail art service by

Removing existing nail polish to assess nail condition

Assessing the condition of the client's skin, nails and cuticles

Question the client on the type of effect and design she would like

Discuss the cost of the service and time involved to achieve the result

Allow extra time if the client's natural nails are in poor condition to enable you to improve the nails' natural appearance

Inviting the client to ask questions. The client should fully understand what the nail art service involves

Recording personal details on the client record card, name, address, etc. Check that there are no contra-indications to nail art service

Checking for contra-indications, do not provide treatment if present. This prevents harm to the client, therapist or other clients for example in the case of a contagious disease

CONTRA-INDICATIONS

The consultation will draw any contra-indications to your attention. If the client has any of the following conditions, nail art service must not be carried out:

- *Tinea unguium*
- *Athletes foot*
- *Paronychia*
- *Cuts* or *abrasions* on the hands or feet
- *Infectious skin diseases*, such as ringworm
- *Warts* on the hands or feet
- *Minor nail separation*
- *Severe psoriasis* of the nail

EQUIPMENT AND MATERIALS

Below is a list of equipment and materials that you may require when offering nail art service:

- *Manicure trolley* – or other surface on which to place everything.
- *Medium-sized clean towels* – freshly laundered for each client.
- *Paper tissue disposable bedroll*.
- *Dry cottonwool and tissues*.
- *Skin cleansing agent* – such as witchhazel or eau de cologne.
- *Emery board*.
- *Orange sticks* – these may be used to apply nail art materials or polish remover to remove excess nail polish.
- *Marbling tool* – this has a small round metal head used to apply dots of colour to the nail, and to mix colours called marbling.
- A *selection of prepared nail designs* – to show the client. These are applied to artificial nails.
- *Base coat*.
- *Top coat or specialised nail art sealer* – which is thicker in consistency.
- *Coloured nail polish* – a selection for the client to choose from.
- *Nail scissors* – to trim the nails and cut nail art materials.
- *Nail polish remover*.
- *Nail polish solvent* – to restore the fluid consistency of nail polish.

> **TIP** ✔
>
> **Nail polish storage**
> Store nail polish stock in a cool, dark place, to avoid separation and fading.

> **TIP** ✔
>
> **Starting off**
> Initially, purchase basic colours of nail paint which can be mixed to create other colours. These include black, red, white, blue, green and yellow.

- *Nail art materials*:
  - Paints, specialist water-based acrylic paints
  - Glitters
  - Glitter dust and mixer, to add shimmer to a design
  - Transfers, these may be either water release or self adhesive
  - Foil strips, strips of metallic foil in various colours and designs, secured with foil adhesive
  - Striping tape
  - Polish secures – jewellery and tiny gems
  - Gem stones such as rhine stones and flat stones
  - Jewellery. This includes sterling silver or 9ct gold nail studs, charms and initials
  - Any other item you choose!

> **TIP** ✔
>
> **Nail studs**
> Nail piercing is used to attach nail jewellery to the free edge. A small hole is made using nail tools a drill and wrench. Posted nail jewellery such as a nail stud or ring may then be fixed, similarly to an earring.
>
>

- *Palette* – to prepare nail art materials such as mixing paints.
- *Brushes* – a selection: *fine* for detail, *liner* brush for creating thick, straight lines, *fan* brush to create a fan effect and to blend colours, *shading* brush to create shades and filling, a *glitter dust* brush to create a sparkle effect on the nails and a *striping* brush, thin and narrow, to create long straight lines.

- *Tweezers* – to place and fix decorations to the nail surface.
- *Nail polish drier* – to increase the speed of the polish hardening process.
- *Bowls or lined pedal bin* – for waste materials.
- *Client's record card*.

Sterilisation and sanitisation

Hygiene must be maintained in a number of ways to prevent secondary and cross-infection:

- ensure that tools and equipment are clean and where applicable sterile before use;
- disinfect work surfaces after each client;
- always follow hygienic working practices;
- clear discarded waste after each client;
- maintain a high standard of personal hygiene.

Preparing the treatment area

Ensure that the area is well ventilated to avoid inhalation of excessive fumes. Ensure that all products are stable to avoid products being knocked over and spilt.

The area must be free of any other previous materials, such as dust created from the application of artificial nails. Dust could spoil the effect of a client's newly painted nails.

Lighting should be good, to enable you to avoid eyestrain, especially when performing intricate art work. It is a good idea to use a table lamp.

Preparation of the therapist

Sitting properly is important. Ideally sit on a properly designed manicure stool or chair which offers adequate back support.

When performing the treatment it is important to sit upright with both feet flat on the floor.

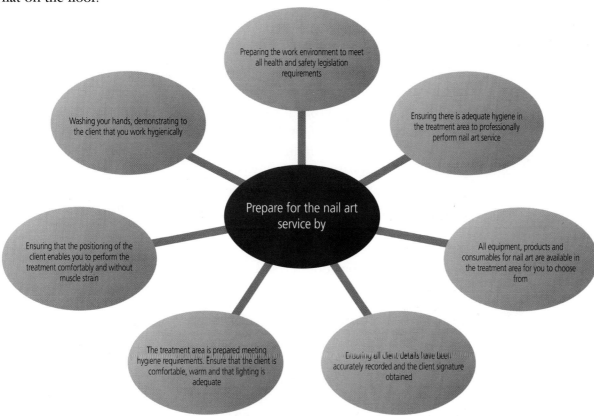

Preparing the work environment to meet all health and safety legislation requirements

Washing your hands, demonstrating to the client that you work hygienically

Ensuring there is adequate hygiene in the treatment area to professionally perform nail art service

Prepare for the nail art service by

Ensuring that the positioning of the client enables you to perform the treatment comfortably and without muscle strain

All equipment, products and consumables for nail art are available in the treatment area for you to choose from

The treatment area is prepared meeting hygiene requirements. Ensure that the client is comfortable, warm and that lighting is adequate

Ensuring all client details have been accurately recorded and the client signature obtained

PREPARING THE CLIENT

1 Confirm the client's choice of nail art.
2 File the nails to achieve the desired shape and length. Ensure the free edge is clean.
3 The cuticles should be neat and smooth. Use the cuticle nippers to trim any uneven, excess cuticle.
4 Ensure the surface of the nail plate is clean and grease free. Wipe with a non-acetone polish remover to prepare the nail. It may be preferable to use a lint-free pad as cottonwool may leave fibres, which may spoil the application of nail polish.
5 Apply the required nail art base. Usually this is a good quality base coat.

TIP	✔
Corrective base coats	
If a corrective base coat is used, such as a nail ridge filler, these have a longer drying time as they tend to be of a thicker formulation.	

Nail Art

Lint-free pads

GENERAL TECHNIQUE

Tips for nail painting

- Ensure the surface of the nail is grease free. If grease is present this will result in nail polish peeling or chipping. Also nail art materials such as foil will not attach securely.

- Select colours that suit the client's nail length and skin colour.

- Dark colours will draw attention to the nails, and will make small/short nails appear smaller/shorter.

- If the nails are very broad leave a margin at the sides of the nail wall free of polish, this will help them to appear slimmer.

- Avoid pearlised polish if the client's nail surface is uneven or ridged. The polish will emphasise the imperfection.

- Always apply a good quality base coat suited to the client's nail condition. This helps to prevent staining from pigment in the polish, and may strengthen the nail or smooth ridges depending on its formulation.

- Apply the base nail polish in strokes, usually three as shown opposite.

- When applying nail polish colour, apply two coats, allowing the nails to dry between each coat to prevent the appearance of brush marks.

Step 1   Step 2   Step 3

Nail polish application

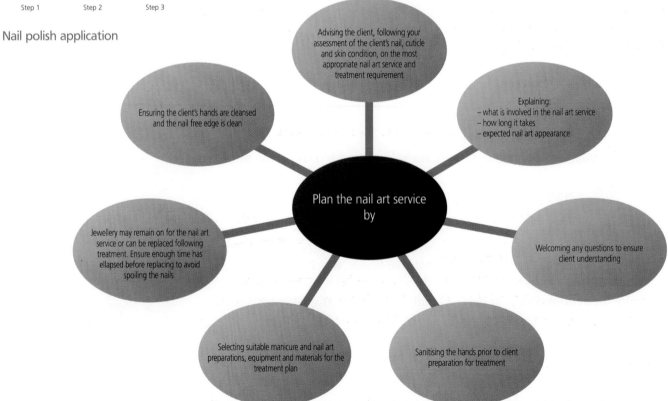

NAIL ART TECHNIQUES

French manicure

This is simple nail art, enhancing the natural appearance of the nails. It is particularly suitable to disguise stained nails. If the free edge is too short then this technique cannot be applied.

Technique

1 Apply base coat.
2 Paint the free edge white, ensuring that the line is even. If the nails are particularly stained you may wish to paint the reverse of the free edge also.
3 Apply a neutral nail polish, suited to your client's nail and skin, in soft beige, pink or clear to evenly cover the nail surface.
4 Apply a further coat of neutral polish to soften the white, or simply apply top coat.

This is a simple freehand technique.

Freehand technique

For freehand techniques you will need to be able to handle your nail art tools and materials confidently. It is important that you support and hold the client's hand, which is at a height and position to ensure that your hand is steady. Posture is also important to avoid muscle strain and future postural problems. The angle of your brush, and pressure of application will influence the result achieved.

Japanese symbol

This is an example of freehand technique which has been created using a fine detail brush.

Technique

1 Apply base coat and two coats of nail polish to each nail, allow to dry.
2 Select a bold contrasting paint, ensure that there is not excessive paint on the brush or 'blobbing' will occur.
3 Apply the symbol of your choice in stages, using light pressure to achieve a fine line and heavier pressure to achieve a thicker line.
4 When dry apply a top coat or nail art sealer to seal the design.

Marbling

Coloured paints are applied using a marbling tool creating a marbled effect.

Technique

Select two or three nail paint colours and a nail polish that complement each other.

1 Apply base coat and two coats of coloured nail polish to each nail.
2 Next, using the large end of the marbling tool place small drops of nail paint onto the polished nail.
3 Clean the marbling tool, and then use it to mix the colours together, creating swirls of colour to achieve a 'marbled' effect.
4 Add more colour using the marbling tool as necessary, until the desired effect and colour is achieved.
5 When dry, apply top coat or nail art sealer.

The marbling tool may also be used to apply small dots of paint, creating designs such as a dog's paw or flowers etc.

1 Apply base coat and two coats of nail polish to each nail.
2 Next, using the small end of the marbling tool place small dots to create different designs.
3 When dry apply top coat or nail art sealer.

Opalescent blending

Opalescent paints are applied over the base nail polish colour, creating an iridescent effect on the nails.

Technique

1 Apply base coat and two coats of the selected coloured nail polish to the nails. This technique is particularly effective when a dark colour is chosen.
2 Apply the opalescent paint in dots down either side of the nail.
3 Using a fan brush sweep the colours from side to side, this blends the colours and achieves the iridescent effect.
4 Apply top coat or nail art sealer when the paint and polish has hardened.

Jefford and Swain

Opalescent blending

Striping design

Different brush sizes make stripes of colour in varying widths.

Technique

1 Apply base coat and two coats of the selected nail polish colour to the nails.
2 Using a striping brush, apply stripes of paint to the nails, in one or several colours, using the sides of the brush not the point.
3 Work across the nails from one side to the other, making some stripes thicker than others. Polish secures or rhinestones can be added to enhance the effect.
4 Apply top coat or nail art sealer when the paint and polish has hardened.

Jefford and Swain

Striping design

tag at top right

Striping tape

Self-adhesive striping tape is applied to create or enhance a design on the nail.

Nail Art

Striping tape

Technique

1 Apply base coat and two coats of the selected nail polish colour to the nails.

2 When dry, apply the striping tape across the nail. Apply gentle pressure and secure the tape to the nail. Trim off any excess tape using nail scissors.

3 A rhinestone may be applied to enhance the effect.

4 Cover the nail with top coat or nail art sealer to seal the design.

Flat stones and rhinestones

These are tiny stones and gems available in differing colours, size and shapes which are secured to the nail polish whilst it is still wet.

Technique

1 Apply base coat and two coats of the selected nail polish colour to the nails.

2 Select a flat stone or rhinestone. Use the end of an orange stick which has been dampened with water to pick it up. Secure the flat stone to the polish. As the polish dries the stone will set in place.

3 Apply top coat or nail art sealer to seal the design. Flat stones and rhinestones may be used to create a design such as a straight line, or alternatively they can be used to enhance a design.

Striping design with rhinestones

Technique

1 Apply basecoat and two coats of the chosen nail polish, allow to dry.

2 Apply a small dot of top coat and attach rhinestones to the nail, to create the design required.

3 Using a striping brush, apply lines of paint, feathering out from the corner of the bottom of the nail to enhance the effect.

4 Apply top coat or nail art sealer to seal the design.

Jefford and Swain

Striping and rhinestone design

Glitter dust (and mixer)

This is a fine sparkly powder available in different colours, applied with a brush.

Technique

1 Apply base coat and two coats of the selected nail polish colour to the nails.

> **TIP** ✔
>
> **Stained glass effect**
> Apply the glitter allowing the base polish colour to show through, creating a stained glass effect.

2 Dip a glitter brush in to the glitter mixer, forming a ball.

3 Dip the end of the brush into the glitter.

4 Apply the tip of the brush to the nail surface and position the glitter. This is achieved by gently moving the glitter over the nail surface using the brush. Apply gentle pressure with the brush to position the glitter.

5 Further colours may be applied. Clean the brush using nail polish remover before each application.

6 Apply top coat or nail art sealer when the paint and polish has hardened, to seal the design.

> **TIP** ✔
>
> **Glitter polish**
> When glitter is suspended in translucent polish, this may be used as a top coat, applied over a coloured polish creating a simple, eye catching effect.

Transfers

These are images that can be secured to the nail creating an instant design. They are available in two forms: *water release* and *self adhesive*.

- **Water release transfers** are dampened using water applied with a damp cottonwool bud on the reverse of the transfer. When dampened sufficiently (approximately 30 seconds), the transfer may be removed from its backing, using your thumb to position it on the nail.
- **Self-adhesive transfers** have a backing that is removed, to provide a sticky surface that adheres to the nail.

Technique

1 Apply base coat and two coats of the selected nail polish colour to the nails.

2 Prepare the transfer, according to which form is chosen.

3 Position in place on the nail, ensuring it is flat and apply gentle pressure.

4 Apply top coat or nail art sealer to seal the design.

Transfers

Foiling

Technique

1 Apply two coats of the selected nail polish colour to the nails.

2 Apply foil adhesive, this is placed where you wish to apply the foil. The adhesive is white on application and becomes clear as it dries.

3 Once clear apply the foil securely to the adhesive with the pattern facing upwards to the nail.

4 Apply top coat or nail art sealer to seal the design.

Foiling

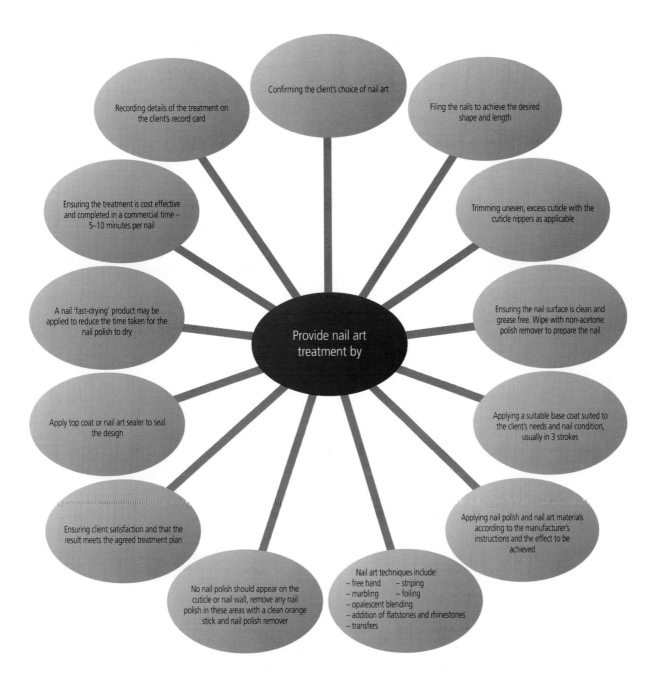

Provide nail art treatment by

- Confirming the client's choice of nail art
- Filing the nails to achieve the desired shape and length
- Trimming uneven, excess cuticle with the cuticle nippers as applicable
- Ensuring the nail surface is clean and grease free. Wipe with non-acetone polish remover to prepare the nail
- Applying a suitable base coat suited to the client's needs and nail condition, usually in 3 strokes
- Applying nail polish and nail art materials according to the manufacturer's instructions and the effect to be achieved
- Nail art techniques include:
  – free hand   – striping
  – marbling   – foiling
  – opalescent blending
  – addition of flatstones and rhinestones
  – transfers
- No nail polish should appear on the cuticle or nail wall, remove any nail polish in these areas with a clean orange stick and nail polish remover
- Ensuring client satisfaction and that the result meets the agreed treatment plan
- Apply top coat or nail art sealer to seal the design
- A nail 'fast-drying' product may be applied to reduce the time taken for the nail polish to dry
- Ensuring the treatment is cost effective and completed in a commercial time – 5–10 minutes per nail
- Recording details of the treatment on the client's record card

CONTRA-ACTIONS

A contra-action is an unwanted reaction to the service. An unwanted reaction to nail art service might include:

- *allergic reaction,* this occurs when a person becomes sensitised to a product ingredient. It is possible to become allergic to a product after having been in contact with it for years. The reaction would be recognised through the skin becoming red, itchy and inflamed.

If an allergic reaction occurs remove all nail products and apply a cool compress and soothing agent to the skin to reduce skin redness and irritation.

HEALTH AND SAFETY

Avoiding a contra-action
Always check at the consultation for any known allergies to substances or ingredients. *Formaldehyde* is used in some base coats to strengthen the nail plate and it can cause an allergic reaction in some people. Always follow the manufacturer's instructions to ensure that products are used correctly and safely.

HEALTH AND SAFETY

Nail tips

If the client has had artificial nail tips applied which have been painted, she may be advised to return to the salon to have them removed, or to soak the nails in acetone-based polish remover which softens the artificial nail – *never* pull these off as this will result in damage to the natural nail.

AFTERCARE AND ADVICE

It is important when carrying out a nail service that the client knows how to care for her nails at home.

When giving aftercare advice it is a good opportunity to recommend retail products, such as nail polish or hand cream, thereby enhancing retail sales and the salon's profits.

Aftercare advice will differ for each client according to individual needs, but generally it will be as follows:

- Wear rubber gloves when washing up
- Wear protective gloves when gardening or doing housework
- Always wear gloves in cold weather
- Dry the hands thoroughly after washing and apply hand cream
- Avoid harsh soaps when washing the hands
- Do not use the fingernails as tools
- Advise on appropriate nail/skin-care products to remedy the problems present, e.g. dry skin, weak nails

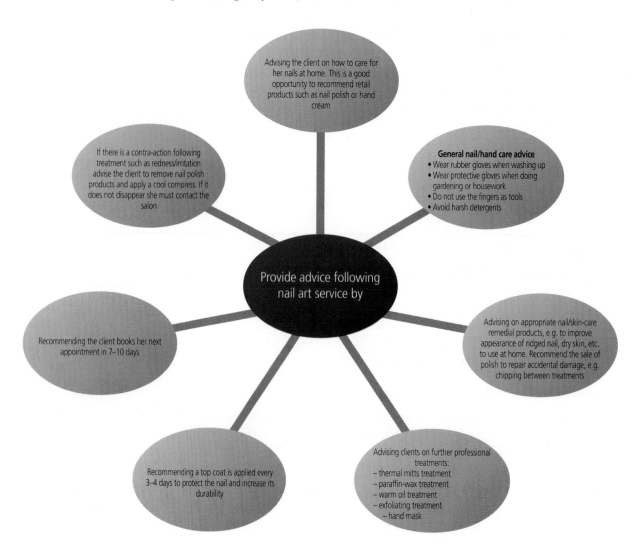

- Advise the client on what other professional treatments you could recommend

- Advise the client on a treatment plan to improve the nail/skin condition and on the time interval recommended between each treatment.

Have retail products available for the client to purchase. These include coloured nail polish, emery boards, nail polish remover and nail/skin treatment products.

It is a good idea to have available the nail polish colours that you have used. The client can then touch up any accidental chip herself.

Recommend the use of a top coat applied every 3–4 days to protect the nail polish, increase its durability and impart shine.

Nail art will last approximately 10 days, so recommend the client books her next appointment after this.

Advise the client as to what to do in the event of a contra-action (see contra-action).

Assessment of knowledge and understanding

You have now learnt about the different nail art techniques available to enhance the nails. These skills will enable you to professionally provide nail art service.

To test your level of knowledge, answer the following short questions. These will prepare you for your summative (final) assessment.

Anatomy and physiology questions required for this unit are found on pages 129–30, 131–2.

Consult with the client

1 Why is it important to discuss and agree the nail art service and outcomes with your client at consultation?

2 What is the benefit of having pre-prepared designs available for the client to view?

3 When deciding on the colour of polish what should you consider?

4 If the nail art service was unrealistic as the client had badly bitten nails, what alternative could you offer her?

Prepare for the service

1 Why is good lighting important?

2 How can you ensure that you have a professional appearance that complies with organisational standards?

3 What different brushes are required for nail art? When are each used?

4 What is the purpose of a marbling tool?

5 How is cross-infection prevented when applying nail art?

6 Name three contra-indications observed at consultation, which would prevent treatment being carried out? (Remember these may be on the hands or the feet.)

Plan for the service

1 Describe how you and the client should be positioned when performing nail art. Why is this important?

2 How would you decide upon the recommended nail art for a client?

3 How does condition of the client's nails influence timing and the choice of nail art?

4 Why is it important to complete the nail art service in the allocated time?

5 What is the commercially acceptable time for nail art?

6 How should the nails be prepared for nail art?

Provide nail art service

1 Name three different nail shapes.

2 Name four nail art techniques.

3 What is the purpose of a nail art base?

4 Why should the cuticle and surrounding skin be kept free of nail polish?

5 How can the quality of nail polish be maintained?

6 Why is it important to confirm that the client is satisfied with the finished result?

7 Why is it important to record all details of the service on the client record card?

Complete the service

1 What aftercare advice should be given to a client following nail art service?

2 What could occur if clients did not receive this specific advice?

3 What is a contra-action? What could be a contra-action to a nail art service?

4 How often should the clients receive this service if they wish to keep the effect maintained?

5 What retail products could be recommended to a client to care for the appearance of her nails and maintain the result?

PIERCE EARS

Learning objectives

This unit describes how to provide the service skin piercing of the earlobe. It describes the competencies to enable you to:

- **consult with the client**
- **prepare for earlobe piercing**
- **plan the treatment**
- **carry out earlobe piercing**
- **complete the treatment**

When providing ear piercing treatment it is important to use the skills you have learnt in the following core mandatory units:

Unit G1 – Ensure your own actions reduce risks to health and safety

Unit G6 – Promote additional products or services to clients

Unit G8 – Develop and maintain your effectiveness at work

THE EARS

Ear piercing is a quick, profitable and popular salon service, which also has the potential to generate further custom. This may be the client's first visit to a beauty salon, and the service she receives may encourage her to return for further treatments.

The structure and function of the earlobe

The external ear collects sound waves and directs these to the inner ear. The part of the ear that is commonly seen pierced is called the **pinna**, which comprises the **helix** and **lobule**. The helix is composed of cartilage, which does not heal quickly and can form lumpy scar tissue; it is therefore considered unsuitable for piercing. The lobule, in contrast, consists of fibrous and fatty tissue with no cartilage, and is therefore suitable for piercing.

pinna
helix
lobule

The earlobe

ACTIVITY

Research ear piercing treatment in three local salons. These may include hairdressing salons as it is a popular treatment to perform in the hair salon.

What is the cost of this service?

RECEPTION

When making an appointment for this service, allow 15 minutes. Although ear piercing is completed quickly, time must be allowed to complete the client's record card and to give clear concise aftercare instructions. Good communication is important. Speak clearly, establish what the client's requirements are and listen to ensure communication is effective and that a professional relationship is developed with the client.

A record card should be prepared for the client, recording just the information that is relevant to the ear-piercing treatment. Whilst completing the record card you will be able to ascertain whether the client is suited to this treatment – if the client is under 16 years of age, for example, it is necessary for a parent or guardian to accompany them and sign a **consent form** containing a disclaimer in the event of contra-indications.

Contra-indications to ear piercing should be checked for. If the area for piercing is unsuitable, politely explain to the client why this is so. All details recorded on the client record card are confidential and should be stored in a secure area following treatment. Access to this information will require written consent from the client. This is enforced through the Data Protection Act 1984 – legislation designed to protect the client's privacy and confidentiality. These records should be kept for at least three years, and be available for inspection as required. This may be by an authorised officer from the local health authority.

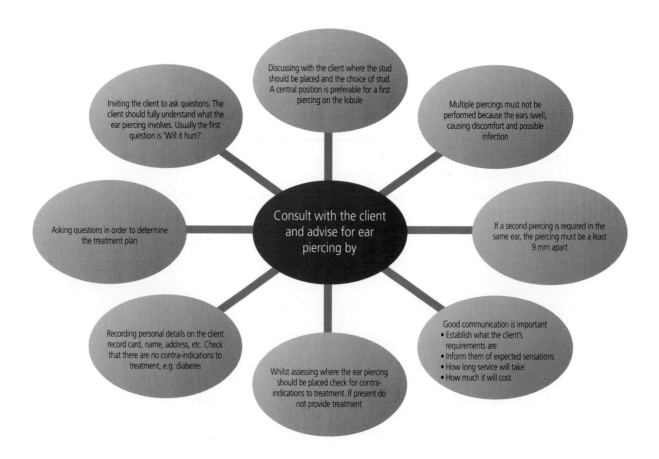

Explain the simple treatment procedure. Most clients will be interested to know what to expect – usually the client's first question is 'Will it hurt?'

Prepare the equipment required for ear piercing, and show the client the range of studs available.

Some salon receptionists are trained to carry out this service. This is practical: many clients will be acting on impulse in deciding to have their ears pierced, and will not have made an appointment.

CONTRA-INDICATIONS

In certain circumstances you should not carry out the ear-piercing treatment. Use your professional judgement to assess the suitability of each client.

- *If a client is particularly nervous* it would be inadvisable to pierce her ears – she might faint or jump whilst the treatment was being carried out, causing incorrect placement of the earring.

If any of the following are present, do not proceed with ear piercing:

- *Diabetes* – the skin is very slow to heal, so infection of the area would be a strong possibility.
- *Epilepsy* – the stress before the treatment and the possible shock incurred during it might induce a fit.
- *Skin disease or disorder*.
- *Hepatitis B or HIV (Human Immunodeficiency Syndrome)* – though the client may not know that she is a carrier, or may choose not to disclose the fact if she does (hygienic practice is vital, for this reason).
- *Inflammation of the ear*.
- *Open wounds, cuts or abrasions* in the area.
- *Moles or warts* in the area.
- *Circulatory disorders*, such as high or low blood pressure.
- *A predisposition to keloid scarring* – lumpy scar tissue (black skin often forms keloid scar tissue following skin healing).
- *Following an operation* – piercing must not be carried out at the site of a recent operation.

Where there is any contra-indication to ear piercing, the client must seek written permission from her GP before treatment can be carried out.

ACTIVITY
Safety and hygiene Research the ear-piercing systems available. Which ones are designed to protect the client's ear, and the gun, from contamination?   Display the literature you have collected in your log book, explaining the various systems' safety features.

BEAUTY WORKS

Date	Beauty therapist name

Client name	Date of birth (identifying client age group)

Address	Postcode

Evening phone number   Day phone number

Name of doctor   Doctor's address and phone number

Related medical history (conditions that may restrict or prohibit treatment application)

Are you taking any medication (this may affect the sensitivity of the skin and reaction to the treatment)

CONTRA-INDICATIONS REQUIRING MEDICAL REFERRAL
(Preventing ear piercing treatment)

- ☐ bacterial infection
- ☐ viral infection
- ☐ fungal infection
- ☐ severe skin conditions
- ☐ diabetes
- ☐ keloid scar tissue
- ☐ ear infections
- ☐ cardio-vascular problems
- ☐ dysfunction of the nervous system
- ☐ allergies to metals
- ☐ epilepsy

EQUIPMENT, MATERIALS AND PRODUCTS

- ☐ ear piercing gun
- ☐ surgical skin marker pen
- ☐ sterile pre-packed alcohol skin-cleansing wipes
- ☐ personal protective equipment
- ☐ sterile pre-packed ear studs
- ☐ consumables
- ☐ aftercare products
- ☐ mirror
- ☐ sharps disposal box (for use in the event of disposing of a contaminated ear stud)

CONTRA-INDICATIONS WHICH RESTRICT TREATMENT
(Treatment may require adaptation)

- ☐ cuts and abrasions
- ☐ bruising and swelling
- ☐ recent scar tissue
- ☐ skin disorders
- ☐ moles
- ☐ skin inflammation
- ☐ keloid scar tissue

AREAS TREATED

- ☐ ear lobe

Beauty therapist signature (for reference)

Client signature (confirmation of details)

TREATMENT ADVICE

This information includes

- advice re after care products that would be suitable for a client to apply at home to soothe and care for her ears to reduce redness and irritation and prevent secondary infection
- advice re avoidance of activities, actions and treatments that may cause irritation and poor skin healing. These include:
  – avoidance of touching the treated area to prevent skin infection
  – avoidance of swimming and other exercise to avoid skin irritation (24–48 hours following piercing treatment)
  – care to be taken when washing hair
- how and when to turn the ear stud
- how and when to remove the ear stud
- recommended replacement of the ear stud used for piercing
- contra-action advice, action to be taken in the event of an unwanted skin reaction
- recommendations for further ear piercing treatments
- the recommended time intervals between ear piercing treatments

EQUIPMENT AND MATERIALS

You will need the following equipment and materials:

- *Ear-piercing gun* – one that complies with current health and safety legislation.
- *Studs* – a variety of styles and designs to accomodate differing client preferences. Preferably of hypo-allergenic metal to minimise allergic reactions in people with metal allergies, e.g. nickel.
- *Surgical skin-marker pen*.

HEALTH AND SAFETY +

Marker pens
Keep the marker pen in a safe hygienic place – if left out, somebody might mistake it for an ordinary felt-tip pen!

- *Pre-packed alcohol-based sterile tissues (2) or manufacturer's cleansing solution* – used to cleanse the ear area.
- *Surgical spirit* – for cleaning the gun after use.
- *Clean cottonwool* – to apply the surgical spirit.
- *Single use disposable gloves* – to ensure a high standard of hygiene and to reduce the possibility of contamination.
- *Waste bowl*.
- *Pedal bin (with liner)*.
- *Headband (clean) or clip* – to hold the hair away from the ear during ear piercing.
- *Hand mirror (clean)* – to show the client the proposed placement of the earrings, after marking and after the ear piercing.
- *Client's record card*.
- *Aftercare solution* – either to offer for sale or to include as part of the cost of the service.

EQUIPMENT LIST

ear piercing gun

studs

surgical skin marker pen

pre-packed alcohol-based sterile tissues or manufacturer's cleansing solution

surgical spirit

aftercare solution

aftercare instruction leaflet

see opposite for complete list of materials required

Medi swabs (sterile tissues)

Ellisons

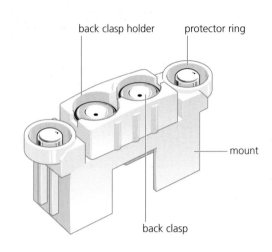

back clasp holder   protector ring

mount

back clasp

System 2000 cassette and instrument

slot for back clasp holder   barrel   plunger knob

trigger

- *Aftercare instruction leaflet* – for the client to keep.
- *Ultraviolet light cabinet* – to store the ear-piercing gun between piercing treatments; helps avoid the risk of contamination.
- *Hand disinfectant* – containing chlorhexidine.

Sterilisation and sanitisation

The premises should be kept clean and hygienic. The floor covering should be such that the surface can be cleaned with a disinfectant and hot soapy water; work surfaces likewise should be washed regularly with hot soapy water and wiped with a disinfectant.

The **Local Government (Miscellaneous Provisions) Act 1982** requires that salons offering any form of skin piercing be registered with the local health authority. This registration includes both the operators who will be carrying out the treatment and the salon premises where the treatment will be carried out.

Premises are inspected by a local authority authorised officer, who checks that relevant local bye-laws are being followed. (The bye-laws are to ensure that treatment is carried out in a healthy, safe and hygienic manner.)

If the inspector is satisfied, the salon will be issued with a **certificate of registration**; this should be displayed in the reception area. Any breach of the Act or the bye-laws could result in a fine, and permission to carry out the treatment could be withdrawn.

HEALTH AND SAFETY

Ear piercing guidelines
The Chartered Institute of Environmental Health has developed useful best practice guidance for those employed as operators in body art, cosmetic therapies and other special treatments.

TIP

Disposable ear-piercing gun
Available for ear-piercing is a sterile disposable ear gun. This ensures a sterile gun with preloaded ear studs and clasp.

ACTIVITY

Personal cleanliness
Personal cleanliness is a fundamental requirement of the Local Government (Miscellaneous Provisions) Act 1982. Discuss how a high standard of personal cleanliness can be guaranteed. The Local Government (Miscellaneous Provisions) Act 1982 is currently under review and it is important to check any updates to the Act on a regular basis to ensure compliance.

Some salons that offer the ear-piercing service also sell earrings. Those designed for pierced ears should not be tried on by a client, in the interest of health and hygiene. (Although there have been no reported cases of transmission of hepatitis B or HIV in this way, all possible risks should be avoided.) Such earrings may instead be attached to a special perspex slide which can be held against the ears to assist in selection.

The gun approved for ear piercing is designed so that it does not come into contact with the client's skin, and is used with pre-sterilised ear studs and ear clasps.

The studs are provided in sterile packs. Many give a date after which their sterility can no longer be assumed; others have a seal that changes colour when the expiry date has been reached. Only use studs that come from a sealed package.

Preparing the cubicle

Ear piercing can be carried out either in a private cubicle or at reception. Use your discretion to decide which would be more appropriate.

Good ventilation and lighting is important – some clients may feel faint following the treatment. The client should sit on a chair at a comfortable height for you.

Check the positioning of the client when performing the treatment. The ear lobe should be easily accessible without risk of injury to the client.

PREPARING THE CLIENT

If the position of the stud has not already been marked, do this now with the surgical skin-marker pen.

1 Wash your hands using a hand disinfectant that contains chlorhexidine as an active ingredient and apply a fresh pair of disposable gloves.
2 Thoroughly cleanse the back and the front of the client's earlobes. Allow the skin to dry. (If moisture is present, the mark will blur.)

HEALTH AND SAFETY +

Cross-infection
If you have any cuts on your hands or fingers, these should be covered with a clean dressing before you treat the client. It is preferable to wear disposable gloves.

Marking the ear prior to piercing

HEALTH AND SAFETY +

Secondary infection
As you cleanse the client's earlobes, you may notice that her skin, ear or hair is dirty. You may proceed, but when giving her the aftercare instructions politely and tactfully point out the importance of cleanliness in preventing secondary infection.

HEALTH AND SAFETY +

Piercing ears
Never perform multiple piercing in each ear. The ears will swell, causing discomfort and possible infection.
  If more than one hole is required in the same ear, the piecing must be at least 9 mm apart.

TIP ✔

If the client has fat lobes explain that the studs may feel a little tight.

Ear studs
Studs are preferable to hooped earrings or sleepers, as dirt is less likely to cling to the stud and infect the ear. Select studs that are manufactured from hypo-allergenic material.

3 Holding a mirror in front of the client, discuss with her where the stud should be placed. Mark the position using the sterile pen.

Remember that the ears are not at the same level on each side of the head, and may protrude at different angles. Take time when marking the position of the studs, to ensure that the final appearance is balanced.

TIP ✔

Try to aim for a central position on the earlobe – this will achieve the best result.

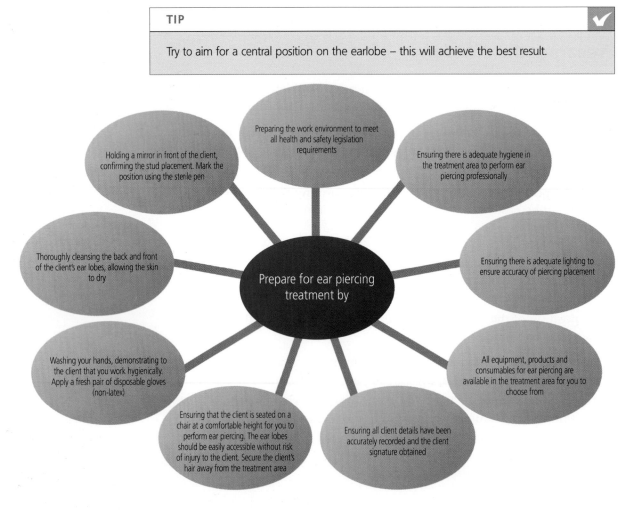

PIERCING THE EARS

The following procedure illustrates the general technique. The details differ according to the ear-piercing gun you are using. Always follow the manufacturer's instructions.

1 Holding the stud pack firmly, remove the backing paper. Take care not to drop the cartridge on the floor! (If you do drop it you will have to throw it away.)

Removing the studs from the
sealed pack

Preparing the gun

Removing the plastic
cartridge

Positioning the back clasps

Loading the studs

Piercing the ear

Reversing the cartridge to reload

2 Pull back the plunger knob on the back of the gun, until it is fully
extended – you will hear it click.

3 Remove the plastic cartridge from the package, holding it by the plastic
mount. To avoid contamination, make sure that you do not touch the
stud or backing clasp.

TIP

Always hold the gun either horizontally or upwards. Never point the gun downwards once it has been loaded – if you do, the studs will fall out.

TIP

The gun should not point down or up when piercing. If the angle of piercing is incorrect, the earring will hang forward, sideways or backwards.

TIP

Gun malfunction
If the piercing is successful but the clasp fails to attach to the post, firmly attach this manually without causing the client unnecessary distress.

If the ear stud needs adjustment following piercing, rewash your hands and apply a fresh pair of gloves before touching the pierced ear.

There are two parts, which must be separated. One part holds the back clasps: this is positioned in the slot. Push the cartridge down until it will go no further. The second holds the studs: position this against the stud barrel of the gun, which places a protective plastic ring around the barrel of the gun and stud.

Gently pull the holder upwards, away from the barrel: this will deposit the stud in the barrel.

4 Gently hold the first ear to be pierced in the non-working hand.

Holding the gun horizontally, position the stem of the stud so that it is accurately placed over the mark on the earlobe.

Gently squeeze the trigger until it stops. Check that the point of the stud is still in the correct position. If it is, squeeze the trigger again. The ear will be pierced, with the back clasp placed onto the back of the stud.

Check that the earring and back clasp are securely connected.

Holding the ear gently, move the gun down from the lobe.

5 Hold the gun upside down and discard the plastic ring into the waste bin.

6 Pull back the plunger knob and insert the next stud and protective ring.

Holding the gun in one hand, grip the back-clasp holder (using the mount in the other hand) and remove the holder from the gun. Invert the holder and place it back into the gun, with the remaining clasp in the top position.

7 Now pierce the second ear, repeating stage **4**.

8 Using the hand mirror, show the client her pierced ears.

TIP

To avoid anxiety to the client, pierce the second ear without hesitation, yet safely.

TIP

Allow the client to sit still for a few minutes following the treatment. Offer her tea or coffee. Some clients may be very anxious and need time to relax.

9 Discuss the aftercare instructions with the client (see below).

10 When the service has been completed, invert the gun, eject the protective ring, and remove the empty back-clasp holder. Dispose of the plastic cartridges into the waste bin.

11 Clean the gun using clean cottonwool and surgical spirit, and place it in the ultraviolet sterilising cabinet.

12 Dispose of all used products in the covered waste bin.

13 Any article that has been used on a client must be sterilised before use on another client to prevent *secondary*, or *cross-infection*.

Any article that has penetrated the skin must be disposed of hygienically immediately.

ACTIVITY

Differing procedures

The procedure for loading the different ear-piercing guns varies. The procedure given above is one example. Referring to the literature you have collected on the different guns, note ways in which the various treatment procedures differ.

CONTRA-ACTIONS

Redness, swelling, inflammation and the exudation (oozing) of serum (weeping) all signify that the ear is infected. If this occurs, the client should contact the salon. Depending on what she describes, it may be possible to give her adequate instructions over the telephone, or it may be necessary to make an appointment for the therapist to look at the ear. If, following action by the therapist, the infection persists, the client should be advised to contact her GP. Infection usually results from incorrect aftercare, removing the studs too early, or wearing cheap earrings.

Closed holes are caused by removing the studs too early, or by not continuing to wear earrings after the removal of the original studs.

Keloids – overgrowths of scar tissue – sometimes occur at the site of ear piercing. If a client suffers from keloids, advise her not to have her ears pierced more than once – further keloid tissue could develop, giving an unsightly appearance.

Fainting may occur if the client was particularly nervous beforehand. The shock of the ear-piercing treatment may cause a short period of unconciousness due to insufficient blood flow to the brain.

AFTERCARE AND ADVICE

After the ear-piercing, complete details of the treatment on the client's record card. The client should be given clear instructions on how to care for her ears to prevent secondary infection. The studs must not be removed for five to six weeks to enable effective skin healing and prevent infection. Invite the client to return to the salon after this period for you to remove the studs.

Remind the client always to wash her hands before cleaning the ear area. (If someone else is going to clean the ears, she also must wash her hands with soap and warm water before touching the client's ears.) The ears should be cleaned twice daily, using an **aftercare lotion**. The lotion may be applied as directed by the manufacturer. This should be applied to clean cottonwool, and the cottonwool squeezed to allow the lotion to run around the stud, at the front of the ear and then at the back. Whilst the ears are being bathed with the cleansing solution, the stud should be rotated by holding it firmly at the front.

Even if the client cleanses her ears effectively, infection could still occur in other ways. These include the following:

- Long nails harbour germs. Infection of the ear can occur whilst the client is turning the stud.
- The client may touch the stud and ear at times other than when cleaning the ear.

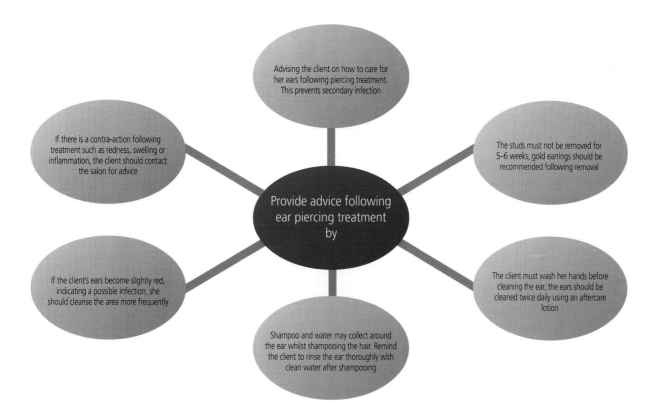

Advising the client on how to care for her ears following piercing treatment. This prevents secondary infection

The studs must not be removed for 5–6 weeks, gold earrings should be recommended following removal

If there is a contra-action following treatment such as redness, swelling or inflammation, the client should contact the salon for advice

Provide advice following ear piercing treatment by

The client must wash her hands before cleaning the ear, the ears should be cleaned twice daily using an aftercare lotion

If the client's ears become slightly red, indicating a possible infection, she should cleanse the area more frequently

Shampoo and water may collect around the ear whilst shampooing the hair. Remind the client to rinse the ear thoroughly with clean water after shampooing

HEALTH AND SAFETY

Antiseptic lotions
Remind the client that if an antiseptic lotion is applied to the ear area, it must be diluted as directed or skin burning may occur.

- Shampoo and dirty water may collect around the ear whilst shampooing the hair. Remind the client to rinse the ear thoroughly with clean water after shampooing.
- The client should protect her ears when applying hair lacquer or perfume, to avoid sensitising the ear.
- Following the removal of the studs, the client should only wear gold earrings. Cheap fashion earrings should be worn only for short periods of time, or allergic reactions and ear infections may occur.

After oral instructions have been given, the client should be provided with an aftercare leaflet containing these instructions.

BODY PIERCING

Body piercing is currently very fashionable. Common areas for piercing include the nipples, the eyebrows, the nose and the navel. Note that body piercing is inappropriate for clients under 17 years of age, as the body is still growing.

TIP

Always check with your insurance company which areas of the body you are able to pierce.

HEALTH AND SAFETY

Body piercing
Before performing body piercing, get approval from your local environmental health authority.
  Remember that body piercing is inappropriate to clients under 17 years of age.

Beauty therapy salons that offer ear piercing are often asked for body piercing also. Body piercing should be undertaken only if you have had thorough training, however, and only if you have the necessary specialised equipment and appropriate insurance cover.

Equipment

The equipment for piercing is either a **body-piercing gun**, which inserts a hollow reed, or the **needle and clamp** method. With the latter, the clamp reduces circulation in the area, thereby anaesthetising it, and the needle is inserted into the skin. The opening made by the needle is then filled with a ring of high-quality non-reactive surgical steel or gold (above 16 carat).

Aftercare

Special care should be taken of the area for one month following piercing. Ideally the jewellery must not be changed for 4–6 months to avoid tissue damage and possible infection. If infection occurs, causing excessive redness, swelling or a discharge, the client should return to the salon.

Assessment of knowledge and understanding

You have now learnt about the service skin piercing of the earlobe. This will enable you to professionally pierce ears.

To test your level of knowledge, answer the following short questions. These will prepare you for your summative (final) assessment.

Consult with the client

1 Which part of the ear is recommended for ear piercing?

2 Which parts of the earlobe are considered unsuitable and why?

3 How would you describe the procedure of ear piercing to ensure a client was confident both about the procedure and your expertise?

4 Why is it necessary to obtain parental/guardian consent for children under the age of 16 years?

2 PIERCE EARS (BT14)

5 How long should be allowed when booking for this treatment?

6 Why should only one pair of studs be fitted at once?

Prepare for earlobe piercing

1 What does the Local Government Miscellaneous Provisions Act 1982 require of those who perform ear piercing?

2 What personal protective equipment must be worn when carrying out the ear piercing treatment?

3 What conditions would contra-indicate an ear piercing treatment?

4 How should the client be positioned for ear piercing treatment? Why is this important?

5 What factors should be considered when piercing the earlobes of the following clients?
- a client who has previously suffered from keloid scarring
- a particularly nervous client
- a client with fat earlobes
- a client with diabetes
- a client who is allergic to nickel
- a client who has had her earlobes pierced previously, and this is a second piercing.

6 How can you ensure that the position of the ear stud will be correct?

7 How is the ear sanitised for treatment?

8 What salon environmental factors should be considered to ensure that the piercing is carried out competently?

Carry out earlobe piercing

1 How can you prevent infection when carrying out an ear piercing treatment?

2 What is the normal reaction following ear piercing treatment? You may wish to discuss this with the client at consultation

3 What should be recorded on the client's record card following the ear piercing treatment, and is this of importance?

4 If the ear piercing gun malfunctioned, what action should be taken?

5 How should waste be disposed of safely and correctly?

Complete the treatment

1 What aftercare instructions should be given following ear piercing?

2 If the client failed to follow the aftercare instructions, what complications could occur?

3 How would infection of the earlobe be recognised?

4 If an infection of the earlobe were to occur, what action should a client take?

5 If a second piercing to the lobe was requested when would you recommend this?

chapter 15

ASSIST WITH SPA TREATMENTS

BT15

Learning objectives

This unit describes how to assist with spa treatments. It describes the competencies to enable you to:

- **prepare work areas for water, temperature and spa treatments**
- **clean, maintain and monitor the spa environment**
- **assist with monitoring water, temperature and spa treatments**
- **assist with the shutdown of treatment areas**

When providing spa treatment it is important to use the skills you have learnt in the following core mandatory units:

Unit G1 – Ensure your own actions reduce risks to health and safety

Unit G6 – Promote additional products or services to clients

Unit G8 – Develop and maintain your effectiveness at work

INTRODUCTION

Spa treatments are used for their beneficial effects upon the whole body. The spa environment and spa treatments induce a physical and mental sense of wellbeing.

The term spa is said to be derived from a village near Liege, in Belgium called *Spau*. It had mineral hot springs which people would visit to improve their health and ailments.

The choice of spa treatments offered in the workplace will depend on the space available and the nature of other treatment services offered. Health farms commonly offer a comprehensive range of spa treatments whereas leisure centres and gyms popularly offer heat treatments such as sauna, steam and spa pools.

> **TIP**
>
> Before adding spa treatments to the services available, consider client usage and profitability. If you do not have a shower facility you will be limited in the range of spa services you can offer.

> **TIP**
>
> **Spa treatments as a preparatory service**
> Spa treatments are beneficial when applied before other body treatments as they make the body tissues and systems more receptive.
>
> **Spa treatments as a rehabilitation service**
> Water is used for the treatment of medical conditions such as rheumatism and rehabilitation after injury.

Spa treatments studied include:

- **Sauna** – a dry heat treatment where air is heated
- **Relaxation room** – sometimes referred to by the Latin name *tepidarium*, a room of ambient temperature (close to body temperature)
- **Steam** – a wet heat treatment where water is heated
- **Hydrotherapy** – where water is used for its therapeutic effect
- **Flotation** – the body is suspended (wet flotation), or supported (dry flotation), inducing relaxation
- **Body wrapping** – the body is wrapped in bandages, plastic sheets or thermal blankets for different therapeutic effects.

Ingredients such as marine minerals or clay are applied to the bandages or directly to the skin to achieve different results.

> **TIP**
>
> **History of spa treatments**
> The therapeutic effects of spa treatments including steam, sauna and spa pools have been recognised throughout the ages.
>
> During the Roman Empire baths were used for their healing, health benefits and as a social meeting place. Examples of these original bath houses can still be seen today in the city of Bath, England.
>
> For thousands of years people from all cultures including Europe, Russia, the Middle East and India have used steam baths, and the medical benefits of the Turkish or Middle Eastern *hamman* steam baths date back to 200BC. Hippocrates, the founder of Western medicine more than 2000 years ago said, *'Give me the power to create a fever and I will cure any disease'*.
>
> Water is still used in medicine today for the treatment of sport injuries, rehabilitation and rheumatic disease.

GENERAL EFFECTS OF SPA THERAPY TREATMENTS

Spa heat treatments and therapeutic skin-conditioning treatments have the following effects.

- Relaxation is induced through treatments which raise the body temperature, increasing the blood circulation generally, which soothes sensory nerve endings and causes muscle relaxation. Heat therapy is a popular de-stressing treatment.
- Blood pressure falls as the superficial capillaries and vessels dilate.
- Heart rate and pulse rate increase.
- Blood circulation is improved. Vasodilation occurs which increases the blood flow through the area, supplying oxygen and nutrients to the cells.
- Lymphatic circulation is increased, assisting with the elimination of toxins and waste materials.

- Desquamation – the removal of surface dead skin cells from the stratum corneum is increased.
- Increased activity of the sebaceous and sudoriferous glands improves skin condition. This also creates a deep-cleaning action.
- Metabolism may be increased or decreased depending upon the treatment received.
- Flotation treatment causes a fall in heart and pulse rate due to its relaxation effect.
- Body wrapping treatments cause a rise in pulse rate due to an increase in body temperature.

ANATOMY AND PHYSIOLOGY

Heat treatments: sauna, steam and relaxation room

When heat treatments are applied, there is an increase in body temperature generally of about 1–2°C. Vasodilation of the blood capillaries occurs to lower the body temperature by increasing heat loss. This vasodilation effect causes erythema, where the skin becomes reddened. This effect soon subsides after application.

The increase in body temperature causes a corresponding increase in the heart and pulse rates. There is a fall in blood pressure as the resistance of the capillary walls is reduced when the capillaries dilate.

The dilation of the blood capillaries enables the blood to transport increased nutrients to the skin, enhancing its function and appearance.

The maximum temperature that the body can tolerate varies according to the type of treatment – dry or wet. Dry air holds less heat than water vapour, and body sweat is able to evaporate in dry heat, thus cooling the skin. This enables the body to tolerate a higher temperature.

Air which is saturated with water vapour is able to hold more heat, and body sweat is unable to evaporate so the body cannot cool itself. The body therefore cannot tolerate very high temperatures in wet heat.

HEALTH AND SAFETY

Sweat loss during heat treatments
The amount of sweat lost during heat treatments can vary from 0.15 to 1.5 litres.
It is important that the client is given water during and after heat treatment as necessary to rehydrate.

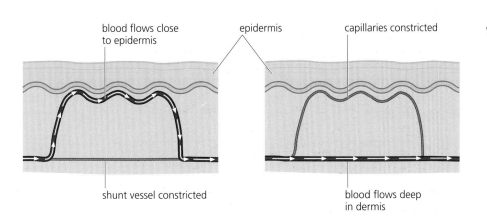

blood flows close to epidermis

epidermis

capillaries constricted

shunt vessel constricted

blood flows deep in dermis

Vasodilation and vasoconstriction

Hydrotherapy treatment

Hydrotherapy uses water to induce physical and mental well-being.

Hydrotherapy treatments include:

- spa pools;
- hydro baths and foam baths.

Spa pool

Also known as a whirlpool and jacuzzi bath, a spa pool will increase blood and lymphatic circulation due to the thermal and mechanical stimulating effect of the water. The rise in body temperature causes the pulse to increase.

Air is forced by a compressor through the water, passed through small openings in the bath. Water jets striking the skin's surface create a skin toning effect. Muscular pain and fatigue is reduced as accumulated toxins and waste are dispersed in the improved lymphatic circulation.

Hydro bath

The hydro bath is fitted with air and water jets that massage the tissues of the body as an air compressor aerates the water. These can be pressure controlled to achieve different effects. A hose may also be used to manually direct air over the body. This can be used to improve the skin tone in specific areas and can relieve muscular aches and pains by the heating effect and improved circulation.

Body temperature is increased which causes muscles to be relaxed due to increased blood circulation. Metabolism is increased.

Foam bath

An air compressor creates foam when air is passed through a shallow bath of water containing a foaming agent. The foam surrounds the body of the client and has a thermal effect, insulating the body and keeping it warm. The heating effect on the body induces perspiration but this cannot evaporate as the surrounding air is saturated with water vapour.

Increased perspiration aids elimination of waste products and toxins from the skin. Muscles are relaxed due to the rise in body temperature and increased blood circulation.

Flotation treatments

During flotation treatment total relaxation occurs and this affects the autonomic nervous system. It has two divisions: the *parasympathetic* and the *sympathetic*.

- The parasympathetic division is stimulated in periods of relaxation
- The sympathetic division is stimulated in periods of stress

During flotation treatment, the sympathetic system is deactivated and the parasympathetic division is stimulated. A calming effect on the body occurs

TIP ✔

Metabolism
Metabolism is a series of chemical reactions which utilises the nutrients required for growth and body repair.

Floataway

Flotation treatment

as pulse rate slows, metabolism reduces, and there is a relaxation of the muscles.

Body wrapping

Body wrapping results in an increase in body temperature, blood circulation generally and pulse rate.

The dilation of the blood capillaries enables the blood to transport increased nutrients to the skin, enhancing its function and appearance. As the skin warms, therapeutic ingredients are absorbed by the skin and have a skin conditioning effect. They are absorbed through the pores, hair follicles and the epidermis (stratum corneum).

The increase in body temperature also increases perspiration and waste elimination. Ingredients such as clay are used to help to draw out toxins.

The lymphatic circulation increases, which aids the elimination of excess fluid and toxins in the improved circulation.

Where heating is an effect of the body wrap this helps to relax tense muscles.

Body wrapping

Spa operation

Sauna – dry heat treatment

Sauna is a dry heat treatment. There are alternative methods of sauna including traditional Finnish or Tyrolean sauna, and the Laconium sauna.

Finnish or Tyrolean sauna
The sauna is usually a timber construction, often made from pine, which is a porous wood. This allows the condensation created to be absorbed and the internal furnishing walls to breathe. The sauna air is usually heated by an electric stove to between 70°–110°C.

The sauna is heated by a stove which contains coals. The coals get very hot and steam is created by pouring water onto them. An air inlet is situated at floor level and an outlet is found near the top of the cabin.

This high temperature is tolerable because the heat is reduced on contact with the skin and the sweat induced rapidly reduces the skin temperature.

Sauna (traditional wood)

HEALTH AND SAFETY	+
Sauna temperature High temperatures are only recommended in larger saunas where there is a greater volume of air.	

Laconium sauna
This sauna creates an evenly distributed mild dry heat. The temperature in the laconium sauna is approximately 55°C, generated by underfloor heating as opposed to heat created from a stove.

TIP

Infrared sauna
An infrared sauna heats the body directly, rather than heating the air which in turn heats the body. Infrared radiators penetrate the body tissues and this stimulates the cardio-vascular system which improves cellular metabolism and improves muscular fatigue and tension.

The positive effect of colour as a therapy – called *phototherapy* – can be combined with this treatment.

HEALTH AND SAFETY

Humidity in the sauna
Water can be sprinkled onto the stones in the sauna to raise moisture content (humidity).

Laconium is suitable for gently heating the skin for the purpose of cleansing and purifying. Some clients will prefer this sauna type as the heat is less intense.

Electricity is used to produce the heat and a sauna is operated by the mains supply because of the high power rating used.

Additional therapeutic effects of dry heat:

- elimination of metabolic waste is increased;
- skin cleansing occurs as the pores dilate, secreting sweat onto the skin's surface, thereby eliminating waste products;
- respiratory congestion can be relieved;
- increased sweating can cause temporary weight loss. However, this loss is quickly replaced with fluids consumed following treatment;
- muscles are relaxed due to the rise in body temperature and increased blood circulation.

Relaxation room The relaxation room enables the client to rest between experiencing different spa treatments, which allows the body temperature and blood pressure to lower. The air is ambient, the same as the body's temperature. The air in the room is dry to enhance the body's immune system and relieve stress. It is important that this area is very quiet to induce relaxation. Heated couches may be found in this room which are warmed by a heat-conducting hot mortar. These are ideal for clients unsuitable to receive heat treatment, which significantly increases blood circulation, e.g. sauna treatment.

Additional therapeutic effects of the relaxation room:

- heating effect soothes the sensory nerve endings;
- relieves muscular aches and pains;
- increases blood flow and removes waste products;
- the relaxing environment reduces stress and tension.

Electricity is used to produce the heat. The room is operated by the mains supply because of the high power rating used.

Steam – a wet heat treatment

Steam treatment can be received individually in a steam bath, or communally in a steam room. To produce steam, water is heated to 100°C. This then mixes with air to produce water vapour.

Steam bath This is constructed from fibreglass. A hinged door allows access and encloses the client; an opening at the top of the bath exposes the client's head. The client sits on a seat inside the bath which is adjustable for the height of each client and for her comfort.

Water is heated in a small tank inside the bath, situated underneath the seat. On boiling, the water produces steam. The steam mixes with the air in the bath and produces water vapour, which circulates inside the cabinet. The temperature inside the cabinet is most comfortable at between 45°–50°C.

Steam room To provide steam for a room, the water is heated in a boiler. The steam created is passed through tubes and the water vapour created circulates inside the room.

The *caldarium* is a steam room that uses natural herbal essences to create an aromatic steam room.

The *hamman* is a communal steam bath with a hot, moist aromatic atmosphere to purify and detox. The hamman bath traditionally has a dome-shaped central chamber with further chambers, of differing temperatures, leading from it. The hottest room is heated from the floor.

Additional therapeutic effects of steam heat:

- Muscles are relaxed due to the rise in body temperature and increased blood circulation.

> **TIP**
>
> **Steam cubicles**
> These are filled with steam and offer an alternative to the steam bath. The air is gently heated to 45°C and usually infused with herbal aromatic oils for their therapeutic effect.

> **HEALTH AND SAFETY** +
>
> **Temperature in the steam room**
> The air in the steam bath/room is saturated with water vapour (that is, it is unable to hold more water) and sweat on the skin's surface is unable to evaporate to create the skin cooling effect. For this reason, the temperature for steam treatment is lower than that for sauna to avoid the body overheating.

> **TIP**
>
> Bath houses have been used for thousands of years – the ancient Romans had hot rooms.

Hydrotherapy

In hydrotherapy, water is used for its therapeutic effect.

> **TIP**
>
> Hydrotherapy bath water may have seaweed, sea salt or essential oils added to enhance its therapeutic effect.

Spa pool A spa pool is full of heated warm water in which the client sits. It is constructed from shaped, durable acrylic, or tiled concrete. Provided with an electric power supply, air is forced through small openings and jets of air pass through the water, creating bubbles. These bubbles massage the surface of the skin from all directions, which has a stimulating effect.

The pool may incorporate features such as jets placed to massage different body parts, for example the lower back, and water fountains which can massage the neck with the power of the water flow.

Hydro baths and foam baths The hydro bath is usually made of acrylic and is filled with warm water. Operated by electricity, an air compressor provides underwater massage through high-powered jets. The air is forced through perforations in a duckboard or through outlet holes in the bath. A hose can also be used to manually direct water to stimulate circulation in specific areas.

The bath may be used to maintain well-being or as a rehabilitation treatment. Features include preset massage programmes to achieve different effects.

Foam baths are usually made of acrylic. A plastic duckboard perforated with small holes is located at the bottom of the bath. Operated by electricity, an

Floataway

Activewise

Flotation bath (wet)

Flotation bath (dry)

air compressor forces air through the holes which mixes with water and a foam agent to create the foam bath.

Additional therapeutic effects of hydrotherapy treatment:

- relaxation – the body weight is supported by the warm water and gently massaged;
- skin cleansing – as the water massages the skin's surface, desquamation is increased;
- skin toning when using jets of water to massage the body tissues;
- muscle fatigue and joint pain can be relieved by the increased blood and lymph circulation and increased cellular metabolism.

Flotation, wet and dry

The body is suspended, floats, or is supported inducing physical and mental relaxation.

Wet flotation in a bath or tank

Flotation baths or tanks are commonly capsule-shaped and constructed from fibreglass. The inside is lined with plastic resin.

Flotation pools are also available.

The treatment uses epsom salts diluted in water at high concentration which enables the body to float, and be suspended in the water. Approximately 280 kilogrammes of epsom salts are diluted in 500 litres of water, which is maintained at body temperature. This is approximately 570g of epsom salts to 1 litre of water.

Due to the high salt content, the skin does not lose body salts, and does not wrinkle, as would commonly occur when exposed to warm water for long periods of time.

Dry flotation

Here the client lies on a warmed tank of water, protected by a polymer flexible membrane covering protected by paper roll. The client lies on a bench which is lowered by the therapist so that the client is suspended by the water but has no direct contact with it.

The client may have specific therapeutic skin-care products applied to the skin to nourish or purify and detoxify. The body is then wrapped to maintain heat and absorb the products.

Additional therapeutic effects of flotation treatment:

- stress is reduced as blood pressure is lowered;
- skin conditioning occurs as circulation is increased, or in dry flotation the skin benefits from the therapeutic skin products applied;

- beneficial to those with back injuries, as the water supports the body taking pressure off the back;
- rheumatic conditions are relieved as there is improved blood circulation between the affected joints and relief of muscular tension;
- slower brain wave patterns, known as theta waves, occur in wet flotation.

Body wrapping A manual treatment. A small electrical heater may be used to heat the towels before use.

Additional therapeutic effects of body wrapping treatment:

- cellular regeneration is increased;
- waste products and toxins are eliminated;
- temporary weight loss through increased sweating and increased loss of body fluids;
- the therapeutic effect of body products helps balance the skin and body by skin stimulation caused by the cleansing, heating action.

RECEPTION

Heat treatments can be offered as individual treatments, but are also beneficial when given before other body treatments to increase their therapeutic effects. If you offer communal sauna, steam or other spa treatments, there will be a recommended number of clients who can use these facilities at once. Make sure you are aware of this to avoid overbooking.

For the client's first heat treatment, treatment time is shorter to monitor their physiological and psychological response to treatment.

Sauna	Treatment may be received 2–3 times per week Treatment duration 15–20 minutes
Relaxation room	Treatment may be received 2–3 times per week Treatment duration 30 minutes
Steam room	Treatment may be received 2–3 times per week Treatment duration 10–15 minutes
Steam bath	Treatment may be received 2–3 times per week Treatment duration 10–20 minutes
Hydrotherapy spa pool	Treatment may be received daily Treatment duration 10–15 minutes.
Hydrotherapy/foam bath	Treatment may be received 2–3 times per week Treatment duration 15–20 minutes
Flotation	Treatment may be received 1–2 times per week Wet flotation treatment duration 50–60 minutes Dry flotation treatment duration 40 minutes
Body wrap	Treatment may be received 2–3 times per week Treatment time 45–60 minutes, depending on the technique used

BEAUTY WORKS

Date	Beauty therapist name

Client name	Date of birth
Address	Postcode

Evening phone number	Day phone number

Name of doctor	Doctor's address and phone number

Related medical history (conditions that may restrict or prohibit treatment application)

Are you taking any medication (this may affect the sensitivity of the skin and reaction to the treatment)

CONTRA-INDICATIONS REQUIRING MEDICAL REFERRAL
(Preventing spa treatment application)
(Temporary CI are listed*)

☐ bacterial infection, e.g. impetigo*
☐ viral infection, e.g. verruca*
☐ fungal infection, e.g. tinea corporis/pedis*
☐ skin disorders
☐ skin disease, e.g. malignant melanoma
☐ high or low blood pressure
☐ heart disease/disorder
☐ medical conditions under supervision
☐ history of thrombosis/embolism
☐ recent scar tissue
☐ dysfunction of the nervous system
☐ epilepsy   ☐ respiratory conditions
☐ liver/kidney or pancreatic conditions
☐ lymphatic disorders   ☐ recent alcohol consumption*
☐ recent heavy meal – temporary*
☐ recent UVL exposure – temporary*

LIFESTYLE

☐ dietary and fluid intake   ☐ exercise habits
☐ smoking habits   ☐ sleep patterns
☐ hobbies, interests, means of relaxation

EQUIPMENT

☐ sauna
☐ steam room   ☐ steam cabinet
☐ flotation bath   ☐ flotation pool dry/wet
☐ body wrapping
☐ relaxation room

CONTRA-INDICATIONS WHICH RESTRICT TREATMENT
(Treatment may require adaptation)

☐ cuts and abrasions*
☐ bruising and swelling*
☐ recent scar tissue (avoid area)
☐ undiagnosed lumps, bumps, swellings
☐ recent injuries to the treatment area*
☐ mild psoriasis/eczema   ☐ medication
☐ high/low blood pressure   ☐ pregnancy*
☐ body piercings   ☐ highly anxious client
☐ allergies   ☐ claustrophobia
☐ menstruation   ☐ migraine

TREATMENT OBJECTIVES

☐ improved skin and body condition
☐ lymphatic drainage
☐ slimming – improved contours
☐ relaxation

TREATMENT AREAS

☐ trunk – body wrap   ☐ limbs – body wrap
☐ body – general

CLIENT PREPARATION

☐ exfoliation   ☐ skin cleansing
☐ showering

PREPARATION FOR AND MONITORING OF TREATMENT ENVIRONMENT

☐ heat   ☐ humidity
☐ water levels   ☐ chemical concentrations
☐ treatment time   ☐ ventilation
☐ consumables   ☐ ambiance of environment

Beauty therapist signature (for reference)

Client signature (confirmation of details)

TREATMENT ADVICE

This information includes

- advice re products that would be suitable for the client to use at home
- advice on how to gain maximum benefit from product use
- record samples provided, to evaluate effectiveness at next treatment with the client.
- advice to enhance the effectiveness of the treatment including:
  - rest and relaxation advice
  - exercise advice
  - dietary advice
- advice to follow immediately following the treatment to include:
  - possible reactions to the treatment and recommended action to take
  - suitable rest period following treatment
  - general advice re food and fluid intake
  - avoidance of stimulants
- contra-action advice, action to be taken in the event of an unwanted reaction (e.g. skin reaction, nausea, dizziness)
- recommendations for further spa treatments and the benefits of continuous treatments
- the recommended time intervals between treatments.

CONSULTATION

Advise the client that a bathing costume may be worn if preferred for heat treatments. Inform the client beforehand that jewellery should not be worn during heat treatments and may have to be removed for body wrapping. She may prefer to not wear it for her appointment, for reasons of security.

If the client is attending for a body wrap which contains iodine, check that the client does not have an allergy to it. If unsure the client may receive a patch test to assess skin reaction before treatment.

Heat and hydrotherapy treatments generally may be received 2–3 times per week.

Body wraps should be recommended as a course if the client's aim is slimming; these may be received twice a week. Otherwise once a week would be appropriate. Advise the client that the slimming effect lasts 4–5 days.

Allow time for client questions when booking or advising on any spa treatment.

Complete personal details on the client's record card. Question the client to check for contra-indications.

CONTRA-INDICATIONS

If whilst completing the record card or on visual inspection of the skin you find the client to have any of the following, heat treatment may not be carried out:

Severe skin conditions

- e.g. acute eczema

HEALTH AND SAFETY

Patch test for allergies
If a client has allergies or hypersensitive skin, assess skin tolerance by applying a small amount of the treatment product to the skin behind the ear or at the inner elbow.

Skin allergy will be recognised by skin irritation itching, redness and swelling.

Record this on the client's record card and do not perform the treatment.

TIP

Data Protection Act 1998
Remember client records should be stored securely and viewed only by those authorised to do so.

HEALTH AND SAFETY

Flotation treatment and skin disorders
Some skin disorders can become aggravated by the salt used in wet flotation treatment. If unsure refer your client to their GP for approval to treat.
Alternatively, if available, dry flotation treatment may be offered.

HEALTH AND SAFETY

Increase in pulse
The heart works much faster during heat treatments. It needs to pump the blood to the surface of the skin to regulate body temperature and can increase from 72 beats per minute to 150 beats per minute.
Because there is an increase in pulse rate with a body wrap it is necessary to gain a GP's permission to treat if the client has high or low blood pressure.

TIP

Claustrophobia
To enable clients to become accustomed to the enclosed environment of the flotation bath, some models have a door which may be kept open during treatment.

Systemic medical conditions

- High/low blood pressure
- Thrombosis, a clot in the blood vessel or heart
- Phlebitis, inflammation of the vein
- Lymphatic disorders such as medical oedema
- Epilepsy, a disorder of the nervous system
- Respiratory conditions i.e. bronchitis/asthma
- Diabetes, decreased insulin secretion which causes excess glucose (sugar) to accumulate in the bloodstream. Increased urination occurs to excrete the excess glucose
- Liver, kidney or pancreatic conditions
- Viral, bacterial or fungal skin disorders such as verrucas and athlete's foot

HEALTH AND SAFETY

Preventing cross-infection
Disposable paper slippers may be worn to prevent cross-infection for spa therapy treatments such as body wrapping.
Verruca socks may be worn for hydrotherapy treatments.

- Disorders requiring medication
- Allergy to iodine, found in seaweed-based skin preparations. This must be checked when performing body wraps.
- Varicose veins (heat treatment and body wrap to the lower limb)
- Claustrophobia. Unsuitable treatments for clients with a fear of being in a confined area include flotation treatment, heat treatments such as the sauna and steam room.

HEALTH AND SAFETY

Treating a client with a contra-indication
Certain contra-indications, if mild or under GP control, may be treated. A GP's permission must be sought before a contra-indicated treatment can be given.

Other contra-indications may be temporary and include:

- Pregnancy
- Menstruation, first days
- Not having eaten for several hours, fainting may occur
- A recent heavy meal
- Recent active exercise, wait approximately 20–30 minutes
- Recent alcohol consumption
- Recent drug use
- Recent over-exposure to UV light

- Recent wax depilation, electrical epilation treatment (24–48 hours before a spa treatment) to avoid skin sensitivity and possible secondary infection
- Migraine
- Severe bruising
- High body temperature with infections such as influenza

TIP ✔

Your work role
Your role is to assist with spa treatments and you must work within your job responsibilities. However, it is important to respond courteously to requests for assistance from colleagues and anticipate their needs to ensure the smooth running of the spa.

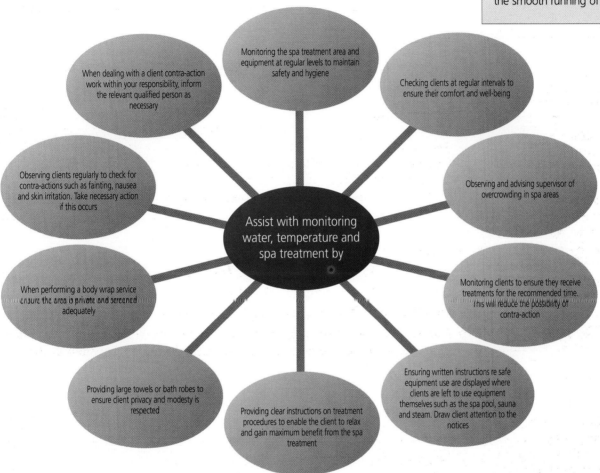

Assist with monitoring water, temperature and spa treatment by

- When dealing with a client contra-action work within your responsibility, inform the relevant qualified person as necessary
- Monitoring the spa treatment area and equipment at regular levels to maintain safety and hygiene
- Checking clients at regular intervals to ensure their comfort and well-being
- Observing clients regularly to check for contra-actions such as fainting, nausea and skin irritation. Take necessary action if this occurs
- Observing and advising supervisor of overcrowding in spa areas
- When performing a body wrap service ensure the area is private and screened adequately
- Monitoring clients to ensure they receive treatments for the recommended time. This will reduce the possibility of contra-action
- Providing large towels or bath robes to ensure client privacy and modesty is respected
- Providing clear instructions on treatment procedures to enable the client to relax and gain maximum benefit from the spa treatment
- Ensuring written instructions re safe equipment use are displayed where clients are left to use equipment themselves such as the spa pool, sauna and steam. Draw client attention to the notices

SPA EQUIPMENT AND MATERIALS

Sauna treatment

- *Sauna* – there must be adequate space for the air to circulate around the sauna.
- *Client record card* – to assess client and record details of treatment.
- *Client guidance instructions* – clearly sited.
- *Appropriate ventilation*.
- *Shower* – to cleanse the skin and regulate body temperature; body and hair shampoos may be provided.

- *Protective footwear* – to avoid cross-infection.
- *Clean towels for each client* – to drape the body after showering and to protect the hair.
- *A wooden pail containing purified water to ladle over the coals* – the water boils when poured onto the heated coals which increases the humidity (water vapour content of the air), cooling the air and making breathing more comfortable. This raising of humidity also makes the sauna feel hotter.

- *Temperature gauge* – to record the heat of the sauna, 70°C for a mild sauna, 110°C for a hot sauna.
- *An electric stove* – which heats the stones or coals, protected by a guard.
- *Hygrometer* – an instrument to measure relative humidity – generally the reading should be between 45–50 per cent.
- *Water* – to rehydrate following treatment.
- *Relaxation area* – to use following treatment.

Steam treatment

- *Steam bath or steam room*.
- *Distilled water* – to fill the water tank.
- *Essence* – to introduce into the steam room, e.g. pine.
- *Appropriate ventilation*.
- *Client guidance instructions* – clearly sited.
- *Client record card* – to assess client and record details of treatment.
- *Shower* – to cleanse the skin and regulate body temperature.
- *Body and hair shampoos* – may be provided.
- *Protective footwear* – to avoid cross-infection e.g. disposable paper slippers.
- *Clean towels for each client* – to drape over the seat and over the floor to protect the back of the client's legs from scalding by the steam; to provide modesty, dry the body after showering and to protect the hair. Also a small towel may be draped around the opening of the cabinet during treatment to prevent moist heat escaping.
- *Water* – to rehydrate following treatment.
- *Relaxation area* – to use following treatment.

Spa pool

- *Spa pool* – with filtration system to maintain water quality; the floor area must be reinforced to withstand the weight of the water.
- *Plant room* – within 5 metres of the pool with appropriate power supply and ventilation.
- *A heavy duty control panel* – all fittings should be strong, safe and reliable.
- *Water testing equipment*.
- *Water temperature should be between 37–40°C*.
- *Client guidance instructions* – clearly sited.
- *Client record card* – to assess client and record details of treatment.
- *Shower* – to cleanse the skin and regulate body temperature.
- *Body and hair shampoos* – may be provided.
- *Protective footwear* – to avoid cross-infection e.g. disposable paper slippers.
- *Water* – to rehydrate following treatment.
- *Clean towels* – for each client to dry the body after showering.
- *Relaxation area* – to use following treatment.

Hydro bath

- *Water temperature should be between 37–40°C*.
- *Position duckboard* – (if used).
- *Client record card* – to assess client and record details of treatment.
- *Shower* – to cleanse the skin and regulate body temperature.
- *Body and hair shampoos* – may be provided.
- *Protective footwear* – to avoid cross-infection e.g. disposable paper slippers.
- *Clean towels* – for each client to dry the body after showering.
- *Water* – to rehydrate following treatment.
- *Relaxation area* – to use following treatment.

Foam bath

- *Water temperature 37–40°C*.
- *Foam agent* – to add to the water.
- *Position duckboard*.
- *Client record card* – to assess client and record details of treatment.
- *Shower* – to cleanse the skin and regulate body temperature.
- *Body and hair shampoos* – may be provided.
- *Protective footwear* – to avoid cross-infection e.g. disposable paper slippers.
- *Clean towels* – for each client to dry the body after showering.
- *Water* – to rehydrate following treatment.
- *Relaxation area* – to use following treatment.

Flotation – wet

- *Flotation tank/pool.*
- *Epsom salts.*
- *Chemicals* – to maintain water cleanliness.
- *Client record card* – to assess client and record details of treatment.
- *Client guidance instructions* – clearly sited.
- *Water temperature preheated to 33°C.*
- *Shower* – to cleanse the skin.
- *Petroleum jelly* – to cover any small abrasions.
- *Ear plugs* – to prevent water entering the ears.
- *Neck support* – if required.
- *Clean towels* – for each client to dry the body after showering.
- *Treatment gown* – for client modesty.
- *Protective footwear* – to avoid cross-infection e.g. disposable slippers.
- *Shower facility* – to use following treatment.
- *Water* – to rehydrate following treatment.
- *Relaxation area* – to use following treatment.

> **TIP**
>
> **Body temperature**
> The temperature of the skin's surface is 33°C.
>   Temperatures above 33°C heat the body – the *hyperthermal effect.* Temperatures below 33°C reduce body temperature – *hypothermal effect.*

Flotation – dry

- *Flotation bed.*
- *Paper roll* – to cover the polymer membrane covering.
- *Treatment product* – to apply to the skin during dry flotation if required.
- *Clean towels* – for the client to dry the body after showering to cleanse the skin.
- *Client record card* – to assess client and record details of treatment.
- *Client guidance instructions* – clearly sited.
- *Clean towels* – for each client to dry the body after showering.
- *Treatment gown* – for client modesty.
- *Protective footwear* – to avoid cross-infection e.g. disposable slippers.
- *Shower facility* – to remove treatment product.
- *Steamed towels* – should be used to cleanse the skin if there is no shower facility.
- *Water* – to rehydrate following treatment.
- *Relaxation area* – to use following treatment.

> **TIP**
>
> **Flotation treatment environment**
> The treatment may be received in silence or meditation/relaxation tapes may be played according to client choice.

Body wrapping

There are various treatment techniques used in body wrapping according to the effect to be achieved or the treatment product used. Always refer to manufacturer's instructions.

The skin may be prepared for treatment by applying an exfoliating treatment or by body brushing which stimulates the circulation, both blood and lymphatic.

The body may be wrapped in hot linen bandages which have been soaked in therapeutic ingredients.

Alternatively treatment products using ingredients such as marine minerals or clay may be applied to the skin to achieve different skin conditioning results, including detoxification.

The body can then be wrapped in a thermal blanket, foil, plastic or bandages to maintain and increase body heat which increases lymphatic circulation and fluid loss, achieving a slimming effect.

- *Treatment couch*.
- *Paper briefs* – for the client to wear.
- *Treatment gown* – for client modesty.
- *Headband* – to protect the hair.
- *Clean bandages, plastic, metallic spa sheet* – (dependent upon system used). There must be sufficient bandages available for demand.
- *Bowls* – to mix products as applicable.
- *Water* – used to mix with powder mask ingredients (as applicable).
- *Treatment products* – herbal; essential oils; sea clay; marine algae; seaweed.
- *Spatulas/brushes* – to apply treatment products.
- *Thermal blankets* – to maintain heat (if required).
- *Tape measure* – to measure the client before and after treatment if performing a slimming body wrap.
- *Client record card* – to assess client and record details of treatment.
- *Shower facility* – to cleanse the skin before treatment and remove treatment products following treatment.
- *Hot, steamed towels* – may be used to remove product if the workplace does not have a shower facility.

Relaxation room

- *Neutral calm decor*.
- *Seating* – to allow the client to sit or lie down.
- *Treatment gown* – for client modesty and to maintain warmth.
- *Water facility* – to rehydrate.

STERILISATION AND SANITISATION

Where the spa treatments are communal and involve heat and moisture they provide ideal breeding conditions for harmful micro-organisms. It is important that all furnishings are regularly cleaned and disinfected as

TIP

Spa products
Seaweed is particularly high in minerals and is a key ingredient of many spa products. Sea water can be used on its own or mixed with seaweeds, muds and essential oils. Marine minerals include sodium, copper, magnesium, zinc, potassium and iron.

TIP

Headband
The headband may be removed following treatment product application, especially if a scalp massage is to be given whilst the treatment takes effect.

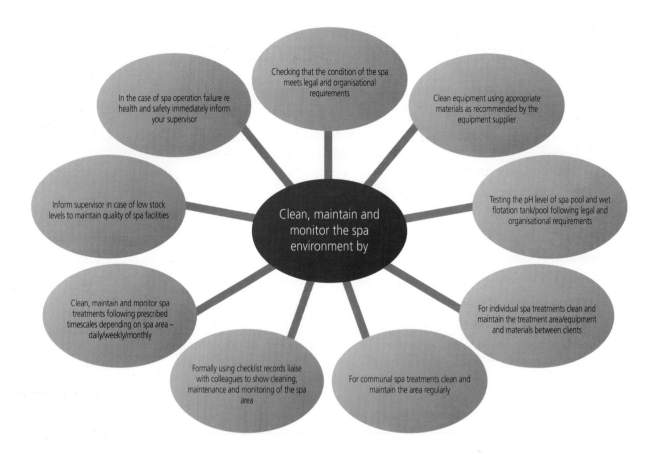

recommended by the manufacturers. This will also avoid stale smells occurring.

Written instructions should be displayed in the treatment area and hygiene practice brought to the attention of the client, e.g. showering thoroughly before using the spa pool etc.

Staff should make regular safety checks to ensure that the facilities are clean, safe and hygienic. These checks may need to be made on a daily, weekly or monthly basis.

HEALTH AND SAFETY

- All chemical storage areas should be clearly identified and accessible to authorised persons
- Keep all chemicals stored as directed
- Handle the chemicals wearing protective clothing to avoid skin contact and potential injury. Protective eye goggles which conform to the relevant British Safety Standard may also be a requirement
- Follow manufacturer's instructions when carrying out sanitisation procedures
- Emergency first aid procedures must be operative and adequate
- First aid resources must be readily available in a designated place
- Fire alarm systems may be available depending upon legal requirements and fire-fighting equipment should be available. Regular training is important to ensure staff are familiar with evacuation procedures

DAILY SAFETY CHECKS

CLUB: _____   DATE: Mon ____ to Sun ____ of ____ 20 ____

AREA	CONTROL MEASURES/ OBSERVATION POINTS	INITIALS AS CHECKED Please link to action required with an *							ACTION REQUIRED	URGENT YES/NO	DATE ACTIONED
		M	T	W	T	F	S	S			
Spa pool	No surround slip/trip hazards										
	No damaged surfaces										
	Access ladder/handrail secure										
	Air temperature and environment satisfactory										
	Water temperature set to appropriate level with temperature details on display										
	Emergency call button working/tested										
	Water test carried out every 2 hours										
Plant room	Doors kept locked										
	Hazardous substances stored in correct areas										
	Pool dosing controls working and set to correct levels										
	Pool pumps operating correctly										
	Chemical dosing tanks full										
	Chemical injectors not blocked										
	No leaks evident										
	Emergency call button working/tested										
	Evacuation routes/Fire exits clear and freely opening										

DATE	NUMBER OF WASTE BAGS TAKEN OUT DAILY	NAME OF STAFF MEMBER WHO TOOK OUT THE WASTE	DATE	NUMBER OF WASTE BAGS TAKEN OUT DAILY	NAME OF STAFF MEMBER WHO TOOK OUT THE WASTE
M			F		
T			S		
W			S		
T					

DAILY SAFETY CHECKS

CLUB: _____   DATE: Mon ____ to Sun ____ of ____ 20 ____

AREA	CONTROL MEASURES/ OBSERVATION POINTS	INITIALS AS CHECKED Please link to action required with an *							ACTION REQUIRED	URGENT YES/NO	DATE ACTIONED
		M	T	W	T	F	S	S			
Steam room	No slip/trip hazards										
	No damaged floors										
	Door in safe condition, including hinges										
	Light working and in safe condition										
	Wall thermostat in safe condition										
	Steam outlet cover secure, in place/properly guarded										
	Temperature set to appropriate level										
	Seating in safe condition										
	Guidance notes on display in the area										
	Emergency call button working/tested										
	Plant room door locked										
Office	No trip hazard from trailing cables										
	No damaged floor surfaces										
	Air temperature satisfactory										
	Equipment/files/stationery stored safely										
	Evacuation routes/Fire exits clear and freely opening										
	Waste bins emptied										

Daily safety checks courtesy of Spirit Health Club, Holiday Inn Hotel, Newton-le-Willows

DAILY SAFETY CHECKS

CLUB: _____   DATE: Mon ____ to Sun ____ of ____ 20 ____

AREA	CONTROL MEASURES/ OBSERVATION POINTS	INITIALS AS CHECKED Please link to action required with an *							ACTION REQUIRED	URGENT YES/NO	DATE ACTIONED
		M	T	W	T	F	S	S			
Reception and foyer area	No slip/trip hazards										
	No damaged floor surfaces										
	Hazardous substances stored in secure locations										
	Furniture in safe condition										
	Electrical sockets covered										
	Glazing in safe condition										
	Air temperature satisfactory										
	Waste bins emptied										
	Emergency call button working/tested										
	Evacuation routes/Fire exits clear and opening freely										
Sauna	No slip/trip hazards										
	No damaged floor surfaces										
	Evacuation routes/Fire exits clear and freely opening										
	Walls and benches free from damage										
	Stove guarded and secure										
	Light working, in safe condition and properly guarded										
	Benches secure and stable										
	Door in safe condition, including hinges										
	Temperature set to appropriate level 80–100										
	Emergency call button working/tested										
	Guidance notes on display in area										

DAILY SAFETY CHECKS

CLUB: _____   DATE: Mon ____ to Sun ____ of ____ 20 ____

AREA	CONTROL MEASURES/ OBSERVATION POINTS	INITIALS AS CHECKED Please link to action required with an *							ACTION REQUIRED	URGENT YES/NO	DATE ACTIONED
		M	T	W	T	F	S	S			
Female changing rooms and toilets	Hairdryers in safe condition										
	Storerooms locked										
	No hazardous substances left out/unattended										
	No slip/trip hazards										
	No damaged floor surfaces										
	All mirrors in safe condition										
	No damaged lockers										
	No damaged benches										
	No damaged wash basins										
	No damaged toilets										
	No damaged showers/shower areas										
	Temperature of showers/hot water taps not scalding										
	Waste bins emptied										
	Evacuation routes/Fire exits clear and freely opening										
Male changing rooms and toilets	Hairdryers in safe condition										
	Storerooms locked										
	No hazardous substances left out/unattended										
	No slip/trip hazards										
	No damaged floor surfaces										
	All mirrors in safe condition										
	No damaged lockers										
	No damaged benches										
	No damaged wash basins										
	No damaged toilets										
	No damaged showers/shower areas										
	Temperature of showers/hot water taps not scalding										
	Waste bins emptied										
	Evacuation routes/Fire exits clear and freely opening										

Daily safety checks courtesy of Spirit Health Club, Holiday Inn Hotel, Newton-le-Willows

DAILY SAFETY CHECKS

CLUB: _____   DATE: Mon ____ to Sun ____ of ____ 20 ____

AREA	CONTROL MEASURES/ OBSERVATION POINTS	INITIALS AS CHECKED Please link to action required with an *							ACTION REQUIRED	URGENT YES/NO	DATE ACTIONED
		M	T	W	T	F	S	S			
Children's playroom/ crèche	No slip/trip hazards										
	No damaged floor surfaces										
	No hazardous substances in the area										
	Furniture in safe condition and appropriate to children										
	Electrical items in safe condition/out of childs reach										
	Electrical sockets covered										
	Mirrors in safe condition										
	Air temperature satisfactory										
	Toilets clean, safe and undamaged										
	Wash basins clean, safe and undamaged										
	Temperature of hot water not scalding										
	Toys clean and in safe condition										
	Waste bins emptied										
	Emergency call button working/tested										
	Evacuation routes/Fire exits clear and freely opening										
Outside areas	Emergency access routes/Fire exits clear										
	Waste stored in containers										
	Chemical storage secure										
Other											

WEEKLY SAFETY CHECKS

CLUB: _____   DATE: _____

AREA	CONTROL MEASURES/ OBSERVATION POINTS	DATE CHECKED	INITIALS AS CHECKED	ACTION REQUIRED	URGENT YES/NO	DATE ACTIONED
Office	Wall surfaces in safe condition					
	Ceilings free from leaks or damage					
	Light fittings secure and working					
	Electrical sockets and wiring safe and undamaged					
	Electrical equipment safe and undamaged					
	All equipment used as intended and correctly stored					
Plant room	Wall surfaces in safe condition					
	Ceilings free from leaks or damage					
	Light fittings secure and working					
	Electrical sockets secure, not exposed to water					
	All glazing undamaged					
	All cables and wires not exposed					
	All electrical distribution boards locked					
	Area clean, tidy and secure					
	Day tanks sufficiently apart or partition separation is in place					
Reception and foyer area	Wall surfaces in safe condition					
	Ceilings free from leaks or damage					
	Light fittings secure and working					
	Electrical sockets secure					
	Reception/foyer furniture in safe condition					
	Sufficient supply of sunbed goggles or winkies					

Daily safety checks courtesy of Spirit Health Club, Holiday Inn Hotel, Newton-le-Willows

WEEKLY SAFETY CHECKS

CLUB: _____   DATE: _____

AREA	CONTROL MEASURES/ OBSERVATION POINTS	DATE CHECKED	INITIALS AS CHECKED	ACTION REQUIRED	URGENT YES/NO	DATE ACTIONED
Outside areas	Walkways around Club are safe and free from potholes					
	Lighting sufficient, secure and working					
	Area around Club free from debris					
	External cables, wires or power sources safe, not dangerous					
Spa pool	Light fittings secure and working					
	All jets working properly					
Children's playroom/ crèche	Procedure in place to protect the children					
	All paper work in place for each child					
General	First Aid boxes checked and recorded					
	Check waste collection has been carried out					
	Fire alarm test carried out and recorded					
Circulation areas	Wall surfaces in safe condition					
	Ceilings free from leaks or damage					
	Light fittings secure and working					
	Glazing/mirrors secure and safe					
	Electrical sockets safe and covered					
	Notice boards secure and safe					
	Furniture safe and free from damage					

WEEKLY SAFETY CHECKS

CLUB: _____   DATE: _____

AREA	CONTROL MEASURES/ OBSERVATION POINTS	DATE CHECKED	INITIALS AS CHECKED	ACTION REQUIRED	URGENT YES/NO	DATE ACTIONED
Female changing rooms and toilets	Wall surfaces in safe condition					
	Ceilings free from leaks or damage					
	Light fittings secure and working					
	Lockers in working condition					
	Cubicles, benches and vanity units undamaged					
Male changing rooms and toilets	Wall surfaces in safe condition					
	Ceilings free from leaks or damage					
	Light fittings secure and working					
	Lockers in working condition					
	Cubicles, benches and vanity units undamaged					
Relaxation/ lounge areas	Wall surfaces in safe condition					
	Ceilings free from leaks or damage					
	Furniture in safe condition					
	Electrical sockets covered					
	Light fittings secure and working					
Sauna	Walls and benches free from damage					
	Light fitting secure and undamaged					
	Door in safe condition					
Steam room	Walls and benches undamaged, all areas sealed					
	Ceilings free from damage					
	Light fitting secure and undamaged					
	Essence tank full					

Daily safety checks courtesy of Spirit Health Club, Holiday Inn Hotel, Newton-le-Willows

WEEKLY SAFETY CHECKS

CLUB: _____   DATE: _____

AREA	CONTROL MEASURES/ OBSERVATION POINTS	DATE CHECKED	INITIALS AS CHECKED	ACTION REQUIRED	URGENT YES/NO	DATE ACTIONED
Treatment/ beauty rooms	Wall surfaces in safe condition					
	Ceilings free from leaks or damage					
	Light fittings secure and working					
	Sharps disposal containers provided for the disposal of sharps (if applicable)					
Storage rooms	Wall surfaces in safe condition					
	Ceilings free from leaks or damage					
	No damaged floor surfaces					
	Light fittings secure and working					
	Electrical sockets safe and covered					
	Items in area stored in a safe location					
	Chemicals stored safely					
Others						

MONTHLY SAFETY CHECKS

CLUB: _____   DATE: _____

AREA	CONTROL MEASURES/ OBSERVATION POINTS	DATE CHECKED	INITIALS AS CHECKED	ACTION REQUIRED	URGENT YES/NO	DATE ACTIONED
General	Emergency lighting tested and recorded					
	Fire extinguishers checked and recorded					
	Personal Protective Equipment checked and recorded					
	Monthly eye wash station checked and recorded					
	Monthly ladder/stepladder checked and recorded					
	Monthly water analysis samples taken for pool/spa					
Female changing rooms and toilets	Monthly showerhead descale					
	Sanitary bins changed by contractor					
Male changing rooms and toilets	Monthly showerhead descale					
Plant room	Plant room safety signage in place					
	PPE available in area for use					
Sauna	Sauna guidance notices in place					
	Check temperature settings					
Steam room	Steam room guidance notices in place					
	Check temperature settings					
Outside areas	Check for damage/deterioration to perimeter walls/ fences					
Spa pool	Guidance notes on display					
	Handrails free from excessive movement					
	Check temperature settings					

Daily safety checks courtesy of Spirit Health Club, Holiday Inn Hotel, Newton-le-Willows

Sauna

- Clean the sauna furnishings and floor regularly with a disinfectant
- Check that the internal shelving is smooth to avoid splinters entering the skin and also harbouring germs
- Empty the wooden bucket of water when not in use to avoid mould formation
- When not in use, keep the sauna door open to allow fresh air to enter

Steam

- Clean the steam cabinet/room internal walls and floor furnishings regularly with a disinfectant that removes surface grease. This also prevents unpleasant smells created by stale body odours

Shower

- Check after each client use, clean to remove residue body skin treatment products such as marine clay etc.
- Ensure there are adequate consumables, body shampoo etc.

HEALTH AND SAFETY

All electrical equipment must be protected from contact with water. There should be sufficient drainage around the spa to avoid flooding.

Hydrotherapy spa pool

- The spa is not drained and filled after every use, but relies on the water being continually filtered and chemically treated
- The edge of the spa pool should be cleaned daily to remove body oils and dead skin cells, which would otherwise form a scum

Water testing

It is essential in the spa to ensure that this damp and warm environment is as free from contamination as possible. Diseases such as legionaires' could prove fatal. This is controlled by following stringent cleaning and water tests to check for water balance.

Back washing is important to filter out harmful organisms not killed by disinfectant.

An integral strainer removes hair and other debris from the water such as hair, skin flakes and plasters and this should be routinely cleaned to maintain its efficiency.

Water is kept free from potential hazard by the use of chemical disinfectants such as sodium and calcium hypochlorite. The normal operating range of the chemical will depend upon the disinfectants used. The water is tested according to the chemical disinfectant selected to ensure it is safe, effective and balanced. This will also assess the water to prevent water corrosion, staining and scaling.

Water is regularly tested for the following:

- pH (acidity/alkalinity)
- hardness (calcium content)
- temperature

Using a thermometer to check the temperature of the water

A spa pool water sample is taken. A phenol red tablet is added to the water which develops in colour according to the chemical content. The resulting colour is compared against the colour metric system to identify the reading for pH. This indicates pH chemical level, which should read between 7.2–7.8.

Calculate free chlorine level by adding DPD1 tablet to a pool sample.

Rotate disc until a colour match is found, then record the reading.

A total chlorine reading is taken by the addition of a DPD3 tablet to the coloured DPD1 sample. The tablet should be crushed and stirred into the water sample thoroughly.

Wait 2 minutes for the colour to develop.

Rotate disc until a colour match is found then record the reading.

When performing water testing ensure your hands are clean and always avoid touching the tablets.

Outdoor shoes must not be worn beside the pool, protective coverings must be worn.

To calculate the combined chlorine levels subtract the reading using the DPD1 tablet from the reading obtained from the DPD3 tablet.

Ideally, the free chlorine reading should be twice as much as combined chlorine.

HEALTH AND SAFETY +

Because of lower water levels in the spa pool it is important to avoid introducing high chemical levels.
The pH of water will be affected by any substance introduced into it. Above pH 7 skin and eye irritation occurs.

Regular testing of water and maintenance of records is an essential part of spa operation.

These measurements are known as **Langelier index** or **Palintest balanced water index**. Water samples are compared against acceptable operating levels. The quantity of disinfectant agents required will depend upon the hydrotherapy pool usage and the results of the water testing.

The amount of available free chlorine (that available to neutralise contaminants in the water) and the pH value need to be controlled and the amount and the effectiveness of the sterilising agent determined. Further chemicals may also need to be added to raise or lower alkalinity or calcium levels. Chemicals used to control the pH of water include sodium bicarbonate and carbon dioxide (CO_2).

A record of tests carried out by an authorised person must be kept for inspection by the local Health Authority. Failure to carry out this legally required duty by a responsible staff member can result in disciplinary action being taken. The Environmental Health Officer (EHO) will make regular checks to ensure that effective maintenance/hygiene is being enforced and will check standards.

Ventilation

The spa pool will create heat, humidity and chemical smells. Adequate ventilation is necessary. High levels of humidity can cause discomfort as the body cannot cool and becomes overheated but on contact with colder surfaces condensation occurs. This may result in a corrosive action as chemicals are deposited in the air. A relative humidity of 50–70 per cent is recommended. Air must be transported into the area through fan units fitted with filters and then heated.

HEALTH AND SAFETY

Heat treatments for use by the public are subject to inspection by the Environmental Health Authority. In spa treatment, the water is checked for safe bacterial levels and the presence of *E.coli* and coliform organisms.

HEALTH AND SAFETY

pH levels in the water affect the efficiency of disinfection. The pH should always be at a level which renders the water safe. Risks to bathers from chemicals used in disinfection include sore eyes and skin irritation. All bathers must be instructed to have a thorough pre-pool shower to cleanse the skin and avoid water contamination which will affect the pH level.

HEALTH AND SAFETY

When chlorine oxidises contaminants (chloramines) form. High levels of chloramines will produce an unpleasant smell and caused irritated eyes, making those using the bather think chlorine levels are high. In fact, there is sufficient free chlorine available.

Hydro baths and foam baths

- These should be drained and cleaned after each client use
- Specialised cleaning agents should be used as directed by the manufacturer. These will help prevent discolouration, algae formation and limescale build-up
- The surrounding floor should be dry
- Dirty towels in the area should be removed
- All waste should be disposed of in a covered, lined waste bin

Flotation – wet

- The water should be checked to see that it looks clear; hair etc. should be removed
- The surface of the flotation tank should be cleaned regularly to remove body oils and dead skin cells which would otherwise form a scum. Use sodium hypochlorite solution mixed as per manufacturer's instructions.
- Chemicals are added to maintain water cleanliness
- The pH of the water is tested daily – a pH of 7.2–7.4 is normal
- The water is filtered between each session
- All waste should be disposed of in a covered, lined waste bin
- The water depth should be 25cm
- Epsom salts need to be added regularly to maintain water density. Add these as guided by the manufacturer.

Flotation – dry

- Wipe the vinyl surface of the flotation bed with a proprietary disinfectant cleaner following the manufacturer's instructions
- Ensure the floor area is clean and dry
- All waste should be disposed of in a covered, lined waste bin

Body wrapping

- Wipe the surface of the treatment couch with a proprietary disinfectant cleaner following manufacturer's instructions
- Boil wash the bandages using a detergent or as directed by manufacturer's instructions
- Thoroughly clean bowls used to mix treatment products
- Brushes used to apply products should be washed in warm soapy water, rinsed, dried and sanitised e.g. placed in the ultraviolet cabinet
- All waste should be disposed of in a covered, lined waste bin

Relaxation room

- Seating should be cleaned regularly
- Used towels should be collected
- Ensure there are no spillages from drinks etc.
- Replenish drinking cups and maintain water facility to rehydrate
- Empty waste bins

PREPARATION OF THE TREATMENT AREA

HEALTH AND SAFETY

All equipment should be serviced as recommended by the manufacturers. A trained member of staff should regularly check all electrical equipment for safety, usually on a weekly basis, although daily safety checks occur.

This will follow compliance with the **Electricity at Work Regulation 1989**.

In many cases the spa treatments such as sauna, steam and hydrotherapy and relaxation room will be used on a continuous basis.

Ensure the area is hygienically maintained, any waste such as disposable paper drinking cups removed, floor areas cleaned regularly and any water spillage dealt with to prevent slippage and accidents.

There are checks to be made on a daily, weekly and monthly basis. These ensure that the condition of the spa meets legal and organisational requirements.

Everyday consumables should be checked and replenished daily. Shortages should be reported to the supervisor.

PROVIDING SPA TREATMENT

Sauna

- Switch the sauna on at the mains
- Heat the sauna adequately before use to allow the heat to evenly penetrate the timber surfaces. This will be between 1 hour and 1 hour 30 minutes depending on the size of the sauna
- Select the preferred temperature – 70–110°C for a Finnish/Tyrolean sauna, 55°C for a Laconium sauna

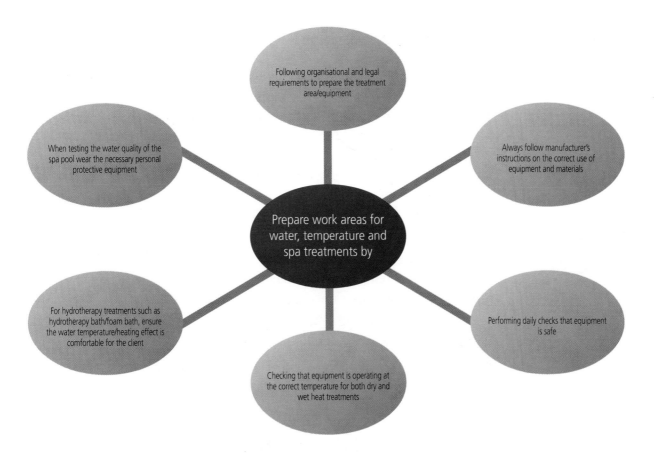

- Ensure air vents are open and clear from obstruction
- Ensure that there is no metal exposed which would burn the client's skin on contact
- Fill the wooden bucket with water if used. Water poured on the sauna coals raises the humidity of the sauna atmosphere
- Clean towels may be provided for the client to place over the seating

Steam bath

- Drape clean towels over the seat of the bath and the floor
- Fill the tank with water to cover the heating element. There should be at least 5 cms of water above the heating element
- Cover the opening of the bath with a clean towel to prevent heat loss
- Switch the machine on at the mains
- Set the temperature of the bath with the temperature dial and set the control for 15 minutes to preheat the cabinet

> **TIP** ✔
>
> The steam bath is less claustrophobic for clients than a steam room, as the head remains exposed. It also offers a more private treatment and the temperature may be adjusted to suit the client.

Steam room

- The preheating time will depend on the size of the steam room
- The recommended temperature is 40°C
- Provide water for the clients to pour over their skin in the hamman steam room

Hydrotherapy spa pool

- The water in the spa should be regularly tested to ensure that it has a balanced pH of 7.2–7.8
- The operating temperature is usually 36–40°C
- Check the water levels at the beginning of each day and regularly throughout the day

Hydrobath

- Fill the bath with warm water; ensure the water level covers all jets before operation
- Add ingredients to the bath for their therapeutic properties
- The operating temperature is usually 36–40°C
- Switch the compressor on after the client has got into the bath. Air aerates the bath water creating bubbles through the duckboards' perforated holes, or jets situated in the bath

Foam bath

- Cover the duckboard with hot water, approximately 38–43°C, to a depth of approximately 10–15 cms
- Add a foam ingredient to the water in the quantity directed by the cosmetic manufacturer
- Switch on the compressor which aerates the water causing the foam to rise. When near the top of the bath, approximately 15 cms, the compressor is switched off

HEALTH AND SAFETY

Underwater massage
The hose attachment, when used, should be kept under water at all times to prevent injury and unnecessary water spillage.

Flotation – wet

- The water should be filtered between each use and the level checked daily
- The temperature should be checked and maintained at surface body temperature (34.5–35.5°C)
- The condition of the water should be regularly monitored and should be clear at all times
- The water should be regularly tested to ensure it has a balanced pH of 7.2–7.4
- Test the alkalinity and free chlorine as per manufacturer's guidelines for usage
- Ensure the lighting is working in the room
- Gentle meditation music may be played
- Check the panic alarm is working

Flotation – dry

- Heat the water to the correct temperature as advised by the manufacturer
- Atmospheric mood music may be played to relax the client
- Raise the board to the top of the tank. Protect the polymer membrane covering with paper roll
- Ensure the floor is protected adequately to avoid marking from the skin treatment product mask if used

Body wrapping

- Ensure the room is warm, clean and aromatic to enhance the sensory experience
- Atmospheric mood music may be played to relax the client
- Prepare the bandages, if used, as appropriate. This may include soaking the bandages in the treatment product
- Ensure there are sufficient bandages to cover the body treatment area adequately

Relaxation room

- Ensure the room is at an ambient temperature (close to body temperature) of 30–40°C
- Ensure that any waste is removed on a regular basis

> **TIP**
>
> **Music**
> Music selection is important for inducing the relaxation atmosphere of the spa. Meditational, peaceful background music is an appropriate choice.

> **TIP**
>
> **Fibre-optic lighting**
> Colour influences the senses through the autonomic nervous system. This can affect the client's mental and physical state. Importantly it reinforces the effects of the spa treatment, inducing relaxation and a feeling of well-being.

PREPARATION OF THE THERAPIST

Ensure that all equipment and materials are regularly maintained. Prepare equipment and materials for specific treatments as required, e.g. foam baths, body wrapping. Ensure operating temperatures of heat and flotation treatments are correct.

Hair, if long, should be secured for reasons of hygiene.

For body wrapping a protective apron may be worn to prevent the treatment mask marking the protective workwear.

Protective clothing may need to be worn when performing tasks such as water testing.

PREPARATION OF THE CLIENT

Complete a consultation explaining the treatment thoroughly. This will enable the client to gain maximum relaxation from the treatment.

- Complete the client record card and check for contra-indications.
- Explain the treatment procedure to the client, its effects and use of equipment as applicable.
- Explain expected skin sensations, treatment effects and contra-actions that she must inform you of as necessary.
- Long hair should be secured and protected. If chemically treated it is advisable to protect the hair with a towel when receiving heat treatments or with a bathing cap for hydrotherapy.
- The client should remove all outside clothing in a private changing area.

- A secure area should be provided for the client to store clothing and personal possessions.

- Contact lenses, glasses and jewellery should be removed.

- Provide the client with clean towels and disposable slippers.

- Paper briefs may be provided to the client receiving body wrapping or dry flotation body mask treatment.

- It is important to encourage the client to ask questions; allow time for this.

- Encourage the client to visit the toilet before treatment as spa treatments may have a diuretic effect.

- Instruct the client to shower before treatment, to remove any cosmetics from the skin's surface. Shower facilities are essential in the spa to cleanse before, during and after spa therapy treatments to remove exfoliating products and body masks from the skin such as those with a mud, marine algae or seaweed base.

- Ensure that the shower is at a comfortable temperature and instruct on shower operation. A non-slip mat must be placed in the shower to prevent the client slipping.

- Pre-treatment the client may receive an exfoliating treatment such as a salt, herb or enzyme scrub. This removes dead skin cells, increases blood and lymph circulation and increases cellular metabolism.

TREATMENT APPLICATION

Sauna

1 Before the client enters the sauna:
   - check the temperature of the sauna by reading the thermometer;
   - check the relative humidity by reading the hygrometer.

2 The client then enters the sauna. New clients should be advised to sit on the lower benches where the air temperature is cooler. Existing clients may move to higher positions.

3 Check client comfort and close the sauna door.

4 After a 10–12 minute period the client should take a shower to cool the skin.

5 The client may return to the sauna for a further 10 minutes. During this time water may be poured onto the coals. The client then takes a final shower.

6 Treatment time is approximately 30 minutes.

7 Record details of the treatment on the client record card.

8 The client should rest after the final shower to allow the blood pressure to return to normal.

Steam bath/room

1 Treatment time is normally 15–20 minutes.

2 Check the temperature in the steam/cabinet room.

3 In the steam bath, adjust the seating height for the height of the client. Close the hinged door.
- In the *steam room* the client sits in the steam atmosphere.
- In the *hamman steam room* the client must acclimatise to the heat in different chambers before entering the hottest room.

4 Drape a towel around the neck of the steam bath to avoid loss of steam.

5 The client should be supervised at all times in the steam bath.

6 A shower should be taken at the end of the treatment to cleanse and cool the skin.

7 Record details of the treatment on the client record card.

Hydrotherapy spa pool

1 A bathing time of 15–20 minutes is recommended.

2 The client should be monitored during treatment.

3 A shower should be taken at the end of the treatment.

4 Provide the client with water for rehydration.

5 Allow the client to rest following treatment.

6 Record details of the treatment on the client record card and provide aftercare advice.

Hydrobaths

1 The client may be advised to hold onto the handles for balance and support during the underwater massage.

2 The therapist may use the hose feature to direct water over the muscle groups. This helps improve muscle tone. It also helps improve the appearance of soft fat.

3 At conclusion of treatment – 15–20 minutes – switch the compressor off.

4 Assist the client from the bath if required.

5 Provide the client with water for rehydration.

6 Allow the client to rest following treatment.

7 Record details of the treatment on the client record card and provide aftercare advice.

HEALTH AND SAFETY

Client safety
If at any time during a heat treatment the client feels light-headed, faint or nauseous, the therapist must be informed. Advise the client of this at consultation and monitor her reaction during the treatment. The client should never be left unattended, to avoid over-exposure to the effects of heating which could lead to fainting etc.

TIP

Hamman steam room
Traditionally hamman steam treatment is followed by a body exfoliation and massage.

HEALTH AND SAFETY

Spa pool
Monitor the communal spa area during use to avoid overcrowding and over-treatment as well as to remove water spillages. It is recommended that clients do not stay in the spa pool for more than 10–15 minutes. Although spa pools have an automatic operation time usually of 10 minutes, some can be switched back on by the client. This could result in client heat exhaustion and dehydration.

TIP

Sea water therapy
Thalassotherapy is the therapeutic benefit of bathing in fresh sea water.

The word is derived from the Greek *thalassa* meaning sea and *therpea* to treat.

By the addition of marine salts and algae to a hydrotherapy bath a thalassotherapy effect can be achieved.

Foam bath

1 The client should lie in the shallow water with her head exposed and her body covered with foam.

2 The client should be allowed to relax but monitored regularly.

3 At the end of the treatments – approximately 15–20 minutes – assist the client from the bath if required.

4 A shower should be taken at the end of the treatment.

5 Provide the client with water for rehydration.

6 Allow the client to relax.

7 Record details of the treatment on the client record card and provide aftercare advice.

Flotation – wet

1 The client should take a cleansing shower and make-up, if used, should have been removed. This would contaminate the water.

2 Advise the client on how long they will be in the flotation room.

3 Explain how to operate the door, demonstrate this and then observe them to confirm understanding.

4 Explain how to alter the lighting level, adjust the audio level, operate the panic alarm.

5 Explain how they should position themselves in the water. These procedures will facilitate relaxation.

6 The client may then apply the earplugs to prevent water entering the ears.

7 A neck cushion may be provided to support the client's neck.

8 Check on the client during treatment as necessary. If the client is enclosed in a room or capsule this may be through the intercom system. This is an important feature to reassure a highly nervous/anxious client.

9 Following treatment the client showers to remove excess salt and toxins from the skin's surface.

10 Provide the client with water for rehydration.

11 The client should take time to relax following treatment. A suitable area should be provided for this purpose.

12 Record details of the treatment on the client record card and provide aftercare advice.

Flotation – dry

1 The client should take a cleansing shower and make-up, if used, should have been removed.

2 A body spa treatment product may be applied before the treatment is received.

3 Advise the client on how long the flotation treatment will take.

4 The client lies on top of the board which is then lowered, controlled by the therapist.

5 A head and scalp massage may be offered whilst the client relaxes.

6 At the end of the treatment the board is raised.

7 The client may shower, specifically if a treatment product has been applied.

8 Provide the client with water for rehydration.

9 The client should take time to relax following treatment. A suitable area should be provided for this purpose.

10 Record details of the treatment on the client record card and provide aftercare advice.

HEALTH AND SAFETY

Client care
During treatment it is important to check the client at regular intervals. This reassures the client and ensures that the client is not suffering from a contra-action.

Body wrapping

Ensure the room is warm, clean and aromatic to enhance the sensory experience. Atmospheric mood music may be played to relax the client.

Treatment will vary depending upon the body wrapping system used. The client may receive a pre-treatment before the body wrap such as a heat treatment, shower and exfoliation or dry body brush.

Body wrapping using bandages to induce a slimming, detoxification effect

1 Measure the client from specific areas, record these measurements on the client record card.

2 a. Apply the treatment product to the skin and then unfold and wrap the bandages around the body part.
   or
   b. Unfold and wrap the bandages around the body part that have already been soaked in active treatment ingredients.

3 The client lies on the treatment couch, covered by a thermal blanket to maintain heat.

4 After the recommended treatment time, dependant upon the treatment system but usually 60 minutes, remove the bandages and excess treatment product.

5 Re-measure the client and advise her of inch loss. Record the results on her record card. When the client re-dresses they will usually find their clothes much looser.

6 Provide the client with water for rehydration.

7 Provide aftercare advice and re-book the client if part of a slimming course.

Body wrapping to induce a skin conditioning/detoxification effect

1 Apply a specialist treatment product to body parts to intensify the effect.

2 Mix and apply the treatment product to the skin using a brush.

TIP

Foot massage
With some body wrap systems a foot massage is given to the client whilst the body wrapping treatment takes effect.

TIP ✔

Body wraps may be applied to specific body parts only such as the foot and lower leg.

Photos: Finders International Ltd

3 The body may then be wrapped in plastic film and foil or blanket to induce a heating effect depending on the system used.

4 After the recommended time (usually 20 minutes), remove any coverings and treatment product.

5 Further treatment may follow such as massage to the area.

6 Provide the client with water for rehydration.

7 Provide aftercare advice.

HEALTH AND SAFETY

Ensure that the bandage application is not too tight or circulation will be poor in the area, resulting in loss of skin sensation and discomfort.

Relaxation room

1 Guide the client on facilities and use of the room.

2 Explain the importance of drinking water to rehydrate.

3 Check on the client's well-being at regular intervals.

HEALTH AND SAFETY

Spa cosmetic products
Always check to ensure that you are storing spa products correctly and that the use by date is clearly identified.

TIP

Body brushing
Body brushing may be provided before a body treatment mask. This will remove dead skin cells, stimulate lymphatic circulation and aid the absorption of the product.

CONCLUSION

When you have been using the spa for treatments it is important that it is prepared for subsequent treatments.

Hygiene and cleaning of the spa areas should occur following legal and organisational procedures.

Treatment areas should be shut down in accordance with manufacturer's instructions and legal and organisational procedures.

Following treatments such as a hydrotherapy bath or foam bath, equipment, water supplies and electricity at the mains should be switched off.

Following flotation treatment and heat therapy treatments switch off the equipments at the mains.

The spa boosters that create the aeration of the spa pool are switched off at the end of the working day (the switch is located in the plant room). The pump which circulates the water is left on. A back wash, which reverses the flow of water through the filter removing waste particles and debris, may occur.

A final water test is recommended before pool shutdown in order that any problems with water quality can be rectified before the next working day. Regular testing and the maintenance of records is an essential part of spa plant operation and health and safety maintenance.

It is important to work within your responsibilities when operating shutdown of the spa area.

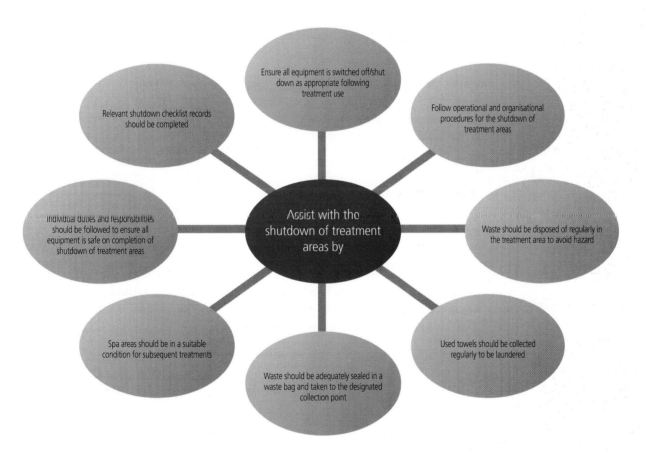

Aftercare

- Heat treatments and body wraps cause a loss of body fluids through perspiration. Clients must be provided with still water or fruit juices to rehydrate following treatment. Water imbalances of only 1–2 per cent can lead to ill health. Increased water consumption aids toxin elimination.

- Following heat treatments and those that induce relaxation, such as flotation treatment, the client should rest for 20–30 minutes. In the case of heat treatments this is to allow body temperatures and blood pressure to return to normal. Sudden movements can cause dizziness and fainting.

- Avoid infrared or ultraviolet light treatments following heat treatments as the skin will be sensitised.
- Other treatments may follow the service, such as exfoliation and body massage, depending on the service that has been received.
- If the client's aim is weight reduction, give advice on healthy eating habits and increased, regular exercise to raise metabolism, increase fitness and muscle tone. An aftercare leaflet may be given to your client suggesting health advice tips.
- Advise the client about other treatments that can be given.
- The client may be encouraged to recreate the benefits of spa mineral treatments at home through the sale of retail products. These contain ingredients such as seaweed, sea salts, algae and mud.

CONTRA-ACTIONS

In the case of any contra-action to treatment it is important to discontinue treatment if it occurs while the client is receiving the treatment. You should take the appropriate remedial action or contact the relevant member of staff trained to deal with the situation.

Aftercare advice should always be given to the client in the case of a contra-action occurring following the treatment.

Heat treatments

Treatment duration too long:

- Low blood pressure and loss of water from the body. Dehydration will occur, causing the cells to absorb fluid from other organs in the body. This may also cause the client to feel faint.

Sauna treatments – relative humidity too low:

- Excessive water loss may occur, leading to dehydration. Also, breathing difficulties may be experienced due to lack of moisture in the air. The temperature of the air will also be higher, causing discomfort when breathing.
- Nausea and dizziness caused by heat exhaustion. This can also be caused by the heat and motion in the spa pool.

Action:

- The client should lie down and rest. Raise the legs to avoid fainting.
- Water should be given to rehydrate.
- Seek medical attention if necessary.

Heat exhaustion caused by loss of fluids and sodium chloride (body salt).

This results in symptoms such as dizziness, sickness, headaches and fainting.

Action:

- The client should lie down and rest, raise legs to avoid fainting.
- Fruit juices or sports drinks may be taken.
- Seek medical attention if necessary.
- Salt tablets may be recommended by the GP to replace lost salts.

Cramp caused by excessive perspiration.

Action:

- Stretch the muscle and massage the area.
- Encourage the client to drink water. Salts may be added to replace lost body salts.

Burning/scalding the skin.

- Through not ladling the water over the coals in the sauna with an outstretched arm, causing the skin to come into contact with the rising steam.
- Skin contact with the heated metal in the sauna.

Action:

- Cool the area with cold water immediately.
- Apply a dry dressing which will not stick to the skin injury. This will protect the skin against infection.
- Medical treatment may be advisable dependant upon the severity of the burn.

Nosebleed due to irritation of the mucous membranes and the effect of the high temperature upon the circulatory system.

Action:

- Bend the head forwards. The client should breathe through her mouth.
- The nose should be gently but firmly pinched for about 10 minutes.
- If the bleeding does not cease after 30 minutes seek medical attention.

Skin reaction.

- Skin irritation due to chemicals in the spa pool.
- Skin irritation due to high temperatures in the steam or sauna room and irritant effect of the dry heat in the sauna room.

Action:

- The client should take a cool shower to remove the products/chemicals from the skin or lower skin temperature.
- Apply a soothing cream to reduce irritation.
- Medical treatment may be advisable if skin irritation continues.

Respiratory disorders may be aggravated due to the heat of the sauna or steam room.

Clients with respiratory disorders should avoid heat treatments where they have to breathe hot air directly.

Action:

- Sit the client down, and if she has medication with her, allow her to use it.
- Seek medical assistance if necessary.

Assessment of knowledge and understanding

You have now learnt about the different spa treatments that are available. To be effective in your role it is necessary for you to be able to prepare, monitor, maintain and assist with the shut down of the different spa areas. This enables you to effectively assist with spa treatments.

To test your level of knowledge and understanding, answer the following short questions. These will prepare you for your summative (final) assessment.

Prepare work areas for water, temperature and spa treatments

1 Who enforces and monitors local by-laws with regard to water, temperature and quality for spa treatments?

2 How can cross-infection be avoided in the spa area? State three examples of cross-infections and what can be done to avoid them.

3 What health and safety legislation should be complied with in the spa environment?

4 Where and why should written instructions about treatment usage be displayed?

5 For each of the following treatments explain how you would ensure the spa equipment was safe, clean and hygienic for each client:
   - wet flotation
   - sauna
   - foam bath
   - steam cabinet.

6 How is humidity measured in the sauna room?

Clean and maintain spa environment

1 How are water and chemical concentrations checked for the spa pool?

2 What Health and Safety legislation states how chemicals required for spas should be stored and used?

3 Which treatments are referred to as dry heat?

4 Which treatments are referred to as wet heat?

5 Why should up-to-date records be kept for clients receiving spa treatments?

6 Why should a client shower before entering the spa pool area?

7 Which heat treatment would be most suitable for a client with a dry, mature skin? Discuss the reasons for your choice.

8 When planning a slimming treatment what advice would you give to a client requiring a body wrap?

9 If a client was suffering from stress, what benefits would heat therapy have? Discuss how you would design a treatment plan for such a client. Explain the spa treatment selected, its benefits, and what other treatment could be received by the client.

10 How would you ensure the client's understanding of spa treatment at the consultation?

11 Name six contra-indications to heat therapy treatments.

Assist with monitoring water, temperature and spa treatments

1 What are the recommended operating temperatures of a:
- spa pool
- hydrotherapy bath
- wet flotation
- mild sauna
- steam cabinet treatment?

2 What is the recommended pH level for a:
- spa pool
- wet flotation.

3 What information should be recorded following a body wrap treatment?

4 What dangers can occur if the chemical pH concentrations in the spa pool are not checked regularly?

5 Why must you check a client regularly when they are receiving spa treatments?

6 What should be checked on a daily basis in the spa environment? How is this check recorded?

7 How often should electrical equipment be serviced?

8 What Health and Safety legislation does this comply with?

9 How often may heat treatment be received per week?

10 How long is allowed for the following treatments:
- dry flotation
- body wrap
- spa pool
- hydrotherapy bath?

11 Why is it important for the client to relax following treatment?

12 How can you ensure the client's modesty and privacy is respected when receiving spa treatment?

13 How would you deal with the following contra-actions:
- fainting
- allergic reactions
- breathing difficulties?

14 Give three examples of aftercare advice that may be given following spa treatment.

Assist with the shut down of spa areas

1 How are the following treatments shut down at the end of the working day?
- spa pool
- sauna room
- steam room?

2 Why is it important to follow organisational procedures for assisting with shut down of the treatment areas?

3 How are the bandages used in the body wrap cleaned and prepared for the next client?

4 How should waste be disposed of?

glossary

Acid mantle the combination of sweat and sebum on the skin surface, creating an acid film. The acid mantle is protective and discourages the growth of bacteria and fungi.

Aftercare advice recommended advice given to the client following treatment to continue the benefits of the treatment.

Allergen a substance that the skin is sensitive to, and causing an allergic reaction.

Anagen the active growth stage of the hair growth cycle.

Antiseptic a chemical agent that prevents the multiplication of micro-organisms.

Appraisal a process whereby a supervisor identifies and discusses with an individual their performance and achievements in their job role, against previously set targets.

Arrector pili a small muscle attached to the hair follicle and base of the epidermis. When the muscles contracts (shortens) it causes the hair to stand upright in the hair follicle.

Autoclave an effective method of sterilsation, suitable for small metal objects and beauty therapy tools, where water is boiled under increased pressure and reaches temperatures of 121–134°C.

Bacteria minute single-celled organisms of various shapes. Large numbers live on the skin's surface and are not harmful (non-pathogenic). Others, however, are harmful (pathogenic) and can cause skin diseases.

Blood nutritive liquid circulating through the blood vessels. It transports essential nutrients to the cells and removes waste products. It also transports other important substances such as oxygen and hormones.

Body language communication involving the body instead of verbal communication.

Body wrapping a body treatment where the body is wrapped in bandages, plastic sheets or thermal blankets to achieve different therapeutic effects including skin toning and weight loss.

Bone the hardest structure in the body. It protects the underlying structures, gives shape to the body and provides an attachment point for muscles.

Buffer a manicure tool with a handle made of plastic and a pad with a replaceable cover. Used on the nail to give a sheen, increase blood supply to the area, and if used with the gritty cream buffing paste, to help smooth out nail surface irregularities.

Cash float a small sum of money to provide change at the beginning of each day.

Catagen the stage of the hair growth cycle where the hair becomes detached from its sources of nourishment, the dermal papilla, and stops growing.

Cell the smallest and simplest unit capable of life.

Cheque an alternative form of payment to that of using cash. A cheque must be accompanied by a cheque guarantee card.

Circulatory system transports material around the body.

Cleanser a skin care preparation that removes dead skin cells, excess sweat and sebum, make-up, and dirt from the skin's surface to maintain a healthy skin complexion.

Communication the exchange of information and the establishment of understanding between people.

Consultation assessment of client's needs using different assessment techniques, including questioning and natural observation.

Consumer Protection (Distance Selling) Regulations 2000 these regulations are derived from a European Union Directive and cover the supply of goods/services made between suppliers acting in a commercial capacity and consumers. They are concerned with purchases made by telephone, fax, internet, digital television and mail order.

Consumer Protection Act 1987 this act follows European Union (EU) Directives to protect the customer from unsafe, defective services and products that do not reach safety standards.

Consumer Safety Act 1978 this act aims to reduce risks to consumers from potentially dangerous products.

Contra-action an unwanted reaction occurring during or after a treatment application.

Contra-indication a problematic symptom which indicates that treatment may not proceed.

Control of Substances Hazardous to Health (COSHH) 1999 these regulations require employers to identify hazardous substances used in the workplace and state how they should be stored and handled.

Credit card an alternative form of payment to that of using cash. These cards are held by those who have a credit account, where there is a pre-arranged borrowing limit. These can only be used if your business has an arrangement to deal with the relevant credit card company.

Cross-infection the transfer of contagious micro-organisms.

Data Protection Act 1998 legislation designed to protect client privacy and confidentiality.

Debit card an alternative method of payment where the card authorises immediate debit of the cash amount from the client's account.

Dermal papilla an organ that provides the hair with blood, necessary for hair growth.

Dermis the inner portion of the skin, situated underneath the epidermis.

Disability Discrimination Act 1995 implemented to prevent disabled persons being discriminated against during recruitment and employment. Employers have a responsibility to remove physical barriers and to adjust working conditions to prevent discrimination on the basis of having a disability.

Disinfectant a chemical agent that destroys most micro-organisms.

Ear piercing is the piercing of the lobule part of the ear, which is composed of fibrous, fatty tissues. An ear piercing system is used to pierce the ear, and insert a stud to adorn the ear.

Electricity at Works Regulations 1989 these regulations state that every piece of equipment in the workplace should be tested every 12 months by a qualified electrician. It is the responsibility of the employer to keep records of the equipment tested and the date it was checked.

Employers' Liability (Compulsory Insurance) Act 1969 this provides financial compensation to an employee should they be injured as a result of an accident in the workplace.

Epidermis the outer layer of the skin.

Equal opportunity non-discrimination on the basis to sex, race, disability, age, etc.

Equal Opportunities Policy the Equal Opportunities Commission (EOC) states it is best practice for the workplace to have a written Equal Opportunities Policy. This will include a statement of the commitment to equal opportunities by the employer and the structure for implementing the policy.

Erythema reddening of the skin.

Exfoliant a cosmetic treatment preparation of chemical or vegetable origin to accelerate the process of natural skin loss called desquamation. It is normally applied to the face after facial cleansing and steaming. Exfoliants may also be applied to the skin of the hands and feet, which tend to be coarser in texture than skin elsewhere.

Exfoliation a salon treatment used to remove excess dead skin cells from the surface of the skin, which has a skin cleansing action. This process can be achieved using a specialised cosmetic, or mechanically by using facial equipment where a brush is rotated over the skin surface.

Eyelash and eyebrow tinting definition of the brow and lash hair, achieved by the application of a permanent dye, especially formulated for use around the delicate eye area.

Eyebrow shaping involves the removal of eyebrow hair to create a new shape or to remove stray hairs to maintain the existing brow shape. Small metal tools called tweezers are used to remove the hairs, or alternatively wax depilation may be used.

Eyelash perming a chemical treatment applied to the eyelashes to permanently curl the lashes, which enhances the appearance of the eyes.

Face shape the size and shape of the client's facial bone structure. Face shapes include: oval, round, square, heart, diamond, oblong and pear.

Facial a treatment to improve the appearance, condition and functioning of the skin and underlying structures.

Facial features the size and shape of a person's nose, eyes, forehead, chin, neck, etc. When applying make-up products, make-up application can emphasise or minimise the facial features.

False eyelashes threads of nylon fibre or real hair attached to the clients natural eyelash hair. There are two main types: individual or strip.

Fibreglass nail extensions a nail extension system using fibreglass in conjunction with a nail tip.

Fire Precautions Act 1971 legislation that states that all staff must be familiar with and trained in fire and emergency evacuation procedures for their workplace.

Fire Precautions (Workplace) Regulations 1997 this legislation requires that every employer must carryout a risk assessment for the premises in relation to fire evacuation practice and procedures, under the Management of Health and Safety Regulations 1999.

Flotation a spa treatment where the body is suspended (wet flotation) or supported (dry flotation), inducing relaxation.

Foam baths a shallow bath of water containing a foaming agent surrounding the body achieving a thermal effect. Increased perspiration caused by this effect aids the elimination of waste and toxins.

Fungus microscopic plants, which are parasites. Fungal diseases of the skin feed off the waste products of the skin. They are found on the skin's surface or they can attack deeper tissues.

Gift voucher a prepayment for beauty therapy services or retail sales.

Hair follicle an appendage (structure) in the skin formed from epidermal tissue. Cells move up the hair follicle from the bottom (the hair bulb), changing in structure, to form the hair.

Hazard something with potential to cause harm.

Health and Safety (Display Screen Equipment) 1992 these regulations cover the use of visual display units (VDUs) and computer screens. They specify acceptable levels of radiation emissions from the screen and identify correct posture, seating position, permitted working heights and rest periods.

Health and Safety (First Aid) Regulations 1981 legislation that states that workplaces must have first aid provision.

Health and Safety at Work Act 1974 legislation which lays down the minimum standards of health, safety and welfare requirements in each workplace.

Highlighter a make-up product that draws attention to – emphasises.

Hirsutism a term used to describe a pattern of growth that is abnormal for a person's sex, such as when a woman's hair follows a male growth pattern.

Histamine a chemical released when the skin comes into contact with a substance that it is allergic to. Cells called 'mast cells' burst, releasing histamine into the tissues. This causes the blood capillaries to dilate, which increases blood flow to limit skin damage and begin repair.

Hot wax a system of wax depilation used to remove hair from the skin. Hot wax cools and sets on contact with the skin. They are a blend of waxes, such as beeswax and resins, which keep the wax flexible. Soothing ingredients are often included to avoid skin irritation.

Hydrotherapy spa treatments where water is used for its therapeutic effect.

Hygiene the recommended standard of cleanliness necessary in the salon to prevent cross-infection and secondary infection.

Hyperpigmentation increased pigment production.

Hypertrichosis abnormal excessive hair growth. It is usually due to abnormal conditions in the body caused by disease or injury.

Hypopigmentation loss of pigmentation.

Infestation a condition where animal parasites invade and live off a host

Job description written details of a persons specific work role, duties and responsibilities.

Legislation laws affecting the workplace in relation to treatments and services, systems and procedures, the premises, employers and employees.

Local Government Miscellaneous Provisions Act 1982 legislation that requires that salons offering any form of skin piercing be registered with the local health authority. This registration includes both the operators who will be carrying out the treatment and the salon premises where the treatment will be carried out.

Lymph a clear straw coloured liquid circulating in the lymph vessels and lymphatics of the body, filtered out of the blood plasma.

Lymphatic system closely connected to the blood system. Its primary function is defensive: to remove bacteria and foreign materials to prevent infection.

Make-up cosmetics applied to the skin of the face to enhance and accentuate the facial features. Make-up products create balance in the face to reduce or emphasise.

Make-up products different cosmetics available to suit skin type, colour and condition, i.e. sensitive/mature. Make-up products include: concealing and contour cosmetics, foundations, translucent powders, eyeshadows, eyeliners, brow liners, mascaras, lipsticks, lip glosses; lipliners.

Management of Health and Safety at Work Regulations 1999 this legislation provides the employer with an approved code of practice for maintaining a safe, secure working environment.

Manicure a treatment to improve the appearance and condition of the skin and nails of the hands.

Manual Handling Operations Regulations 1992 legislation that requires the employer to carry out a risk assessment of all activities undertaken which involve manual handling (lifting and moving objects).

Mask a skin cleansing treatment preparation applied to the skin which may contain different ingredients. It can have a deep cleansing, toning, nourishing or refreshing effect. It may be applied to the hands, feet and face.

Massage manipulation of the soft tissues of the body, producing heat and stimulating the muscular, circulatory and nervous system.

Massage manipulations movements which are selected and applied according to the desired effect, which may be stimulating, relaxing or toning. Massage manipulations include effleurage, petrissage, percussion (also known as tapotement) and vibrations.

Melanin a pigment in the skin that contributes to skin colour.

Melanocytes cells that produce the skin pigment melanin that contributes to skin colour.

Moisturiser a skin care preparation whose formulation of oil and water helps maintain the skins natural moisture by locking moisture into the skin, offering protection and hydration.

Muscle contractile tissue responsible for movement of the body.

Muscle tone the normal degree of tension in healthy muscle.

Nail art nail decoration applied to the natural nail plate or artificial nail, using nail art materials including: nail polish, transfers, gemstones, glitter and foil.

Nail forms made of paper or metal, these are placed at the end of the nail. The natural nail is lengthened onto the nail form using nail extension product.

Nail tips plastic nail tips used to extend the length of the natural nail.

Nail wrap a material such as silk or fibreglass is attached to the nail to repair or strengthen the natural nail.

Nails hard, horny epidermal cells that protect the living nail bed of the fingers and toes.

Nerve a collection of single neurones surrounded by a protective sheath through which impulses are transmitted between the brain or spinal cord and another part of the body.

Nervous system co-ordinates the activities of the body by responding to stimuli received by sense organs.

Neurones nerve cells which make up nervous tissue.

Nutrition the process of nourishment derived from food, required for the bodies growth, energy, repair and production.

Oedema extra fluid in an area causing swelling.

Overlay a thin coating applied to the natural nail or an application over the natural nail and tip.

Palintest balanced water index the method of regular testing and maintenance of water quality in the spa whirlpool/swimming pool.

Pedicure a treatment to improve the appearance and condition of the skin and nails of the feet.

Personal Protective Equipment (PPE) at Work Regulations 1992 this legislation requires managers to identify through a risk assessment those activities which require special protective equipment to be worn.

Petrissage massage manipulation which applies intermittent pressure to the tissues of the skin, lifting them away from the underlying structures. Often known as compression movements.

Posture the position of the body, which varies from person to person. Good posture is when he body is in alignment. Correct posture enables you to work longer without becoming tired. It prevents muscle fatigue and stiff joints.

Prices Act 1974 this act states that the price of products has to be displayed in order to prevent the buyer being misguided.

Provision and Use of Work Equipment Regulations (PUWER) 1998 this regulation lays down important health and safety controls on the provision and use of equipment.

Public Liability Insurance protects employers and employees against the consequences of death or injury to a third party while on the premises.

Punctuality arriving at the correct time.

Reception the area where clients are received.

Receptionist person responsible for maintaining the reception area, scheduling appointments, and handling payments.

Record cards confidential cards recording personal details of each client registered at the salon.

Relaxation room of ambient temperature (close to the body's temperature) often referred to by the latin name *tepidarium*.

Reporting of Injuries, Diseases and Dangerous Occurences Regulations (RIDDOR) 1995 RIDDOR requires the employer to notify the local enforcement officer in writing, in cases where employees or trainees suffer personal injury at work.

Resale Prices Act 1964 and 1976 this act states that the manufacturer can supply a recommended price (MRRP), but the seller is not obliged to sell at the recommended price.

Roller wax a warm wax system used to remove hair from the skin. The wax is contained in a cartridge container with a disposable applicator, which rolls the wax onto the skins surface. The applicator is renewed for each client.

Sales and Supply of Goods Act 1994 this act has replaced the Sales of Goods Act 1982. Goods must be as described, or merchantable quality, and fit for their intended purpose.

Sanitisation the destruction of some, but not all living micro-organisms.

Sauna timber construction where the air inside is heated to produce a therapeutic effect on the body.

Sculptured nails artificial nails formed using a liquid and powder system or a gel. The mixture is sculpted and built-up over the natural nail plate and extends past the end of the nail onto a nail form.

Sebaceous gland a minute sac-like organ usually associated with the hair follicle. The cells of the gland decompose and produce the skin's natural oil sebum. Found all over the body, except for the soles of the feet and the palms of the hands.

Sebum the skin's natural oil which keeps the skin supple.

Secondary infection bacterial penetration into the skin causing infection.

Shader a make-up product that draws attention away – minimises.

Skin allergy if the skin is sensitive to a particular substance an allergic skin reaction will occur. This is recognised by irritation, swelling and inflammation.

Skin analysis assessment of the client's skin type and condition.

Skin appendages structures within the skin including sweat glands (that excrete sweat), hair follicles (that produce hair), sebaceous glands (produce the skin's natural oil sebum) and nails (a horny substance that protects the ends of the fingers/toes).

Skin test method used to assess skin tolerance to substances or treatments.

Skin tone the strength and elasticity of the skin.

Skin type the different physiological functioning of each person's skin dictates their skin type. There are four main skin types normal (balanced), dry (lacking in oil), oily (excessive oil) and combination (a mixture of 2 skin types, i.e. dry and oily).

Spa pool a pool of warm water in which the client sits with jets of air passing through to create bubbles which massage the skin.

Steam treatment water is heated to create steam, which is applied to the body for its therapeutic purposes.

Sterilisation the total destruction of all micro-organisms.

Strip sugar a system of wax depilation similar to warm wax technique, used to remove hair from the skin. Made from sugar, lemons and water, the paste is applied to embed the hair, which is then removed from the skin using a wax removal strip.

Subcutaneous tissue a layer of fatty tissue situated below the epidermis and dermis.

Sugar paste, a system of wax depilation, used to remove hair from the skin. An organic paste made from sugar, lemons and water, is used to embed the hair, which is then removed in the paste from the skin.

Sugaring an ancient popular method of hair removal using organic substances of sugar and lemon.

Superfluous hair (excess hair) this hair growth is perfectly normal at certain parts in a woman's life, such as puberty and pregnancy, when there is a hormone disturbance in the body. New hairs, which grow at these times, usually disappear once hormone balance returns.

Systemic medical condition a medical condition caused by a defect in one of the bodies organs i.e. the heart.

Tapotement also known as percussion. A massage manipulation which is used for its general toning and stimulating effect.

Target a goal or objective to achieve, usually set within a timescale.

Telogen the resting stage of the hair growth cycle where the hair is finally shed.

Terminal hair deep rooted, thick, coarse, pigmented hair found on the scalp, underarms, pubic region, eyelash and brow areas.

Tips and overlays a nail tip is applied, blended to remove the visible line, and is overlayed by acrylic, gel or fibreglass.

Toning lotion a skin care preparation to remove all traces of cleanser from the skin. It produces a cooling effect on the skin and has a skin tightening effect.

Towel steaming an alternative to facial steaming using an electrical vapour unit. Small, clean facial towels are heated in a bowl of warm water or specialised heater, before application to the face to warm, cleanse and stimulate the skin.

Trades Description Act 1968 and 1972 legislation that states that information when selling products both in written and verbal form should be accurate.

Treatment plan after the consultation suitable treatment objectives are established to treat the client's condition and needs.

Tweezers small metal tools used to remove body hair, by pulling it from the bottom of the hair follicle (small openings in the skin where the hair grows from). There are 2 types: *automatic* – designed to remove the bulk of the hair and *manual* – designed to remove stray hairs.

Ultraviolet light invisible rays of the light spectrum with a wavelength shorter than visible light rays.

Ultraviolet light (UVL) cabinet a unit which uses UVL to *sanitise* small objects. Objects need to be clean before placing in the cabinet, and must be turned, in order that the UVL rays effectively strike each surface of the object.

Vapour unit an electrical unit that heats water to produce steam, which is applied to the skin of the face and neck, to warm, cleanse and stimulate the skin.

Vellus hair hair which is fine, downy and soft – found on the face and body.

Vibrations massage manipulation applied on a nerve centre. They stimulate the nerves and can produce a relaxation effect. The movements are firm and trembling, performed with one or both hands.

Virus the smallest living bodies, too small to see under an ordinary microscope. They are considered to be *parasites*, as they require living tissue to survive. Viruses invade healthy body cells and multiply within the cell. Eventually the cell walls break down and the virus particles are freed to attack further cells.

Warm wax a system of wax depilation used to remove hair from the skin. Warm wax remains soft at body temperatures. It is frequently made of mixtures of glucose syrup and zinc oxide. Honey can be used instead of glucose syrup – referred to as honey wax.

Wax depilation the temporary removal of excess hair from a body part using wax.

Workplace (Health, Safety and Welfare) Regulations 1992 these regulations provide the employer with an approved code of practice for maintaining a safe, secure working environment.

Wrap a fibreglass or silk nail system to overlay natural nails.

index